Preface

The effective management of supply is continuing to be a major challenge for practitioners and academics alike. Economic, political, and social changes in the world create both problems and opportunities for the field of purchasing and materials management. Increasing world competition is forcing supply managers to rethink traditional concepts and to develop new strategies congruent with the short- and long-term needs of their organizations.

The increasing emphasis on viewing the supply function in a strategic sense is a healthy trend. This requires not only a reeducation of current purchasing practitioners, but also of those concerned with general and functional areas of management, who used to view the supply function in a service perspective. A completely new strategy chapter has, therefore, been included in this text, reinforced by the cases at the end of all chapters.

Current management trends toward increased emphasis on world class status and world competitiveness, continuing improvement, focused operations, inventory and waste reduction, longer term perspective, greater customer awareness, and participative management all impact on the purchasing and materials management area in a variety of ways. Typical examples include not only the renewed emphasis on a strategic perspective, but also the quality movement, inventory reduction, just-in-time (JIT), material requirements and resource planning, vendor rationalization, electronic data interchange (EDI), longer term contracts, international procurement, reverse marketing, and team purchasing. Each of these topics is included in the revised chapters of this book, along with case material involving organizations grappling with the implementation of these ideas. The growing trend to a service economy is reflected in the growing references to acquisition management in a service context, as well as in a new chapter on the acquisition of services.

Professor John Haywood-Farmer was the prime author of the quantitative chapter and also gave valuable insights on the new chapter for the acquisition of services.

Many helpful suggestions for improvements from teachers using this text are gratefully acknowledged. In particular, detailed reviews from Charles Bimmerle, North Texas State University; Stephen N. Chapman, University of Iowa; E. A. Hale, San Diego State University; Gene Mangold, Corpus Christi State University; Jean Nollet, Ecole Des Hautes Etudes

Commerciales; and Glenn Thiel, Robert Morris College were most welcome. We would also like to thank Elaine Whittington for contributing to the subcontracting section.

The assistance from practitioners whose cases have been included is always invaluable. Every case in this text was contributed by a person actually wrestling with a supply issue, decision, or problem. Their situations and insights in the form of cases form a most useful addition to the text.

Contributors of cases and case writers other than the authors of this text included Doug Clark and Michael Watkins and Professors Jean Nollet, John Patterson and Morton Fox. Loretta Peregrina, Carol L. Ketchum and Cheryl T. DeLaura provided most welcome secretarial support. Sheila Smith at R.D. Irwin supplied the editorial strength and worried about those minor details of production with which authors could not be trusted anyway.

Our concluding thanks go to our spouses, Louise, Dottie, and Ruth and to our families for their loving support.

Michiel R. Leenders
Harold E. Fearon
Wilbur B. England

Contents

6 Supplier Selection and Supplier Relations 225

Make or Buy. Reasons for Make instead of Buy. Dangers Involved in Decision to Manufacture. The Grey Zone in Make or Buy. Subcontracting. The Supplier Selection Decision: *Good or Preferred Suppliers. Supplier Goodwill. Sources of Information about Suppliers. Narrowing the List.* Supplier Evaluation: *Existing and Potential Sources. Informal and Formal Evaluation of Current Suppliers.* Purchaser-Supplier Relations: *Perceptions. Congruent Situations. Noncongruent Perceptions. Using the Framework. Tools and Techniques for Moving Positions. Supplier Management.* The Evaluation of Potential Sources: *Technical, Engineering, and Manufacturing Strengths. Management and Financial Evaluation. Additional Source Selection Considerations. Concentration of Purchases with One Source. Purchase from Manufacturer or Distributor. Geographical Location of Sources. Trade Relations. Attitude toward Gratuities. Joint Purchasing with Supplier. Purchasing for Company Personnel. Social, Political, and Environmental Concerns. Overall Vendor Selection Consideration. Reverse Marketing/Supplier Development.*
CASES: 6-1 Unifood Inc.   6-2 Davidson Equipment
6-3 Stevens Construction, Inc.   6-4 Plastic Cable Clips

7 Price Determination 287

Relation of Cost to Price: *Meaning of Cost. How Vendors Establish Price. The Cost Approach. The Market Approach. Governmental Influence on Pricing. Legislation Affecting Price Determination.* Types of Purchases and Methods of Price Determination: *The Use of Quotations and Competitive Bidding. Firm Bidding. Determination of Most Advantageous Bid. Collusive Bidding. The Problem of Identical Prices. Negotiation as a Method of Price Determination. Cost/Price Analysis. The Learning Curve. Negotiation Strategy and Practice. Ground Rules for Successful Negotiation. Provision for Price Changes: Discounts. The Price Discount Problem. Quantity Discounts and Source Selection. Contract Cancellation.* Forward Buying and Commodities: *Forward Buying versus Speculation. Speculation versus Gambling. Organizing for Forward Buying. Control of Forward Buying.* The Commodity Exchanges: *Limitations of the Exchanges. Hedging. Sources of Information regarding Price Trends.*
CASES: 7-1 Seatide Crafts, Inc. (A)   7-2 Seatide Crafts, Inc. (B)
7-3 Seatide Crafts, Inc. (C)   7-4 The Morrison Institute
7-5 Clarebrook Hospital   7-6 Price Forecasting Exercise
7-7 Commodity Purchasing Game

*Evaluation. Procedure to Be Used by an Outside Consultant. Points
for Judgment in Appraisal. Review of Personnel Policy. Extent and
Areas of Current Performance Measurement.*
CASES: 11-1 Arden Foods, Inc.   11-2 Maral Pharmaceuticals
11-3 MEC Corporation (R)

12   Foreign Purchasing   480

Why the Concern with Foreign Purchasing? *U.S. Imports.* Reasons
for Foreign Buying: *Price. Quality. Unavailability of Items
Domestically. Faster Delivery and Continuity of Supply. Better
Technical Service. Technology. Marketing Tool. Tie-In with Foreign
Subsidiaries. Competitive Clout.* Potential Problem Areas: *Source
Location and Evaluation. Lead/Delivery Time. Expediting. Political
and Labor Problems. Currency Fluctuations. Payment Methods.
Quality. Rejects. Tariffs and Duties. Paperwork Costs. Legal
Problems. Transportation. Language. Cultural and Social Customs.*
Information Sources for Locating and Evaluating Foreign Vendors.
Organization for Foreign Purchasing: *Import Broker or Sales Agent.
Import Merchant. Trading Company. Assignment within the
Purchasing Department. Foreign Buying Office.* Countertrade
Cooperative. Country Considerations. Countertrade: *Pure Barter.
Mixed Barter. Offset Arrangements. Co-Production.* Foreign Trade
Zones: *Foreign Trade Zones Compared with Bonded Warehouses.
TIBs and Duty Drawbacks.*
CASES: 12-1 Mirror Stainless Steel   12-2 Surpil, Inc.

13   Public Purchasing   512

Characteristics of Public Buying: *Source of Authority. Budgetary
Restrictions/Limitations. Outside Pressures. Greater Support of
Public Service Programs. Absence of Interest Costs. Absence of
Inspection. Lack of Traffic Expertise. Time Required to Modify the
Organization. Salary Levels. Information Cannot Be Kept
Confidential. Importance of Specifications. Emphasis on the Bid
Process.* Federal Government Purchasing: *History. Small Business
Favoritism. Labor Surplus Area Favoritism. Buy American Act.
Renegotiation. General Services Administration (GSA). Military
Purchasing.* State and Local Government Purchasing: *History.
Participation in GSA Contracts. Prison-Made Goods. Cooperative
Purchasing. Local-Bidder Preference Laws. Innovations in
Government Purchasing. Health Care Purchasing. Model
Procurement Code.*
CASES: 13-1 Folan City   13-2 City of Hampton (B2)   13-3 The
Eastern Counties Region

in Purchasing, Major Purchasing Functional Strategy Areas,
Strategic Components: *What? Quality? How Much? Who? When?
What Price? Where? How? Why?* The Future: *Research Needs.*
References, Questions for Review and Discussion:
CASES: 16-1 Diprod (R)   16-2 Locar Corporation (R)

CHAPTER 1

The Challenge of Purchasing and Materials Management

These are exciting times for those concerned with the effective and efficient management of supply and materials functions. Materials requirements planning, just-in-time production, and a renewed emphasis on quality and productivity have required a reexamination of many traditional supply concepts. For example, the traditionally held view that multiple sourcing increases supply security has been challenged by a trend toward single sourcing. Close vendor relations and cooperation on scheduling and quality assurance systems question the wisdom of the traditional arm's length dealings between the purchaser and supplier. Negotiation is receiving increasing emphasis as opposed to competitive bidding and longer term contracts are replacing short-term buying techniques. All of these trends are a logical outcome of increased managerial concern with value and increasing procurement aggressiveness in developing suppliers to meet specific supply objectives of quality, quantity, delivery, price, service, and continuity.

Effective management of materials and purchasing can contribute significantly to the success of most modern organizations. This text will explore the nature of this contribution and the management requirements for effective and efficient performance. The acquisition of materials, supplies, services, and equipment—of the right qualities, in the right quantities, at the right prices, at the right time, and on a continuing basis—long has occupied the attention of many managers in both the public and private sectors. The rapidly changing supply scene, with cycles of abundance and shortages, varying prices, lead times, and availabilities, provides a continuing challenge to those organizations wishing to obtain a maximum contribution from this area.

Although interest in the performance of the purchasing function has been a phenomenon primarily of the 20th century, it was recognized as an independent and important function by many of the nation's railroad organizations well before 1900. The first book devoted specifically to purchasing, *The Handling of Railway Supplies—Their Purchase and Disposition,* published in 1887, was authored by an executive with the Chicago and

1

Northwestern Railway, Marshall M. Kirkman.[1] Growth of interest in and attention to purchasing was rather uneven in the early 1900s, but by 1915 several books on purchasing had appeared and several articles had been published in the trade press, primarily in the engineering journals.[2]

Yet, prior to World War I, most firms regarded the purchasing function primarily as a clerical activity. However, during the time periods of World War I and World War II, the success of a firm was not dependent on what it could sell, since the market was almost unlimited. Instead, the ability to obtain from vendors the raw materials, supplies, and services needed to keep the factories and mines operating was the key determinant of organizational success. Attention was given to the organization, policies, and procedures of the purchasing function, and it emerged as a recognized managerial activity. During the 1950s and 1960s, purchasing continued to gain stature as the techniques for performing the function became more refined and as the supply of people trained and competent to make sound purchasing decisions increased. Many companies elevated the chief purchasing officer to top management status, with titles such as vice president of purchasing, director of materials, or vice president of purchasing and supply.

As the decade of the 70s opened, organizations faced two vexing problems—an international shortage of almost all the basic raw materials needed to support operations and a rate of price increases far above the norm since the end of World War II. The Middle East oil embargo during the summer of 1973 intensified both the shortages and the price escalation. These developments put the spotlight directly on purchasing departments, for their performance in obtaining needed items from vendors at realistic prices spelled the difference between success or failure. This emphasized again to top management the crucial role played by purchasing. As we move into the decade of the 1990s, it has become clear that organizations must have an efficient and effective purchasing and materials function if they are to compete successfully with both domestic and foreign firms. In the words of one author, "Upgrading the purchasing function is another route to permanent cost control. In many companies, outlays for purchased materials vastly exceed labor or other costs."[3]

The purchasing department has the potential to, and should, play a key role in developing and operationalizing a strategy leading to sharpened efficiency and heightened competitiveness, through actions such as (1) combating inflation by resisting unwarranted price hikes, (2) significantly reducing dollar investment in materials inventory, through better planning

---

[1]Harold E. Fearon, "The Purchasing Function within Nineteenth Century Railroad Organizations," *Journal of Purchasing,* August 1965, pp. 18–30.

[2]Harold E. Fearon, "Historical Evolution of the Purchasing Function," *Journal of Purchasing,* February 1968, pp. 43–59.

[3]A. Gary Shilling, "We're Out of Choppy Waters, but Keep Cost Hatches Battened," *The Wall Street Journal,* April 23, 1984, p. 28.

FIGURE 1-1   Evolution of Purchasing/Materials Management Function

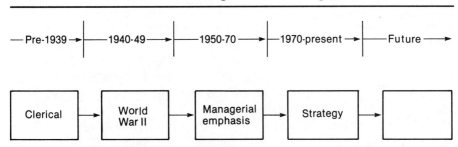

and vendor selection, (3) raising the quality level of purchased materials and parts inputs, so that the quality and consistency of end product/service outputs can be improved, (4) reducing the materials segment of cost-of-goods-sold, and (5) effecting product and process improvements through encouraging and facilitating open communication between buyer and seller, to the mutual benefit of both parties.

Figure 1-1 depicts the movement of the purchasing/materials management function through time as it moved from the clerical era to today's strategic era. The future will see a gradual shift from predominantly defensive strategies, resulting from the need to change in order to remain competitive, to aggressive strategies, in which firms take an imaginative approach to achieving supply objectives to satisfy short-term *and* long-term organizational goals.[4] This text will discuss what organizations should do today to remain competitive as well as what strategic purchasing management will focus on tomorrow.

Growing management interest through necessity and improved insight into the opportunities in the materials area has resulted in a variety of organizational concepts. Terms such as *purchasing, procurement, supply, materiel, materials management,* and *logistics* are used almost interchangeably. No agreement exists on the definition of each of these terms, and managers in public and private institutions may have identical responsibilities but substantially different titles. The following definitions may be helpful in sorting out the more common understanding of the various terms.

In general usage, the term *purchasing* describes the process of buying: learning of the need, locating and selecting a supplier, negotiating price and other pertinent terms, and following up to ensure delivery. *Procurement* is a somewhat broader term and includes purchasing, stores, traffic, receiving, incoming inspection, and salvage.

Supply is often used in North America by industrial concerns to cover

[4]Michiel R. Leenders and David L. Blenkhorn, *Reverse Marketing: The New Buyer-Supplier Relationship* (New York: The Free Press, 1988), p. 2.

the stores function of internally consumed items such as stationery and office supplies. However, in the United Kingdom and Europe, the term *supply* has a broader meaning to include at least purchasing, stores, and receiving. The governmental sector also uses this broader interpretation. In Canada, for example, the Department of Supply and Services is responsible for procurement in the federal government. *Materiel* has a military or governmental connotation and often includes the same functions as those identified under materials management.

An organization which has adopted the materials management organizational concept will have a single manager responsible for the planning, organizing, motivating, and controlling of all those activities principally concerned with the flow of materials into an organization. Materials management views material flows as a system. Another way to look at materials management is to indicate its major activities:

1. Anticipating material requirements.

2. Sourcing and obtaining materials.

3. Introducing materials into the organization.

4. Monitoring the status of materials as a current asset.

The specific functions which might be included under the materials manager are material planning and control, production scheduling, material and purchasing research, purchasing, incoming traffic, inventory control, receiving, incoming quality control, stores, in-plant materials movement, and scrap and surplus disposal. Not all 11 functions are necessarily included; the ones often excluded are production scheduling, in-plant materials movement, and incoming quality control.

Adoption of the materials management concept largely grew out of problems in the airframe industry during World War II. Production of an aircraft requires a large number of individual items, many of which are quite sophisticated and must meet stringent quality standards, procured from thousands of vendors located over a wide geographic area. Many of the items are vital to the total functioning of the end product. The objectives of materials management are to solve materials problems from a total company viewpoint (optimize) by *coordinating* performance of the various materials functions, providing a *communications* network, and *controlling* materials flow. As the computer was introduced into organizations, this provided a further reason to adopt materials management, for the materials functions have many common data needs and can share a common data base.

Logistics has its origin near the year 1670, when a new staff structure proposed for the French army included the position of "Marechal General des Logis," who was responsible for supply, transportation, selecting camps, and adjusting marches.[5] Although *logistics* long has been a military term, its application to nonmilitary management occurred primarily in the 1960s and included "the optimum co-ordination of the inbound raw material movements, raw material storage, work in process handling, and of the outbound packaging, warehousing of finished products, and movements of finished products to the customer."[6] A recent definition of logistics, adopted in 1985 by the Council of Logistics Management, is "the process of planning, implementing, and controlling the efficient, cost-effective flow and storage of raw materials, in-process inventory, finished goods, and related information from point of origin to point of consumption for the purpose of conforming to customer requirements."[7]

Although the logistics concept is attractive from a theoretical point of view, encompassing the complete systems approach, two major problems of implementation still exist: first is the ability of a logistics manager to handle a job with this scope, crossing so many traditional lines of organizational authority and responsibility, and second is the current state of computer software systems. This text will cover primarily those functions normally included in the purchasing and materials management definitions. The activities usually included in physical distribution management, such as determining finished goods inventory levels, finished goods warehouse locations and levels of inventory, outbound transportation, packaging, and customer repair parts, warranty, and installation service, will receive no special coverage. Our main concern is the inflow of goods and services, rather than the outflow. Even within the materials management area, greater emphasis will be placed on areas like source selection and determining the price to be paid than on inventory control and traffic.

What is currently feasible or desirable in one organization may not be applicable in another, for sound reasons. The relative importance of the area compared to the other prime functions of the organization will be a major determinant of the management attention it will receive. How to assess the materials needs of a particular organization in context is one of the purposes of this book. Cases are provided to illustrate a variety of situations and to give practice in resolving managerial problems.

SIGNIFICANCE OF MATERIAL DOLLARS

U.S. manufacturing firms purchased materials totaling $1 trillion, 276 billion, 13 million in 1985, which was over 2.1 times the $597 billion

---

[5] J. D. Little, *The Military Staff, Its History and Development*, 3rd ed. (Harrisburg, Pa.: Stackpole Co., 1961), pp. 48–49.

[6] E. G. Plowman, *Elements of Business Logistics* (Stanford, Calif.: Stanford Graduate School of Business, 1964).

[7] Ernst & Whinney, *Corporate Profitability and Logistics: Innovative Guidelines for Executives* (Oak Brook, Ill.: Council of Logistics Management, 1987), p. 2.

TABLE 1-1 Cost of Materials—Value of Industry Shipments Ratios for Manufacturing Firms, 1985

Standard Industrial Code	Industry	Cost of Materials (millions)*	Capital Expenditures, New (millions)†	Total Material and Capital Expenditures (millions)	Value of Industry Shipments (millions)‡	Material/ Sales Ratio	Total Purchase Sales Ratio
20	Food and kindred products	197,275	7,049	204,324	301,562	65	68
21	Tobacco products	6,626	669	7,295	18,507	36	39
22	Textile mill products	32,258	1,863	34,121	53,277	61	64
23	Apparel and other textile products	29,130	697	29,827	56,993	51	52
24	Lumber and wood products	33,169	1,664	34,833	54,185	61	64
25	Furniture and fixtures	14,764	763	15,527	31,294	47	50
26	Paper and allied products	53,039	6,276	59,315	93,414	57	64
27	Printing and publishing	39,104	4,715	43,819	111,885	35	39
28	Chemicals, allied products	101,696	8,269	109,965	197,311	52	56
29	Petroleum and coal products	161,291	3,438	164,729	179,135	90	92
30	Rubber, miscellaneous plastics products	35,754	3,430	39,184	71,324	50	55
31	Leather, leather products	4,444	103	4,547	8,567	52	53
32	Stone, clay, glass products	26,179	2,780	28,959	55,064	48	53
33	Primary metal	70,603	4,755	75,358	110,301	64	68
34	Fabricated metal	70,490	4,346	74,836	139,580	51	54

35	Machinery, except electric	102,831	8,323	111,154	215,080	48	52
36	Electric, electronic equipment	83,079	10,471	93,550	192,732	43	49
37	Transportation equipment	180,856	10,377	191,233	301,386	60	64
38	Instruments and related products	20,982	2,581	23,563	61,008	34	39
39	Miscellaneous manufacturing	12,442	667	13,109	26,527	47	49

All Operating Manufacturing Establishments

1971	356,016	20,940	376,956	670,970	53	56
1973	478,169	26,978	505,147	875,443	55	58
1975	597,327	37,262	634,589	1,039,377	57	61
1977	782,417	47,459	829,876	1,358,526	58	61
1979	999,157	61,533	1,060,690	1,727,214	58	61
1981	1,193,969	78,632	1,272,601	2,017,542	59	63
1983	1,170,238	61,931	1,232,169	2,054,853	57	60
1985	1,276,013	83,237	1,359,250	2,279,132	56	60

*Refers to direct charges actually paid or payable for items consumed or put into production during the year, including freight charges and other direct charges incurred by the establishment in acquiring these materials. Manufacturers included the cost of materials or fuel consumed regardless of whether these items were purchased by the individual establishment from other companies, transferred to it from other establishments of the same company, or withdrawn from inventory. It excludes the cost of services used, such as advertising, insurance, telephone, etc., and research, developmental, and consulting services of other establishments. It also excludes materials, machinery, and equipment used in plant expansion or capitalized repairs which are chargeable to fixed assets accounts.

†Includes funds spent for permanent additions and major alterations to manufacturing establishments, and new machinery and equipment used for replacement purposes and additions to plant capacity if they are chargeable to a fixed asset account.

‡The received or receivable net selling values, FOB plant, after discounts and allowances, and excluding freight charges and excise taxes. However, where the products of an industry are customarily delivered by the manufacturing establishment, e.g., bakery products, the value of shipments is based on the delivered price of the goods.

SOURCE: U.S. Bureau of the Census, *1985 Annual Survey of Manufactures* (Washington, D.C.: U.S. Government Printing Office, Statistics for Industry Groups and Industries, M85(AS)–1, pp. 1–8, 1–9, and Appendix.

purchased 10 years earlier (1975) and about 3.6 times the amount purchased in 1971. Capital expenditures amounted to $83 billion in 1985, over twice the $37 billion in 1975. (See Table 1–1). The magnitude of these figures emphasizes the importance to the U.S. economy of performing the purchasing function in the most effective manner possible.

Purchasing is the largest single dollar control area with which most managements must deal. Obviously, the percent of the sales or income dollar which is paid out to vendors will vary greatly from industry to industry. For example, in a hospital or bank, purchasing dollars as a percent of operating income will be less than 20 percent, since these industries are labor, rather than material, intensive. But in the manufacturing sector, material dollars typically account for well over half of the sales dollar. When an automobile producer sells a new car to a dealer for $12,000, it already has spent over $6,000 (over 50 percent) to buy the steel, tires, glass, paint, fabric, aluminum, copper, and electronic components necessary to build that car. When a soft drink producer sells $1,000 of packaged beverage to the supermarket, it already has paid to vendors close to $750 for the sweetener, carbonation, flavoring, bottles, caps, and cardboard or plastic containers necessary to make the end product.

Table 1–1, using data collected by the U.S. Bureau of the Census for their *1985 Annual Survey of Manufactures,* presents aggregate purchase/sales data for the entire U.S. manufacturing sector, broken down by type of industry. These figures show that in the average manufacturing firm, materials account for 56 percent of the sales dollar; if expenditures for capital equipment are included, this goes up to 60 percent. This is about one-and-a-half times the remaining 40 percent available to pay salaries, wages, other operating expenses, taxes, interest, and dividends. And, when compensation (wages, salaries, and fringe benefits) of *all* employees in the manufacturing sector for 1985 is compared to total purchases, it amounts to only about one third of the purchase percentage. In other words, the average manufacturing firm spends three times as much for purchases as for all wages, salaries, and fringe benefits.

The material/sales ratio varies dramatically among industries. For example, in standard industrial classification 38, "Instruments and related products" it is only 34 percent, but this industry includes firms making items such as the autopilot used on large commercial aircraft, which require a high percentage of engineering, quality control, research and development, and direct assembly labor. On the other hand, in SIC 20, "Food and kindred products," it is 65 percent. This industry includes commercial bread bakeries and beverage producers, whose production process is material intensive and requires a minimum amount of labor cost due to use of highly mechanized/automated manufacturing processes. Table 1–1 shows that the average material/sales ratio in manufacturing has moved up from 53 percent in 1971 to 56 percent in 1985, as manufacturing processes have become more material and capital intensive and less labor intensive. As firms respond to the mandate to become more efficient if they are to compete effectively with foreign manufacturers, it seems likely that additional labor costs will be designed out of the processes used; thus the material/sales ratio will further increase. Any function of the firm which accounts for well over half of its receipts certainly deserves a great deal of managerial attention.

Decision Making in the Materials Management Context

One of the challenging aspects of the materials management function to its practitioners is the variety and nature of the decisions encountered. Should we make or buy? Must we inventory materials and how much? What price shall we pay? Where shall we place this order? What should the order size be? When will we require this material? Which alternative looks best as an approach to this problem? Which transportation mode and carrier should we use? Should we make a long- or a short-term contract? Should we cancel? How do we dispose of surplus material? Who will form the negotiation team and what shall its strategy be? How do we protect ourselves for the future? Shall we change operating systems? Should we wait or act now? In view of the trade-offs what is the best decision? What stance do we take regarding our customers who wish to supply us? Do we standardize? Is systems contracting worthwhile here? Should we use one supplier or multiple suppliers? Decisions like these will have a major impact on the organization. What makes the decisions exciting is that they are almost always made in a context of uncertainty.

Advances in management science in recent decades have substantially enlarged the number of ways in which materials decisions can be analyzed. The basic supplier selection decision is a classical decision tree model as shown in Figure 1–2. This is a choice between alternatives under uncertainty. In this example, the uncertainty relates to our own demand: we are not sure if it will be high, medium, or low. The outcome is concerned with both price and ability to supply. Does the decision maker wish to trade a higher price against supply assurance under all circumstances? That it is difficult to quantify all consequences reinforces the need for sound judgment in key decisions. It also means that the decision maker's perception of the risk involved may in itself be a key variable. Thus, the opportunity is provided to blend managerial judgment, gained through experience and training, with the appropriate decision concepts and techniques.

THE DIFFERENCES BETWEEN COMMERCIAL AND CONSUMER ACQUISITION

Purchasing is a difficult function to understand because almost everyone is familiar with another version, that of personal buying. It is easy for one to presume a familiarity or expertise with the acquisition function for this

FIGURE 1–2   Simplified One-Stage Decision Tree Showing a Supplier Selection Decision

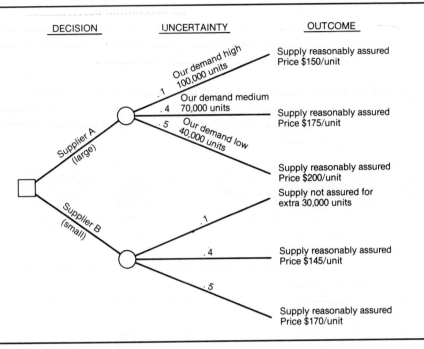

reason. A consumer point of view is characterized by a shopping basket philosophy. It assumes a retail type of marketing operation where there are many suppliers of relatively common items. Every customer buys on a current need basis and also is the final consumer of the product or service acquired. Some price variation may occur from supplier to supplier depending on what marketing strategy the supplier chooses to follow. The consumer has the freedom to choose the nature and quality of items required and to choose the appropriate supplier. With few exceptions the individual consumer has no power to influence the price, the method of marketing, or the manufacturer chosen by the supplier's management. The individual consumer's total business is a very small portion of the supplier's total sales.

Commercial materials management presents a totally different picture. The needs of most organizations are often specialized and the volumes of purchase tend to be large. The number of potential sources may be small and there may be few customers in the total market. Many organizations acting as buyers are larger than their suppliers and may play a multiplicity of roles with respect to their sources. Because large sums of money are involved, suppliers have a large stake in an individual customer and frequently will resort to many kinds of strategies to secure the wanted business. In such an environment, the right to award or withhold business represents real power. Special expertise is required to assure proper satisfaction of needs on the one hand and the appropriate systems and procedures on the other to assure a continually effective and acceptable performance.

Suppliers spend large sums annually to find ways and means of persuading their customers to buy. Purchasing strength needs to be pitted against this marketing strength to assure that the buying organization's needs of the future are adequately met. The materials function should be staffed with people who can deal on an equal basis with this marketing force. It is not sufficient in this environment to be only reactionary to outside pressures from suppliers. Foresight and a long-range planning outlook are vital so that future needs can be recognized and met on a planned basis.

CONTRIBUTION OF THE PURCHASING/MATERIALS MANAGEMENT FUNCTION

Performance of the materials function can be viewed in two contexts: *trouble avoidance* and *opportunistic.* The trouble avoidance context is the most familiar. Many people inside the organization are inconvenienced to varying degrees when the materials function does not meet with minimum expectations. Improper quality, wrong quantities, and late delivery may make life miserable for the ultimate user of the product or service. This is so basic and apparent that "no complaints" is assumed to be an indicator of good materials performance. The difficulty is that some users never expect anything more and hence may not receive anything more.

The second context is that of potential contribution to organizational objectives. At least eight major areas of potential contribution are possible: profit leverage, return on assets, information source, effect on efficiency, effect on competitive position, image, training provided, and management strategy and social policy.

Profit-Leverage Effect

If, through better purchasing, a firm saves $100,000 in the amounts paid to vendors for needed materials supplies and services, that $100,000 savings goes directly to the bottom line (before tax) account on its profit and loss (P&L) statement. If that same firm sells an additional $100,000 of product, the contribution to profit, assuming a 5 percent before-tax profit margin, would be only $5,000. Purchase dollars are high-powered dollars!

Perhaps an example, using a hypothetical manufacturer, would help:

Gross sales	$1,000,000
Purchases (assuming purchases account for 50 percent of the sales dollar)	500,000
Profit (assuming a before-tax profit margin of 5 percent)	50,000

Now, assume this firm were able to reduce its overall purchase cost by 10 percent through better management of the function. This would be a

FIGURE 1–3   Return-on-Assets Factors

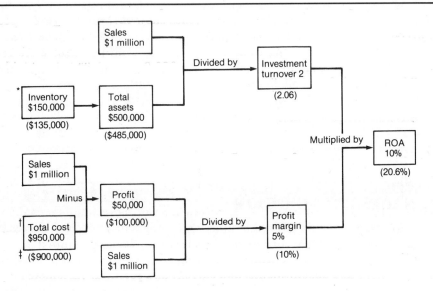

*Inventory is approximately 30 percent of total assets.
†Purchases account for half of total sales, or $500,000.
‡Figures in parentheses assume a 10 percent reduction in purchase costs.

$50,000 additional contribution to before-tax profits. To increase before-tax profits by $50,000 solely through increased sales would require an additional $1,000,000, or a doubling, of sales.

This is not to suggest that it would be easy to reduce overall purchase costs by 10 percent. In a firm which has given major attention to the purchasing function over the years it would be difficult, and perhaps impossible to do. But, in a firm which has neglected purchasing, it would be a realistic objective. Because of the profit-leverage effect of purchasing, large savings are possible relative to the effort that would be needed to increase sales by the much larger percentage necessary to generate the same effect on the P&L statement. Since, in many firms, sales already has received much more attention, purchasing may be the last untapped "profit producer."

Return-on-Assets Effect

Firms are increasingly more interested in return on assets (ROA) as a measure of performance. Figure 1–3 shows the standard ROA model, using the same figures as in the previous example, and assuming, realistically, that inventory accounts for 30 percent of total assets. If purchase costs were reduced by 10 percent, that would effect a 10 percent reduction in the inventory asset base. The numbers in the boxes show the initial figures used in arriving at the 10 percent ROA performance. The numbers below each box are the figures resulting from a 10 percent overall purchase price reduction, and the end product is a new ROA of 20.6 percent. This is a highly feasible objective for many firms.

Information Source

The contacts of the purchasing function in the marketplace provide a logical source of information for various functions within the organization. Primary examples include information about prices, availability of goods, new sources of supply, new products, and new technology, all of interest to many other parts of the organization. New marketing techniques and distribution systems used by suppliers may be of interest to the marketing group. News about major investments, mergers, acquisition candidates, international political and economic developments, pending bankruptcies, major promotions and appointments, and current and potential customers may be relevant to marketing, finance, research, and top management. Purchasing's unique position vis-à-vis the marketplace should provide a comprehensive listening post.

Effect on Efficiency

The effectiveness with which the purchasing function is performed will show up in other operating results. While the firm's accounting system may not be sophisticated enough to identify poor efficiency as having been caused by poor purchase decisions, that very often is the case. If purchasing selects a vendor who fails to deliver raw materials or parts which measure up to the agreed-on quality standards, this may result in a higher scrap rate or costly rework, requiring excessive direct labor expenditures. If the vendor does not meet the agreed-on delivery schedule, this may require a costly rescheduling of production, decreasing overall production efficiency, or in the worst case it will result in a shutdown of the production line—and fixed costs continue even though there is no output.

Effect on Competitive Position

A firm cannot be competitive unless it can deliver end products or services to its customers when they are wanted and at a price the customer feels is fair. If purchasing doesn't do its job, the firm will not have the required materials when needed and at a price which will keep end-product costs under control.

Some years ago, one of the major automobile producers decided to buy all its auto glass from one firm (a single source). Some months into the supply agreement, it became evident that the forthcoming labor-contract negotiations might result in a deadlock and a long strike. To protect themselves, the auto company built up a 90-day glass stockpile, even though the inventory carrying costs were high and they had problems finding the physical storage facilities for that much glass. They were right; there was a strike in the glass industry, but the union struck only the glass firm supplying that auto producer. The strike lasted 118 days and the auto producer had to shut down their production lines for over a month.

The auto producer had a large net financial loss that year, since that sales loss dropped them below their break-even point. The president explained to the stockholders that the glass strike cost them the sale of about 100,000 cars (a month's sales). Auto customers evidently were not willing to wait until the strike ended, and they "went across the street" and bought a car made by a competitor. The dealer can tell a customer, "Here's the car. Bring it back in a month and we'll put the hubcaps on for you," and he'll make the sale. But it's difficult to convince the customer to take the car now and bring it back later for the windshield! Actually, they probably lost closer to 500,000 future auto sales, because if a customer bought another maker's car, and liked the different make, this person probably went back to the new dealer for future purchases.

Effect on Image

The actions of the purchasing department influence directly the public relations and image of a company. If actual and potential vendors are not treated in a businesslike manner, they will form a poor opinion of the entire organization and will communicate this to other firms. This poor image will adversely affect the purchaser's ability to get new business and to find new and better vendors. Public confidence can be boosted by evidence of a sound policy and fair implementation.

Training Ground

The purchasing area is also an excellent training ground for new managers. The needs of the organization may be quickly grasped. Exposure to the pressure of decision making under uncertainty with potentially serious consequences allows for evaluation of the individual's ability and willingness to take risk and assume responsibility. Contacts with many people at various levels and a variety of functions may assist the individual in charting a career plan and will also be of value as the manager moves up the organization. Many organizations find it useful to include the purchasing area as part of a formal job rotation system for high potential employees.

Management Strategy and Social Policy

The materials function also can be used as a tool of management strategy and social policy. Does management wish to introduce and stimulate competition? Does it favor geographical representation, minority interest, and environmental and social concerns? For example, are domestic sources preferred? Will resources be spent on assisting minority suppliers? As part of an overall organization strategy, the materials function can contribute a great deal. Assurance of supply of vital materials or services in a time of general shortages can be a major competitive advantage. Similarly, access to a better quality or a lower priced product or service may represent a substantial gain. These strategic positions in the marketplace may be gained through active exploration of international and domestic markets, technology, innovative management systems, and the imaginative use of corporate resources in the materials area. Vertical integration and its companion decision of make or buy are ever present considerations in the management of materials.

The potential contribution to strategy is obvious. Achievement depends on both top executive awareness of this potential and the ability to marshall corporate resources to this end. At the same time, it is the responsibility of those charged with the management of the materials function to seek strategic opportunities in the environment and to draw top executive attention to them. This requires a thorough familiarity with organizational objectives, strategy, and long-term plans and the ability to influence these in the light of new information. Chapter 16 discusses both the potential purchasing contributions to business strategy *and* the major strategy areas within the purchasing function.

This is a capsule of the potential contributions of the function. It does not just happen, however. In some organizations the materials function is not management's prime concern. Continued lack of management interest and commitment can defeat the objectives of competent purchasing performance, causing a weak link in the total chain. The experience of many companies has shown that a relatively small amount of time and effort in the materials area will provide a substantial return on investment. This is an opportunity which should be brought to the attention of the key decision makers.

An effective materials function can and must be highly responsive to the users' needs in terms of quality, quantity, price, and delivery. It also can contribute to policy objectives as well as the overall public image of the organization. Those in the materials function cannot accomplish this without assistance and cooperation from suppliers, users, and others involved in the total process.

Progressive managers have recognized these potential contributions of the materials area and have taken the necessary steps to assure results. The most important single step in successful organizations has been the elevation to top executive status of the purchasing/materials manager. This, coupled with high-caliber staff and the appropriate authority and responsibility, has resulted in an exciting and fruitful realization of the potential of the materials function.

PROFESSIONALISM IN PURCHASING

Certainly the changes which have occurred over the past several decades have caused top management, in general, to recognize the importance of effective and efficient performance of the purchasing/materials management function. How has this changed the people who perform the purchasing function? How have they grown? While it is not possible to provide any specific single-number measure of this change, six of the indicators are:

New Assignments.   The profession and those persons performing in the activity have taken on several new responsibilities. A 1988 study, based on data collected from 297 major U.S. organizations, by the Center for Advanced Purchasing Studies found that the following functions had been *newly assigned* to purchasing since 1980 (percent of the organizations in which it was newly assigned): personnel travel, 14 percent; traffic-transportation, 13 percent; countertrade–offset planning/execution, 12 percent; and strategic planning, 9 percent. The functions in which purchasing had assumed an *increased role or responsibility* since 1980 were: strategic planning, 43 percent; providing economic forecasts-indicators, 41 percent; capital equipment buys, 37 percent; product development, 31 percent; new product evaluation, 26 percent; traffic-transportation, 23 percent; personnel travel, 16 percent; countertrade–offset planning/execution, 15 percent; and cash flow planning, 13 percent. The high percentages in traffic-transportation and personnel travel are a direct result of the transportation deregulation changes which now permit the application of established purchasing techniques to these buys. The activity in countertrade–offset planning/execution is a flow down of responsibilities necessitated by the increased dollar sales made by U.S. firms into foreign markets. The increased and new roles in strategic planning, economic forecasting, capital equipment buys, product development and evaluation, and cash flow planning are a result of the increasing long-term orientation of purchasing as a major contributor to the overall mission of the organization.[8]

Education.   Although there are no universal educational requirements for entry-level jobs, most large organizations require a college degree

---

[8]Harold E. Fearon, *Purchasing Organizational Relationships* (Tempe, Ariz.: Center for Advanced Purchasing Studies/National Association of Purchasing Management, 1988), pp. 15–16.

in business administration or management.[9] Several major educational institutions, such as Arizona State University, Bowling Green State University, Florida State University, George Washington University, Miami University, and Michigan State University, now offer an undergraduate major in Purchasing/Materials Management (or Materials/Logistics) as part of the B.S. in Business Administration degree. In addition many schools offer some coursework in purchasing, for either full- or part-time students.[10]

A 1987 survey by *Purchasing* found that 59 percent had a bachelor's degree (for persons with the title of vice president or director of purchasing, 73 percent held a B.S. degree). Fifty-three percent of those holding a B.S. degree majored in business. Twenty-two percent of the B.S. degree holders also had completed an advanced degree.[11] In the 1988 study by the Center for Advanced Purchasing Studies, 94 percent of the chief purchasing officers in the 295 organizations that supplied data were college graduates, and 39 percent held an advanced degree in addition to the bachelor's degree. Fifty-five percent of the B.S. degree holders majored in business and 19 percent in engineering.[12]

College Recruitment.   Many of the major companies now look to the campus for their input of junior-level personnel into the purchasing/materials management department. This is based on the belief that if persons recruited today will be expected to move into purchasing management responsibilities five years from now, it is essential to start out with the best possible personnel raw material. Their experience has been that this source of entry-level personnel has the highest probability of providing well-rounded, aggressive, successful new hires.

Training Programs.   The better managed firms now provide continuing education/training for their purchasing professionals. This training is organized on a formal, in-house seminar basis in which a given individual may participate in a full-week training session over each of several years, or the firm may use a planned combination of seminars/courses offered by universities, associations, or private training organizations. This purchasing training then is supplemented by various general management courses and seminars.

Salary Levels.   While salaries vary widely for purchasing personnel,

---

[9]"Purchasing Agents," *Occupational Outlook Handbook,* 1982–83 edition (Washington, D.C.: U.S. Department of Labor, Bulletin 2200), p. 46.

[10]Caroline Reich, "It's Back to School for Purchasing Pros," *Purchasing World,* September 1987, pp. 59–62.

[11]Somerby Dowst, "Profile of the Purchasing Pro: 1987," *Purchasing,* October 22, 1987, p. 64.

[12]Fearon, *Purchasing Organizational Relationships,* p. 9.

since duties and responsibilities vary from company to company, some rough indications of compensation levels can be obtained from the annual salary surveys done by *Purchasing* and *Purchasing World* magazines.

The 1986 salary survey by *Purchasing,* using a survey sample of 4,718, found an average salary of $35,700, which was up $2,100 from the 1985 average. Thirty-one percent said they receive an annual bonus (which was included in the annual compensation figure).[13] The 1986 survey by *Purchasing World,* using data from 6,414 positions in 1,069 firms, found that the "average" purchasing manager was 39 years old, had a bachelor's degree in business, had 11 years of experience in purchasing, and earned $51,000 a year. A 6.8 percent raise was received in 1986. Nonsalary compensation accounted for 19 percent of total compensation.[14] Their 1983 survey found "the average income of $34,000" was some $9,000 higher than in 1981.[15] Obviously, purchasing salaries have risen markedly over the past several years, more than keeping pace with inflation.

The *Purchasing World* survey also presented median salaries in 1986, by title: vice president, purchasing, $88,600; vice president, materials, $103,800; purchasing director, $72,500; materials director, $73,700; purchasing manager, $54,000; materials manager, $61,300; purchasing agent, $44,200; senior buyer, $40,700; buyer, $34,000; junior buyer, $25,700; expediter, $25,200; and trainee, $22,800.[16] Over the past several years, compensation levels have gone up, to reflect greater responsibilities.

Professional Associations.   As any profession matures, its professional associations emerge as focal points for efforts to advance professional practice and conduct. In the United States, the major professional association is the National Association of Purchasing Management, Inc., founded in 1915 as the National Association of Purchasing Agents (NAPM).[17] NAPM is organized as an educational and research association; it has some 27,000 members, who belong to NAPM through its over 161 local purchasing management associations.

In addition to regional and national conferences, NAPM sponsors seminars for purchasing people. It publishes a variety of books and monographs and the leading scholarly journal in the field, *Journal of Purchasing and Materials Management,* which it began in 1965. Since the early 1930s NAPM has conducted the monthly "NAPM Report on Business," which is

---

[13]Somerby Dowst, C.P.M., "Purchasing's 1986 Salary Survey," *Purchasing,* December 11, 1986, pp. 59–61.

[14]Robert R. Blumel, "Pull Your Pay Stub and See How You're Faring," *Purchasing World,* December 1986, pp. 33–39.

[15]"Profile of the Purchasing Professional—1983," *Purchasing World,* November 1983, p. 54.

[16]Blumel, *Purchasing World,* p. 34.

[17]The address of the National Association of Purchasing Management is 2055 East Centennial Circle, P.O. Box 22160, Tempe, Ariz., 85282–0960.

one of the best recognized current barometers of business activity. The survey results normally appear the first Monday of each month on the front page of *The Wall Street Journal.* Additionally, it works with colleges and universities to encourage and support the teaching of purchasing and related subjects and provides financial grants to support faculty and graduate student research.

In 1974 the National Association of Purchasing Management initiated the Certified Purchasing Manager (C.P.M.) program, which tests purchasing people. On successful completion of the program it certifies by award of the C.P.M. designation that the recipient has met the established knowledge, education, and experience standards. Currently over 14,000 people have earned the C.P.M. designation, by passing four written examinations, completing specific education and seminar requirements, and meeting an experience requirement. To retain the C.P.M., evidence of additional education must be provided every five years (recertification). Of the 14,000 people who have earned the C.P.M., it is estimated that between 11 to 12,000 now hold a valid C.P.M. The most recent major innovative professional activity of the National Association of Purchasing Management was the establishment of a Center for Advanced Purchasing Studies (CAPS) in late 1986 as a national affiliation agreement between NAPM and the College of Business at Arizona State University.[18] The center has three major goals to be accomplished through its research program: (1) to improve purchasing effectiveness and efficiency, (2) to improve overall purchasing capability, and (3) to increase the competitiveness of U.S. companies in a global economy. The initial research projects include the purchasing process in the service, government, institutional, retail/trade/purchasing; and world-class purchasing organizations and practices.

In Canada, the professional association is the Purchasing Management Association of Canada (PMAC), formed in 1919.[19] Its membership of approximately 6,000 is organized in some 42 districts from coast to coast. Its primary objective is education, and in addition to sponsoring national and regional conferences, it has designed and offers a series of purchasing and purchasing management seminars, some by correspondence. It also sponsors the Professional Purchaser (P.P.) program, which awards the P.P. diploma on successful completion of a specified series of seminars and courses and an oral examination before the PMAC Board of Examiners. The P.P. program was started in 1963; some 1,100 purchasing professionals have earned the P.P. designation.

In addition to NAPM and PMAC, there are several other professional

---

[18]The address of the Center for Advanced Purchasing Studies is the Arizona State University Research Park, P.O. Box 22160, Tempe, Ariz., 85282–0960.

[19]The address of the Purchasing Management Association of Canada is 2 Carlton Street, Suite 815, Toronto, Ontario, Canada M5B 1J3.

purchasing associations, such as the National Institute of Governmental Purchasing (NIGP), National Association of State Purchasing Officials (NASPO), and the National Association of Hospital Purchasing Management. Several of these associations offer their own certification program. Most industrialized countries have their own professional purchasing association, for example, Institute of Purchasing and Supply Management (Australia), Institute of Purchasing and Supply (Great Britain), Confederación Mexicana de Asociaciones de Ejecutivos de Compras y Abastecimiento (Mexico), and Japan Materials Management Association. These national associations are loosely organized into the International Federation of Purchasing and Materials Management (IFPMM), which has as its objective the fostering of cooperation, education, and research in purchasing on a worldwide basis among the 39 member national associations.[20] As of 1987 the IFPMM was investigating the possibility of beginning a program to provide international certification of purchasing professionals around the world who meet a prescribed standard.[21] Purchasing truly has become an internationally recognized profession.

QUESTIONS FOR REVIEW AND DISCUSSION

1. "In the long term, the success of any organization depends on its ability to create and maintain a customer." Do you agree? What does this have to do with purchasing and materials management?

2. Differentiate between purchasing, procurement, materials management, and logistics.

3. What is the profit-leverage effect of purchasing? Is it the same in all organizations?

4. How does purchasing and materials management affect return on assets (ROA)? In what specific ways could you improve ROA through purchasing/materials management?

5. How has the purchasing function changed over the last several years? What factors have influenced this evolution? How will it change over the next 10 years?

6. What are the various professional associations in purchasing trying to accomplish?

7. "Purchasing is not profit making; instead, it is profit taking since it spends organizational resources." Do you agree?

---

[20]Michael Taylor, "The Nature and Purposes of the IFPMM," *Journal of Purchasing and Materials Management*, Summer 1984, pp. 2–6.

[21]The address of the IFPMM as of 1988 was P.O. Box 87, CH–5001, Aarau, Switzerland.

8. Is purchasing a profession? If not, why not? If yes, how will the profession, and the people practicing it, change over the next decade?

REFERENCES

Burt, David N. *Proactive Procurement: The Key to Increased Profits, Productivity, and Quality.* Englewood Cliffs, N.J.: Prentice-Hall, 1984.

Cavinato, Joseph L. *Purchasing and Materials Management.* St. Paul, Minn.: West Publishing, 1984.

Dobler, Donald W.; Lamar Lee, Jr.; and David N. Burt. *Purchasing and Materials Management.* 4th ed. New York: McGraw-Hill, 1984.

Farrell, Paul V., coordinating editor. *Aljian's Purchasing Handbook.* 4th ed. New York: McGraw-Hill, 1982.

Heinritz, Stuart F.; Paul V. Farrell; and Clifton L. Smith. *Purchasing: Principles and Applications.* 7th ed. Englewood Cliffs, N.J.: Prentice-Hall, 1986.

Leenders, Michiel R., and David L. Blenkhorn. *Reverse Marketing.* New York: The Free Press, 1988.

Shealy, Robert. "The Purchasing Job in Different Types of Businesses." *Journal of Purchasing and Materials Management,* Winter 1985.

Taylor, Michael. "The Nature and Purposes of the IFPMM." *Journal of Purchasing and Materials Management,* Summer 1984.

Zenz, Gary J. *Purchasing and the Management of Materials.* 6th ed. New York: John Wiley & Sons, 1987.

Case 1–1

LDT CORPORATION

In early April, Jim Smith, purchasing manager at LDT, reviewed his vendor files on Olson Steel, the current supplier of all LDT's raw steel. Although the past relationship between the two firms was good, a recent quotation by a competitive steel company had come in at a substantially lower price. Top management at LDT was eagerly awaiting Jim's recommendation regarding the choice of a steel supplier.

LDT Corporation was a privately owned business with sales of $15 million. The product line consisted of dump trucks and other industrial vehicles and the total employee complement was 180.

This case was written by Leanne C. Nelson during the 1987 Case Writing Workshop.

Case Material of the School of Business Administration is prepared as a basis for classroom discussion.

Purchasing

The purchasing function was considered a key success factor in the running of the business since 54 percent of the total cost of production consisted of purchased goods. In particular, the purchasing of raw steel was considered critical and was monitored closely. The dollar value of steel purchased was just over $1 million, and, currently, inventory of raw steel valued at near $250,000 was recorded on the company's books.

A partial organization chart depicting the reporting relationships within the purchasing department is shown below. Conflicting goals between some of these people existed. The vice president, operations was concerned with keeping price and inventory levels down, whereas the purchasing manager, who was responsible for ensuring inventory was in stock as needed, was more concerned over reliable sourcing and maintenance of strong vendor/supplier relations.

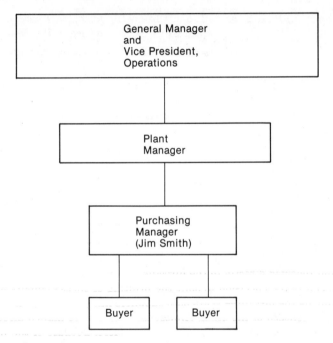

The Olson Contract

For the past eight years, LDT had been purchasing raw steel exclusively from Olson Steel Corp. Over the years, Olson had worked with LDT to develop steels for special applications. Recently however, LDT had some concerns with regard to their steel supplier:

1. Olson was producing at capacity. Since they had more orders than available production time, allocation amongst customers was common. Because LDT's annual steel volumes only represented one-half day's production for Olson, concern was raised as to whether LDT's supply was guaranteed.

2. Despite large order backlogs, Olson was experiencing financial difficulty.

3. Olson's labor contract expired the end of July and a strike, which could potentially cut off LDT's steel supply, was a distinct possibility.

The Teral Alternative

Teral, a small, relatively unknown, Western-based steel producer, represented an alternative supply source for LDT. Teral had recently quoted a price on the LDT steel contract representing a $400–$500 savings off the bottom line on the sale of a $20,000 piece of machinery. Additionally, LDT would likely become a preferred customer since their volume would comprise a larger part of Teral's total sales than they represented to Olson.

Despite these facts, LDT management was nervous about the reliability of such a young company and had to consider the fact that Teral could only supply 90 percent of their steel needs. Although negotiation on specific contract details would have to wait until Teral steel passed certain testing procedures, Jim Smith wondered what the effect of such negotiations would have on relations.

The thought of dual suppliers was appealing; however, the way to get necessary discounts in the steel purchasing procedure was strictly through volume, and sourcing steel from both companies was thus impractical. Selecting and weighting the criteria for decision making became Jim Smith's immediate task.

Case 1–2

THE TRAGA BANK

The Traga Bank, a large Western financial institution, was well known for its active promotional efforts to attract consumer deposits. The bank provided standard personalized consumer checks free of charge, a substantial printing order, totaling about $4 million per year. Betty Small was a purchasing agent in charge of all printing for Traga and reported directly to the director of purchasing.

It had been Betty's decision to split the printing of checks equally among two suppliers. During the last three years both suppliers had provided quick and quality service, a vital concern of the bank. Almost all checks were mailed directly to the consumer's home or business address by the suppliers. Because of the importance of check printing, Betty had requested a special cost analysis study a year ago, with the cooperation of both suppliers. The conclusion of this study had been that both suppliers were receiving an adequate profit margin, were efficient and cost conscious, and that the price structure was fair.

Two weeks ago, Betty received an unsolicited, unofficial quotation from a third printing supplier, Killoran, Inc., at a price 10 percent below that of the current sources. Betty believed that Killoran was underbidding to gain part of the check printing business. This in turn would give Killoran access to Traga's customers' names. Betty suspected that Killoran might then try to pursue these customers more actively than the current two suppliers to sell special "scenic checks" which customers paid for themselves.

Betty was not sure how she should react and wondered what action to take now.

CHAPTER 2

Objectives and Organization for Effective Purchasing and Materials Management

Every organization in both the public and private sector is in varying degrees dependent on materials and services supplied by other organizations. Even the smallest office needs space, heat, light, power, communication and office equipment, furniture, stationery, and miscellaneous supplies to carry on its functions. No organization is self-sufficient. Purchasing is, therefore, one of the basic, common functions of every organization. Structuring the purchasing/materials management function to obtain effective contribution to objectives is one of the challenges of management.

OBJECTIVES OF PURCHASING/MATERIALS MANAGEMENT

The standard statement of the overall objectives of the purchasing function is that it should obtain the *right materials* (meeting quality requirements), in the *right quantity*, for delivery at the *right time* and *right place*, from the *right source* (a vendor who is reliable and will meet its commitments in a timely fashion), with the *right service* (both before and after the sale), and at the *right price.* The purchasing decision-maker might be likened to a juggler, attempting to keep several balls in the air at the same time, for the purchaser must achieve several goals simultaneously—the seven *rights* previously listed. It is not efficient to buy at the lowest price, if the goods delivered are unsatisfactory from a quality/performance standpoint, or if they arrive two weeks behind schedule, causing a shutdown of a production line. On the other hand, the *right* price may be a much higher than normal price if the item in question is an emergency requirement on which the buyer cannot afford the luxury of adhering to the normal lead time. The purchasing-decision-maker attempts to balance out the often conflicting objectives and makes trade-offs to obtain the optimum mix of these seven rights.

A more specific statement of the overall goals of purchasing would include the following nine items:

1. *Provide an uninterrupted flow of materials, supplies, and services required to operate the organization.* Stockouts of raw materials and production parts would shut down an operation and be extremely costly in terms of lost production, escalation of operating costs due to fixed costs, and inability to satisfy delivery promises to customers. For example, (1) an automobile producer cannot complete the car without the purchased tires; (2) an airline cannot keep its planes flying on schedule without purchased fuel; and (3) a hospital cannot perform surgery without purchased IV (intravenous) solutions.

2. *Keep inventory investment and loss at a minimum.* One way to assure an uninterrupted material flow is to keep large inventory banks. But inventory assets require use of capital which cannot be invested elsewhere; the cost of carrying inventory may be 20 to 36 percent of value per year. If purchasing can support operations with an inventory investment of $10 million instead of $20 million, at an annual inventory carrying cost of 30 percent, the $10 million reduction in inventory represents a saving of $3 million.

3. *Maintain adequate quality standards.* To produce the desired product or service, a certain quality level is required for each material input; otherwise the end product or service will not meet expectations or will result in higher-than-acceptable production costs. The internal cost to correct a substandard-quality material input can be huge. For example, an unsatisfactory spring assembled into the braking system of a diesel locomotive costs only 93 cents, but if the defective spring shows up when the locomotive is in service, the replacement cost is in the thousands of dollars, caused by teardown required to replace the spring, the lost revenue to the railroad because the locomotive is not in service, and the possible loss of locomotive reorders. The need to improve quality to compete effectively on a worldwide basis has caused renewed attention to purchasing's quality objective.

4. *Find or develop competent vendors.* In the final analysis, the success of the purchasing department depends on its skill in locating or developing vendors, analyzing vendor capabilities, and then selecting the appropriate vendor. Only if the final selection results in vendors who are both responsive and responsible will the firm obtain the items it needs at the lowest ultimate cost. For example, if the purchase of a complex computer system is made from a vendor who later goes out of business and is not able to perform the long-term maintenance, modification, and updating of the system, the initial favorable price turns out to be a very high price, due to the vendor's inability to make good on the original commitment.

5. *Standardize, where possible, the items bought.* The best item possible, from an overall company viewpoint, for the intended application should be bought. If purchasing can buy a quantity of one item to do the job that two or three different items previously did, the organization may gain efficiency advantages through a lower initial price resulting from a quantity discount, lower total inventory investment without lowering service levels, reduced costs of personnel training and maintenance costs in the use of equipment, and increased competition among suppliers.

6. *Purchase required items and services at lowest ultimate price.* The purchasing activity in the typical organization consumes the largest share of that organization's dollar resources. In addition, the profit-leverage effect of the purchasing activity, as discussed in the previous chapter, can be very significant. While the term *price buyer* has a derogatory connotation, suggesting that the only factor purchasing considers is price, the purchasing department should strive to obtain needed items and services at the lowest possible price, assuming that the quality, delivery, and service requirements also are satisfied.

7. *Improve the organization's competitive position.* An organization will be competitive only if it can control costs in order to protect profit margins. Purchase costs are the largest single element in the operation of many organizations. Additionally, product design and manufacturing methods changes are needed to keep pace with changing technology and production environments; the purchasing department can supply information to product design and manufacturing engineering on new products available and what changes are occurring and are likely to occur in production technology. Finally, the purchasing department is responsible for assuring the smooth flow of materials necessary to enable the production of products and provision of services as required to meet delivery commitments to customers; in the long run, the success of any organization is dependent on its ability to create and maintain a customer. Chapter 16 discusses the potential contributions of purchasing to the overall strategy of an organization and specific internal purchasing strategies for strengthening an organization's competitive position.

8. *Achieve harmonious, productive working relationships with other departments within the organization.* Purchasing actions cannot be effectively accomplished solely by the efforts of the purchasing department; cooperation with other departments and individuals within the firm is vital to success. For example, the using departments and production control must provide information on material requirements in a timely fashion if purchasing is to have the lead time needed to locate competent vendors and make advantageous purchase agreements. Engineering and production must be willing to consider the

possible economic advantages of using substitute materials and different vendors. Purchasing must work closely with quality control in determining inspection procedures for incoming materials, in communicating to vendors the changes needed in the event that quality problems are found, and assisting in evaluating the performance of current vendors. Accounting must pay vendors in a timely fashion, to take advantage of quantity discounts and maintain good long-term vendor relations. If there is a problem with information flow from purchasing, receiving, or incoming inspection which is necessary for making payment to vendors, purchasing is responsible for correcting the problem since the vendor does not deal directly with accounting, receiving, or incoming inspection. Instead, the vendor deals with purchasing and expects to be paid on schedule.

9. *Accomplish the purchasing objectives at the lowest possible level of administrative costs.* It takes resources to operate the purchasing department: salaries, telephone and postage expense, supplies, travel costs, computer costs, and accompanying overhead. If purchasing procedures are not efficient, purchasing administrative cost will be excessive. The objectives of purchasing should be achieved as efficiently and economically as possible, which requires that the purchasing manager continually review the operation to assure that it is cost effective. If the firm is not realizing its purchasing objectives due to inadequate analysis and planning, perhaps additional personnel are needed. But the firm should be continually alert to improvements possible in purchasing methods, procedures and techniques. Perhaps unneeded steps in processing purchasing paperwork could be eliminated; perhaps the computer could be used to make the storage and recall of necessary data more efficient.

ORGANIZATION FOR PURCHASING/MATERIALS MANAGEMENT

The process of building effective organizations involves many activities, but none are more important at the outset than the relationship between strategies, structures, and delegation. Strategies, once devised, must be carried out in some structural framework; and no matter what organizational design is chosen, delegation takes place within it. Whether the organization structure is based on building blocks, information flows, or people-oriented concepts is immaterial; what really matters is that work must be assigned and executed in accordance with strategic plans and organizational goals. It follows logically that organizational planning and delegation procedures are important segments of the integration of strategic goals and organizational designs.

What makes the task of organizing the materials function particularly difficult is that not only corporate strategy and internal needs have to be considered but the outside world as well. Both the purchasing and traffic functions have daily contact with the marketplace and have to be responsive to market developments. If suppliers place high emphasis on marketing, and staff the area with well-qualified, aggressive, and imaginative personnel with high status, buying organizations must find a suitable way to counterbalance this outside force.

Purchasing Department Responsibilities

As the complexity of organizations increased in the 1980s, due to growth, acquisitions, and mergers, supply lines became more uncertain, foreign buying activity heated up, purchased material quality received heightened attention, and emphasis on obtaining the profit leverage of purchasing as a means of maintaining or increasing the organization's competitive position intensified. Purchasing departments have assumed larger, and different, responsibilities.

An indication of the magnitude of change over the last 20 years is shown by the results of a 1983 *Purchasing World* survey:

98 percent have primary responsibility for developing new supply sources (up from 68 percent in 1963).

89 percent manage value analysis activities (compared to 40 percent in 1963).

87 percent are responsible for the make-or-buy decision (only 18 percent in 1963).

86 percent select the in-bound transportation carrier (up from 64 percent in 1963).

81 percent now control inventories (47 percent in 1963).[1]

The 1988 *Purchasing Organizational Relationships* study done by the Center for Advanced Purchasing Studies (CAPS) shows that the specific purchasing related activities that report to the purchasing function vary widely between different organizations. The percent of the 297 organizations in which each of the following functions reports to the purchasing departments was:[2]

---

[1]Richard L. Dunn, "You're Not Getting Older, You're Getting Better," *Purchasing World*, June 1983, p. 138.

[2]Harold E. Fearon, *Purchasing Organizational Relationships* (Tempe, Ariz. Center for Advanced Purchasing Studies/National Association of Purchasing Management, 1988), p. 14.

Scrap/surplus disposal	57%	Outbound traffic	32%
Inbound traffic	41	Receiving	26
Inventory control	37	Incoming inspection	16
Warehousing or stores	34		

TABLE 2–1   Activity Areas Newly Assigned, and Activity Areas in Which Purchasing Has Assumed a New Role/Responsibility since 1980 (292 responding organizations)

	Percent of Organizations in Which	
Activity Area	*Newly Assigned*	*Increased Role/ Responsibility*
Strategic planning	9%	43%
Product development	3	31
Traffic, transportation	13	23
New product evaluation	4	26
Capital equipment buys	7	37
Personnel travel	14	16
Marketing planning	1	9
Providing economic forecasts or indicators	6	41
Commodity futures trading	3	6
Cash flow planning	4	13
Countertrade–offset planning/execution	12	15

In addition, the CAPS study examined the changes in purchasing responsibilities which have taken place since 1980. Table 2–1 shows the trends that are taking place in the evolution of the purchasing function. The 292 responding organizations (most were very large in terms of 1986 sales revenues: 81 had sales of under $500 million, 44 were in the $500 million to $1 billion category, 108 had sales of $1.1 to $5 billion, 31 from $5.1 to $10 billion, and 28 had sales of over $10 billion) indicated both activity areas newly assigned (since 1980) to purchasing, and activity areas in which purchasing has assumed an increased role or responsibility since 1980.[3]

With transport deregulation (which began in 1977) purchasing has assumed a new responsibility in many organizations for buying personnel travel services for company employees and for freight services. Countertrade, often thought to be solely a marketing activity, now involves purchasing in many organizations as buybacks became a way of life in selling outside the United States. The increased role of purchasing in strategic

---

[3]*Ibid.,* pp. 15–16.

planning, providing economic forecasts, capital equipment buys, and product development recognizes the movement to a top-level corporate support position, as opposed to only a material-acquisition-and-flow interest. This implies that the people in purchasing must have broader abilities and an understanding of the overall mission and functioning of the organization.

Centralization versus Decentralization

If a firm approaches purchasing on a _decentralized_ basis, individual department managers will handle their own purchasing. The advantage to this approach is that the user probably knows departmental needs better than anyone else. Also, it may be faster, since when a department needs something, the manager simply picks up the phone and orders it.

However, the advantages of _centralized purchasing_ are so great in comparison with decentralized purchasing that almost all but the smallest of firms are centralized. In centralized purchasing, a separate individual or department is established and given authority to make all (except, perhaps, the very unusual buy, such as a new company aircraft) purchases. The advantages to be gained from centralized purchasing are:

1. It is easier to standardize the items bought if purchasing decisions go through one central control point.

2. It cuts down on administrative duplication. Instead of each department head writing a separate PO for lightbulbs, the purchasing department writes only one PO for the firm's total requirement. More than likely, purchasing will enter into an annual contract, providing for pricing based on the organization's total requirements for the entire year (or a multiyear agreement).

3. By combining requirements from several departments, purchasing can go to a vendor and discuss an order quantity that is large enough to really get the vendor's interest. This is called _clout,_ and often the purchasing department can persuade the vendor to give concessions, such as faster delivery or a quantity discount. There also may be freight savings, because shipment now can be made in carload quantities.

4. In periods of materials shortage, one department does not compete with another department for the available supply and by this action drive up the price.

5. It is administratively more efficient for vendors, since they need not call on several people within the company. Instead, they "make their pitch" to the purchasing manager.

6. It provides better control over purchase commitments. Since a large percent of a firm's cash outflow goes for material purchases, a central control point is needed to monitor the aggregate commitment amount at any specific point in time. Also, purchasing decisions about

placement of orders with vendors are sensitive in that the opportunity for kickbacks and bribery is great if POs are issued to unscrupulous vendors. It is easier to prevent such illegal or unethical practices if all decisions on the flow of purchase commitments go through one central "funnel," for the spotlight can be focused on the purchasing department instead of attempting to monitor purchase decisions that are scattered throughout the various departments of the firm.

7. It enables the development of specialization and expertise in purchasing decisions and is a better use of time. If a department head acts as the purchasing agent, the time spent on purchasing probably could better be used in managing the department. Additionally, the department manager will not spend enough time in purchasing to develop any real expertise. A full-time buyer, who can devote undivided attention to purchasing, will rapidly develop expert knowledge of purchasing techniques, sources of supply, available and new materials and manufacturing processes, markets, and prices. This *development of expertise is the primary reason why almost all firms have gone to centralization of the purchasing function.*

If the contention that purchasing is a major function holds, then it must be recognized in its organization structure. There can be no more justification for investing the authority to make purchases in a dozen or more individuals in a company than there is for diffusing the responsibility for production or sales or finance among a similar number of persons. The manager's responsibilities may be divided and apportioned among subofficials and departments, but the functional responsibility and authority of any department head should be definitely recognized. Moreover, functionalization implies that all the responsibilities reasonably involved in the purchasing function must be given to the purchasing officer as a major official. It is not sufficient to make the purchasing officer's sole responsibility the placing of orders as a matter of clerical routine. There should be a clear and definite understanding of the officer's responsibilities and authority. The purchasing officer must be given adequate assistance and must have the backing of executive management.

The difficulty, of course, is in determining exactly what are the purchasing officer's responsibilities and in defining the officer's authority. Certain duties are, for example, to interview all salespeople before they call on other members of the company personnel, to see that the goods purchased conform with the requirements or specifications, to select the source from which the purchase is to be made, to conduct all intermediate negotiations between the vendor and the buyer, and to consummate the purchase by actually placing the order. Additional responsibilities and duties may depend largely on circumstances. The essential principle is that there are certain universally recognized duties pertinent to this function and that these duties should be definitely placed in a separate department coordinate in status with the other major departments of business.

Where purchasing is organized under a competent director and where full cooperation with other departments is enjoyed, definite advantages may and do follow. Responsibility is placed on officials who have the interest and the skill to do the work properly and whose primary concern is in the performance of this special task. It aids in fixing responsibility and in measuring the consequences of any given purchasing policy. It permits setting up uniform policies for vendor relationships. It facilitates prescribing procedures, records and routine, and also expedites inspection and approval of materials and payment. It encourages market analysis, study of price trends, and analysis of vendor's production costs, with the result that purchases are made under the most favorable conditions and at the most favorable times. It promotes economy by consolidating requirements and by setting up material standards for inventories. Through searching for substitute materials and materials exactly suited to the requirements demanded, it encourages cost reduction without impairing the quality of the product.

SPECIALIZATION WITHIN THE PURCHASING FUNCTION

Within the purchasing department itself, the overall purchasing function often is organized on the basis of further specialization and the development of expertise which results from specialization. Obviously, in a small firm, where there is a one-person purchasing department, no specialization is possible and the one person must be a "jack of all trades"—a difficult assignment. But in the larger purchasing organization, the usual functional breakout identifies the four specialized activities shown in Figure 2–1.

Buying and Negotiation.   These personnel locate potential vendors, analyze vendor capabilities, select vendors, and determine prices, terms, and conditions of the agreements made with vendors. This activity normally is further specialized by type of commodity to be purchased; that is, raw materials (which may be further specialized); fuels; capital equipment; office equipment and supplies; and maintenance, repair, and operating (MRO) supplies. Figure 2–2 presents typical job descriptions for a buyer and an expediter.

A variation of this is project buying, where the specialization of buying and negotiation is based on specific end products or projects, because of the supposed advantage of the buyer concentrating on and becoming intimately familiar with all aspects of the project from beginning to end. At the completion of the project, the buyer then would be reassigned to another project. Project buying might be used in the purchasing organization of a large general contractor, where each construction job and the purchasing for that job is set up with its own self-contained, temporary organization.

FIGURE 2–1   Organization Structure of a Typical Large Purchasing
Department

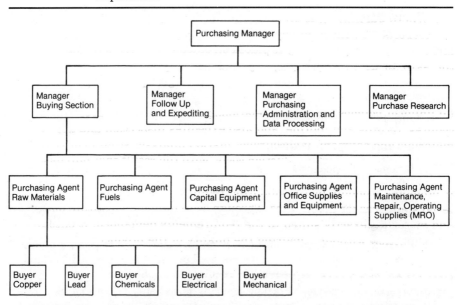

Follow Up and Expediting. This group takes the purchase agreement and keeps track of how the vendor is doing in meeting its delivery and quality commitments, so as to avoid any disruptive surprises. If problems develop, this group pressures and assists the vendor to resolve them. (See Figure 2–3.)

Administration. This group handles the physical preparation and routing of the formal purchase documents, keeps the necessary data required to operate the department, and prepares those periodic reports needed by top management and materials personnel. Operation of the integrated materials computer data system, if in use, will be handled by these personnel.

Purchase Research. This individual or group works on special projects relating to the collection, classification, and analysis of data needed to make better purchasing decisions. Studies on use of alternate materials, price and supply forecasts, analysis of what it should cost an efficient vendor to produce and deliver an item, or studies to develop a more effective system of rating vendor performance are the types of special studies done.

PURCHASING PREROGATIVES

The purchasing department must have four key prerogatives, if it is to meet the objectives of good purchasing:

FIGURE 2–2   Buyer Job Description

Job Summary:

Responsible for meeting purchasing needs in an assigned area of commodities and/or services, including planning, requisition review, supplier selection, order placement, and follow up.

Dimensions:

Volume of annual purchases—$10 million

Nature and Scope of Position:

1. Becomes knowledgeable of specific company unit, divisional unit, or specific commodity group of material, service, and transportation requirements, their uses and application, their sources of supply and availability, and the price, quality, vendor performance, and market conditions of specified requirements.
2. Becomes knowledgeable about laws and regulations that pertain to the procurement of these requirements as they pertain to the delivery and usage of the specified item at the required location of use.
3. Becomes knowledgeable about company purchasing policy and local requisition and purchasing procedures and recognizes, coordinates, and communicates required commodities which more economically can and should be geographically centrally purchased.
4. Reviews all received requisitions of required material and services for completeness, description, appropriate approval, delivery date, and designated receipt point.
5. Reviews all confirmed commitments received with respect to the overall value to the company as to delivery, price, payment terms, and vendor selection quality, so as to report any loss of value to the company both to purchasing and management.
6. Communicates purchasing policies and requisition procedures to all requisitioners and potential requisitioners in the designated area of responsibility.
7. Establishes and maintains rapport and business association with suppliers and appropriate salesmen, and directs and procures vendor technical and operating expertise as required to appropriate internal personnel.
8. Negotiates, places orders, and enters into contracts for procurement as necessary for required materials and services to ensure timely delivery with maximum company benefit.

Right to Select the Vendor. Purchasing should be the expert in knowing who has the capability to produce needed items and how to analyze

FIGURE 2-2 *(concluded)*

---

9. Monitors open transactions through completion and closing and informs as necessary, vendor, requisitioners, appropriate management, geographically central purchasing personnel on order status and delivery. Provides as necessary, reports summarizing selected purchasing activities relating to the given area of buying responsibility.

10. Monitors designated item inventory for adherence to appropriate approved levels and disposes of surplus material, junk, or other excess material by transfer, usage, or sale.

11. Continually monitors, via day-to-day application, the purchasing procedures for compliance. Also recommends changes as appropriate to corporate purchasing management in policies and procedures that enhance the activity of purchasing or enhance the accomplishment of the core business.

12/1/87

---

vendor reliability. If someone else selects the vendor, purchasing then is in a sole source situation and can do little to bargain for an advantageous purchase agreement.

Right to Use Whichever Pricing Method Is Appropriate. This also includes determining the price and terms of the agreement. This is one of the main expertise areas of purchasing; it must have room to maneuver if it is to achieve lowest ultimate price.

Right to Question the Specifications. Purchasing often can suggest substitute or alternate items which will do the same job and it has the responsibility of bringing these items to the attention of the requisitioner. The final decision on accepting a substitute is made by the user.

Right to Control All Contacts with Potential Vendors. Communication with potential vendors must flow through purchasing. If users contact vendors directly, this encourages *back door selling,* in which a potential vendor will influence the specifications so that it will be in a sole source situation. Or the requisitioner will make commitments to vendors which prevent purchasing from arriving at agreements that will give the buying firm the lowest ultimate price. If vendor technical personnel need to talk directly with engineering or operating personnel in the buyer's firm, purchasing will arrange for such discussions and monitor their outcome.

These purchasing prerogatives should be established as matters of company policy, approved by the chief executive officer.

FIGURE 2–3   Expediter Job Description

Job Summary

Under general supervision monitors, reports, and takes authorized corrective action to coordinate the timely delivery of purchased parts and materials. May provide general administrative support to the purchasing department as required.

Minimum Qualification

Educational: Must be able to communicate verbally and in writing and possess basic arithmetic skills normally associated with high school training.

Experience: Two years in production control, material control, or equivalent combination of training and closely related administrative experience.

Special qualifications:

Must be capable of:
—exercising initiative, common sense, and ability to interpret data
—maintaining effective internal and external working relationships
—establishing and maintaining purchasing records
—recognizing and identifying errors or inconsistencies and requesting contingency plans.

Must have knowledge of:
—basic electronic terms.

Must have an understanding of:
—production cycle
—basic human relations in the art of motivation
—purchasing cycle.

Significant Duties

1. Contacts vendor by telephone, letter, or wire and/or responds to inquiries from vendors regarding delivery status of purchased material or company supplied materials and specifications.
2. Identifies actual or potential delivery or documentation problems, and takes authorized corrective action or refers to higher authority.
3. Obtains and maintains records on specifications, delivery status, and vendor performance and presents higher authority with timely reports on status.
4. Maintains contacts with user departments and responds to inquiries on delivery status.
5. Performs other duties of a similar or related nature.

Reporting and Relations with Other Departments

The executive to whom the purchasing manager reports gives a good indication of the status of purchasing and the degree to which it is emphasized within the organization. If the chief purchasing officer has vice pres-

TABLE 2–2   Purchasing Reports (to whom)

Direct Report	Percent
President	16%
Executive vice president	18
Financial vice president	7
Mfg/prod/opns vice president	24
Materials management vice president	8
Engineering vice president	1
Administrative vice president	13
Other	12
Total (less than 100 percent, due to rounding)	99%

idential status and reports to the CEO, this indicates that purchasing has been recognized as a top management function.

However, in many firms, purchasing reports to the executive immediately in charge of the manufacturing function, since the major share of purchasing activity is directed at buying items needed to support production. In other firms, purchasing might report to an administrative support vice president due to purchasing's role in providing service to all functional areas of the organization. Or purchasing may report to the chief financial officer, based on its immediate impact on cash flows and the large number of dollars tied up in inventory. In a heavily engineering-oriented firm, the reporting relationship might be to the chief of engineering, to get closer communication and coordination on product specification and quality control matters. Table 2–2 presents the results from the study by the Center for Advanced Purchasing Studies, presenting the reporting relationship of purchasing in 291 major organizations.[4]

The factors which influence the level at which the purchasing function is placed in the organization structure cover a broad spectrum. Among the major ones are:

1. The amount of purchased material and outside services costs as a percentage of either total costs or total income of the organization. A high ratio emphasizes the importance of effective performance of the purchasing function.

2. The nature of the products or services acquired. The acquisition of complex components or extensive use of subcontracting represents a difficult purchasing problem.

[4]*Ibid.*, p. 13.

3. The conditions in the marketplace for those products and services of vital importance to the organization.
4. The talent available for assignment.
5. The problems and opportunities present in the purchasing area to achieve organizational objectives.

The important consideration in determining to whom purchasing will report relates to where it will be most effective in realizing the organization's objectives. Certainly, purchasing should be at a level high enough that it can be "heard," and that the purchasing aspects of key managerial decisions will receive proper consideration.

Purchasing must have a close working relationship with several other areas of the firm. It depends on production to supply realistic plans so that purchases can be made within normal vendor lead times to obtain best ultimate value. It depends on engineering to evaluate the cost advantages of using alternate materials. It depends on marketing for long-term market plans, so that realistic material-supply strategies can be developed. It depends on accounting to pay invoices in a timely fashion to take advantage of cash discounts and maintain good vendor relationships. In addition, if organized as separate departments and not a responsibility of purchasing, close cooperation is needed between receiving, stores, inventory control, traffic, and scrap disposal, since they all impact on the ability of purchasing to do an effective job.

This is not a one-way street. The other functions within the firm have a right to expect that their material needs will be met in a timely and cost-effective manner. Also, they expect to get reliable and timely information, as needed, from purchasing.

Purchasing in the Multiplant Organization

A variation of centralized purchasing often is present in the multiplant organization. Here the firm operates several different producing divisions which often make different products requiring a different mix of purchased items. The firm often uses a profit-center management motivation and control technique in which the division manager is given total responsibility for running the division, acts as president of an independent firm, and is judged by profits made by the division. Since material purchases are the largest single controllable cost of running the division and have a direct effect on its efficiency and competitive position, the profit-center division manager insists on having direct authority over purchasing. It would be difficult to hold the division manager responsible for results without having decision-making power over the major expenditure area. This has led firms to adopt decentralized-centralized purchasing in which the purchasing function is centralized on a division or plant basis but decentralized on a corporate basis. Often there is a corporate purchasing organization which operates in a staff capacity and assists the division purchasing departments in those tasks which are more effectively handled on a corporate basis: (1) establishment of policies, procedures, and controls, (2) recruiting and training of personnel, (3) coordinating the purchase of common-use items in which more "clout" is needed, and (4) auditing purchasing performance. Figure 2–4 is a job description for a central staff purchasing manager position. Figure 2–5 presents a simplified organization chart for a firm organized on a profit center basis.

To what extent the purchasing function should follow this trend is an interesting question. Today so many organizations are spread geographically and have a variety of products and services to offer through subunits that centralized purchasing may not be compatible with the general corporate philosophy. This raises questions such as:

1. Should there be a headquarters purchasing organization and what should be its role?

2. Should a headquarters purchasing organization buy the major raw materials for several or all of the divisions?

FIGURE 2–4   Director of Procurement Management Job Description

---

Summary Statement

Develops, maintains, and promulgates procurement and materials management policies, procedures, and practices for the company. Assesses the efficiency of purchasing functions performed throughout the company in parameters of cost effectiveness, maximizing purchasing leverage, and assignment of purchasing responsibility. Develops and maintains a data system which ensures a central point of cognizance in determining what is being purchased, by whom, from whom, in what quantity, and at what cost. Accomplishes negotiation and central purchasing of appropriate items and commodities. Provides staff support which ensures a full-service capability to deal with all procurement or purchasing problems which may be identified for solution by or referred to the corporate staff level. Works closely with purchasing personnel at all levels in the operating groups and divisions to ensure the continuity and full integration of purchasing functions. Maintains a strategic awareness and macro-overview of domestic and international availability of materials and procurement management concepts. Develops contacts with industrial counterparts, trade associations, and suppliers in assessing the materials market and developing company strategy, both short-range and long-range.

Key Responsibilities

1. Ensure that primary items and commodities are available in sufficient supply to continue production and services at required consumption rates.

FIGURE 2–4 (*concluded*)

2. Direct and assist the operating groups, divisions, regions, and activities in maximizing the efficiency of their respective purchasing functions.
3. Develop and maintain a procurement/purchasing data system which is compatible with and integrated into similar systems within the company. Ensure that this composite system provides all management data necessary to determine materials requirements, sources of purchasing, and associated costs. Direct and assist group, division, region, and plant purchasing activities, respectively, in developing a compatible information system.
4. Accomplish the purchase of commodities and items which should be centrally procured, such as fuels, mobile equipment, and automobiles. Negotiate national contracts as appropriate.
5. Assign the responsibility for procurement of those items, materials, and appropriate services purchased at other than corporate level.
6. Compile the total requirements from all operating groups and divisions for those commodities or items for which the group has been assigned the purchase responsibility and arrange for communication of these requirements to the appropriate group purchasing director on a timely basis consistent with meeting contract negotiation schedules.
7. Direct the training and upgrading of purchasing skills throughout the company. Maintain appropriate data for a central point of awareness of the qualifications and progress of all key purchasing employees so as to facilitate hiring, transferring, and promoting of employees in conjunction with the requirements of the operating groups. Be directly involved in the corporate review of all such personnel actions as they pertain to key purchasing employees.
8. Direct and assist purchasing personnel at all levels in awareness, understanding, and application of procurement, legal (particularly FTC), audit, and EEOC policies and procedures.
9. Direct and assist the purchasing personnel at all levels in establishing inventory control systems, reserve levels, reorder points, and general materials management administrative effectiveness.
10. Coordinate closely with the director of energy conservation for assuring the effective use of corporate resources attendant to energy procurement.

3. Where one division uses products manufactured by another division, should the using division be required to buy from the making division when an outside supplier can supply proper quality at a substantially lower price?
4. How far should the organization's chief purchasing officer go in evaluating the performance of a divisional purchasing executive?

Obviously, there are no ready-made answers to such decisions—much

FIGURE 2–5 Multidivision Organization Structure for Purchasing

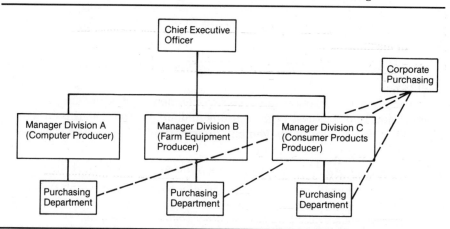

depends on the abilities and personalities of the executives in such an organization.

The evidence seems to indicate a gradual movement to greater centralization of the purchasing function in the multiplant organization. In a study conducted among 39 large U.S. manufacturing companies with annual purchases ranging from $100 million to $6 billion per year, with an average of $1.1 billion per year, and an average of 54 manufacturing locations, it was found that:

33 (85 percent) had a corporate-wide purchasing office.

23 (59 percent) had regional or group purchasing offices.

23 (59 percent) had regional or national purchasing councils.

50 percent of the firms have seen their purchasing become more centralized over the past 10 years.

65 percent predict greater centralization over the next 10 years.

The most important reasons cited for greater centralization were better prices and better service.

Specialization of manpower, research and planning, efficiency in developing policies, and the need for better control and evaluation systems also were cited as reasons why greater centralization would occur.[5]

---

[5]George F. Bernardin, "Centralized/Decentralized Purchasing: The Quest for a Perfect Mix," in *The Purchasing Function: From Strategy to Image* (Washington, D.C.: Machinery and Allied Products Institute, 1982).

An earlier study of three companies in which a major purchasing reorganization had taken place (General Motors, PPG Industries, and General Foods) found that four principal factors had prompted the move to greater centralization:

1. Coping with supply shortages and the need to assure long-term availability.
2. Responding to a changed business environment, including the growth in multinational business organizations and supply sources, the growth in use of computerized management information systems, and increasing government regulation and control.
3. Emphasizing purchasing as a means of obtaining profit leverage.
4. Realizing the need for professional development of purchasing personnel and using scarce personnel resources as effectively as possible.[6]

This study also found that the headquarters purchasing organization typically is involved in (1) monitoring developments in key supplying industries, (2) establishing purchasing policies and procedures, (3) auditing performance, (4) measuring purchasing performance, and (5) working with division purchasing managers to develop and train purchasing personnel.[7]

The 1988 CAPS study found that most of the 296 major organizations use some combination of a centralized–decentralized organization (Table 2–3).[8] The centralized form of organization, in which all or almost all purchasing is done at one central location for the entire firm, is a less used arrangement as organizations grow in size. It goes from 44 percent of organizations in the smallest size category (sales under $500 million) to only 15 percent in the largest category (over $10 billion). The decentralized form of organization is used by 11 to 14 percent of organizations in all size categories. Centralized/decentralized organization is used by 59 percent of organizations overall, and it increases in use from the smallest (42 percent) to the largest (74 percent) size organizations. This form of organization combines the advantages of having some purchasing decisions made at the location of the requirements with the advantages of volume buying which come from handling common requirements on a centralized (aggregate) basis.

Insofar as divisions or geographically dispersed units are uniform in terms of common needs and services and deal with the same suppliers, centralized purchasing may well make sense. It is important, however, that the purchasing function fits reasonably with organizational policies regarding divisionalized responsibilities. Obviously, the greater the geographical

---

[6]E. Raymond Corey, "Should Companies Centralize Procurement?" *Harvard Business Review,* November–December 1978, p. 103.

[7]*Ibid.,* p. 107.

[8]Fearon, *Purchasing Organizational Relationships,* p. 13.

TABLE 2–3 Centralization and Decentralization of the Purchasing Function, by Organization Size (1986 sales dollars)

Organization Structure	Number of Organizations Responding		Under $500 Million		$500 Million to $1 Billion		$1.1–5 Billion		$5.1–10 Billion		Over $10 Billion	
	No.	%	No.	%	No.	%	No.	%	No.	%	No.	%
Centralized—all, or almost all, purchasing done at one central location for entire firm	83	28	37	44	15	33	22	20	5	16	4	15
Centralized/Decentralized—some purchasing done at the corporate headquarters; purchasing also done centrally at major operating divisions/plants	175	59	35	42	24	53	73	67	23	74	20	74
Decentralized—purchasing done on a division/plant basis	38	13	12	14	6	13	14	13	3	10	3	11
Totals	296	100	84	100	45	99	109	100	31	100	27	100

Percent may not add to 100, due to rounding.

TABLE 2–4   Number of Professional Purchasing Personnel, by Organization
Size (1986 sales dollars)

Size	Average Number of Professionals
Under $500 million	14
$500 million to $1 billion	42
$1.1 to $5 billion	71
$5.1 to $10 billion	366
Over $10 billion	485
All organizations	118

spread and the greater the divergence in organizational needs, the stronger
the argument for purchasing decentralization to distinct subunits becomes.

Size of Professional Staffs

Table 2–4 shows the number of professional personnel, by organization
size.[9] The average for the total 290 organizations that supplied data was
118 persons. The number of personnel increases steadily as organizations
grow in size. Five of the organizations employed over 1,000 professional
purchasing people.

Purchasing Problems in Conglomerate Organizations

Conglomerate types of organizations are usually large groupings of
companies which have been acquired by a parent organization. In many
instances, no direct relationship is found among the types of industries
represented by the acquired companies, although there may be an underlying relationship centering on an area of science or technology. Because of
the diversity of the member companies of a conglomerate corporation and
in many cases the large size of each member company, the problems of
developing any meaningful concept of corporate purchasing are immense.

Any solution to the problem must be developed over long time periods
to have any chance for success. Some conglomerate companies have found
that one way to start to develop sound purchasing policies and coordination
among the member companies is to have a small headquarters group of
highly competent purchasing executives who are available to act as consultants on purchasing problems when called on by the appropriate division
executives. Needless to say, the success of the consultants will depend as

---

[9]*Ibid.*, p. 12.

much on their abilities in the human relations field as on their competence in the purchasing function.

Several problems are associated with complete functional decentralization without a corporate headquarters group. Where the decentralized units are small in size, they may become so involved in operating matters that the impetus for change and planning is overlooked. Status of such decentralized units also may be relatively low, with the resulting problems of quality of personnel and identification of supply opportunities. No subunit may be large enough to justify functional expertise in areas such as customs, traffic, warehousing, inventory management, purchasing research, materials handling, and value analysis. Corporate benefits may be lost, because of a low level of performance and lack of coordination in each of these areas. Even in those organizations where the individual units are large enough in size that the above problems are not serious, they may compete with one another in the marketplace for the same suppliers or materials without knowing it.

ORGANIZATION FOR MATERIALS MANAGEMENT

The rationale of materials management may be better comprehended through understanding of the growth of a small firm through three separate stages. These stages are complete integration, evolution of independent functions, and reintegration of related activities.

Complete Integration

When an organization initially is established, almost all functions are performed by the chief executive (often the owner) or by a few key individuals who make up the management team. For example, the purchasing function might be performed by the chief executive who also handles the scheduling of production and watches inventory levels closely so that there will be no problem of coordination or control. This system works reasonably well, for the evidence shows that the materials-type functions (for example, purchasing, inventory control, stores, and traffic) typically are grouped together and assigned to one person.

Evolution of Independent Functions

As the firm's business increases and additional personnel are added to the organization, it becomes evident that certain advantages would accrue if individual functions, such as purchasing, stores, traffic, production scheduling, inventory control, and quality control were separated and made full-time managerial assignments. The primary advantage, assuming the workload is sufficient to justify a full-time job assignment, is that of occupational specialization. The purchasing agent and later on the buyers that are added to the purchasing department (using that function as an example) become professional specialists. They bring to their function an expertise available only when an individual can devote all energies solely to one job. But with the emergence of these independent functions a problem of coordination develops.

The organizational assignment of individual functions to other major activities normally will be done on a "most use" criterion. Thus, purchasing might be assigned to the operations or production manager, since the major dollars are spent for raw materials; traffic might be assigned to the sales manager, since he would be responsible for delivery of finished items to customers. The "critical relationship" is a second criterion which might be used to assign certain functions. For example, inventory control might be assigned to finance, in view of the dollar investment involved. Other functions might be assigned on an "executive interest" basis. For example, the value analysis/engineering function might be assigned to engineering, since the engineering manager may be the one who has promoted and pushed this activity. The point is that the responsibility for different, but interrelated, functions becomes widely dispersed throughout the organization structure, creating very real problems of coordination and communication which prevent the organization from effectively and efficiently achieving its overall goals.

Reintegration of Related Activities

Eventually it becomes clear that substantial advantages, through the reduction of communication and coordination problems, could be obtained by bringing together again, under one responsible individual, all those functions which clearly are interrelated. This reintegration of interrelated materials functions is the basis of the materials management concept.[10]

If an organization adopted a "full-blown" materials management concept, following the principle of homogeneous assignment, the organizational structure might appear as in Figure 2–6.

The single-manager materials concept overcomes the shortcomings of the conventional organization, in which the various materials functions are organizationally splintered, by recognizing (1) that materials decisions are additive and not independent of actions elsewhere, (2) the self-interest and potentially conflicting objectives of the individual materials functions, and (3) the need to concentrate authority and responsibility for materials decisions to avoid "buck passing." Materials management in a formal organization sense is not needed in the small organization, for there the chief executive (normally the owner) makes all the materials decisions and can provide the needed coordination and control.

---

[10]Harold E. Fearon, "Materials Management: A Synthesis and Current View," *Journal of Purchasing,* February 1973, pp. 35–36.

FIGURE 2–6   Organization Structure for Materials Management

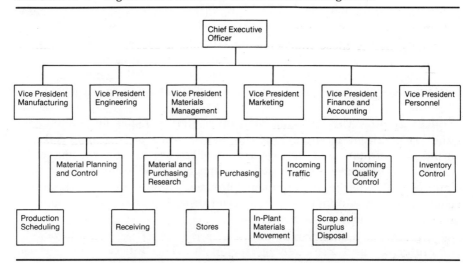

Functions Included in Materials Management

Material Planning and Control.   This is the aggregate planning of material requirements to meet the broad, overall production plan. It is concerned with the approximate quantities of the key and critical purchased materials needed to produce the approximate quantities of end products needed in specific time periods (probably by weeks). If problems in obtaining needed quantities are apparent, the aggregate production plan must be adjusted.

Production Scheduling.   The production scheduling manager plays an important part in establishing the total production schedule. Working with information inputs which either estimate future demands for a company's products or are based on the receipt of actual orders or are a combination of both, production control develops the specific time and quantity schedules for parts and materials needed to facilitate the production schedule.

Production scheduling is concerned with numbers of units to be produced, the time intervals over which production will occur, and the availability of materials and machines to produce the number of units specified within the schedule time constraints.

Once the number of units to be produced within a specified time period is determined, production scheduling is in a position to figure detailed requirements for parts and materials, both purchased and manufactured, by using bills of materials and specifications supplied by engineering. Companies with integrated data processing systems which have incorporated bills of material and specification requirements within the system can determine material requirements for any production schedule with great rapidity. Materials requirements planning (MRP) fits in well with the materials management concept.

A good production scheduling department should provide for follow-up activities to make certain that its schedules are met. If records are kept of materials in various stages of fabrication, it is helpful in limiting losses from spoilage, pilferage, or obsolescence and in maximizing turnover.

Receiving.   The receiving department is responsible for the physical handling of incoming shipments, the identification of such material, the verification of quantities, the preparation of reports, and the routing of the material to the place of use or storage. In some organizations, the responsibilities for the packaging of finished products for shipment, the stenciling or labeling of the shipping instructions on the shipping containers, and the delivery to the carrier also are included.

Materials and Purchasing Research.   This function is concerned with the collection, classification, and analysis of data necessary to find alternate materials; forecasts of supply, demand, and price of major purchased commodities; analysis of vendor costs and capabilities; and devising new and more effective methods for processing the paperwork necessary to operate the materials system.

Stores.   This function physically controls and maintains all inventory items. Appropriate physical safeguards must be established to protect items from damage, unnecessary obsolescence due to poor stock rotation procedures, and theft. Records must be maintained which enable immediate location of items.

Purchasing.   The purchasing department has the responsibility of buying the kinds and quantities of materials authorized by the requisitions issued by production scheduling, inventory control, engineering, maintenance, and any other department or function requiring materials. Where the purchasing department has the right and the duty to advise, question, and even to challenge other departments on matters of material specification and selection, a dynamic value is added to the operation of the purchasing function and the firm.

The basic activities of purchasing can be grouped as follows:

1. Checking the specifications of materials which are requisitioned in an endeavor to standardize where possible and to buy the materials which are the best values for the purposes intended.

2. Selecting the best available sources of supply, negotiating the terms of purchase, including delivery and performance, and preparing the proper

purchase orders. Maintaining the necessary records to provide historical data on price trends, vendor performance, and the like.

3. Follow-up to ensure on-time delivery and receipt of the proper quality and quantity.

4. Acting as the company's "G2" or intelligence unit in the marketplace, constantly searching for new and more effective suppliers and new materials and products with the objective of reducing costs or improving the company's product.

5. Supervising or conducting all contacts between suppliers and all other company departments on all matters relating to the purchase of materials.

In-Plant Materials Movement.   This includes all those activities involved in moving materials from their point of receipt or storage to the point of usage. This involves the physical handling and transportation of materials from their storage area to the point where they will be employed; issuance of material to using departments; maintenance of records necessary to transfer accountability from the materials function to the user; and provision of information which will enable preparation of useful accounting reports. The "kitting" of parts for the production floor would be performed in this activity.

Traffic.   Transportation costs have had an increasing influence on material costs in recent years. Also, types of transportation have had a major influence on inventory policy; for example, the use of air freight and air express has reduced size of inventory stocks for certain items. There are two basic traffic activities:

1. Traffic control involves the selection of carriers, documentation of shipments, study of carrier services and rates, tracing shipments, audit and approval for payment of carrier charges, and the evaluation of carrier performance.

2. Traffic analysis is concerned with assessing the total cost of transportation, including loading and unloading, methods of packaging, transit time, thefts and other losses, and with developing techniques for reducing overall transportation costs.

Disposal of Scrap and Surplus.   Traditionally this has been a function included with the responsibilities of purchasing. Aside from the desire to obtain good value for disposals, two major additional concerns stem from protection of the environment and shortages of critical materials.

Quality Control.   Quality control continues to be a difficult function to place in many organizations. The responsibility for inspection of incoming raw materials and supplier's operations places it directly with materials management.

Inventory Control.   The inventory control function is responsible for keeping detailed records of parts and materials used in the production process. Records of parts and materials on order are maintained and periodic physical inventories are taken to verify or adjust the records. Material requirements determined by production control are checked against the inventory records before requisitions detailing needs are sent to the purchasing department.

In addition to the control of production inventories, there is need to control the nonproduction materials such as expendable tools, office supplies, and maintenance, repair, and operating supplies. The specific control methods include:

1. Maintenance of records of items on hand, on order, and total usage. Establishment of controls to minimize losses from spoilage and theft and to prevent stockouts or duplication.

2. Handling the physical stocks of MRO (maintenance, repair, and operating supplies) items to be issued as needed for operations or maintenance.

3. Issuing requisitions to the purchasing department when stocks reach the reorder point or special needs arise.

Both production and nonproduction parts, materials, and supplies can be controlled through one inventory control department, or they can be organized into two separate departments.

MATERIALS MANAGEMENT USE

How common is the materials management (MM) concept in actual usage in organizations today? The answer is that well over two thirds of large organizations use it. The study by the Center for Advanced Purchasing Studies defined MM as an organization in which at least *three* of the functions of purchasing, inventory, production scheduling and control, inbound traffic, warehousing and stores, and incoming quality control report to a single responsible individual. It found that 204 of the 291 reporting organizations, or 70 percent, are organized on a MM basis. It was used by at least two thirds of the organizations in all size categories, but by an even larger percentage of the very large organizations. Table 2–5 presents the data. In three of the industry groups, Apparel, Furniture and Fixtures, and Aerospace, all firms were organized on a MM basis. Ninety-three percent of the firms in the Machinery, except Electrical, industry used MM and 92 percent in Transportation Equipment.[11]

---

[11]Fearon, *Purchasing Organizational Relationships,* p. 17.

TABLE 2–5 Use of Materials Management, by Organization Size (1986 sales dollars)

	Total		Under $500 Million		$500 Million to $1 Billion		$1.1–5 Billion		$5.1–10 Billion		Over $10 Billion	
	No.	%	No.	%	No.	%	No.	%	No.	%	No.	%
Organization does use materials management	204	70	58	70	29	66	71	67	24	80	22	78
Organization does not use materials management	87	30	25	30	15	34	35	33	6	20	6	22
Totals	291	100	83	100	44	100	106	100	30	100	28	100

TABLE 2–6

Functions Included under the Materials Manager	By Percentage of the 204 MM Organizations
Inventory	90%
Purchasing	86
Warehousing and stores	84
Inbound traffic	67
Production scheduling and control	59
Incoming quality control	25

PURCHASING IN THE MATERIALS MANAGEMENT CONTEXT

What happens to the purchasing function when it becomes part of a materials management organization? Will the purchasing manager become the materials manager if an organization goes to MM?

The 1988 organization study by the Center for Advanced Purchasing Studies showed that in the 204 large organizations that used the materials management concept, the purchasing, inventory, and warehousing and stores functions are included in the MM organization by an almost equal number of firms (see Table 2–6).[12]

These figures are generally higher than those from an earlier, 1979 study conducted among 137 manufacturing companies (average sales of $200 million annually) that found that when a firm uses the materials management organizational concept, in 69 percent of the firms the purchasing function reports to the materials manager, which is substantially less than found in the CAPS study.

The figures for other key functions reporting to the materials manager were production planning, 77 percent; distribution, 39 percent; and traffic, 55 percent. This study also found that manufacturing is the most common home for materials management, with 43 percent of the materials managers reporting to a manufacturing manager. Twenty-two percent reported to the general manager or president, 4 percent reported to control or finance; and 31 percent reported to various positions, such as executive vice president or vice president of administration.[13]

Certainly purchasing people are most interested in how the materials management concept develops and evolves in organizations, if for no other reason than that it will affect their own situations. For example, the 1986

---

[12]*Ibid.*

[13]Jeffrey G. Miller and Peter Gilmour, "Materials Managers: Who Needs Them?" *Harvard Business Review,* July-August 1979, p. 151.

salary survey by *Purchasing World* magazine found that the median salary for persons with the title of "materials" was higher than for someone with the title of purchasing; for example, materials manager, $61,300 compared to purchasing manager, $54,000; materials director, $73,700 compared to purchasing director, $72,500; and vice president of materials, $103,800 compared to vice president of purchasing, $88,600.[14]

Originally, it was argued that the purchasing manager was the logical candidate to become the materials manager in the organization that decided to adopt MM. However this does not appear to be the case in practice. As two purchasing professionals see it,

> As an increasing number of companies adopt the materials management concept, many early fears that the purchasing function would be removed one more step from top management indeed appear to have been well founded. . . . In recent years . . . with utilization of sophisticated computer-based material requirements planning systems (MRP) for production and inventory planning purposes, an increasing number of materials managers have been drawn from the production function. Presently it is estimated that at least as many materials managers are coming from the production area as from the purchasing function.[15]

The Buyer/Planner

A takeoff on the materials management approach is the buyer/planner concept. The traditional approach is to divide materials responsibilities into two job parts: (1) planners, who determine what materials are needed to keep production moving, and (2) buyers, who handle the actual sourcing and buying.

Thus the planner controls inventory levels, schedules purchased and internally fabricated parts, and expedites to assure that items are available when and where needed. The buyer selects suppliers, negotiates, and expedites past due shipments from vendors. However, due to the overlap of responsibilities, three conflicts often arise:

1. Inventory level/best price conflict: to minimize inventory level often dictates quantities too small to qualify for the best price break.

2. Lead time conflict: the planner wants short lead times, since that will necessitate fewer, expensive schedule changes. Purchasing, on the other hand, can get better prices if it makes long-term commitments.

3. Processing conflict: the planner tends to blame purchasing for

---

[14]Robert R. Blumel, "Pull Your Pay Stub and See How You're Faring," *Purchasing World,* December 1986, p. 34.

[15]Harold Bloom and James M. Nardone, "Organizational Level of the Purchasing Function," *Journal of Purchasing and Materials Management,* Summer, 1984, p. 17.

delays in obtaining the materials needed to fill requisitions; purchasing blames inventory control for short lead time requisitions and forecasts that change too often.

The buyer/planner solution is to combine the planning and purchasing functions into one position, the buyer-planner, who is in charge of a specific line of inventory. Hopefully this will 'minimize the conflicts. The buyer-planner is responsible for the inventory level of the assigned product group, as well as getting product at the best price. This person establishes schedules, issues and analyzes quotations, places orders, monitors supplier performance, and keeps abreast of market trends, vendor capacities, and changes in technology. These procedures are based on the idea that the same person should have the authority and responsibility for *both* the inventory control *and* the purchasing decisions.[16] This is the same approach, on an individual task level, that the materials management concept applies at the organizational level.

Without question, the materials management concept has had a major impact on purchasing and will likely further impact it in the future.

LOGISTICS MANAGEMENT

Over the past 10 or so years, the activity known as logistics has been the focus of much attention. A 1985 definition of logistics by the Council of Logistics Management states that it is "the process of planning, implementing, and controlling the efficient, cost-effective flow and storage of raw materials, in-process inventory, finished goods, and related information from point of origin to point of consumption for the purpose of conformity to customer requirements."[17] Logistics includes the flow and storage of items, from raw materials to customer delivery.

Figure 2–7 is a simplified organization chart showing the logistics organization. The attractiveness of this concept is that it looks at the material flow process as a complete system, from initial need for materials to delivery of finished product or service to the customer. It attempts to provide the communication, coordination, and control needed to avoid the potential conflicts between the physical distribution and the materials management functions. While the logistics concept is attractive from a theoretical point of view as a means of recognizing and facilitating the interfaces and interdependencies between the inbound and outbound material flows, the problems in its implementation are many: the self-interest and vested interests of the people in the individual functions, the shortage of managers who can provide the required coordination, and the lack of total computer software

---

[16]Mark S. Miller, "The Buyer/Analyst Concept," *Purchasing World,* March 1986, pp. 62–63.

[17]Ernst & Whinney, *Corporate Profitability & Logistics* (Oak Brook, Ill.: Council of Logistics Management, 1987). p. 2.

FIGURE 2–7 Typical Logistics Organization

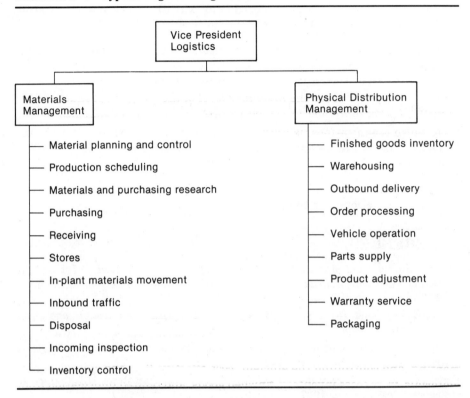

to facilitate the needed data flows. However, as our knowledge of management and systems in the material areas grows over the next decade, and as organizations experiment with advanced systems, it seems likely that the logistics concept will gain greater acceptance and usage.

QUESTIONS FOR REVIEW AND DISCUSSION

1. What are the specialized functions within purchasing? Is this idea used in a very small organization? How?

2. Why do almost all organizations use centralized purchasing? How might a large, multiplant organization set up its purchasing function?

3. Where should the purchasing function report in the organization structure?

4. What is included in the buyer/planner position and why is it used?

5. Discuss the specific objectives of purchasing and materials management. Relate these to (1) a company producing washing machines, (2) a large, fast food restaurant chain, and (3) a hospital.

6. What is materials management; how is it used; and why is it used?

7. What prerogatives must purchasing have, if it is to be truly effective? What will happen if purchasing does not have these "rights"?

8. In large organizations, is the trend toward greater centralization of purchasing or is it to decentralization? What are the factors that will affect this decision?

9. How is the materials management concept likely to impact the purchasing function over the next decade?

REFERENCES

Bloom, Harold, and James M. Nardone. "Organizational Level of the Purchasing Function." *Journal of Purchasing and Materials Management.* Summer 1984.

Corey, E. Raymond. *Procurement Management: Strategy, Organization, and Decision-Making.* Boston: CBI Publishing, 1978.

Corey, E. Raymond. "Should Companies Centralize Procurement?" *Harvard Business Review.* November-December 1978.

Ernst & Whinney. *Corporate Profitability & Logistics.* Oak Brook, Ill. Council of Logistics Managment, 1987.

Fearon, Harold E. "Materials Managment: A Synthesis and Current View." *Journal of Purchasing and Materials Management.* Summer 1975.

Fearon, Harold E. *Purchasing Organizational Relationships.* Tempe, Ariz.: Center for Advanced Purchasing Studies/National Association of Purchasing Management, 1988.

Miller, Jeffrey G., and Peter Gilmour. "Materials Managers: Who Needs Them?" *Harvard Business Review.* July-August 1979.

Zenz, Gary J. "Materials Management and Purchasing: Projections for the 1980s." *Journal of Purchasing and Materials Management.* Spring 1981.

Case 2–1

DRYDEN INKS

Jane Waterman was reviewing her first year on the job as purchasing agent for Dryden Inks. There were a number of matters that caused her concern, not the least of which was the excessive overtime she had put in during the last six months. Dryden Inks was a producer of printing inks and varnishes. The company had started as a small family business over 80 years earlier. Most of its growth had occurred over the past two decades. Dryden enjoyed a good reputation for quality in the trade. However, competition had become much stronger, so that prices had been under considerable pressure. Dryden's profits over the past few years had been minimal.

Jane Waterman had been hired by the purchasing manager at Dryden to assist him in both the buying and the paperwork. However, after six months the purchasing manager left for a better paying position with another company. Jane was promoted to purchasing agent, reporting to the manufacturing manager who was in charge of production and inventory control and had no personal interest in or familiarity with the procurement function. This arrangement lasted for about four months. Then, because of an organizational shuffle, Jane was asked to report to the plant manager instead.

It seemed to Jane that the company was using old methods with long-term staff (the average employment of the office staff amounted to about 25 years). It was possible that these methods might have been appropriate when the company was smaller and the industry less competitive. For example, the order quantities and order points in the company's computerized inventory control system had never been changed since the system was installed about eight years earlier. Pigment, a high-value, high-use purchase item was brought into raw material inventory in very large quantities. Inventory records were never accurate and it was normal for production foremen to rush into Jane's office explaining the need for a purchase in a hurry because they could not find the materials that were supposed to be in stock. Sales and production did not work to a forecast and order schedule and hence Jane was almost never given enough lead time. Most orders were on a rush basis and Jane could feel the frustration of vendors when she called for "another favor."

Jane, herself, did all of the buying as well as the paperwork associated, such as opening mail, filing, typing, and distribution of purchase orders, and matching invoices. To get everything done, she worked every day from 7 A.M. to 8 P.M. and often also on Saturdays. She felt she was just "putting out fires" and not really accomplishing anything constructive in a purchasing sense. She did not consider herself a complainer and wanted to contribute to the company in a more substantial manner. She was not sure, however, where and how to start. She realized if she did not have a definite plan the daily grind of emergencies would automatically take precedence.

Case 2–2

NORTHWEST DIVISION

Alec Perrin, manager of corporate purchases for Northwest Division, had long been concerned about the engineering/purchasing relationship in Northwest Division. He had asked his assistant to prepare a set of suggestions on how the two functions might cooperate better in the future. His assistant, Ted MacDonald, had prepared a set of guidelines and had given these to Alec with the words: "If these rules can't fix it up, nothing can." Alec was not sure how he might assess the guidelines and what action to take subsequently.

Company Background

Northwest Division was the agricultural and forest products branch of ATA Chemical Corporation, a large multinational concern with consolidated sales exceeding $1.7 billion. Northwest Division has annual sales exceeding $200 million and, like all divisions of ATACC, operated in a reasonably autonomous manner. Engineering had traditionally held a strong position at Northwest. The division had a reputation as a market leader in technological advances, new products, and high quality. (For organization chart see Exhibit 1.)

Engineering and Purchasing

Annual purchases for Northwest exceeded $80 million and were growing rapidly. Alec Perrin had been manager for two years, having transferred from the forest products sales group to purchasing. The former manager of purchases had held the position for 37 years. He had not been successful in obtaining engineering cooperation. During his stay in forest products sales, Alec Perrin had gained the impression that engineers preferred to bypass purchasing because they thought they could cut the red tape and do a better job.

As manager of purchasing, Mr. Perrin had spent the first two years becoming better acquainted with the job, looking after the most pressing crises, and building a stronger and more capable staff. The new group consisted primarily of university graduates in science, engineering, or business administration. About half had worked in other areas of Northwest Division prior to joining the new purchasing team. He found that his personnel resented the engineering bypass attitudes, and a number of incidents had occurred during the last two years to convince Alec Perrin that purchasing had a legitimate role to play in matters now apparently viewed as in the engineering domain.

The ability to influence specifications, early involvement in capital project planning, and awareness of engineering supplier contacts were three typical areas of major concern.

For example, in a recent incident a design engineer had specified an expensive alloy tank for an application where a standard stainless steel would have sufficed at savings of about $20,000. Despite the courteous attempts at questioning by the

EXHIBIT 1 Organization Chart

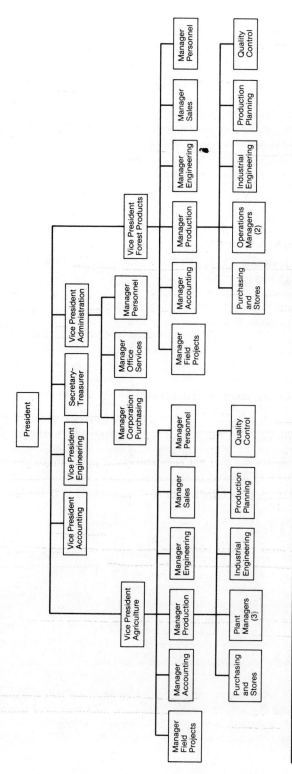

equipment buyer, an experienced engineer himself, the design engineer refused to discuss the matter saying: "My job is to design the equipment, yours is to buy what I tell you to get, where I want it and to look after the necessary paperwork. And if you don't like it that way, I'll be happy to look after the whole thing myself."

Purchasing was seldom aware of new capital projects until engineering sent the necessary details for the final purchase orders. Frequently, by that time there was considerable pressure to get the paperwork out quickly to avoid delaying the project. A recent purchase involving a $750,000 mixer unit was typical. Engineering handled all preliminary supplier contacts and price estimates without purchasing's knowledge. One of the design engineers involved had an automobile accident which delayed engineering planning about three months. When purchasing finally received instructions to purchase the mixer from a supplier chosen by engineering, a $100,000 premium had to be paid to assure on-time delivery, and there was no opportunity at all to search for alternate sources.

Alec Perrin was aware that the engineering group had traditionally made a significant contribution to Northwest because of its innovative role, strong expertise, and ability to maintain a high-quality consumer product. He, nevertheless, thought that purchasing had its own contribution to make which could not be achieved with current engineering attitudes and practices.

After a particularly touchy deal in February, involving an engineering commitment to a supplier without the knowledge of purchasing, Alec Perrin had asked his assistant, Ted MacDonald, a recent business school graduate, to see what he could recommend. Ted immediately went to work. He talked with purchasing department personnel, supplier personnel, production people and engineers. He contacted purchasing people in other ATACC divisions to see what they had done. He also did a library search on books and periodicals. His findings were summarized in the following set of guidelines.

Alec wished to review the guidelines carefully. He had a high regard for Ted MacDonald and knew that Ted expected action quickly. Nevertheless, he wanted to be absolutely sure he had a sound plan and approach before he committed himself.

Guidelines for Engineering/Purchasing Relationship

Project Planning and Estimates.   Collection of data and prices for project planning and preliminary estimating requires flexibility and cooperation between the engineering and the purchasing departments. Care should be taken to prevent individual suppliers from doing considerable work to supply initial estimates to us. Care should also be taken that specifications are not written to fit one supplier's product to the exclusion of other suppliers in the field.

All requests by engineering for commercial information from suppliers will be made through the purchasing department on form "Request for Information," copy attached. The proper use of this form will ensure that all of the data required for estimating and purchasing are obtained from the vendor.

Vendor Contacts.   Vendor contacts by the engineering department prior to the awarding of a contract or the placing of a purchase order require cooperation between the two groups. It is recognized that at times the engineering department will, of necessity, discuss preliminary information or technical aspects with a vendor.

EXHIBIT 2

REQUEST FOR INFORMATION

TO: Mr./Ms._____   FROM:_____
Purchasing Department   Engineering Department

DATE:_____   SUBJECT:_____

_____

Project_____W.O._____

Please obtain the following information on the subject item(s):

_____

_____

FOR ESTIMATING PURPOSES ☐   FOR PURCHASE ☐

Secure bids   ☐

Price   ☐

Shipping weight   ☐

Estimated freight   ☐

Taxes applicable   ☐

Duty (if imported)   ☐

Current delivery   ☐

Literature   ☐

Sample(s)   ☐

Arrange meeting with representative   ☐

List of recommended spare parts   ☐

Time required to supply approval drawings   ☐

Time required to supply certified drawings   ☐

Enclosed are_____ sets of specifications and/or drawings.

SUGGESTED VENDORS

_____   _____

_____   _____

_____   _____

INFORMATION/BIDS REQUIRED BY_____

ESTIMATED VALUE $_____

Copies to: Signature_____

It is the responsibility of the engineering department to keep the purchasing department informed of the discussion and direct the vendor to send a copy of any pertinent correspondence to the purchasing department. The engineering department must not solicit bids from the representatives. If a quotation is required, a Request for Information should be filled out and the vendor's representative referred to the purchasing department (see Exhibit 2).

After awarding of the contract, technical contacts may be made by engineering with a copy of any pertinent correspondence to purchasing. All commercial contacts must be made by the purchasing department with a copy of any pertinent correspondence to engineering. Assigned inspectors or expediters may contact the supplier in carrying out their respective responsibilities.

Bid Lists

Bid Lists for Engineering Consultants.   The engineering department has the prime responsibility for the bid lists for engineering consultants after evaluating their personnel, facilities, and experience. If the project is particularly large or includes an arrangement for the consultant to do project purchasing, the purchasing department should be involved.

Bid Lists for Contractors.   Preparation of bid lists for contractors is a joint responsibility of engineering and purchasing. Engineering should investigate technical ability, experience, and personnel. The purchasing department should investigate commercial standing, obtain financial data and suitability from past performance.

Bid Lists for Major Equipment.   Preparation of bid lists for major equipment is the joint responsibility of engineering and purchasing. Engineering will prepare detailed specifications of their requirements and provide purchasing with a list of suggested suppliers. Purchasing should take this original list and endeavor to find or develop other sources of supply until an adequate number for competitive bidding is obtained. In the case of noncompetitive or single supplier products, the engineering department must provide the purchasing department with the reason for handling in this manner. Purchasing may suggest that engineering rewrite specifications to enable them to obtain competitive bids.

Bid Lists for Minor Equipment and Construction Supplies.   The engineering department will prepare specifications for miscellaneous equipment and supplies. The preparation of the bid list is the prime responsibility of the purchasing department. Engineering department will comment, if necessary, on any particular item and supplier.

Bid Transmittal and Comparison.   Purchasing will prepare for engineering a "Bid Transmittal and Comparison" and "Engineering Equipment Comparative Bid Sheet" (see Exhibits 3 and 4). After complete technical analysis by engineering, the Bid Transmittal and Comparison form will be returned to purchasing—the bottom half completed, accompanied by an approved purchasing requisition. Engineering will make recommendations for preferred supplier and reason for same. Purchasing will negotiate the best commitment for the item or service.

Supplier Selection.   Recommendation of the contractor, consultant, and supplier of major equipment and justification for the recommendations will be pro-

EXHIBIT 3

Project:_____

Item No._____

360 Work Order:_____

BID TRANSMITTAL AND COMPARISON

TO: Engineering – Attention:

Attached are Bids and Bid Comparisons covering

Buyer:_____

To be completed by Engineering

RECOMMENDATION FOR PURCHASE

TO: Purchasing – Attention

c.c.

Attached is approved Requisition No.

Recommended Vendor:

Reason:

Engineer:_____

EXHIBIT 4

ENGINEERING EQUIPMENT

COMPARATIVE BID SHEET

BIDDERS

QTY.	ITEM					
	QUOTED PRICE					
	F.O.B.					
	TAXES					
	DUTY					
	ESTIMATED FREIGHT					
	TERMS					
	DELIVERED PRICE					
	DELIVERY					

COMMENTS:

PREPARED BY: DATE:

vided by the engineering department. The final decision on the contractor, consultant, or supplier is a joint responsibility of the two departments.

Notification.   The purchasing department will notify, in writing, the unsuccessful bidders on all major items and contracts.

Specifications.   Engineering specifications must be precise to prevent misunderstanding after the contract is let. In addition to details of buildings and equipment, items such as company's safety policies, work rules and restrictions, availability of utilities, and other items affecting contractor's cost should be included in the specifications. Care should be taken to see that items placed in the specifications conform with the requirements of standard Northwest Division documents such as contract forms, purchase orders, and so on, to prevent undue costs due to ambiguity in specifications. Specifications should be reviewed by the plant management for the areas affected by the construction or installation. This is an engineering department responsibility.

Contract Preparation.   It is the responsibility of the purchasing department to prepare contracts. Contracts should include warranties, guarantees, payment schedules, holdbacks, bonus/penalty clauses, and so on. Purchasing department must consult with engineering, legal department, and so on, regarding their phases of the contract.

Commitments.   All commitments must take the form of a purchase order or purchase contract placed by the purchasing department. Field change orders may be committed in writing by the designated project engineer/manager. All additions or deletions including field changes must be confirmed by the purchasing department on a purchase order change notice.

Noncompetitive Purchasing Policy.   Lowest cost, commensurate with quality and service, can only be achieved by competitive bidding from qualified suppliers. Vendors' qualifications and performance must be continually updated and new suppliers sought out and evaluated from three viewpoints: quality, price, and service, which includes meeting schedules. The purchasing organization and the engineering department share the evaluation requirements, with purchasing being responsible for permanent files.

There are occasions when noncompetitive purchases must be made; for example, compressor parts, custom machine parts, instruments parts. However, ball bearings, seals, packing, gaskets, etc., do not normally fall in this category. Requisitions for noncompetitive materials must clearly identify the vendor's part number, vendor's serial or shop number, and Northwest's original purchase order number if needed by the vendor for identification purposes. The purchasing organization is authorized to make these purchases with normal approvals.

Any purchase requisition originating in the engineering department limiting the purchase to one supplier, other than materials in the above statement, will require the approval of the engineering manager if the purchase value exceeds $500. Multiple requisitions will not be used to circumvent this policy, and this aspect will be monitored by purchasing.

The local purchasing manager will define the approval requirements for noncompetitive purchases less than $500. This may vary with locations in order to be compatible with the staffing at that location. The purchasing managers will also establish a maximum purchase value, whereby it costs more to obtain competitive prices than the potential saving of competitive bids.

EXHIBIT 5

CONTRACTOR'S PERFORMANCE REPORT	Contractor's Name
Product group and location	Contractor's representative

Project identification

Type of contract

☐ Lump sum   ☐ Unit price   ☐ Cost plus fixed fee   ☐ Cost plus percentage fee

Contract amount	Final total payments	Reason for additional payments in excess of contract amount
$	$	

Contractor's claims for extras reasonable   Unreasonable number of petty extras submitted

☐ YES   ☐ NO   ☐ YES   ☐ NO

Job progress – scheduled start	Scheduled completion	Actual start	Actual completion

Cause of delays (if any)

PERFORMANCE RATING	EXCELLENT	ADEQUATE	UNSATISFACTORY
Quality of subcontractors			
Scheduling and coordination			
Workers			
Labor relations			
Materials procurement and delivery			
Quality and supply of tools and equipment			
Cooperation with owner and/or owner's rep.			
Cooperation with other contractors			
Safety record			
Quality of field supervision			
General housekeeping of construction site			

Contractor recommended for future work   ☐ Yes   ☐ No (if no, give reason)

Submitted by	Date	Title

Contractor's Performance Report.   The manager of engineering or a designated substitute will prepare a "Contractor's Performance Report" (see Exhibit 5) at the completion of the contract and forward to the local purchasing department. This department will make comments on commercial matters and forward a copy to the head office purchasing and engineering department.

Equipment Performance Report.   Due to the wide variety of equipment and applications it is not practical to have a standard single report. The local purchasing and engineering departments are responsible to report supplier and equipment performance in a similar fashion to contractor's performance. Such report would include all types of performance such as delivery, quality, service facilities, and costs of spare parts, and so on.

Expediting/Inspection.   The importance of expediting depends on the need for the particular item. Expediting of major or long-term items should be combined with inspection. It is usually necessary to inspect the fabrication or construction to assess properly accuracy of the vendor's delivery promise. On large projects, expediting and inspection may be a full-time job for a member of the project team. Outside inspectors and/or expediters may be hired for these projects by the project manager.

On all other items, expediting will be done by the purchasing department on an exception basis. These exceptions are in two classes:

1. When the time is late.

2. On a special request basis.

Request for expediting should accompany the purchase requisition to the purchasing department and indicate the minimum frequency of the expediting contacts.

Purchasing, with the approval of the engineering manager, may retain outside expediting/inspection services on major project items or on any items where delivery could affect the manufacturing operation. Purchasing should also notify the engineering manager when, in its opinion, expediting and inspection may be required.

Equipment Delivery.   Purchasing will endeavor in all cases to procure equipment when stated on requisition and will advise engineering prior to placing order if the requested delivery date is unattainable.

CHAPTER 3

Procedures and Information Flows

The purchasing/materials management area requires a wide range of standard operating procedures to deal with the normal daily tasks. The large number of items, the large dollar volume involved, the need for an audit trail, the severe consequences of unsatisfactory performance, and the potential contribution to effective organizational operations inherent in the function are five major reasons for developing a sound system. The acquisition process is closely tied to almost all other functions included in an organization and also to the external environment, creating a need for complete information systems. The introduction of the computer has had a substantial impact on the acquisition process and its management. Considerable management skill is required to assure continuing effectiveness.

STEPS IN THE PURCHASING SYSTEM

Only a brief statement of the broad outlines of any system of sound purchasing procedure will be presented.

The essential steps in the purchasing procedure are:

1. Recognition of need.

2. Description of the need, with an accurate statement of the characteristics and amount of the article or commodity desired.

3. Determination and analysis of possible sources of supply.

4. Determination of price and terms.

5. Preparation and placement of the purchase order.

6. Follow-up on and/or expediting the order.

7. Receipt and inspection of goods.

8. Clearance of the invoice and payment of the supplier.

9. Maintenance of records.

1. Recognition of Need

Any purchase originates with the recognition of a definite need by someone in the organization. The person responsible for a particular activity should know what the individual requirements of the unit are—what, how much, and when it is needed. This may result in a material requisition on the stores department. Occasionally, such requirements may be met by the transfer of surplus stock from another department. Sooner or later, of course, the purchase of new supplies will become necessary. Some purchase requisitions originate within the production or using department. Requests for office equipment of all sorts might come from the office manager or from the controller of the company. Some requests may come from the sales or advertising departments or from research laboratories. Frequently, special forms will indicate the source of requisitions; where this is not the case, distinctive code numbers for each department may be used. A typical requisition is shown in Figure 3–1.

The purchasing department is responsible for helping to anticipate the needs of using departments. The purchasing manager should urge not only that the requirements be as nearly standard in character as possible and that a minimum of special or unusual orders be placed, but also that requirements be anticipated far enough in advance to prevent an excessive number of "rush" orders. Also, since the purchasing department is in touch with price trends and general market conditions, the placing of forward orders may be essential to protect against shortage of supply or increased prices. This means that purchasing should inform using departments of the normal lead time, and any major changes, for all standard purchased items.

Emergency and Rush Orders

Frequently an excessively large number of requisitions will be received marked "rush." Rush orders cannot always be avoided; emergencies do arise which justify their use. Sudden changes in style or design and unexpected changes in market conditions may upset a most carefully planned material schedule. Breakdowns seemingly are inevitable, with an accompanying demand for parts or material which it would be unreasonable to carry in stock regularly.

There are, however, so-called rush orders that cannot be justified on any basis. They consist of those requisitions which arise because of *(a)* faulty inventory control, *(b)* poor production planning or budgeting, *(c)* an apparent lack of confidence in the ability of the purchasing department to get material to the plant by the proper time, and *(d)* the sheer habit of marking the requests "rush." Whatever the cause, such orders are costly. This higher cost is due in part to the greater chance of error when the work is done under pressure. Rush orders also place an added burden on the seller, and this burden must directly or indirectly find its way into the price paid by the buyer.

FIGURE 3–1   Purchase Requisition

Purchase Requisition		
Department requisitioning _____ Number _____		
Budget account _____ Date _____		

Quantity required	Unit	Description

Required date _____

Notify in event of problems _____

Special delivery instructions _____

_____
Requisitioning authority

Instructions: Complete in duplicate. Send original to Purchasing Department, requisitioner keep file copy.

What can be done to reduce the seriousness of the problem? For an excessive number of rush orders that are not actually emergency orders, the solution is a matter of education in the proper purchasing procedure. In one company, for example, a ruling has been made that when a rush requisition is sent to the purchasing department, the department issuing such an order has to explain to the general manager the reason for the emergency requirement and secure approval. Furthermore, even if the requisition is approved, the extra costs, so far as they can be determined, are charged to the department ordering the material. The result has been a marked reduction in the number of such orders.

Small Orders

Small orders are a continuing matter of concern in every organization. Most requisitions follow Pareto's law, which says that about 70 percent of all requisitions only amount to about 10 percent of the total dollar volume. One important consideration then becomes the cost of the system set up to handle small orders versus the cost of the items themselves. Since the lack of a small item may create a nuisance totally out of proportion to its dollar value, assured supply is usually the first objective to be met. Many approaches can be used to address the small order question. A few examples are:

1. If the fault lies with the using department, perhaps persuasion may be employed to increase the number of standardized items requested.

2. Another possibility is for the purchasing department to hold small requisitions as received until a justifiable total, in dollars, has been accumulated.

3. A third method is to establish a requisition calendar, setting aside specific days for the requisitioning of specific supplies, so that all requests for a given item are received on the same day. The calendar also may be so arranged that practically all the supplies secured from any specific type of vendor are requisitioned on the same day.

4. Still another method is to make use of the "stockless buying" or "systems contracting" concept. This has been used most widely in the purchase of MRO (maintenance, repair, and operating supply) items. (See explanation later in this chapter.)

Blank Check Purchase Order

This method for combating the small order problem often is referred to as the "Kaiser Purchase Order Draft" system. Some years ago when the Kaiser Aluminum and Chemical Corporation analyzed their purchasing paperwork, they found that 75 percent of their purchase orders (POs), had a face value of $200 or less but accounted in total for only 5 percent of total purchase dollars; further, 92 percent of their POs were for a face value of $1,000 or less but accounted for only 6 percent of total purchase dollars. To handle these small orders, they devised the blank check buying procedure.

The blank check PO is a special form, in which the vendor is sent a check along with the PO (see Figure 3–2). When the merchandise is shipped, the vendor enters the amount due on the check and cashes it. This system has certain built-in safeguards: the check can be deposited only to the ven-

FIGURE 3–2 Blank Check Form

FUND	DEPT.	DIV.	C C	W O	ACCT. NO.

MARICOPA COUNTY ARIZONA

CASH PURCHASE ORDER
This number MUST appear on ALL documents.

C.P.O. No.
X 00057

CASH PURCHASE ORDER
MARICOPA COUNTY
DEPARTMENT OF MATERIALS MANAGEMENT
MATERIALS MANAGEMENT CENTER, 320 W. LINCOLN
PHOENIX, ARIZONA 85003

SEE ATTACHED INSTRUCTIONS

V E N D O R

DATE

CONTRACT NO.

DELIVERY INSTRUCTIONS

SHIP TO

ON OR BEFORE

I T M	CATALOG NO. REQ/ITEM NO.	DESCRIPTION	QUANTITY AND UNIT OF ISSUE	UNIT PRICE	EXTENDED PRICE

IMPORTANT

TO AVOID INVOICING, THE VENDOR MUST ITEMIZE THIS SALE IN THE SPACE PROVIDED BELOW.

ALL DISCREPANCIES MUST BE RECONCILED WITH THE DEPARTMENT OF MATERIALS MANAGEMENT BEFORE THIS ORDER IS FILLED. PLEASE CALL—
(602) - 262-3244

LESS CASH DISCOUNT		%	—
ON $	TAX	%	+
BUYER		TOTAL	

NEW 6-78 20-05-11

91-170
1221

▼ **VENDOR MUST COMPLETE THIS SECTION** ▼

ITM	QUANTITY	UNIT PRICE	AMOUNT
INVOICE #	CASH DISCOUNT ____ %	—	
	TAX ____ %	+	
	TOTAL		

TREASURER OF MARICOPA COUNTY
PHOENIX, ARIZONA
CASH PURCHASE ORDER

WARRANT & CLAIM NO.
X 00057

FUND   VOID 90 DAYS AFTER   DATE   AMOUNT
$
NOT VALID FOR MORE THAN $500.00

PAY TO THE ORDER OF

DRAWN BY MARICOPA COUNTY BOARD OF SUPERVISORS

MATERIALS MANAGEMENT DEPARTMENT
AUTHORIZED SIGNATURE

CONTROLLER'S DEPARTMENT
AUTHORIZED SIGNATURE

⑈900000 57⑈ ⑆1221017 06⑆ 212 001⑈000 212⑈

dor's account; it must be presented for deposit within a set number of days (normally 60 or 90 days); and the check (it's really a bank draft) clearly is marked "not good for an amount over $1,000." Obviously the maximum amount limit is set to fit the particular buying organization's needs; typically it is $1,000 but some companies set a lower amount, for example, $500, and some go as high as $5,000. The risk to the buyer is small under these restrictions. The advantages are that it cuts down paperwork on the low-dollar purchases; it saves postage, for the check goes in the same envelope with the PO; it saves envelopes; the buyer can negotiate a larger cash discount in return for instant payment; and it saves time (and personnel) in the accounts payable function. But probably the major advantage is that this system requires complete shipment—*no back orders are allowed* (referred to as "fill or kill"), and the vendor is notified either by the PO or by an attached instruction sheet that whatever amount is shipped closes the order and the vendor pays itself only for that amount actually shipped. Thus the vendor has a real incentive to ship the order complete—and most normally do—since payment is immediate for items shipped. This cuts down on the number of receiving reports, inventory entries, and payments.

2. Accurate Description of Desired Commodity

No purchaser can be expected to buy without knowing exactly what the using departments want. For this reason, it is essential to have an accurate description of the need, the article, the commodity, or the service which is requested.

The purchaser should question a specification if it appears that the organization might be served better through a modification. An obvious case is the one where market shortages exist in the commodity requested and a substitute is the only reasonable alternative. Since future market conditions play such a vital role, it makes sense to have a high degree of interaction between the purchasing and specifying groups in the early stages of need definition. At best, an inaccurate description may result in some loss of time; at worst it may have serious financial consequences and cause disruption of supply, hard feelings internally, and loss of supplier respect and trust.

Since the purchasing department is the last one to see the specification before it is sent on to the supplier, the need for a final check here is clear. Such a check is not possible if purchasing department personnel have no familiarity with the product or service requested. Any questions regarding the accuracy of the requisition should be referred back to the requisitioner and should not be settled unilaterally in the purchasing department.

The terms used to describe desired articles should be uniform. The importance of proper nomenclature as a means of avoiding misunderstanding cannot be overemphasized. The most effective way to secure this uniformity is to maintain in the purchasing office a file listing the articles usually purchased. Such files may be kept in various ways. Some organizations have found it worthwhile to maintain a general catalog, which lists all the items used, and a stores catalog, which contains a list of all of the items carried in stock. Such catalogs may be kept in loose-leaf form, in a card index, or by a computer listing. If such catalogs are adequately planned and properly maintained, they tend to promote the uniformity in description. They also tend to reduce the number of odd sizes or grades of articles requisitioned, and they facilitate accounting and stores procedures. However, unless such catalogs or their equivalents are properly planned, maintained, and actually used, they can be confusing and expensive beyond any benefits which could be derived from them.

The following information should be included on the requisition (see Figure 3–1):

1. Date.
2. Number (identification).
3. Originating department.
4. Account to be charged.
5. Complete description of material desired and quantity.
6. Date material needed.
7. Any special shipping instructions.
8. Signature of authorized requisitioner.

Some organizations include spaces on the requisition form for "Suggested vendor" and "Suggested price." However, the requisitioner should not need to supply these items of information. The purchasing department should be the expert in obtaining source and price information and can determine these aspects of the purchase much more efficiently than can the requisitioner. Additionally, when this information is requested from the requisitioner, it encourages that person to begin contacting possible vendors, which opens the door to "backdoor selling"—that is, bypassing the purchasing department—resulting in embarrassing commitments to a vendor and/or a set of specifications written so that only one vendor will qualify, thus putting that vendor in a sole source position.

Flow of the Purchase Requisition

At a minimum, at least two copies of the requisition should be made: the original to be forwarded to the purchasing department and the duplicate retained by the issuer. It is a common practice to allow only one item to appear on any one purchase requisition, particularly on standard items. In the case of some special items, such as plumbing fittings not regularly carried in stock, several items may be covered by one requisition, provided they are likely to be purchased from one vendor and for delivery at the same time. This simplifies record keeping, since specific items are secured from various suppliers, call for different delivery dates, and require separate purchase orders and treatment. In the case of firms operating with a computerized material requirements planning (MRP) system, the requisitions will be automatically computer generated.

It is important for the purchasing department to establish definitely who has the power to requisition. Under no circumstances should the purchasing department accept requisitions from anyone other than those specifically authorized. Just as important is that all sales personnel know definitely that a requisition is not an order.

All requisitions should be checked carefully before any action is taken. The requested quantity should be based on anticipated needs and should be compared to economical purchasing quantities. The delivery date requested should allow for sufficient time to secure quotations and samples, if necessary, and to execute the purchase order and obtain delivery. If insufficient time is allowed, or the date would involve additional expense, this should be brought to the attention of the requisitioner immediately.

The procedure for handling requisitions on receipt in the purchase office is of sufficient importance to warrant citing an example: On receipt of the requisitions in the purchasing office, after being time stamped, all requisitions are turned over to the order typist or clerk, who has the specification cards and who will attach the proper specification card to each individual requisition. The requisitions then are turned over to the buyer, who will mark all contract items, placing on the requisition the word *contract,* the name of the firm with which the order is to be placed, the price, terms, the FOB point, the total value, and the payment date, for the controller's information. The requisitions then will be turned back to the order typist, who will type the order, after which it will be carefully checked with the specification card, the price, terms, and so on, before the order is finally mailed to the vendor.

When items are not covered by contract, requests for quotations will be sent out on standard inquiry blanks provided for this purpose. Where quotations are to be requested, a list of the names of potential vendors will be written on the back of the requisitions. The requisitions then will be turned over to the typist, who will make out standard inquiry forms and turn them over to the buyer, who will check and sign before mailing.

When the quotations are received from the various vendors, they will be entered on the quotation sheet by the clerk and then turned over to the buyer, who will determine the vendor with whom the business is to be placed. The buyer then initials the requisition and turns it over to the order typist who will type the purchase order.

Use of the Traveling Requisition

In the search to reduce operating expenses, some companies have found it desirable to use the so-called traveling requisition for recurring requirements of materials and standard parts. The traveling requisition is a cardboard form used when a particular item must be purchased frequently for a given department. The traveler contains a complete description of the item and is sent to purchasing when a resupply of the item is needed by the user, indicating quantity and date needed. Purchasing writes the PO, enters data on vendor, price, and PO number on the traveler, and sends it back to the requisitioner, who puts the card in the files until a subsequent resupply is needed. As many as 24 to 36 purchases can be triggered by this traveler card. Use of the traveler eliminates the recopying of routine description data and substitutes for 24 to 36 individual purchase requisitions, saving paperwork and clerical time. It also provides a complete, cumulative purchase history and use record on one form.

When parts or material covered by the traveling requisition are being ordered, the inventory control clerk inserts the date, the date required, the name of the department for which the request is made and the quantity, and obtains an authorized signature prior to sending the requisition to the purchasing department. After selecting the vendor, the buyer fills in the vendor's code number, quantity, required date, unit price, and his or her name and date, and returns the card to the using department or inventory control department after the PO is issued, where it is filed until another requisition is needed.

Use of the Bill of Materials Requisition

A second variation is the bill of material (B/M). It is used by firms who make a standard, manufactured item over a relatively long period of time, as a quick way of notifying purchasing of production needs: A B/M for a toaster made by an appliance manufacturer would list the total number or quantity, including an appropriate scrap allowance, of parts or material to make one end unit (for example, one cord set). Production scheduling then merely notifies purchasing that it has scheduled 18,000 of that model into production next month. Purchasing then will "explode" the B/M (normally by a computerized system) by multiplying through by 18,000 to determine the *total* quantity of material needed to meet next month's production schedule. Comparison of these numbers with quantities in inventory will give purchasing the open-to-buy figures. In a firm which has developed a totally integrated materials computer system, in which long-term agreements containing vendor and pricing information have been entered into the data base, the computer will generate order releases to cover the open-to-buy amounts. Use of the B/M system is a means of simplifying the requisitioning process where a large number of frequently needed line items is involved.

Stockless Buying or Systems Contracting

This technique has been used most frequently in buying stationery and office supplies, repetitive items, maintenance and repair materials, and operating supplies (MRO). This latter class of purchases is characterized by many different types of items, all of comparatively low value and needed immediately when any kind of a plant or equipment failure occurs. The technique is built around a blanket-type contract which is developed in great detail regarding approximate quantities to be used in specified time periods, prices, provisions for adjusting prices, procedures to be followed in picking up requisitions daily and making delivery within 24 hours, simplified billing procedures, and a complete catalog of all items covered by the contract.

Generally the inventory of all items covered by a contract is stored by the supplier, thus eliminating the buyer's investment in inventory and space. Requisitions for items covered by the contract go directly to the supplier and are not processed by the purchasing department. The requisition is used by the supplier to pull stock, to pack, to invoice, and as a delivery slip. The streamlined procedure reduces paper handling costs for the buyer and the seller and has been a help in solving the small-order problem.

Some organizations use a special phone system in systems contracting which requires a data transmission terminal in the purchasing department. The buyer simply inserts a prepunched card for each item needed and indicates the quantity required, which is transmitted electronically to the vendor's computer, which types out the purchase order, at the previously agreed-on contract price for each item.

In some firms with large volume requirements from a specific vendor, that vendor stores items in the customer's plant, as though it were the vendor's warehouse. The buyer's contact with the vendor is by computer, using a printer, through a computer modem (which changes computer impulses so they can be communicated over a telephone line). The system works as follows:

1. The buyer places the blanket order for a family of items, such as fasteners, at firm prices.

2. The vendor delivers predetermined quantities to the inventory area set aside in the buyer's plant. The items are still owned by the vendor.

3. Buyer inspects the items when they are delivered.

4. The computer directs storage to the appropriate bin or shelf.

5. Buyer places POs through the computer terminal, thus relieving the vendor's inventory records.

6. Pick sheets are computer prepared. Buyer physically removes the items from the vendor's inventory.

7. Vendor submits a single invoice monthly for all items picked.

8. Buyer's accounting department makes a single monthly payment for all items used.

9. Computer prepares a summary report, at predetermined intervals, show-

ing the items and quantity used, for both the buyer's and vendor's analysis, planning, and restocking.[1]

Systems contracting has become popular in nonmanufacturing organizations as well. It is no longer confined to MRO items and may well include a number of high-dollar volume commodities. The shortening of the time span from requisition to delivery has resulted in substantial inventory reductions and greater organizational willingness to go along with the supply system. The amount of red tape has become minimal. Since the user normally provides a good estimate of requirements and compensates the supplier in case the forecast is not good, the supplier risks little in inventory investment. The degree of cooperation and information exchange required between buyer and seller in a systems contract often results in a much warmer relationship than is normally exhibited in a traditional arms-length trading situation.

3. Selection of Possible Sources of Supply

Supplier selection constitutes an important part of the purchasing function, and involves the location of qualified sources of supply and assessing the probability that a purchase agreement would result in on-time delivery of satisfactory product and needed services before and after the sale. This step is discussed in detail in Chapter 6.

Among the basic records in a well-organized purchasing office should be:

1. Outstanding contracts against which orders are placed as required.
2. A commodity classification of items purchased.
3. A record of vendors.

With many commodities which are in constant use by an organization, particularly those for which there is an open and free market on which quotations can be obtained at practically any hour of the day, no problem is involved. Bids are often called for, however, on merchandise of common use, such as stationery. A typical bid form is illustrated by Figure 3–3.

4. Analysis of Bids

Analysis of the quotes and the selection of the vendor lead to the placing of an order. Since analysis of bids and the selection of the vendor are matters of judgment, it is necessary only to indicate here that they are logical steps

---

[1] Morris Epstein, "You Can Make Stockless Purchasing Work," *Purchasing World*, April 1983, pp. 50–52.

FIGURE 3–3 Quotation Request

3M COMPANY

REQUEST TO QUOTE

THIS IS NOT AN ORDER

DATE OF REQUEST (MO. | DAY | YR.) | OUR FILE NO. | REQUESTED BY | TENDERS CONSIDERED ONLY IF REC'D. NOT LATER THAN | MAIL REPLIES TO ATTENTION OF

COMPLETE THE SECTION OPPOSITE YOUR FIRM NAME

A	SALES TERMS	SHIPPING POINT	LEAD TIME REQUIRED	F.O.B. POINT
	FREIGHT TERMS	CURRENCY OF PAYMENT	MANUFACTURING SOURCE	OFFER TO EXPIRE ON DATE OF:
B	SALES TERMS	SHIPPING POINT	LEAD TIME REQUIRED	F.O.B. POINT
	FREIGHT TERMS	CURRENCY OF PAYMENT	MANUFACTURING SOURCE	OFFER TO EXPIRE ON DATE OF:
C	SALES TERMS	SHIPPING POINT	LEAD TIME REQUIRED	F.O.B. POINT
	FREIGHT TERMS	CURRENCY OF PAYMENT	MANUFACTURING SOURCE	OFFER TO EXPIRE ON DATE OF:

ITEM	QUANTITY	UNIT	CODE NO. DESCRIPTION	PRICE A	PRICE B	PRICE C	UNIT

FORM NO. 132-1

FILE COPY

in purchasing. Some organizations use a simple bid analysis form (see Figure 3–4) to assist in analyzing the proposals, but there is no uniform practice. And many POs are placed through other than bidding, for example, price lists or negotiation. Determination of price and terms is discussed in detail in Chapter 7.

5. Preparation of the Purchase Order

The placing of an order usually involves preparation of a purchase order form (see Figure 3–5) unless the vendor's sales agreement or a release against a blanket order is used instead. Failure to use the proper contract form may result in serious legal complications. Furthermore, the transaction may not be properly recorded. Therefore, even where an order is placed by telephone, a written order should follow for purposes of confirmation. At times, when emergency conditions arise, it may be expedient to send a truck to pick up parts without first going through the usual procedure of requisition and purchase order. But in no instance—unless it be for minor pur-

FIGURE 3-4 Bid Analysis Form

TELEPHONE BID RECORD
ARIZONA STATE UNIVERSITY

DATE | BY | PURCHASE REQUISITION

VENDOR | QUOTED BY | BID AMOUNT

VENDOR | QUOTED BY | BID AMOUNT

VENDOR | QUOTED BY | BID AMOUNT

QUANT. | DESCRIPTION

TOTAL
DELIVERY TIME
TERMS
F. O. B. POINT

101422-9 2/80

FIGURE 3–5   Purchase Order

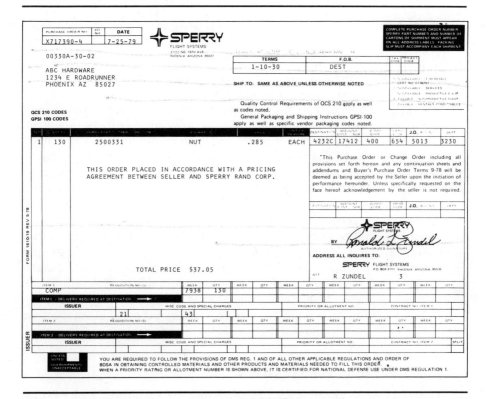

chases from petty cash—should the materials be bought without a written order of some sort.

All companies have purchase order forms; in practice, however, all purchases are not governed by the conditions stipulated on the purchase order but many are governed by the sales agreement submitted by the seller. A comparison of the sales agreements and the purchase order forms may be interesting. Since every company naturally seeks to protect itself as completely as possible, responsibilities which the purchase order form assigns to the source of supply are, in the sales agreement, often transferred to the buyer. Naturally, a company is anxious to use its own sales agreement when selling its products and its own purchase order form when buying.

Some purchasing officers assert that they will not make any purchase except on their own order form. If the seller strenuously objects to any of the conditions contained in the order form and can present good reasons for the modification of such provisions, a compromise is effected. In a strong sellers' market, however, it may be difficult to adhere to this rule. Also, some suppliers refuse to sell except when the buyer signs their sales order form. If there is no alternative source, as, for example, when a company holds a patent on an article, the value of which is so outstanding that no substitute is acceptable, then the purchasing officer has no choice in the matter. But ordinarily the choice as to which document shall actually be used depends somewhat on the comparative strength of the two parties, the character of the commodity being purchased, the complexity of the transaction, and the strategy used in securing or placing the order.

A good deal of confusion seems to prevail on this whole matter. A purchasing agent may freely sign a salesman's order form (which, though it may bind the purchaser, legally is not likely to be binding on the vendor until later confirmed by its home office) and then send a purchase order to the vendor, expecting it to govern. Or a purchasing agent, subsequent to the mailing of a purchase order, may receive in reply not an acceptance but a sales order, which really is a counteroffer, and not an acceptance.

However, in the case of low-dollar-value POs, having a legally binding agreement may not be of great importance, for the likelihood of subsequent legal action is slight. For this reason, and to save the cost of handling extra paperwork, many firms do not even use an acknowledgment or acceptance copy as part of the purchase order packet on orders under a certain dollar amount, for example, $5,000. This means that they do not have a legally binding contract until the materials arrive. However, the cost of legal action to force delivery on small value POs would not be feasible.

Form of the Purchase Order

Purchase order forms vary tremendously as to format and routing through the organization. The movement to secure a standard purchase order form has not gained much headway.

The essential requirements on any satisfactory purchase order form are the serial number, date of issue, the name and address of the firm receiving the order, quantity and description of the items ordered, date of delivery required, shipping directions, price, terms of payment, and conditions governing the order.

These conditions governing the relations between the buyer and the seller are extremely important and the question of what should and what should not be included is subject to a good deal of discussion. What actually appears on the purchase order form of any individual company is usually the result of experience. The items included in the conditions might:

1. Contain provisions to guard the buyer from damage suits caused by patent infringement.

2. Contain provisions concerning price, such as "If the price is not stated on this order, material must not be billed at a price higher than last paid without notice to us and our acceptance thereof."

3. Contain clauses stating that no charges will be allowed for boxing, crating, or drayage.

4. Stipulate that the acceptance of the materials is contingent on inspection and quality.

5. Require in case of rejection that the seller receive a new order from the buyer before replacement is made.

6. Mention rejection because of quality.

7. Provide for cancellation of the order if deliveries are not received on the date specified in the order.

8. Contain conditions stating that the buyer refuses to accept drafts drawn against the buyer.

9. Have some mention of quantity, relating to overshipments or undershipments of the quantities called for. In certain industries it is hard to control definitely the amount obtained from a production run, and in such instances, overruns and underruns are usually accepted within certain limits.

10. Provide for matters of special interest to the companies issuing the forms, governing such matters as arbitration and the disposition of tools required in making parts.

Individual companies differ widely both in the number of copies of a purchase order issued and in the method of handling these copies. In a typical example, the distribution may be as follows: The original is sent to the supplier, sometimes accompanied by a duplicate copy to be returned by the vendor as an acceptance copy to complete the contract.

One copy is filed in the numerical PO file maintained by the purchasing department; another may be maintained in the vendor file. In some companies, the purchasing department does not maintain hard copies of POs; instead the copies are photographed and kept in microfilm or microfiche form. One copy is sent to the accounting department for use in the accounts payable process. A copy is sent to the stores department so it can plan for the receipt of the materials. A separate copy may be sent to the receiving department (if receiving and stores are organizationally separate) where it will be filed alphabetically by vendor and used to record quantities actually received when the shipment arrives. If the material is to go through incoming inspection (which normally would be raw material and production parts) a copy would be routed there also.

All the copies of the purchase order, though essentially identical and all typed at one operation, are by no means identical in form. For instance, the vendor's acceptance copy may contain an acceptance statement not reproduced on any of the other copies. Only the receiving department's copy may provide for entering the receiving data. The purchasing department copies may provide space for data regarding delivery promise, invoices, and shipments. Pricing information normally is eliminated from the receiving copy, due to its confidential nature.

As might be expected, purchase orders are filed in various ways. The really important thing is to be able to locate the documents any time they are wanted. So far as possible, too, all papers relating to a particular purchase order should be attached to one copy or, if necessary to file some elsewhere, cross-referenced so they can be found quickly. Nothing reflects more unfavorably on a purchasing department than to have inquiries made by users, production, stores, engineering, or accounting personnel concerning information answerable only from the purchase order and to find the purchasing personnel cannot answer the questions promptly and authoritatively.

One method of filing the purchase orders, where two are kept, is to file one numerically by the purchase order number, and to file the second, together with the accompanying requisition and correspondence, alphabetically by vendor's name.

Still another procedure is to file one alphabetically by vendor, and the second copy in a tickler file under the date the acceptance copy should be received from the vendor. In case acceptance is not received according to the time due, this fact is noted on this copy of the purchase order, follow-up is instituted in an effort to get the acceptance, and the purchase order is moved ahead to a second "acceptance date." When the order is finally accepted, the tickler copy is again moved; this time being filed under the date either by which final follow-up is desirable or by which the shipment is due.

Giving or sending a purchase order does not constitute a contract until it has been accepted. The usual form of acceptance requested is that of an "acknowledgment" sent by the vendor to the purchasing department. Just what does constitute mutual consent and the acceptance of an offer is primarily a legal question. Generalizations concerning the acceptance of offers, as any lawyer will indicate, are likely to be only generalizations with many exceptions.

One further reason for insisting on securing an acceptance of the purchase order is that, quite aside from any question of law, unless the order is accepted, the buyer can only assume that delivery will be made by the requested date. When delivery dates are uncertain, definite information in advance is most important if the buyer is to plan operations effectively.

Blanket and Open-End Orders

The cost of issuing and handling purchase orders may be reduced when conditions permit the use of blanket or open-end orders. A blanket order usually covers a variety of items. An open-end order allows for addition of items and/or extension of time. MRO items and production line require-

FIGURE 3-6 Blanket Order Release

RAYTHEON	RAYTHEON COMPANY SORENSEN OPERATION SOUTH NORWALK, CONN.				BLANKET ORDER RELEASE
					THIS NUMBER MUST APPEAR ON ALL DOCUMENTS AND PACKAGES

REQUISITION NO.	REQUISITIONED BY:	UNIT	RELEASE DATE	PURCHASE ORDER NO.	RELEASE NO.
TO		SHIP VIA UPS		ACCOUNT NO.	
		SHIP MATERIAL TO ABOVE ADDRESS UNLESS INDICATED OTHERWISE BELOW		PROD. SHOP ORDER NO.	
		SORENSEN		DELIVER MATERIAL TO (INTERNAL)	

DELIVERY AT DESTINATION		VENDOR CODE 620393	MATERIAL CODE	TAX– ABLE	YES	NO X	EXEMPTION NO. 5151175		

RECEIVED Date	Quantity	Item	Quantity Ordered	D E S C R I P T I O N	Part Number	Dev	Net Unit Price	

x INDICATES CONFIRMING ORDER		BLANKET ORDER TERMS AND CONDITIONS APPLY		Total
DATE	YOUR			
RECEIVING DEPARTMENT USE ONLY				

ments used in volume and purchased repetitively over a period of months may be bought in this manner.

All terms and conditions involving the purchase of estimated quantities over a period are negotiated and incorporated in the original order. Subsequently, releases of specific quantities are made against the order. In some instances, it is possible to tie the preparation of the releases into the production scheduling procedures and forward them to the purchasing department for transmission to the vendor. It is not unusual for an open-end order to remain in effect for a year, or until changes in design, material specification, or conditions affecting price or delivery make new negotiations desirable or necessary. Figure 3-6 shows a form used to authorize release of materials on a blanket order.

6. Follow-Up and Expediting

After a PO has been issued to a vendor, the buyer may wish to follow up and/or expedite the order. At the time the order is issued, an appropriate follow-up date is indicated. In some firms, purchasing has full-time follow-up and expediting personnel.

Follow-up is the routine tracking of an order to assure that the vendor

FIGURE 3–7   Follow-Up Form

aps.

PURCHASE ORDER FOLLOW-UP
(Please Rush Reply)
PURCHASING DEPARTMENT · P.O. BOX 21666 · PHOENIX, ARIZONA 85036

Date _____

This is our _____ Request

Please Answer Immediately

REPLY TO ITEMS CHECKED BELOW BY
☐ This Form   ☐ Wire   ☐ Phone

Our Purchase Order No.	Request for Quotation No.	Your Invoice No.	Date	Amount	Your Reference

☐ 1. RUSH SHIPMENT. ADVISE EARLIEST DATE.
☐ 2. WHEN WILL SHIPMENT BE MADE? IF SHIPPED, ADVISE METHOD.
☐ 3. PLEASE TRACE SHIPMENT.
☐ 4. IF SHIPMENT HAS BEEN MADE, MAIL INVOICE, TODAY.
☐ 5. PLEASE MAIL RECEIPTED FREIGHT BILL.
☐ 6. WHY DID YOU NOT SHIP AS PROMISED? ADVISE WHEN YOU WILL SHIP.
☐ 7. WILL YOU SHIP ON DATE SHOWN ON PURCHASE ORDER?
☐ 8. RELEASE SHIPMENTS AS SHOWN UNDER REMARKS.
☐ 9. PLEASE MAIL US ACCEPTANCE COPY OF OUR PURCHASE ORDER.
☐ 10. PLEASE ACKNOWLEDGE OUR ORDER.
☐ 11. PLEASE MAKE YOUR SHIPPING DATE MORE SPECIFIC.
☐ 12. WHEN WILL BALANCE OF ORDER BE SHIPPED.
☐ 13. WHEN WILL PRICES BE SUBMITTED? PLEASE RUSH.
☐ 14. PLEASE MAIL SHIPPING NOTICE.
☐ 15. PLEASE INDICATE OUR PURCHASE ORDER NUMBER ON PAPERS REFERRED TO OR ATTACHED.

☐ 16. WE HAVE NO RECORD OF TRANSACTION COVERED BY INVOICE. ADVISE DATE OF SHIPMENT, NAME OF PERSON PLACING ORDER AND FURNISH SIGNED DELIVERY RECEIPT COPY.
☐ 17. INVOICE RETURNED HEREWITH.
☐ 18. INVOICE IS REQUIRED IN _____ COPIES.
☐ 19. PRICE OR DISCOUNT IS NOT IN ACCORDANCE WITH QUOTATION.
☐ 20. TERMS ON INVOICE ARE NOT IN ACCORDANCE WITH THE PURCHASE ORDER.
☐ 21. ENCLOSED INVOICE SENT TO US IN ERROR.
☐ 22. DIFFERENCE IN QUANTITY.
☐ 23. UNIT PRICE INCORRECT.
☐ 24. EXTENSION INCORRECT.
☐ 25. PURCHASE ORDER NO. LACKING OR INCORRECT.
☐ 26. SALES TAX DOES NOT APPLY — See reverse side of Purchase Order.
☐ 27. SHOULD BE BILLED F.O.B. DESTINATION.
☐ 28. HAVE YOU CONSIDERED THIS ORDER COMPLETE?
☐ 29. _____

Reply: _____

Vendor
By _____

Purchasing
By _____

510-00J

SEND WHITE AND PINK COPIES WITH CARBON INTACT. WHITE COPY IS RETURNED WITH REPLY.

will be able to meet delivery promises. If problems—for example, quality or delivery—are developing, the buyer needs to know this as soon as possible, so that appropriate action can be taken. Follow-up, which requires frequent inquiries of the vendor on progress and possibly a visit to the vendor's facility, will be done only on large-dollar and/or long lead-time buys. The follow-up often is done by phone, to get immediate information and answers, but some firms use a simple form, often computer generated, to request information on expected shipping date or percentage of the production process completed as of a certain date. Figure 3–7 shows one follow-up form.

Expediting is the application of pressure on vendors to get them either to meet the original delivery promise or to deliver ahead of schedule. It may involve the threat of order cancellation or withdrawal of future business if the vendor cannot meet the agreement. Expediting should be necessary on only a small percentage of the POs issued, for if the buyer has done a good job of analyzing vendor capabilities, only reliable vendors—ones who will perform according to the purchase agreement—will be selected. And if the firm has done an adequate job of planning its material requirements, it should not need to ask a vendor to move up the delivery date except in unusual situations. Of course, in times of severe material scarcity such as in the early 1970s, the expediting activity assumes greater importance.

7. Receipt and Inspection of Goods

The proper receipt of materials and other items is of vital importance. The great majority of firms have, as a result of experience, centralized all receiving under one department, the chief exceptions being those large companies with multiple plants. Receiving is so closely related to purchasing that, in probably 70 percent of the cases, the receiving department is directly or indirectly responsible to the purchasing department.

The arrival of the goods always involves one additional step and sometimes two. All incoming shipments should be checked by the receiving department, except in the case of some small-value MRO items, which purchasing may instruct the supplier to mark for direct shipment to the requisitioner. That individual may complete a separate receiving form, or to reduce paperwork, payment may be made simply by comparing the vendor invoice with the PO. If they agree, payment is made. This system depends on the requisitioner notifying purchasing if the requested item never was received; in this case, the vendor is asked to supply proof of delivery; lacking such proof, the vendor is told to make a replacement shipment. Admittedly, this is a novel approach, and is used only for nonproduction, noninventory purchases of small value, for example, under $200.

Normally one copy of the PO form, often with the quantity column masked out to force a count, is used for receiving. This information then must be supplied to the purchasing department to close out the order, to inventory control to update the inventory files, and to accounts payable for the invoice clearance and payment. Some firms use a separate receiving slip form, rather than a copy of the PO, on which receiving records the date of receipt, vendor name, description of materials, and the receiving count. In companies with an integrated computer materials system, receiving counts are entered directly into the computer data file.

Sometimes suppliers are negligent about invoicing goods shipped, and it may be necessary to request the invoice to complete the transaction. On the other hand, payment of an invoice prior to the receipt of material is often requested. The question then is: When invoices provide for cash discounts, do you pay the invoice within the discount period, even though the material may not actually have been received, or do you withhold payment until the material arrives, even at the risk of losing cash discounts?

The arguments for withholding payment of the invoice until after the goods have arrived are as follows:

1. Frequently the invoice does not reach the buyer until late in the discount period and, on occasion, may even arrive after it. This situation arises through a failure on the part of the vendor *(a)* to mail the invoice promptly, especially where due allowance is not made for the Saturdays, Sundays, or holidays which elapse between the dating of the invoice and the processing and mailing of it, and *(b)* where the vendor is, in terms of mailing time, several days away from the buyer.

2. It is unsound buying practice to pay for anything until an opportunity has been given for inspection. The transaction has not, in fact, been completed until the material or part has actually been accepted, and payment prior to this time is premature. In fact, legally, the title to the goods may not have passed to the buyer until acceptance of them.

3. In any event, the common practice of dating invoices as of the date of shipment should be amended to provide that the discount period runs from receipt of the invoice or the goods.

The arguments in favor of passing the invoice for payment without awaiting the arrival, inspection, and acceptance of the material are several:

1. The financial consideration may be substantial.

2. Failure to take the cash discounts as a matter of course reflects unfavorably on the credit standing of the buyer.

3. When purchasing from reputable vendors, mutually satisfactory adjustments arising out of unsatisfactory material will easily be made, even though the invoice has been paid.

Obviously, the problem of payment to take cash discounts before material actually is received can be solved if purchasing is successful in negotiating cash discount terms "from receipt of invoice or material, whichever occurs later."

Some firms, particularly those with integrated computer purchasing systems, are beginning to question whether they need to receive an invoice at all, since the invoice provides no information that they do not already have and it is another piece of paperwork that costs money to handle. These firms then notify their vendors that payment, under the agreed-on cash discount schedule, will be made in a set number of days from receipt of satisfactory merchandise (and they may specify that payment will be made only after the complete shipment has been received). They simply then compare, in their computer system, the PO, the receiving report, and the inspection report; if they agree then the computer simply prints a check at the receipt date plus the agreed-on payment term. Obviously, this requires that the receiving report be accurate; that the PO be fully priced, including taxes and cash discount terms; and that purchases be made FOB destination, since there is no way to enter in freight charges. The PO then is the controlling document. An additional enhancement is use of an electronic funds transfer system (EFT) where the buyer simply provides its bank with a computer tape (or transmits payment information from its computer through a telephone modem to the bank's computer), and the funds are transferred to the vendor's bank account by account number and PO number.

Aside from checking the quantity of goods received, there is the problem of inspection. Inspection for quality is handled differently by various concerns. Some merchandise is not inspected for quality at all; some is inspected only by sampling; some is 100 percent inspected; and some is checked by a laboratory or an independent testing agency. A concern may have a quality control department which determines how much and how frequently and in what manner inspection shall be made. Following inspection, it may be necessary to return some of the material to the supplier. The problem of inspection is discussed in more detail in Chapter 4.

In checking the goods received, it sometimes will appear that shortages exist either because material has been lost en route or because it was short shipped. Occasionally, too, there is evidence that the shipment has been tampered with or that the shipment has been damaged in transit. In all such cases, full reports are called for, going to both the traffic department and the purchasing department.

8. Clearing the Invoices and Payment

Invoices usually arrive before the goods, except on local deliveries, in which case they arrive almost simultaneously with them. Since the invoice constitutes a definite claim against the buyer, it needs to be handled with great care. Invoices are commonly requested in duplicate. In addition, it is not uncommon to find such statements as "invoices must show our order number and itemized price for each article invoiced."

Procedure relating to invoice clearance is not uniform. In fact, there is difference of opinion on whether the checking and approval of the invoice is a function of the purchasing department or of the accounting department. Clearly, the invoice must be checked and audited. Many concerns maintain that since the work is accounting in character, the accounting department should do it. In such companies, verification of delivery is given by the receiving department; inspection verifies quality; and prices, terms, and extensions are checked in accounts payable. For this purpose a copy of each purchase order is filed in accounts payable. The arguments for this procedure are that such checking is essentially an accounting function; that it relieves the purchasing department of the performance of a task not essential to purchasing; that it concentrates all the accounting work in a single office; and that it provides a check and balance between the commitment to buy and the payment to the supplier.

The prime reason for having invoices checked in the purchasing department is that this is where the original agreement was made. If discrepancies exist, immediate action can be taken by purchasing. However, since the desired check and balance is lost under this approach, it normally is done this way only in the relatively small organization where one person wears both purchasing and receiving hats.

Where the invoice is normally handled by the accounting department, the following procedure is typical:

1. All invoices are mailed in duplicate by the vendor directly to the accounts payable department, where they are promptly time stamped. All invoices are then checked and certified for payment, except where the purchase order and the invoice differ.

2. Invoices at variance with the purchase order on price, terms, or other features are referred to the purchasing department for approval.

Since the time required in purchasing to resolve minor variances might be more valuable to the organization than the dollar amount in dispute, many organizations use a decision rule that calls for payment of the invoice as submitted, providing the difference is within prescribed limits, for example ±5 percent or $25, whichever is smaller. Of course, accounts payable should keep a record of the variances paid by vendor account to identify vendors who are intentionally short shipping.

If any of the necessary information is not on the invoice or if the information does not agree with the purchase order, the invoice is returned to the vendor for correction. Ordinarily, the buyer insists that, in computing discounts, the allowable period dates from the receipt of the corrected invoice, and not from the date originally received.

In every instance of cancellation of a purchase order involving the payment of cancellation charges, accounting requires from the purchasing department a "change notice" referring to the order and defining the payment to be made before passing an invoice for such payment. The director of purchases must approve cancellation charges if the amount is over a specified figure.

In cases where purchasing does the invoice checking, the following procedure applies: after being checked and adjusted for any necessary corrections, the original invoice is forwarded to the accounting department to be held until the purchasing department authorizes its payment. The duplicate invoice is retained by the purchasing department until the receiving department notifies it of the receipt of the materials. As soon as the purchasing department obtains this notification in the form of a receiving report, it checks that report against the invoice. If the receiving report and the invoice agree, the purchasing office keeps both documents until it receives assurance from inspection that the goods are acceptable. The purchasing department then forwards its duplicate copy of the invoice and the report from the receiving department to the accounting department, where the original copy of the invoice is already on file.

9. Maintenance of Records

After having gone through the steps described, all that remains for the disposal of any order is to complete the records of the purchasing department. This operation involves little more than assembling and filing the purchasing department's copies of the documents relating to the order and transferring to appropriate records the information the department may wish to keep. The former is largely a routine matter. The latter involves judgment as to what records are to be kept and also for how long.

Most companies differentiate between the various forms and records as to their importance. For example, a purchase order constitutes evidence of a contract with an outside party and as such may well be retained much longer than the requisition, which is an internal memorandum.

The minimum, basic records to be maintained, either manually or by computer, are:

1. PO log, which identifies all POs by number and indicates the open or closed status of each.
2. PO file, containing a copy of all POs, filed numerically.
3. Commodity file, showing all purchases of each major commodity or item (date, vendor, quantity, price, PO number).
4. Vendor history file, showing all purchases placed with major large-total-value vendors.

Some of the optional record files are:

1. Labor contracts, giving status of the union contracts (expiration dates) of all major suppliers.
2. Tool and die record showing tooling purchased, initial life (or production quantity), usage history, price, ownership, and location. This information may avoid the buyer being billed more than once for the same tooling.
3. Minority and small business purchases, showing dollar purchases from such vendors.
4. Bid-award history file, showing suppliers asked to bid, amounts bid, number of no bids, and the successful bidder, by major items. This information may highlight vendor bid patterns and possible collusion.

POLICY AND PROCEDURE MANUAL

Carefully prepared, detailed statements of organization, of duties of the various personnel, and of procedures and filing systems (including illustrative forms, fully explained) are of value not only to the senior members of the department but even more so to newcomers. A manual is almost an essential for the well-conceived in-company training program for junior members. Furthermore, it adds an element of flexibility in facilitating the transfer of personnel from one job to another in case of vacation, illness, or the temporary overburdening of a particular segment of the organization. Finally, the manual is useful in explaining to those not in the department what and how things are done.

Some managers feel that because their departments are not so large as those in bigger companies, there is no special need for a manual. They feel that everyone knows all that would commonly be put in a manual anyway and that hence there is no need for writing it all down. This argument overlooks the benefits gained in the actual task of preparing the manual.

The preparation of a manual is time consuming and somewhat tedious, to be sure, but one well worth the cost. It is well to bear in mind that unless the work is carefully planned and well done, accurate, and reasonably complete, it might almost as well not be done at all. Careful advance planning of the coverage, emphasis, and arrangement is essential, to include a clear definition of the purposes sought in issuing the manual and the uses to which it is to be put, for both of these have a bearing on its length, form, and content.

Very early in the project, the preparer must decide whether the manual is to cover only policy or is to include also a description of the organization and the procedure, and if the latter, in how much detail. A collection of manuals now in use should be the starting point. Fortunately, excellent sample manuals that will serve as guides can be obtained from any number of companies.

When the general outlines have been determined, the actual writing may be undertaken. This work need not be done all at one time but section by section as the opportunity presents itself. It also is well to have the work thoroughly discussed and carefully checked, not only by those within the department itself but by those outside, such as engineering and production personnel, whose operations are directly affected. When a section is completed, that portion may provide the basis for a department discussion forum, not only for the sake of spotting errors and suggesting modifications before the material is actually reproduced but also to ensure that everyone understands its contents. This should be done prior to issue. When reproduced, a loose-leaf form may be found preferable, since it allows for easy revision. Another worthwhile step is to have the chief executive of the company write a short foreword, endorsing the policy and practices of the department and defining its authority.

While many subjects might be covered in the manual, some of the more common are authority to requisition, competitive bidding, approved vendors, vendor contacts and commitments, authority to question specifications, purchases for employees, gifts, blanket purchase orders, confidential data, rush orders, vendor relations, lead times, determination of quantity to buy, over and short allowance procedure, local purchases, capital equipment, personal service purchases, repair service purchases, authority to select vendors, confirming orders, unpriced purchase orders, documentation for purchase decisions, invoice clearance and payment, invoice discrepancies, freight bills, change orders, samples, returned materials, disposal of scrap and surplus, determination of price paid, small order procedures, salesperson interviews, and reporting of data.

USE OF THE COMPUTER IN PURCHASING

Up to this point, the discussion and the analysis of the procedures needed and used in performing the purchasing function have been based on the use of traditional office equipment and clerical methods. Within the past 30 years, however, we have witnessed a remarkable development of data processing equipment use in aiding the recording, analysis, and reporting of information in the operation of complex business systems. There are many potential areas of computer application in purchasing.[2]

When a computer system is installed to assist in performing the purchasing function, the essential steps of good purchasing remain much the same as those of the manual methods. The change occurs only in the way the essential steps are performed. When it is economically feasible to introduce a computer system, four basic benefits are obtained:

1. The electronic handling of procedures reduces clerical manual effort to a minimum.

2. Information from records becomes available almost instantly.

3. Control over operations is improved, not only by the timely availability of the information for sound decision making but also by the flexibility afforded by the ease of handling vast quantities of detail, thus providing new tools for the buyer and manager.

4. Operating performance is improved by the availability of information and the improved control of operations.

At the beginning of this chapter, the nine essential steps of purchasing were listed and then discussed. Now we will consider briefly how the power of the computer can be applied to each step.

1. Recognition of Need. When used properly, computers can be of great assistance in analyzing information pertaining to past usage, markets,

---

[2]Robert B. Vollum, "43 Ways Computers Can Help You," *Purchasing World,* June 1983, pp. 81–82; and John Herrmann, "How Chemical Bank Uses Computers to Drive Hard Bargains," *Management Technology,* March 1984, pp. 42–46.

economic factors, prices, and expected usage, to the end that forecasts can be made with promptness and improved accuracy. Computers can assist in translating forecasts into estimates of requirements and needed materials, quantities, and delivery dates.

2. Description of the Need. The responsibility for developing an accurate statement or specification for the article or the commodity used in the firm normally rests with the engineering or the using department. After determination, the specification can be made readily available by recording the specification in a computer data file. The quantities of the items required to be purchased are determined after obtaining the breakdown of the information mentioned in Step 1 and exploding the bill of materials to determine the effect of existing inventories and open orders on the specific requirements. The requisition for specific requirements can be fed into the computer for an economical purchasing quantity analysis to consider such things as acquisition costs (including costs of placing an order, quantity discounts, and transportation costs) against inventory carrying costs.

3. Determine and Analyze Possible Sources of Supply. As the requisition is processed by the computer, information regarding suppliers, previously stored in the computer's memory, can provide lists of vendors and their past prices and record of performance and prepare bid request forms.

4. Determine Price and Terms. Vendors' proposals can be programmed into the computer data base, allowing the computer to arrive at the most efficient placement of business in situations when many variables are present, such as quantity discounts, payment terms, learning curves, transportation rates and allowances, multiple plants to be supplied, opportunities to group orders, and numerous suppliers scattered geographically.

5. Prepare and Place the PO. Human judgment must be used in the final selection of the vendor(s). But once the selection is made and the pricing determined, the computer can produce the purchase order or blanket order release automatically.

6. Follow Up and/or Expedite the Order. When the PO is placed, an order status record is created. This record is kept up to date by recording the receipts of the ordered material, the invoices, the change orders, and the expediting data, thus providing the current status of each open order. This record becomes the basic file for the invoice and receiving audit, and the follow-up and expediting procedures. It can automatically produce the follow-up paperwork, following a predetermined schedule. If a materials requirements planning (MRP) system is used, when schedule changes occur the computer can determine where and when expediting or de-expediting action is needed.

7. Receipt and Inspection of Goods. Receiving and inspection reports can be fed into the order status record as completed and used in auditing the invoice, in keeping inventory records, and in compiling quality reports.

8. Clear the Invoice and Pay the Supplier. When invoices are received, the computer matches the invoices to the purchase orders, and the computer can be programmed to audit price, quantity, extension, discounts if any, routing, and transportation terms. Where everything is in order, a check for the proper payment can be written automatically and held for the payment due date.

9. Maintenance of Records. Closed orders usually are carried in the order status record for a period of time (perhaps six months) to allow adequate time for any rejections or adjustments. The PO log, data on vendor performance, vendor history, commodity history, labor contracts, tool and die record, minority and small business purchases, and bid-award history file can be maintained in the computer and called up on a cathode ray tube (CRT) in a matter of seconds. Many of the management and operations reports can be computer generated.

Figure 3–8 shows a simple flow chart of a computerized purchasing system. There are a larger number of potential uses to which the computer may be put and a number of research studies have attempted to determine the nature of current applications. The first question concerns how (where) the computer can be used in purchasing. The second question deals with what is now being done.

Computer Applications Potential

While we have not yet explored all of the potential applications of the computer in purchasing, the three general areas are:

1. Purchasing Operating Systems. These process data for the routine operations of the department, such as maintaining the status of purchasing actions; typing POs, change orders, and requests for quotation; filing and sorting vendor lists; and maintaining commodity, price, and vendor history files. Typically those purchasing functions having large volumes of repetitive data are most likely to use these systems. The greater accuracy of high quality data throughput and turnaround effectiveness justify their use. These systems also feed information from a common data base to the other two systems.

FIGURE 3–8   Simplified Flow Chart of an Automated Purchasing System

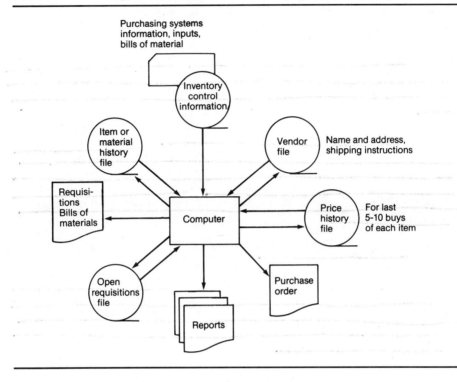

2. Management-Reporting Systems. These systems process data, often drawing on data files set up for the purchasing operating systems files, and then report these data to management. Examples are the vendor and buyer performance evaluation reports.

3. Decision-Assisting (Decision-Support) Systems. These systems process data to assist purchasing management in selecting from among alternatives. While all three systems (operating, management-reporting, and decision-assisting) can be directly or indirectly useful to the organization by providing more timely or accurate information on which to base choices, decision-assisting systems have further refinements. They do not merely present or analyze data, but rather they incorporate information into an analytical framework utilizing techniques such as mathematical relationships, simulations, or other algorithms. The outcome is definitive in nature and presents the results in either a deterministic or probabilistic fashion. Decision-assisting systems typically select alternative actions; management then considers the recommendation of the model with other variables (that may not be quantifiable) in arriving at a final decision. Examples are quo-

TABLE 3–1   Level of Computerization (percent reporting)

	No Action	In Planning	In Implementation	Online
Requirements generation	29%	23%	3%	45%
Buyer workload scheduling	75	14	2	9
Solicitation generation (RFP)	68	16	4	12
Expediting	43	22	4	31
Purchase order generation	25	29	5	41
Receiving report	24	25	4	47
Cash commitment reporting	44	15	3	38
Buyer workload evaluation	72	15	1	12
Buyer performance evaluation	71	16	1	12
Vendor history recording	29	28	4	39
Vendor performance evaluation	38	35	5	22

tation analysis, price discount analysis, synthetic pricing, forecasting, and forward buying and futures trading models.

Current Computer Applications

A study conducted in 1985, using data supplied by 278 purchasing executives, presented a picture of computer activity across 11 purchasing functions. Table 3–1 presents the results.[3]

A 1987 *Purchasing* magazine survey found that 88 percent of the organizations make some use of the computer in purchasing (up 15 percent from a similar survey two years earlier). Table 3–2 shows the uses made of computer systems.[4]

Those companies that had some form of online purchasing system could collect and store the following information:

---

[3] Bernard J. LaLonde and Margaret A. Emmelhainz, "Electronic Purchase Order Interchange," *Journal of Purchasing and Materials Management,* Fall 1985, p. 4.

[4] "Computers in Purchasing: Buyers Expect More Now," *Purchasing,* July 30, 1987, p. 16.

Purchase orders, 84 percent

Vendors, 83 percent

Parts, 75 percent

Receipts, 73 percent

Change orders, 67 percent

Order releases, 62 percent

Requisitions, 48 percent

TABLE 3–2   Computer Uses (in computerized departments)

	Percent Using
Online decision support system	40%
Online purchase order processing	64
Batch processing of purchase orders	32
Preparation of status reports	66
Offline problem solving	46

The *Purchasing* survey also found that 70 percent share computerized data with other departments in the organization (up from 55 percent in a similar 1985 study). The departments cited as those with which information was shared were accounts payable, inventory control, and production control. Sixty-nine percent (up from 57 percent in 1985) said they planned to expand their computer applications in purchasing.[5]

This study also noted a shift in the hardware being used to process purchasing data. Nearly half the respondents (49 percent) used a centrally controlled mainframe, which was substantially smaller than the 67 percent in 1985. This is a reflection of the increased hardware and software capabilities of the microcomputers (personal computers). Thirty-five percent used microcomputers, either as stand alone units or networked in some way. An additional 16 percent said they used microcomputers for offline processing of data or for running programs that draw on centrally controlled information.[6]

Microcomputers in Purchasing

The microcomputer (desktop, personal computer) has been the primary factor which has brought computer applications to purchasing. The microcomputer arrived on the scene in the early 1980s and, after a slow start,

---

[5]*Ibid.*, pp. 16–17.
[6]*Ibid.*

has become an integral part of many purchasing systems, both large and small. The reasons:

1. For a modest equipment investment in hardware (about $5,000, complete with adequate storage capacity and printer) and perhaps another $2,000 for software programs, the purchasing department can have the same computing power today that only a few years ago required a $1 million mainframe computer system.

2. The "what if" questions—for example, a price increase on a major purchased commodity—can be answered by the computer in a matter of seconds. Thus purchasing can estimate quickly and accurately the effect on the whole system that a change in one of the key variables will cause. This gives purchasing the planning power it so sorely needs.

3. The personal computer is a stand-alone system, which is dedicated for use in purchasing. This means that purchasing is in control of how and when the computer will be used, rather than having to queue up with finance, accounting, engineering, marketing, and operations to get time on the mainframe unit.

4. Data fed to the microcomputer can remain confidential within purchasing, as long as care is taken to safeguard the access codes.

5. The timeliness and accuracy of data and reports can be greatly improved, with resultant time savings for the purchasing decision maker and increased quality of decisions made.

6. Spreadsheet software available "off the shelf" permits applications to routine activities in purchasing, such as monitoring purchase orders, inventories, prices, discounts, raw material usage, delivery dates, and financial and statistical information. Common nonroutine activity applications include bid evaluation, vendor evaluation, transportation cost analysis, inventory control, impact analysis of inflation, and analysis of process costs.[7]

These microcomputers have the data capacity and computational ability, if properly programmed, to handle all the applications discussed under the earlier heading of "Computer Applications Potential": (1) purchasing operating systems, (2) management-reporting systems, and (3) decision-assisting systems. Certainly they can handle all the computer applications in the nine essential purchasing steps discussed earlier.

---

[7]R. E. Mazurak, S. R. Rao, and D. W. Scotton, "Spreadsheet Software Applications in Purchasing," *Journal of Purchasing and Materials Management*, Winter 1985, pp. 8–16.

Computer Software

To operate the computer, two types of software are needed. The first is the *systems software,* a group of programs provided by the computer manufacturer that runs the computer—starts it and makes the components work together. The standard ones for the desktop computers are CP/M and DOS. They do things such as copy information from one storage disk to another and cause the printer to work. The systems software currently is very adequate for the tasks at hand.

Second is the *applications software,* which are the programs that manipulate data for a specific purpose, such as maintaining the open order file or taking vendor performance statistics and formating them into a vendor performance evaluation analysis and report. Over the past few years, several "off-the-shelf" software packages for purchasing have become available. For example, a 1987 *Purchasing* magazine article lists 42 software programs that "deal directly with purchasing either as stand-alone programs or as major modules of larger programs."[8] Prior to the mid-1980s, most firms had to write their own programs, since packaged software was not available. Companies with large purchasing systems, requiring huge amounts of data, still normally must design their own software program.

Electronic Data Interchange (EDI) with Suppliers

Another exciting development in the 1980s, with the growth of microcomputer usage in purchasing, is the capability of direct electronic transmission of data and standard business forms between a buying firm and its supplier. This allows both buyer and seller to obtain and provide much more timely and accurate information, permitting greater administrative efficiency through paperwork reduction, as well as raising the quality level of decisions made. Such applications have been in place for many years, although on a limited scale. For example, for several years Baxter has used an automated ordering system, in which the buyer transmits purchase requirements through a data terminal to a Baxter distribution center. At this center a priced PO and shipping document is automatically printed out, saving time and paperwork for both parties. This system has 5,600 users. A further innovation being tested is a system in which hospitals will be able to purchase from a variety of vendors through one computer system. This should eliminate the need to have a different system for each vendor.

The availability of the microcomputer in purchasing provides the capability of expanding such applications nationwide for any American Standard Code for Information Interchange (ASCII) dumb terminal, including almost all microcomputers, that has appropriate communications software;

---

[8]"Buyers Guide to Software for Purchasing," *Purchasing,* March 26, 1987, pp. 70–74.

and a telephone modem now can communicate over the phone lines to another computer, which may be thousands of miles away. The cost of the communications software and telephone modem that make the computer and telephone signals compatible can be less than $200. The rate of transmission of signals is very rapid; the 300 baud modem transmits at the rate of 300 bits per second (bps). The 1,200 baud modem, which has become the standard, communicates four times faster. Newer systems operate at either 2,400 or 9,600 baud.[9]

With such a direct communications linkup with a supplier, the buyer can obtain price quotes, determine availability of items in a supplier's stock, transmit a PO, obtain follow-up information, provide the supplier information about changes in purchase requirements caused by schedule revisions, obtain service information, and send letters and memos—all instantly. This closer, faster relationship with suppliers likely will become the norm rather than the exception over the next decade. Indeed, the volume of EDI transmissions is predicted to grow 100 percent between 1985 and 1990.[10] It will result in far-reaching changes in the way buyers and suppliers cope with their administrative, paperwork requirements. Electronic data interchange (EDI) will become the preferred way of doing business. And because the cost of buying and operating a microcomputer has fallen so rapidly in the past few years, EDI is not limited to only large organizations. It is well within reach of the small purchaser and supplier as well! There is even a 162-page directory that lists some 1,445 companies using or in the process of using EDI, consultants, and companies selling EDI systems.[11]

Figure 3–9 shows a conventional purchase order, and Figure 3–10 shows its conversion into an EDI purchase order. In EDI language, each line is called a *segment* and each item within the segment becomes an *element*.[12]

The most complete guide to the implementation of EDI systems between buying and selling firms envisions that it will make five specific contributions to procurement strategy and corporate-wide strategic direction:

1. Reducing paperwork (paperless purchasing) which will provide additional time for purchasers to conduct professional activities with other departments and suppliers.

---

[9]David Gabel, "Update: Modems," *Electronic Buyers' News,* August 31, 1987, pp. 36–39.

[10]Robert M. Monczka and Joseph R. Carter, *Electronic Data Interchange: Managing Implementation in a Purchasing Environment* (East Lansing, Mich: Graduate School of Business Administration, Michigan State University, 1987), p. 3.

[11]"Free Booklet of EDI Listings," *Purchasing,* October 8, 1987, p. 19.

[12]Monczka and Carter, pp. 53–54.

FIGURE 3-9   Original Purchase Order

Purchase Order

Date: 04/23/84   Page 1 of 1

To: Selling Party   40061   Buyer Contact   5KK3-05530
        123 E. West St.   Joan Buyes   This Number Must
        Anytown, USA 99999   Appear on all Boxes,
                                                        Packages, Shipping
                                                        Documents & Invoices.

From: Buying Party   162   Ship: Ship To Party   1100
        444 W. East Ave.   Receiving Dock
        Downtown, USA 99999   100 Main St.
                                          Downtown, USA 99999

Ship Truck	FOB Mill	Freignt Allowance Less C/L FA	Terms 2/20LCC	Ship Date 05/13/84	Due Date 05/15/84

Line No.	Your Item No.	Our Item No.	Item Description	Unit Price	Quantity	UOM	Item Due Date
1	20784	1147560	23x25 8100 Shasta Gl Bk Whte	56.75	16 16 16	Ctn Ctn Ctn	05/15/84 05/22/84 05/29/84
2	14096	1124486	23x25 880 Shasta Suede Bk Wh	59.50	16	Ctn	
3	51193	1107820	23/25 Offset Opaq Vellum	46.00	16	Ctn	

2. Reducing the need for people to do work which could be done via EDI. This paperwork administration can vary from 15-40 percent of the time spent by purchasing organizations.

3. Fostering development of integrated and improved procurement and materials management systems. This will enable buyers to act in a commodity management role. They will manage smaller numbers of suppliers and, by being able to use data from a procurement data base in conjunction with EDI, will communicate quickly, accurately, and interactively with suppliers about requirements, schedules, orders, invoices, and so forth.

4. By using third-party networks that have international transmission capabilities and standards, the communication pace between buying and using locations and suppliers throughout the world can be quickened.

5. EDI can enhance the firm's capability to reduce total costs of doing business. EDI makes an important contribution to furthering just-in-time systems with associated lead time and inventory reduction, bar coding system applications, integrated manufacturing between buyer and seller and electronic funds transfer. EDI provides for needed transparency between or-

FIGURE 3–10   Translation of Purchase Order for Electronic Data Interchange

---

Format for EDI

ST*850*8400 N/L

BEG*00*SA*5KK3-05530***840423 N/L

N1*SE*92*40061 N/L

N1*BY**91*162 N/L
PEP*SD*Joan Buyes N/L
N1*ST**91*1100N/L

ITD*01*03*2**20 N/L
SHH*SD*010*840513 N/L
SHH*DD*002*840515 N/L
FOB*PP*M1*Less C/L FA N/L
TD2*O*E N/L
PO1*1*48*CT*56 75*QT*IN*1147560*VN*20784 N/L
SCH*16*CT****002*840515 N/L

SCH*16*CT****002*840522 N/L
SCH*16*CT****002*840529 N/L

PO1*2*16*CT*59 5*QT*IN*1124486*VN*14096 N/L
PO1*3*16*CT*46*QT*IN*1107820*VN*51193 N/L

CTT*3*80 N/L
SE*19*8400 N/L

Related Purchase Order Section

Purchase Order

Date: 04/23/84   5KK3-05530
This Number Must
Appear on all Boxes,
Packages, Shipping
Documents & Invoices.

To: Selling Party   400061
123 E. West St.
Anytown, USA 99999

From: Buying Party   162
444 W. East Ave.
Downtown, USA 99999

Buyer Contact
Joan Buyes

Ship: Ship To Party 1100
Receiving Dock
100 Main St.
Downtown, USA 99999

Terms

2/20LCC

Ship Date   Due Date
05/13/84   05/15/84

FOB   Freight Allowance

Mill   Less C/L FA

Ship

Truck

Line No.	Your Item No.	Our Item No.	Item Description	Unit Price	Quantity	UOM	Item Due Date
1	20784	1147560	23x35 8100 Shasta Gl Bk Whte	56.75	16 16 16	Ctn Ctn Ctn	05/15/84 05/22/84 05/29/84
2	14096	1124486	23x25 880 Shasta Suede Bk Wh	59.50	16	Ctn	
3	51193	1107820	23/25 Offset Opaq Vellum	46.00	16	Ctn	

FIGURE 3–11   EDI Benefits

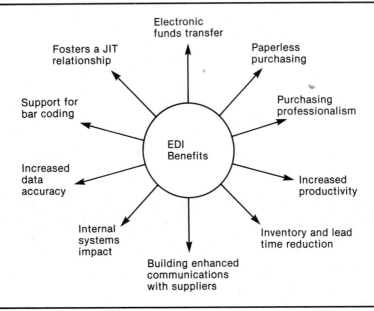

ganizations to further integrate processes in the supply and manufacturing systems.[13]

Figure 3–11 is a schematic showing the benefits to purchasing that can accrue from EDI application.[14]

INFORMATION SYSTEMS

Purchasing procedures are established basically to process inputs of information from outside the purchasing function and to produce outputs of information needed by other functions and institutions outside the purchasing function. Few business functions have the breadth of contacts both within the firm and with the external environment that the well-operated purchasing function has.

Internal Information Flows to Purchasing

Every functional activity within the firm generates information to, and/or requires information from the purchasing system. Figure 3–12 diagrams

---

[13]*Ibid.*, pp. 3–4.
[14]*Ibid.*, p. 7.

FIGURE 3–12   Internal Information Flows to Purchasing

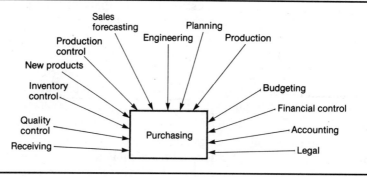

the information flows to purchasing. The information sent to purchasing breaks down into the following two major categories.

1. Statements of needs for materials and services obtained from inside the firm.

2. Requests for information available within purchasing or obtainable from outside the firm.

A brief description of the information flows charted in Figure 3–12 follows.

Planning. This function provides purchasing with information important in obtaining the long-term future requirements of the firm for facilities, materials, and outside services. Competent planning is of special importance in preparing for future construction needs and for raw materials in tight or diminishing supply.

Sales Forecasting. Well-developed sales forecasts are one of the most helpful tools available to purchasing in planning strategies. Business operations usually achieve the greatest degree of operating efficiency when orderly planning permits orderly acquisition and scheduling of requirements. When purchasing has adequate advance notice of kinds of materials likely to be required and approximate quantities, it is in a favorable position to obtain the optimum balance between the conditions in the marketplace and the needs of the firm.

Budgeting and Financial Control. The information provided by the budgeting function helps in coordinating the information from planning and sales forecasting and brings into focus any constraints imposed by the financial control function. Such constraints may apply to the operating expenses of the purchasing system as well as to the possibilities of following other than a buy-as-required inventory policy.

Accounting.   The accounting function supplies information on payments to suppliers, cost studies for make-or-buy decisions, and comparison of actual expenditures to budget.

Legal.   Since the purchasing function is the major activity authorized to commit the firm to contracts for materials and outside services, the legal function provides information regarding contracts and procedures.

Engineering.   The basic responsibility of engineering is to provide information on what types of materials are needed and the specification of the qualities needed. The acknowledged right of purchasing to challenge specifications usually promotes more effective operation of the function for the benefit of the firm.

Production and Production Control.   The production function frequently provides information on the quality requirements for materials. The production control and scheduling function provides information on what materials are needed and in what quantities for a given time period covered by a production cycle. Properly compiled, such information provides a useful tool in planning purchasing operations.

Inventory Control.   This function provides basic information on what needs to be purchased or ordered at any given time. The use of economic order quantities will be determined by the inventory policy which governs the investment in inventory at any given period. An inventory policy may be influenced by the financial resources of the firm, future plans, current market conditions, and lead time in the purchase of materials.

Quality Control and Receiving.   Both of these functions provide information which determines if the suppliers have furnished materials of the quality and quantity specified. Such information is essential to the proper performance of the purchasing function.

New Products.   The importance of new product development to the success of a company has increased greatly in recent years. Unless information about new product development reaches purchasing at the inception of the project, the full contribution possible from purchasing seldom will be realized.

FIGURE 3–13   External Information Flows to Purchasing

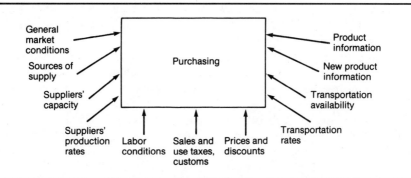

External Information Flows to Purchasing

The efficiently operated purchasing department is one of the firm's major contact points with the external world and as such is a receiving point for a flow of information from sources outside the firm. Much of this information is essential to the operation of the firm. Figure 3–13 shows the nature of the information. A brief explanation of each of the major types of information coming from external sources follows:

General Market Conditions.   Competent purchasing executives and buyers become specialists on general market and business conditions. Suppliers' salespeople, purchasing trade publications, various National Association of Purchasing Management publications and services, and local purchasing association meetings and publications provide a constant stream of information about prices, supply and demand factors, and competitors' actions.

Sources of Supply.   Suppliers' salespeople, advertising media of all types, special promotions, exhibits at trade shows and conventions, and credit and financial reports provide information initiated by vendors and aimed at their customers and potential customers.

Suppliers' Capacity, Suppliers' Production Rates, and Labor Conditions in the Suppliers' Plants and Industries.   Information flows on these factors are of great importance in determining inventory policy and assuring continuity of supply and production.[15]

---

[15]While not all vendors require the same types and amounts of information, some are: order entry, price/cost, availability, specifications, financial position, manufacturing process, capacity, requirements forecasts, delivery dates, quality assurance, and product improvement/innovation. See Joseph R. Carter, "Communicate with Your Vendors," *Journal of Purchasing and Materials Management,* Winter 1986, p. 17.

Prices and Discounts, Customs, Sales and Use Taxes.   Information of any nature regarding prices is important to the effective functioning of purchasing. Much of the price information is obtained directly from suppliers or salespeople representing potential suppliers. The services of consultants specializing in economic trends frequently are useful in determining price trends, particularly of commodities. Both the customs and tax fields are rapidly changing, requiring continuous monitoring.

Transportation Availability and Rates.   The types, availability, and rates of transportation services have had an increasingly important bearing on the cost of materials within recent years. Whether problems involving transportation are the direct responsibility of a traffic department is not the critical point. It is how the information which is of importance in its effect on costs of material is used by purchasing.

New Product and Product Information.   The great emphasis on creating new products has placed a heavy burden on the purchasing function. Purchasing must process the information about products received from the outside in such a way that the appropriate function within the firm will be alerted to any product information, whether it be new or old, which can be useful in improving effectiveness, reducing costs, or aiding in developing new products for the firm.

Internal Information Flows from Purchasing to the Organization

There are very few functions of a business which are not concerned to some degree with the information which flows or can be generated from purchasing. Figure 3–14 diagrams the major types of information which flow from purchasing to the organization:

General Management.   Purchasing personnel have daily contact with a wide spectrum of the marketplace, and if properly qualified by education, ability, and experience are in an advantageous position to collect up-to-the-minute information about current market and business conditions. These data, when correlated and refined, can provide top management with information valuable in the operation of the company.

Engineering.   The engineering function requires much information from the marketplace. While there are situations which warrant the engineers making their own direct contacts with suppliers in order to obtain product and/or price information or place orders, such situations should be the exception. Competent purchasing specialists can provide more effective

FIGURE 3–14   Internal Information Flows from Purchasing

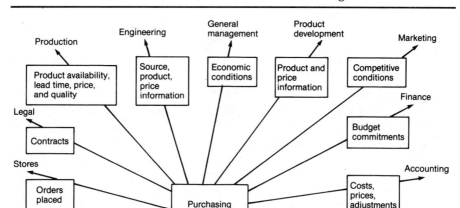

service by better sourcing and negotiation of lower prices than an engineer whose special competence is concerned with an engineering specialty.

Product Development.   Product development departments, regardless of whether they are part of the engineering or the marketing functions, benefit from new materials information and price information which the purchasing function can provide from its contacts in the marketplace. A purchasing function which recognizes its obligation to maximize information flow to new product activities performs a valuable service.

Marketing.   The purchasing department is a target for the sales and promotion plans of many different suppliers from many industries. Perceptive purchasing personnel frequently can provide information on new types of selling campaigns which have value to the marketing function of their own firm.

Production.   The production function depends on purchasing for information about materials, material availability, material delivery lead times, material substitutes, and help in locating sources of supply for production equipment. Production also can be aided by purchasing with information about maintenance, repair, and operating supply items.

Legal.   The purchasing department furnishes the legal department with all the information needed for drawing contracts for all types of materials purchased under a blanket contract, a stockless buying arrangement, and long-term agreements.

Finance and Accounting.   Purchasing is in a position to provide the finance and accounting functions with information basic to budget development and administration and determining cash requirements. Material and transportation costs and trends in costs, need for forward buying because of possible shortages resulting from greater demand, or anticipated interruption of supply such as happens during a major strike are some of the kinds of information purchasing provides to aid in planning financial operations.

Stores.   The formulation of an inventory policy for a store's department is dependent on information concerning lead times and availability of materials, price trends, and substitute materials. The purchasing department is the best source of such information.

QUESTIONS FOR REVIEW AND DISCUSSION

1. Outline and discuss the steps involved in a sound purchasing procedure.
2. Where, and how, should invoices be cleared for payment within an organization?
3. What contribution to purchasing efficiency might be effected through the use of (1) the traveling requisition, (2) the bill of material, and (3) systems contracting?
4. What approaches, other than the standard purchasing procedure, might be used to minimize the small order problem?
5. What records are needed for efficient operation of the purchasing function? Specifically, how can needed data be obtained and maintained?
6. How do follow-up and expediting procedures differ?
7. What items should be covered in a policy manual? Write a proposed policy statement for three of the items.
8. Are rush orders ever justified? When? How should they be handled?
9. What is EDI? How has it changed buyer-seller relationships?
10. In a company not now using the computer for purchasing, where would you start and what would you need to do to develop an integrated computer purchasing/materials management system?
11. How has use of the microcomputer impacted the purchasing function?
12. What kinds of software are needed for computer applications in purchasing? What is presently available?

13. What should be the information flows between purchasing and (1) internal organizational activities and (2) external activities?

REFERENCES

Baker, R. Jerry; Robert S. Kuehne; and Lee Buddress. *Policy and Procedures Manual for Purchasing and Materials Control.* Englewood Cliffs, N.J.: Prentice-Hall, 1981.

Carter, Joseph R. "Communicate with Your Vendors." *Journal of Purchasing and Materials Management,* Winter 1986.

Carter, Joseph R.; Robert M. Monczka; Keith S. Clauson; and Thomas P. Zelinski. "Education and Training for Successful EDI Implementation." *Journal of Purchasing and Materials Management,* Summer 1987.

LaLonde, Bernard J., and Margaret A. Emmelhainz. "Electronic Purchase Order Interchange." *Journal of Purchasing and Materials Management,* Fall 1985.

Mazurak, R. E.; S. R. Rao; and D. W. Scotton. "Spreadsheet Software Applications in Purchasing." *Journal of Purchasing and Materials Management,* Winter 1985.

Monczka, Robert M., and Joseph R. Carter. *Electronic Data Interchange: Managing Implementation in a Purchasing Environment.* East Lansing, Mich: Graduate School of Business Administration, Michigan State University, 1987.

Schonberger, Richard J., and Abdolhossein Ansari. "'Just-In-Time' Purchasing Can Improve Quality." *Journal of Purchasing and Materials Management,* Spring 1984.

Tersine, Richard J.; Marsha H. Nelson; and Susan J. Willer. "Enhancing Productivity with Automated Storage and Retrieval Systems." *Journal of Purchasing and Materials Management,* Fall 1985.

FORMS EXERCISE

1. If you currently work for an organization, please bring a sample of the various forms used in the materials management system in your organization and be ready to explain the function of each form.

2. If you do not work for an organization and you have friends or family members who do, you may ask for assistance in the collection of these forms.

3. If you do not fall into categories 1 or 2, you should go to a library and from the procurement texts available extract a set of forms used in the various stages of the acquisition and materials cycle.

   Notes:
   a. Pay special attention to the number of copies used.
   b. Which of these forms would become obsolete in a fully computerized system?
   c. Which forms could not be collected?

Case 3-1

ICD

Karen Nicholson, purchasing manager for the industrial controls division (ICD), was reviewing the purchasing process for electronic components. She believed ICD should be able to do a better job, but wondered what action to take. She had discussed the situation with Susan Bradley, the buyer involved, and Susan had suggested the possibility of systems contracting.

ICD was a division of Able Holdings, a large multinational involved in a wide variety of industries and products. ICD specialized in industrial controls which normally involved a large number of custom orders.

During the past year ICD had purchased about $300,000 worth of electronic components from six local distributors. ICD maintained good relations with each distributor and had depended on each at one time or another to do some special favors to ICD. Unit values of electronic components ranged from about $0.15 to about $70. According to figures supplied by a purchase analyst, it cost ICD about $54,000 last year to purchase electronic components since each order was triggered by an individual purchase order. ICD also maintained a stock of electronic components averaging about $90,000 with a 20 percent obsolescence rate.

ICD's ordering pattern was highly irregular as shop loads varied considerably. Engineering specifications had to be adhered to 100 percent and, frequently, customers themselves specified the use of certain electronic components. Obsolescence was high because of technological advances as well as feedback from the field on the reliability of past designs.

Karen had called several colleagues in related Able divisions and received sympathy, but not many concrete suggestions. Apparently, nowhere within Able Holdings had anyone ever tried a systems contract on electronic components. And, to her surprise, Karen found that within ICD's production and engineering departments, several individuals expressed strong negative feelings towards it. Susan Bradley, however, had become more enthusiastic about systems contracting as she had investigated it further. Susan believed that ICD could work successfully without most of its current inventory and could cut purchasing cost by at least 50 percent and obtain lower prices by at least 20 percent if ICD were willing to set up a systems contract with only one distributor.

Case 3–2

MEADOWVALE HOSPITAL

In mid-March Mark Norton, Director of the Materials Management Division at Meadowvale Hospital, was drafting a proposal to purchase a materials management computer system.

Meadowvale was a 600-bed, active treatment and teaching hospital affiliated with the University of Kensington Medical School. Introduction of an *exchange-car* delivery system and growth in purchase volumes had placed increasing pressure on the existing purchase control system. In addition, the hospital administration had projected a budget deficit of $2.5 million for the coming year. This had resulted in a strong desire to improve control of departmental budgets, including the major component of purchased goods. The Materials Management Division was using a computer service bureau to maintain inventory records, but Mark felt that the available software could not be used to manage the additional purchasing control tasks effectively.

Mark had solicited proposals from several computer systems supply companies for a materials management system. He was concerned about how to evaluate the relative costs and benefits of a new system. He wondered what he should include in his proposal, which would eventually go to the Finance Committee of the hospital's board of directors for approval.

MEADOWVALE HOSPITAL

The hospital was owned and operated by a nonprofit corporation which also owned a chronic care facility located across the street from Meadowvale, and hospitals in two other nearby cities.

In the past few years, the corporation had been moving toward more corporate, that is, multihospital, decision making. Recently, a single board of directors was appointed to oversee both Meadowvale and the chronic care facility. However, the two hospitals still had separate administrations, although the Materials Management Division at Meadowvale handled about 70 percent of the chronic care facility's purchasing. An organization chart of the Meadowvale administration is shown in Exhibit 1. Construction was planned for Meadowvale and the chronic care facility two years hence. The functional plan called for the demolition of the old northwest wing of Meadowvale and its replacement with a new structure.

Case material of The University of Western Ontario School of Business Administration is prepared as a basis for classroom discussion. This case was written by Michael Watkins, under the direction of John Haywood-Farmer. The authors thank the Purchasing Management Association of Canada for their generous financial support.

EXHIBIT 1 Administration Organization Chart

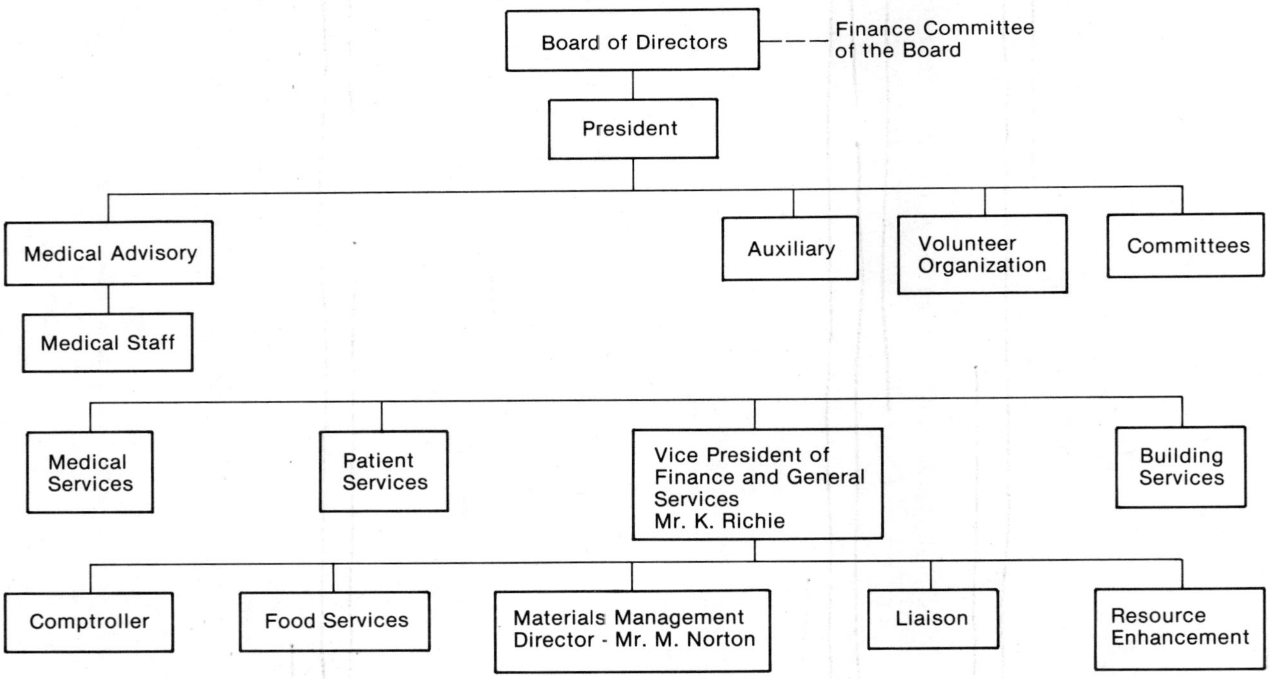

Board of Directors

Finance Committee of the Board

President

Medical Advisory

Medical Staff

Auxiliary

Volunteer Organization

Committees

Medical Services

Patient Services

Vice President of Finance and General Services
Mr. K. Richie

Building Services

Comptroller

Food Services

Materials Management Director - Mr. M. Norton

Liaison

Resource Enhancement

MATERIALS MANAGEMENT SYSTEM OVERVIEW

As director of the materials management division, Mark Norton reported to the hospital's vice president of finance and general services, Mr. Ken Richie (Exhibit 1). Mark had become manager of the Materials Management Department when the hospital had adopted the materials management concept five years earlier. In the spring of the current year the Materials Management Department was designated a division and Mark became director.

The Materials Management Division was divided into two departments, Purchasing, and Supply Processing and Distribution (SPD), as shown in Exhibit 2. The division supplied goods to 150 hospital departments including 30 nursing units (wards, operating rooms).

The hospital's materials management system could be usefully described in terms of three sets of functions: materials sourcing (procurement), inventory, and delivery, as shown in Exhibit 3. The division was responsible for all purchased and processed goods except for food, which was the complete responsibility of the General Services Division. In addition, certain departments and divisions maintained their own inventories of specialized goods, although materials management did the actual purchasing for them. The operating room and the Plant Operations and Maintenance Division each had separate inventories of this type.

1. Materials Sourcing

Materials sourcing occurred either through internal process or external purchasing of goods. Internally processed goods included reusable sterile supplies (instruments, syringes), linen, and laundered goods. Processing of these materials was the responsibility of the Supply, Processing, and Distribution Department as shown in Exhibit 2.

The Purchasing Department procured goods from external suppliers. These goods were classified into stock and nonstock categories. Commonly used items were purchased for inventory (stock). Nonstock items were purchased as requisitioned by individual departments.

2. Inventories

Inventory was held at several locations in the system. Externally purchased stock items were received and held in a bulk stores location in the basement of the hospital. Space constraints had limited the available area to 3,000 square feet. In addition, the hospital rented 1,000 square feet of off-site storage area which was used to hold bulk hospital forms. No increase in storage space was expected until the construction program was completed three years from now.

Nursing units were supplied with all stock goods, with the exception of intravenous (IV) solutions, via an *exchange-cart* system (see below). The exchange cart system required a cart replenishment area called central supply. It was a separate area of approximately 3,000 square feet located on the ground floor of the hospital.

EXHIBIT 2 Materials Management Organization

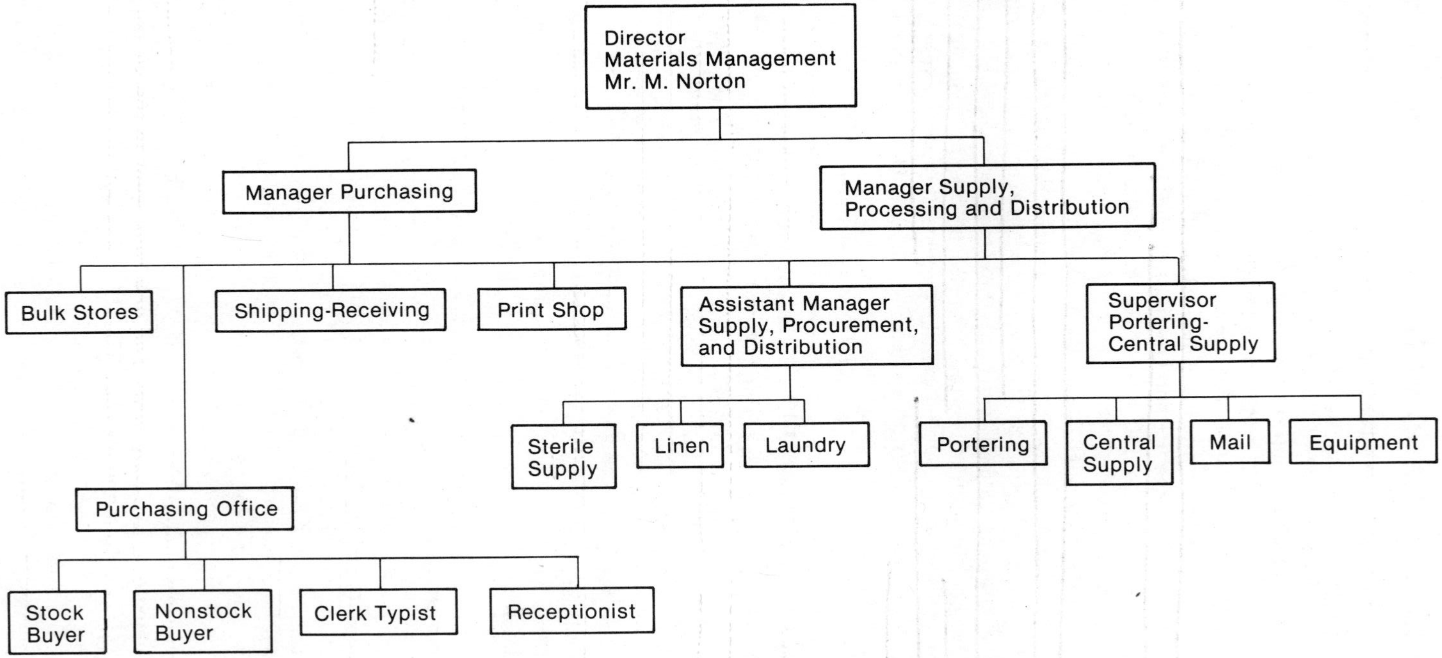

Director
Materials Management
Mr. M. Norton

Manager Purchasing

Manager Supply,
Processing and Distribution

Bulk Stores

Shipping-Receiving

Print Shop

Purchasing Office

Stock Buyer

Nonstock Buyer

Clerk Typist

Receptionist

Assistant Manager
Supply, Procurement,
and Distribution

Sterile Supply

Linen

Laundry

Supervisor
Portering-
Central Supply

Portering

Central Supply

Mail

Equipment

3. Delivery

Delivery consisted of several stages of goods transfer, depending on the type of good and the end user involved.

Bulk stores personnel delivered all nonstock items directly to the requisitioning unit after receipt of the goods and processing of the paper work.

The method of delivery for stock items varied with the end user department. Nonnursing departments were supplied on a scheduled delivery basis. These departments submitted orders on a designated day each week. The orders were filled at bulk stores and the supplies delivered to the departments by portering staff (see Exhibit 2).

Nursing units were supplied by the exchange-cart system. In this system, each nursing unit was assigned two mobile carts (approx. $5' \times 2' \times 5'$) of supplies, including purchased and internally processed goods (except IV solutions). One of the carts remained in the nursing unit at all times. Each day the other cart was replenished to a predetermined *par* stock level at central supply and quantities were noted on a weekly cart replenishment record. The replenished cart was then taken to the nursing unit by central supply staff and exchanged for the depleted cart. The depleted cart was returned to the central supply location for the next cycle. The staff that replenished the carts would check the inventory levels visually and transfer goods from bulk stores, or Supply, Processing, and Distribution as required.

The exchange-cart system had replaced a system of scheduled deliveries of purchased goods from bulk stores to the nursing units. Processed goods from Supply, Processing, and Distribution had previously been handed out at a central supply location, and no records had been kept. Implementation of the exchange-cart system had resulted in a doubling of the number of stock items maintained on computer records, as the internally processed goods were added to the inventory control system.

Intravenous solutions were delivered directly to nursing units from bulk stores because of the large volume and size of the containers. Each nursing unit had an IV storage area and designated par stock level which was checked and replenished by stores personnel each day.

PURCHASING CONTROL SYSTEMS

Purchase orders were processed through an interaction of Purchasing, Receiving, Stores and Finance personnel. Two sets of procedures were used, one for stock goods and the other for nonstock items.

1. Stock Items

Four years earlier, Meadowvale had contracted with a computer service bureau, Compupac Ltd., to use their inventory control package. Inventory records for 1,200 stock items were maintained on a computer data base. A purchase order for stock items consisted of a five-copy form. The first copy went to the vendor. The second was the computer input and file copy. The third was sent to the Finance Department where it was held for eventual matching with the vendor invoice prior to payment. The fourth and fifth copies were sent to bulk stores and held in a file pending the arrival of the order. A purchasing clerk held the computer input copies of the out-

EXHIBIT 3 Materials Management

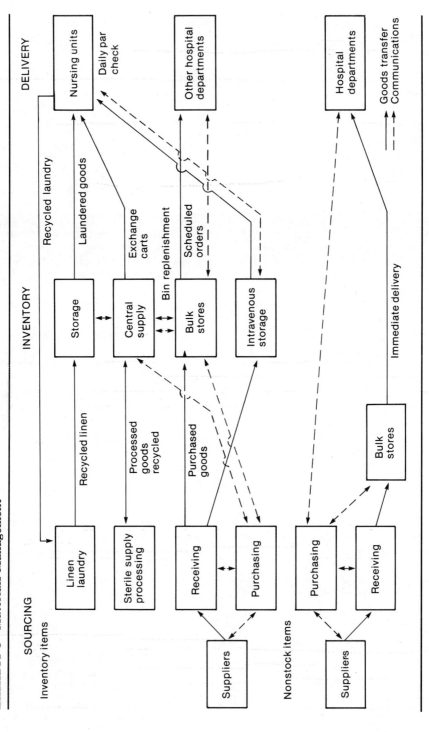

standing purchase orders. Records of orders actually received, and of goods outflows (from cart replenishment records and scheduled delivery orders) were also prepared for computer input. The information was batched and sent to the service bureau once each week. The service bureau updated Meadowvale's outstanding order and inventory record files and produced management control reports each Wednesday night. The reports were delivered to the hospital the following day.

The computer system identified present minimum order levels and produced a list of items to be reordered. However, inventory space constraints necessitated ordering fast-moving goods two or more times per week. Recommended order reports were already out of date when they arrived, except for longer lead time items like bulk multipart forms. Mark had tried having the service bureau do two runs, but this had not resulted in any significant improvement. In addition, the system was relatively expensive to use. Meadowvale was billed a flat rate per run of 13.8 cents for each item input plus additional charges for optional management reports. The cost had averaged $3,641 per month for the past six months. The price per transaction was expected to increase 4 percent annually.

The computer system could maintain inventory records, and was useful for summary reports, but could not generate orders for the majority of stock items. Orders for the fast moving stock were generated in two ways. Personnel in bulk stores would "eyeball" the stock levels as they filled orders. They knew from experience when reorder was required and roughly how much to order. The stock item buyer was contacted and the order was placed. A tag was placed on the goods bin to inform other staff that an order had been placed.

The "eyeball" system had worked well with experienced staff. However, it had become less efficient as staff and the number of stock items had increased with the implementation of the exchange-cart system. Over a period of time, check lists had been developed for multiproduct, high-volume vendors. Stores personnel were given vendor lists on a preset schedule. Two or three times each week, the stores staff checked stock, filled in order quantities, and returned the list to the stock buyer. The tag system was still used to indicate that an order had been made. There were problems with the tagging system when staff failed to notice a tag and double ordered, or failed to remove the tag after the order had arrived.

All goods were received and quantities checked against the vendor packing slip, then moved to bulk stores.

Once the packing slip was checked in stores, it was sent to the Finance Department for matching with their filed purchase order copy. The stores purchase order copies were sent to the purchasing clerk for computer input and filing. Received orders were deleted from the computer's outstanding order file and added to inventory. The majority of Meadowvale's suppliers were located within a 150 mile radius, so delivery was rapid, typically one to two days from order. Because the purchase order had to be on file in bulk stores when the order arrived, it had to be closed rapidly. Each purchase order typically included only a few items, although it could list up to 14 items. A summary of stock purchase order volumes is shown in Exhibit 4. Mark felt that there was a significant problem with purchase order copies being misfiled or not arriving in stores before the order itself.

Mark felt that there was no major problem with stockouts. If a stockout occurred and the item was required immediately, it could be borrowed from one of two other local hospitals that participated in an informal mutual backup arrangement.

A physical inventory count was performed annually. The last, in January, had

EXHIBIT 4 Meadowvale Hospital—Purchase Order Volumes

Inventory Purchase Orders		No. of POs Processed
Three years ago		1,750
Two years ago		2,125
Last year		2,375

Nonstock Purchase Orders	Person Processing	No. of POs Processed
Two years ago	Nonstock Buyer	3,875
	Manager—Purchasing	2,375
	Mark Norton	945
Last year	Nonstock Buyer	5,225
	Manager—Purchasing	1,750
	Mark Norton	1,125
Last 3 months	Nonstock Buyer	1,625
	Manager—Purchasing	375
	Mark Norton	250

revealed a shrinkage of $164,000, a rather unpleasant surprise. Mark wanted to improve the physical inventory control, possibly through implementation of a cycle-counting system. However, he did not have sufficient staff to do so.

Major Problems

2. Nonstock Items

Goods which were not ordered regularly were not held in inventory. Approximately 800 of these nonstock items had been assigned hospital stock numbers, and were purchased when requisitioned by user departments. In spite of the relative infrequency of ordering, nonstock goods were often quite expensive, and represented 80 percent of the annual dollar volume of goods purchased by the hospital.

Hospital departments were not provided with their own catalogs specifying hospital stock numbers, and few departments kept records of nonstock purchases. Thus, requisitions frequently had only vendor catalog numbers or were missing important ordering data. Mark felt that catalogs for each department would be costly to produce and difficult to maintain.

After receipt of a requisition, the nonstock buyer checked it and filled in ordering information as required. The buyer then called the vendor to place the order. Prices, tax codes, and the purchase order number were filled in on the two-copy requisition form, attached to the blank purchase order and sent for typing. Copies of the completed purchase order were forwarded to the Finance Department and to bulk stores as with stock item purchase orders, but no computer input was done. One copy of the requisition was sent back to the requisitioning department. A summary of the volume of nonstock requisitions processed is shown in Exhibit 4.

Mark felt that this system had several problems. There was frequent criticism of the slowness of delivery of nonstock orders. Purchasing received about six order-status check requests each day. A status check involved locating the correct purchase order number, checking back through the system to attempt to locate the goods, and then reporting back to the requesting individual. Often, the person requesting the status check was not the same person who originally requisitioned the goods and few departments kept requisitions on file, and frequently only partial ordering information was available. This necessitated an initial search for the correct PO number. Once the number was obtained, receiving and stores were checked to see if the goods had arrived, but had not yet been delivered. If the material was not found in receiving or stores, the vendor was contacted. The nonstock buyer had become quite efficient at handling status checks, but when the buyer was not available, the manager of purchasing or sometimes even Mark did them. When this happened, a single status check could take up to an hour of management time.

In addition, Mark was concerned that no systematic tracking of the prices of nonstock items was done. The nonstock buyer kept a crude card index of previous purchases, but no automatic calculation and flagging of rapid price increases was done. Thus, the hospital could be subjected to significant price increases for nonstock goods without being aware of it. Also, price comparisons with interchangeable products from other vendors were difficult.

In addition, the monthly management control reports for nonstock purchases which were produced to user departments were very crude. They outlined relatively broad categories of nonstock purchases, but did not provide easy access to details of current purchases or purchase histories for a single item.

History of Hospital Computerization

Meadowvale had an in-house computer system for admitting, discharging, scheduling, order processing, and lab testing. It consisted of a mainframe from a major computer manufacturer and support equipment with terminals and printers at various locations in the hospital. The software had been supplied by a company that specialized in hospital computerization. In addition, the Finance Department ran general accounting programs through a service bureau similar to that used by materials management. The comptroller continued to review future computerization of the finance areas.

Computer acquisition by the hospital was overseen by a computer committee which consisted of the computer systems manager, the comptroller and several members of the staff chosen for their knowledge of computer systems. The committee made recommendations on computerization to the hospital's president.

In addition to the concerns that Mark had about the ability of the existing system to handle increasing purchase order volume, he knew that the hospital administration strongly desired better monitoring and control of departmental budgets to assist in reducing the projected budget deficit.

A major component of any department's budget consisted of goods ordered through materials management. Mark felt that better monitoring and control of departmental purchasing was crucial to improved cost control. Mark concluded that the existing computer system could not be adapted to do this. In October he initiated discussions with Tak Laboratories, Meadowvale's largest supplier, to discuss computerized purchasing control systems. Mark was directed to Halcorp Ltd., a hospital computer systems company that Tak represented for marketing purposes.

Mark traveled to Chicago to inspect a Halcorp system. The system was installed in a 1,000 bed institution that issued 25,000 purchase orders annually. The system consisted of a Texas Instruments business minicomputer, 12 video display terminals, and a Halcorp software package. Mark was also interested in packaged systems from three other companies: Hospital Computing Ltd., Medical Electronics, Inc., and Bryant Systems Ltd. Mark looked particularly hard at the Hospital Computing Ltd. offering because of the previous work they had done for the hospital. He found that the package was not one of the company's stronger offerings and he concluded that it did not incorporate several desirable enhancements which were available on other systems. These included the maintenance of single vendor records for stock and nonstock items, price and volume tracking for nonstock items, and record searches using partial information. In addition, existing hardware did not have the capacity to run the hospital computing package, so no hardware savings would result from its selection.

In late February, Mark requested proposals from Medical Electronics, Bryant, and Halcorp. The system that he specified included a minicomputer, 10 video display terminals, 5 printers, and the software package. He planned to locate the terminals in receiving, bulk stores, central supply, accounts payable (finance), with each of the buyers, the purchasing office clerk-typist, each of the departmental managers, and in his own office. The printers would be located in bulk stores, accounts payable, central supply, and in the purchasing office (2). He eventually hoped to get a terminal for the Operating Room Department to allow them to keep a separate inventory record. In addition, he planned to investigate acquisition of bar coding scanners and support equipment to speed up stock checking in bulk stores.

The software package was a perpetual inventory, online system that automatically calculated EOQs and ROPs from records of past usage. The complete inventory would be run as a single asset. Two or three times each week, the system would produce recommended order lists for each vendor. These lists would be printed in bulk stores, checked by stores personnel for reasonableness, and altered as required. The altered list would then be forwarded to the inventory buyer, who modified the computer file. This modified file became a purchase order, part of a pool of purchase orders that were processed on a daily basis, with copies sent to the vendor, to bulk stores, and to finance.

By early March, he had received proposals from Bryant and Halcorp. Both proposals recommended the same hardware, a top-of-the-line Texas Instruments model minicomputer and similar software, and were therefore easily comparable. The Halcorp proposal totaled $174,000 and the Bryant proposal totaled $166,000. (See Exhibit 5.)

After evaluation of the proposals, Mark planned to seek administrative approval for the capital expenditure. Once approved by the administration, the plan would be presented to the Finance Committee of the Board of Directors for final approval.

Mark was concerned about several factors in the development of his plan:

He was uncertain what the future location of the various departments of materials management would be. In the short-term, the purchasing office might have to be moved out of the hospital and into a nearby building. It would probably be moved into the rebuilt wing of the hospital when it was completed. Mark wondered what effect this might have on the maintenance of communications and paper flows between departments.

The hospitals in Jamestown and Forest Hill were also investigating comput-

EXHIBIT 5   Bryant Proposal Summary

Company Background and Services

- Division of Amtech International (United States).
- Specialists in hospital materials management computer systems.
- Have an established users' group with organized annual meetings and monthly newsletters detailing system enhancements.
- Offer cash incentives to users who find bugs in system.

System Hardware

Texas Instruments Business System including central processing unit with memory, disk drive, and streamer tape drive, ten (10) video display terminals (VDT), five (5) printers, three (3) bar code scanners, two (2) bar code printers boards, one (1) communications modem (all hardware details supplied separately).

System Software

BRY Model 15/16

- Suitable if only current material program to be automated and bulk stores and central supply to be managed as a single inventory.
- Perpetual inventory on line system for inventory items produces recommended order lists for each vendor two to three times weekly.
- Maintains records of outstanding nonstock orders, with order data retrievable by inputing purchase order number, stock number, vendor catalog number or vendor name.
- Records maintained on previous purchases to facilitate price tracking.

Optional: BRY Model 20
Suitable if automation of other inventories planned
(e.g. operating room lab)
or if bulk stores and central supply to be treated as separate assets

Management Reports Generated

- Stock status reports
- ABC analysis
- Cart par stock analysis
- Departmental expense and usage
- Departmental usage histories
- Item usage histories
- EOQ/ROP recommendations
- Excess/No movement item identification
- Index price analysis
- Inventory variance (with physical count input)
- Open orders
- Patient price simulation
- Vendor receipts analysis

---

erization of the materials management function. Jamestown currently used a completely manual system and Forest Hill had contracted with Compupac for the same computer services used by Meadowvale. Mark had discussed the potential for a multisystem purchase with the materials managers of the other hospitals. Such a purchase would involve the same software, but with hardware capacity matched to

EXHIBIT 5   *(concluded)*

System Capital Cost	
Hardware	$110,000
Software—BRY 15/16	40,000
—BRY 20	50,000
Bryant implementation fee (includes structured on-site consulting program of 12 days, and creation of data files by Bryant)	6,000
Cabling to be done at hospital expense.	

Monthly Maintenance Charges	
Hardware	$1,000
Software	400

the individual hospital's needs. Mark believed that a common system design might result in more efficient software support and the advantages of shared operational experience. In addition, he felt that a multiunit purchase might yield a better price. However, the other hospitals were not ready to go ahead, and Mark felt that there would be considerable administrative difficulties in managing a joint purchase. In addition, Mark knew that both Bryant and Halcorp were anxious to enter the local market and were therefore offering incentive prices. He was concerned that he might lose this opportunity if he delayed too long.

Mark wondered how he could get approval for the system. Use of a computer system could result in significant improvements in service levels, both inside the materials management division, and in end user departments. No personnel reductions were anticipated, and this increased efficiency would allow time to be channeled into activities such as improving the physical inventory control. Mark hoped to implement a cycle-counting system in bulk stores if sufficient staff time was available, but worried that maintenance of the computer system might use up more time than anticipated. Mark was certain that the level of service offered to end users would improve, especially the ability to monitor nonstock purchases and to expedite orders. In addition, certain customer departments, especially the operating room, could make use of computer generated data to cost out procedures for budget purposes. However, he wondered how to characterize and value such improvements in service.

In general, Mark worried about promising *any* service level improvements or labor savings, in case they did not materialize. He was concerned that such a failure might reduce his credibility in recommending future changes. However, he also wondered if a plan would be approved simply on the basis of comparative operating costs.

In terms of procedure, Mark had to obtain approval from the hospital's president prior to making a presentation to the Finance Committee of the Board of Directors for final acquisition approval. Mark felt that board approval was virtually certain if he obtained administrative approval. He knew he had the support of his immediate superior, Ken Richie, and of the comptroller. His main concern was the reaction of the computer committee because he knew that it would not recommend a materials management computer system if the payback was in excess of three years. The Finance Department planned to acquire a general ledger-payroll system which would have to be interfaced and compatible with any materials management system. Mark wondered if the system could be justified on the basis of a financial analysis.

CHAPTER 4

Quality, Specification and Inspection

Every acquisition is intended to fill a need inside the purchaser's organization. Effective supply requires a full understanding of the function the acquisition is to fulfill; how the need is described and how its quality is determined and measured. Together these various activities determine *what* is to be acquired and whether what is supplied meets requirements.

Quality has taken on a special meaning in the past decades. While new concepts such as MRP and just-in-time production have revolutionized the quantity, delivery, and inventory aspects of materials management, they have also required a new attitude toward quality. When no safety stock is available and required items arrive just before use, their quality must be fully acceptable. This extra pressure, along with all other good reasons for insisting on good quality, has sparked major efforts by purchasers to seek supplier quality assurance. In many cases these efforts have involved substantial programs of vendor-purchaser cooperation, including the establishment of satisfactory quality control programs at the premises of those who supply the vendors.

Renewed interest in quality has reinforced the need for a team buying approach to purchasing, the trend to vendor rationalization, cooperative buyer-supplier relations, longer-term contracts, and a reevaluation of the role of the price-quality trade-off in purchase decisions.

To understand the role of quality in procurement, it is necessary to determine how needs are defined, what constitutes a "best buy," and what action purchasers take to ensure the right quality is supplied.

Every organization can be viewed as a transformation process with inputs and outputs. Before the input can be acquired effectively and efficiently, it is necessary to identify exactly what is needed and why. This identification is often complicated because different people in the organization share in the responsibility of preparing and questioning specifications

126

and because considerations external to the organization may have a major influence as well. Furthermore, no common agreement exists as to the meaning of ideas, such as function, quality, reliability, and suitability.

It makes sense, therefore, to examine this topic area by first concentrating on what the product or service to be acquired is intended to do. This will permit discussion of terminology and also establish a notion of basic function. This will be followed by the various ways of describing what is to be purchased so that both vendors and purchasers can agree on what is required. Finally, quality assurance, inspection, and quality control will cover the approaches used to assure that what is specified will actually be provided. The challenge for procurement is to assure supply and at the same time achieve good value.

FUNCTION

The first phase in any acquisition is to determine what is needed and why. Actually, this should be a three-step process. First, the organization's needs are established. Second, it is determined what the market can supply. Third, a conclusion is reached as to what constitutes good value under the circumstances. Frequently, steps one and two and, occasionally, all three steps are performed concurrently. The danger in proceeding through these steps too quickly is that vital information and analysis may be lost. Obviously, in complex purchases the process may well go through these steps iteratively before a final decision is reached.

To understand what is needed inside the organization, it is useful to focus on the function to be performed by the needed item or service. It is not easy to think of the basic function the item must perform. We tend to speak of a box instead of something to package this in, a bolt instead of something that fastens. We think of a steak, instead of something to eat, and a bed, instead of something to sleep on.

Why make an issue of this? It seems so simple as to be hardly worth mentioning. But, actually, this is the heart of a sound purchasing system. Here lie the major clues for improving value. A casual bypassing of the function need frequently results in improper specification. For example, a hose will be too short, a lining will shrink, a bolt shear, a motor burn out, a paint peel, a machine vibrate, a vessel burst, a part won't fit, an insurance policy won't cover, and a host of other troubles of this sort arise. Many of these troubles will result from underestimating the function required or from negligence, error, or oversight because certain functional needs have been forgotten or overlooked. It is no coincidence that value analysis and value engineering concentrate on proper function definition as their basis.

The answer to this problem, one will say, is to buy quality. Quality is really part of the function need. If the item is not of sufficient quality to perform the task required of it, it does not fulfill the function. Moreover, quality can be a cloak for various inadequacies. Buying the best quality, high alloy screws will not help if bolts were needed in the first place.

If the basic functional need is defined as a sheet metal screw, instead of a need to fasten together two sheets of metal of certain physical and chemical characteristics, the first basic step in purchasing is missed. Also missed is the opportunity to investigate such alternatives as bolts, rivets, and spot welds, to name just a few.

Describing functions as verb-noun combinations "provide torque, transmit current, contain liquid, and so on," forces clear thinking about the intended function. Separating functions into primary and secondary categories also identifies what is really needed versus what might be deleted. In addition, once the function is properly identified, it is possible to establish its worth by comparison to other ways of achieving the same function. For example, special alloy, custom-shaped fuel tanks for a small navy boat were replaced by four mild steel drums reducing cost by about 90 percent. The four mesh screens on an industrial motor were needed to "exclude matter" and "permit access." The value of these functions was estimated at 20 percent of the existing cost. A more detailed look at value analysis and value engineering is provided in Chapter 11. Nevertheless, at this point the usefulness of functional identification needs to be recognized.

Quality, Suitability, Reliability, and Best Buy

Practitioners often use the term *quality* to describe the notions of function, suitability, reliability, conformance with specifications, satisfaction with actual performance, high price, and best buy. This is highly confusing.

Quality

Quality in the simplest sense should refer to the ability of the vendor to provide goods and services in conformance with specifications. The area of inspection, discussed at the end of this chapter, covers this interpretation. Quality may also refer to whether the item performs in actual use to the expectations of the original requisitioner, regardless of conformance with specifications. Thus, it is often said an item is "no good" or of "bad quality" when it fails in use, even though the original requisition or specification may be at fault. The ideal, of course, is achieved when all inputs acquired pass this use test satisfactorily.

Suitability

Suitability refers to the match between a commercially available material, good, or service and the intended functional use. In a pure sense, suitability ignores the commercial considerations and refers to fitness for use. In reality, that is hardly practiced. Gold may be a better conductor than silver or copper, but is far too expensive to use in all but special applications. That is why chips are wired with gold and houses with copper or aluminum. The notion of "best buy" puts quality, reliability, and suitability into a sound procurement perspective.

Reliability

Reliability is the mathematical probability that a product will function for a stipulated period of time. Complexity is the enemy of reliability because of the multiplicative fact of probabilities of failure of components. The distribution of failures is normally considered to be exponential, with failures occurring randomly. This facilitates calculations by making the reliabilities of the components additive. Testing is also more flexible because of the time-numbers trade-off. The same inference may be drawn from 20 parts tested for 50 hours as for 500 parts tested for 2 hours. Exceptions like the Weibull distribution (which accounts for the aging effect) and the bathtub curve (which recognizes the high probability of early failure, a period of steady state, and a higher probability of failure near the end of the useful life) can also be handled, but they require more complex mathematical treatment.

From a procurement standpoint, it is useful to recognize the varying reliabilities of components and products acquired. Penalties or premiums may be assessed for variation from design standard depending on the expected reliability impact.

"Best Buy"

The decision on what to buy involves more than balancing various technical considerations. The most desirable technical feature or suitability for a given use, once determined, is not necessarily the desirable buy. The distinction is between technical considerations which are matters of dimension, design, chemical or physical properties, and the like, and the more inclusive concept of the "best buy." The "best buy" assumes, of necessity, a certain minimum measure of suitability, but considers cost and procurability, transportation and disposal as well.

If the cost is so high as to be prohibitive, one must get along with an item somewhat less suitable. Or if, at whatever cost or however procurable, the only available suppliers of the technically perfect item lack adequate productive capacity or financial and other assurance of continued business existence, then, too, one must give way to something else. Obviously, too, frequent reappraisals are necessary. If the price of copper increases from $0.70 a pound to $1.50 or more, its relationship to aluminum or other substitutes may change.

The "best buy" is a combination of characteristics, not merely one. The specific combination finally decided on is almost always a compromise, since the particular aspect of quality to be stressed in any individual case depends largely on circumstances. In some instances the primary consideration is reliability; questions of immediate cost or facility of installation or the ease of making repairs are all secondary. In other instances the lifetime of the item of supply is not so important; efficiency in operation becomes more significant. Certain electrical supplies suggest themselves as illustrations. While a long life is desired, it is more important that the materials always function during such life as they may have, than that they last indefinitely. Assuming dependability in operation and a reasonable degree of durability, the ease and simplicity of operation may become the determining factor. For instance, it is well known that the mechanism of the modern calculator makes it dependable under all ordinary usages but that it is not essential for a calculator to last indefinitely. Given these two factors more or less standardized among various types of calculators, the determining factor is the ease with which the calculator can be operated. What constitutes a satisfactory "best buy," therefore, depends largely on what a person is seeking in particular goods.

The decision on what constitutes the best buy for any particular need is as much conditioned by procurement as by technical considerations. It should be clear that neither the engineer or user, on the one hand, nor the purchaser, on the other, is qualified to reach a sound decision on the best buy unless they work closely together. The ability and willingness of all parties concerned to view the trade-offs in perspective will significantly influence the final decisions reached.

Service and "Best Buy"

Sometimes the service the vendor performs is as important as any attribute of the product itself. Service may include installation, training, inspection, repair, advice, as well as a willingness to make satisfactory adjustments for misunderstandings or clerical errors. Some purchasers even include the supplier's willingness to change orders on short notice and be particularly responsive to unusual requests as part of their evaluation of the service provided. To cover some types of service, vendors issue guarantees, covering periods of varying length. The value of such guarantees rests less on the technical wording of the statement itself than on the goodwill and reliability of the seller.

Many vendors specifically include the cost of service in the selling price. Others absorb it themselves, charging no more than competitors and relying on the superior service for the sale. One of the difficult tasks of a buyer is to get only as much of this service factor as is really needed without paying for the excessive service the vendor may be obliged to render to some other purchaser. In many instances, of course, the servicing department of a manufacturing concern is maintained as a separate organization. The availability of service is an important consideration for the buyer in securing the "best buy" at the outset.

Responsibility for Determining the "Best Buy"

It is generally accepted that the final verdict on technical suitability for a particular use should rest with the using, engineering, specifying, or resale department. Thus, questions on the specification of office supplies and equipment may be settled by the office manager, advertising material by advertising personnel, maintenance supplies by maintenance supervisors, and resale items by marketing.

The ultimate responsibility for the specifications of manufactured items should rest primarily with the engineering department charged with design and standards involving raw or semiprocessed materials and component parts. Basically, the immediate decision is an engineering/production decision. The person responsible for converting primary materials or semi-manufactured articles into the finished product is the person who should have the authority to determine what is to be required. It is the purchaser's task to keep the cost of material down to the lowest point consistent with the standard quality required in the completed product. Purchasing's right to audit, question, and suggest must be recognized if this task is to be successful along with early involvement of procurement during the design phase.

Purchasing fails to live up to its responsibility unless it insists that economic and procurement factors be considered and unless it passes on to those immediately responsible for specification suggestions of importance that may come as a result of its normal activities. The buyer is in a key position to present the latest information from the marketplace which may permit modifications in design, more flexibility in specifications, or changes in manufacturing methods which will reduce the cost of materials without detracting from their performance.

Purchasing Engineering Relations

The trend toward securing full and active cooperation between the engineering, using, and procurement departments places a heavy responsibility on purchasing personnel, for unless they are well qualified to make real contributions toward determining the best buy, their suggestions are not likely to be considered seriously.

This responsibility can be met in several ways. All of them seek to ensure that buyers, regardless of the particular items they buy, or the uses to which the items are put, know as much as possible about the products they purchase. Of course, an adequate technical knowledge of some simple supplies is much more easily acquired than that for highly technical products, particularly those still in the developmental stage. The amount and character of the technical background required of a qualified buyer will therefore depend on the nature of the commodities purchased. Likewise, the number of engineering qualified buyers in a department will vary from one type of organization to another.

The purchasing department may seek to increase the ability of its buyers to be of service in selecting the best buy in various ways:

1. *Early involvement in the specification process.* It is far more difficult to change specifications once they have been set, rather than to influence them before they have been decided upon.

2. *Select only persons with engineering training to fill buyers' jobs.* It is argued that an engineer has an advantage over a non-technical person in buying because the basic engineering training and experience have given a thorough knowledge of materials, manufacturing methods, and inspection procedures. Thus equipped, the engineer commands the respect of those in the engineering and production departments and is able to "talk the language" of the designer and vendor.

3. *Employ one or more engineers in the purchasing department.* Such engineers can serve in a staff capacity as advisors to the various buyers in cases in which their advice and help are useful and can serve in a liaison capacity between the purchasing and engineering departments.

4. *Physically transfer some of the purchasing personnel to the engineering department.* Such buyers are assigned desks adjacent to the engineers working on the same class of items as those in which the buyer is interested.

5. *Without making any changes in organization or personnel, buyers, assistant buyers, and others are encouraged to take advantage of night courses in quality control, design, machine tool operations, cost accounting, engineering, materials, and similar studies.* Supervised plant visits, films, and organized reading also may be used to advantage. Many managers think an alert, conscientious person can gain an adequate background in those aspects of engineering and operations necessary for satisfactory performance.

6. *Regular meetings between purchasing and engineering staff.* Weekly, bi-weekly, or monthly meetings can be used to discuss progress on specific activities, as well as resolve any difficulties currently outstanding.

7. *Purchasing representation on task forces, projects, planning committees, etc.* Such purchasing presence not only underlines the legitimacy of purchasing involvement, but also permits the inclusion of purchasing considerations during the evolution of final recommenda-

tions arising from such group activities. In new product design, the traditional steps of research and development, functional design, pilot design, pilot test, manufacturing design, specification, procurement quotes, bid analysis, vendor selection and manufacture created a significant lead-time problem. This is especially true in situations where the organization's effectiveness and competitiveness would be at stake in quick new product introductions. Time compression is possible when there is early involvement of all parties, including manufacturing design, quality control, marketing, purchasing, and vendors before the functional design is decided upon.

Purchasing Relations with Other Specifiers or Users

The suggestions for better purchasing-engineering relations to achieve the "best buy" are also applicable to other key users or specifiers. For example, buyers for resale items would do well to take marketing courses and could be located in the marketing department. In educational institutions, it is common to have one or more buyers located in the physical plant department to serve maintenance, repair, and operating supply needs better. The basic principle underlying such suggestions is that effectiveness in the determination of the "best buy" requires the joint input of a variety of parties inside any organization, including purchasing's. Moreover, effective purchasing participation depends on both early involvement in the need recognition and definition process as well as open and willing exploration of alternatives by all influencers of the "best buy."

DESCRIPTION AND SPECIFICATION

The using, requesting, or specifying department must be capable of reasonably describing what is required to be sure of getting exactly what is wanted. Although the responsibility for determining what is needed usually rests with the using department in the first instance, the purchasing department has the direct responsibility of checking the description given. The purchasing department should, of course, not be allowed to alter arbitrarily the description or the quality. It should, however, have the authority to insist that the description be sufficiently accurate and detailed to be perfectly clear to every potential supplier. The buyer also must call to the attention of the requisitioner the availability of other options which might represent better value.

The description of an item may take any one of a variety of forms or, indeed, may be a combination of several different forms. For our discussion, therefore, *description* will mean any one of the various methods by which a buyer undertakes to convey to a seller a clear, accurate picture of the required item. The term *specification* will be used in the narrower and commonly accepted sense referring to one particular form of description.

The methods of description ordinarily used may be listed as follows and will be discussed in order:

1. By brand.
2. By specification.
   a. Physical or chemical characteristics.
   b. Material and method of manufacture.
   c. Performance.
3. By engineering drawing.
4. By miscellaneous methods.
   a. Market grade.
   b. Sample.
5. By a combination of two or more methods.

Description by Brand

There are two questions of major importance in connection with the use of branded items. One relates to the desirability of using this type of description and the other to the problem of selecting the particular brand.

Description by brand or trade name indicates a reliance on the integrity and the reputation of the supplier. It assumes that the supplier is anxious to preserve the goodwill attached to a trade name and is capable of doing so. Furthermore, when a given requirement is purchased by brand and is satisfactory in the use for which it was intended, the purchaser has every right to expect that any additional purchases bearing the same brand name will correspond exactly to the quality first obtained.

There are certain circumstances under which description by brand may be not only desirable but also necessary:

1. When, either because the manufacturing process is secret or because the item is covered by a patent, specifications cannot be laid down.

2. When specifications cannot be laid down with sufficient accuracy by the buyer because the vendor's manufacturing process calls for a high degree of that intangible labor quality sometimes called *workmanship* or *skill,* which cannot be defined exactly.

3. When the quantity bought is so small as to make the setting of specifications by the buyer unduly costly.

4. When, because of the expense involved or for some similar reason, testing by the buyer is impractical.

5. When users often develop very real, even if unfounded, preferences in favor of certain branded items, a bias the purchaser may find almost impossible to overcome.

On the other hand, there are some definite objections to purchasing branded items, most of them turning on cost. Although the price may often be quite in line with the prices charged by other vendors for similarly branded items, the whole price level may be so high as to cause the buyer to seek unbranded substitutes or even, after analysis, to set its own specifications. There are many articles on the market which, in spite of all the advertising, have no brand discrimination at all. Thus, the purchaser may just as well prefer using trisodium phosphate over a branded cleaning compound costing 50 to 100 percent more.

A further argument, frequently encountered, against using brands is that undue dependence on brands tends to restrict the number of potential suppliers and deprives the buyer of the possible advantage of a lower price or even of improvements brought out by competitors through research and invention.

Description by Specification

Description of desired material specifications constitutes one of the best-known of all methods employed. A lot of time and effort has been expended in making it possible to buy on a specification basis. Closely related to these endeavors is the effort toward standardization of product specifications and reduction in the number of types, sizes, and so on, of the products accepted as standard.

It is also becoming more standard practice to specify the test procedure and results necessary to meet quality standards as part of the specification.

Traditional advantages of buying with specifications include:

1. Evidence exists that thought and careful study have been given to the need and the ways in which it may be satisfied.

2. A standard is established for measuring and checking materials as supplied, preventing delay and waste that would occur with improper materials.

3. An opportunity exists to purchase identical requirements from a number of different sources of supply.

4. The potential exists for equitable competition. This is why public agencies place such a premium on specification writing. In securing bids from various suppliers, a buyer must be sure that the suppliers are quoting for exactly the same material or service.

5. The seller will be responsible for performance when the buyer specifies performance.

Using specifications does not constitute a panacea for all difficulties involving quality. The limitations involved in using specifications fall into eight classes:

1. There are many items for which it is practically impossible to draw adequate specifications.

2. Although a saving may sometimes be realized in the long run, the use of specifications adds to the immediate cost. If, therefore, the requirement is not purchased in large quantities and does not need to conform particularly to any definite standards, it is frequently inadvisable to incur the additional expense.

3. Buyers may request the vendor to quote on the basis of the specifications and at the same time indicate whether or not a standard article closely approaching the one specified is available, and, if so, to quote a price on the standard article, indicating how it differs from the specifications submitted. It may then turn out that the original specification was not the best.

4. Compared with purchase by brand, the immediate cost is also increased by the necessity of testing to ensure that the specifications have been met.

5. One of the difficulties arising from the use of specifications comes from carelessness in drawing them when they are likely to give the purchaser a false sense of security.

6. At the opposite extreme is setting up specifications so elaborate and so detailed as to defeat their own purpose. Unduly elaborate specifications sometimes result in discouraging possible suppliers from placing bids in response to inquiries.

7. Unless the specifications are of the performance type, the responsibility for the adaptability of the item to the use intended rests wholly on the buyer, provided only that the item conforms to the description submitted.

8. The minimum specifications set up by the buyer are likely to be the maximum furnished by the supplier.

Specification by Physical or Chemical Characteristics.   Specification by physical or chemical characteristics provides definitions of the properties of the materials the purchaser desires. They represent an effort to state in measurable terms those properties deemed necessary for satisfactory use at the least cost consistent with quality. They sometimes include information on disposition of material in case of failure to meet requirements.

Specification by Material and Method of Manufacture.   The second type of specification includes those prescribing both the material and method of manufacture. Outside of some governmental purchases, such as those of the armed forces, this method is used when special requirements exist and when the buyer is willing to assume the responsibility for results. Many organizations are not in this position, and as a result, comparatively little use is made of this form of specification.

Specification by Performance.   Performance specification is a method employed to considerable extent, partly because it throws the responsibility for a satisfactory product back to the seller. Performance specification is results and use oriented, leaving the supplier with the decisions on how to make the most suitable product. This enables the supplier to take advantage of the latest technological developments and to substitute anything that exceeds the minimum performance required.

A specification for missile silo doors required that they be able to withstand the impact of a tree or telephone pole that might be moving at hurricane speeds. This required the contractor to construct a telephone-pole hurling machine!

The satisfactory use of a performance specification, of course, is absolutely dependent on securing the right kind of supplier. There are also some buyers who may resort to such specifications as an alibi for not going to the trouble of getting an exact method of description or of locating more satisfactory sources. It should be noted that it may be difficult to compare quotations and the vendor may include in the price a risk allowance.

Description by Engineering Drawing

Description by a blueprint or dimension sheet is common and may be used in connection with some form of descriptive text. It is particularly applicable to the purchase of construction, electronic and electrical assemblies, machined parts, forgings, castings, and stampings. It is an expensive method of description not only because of the cost of preparing the print or computer program itself but also because it is likely to be used to describe an item which is quite special as far as the vendor is concerned and, hence, expensive to manufacture. However, it is probably the most accurate of all forms of description and is particularly adapted to purchasing those items requiring a high degree of manufacturing perfection and close tolerances.

Miscellaneous Methods of Description

Description by Market Grades.   Purchases on the basis of market grades is confined to certain primary materials. Wheat and cotton[1] have already been referred to in this connection; lumber, butter, and other commodities will suggest themselves. Purchase by grade is for some purposes entirely satisfactory. Its value depends on the accuracy with which grading is done and the ability to ascertain the grade of the material by inspection.

The grading, furthermore, must be done by those in whose ability and

---

[1]For agricultural raw materials, such as wheat and cotton, the grades are established by the U.S. Department of Agriculture. These include all food and feed products, the standards and grades for which have been established in accordance with the Federal Food and Drugs Act, the Grain Standards Act, and other laws enacted by Congress. As will be noted later, establishing grades acceptable to the trade is essential to the successful operation of a commodity exchange.

honesty the purchaser has confidence. It may be noted that even for wheat and cotton, grading may be entirely satisfactory to one class of buyer and not satisfactory to another class.

Description by Sample.   Still another method of description is by submission of a sample of the item desired. Almost all purchasers use this method from time to time but ordinarily—there are some exceptions—for a minor percentage of their purchases and then more or less because no other method is possible.

Good examples are items requiring visual acceptance, such as wood grain, color, appearance, and so on.

Combination of Descriptive Methods

An organization frequently uses a combination of two or more of the methods of description already discussed. The exact combination found most satisfactory for an individual organization will depend, of course, on the type needed by the organization and the importance of quality in its purchases. There is no one best method applicable to any single product, nor is there for any particular organization a best method of procedure. The objective of all description is to secure the right quality at the best possible price.

Sources of Specification Data

Speaking broadly, there are three major sources from which specifications may be derived: (1) individual standards set up by the buyer; (2) standards established by certain private agencies, either other users, suppliers, or technical societies; and (3) governmental standards.

Individual Standards.   Individual standards require extensive consultation among users, engineering, purchasing, quality control, suppliers, marketing, and, possibly, ultimate consumers. This means the task is likely to be arduous and expensive.

A common procedure is for the buying organization to formulate its own specifications on the basis of the foundation laid down by the governmental or technical societies. To make doubly sure that no serious errors have been made, some organizations mail out copies of all tentative specifications, even in cases where changes are mere revisions of old forms, to several outstanding suppliers in the industry to get the advantage of their comments and suggestions before final adoption.

Standard Specifications.   If an organization wishes to buy on a specification basis, yet hesitates to undertake to originate its own, it may use one of the so-called standard specifications. These have been developed as a result of a great deal of experience and study by both governmental and nongovernmental agencies, and substantial effort has been expended in promoting them. They may be applied to raw or semi-manufactured products, to component parts, or to the composition of material. The well-known SAE steels, for instance, are a series of alloy steels of specified composition and known properties, carefully defined, and identified by individual numbers.

When they can be used, standard specifications have certain advantages. They are widely known and commonly recognized and readily available to every buyer. Furthermore, the standard should have somewhat lower costs of manufacture. Finally, because they have grown out of the wide experience of producers and users, they should be adaptable to the requirements of many purchasers.

Standard specifications have been developed by a number of nongovernmental engineering and technical groups. Among them may be mentioned the American Standards Association, the American Society for Testing Materials, the American Society of Mechanical Engineers, the American Institute of Electrical Engineers, the Society of Automotive Engineers, the American Institute of Mining and Metallurgical Engineers, the Underwriters Laboratories, the National Safety Council, the Canadian Engineering Standards Association, the American Institute of Scrap Iron and Steel, the National Electrical Manufacturers' Association, and many others.

While governmental agencies have cooperated closely with these organizations, they have also developed their own standards. The National Bureau of Standards in the U.S. Department of Commerce compiles commercial standards. The General Services Administration coordinates standards and federal specifications for the nonmilitary type of items used by two or more services. The Defense Department issues military (MIL) specifications.

Necessity to Meet Government Legal Requirements.   Federal legislation concerning employee health and safety and consumer product safety requires vigilance on the part of purchasing personnel to be sure that products purchased meet government requirements. The Occupational Safety and Health Administration (known as OSHA) of the U.S. Department of Labor has broad powers to investigate and control everything from noise levels to sanitary facilities in places of employment. The Consumer Product Safety Act gives broad regulatory power to a commission to safeguard consumers against unsafe products. Purchasing people have the responsibility to make sure that the products they buy meet the requirements of the legislation. Severe penalties, both criminal and civil, can be placed on violators of the regulations.

Loss Exposure.   Robert S. Mullen, director of purchasing, Harvard

University, adds an extra dimension to the above concerns, drawing attention to loss exposure.

I am not suggesting that purchasing play the role of risk manager, but rather that it be sensitive to those selective buy situations in which loss exposure may be involved, and include this ingredient as a par-for-the-course consideration within the scope of its professional concern in determining "the best buy."

Selective consideration is the appropriate term, since, obviously, purchasing buys a wide range of products and services in which loss exposure is not involved. When it may be, however, and unfortunately, loss which might have been avoided in fact occurs, the consequences, dollarwise, if not also public relations-wise, can be substantial. I can only speak to the issue in the context of experience in an educational institution. For example, in buying mattresses for dormitories, we can make what we think is an excellent buy, namely minimal maintenance, sound construction, long-lasting comfort, and exceptionally low price, *except* that the degree of assured inflammability may not have been given adequate emphasis. Result: a student smoking in bed falls asleep, the cigarette ignites the mattress and a fire ensues, resulting in perhaps $30,000 property damage, but what is far worse, two students die of smoke inhalation. Their deaths would be unthinkable enough, but, in addition, there might well follow two suits for negligence amounting to $3 million brought by parents. The cost of guaranteeing against inflammability as part of the buy might only have been $1,000 additional.

Another concern is that of hazardous waste disposal and the responsibility upon those generating it, under the "cradle to grave" responsibility imposed by the Resource Conservation and Recovery Act of 1976 (RCRA). The vast area of product liability, so prevalent today in our litigation-inclined society, has ramifications which extend to all kinds of components and subcontracted assemblies, many of which by themselves would not be considered to involve aspects of inherent loss exposure.[2]

Another form of loss exposure is related to the possibility of pilferage. The attractiveness of the requirements to consumers and the ease of resale may be reasons for theft. An alert purchaser can significantly cut down on losses by: purchasing in smaller quantities, insisting on tamper-proof packaging, choosing the appropriate transportation mode, following advice of security experts, and making sure that quantities are carefully controlled throughout the acquisition and disposal process.

Standardization and Simplification.   The terms *standardization* and *simplification* are often used to mean the same thing. Strictly speaking, they refer to two different ideas. Standardization means agreement on definite sizes, design, quality, and the like. It is essentially a technical and engineering concept. Simplification refers to a reduction in the number of

---

[2]Robert S. Mullen, "Purchasing's Relationship with Risk Management," *Washington Purchaser,* July 1983, p. 14.

sizes, designs, and so forth. It is a selective and commercial problem, an attempt to determine the most important sizes, for instance, of a product and to concentrate production on these wherever possible. Simplification may be applied to either articles already standardized as to design or size or as a step preliminary to standardization.

The challenge in an organization is where to draw the line between standardization and simplification, on the one hand, and suitability and uniqueness, on the other. Clearly, as economic and technological factors change, old standards may no longer represent the best buy. Frequently, by stressing standardization and simplification of the component parts, rather than the completed end product, production economies may be gained combined with individuality of end product. Simultaneously, procurement advantages are gained in terms of low initial cost, lower inventories, and diversity in selection of sources. The automotive industry, for example, has used this approach extensively to cut costs, improve quality, and still give the appearance of extensive consumer options.

QUALITY

Quality refers to the ability of the supplier to provide goods and services according to specifications. Considerable interest in the use of quality as a competitive tool has reawakened management appreciation of the contribution quality can make in an organization. On the supply side, how well vendors perform may be crucial to the buying organization's own success in providing quality goods and services. A variety of surveys tend to show that in many organizations at least 50 percent of the quality problems stem from goods and services supplied by suppliers. Moreover, new management tools and techniques like MRP, JIT, and stockless purchasing all require that what is delivered by a supplier conforms to specifications. Furthermore, it is not realistic to insist that vendors supply high quality goods without ensuring that the buying organization's own quality performance is beyond reproach. This applies to the procurement organization, its people, policies, systems, and procedures as well. Quality improvement is a continuing challenge for both buyer and seller alike. Moreover, close cooperation between buying and selling organizations is necessary to achieve significant improvement over time.

The old-fashioned management perspective was that the quality-cost curve was similar to the economic order quantity curve, or broadly U-shaped. (See Figure 4–1.) Under this notion, it was considered acceptable to live with a significant defect level, because it was assumed that fewer defects would increase costs.

Thanks to the contribution of leaders like Deming, Juran, and Crosby, as well as Japanese industry, a new perspective on quality and its achievability has emerged. This view of quality argues that every defect is expensive and prevention or avoidance of defects lowers costs. (See Figure 4–2.)

FIGURE 4–1   The Traditional View of the Quality–Cost Trade-off

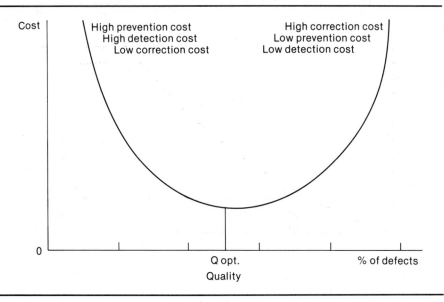

Interestingly enough, it used to be that purchasers were willing to pay more for higher quality products or services, recognizing the benefits to the purchaser's organization, but also assuming that the vendor might have to incur higher costs to achieve better quality. If the quality is "inspected in," this would indeed be a higher-cost solution. Deming argues that the stress in quality should be in making it right the first time, rather than inspecting quality in. Making it right the first time should be a lower-cost solution. Therefore, it is not unreasonable for a purchaser and seller to work together on achieving both improved quality and lower costs!

Quality presents three real challenges for supply. The first is learning how to apply quality principles to purchasing's own performance. The second, how to work cooperatively with vendors on continuing quality improvement. And the third is how to deal with vendor rationalization and all that it implies.

Many of purchasing's policies and procedures have been designed on the principle that competition is at the heart of the buyer-seller relationship. What keeps the seller sharp is the fear that another supplier can take away sales to a particular purchaser by offering better quality, better price, better delivery, better service, or a host of other inducements. The assumption was that a supplier switch was inexpensive for the purchaser and that multiple sourcing gave the purchaser both supply security and control over suppliers. The emergence of quality as a prime purchasing criterion challenges this

FIGURE 4–2   The Current View of the Quality–Cost Trade-off

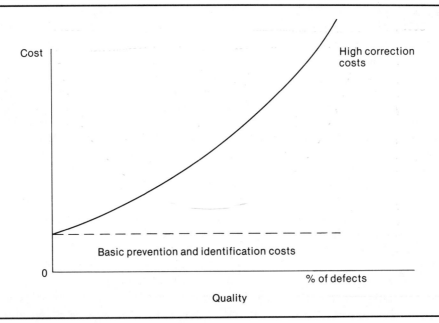

traditional competitive view. It argues that it is very difficult to find a high quality supplier and even more difficult to create a supplier who will continually improve quality. In fact, it may require very extensive work of various experts in the purchasing organization, along with the appropriate counterparts in the selling organization, to achieve continuing improvements in quality. (The description of the Signetics program which follows gives some inkling of how much may be involved.) Under these circumstances it is not realistic to use multiple sources for the same end item, to switch suppliers frequently, and to go out for quotes constantly. But, single sourcing has traditionally created considerable purchaser nervousness. The idea of sharing key organizational information with suppliers so that they can plan, design, and service the purchaser's requirements better is scary for procurement experts whose skills were honed on a competitiveness philosophy. The heart of a new approach to quality centers on understanding the tools, techniques, and mathematics of quality involved. The following section provides a brief summary.

The Cost of Quality

Perhaps the traditional view of quality stems from an economic environment of high demand and low world-wide competition, in which defects were tolerated. Perhaps this was further abetted by an incomplete grasp of the real costs of quality and of poor quality. Unfortunately, in many organizations these costs are well hidden and, therefore, difficult to consider in decision making.

Three major cost categories applicable to quality are detection, prevention, and correction. Detection costs might occur at both the seller's and buyer's organization as each uses a variety of inspection systems to ensure quality conformance. If detection requires setting aside batches, or sending product to a separate inspection department, detection costs should include extra handling and inventory tie-up costs aside from the inspection cost itself in terms of space, people, equipment, materials, and associated reporting systems. (The advantages of using the supplier's QC reports and making it right the first time are evident.)

Prevention costs include such diverse costs as various quality assurance programs, precertifying and qualifying vendors, employee training and awareness programs, machine, tool, material and labor check-outs, preventive maintenance, single sourcing with quality vendors, as well as the associated personnel, travel, equipment, and space costs.

Correction costs have a wide diversity and may include some costs substantially greater than prevention or detection costs. The simplest correction costs are those associated with rework, replacement, or disposal of products or services found unacceptable. Most of these are detailed in the subsequent section on rework and returns. Typical minimum costs for a purchaser include transportation back to the supplier, extra handling, rescheduling, extra inspection, and extra paperwork costs.

Unfortunately, when parts are incorporated in assemblies, disassembly and reassembly costs may far outweigh the cost of the original part itself. When a defective product gets into the hands of customers or their customers, the possibility of consequential damages arises because a paper roll did not meet specifications, the printer missed an important deadline, a magazine did not reach advertisers and subscribers on time, and so on. There may be health or safety consequences from defective quality products. The loss of customers, the inability to secure new customers, the penalties paid to keep existing customers, all are also part of the cost of correction.

One cost seldom recognized in an accounting sense is the morale cost of producing (or having to use) defective products or services. Aside from the obvious productivity impact, it may remove the incentive for the employees in the organization to keep searching for continuing improvement and may develop a laissez-faire attitude.

In fact, it is so unpleasant to detail the costs of defective quality, that the temptation is strong to ignore them. And that is exactly what many organizations have done for many years. They have also built these costs into internally accepted standards. As a consequence, the opportunity to improve quality is great in most organizations.

An attempt has been made in Figure 4–3 to summarize the quality cost perspective including the size of costs and their ease of determination. A high difficulty of cost determination does not at all imply that the cost is not real or not high. Neither does the diagram try to imply that all prevention and identification costs are minor. For a large organization, the mounting of an effective prevention program may run into millions of dollars. At the same time, for a large organization correction costs may run into tens or hundreds of millions of dollars, although many of these costs might not even be identified. For example, potential sales to new customers which were never realized may never be identified on any budget or financial statement of the organization.

Responsibility for Adjustments and Returns

Prompt negotiations for adjustments and returns made necessary by rejections are a responsibility of the purchasing department, aided by the using, inspection, or legal departments.

Any nonconforming product, material, or equipment needs to be locked up to avoid the possibility of inadvertent processing, pilferage, or additional damage while its disposition is being deliberated. Some organizations use a material review board to decide how to deal with specific nonconforming materials.

The actual decision as to what can or should be done with material that does not meet specifications is both an engineering and a procurement question. It can, of course, be simply rejected and either returned at the supplier's expense or held for instructions as to its disposition. In either case the buyer must inform the supplier whether the shipment is to be replaced with acceptable material or to consider the contract canceled. Not infrequently, however, a material may be used for some other than the originally intended purpose or substituted for some other grade. It is also possible that some private readjustment is called for. A third alternative is to rework the material, deducting from the purchase price the cost of the additional processing involved. Also, particularly in the case of new types of equipment or new material to which the purchaser is not accustomed, the vendor may send a technical representative to the buyer's organization in the hope that complete satisfaction may be provided.

A problem growing out of inspection is that of the allocation, between buyer and seller, of costs incurred in connection with rejected material. The following statement indicates the nature of the problem and the various practices in dealing with it:

The costs incurred on rejected materials may be divided into three major classes:

1. Transportation costs.

2. Testing cost.

FIGURE 4–3   The Relationship among Quality Identification, Prevention, and
Correction Costs and the Difficulty in Determining the Nature
and Size of These Costs

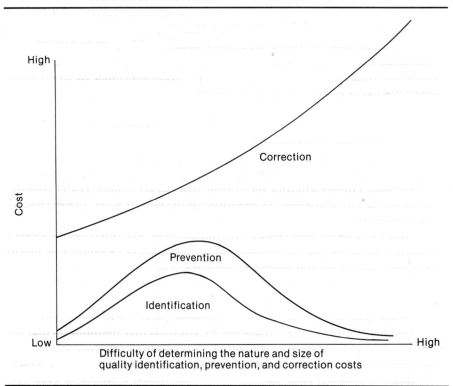

Difficulty of determining the nature and size of
quality identification, prevention, and correction costs

3. Contingent expense.

The practice of allocating these costs varies considerably. The practice
is affected to some degree by the kind of material rejected, trade customs,
the essential economies of the situation, the buyer's cost of accounting procedure, and the positions of strength of each organization.

In practically all cases reported, transportation costs both to and from
the rejection point are charged back to the supplier.

Very few companies report inspection or testing costs as items to be
charged back to the supplier. Such costs are ordinarily borne by the buyer
and are considered a part of purchasing or inspection costs.

In many cases contracts or trade customs provide definitely that the
supplier will not be responsible for contingent expense, yet this is perhaps
the greatest risk and the most costly item of all from the buyer's standpoint.

Incoming materials which are not of proper quality may seriously interrupt production; their rejection may cause a shortage of supply which may result in delay or actual stoppage of production, extra handling, and other expense. Labor may be expended in good faith on material later found to be unusable, and not only the material but the labor thus expended is a total loss to the buyer. It is, in general, however, not the practice of buyers to allocate such contingent costs to the vendor. Some buyers, however, insist on agreements with their vendors to recover labor or other costs expended on the material before discovery of its defective character.

QUALITY ASSURANCE, TESTING, INSPECTION, AND QUALITY CONTROL

No matter how perfect the description of the need, the purchaser still needs to worry about whether the vendor will supply what is really required. Normally, this involves quality assurance programs, testing, inspection, and quality control.

Usually, before a new vendor is given an order, and often before a vendor is allowed to quote, the purchaser conducts a quality capability or quality assurance survey on the vendor's premises. The purpose is to ensure that the vendor is capable of meeting the specifications and quality standards required. Whereas this practice started in the military field, it is now common in all high technology areas and in most larger organizations.

This survey, normally conducted by engineering, manufacturing, purchasing, and quality control personnel, will examine not only the vendor's equipment, facilities, and personnel, but also the systems in place to monitor and improve quality. Also examined are the vendor's efforts to seek cooperation and compliance in quality standards from its suppliers and the suppliers' commitment to ongoing quality improvement.

It is desirable to have continuing involvement with vendors to evolve common quality standards, to agree on inspection methods, and to work out ways and means of improving quality while decreasing inspection and overall cost.

For example, in one high-technology company, the following quality improvement program is in place:

Phase I is complete when Signetics and the vendor agree on inspection measurement procedures and techniques. There is also mutual agreement that inspection of the same product leads to exact correlation. Every supplier completing Phase I is awarded a Certificate of Certification.

During Phase I, the labeling, packaging, transportation, and billing of shipment samples is agreed on. In addition, agreement is also reached on the frequency of maintaining correlation between inspectors and calibration of inspection equipment.

A control chart is developed for each inspection measurement. An upper and lower limit is also established based on equipment and inspection tolerances and differences. The data received from the vendor and the data generated by Signetics must fall within the established percentage of uncertainty. Reasons for any deviations are determined and corrections are made accordingly.

Phase II begins with a material conformance control analysis. This is accomplished by using additional correlation samples. For each measurement taken, control charts track the vendor's performance to specification. When a vendor exhibits consistent control of material conformance for a three-month period, he proceeds into Phase III.

In Phase III the vendor pulls all samples and does a complete outgoing inspection analysis. At Signetics' discretion these samples are used, either in part or in total, to disposition the incoming shipment. A vendor who demonstrates that his quality history and inspection and process certification are in control for a three-month period will move into Phase IV.

Phase IV is the same as Phase III except samples and data are sent ahead of the shipment. This allows Signetics' IQC to operate in an audit mode by using vendor samples and data for preshipment or skip lot inspection. In this phase, the certified vendor supplies certification control samples/data, complete lot inspection samples/data, and a certificate of compliance. Shipments that are skipped have the supplied samples/data and certificate of compliance reviewed for inspection correlation and material conformance. No additional samples are inspected if all are found acceptable.

Continuous monitoring and auditing of Phase I–IV are the responsibility of Signetics' IQC. Nonconformance issues and/or inspection correlation problems result in immediate stoppage of the program. Reinstitution occurs when all issues are resolved. . . .

The vendor communications program permits and encourages open lines of communications between Signetics and all suppliers. Driven by the purchasing department, the program provides reports and graphs to accurately track vendor quality performance. Each month, suppliers receive information including:

Performance summary data—lot acceptance rates, parts per million defective information, and defect mode analysis

Percent defective data for each inspection criteria

Lot acceptance rate/volume/PPM charts, and inspection correlation control charts, and

Vendor certification graphs.[3]

The obvious target in improving quality is to have the right quality by making it right the first time, rather than inspecting the quality in. It is this pressure to create quality at its source that is behind all quality improvement programs. The same philosophy should also apply to the purchasing department itself and the purchaser's own organization. It is very difficult for a purchaser to insist that vendors meet stringent quality requirements when it is obvious to the suppliers that the purchasing orga-

---

[3]Richard Brooks, "A Strategy for Winning the Quality Battle," *Modern Purchasing,* November 1983, pp. 30–33.

nization itself shows no sign of a similar commitment. The smartest thing for any purchasing department wishing to start a quality drive is to apply quality standards to its own performance on all of the phases it is involved in, in the acquisition cycle. Not only will this create familiarity with statistical quality control and quality standards in the purchasing department itself, but it also gives purchasing the right to ask for similar commitment by others.

Inspection and Testing

Inspection and testing may be done at two different stages in the acquisition process. Before commitment is made to a supplier, it may be necessary to test samples to see if they are adequate for the purpose intended. Similarly, comparison testing may be done to determine which product is better from several different sources. After a purchase commitment has been made, inspection may be required to assure that the items delivered conform to the original description.

Testing

Testing products may be necessary before a commitment is made to purchase. The original selection of a given item may be based either on a specific test or a preliminary trial.

When suppliers offer samples for testing, the general rule followed by purchasers is to accept only samples which have some reasonable chance of being used. Buyers are more likely to accept samples than to reject them, since they are always on the lookout for items that may prove superior to those in current use. For various reasons, however, care has to be exercised. The samples cost the seller something, and the buyer will not wish to raise false hopes on the part of the salesperson. Sometimes, too, the buyer lacks adequate facilities for testing and testing may be costly to the buyer.

To meet these objections, some companies insist on paying for all samples accepted for testing, partly because they believe that a more representative sample is obtained when it is purchased through the ordinary trade channels and partly because the buyer is less likely to feel under any obligation to the seller. Some companies pay for the sample when the value is substantial; some follow the rule of allowing whoever initiates the test to pay for the item tested; some pay for it only when the outcome of the test is satisfactory. The general rule, however, is for sellers to pay for samples on the theory that, if sellers really want the business and have confidence in their products, they will be willing to bear the expense.

Use and Laboratory Tests.   The type of test given also varies, depending on such factors as the attitude of the buyer toward the value of

specific types of tests, the type of item in question, its comparative importance, and the buyer's facilities for testing. At times a use test alone is
considered sufficient, as with paint and floor wax. One advantage of a use
test is that the item can be tested for the particular purpose for which it is
intended and under the particular conditions in which it will be used. The
risk that failure may be costly or interrupt performance or production is,
however, present. At other times a laboratory test alone is thought adequate
and may be conducted by a commercial testing laboratory or in the organization's own quality control facility. For retailers, a test may be given in
one or more stores to establish whether consumer demand is sufficient to
carry the product.

The actual procedure of handling samples need not be outlined here. It
is important to make and keep complete records concerning each individual
sample accepted. These records should describe the type of test, the conditions under which it was given, the results, and any representations made
about it by the seller. It is sound practice to discuss the results of such tests
with supplier representatives so that they know their samples have received
a fair evaluation.

Inspection

The ideal situation for inspection is, of course, one in which no inspection
is necessary. This is possible because the quality assurance effort cooperatively mounted by the purchaser and the vendor has resulted in outstanding quality performance and reliable supporting vendor records. Since
not all organizations have reached this enviable goal, examining some
of the more common ideas surrounding inspection and quality control is
useful.

Just as the purpose of adequate description is to convey to the vendor
a clear idea of the item being purchased, so the purpose of inspection is to
assure the buyer that the supplier has delivered an item which corresponds
to the description furnished. When new suppliers are being tried, their
products or services must be watched with particular care until they have
proved themselves dependable. Unfortunately, too, production methods and
skills, even of old suppliers, change from time to time; operators become
careless; errors are made; and occasionally a seller may even try to reduce
production costs to the point where quality suffers. Thus, for a variety of
reasons, it is poor policy for a buyer to neglect inspection methods or procedures. There is no point in spending time and money on the development
of satisfactory specifications unless adequate provision is made to see that
these specifications are lived up to by vendors.

The type of inspection, its frequency, and thoroughness vary with circumstances. In the last analysis, this resolves itself into a matter of comparative costs. How much must be spent to ensure compliance with specifications?

In setting specifications, it is desirable to include the procedure for inspection and testing as protection for both buyer and seller. The vendor cannot refuse to accept rejected goods on the ground that the type of inspection to which the goods would be subjected was not known or that the inspection was unduly rigid.

Vendor and purchaser need to work out both the procedure for sampling and the nature of the test to be conducted. This way both vendor and purchaser should achieve identical test results, no matter which party conducts the test. Whereas in some situations purchasers may be more sophisticated in quality control and, in others, the vendors, it is sensible for both sides to cooperate on this thorny issue.

On-Premise-Buyer Inspection.   Inspection may be conducted by the buyer in the plant of the vendor because the usual methods of inspection of the finished item may not be adequate. Latent defects not determinable may appear only after the purchaser has further processed the material or part. Again, the correction of defects, if attended to as soon as possible, avoids the additional costs of carrying the work on to completion, only to find the end result unacceptable. Furthermore, transportation charges incident to the return to the vendor of rejected material, especially on heavy material or items shipped long distances, can be avoided. On the other hand, such inspection has two definite disadvantages. One is the heavy cost of maintaining such an inspection staff. The second is that the presence of inspectors in the plant may be strongly resented by the supplier.

A different kind of buyer inspection at the seller's premises takes place when selection, rather than production of a commodity, determines the quality and when price varies accordingly. Examples would include, but are not limited to, veneer and saw logs, pulp wood, livestock, land, feed and mixed grains, used equipment, antiques, paintings, scrap, and professional contracts. Furthermore, on-premise-buyer inspection almost always applies in auctions.

Commercial Testing Labs and Services.   The type of inspection required may, in fact, be so complicated or so expensive that it cannot be performed satisfactorily in the buyer's or seller's own organization. In such cases it may be attractive to use the services of commercial testing laboratories, particularly in connection with new processes or materials or for aid in the setting of specifications. Also, the use of an unbiased testing organization may lend credibility to the results. For example, air, water, and soil samples are often sent to commercial labs to test for compliance with EPA standards.

Furthermore, standard testing reports of commonly used items are available from several commercial testing laboratories. They are the commercial equivalent of consumer's reports and can be a valuable aid.

Quality Control

The responsibility of a quality control group is not confined to the technical task of inspecting incoming material or monitoring in-house production. The quality group can initiate material studies. It can be called on to pass on samples left by salespeople. Frequently it must investigate claims and errors, both as to incoming items and as to outgoing or finished products. It may pass on material returned to stores to determine its suitability for reissue. Similarly, it may be called on to examine salvage material and to make a recommendation as to its disposition. Other duties include quality assurance and attendant efforts to help suppliers and their suppliers to design, implement, and monitor continuous quality improvement programs.

The structure and location of the quality control function constitute a relevant problem of administration. In most cases, the work of inspection is performed by a separate department whose work may be divided into three main parts: the inspection of incoming materials, the inspection of materials in process of manufacture, and the inspection of the finished product. The assignment of this work to a separate department is supported partly on the ground that if the inspectors of materials in process and of the finished product report to the executive in charge of production, there may be occasions when inspection standards are relaxed in order to cover up defects in production.

Inspection Methods.   The current high interest in quality fueled by concern for cost, competitiveness, employee morale, and technological requirements reinforces the need for appropriate inspection methods.

A substantial specialized body of literature is available on the subject of quality control and inspection methods. In this text only some of the basic quality control concepts will be raised.

Although the mathematics for statistical quality control have been well established for decades, their application has not been as widespread as might have been desirable. Over the past 30 years, various forms of *zero defects programs* have been initiated. The original efforts were largely attributable to defense and space programs, where the consequences of part failures were obviously very serious. Current thinking on quality reinforces the zero defects target as suppliers and purchasers both seek this goal for mutual benefit. If a purchaser could be certain that everything supplied by a vendor was defect-free, it would eliminate the need for overordering and for further inspection and enable immediate use of the materials or parts supplied. At the same time the purchaser could concentrate its efforts on assuring that its own goods or services meet with desired quality targets. As the earlier example of Signetics Corporation indicated, such an ideal situation does not evolve without extensive management efforts. The procurement role in seeking vendor cooperation in the pursuit of the zero defect objective should not be minimized.

Similarly, it behooves materials personnel to be thoroughly familiar with the inspection methods commonly used inside their organization and by vendors, so that they can reinforce their organization's quality control efforts appropriately.

Inspection is expensive. If a part is of acceptable quality, inspection does not normally add to its value. Inspection represents a delay, a further addition of cost, and a possibility of error or damage in handling. It is obviously preferable to make it right in the first place, rather than "inspect the quality in" by separating the acceptable from the unacceptable parts, which is wasteful. Moreover, experience in organizations that have successfully pursued quality improvement programs shows significant productivity improvements have simultaneously occurred.

It would be ideal if the same inspection methods could be used by both the manufacturer and the purchaser. Since almost all output results from a manufacturing or transformation process of some sort, process quality control will be the first topic discussed. This will be followed by screening and sampling which deal with items already produced. All quality control can be divided further into observations of attributes and variables. Attributes usually observed are whether the product is acceptable or not. For example, for an automobile assembly line, is the paint acceptable or not? In a hotel, have the rooms been properly cleaned or not? This type of yes or no inspection is usually based on the binomial distribution.

Observation by variables tries to determine by how much the sample varies from the specification or from other units. How many paint defects on this car? How many things are wrong with the way this hotel has been cleaned? Observation by variables is usually based on the normal distribution.

Process Quality Control.   In processes using repetitive operations, the quality control chart is invaluable. The output can be measured by tracking a mean and dispersion. The X bar chart is useful for charting the population means and the R bar chart the dispersion.

Dr. W. Edwards Deming, the well-known American quality control specialist, assisted Japanese manufacturers in instituting statistical quality control. Dr. Deming showed that most machines tend to behave in a statistical manner, and that understanding how the machine behaves without operator interference is necessary before controls can be instituted. Upper and lower control limits can be set so that operator action is only required when the process or machine starts to fall outside of its normal desirable operating range. Figure 4–4 illustrates this "wandering" type of behavior for an automatic filling machine. It is important that packages filled by this machine are not sent out significantly under or overweight. The operator in this example, therefore, takes random samples of four packages each and their weights and weight range are plotted on the quality control chart by

FIGURE 4–4 Filler Control Chart, Summary, and Explanations

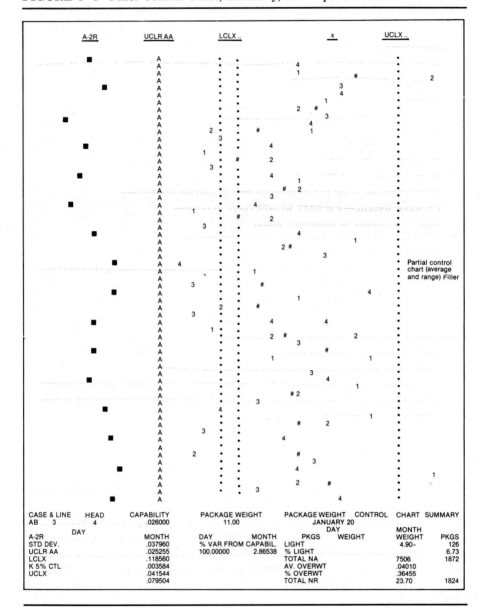

Partial control chart (average and range) Filler

CASE & LINE	HEAD	CAPABILITY	PACKAGE WEIGHT		PACKAGE WEIGHT	CONTROL	CHART	SUMMARY
AB 3	4	.026000	11.00		JANUARY 20			
	DAY					DAY	MONTH	
A-2R		MONTH	DAY	MONTH	PKGS	WEIGHT	WEIGHT	PKGS
STD DEV.		.037960	% VAR FROM CAPABIL.		LIGHT		4.90–	126
UCLR AA		.025255	100.00000	2.86538	% LIGHT			6.73
LCLX		.118560			TOTAL NA		7506	1872
K 5% CTL		.003584			AV. OVERWT		.04010	
UCLX		.041544			% OVERWT		.36455	
		.079504			TOTAL NR		23.70	1824

FIGURE 4–4 (concluded)

Terminology:

A-$2R$—($A_2\overline{R}$) where A_2 is a constant for a sample of 4 and $\overline{X}' \pm A_2\overline{R}$ gives the upper and lower control limits.

$UCLR$—(UCL_R) Upper control limit, range

$LCLX$—(LCL_x) Lower control limit, average

X 5% XTL—($\overline{X}')_1$ point at which average is set to insure that 95 percent of packages will equal or exceed stated net weight (CTL—control limit)

$UCLX$—(UCL_x) Upper control limit, average

Capability—Capability of machine under control conditions

% Var. from capability—A percent by which the daily or month to date capability varies from the capability under control conditions

Package weight—Package weight (net) in ounces

Light—Number of packages under net weight

% Light—Percent of packages under net weight

Total NA—Total sample size

Av overwt.—Total overweight divided by the total sample size (gives average weight over new weight)

% Overwt.—Average overweight divided by the package weight

Total NR—The Total NR figure is similar to the Total NA figure except that the computer rejects samples which have "gone wild." These are removed and the Total NR figure is used to calculate the standard deviation

Note: Figure 4–1 is a composite of two control charts. The two columns on the left refer to the range control chart while the remaining three columns represent the weight control chart. The symbols 1, 2, 3 and 4 on the weight control chart refer to the observation number and the sample average is designated by the symbol #.

the computer. The computer also prepares daily and monthly records of machine performance. The range plot on the left-hand side of the chart shows a wavy curve, well below the upper control limit. The individual weight sample plots on the right-hand side show a significant number of individual packages below the lower control limit, but the mean of the sample of four packages stays within acceptable limits. If the range or mean weights were to fall outside their acceptable limits, the process is stopped and action is taken to determine the cause for the shift so that corrections can be made.

The control chart uses random sampling techniques and is well suited to most manufacturing operations producing large output and where it is not necessary to screen every item produced.

Screening.   There are basically two major types of quality checks on output. One is to inspect every item produced. The other is to sample.

It is traditionally held that 100 percent inspection, or screening, is the most desirable inspection method available. This is not true. Experience shows that 100 percent inspection seldom accomplishes a completely satisfactory job of separating the acceptable from the nonacceptable or measuring the variables properly. Actually, 200 or 300 percent inspection or even higher may have to be done to accomplish this objective. Depending on the severity of a mistake, an error of discarding a perfectly good part may be more acceptable than passing a faulty part. In some applications the use of such extreme testing may increase the cost of a part enormously. For example, in certain high technology applications, individual parts are required to be accompanied by their own individual test "pedigrees." Thus, a part which for a commercial application might cost $0.75 may well end up costing $50.00 or more and perform the identical function.

If the test is destructive, 100 percent testing is impractical. The cost of 100 percent testing is frequently high. The testing is seldom fully reliable, because of worker boredom or fatigue, or inadequate facilities or methods, and, therefore, it is not often used in high-volume situations.

Sampling.   The alternative to inspection of every item produced is to sample. How a sample is taken will vary with the product and process. The purpose is always to attempt to secure a sample that is representative of the total population being tested. Random sampling is one commonly used technique.

The method of taking a random sample will depend on the characteristics of the product to be inspected. If it is such that all products received in a shipment can be thoroughly mixed together, then the selection of a sample from any part of the total of the mixed products will represent a valid random sample. For example, if a shipment of 1,000 balls of supposedly identical characteristics are thoroughly mixed together and a random sample of 50 balls is picked from the lot and inspected and 5 are found to be defective, it is probable that 10 percent of the shipment is defective.

If the product has characteristics which make it difficult or impractical to mix together thoroughly, consecutive numbers can be assigned to each product, and then, through the use of tables of random sampling numbers (of which there are several) or a standard computer program, a sample drawn by number is chosen for detailed inspection.

The general rule which the statisticians believe should be observed when drawing a random sample is: Adopt a method of selection that will give every unit of the product to be inspected an equal chance of being drawn.

Operating Characteristic Curves.   Operating characteristic (OC) curves are used to see how well a sampling plan distinguished between acceptable and nonacceptable product. In procurement the purchaser has to determine what the probability is of accepting goods that do not meet the

FIGURE 4-5   Typical OC Curve

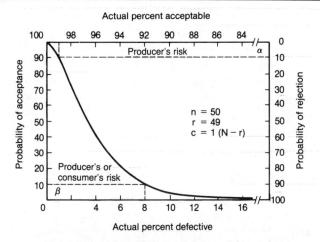

Note: Data showing probability of rejecting good lots by the producer with α = .10 and the probability of accepting bad lots by the purchaser with β = .10.

SOURCE: R. B. Chase and N. J. Aquilano, *Production and Operations Management* (Homewood, Ill.: Richard D. Irwin, 1973), p. 156. © Richard D. Irwin, Inc., 1973.

minimum level of quality specified. This is called the consumer's risk with a percentage β. There is a parallel risk α for the producer that work may be rejected at the plant when it is in reality acceptable (see Figure 4–5).

In the example shown, the purchaser and the producer must select a sampling plan which establishes the appropriate trade-off between risk, accuracy, and inspection cost. Usually, as the number of samples is increased additional accuracy is obtained, but sampling cost is also increased. Theoretically, in the selection of any sampling plan the cost of sampling must be weighed against the losses that would be incurred if no sampling were done. It is unfortunate that the sampling cost is normally easier to determine than the losses arising from not sampling.

Sequential Sampling.   Sequential sampling may be used to reduce the number of items to be inspected in accept-reject decisions without loss of accuracy. It is based on the cumulative effect of information that every additional item in the sample adds as it is inspected. After each individual item's inspection, three decisions are possible: to accept, to reject, or to sample another item. A. Wald, one of the pioneers of sequential sampling development, estimated that, using his plan, the average sample size could be reduced to one half, as compared to a single sampling plan.

In a simple version of sequential sampling, 10 percent of the lot is inspected, and the whole lot is accepted if the sample is acceptable. If the sample is not acceptable, an additional 10 percent may be inspected if the decision to reject cannot be made on the basis of the first sample.

Selective Inspection Computer Programs.   Many quality control computer programs are available. They have resolved the tedium of extensive calculations and provide a range of applications. All computer manufacturers and many service companies maintain these programs for use by customers. Standard programs, for example, select sampling plans, calculate sample statistics and plot histograms, produce random selection of parts, plot OC curves, and determine confidence limits.

QUESTIONS FOR REVIEW AND DISCUSSION

1. What are the various costs associated with quality and why is it difficult to determine the magnitude of some of these costs?
2. Why is Deming so insistent on single sourcing?
3. What are the advantages of using functional specifications?
4. Why should a purchaser be concerned about function?
5. What activities should an inspection department engage in?
6. How could a quality philosophy be applied to a purchasing department?
7. What are the attractions of sequential sampling?
8. Why should a purchaser be familiar with the mathematics of quality control and inspection?
9. What are the responsibilities of a good supplier?
10. What constitutes a best buy?

REFERENCES

Crosby, Philip B. *Quality Without Tears: The Art of Hassle Free Management.* New York: McGraw-Hill, 1984.

Deming, W.E. *Out of the Crisis.* Boston: MIT, 1987.

Gryna, Frank M., Jr. *Quality Circles: A Team Approach to Problem Solving.* New York: AMACOM, 1981.

Juran, Joseph M. and Frank M. Gryna, Jr. *Quality Planning and Analysis.* 2nd ed. New York: McGraw-Hill, 1980.

Leigh, Thomas W. and Rethans, Arno J. "User Participation and Influence in Industrial Buying." *Journal of Purchasing and Materials Management,* Summer 1985.

Schonberger, Richard J. *World Class Manufacturing: The Lessons of Simplicity Applied.* New York: Free Press, 1986.

Treleven, Mark. "Single Sourcing: A Management Tool for the Quality Supplier." *Journal of Purchasing and Materials Management,* Spring 1987.

Case 4–1

Earl's Candies

Louise Moffat, packaging buyer for Earl's Candies, was wondering what to do with Longmore Packaging on an order of misprinted boxes. Eric Svenson, sales representative for Longmore, would be in Louise's office within an hour to discuss the situation.

Louise had already spent several hours with marketing and production to see what could be done with the boxes. She was angry, because this had been Longmore's first delivery on a new contract. It had not been easy to persuade marketing and production to switch suppliers. Imperial Packaging had supplied Earl's with all of its box requirements for years to the full satisfaction of marketing and production. However, in Louise's opinion, although Imperial's quality and delivery performance had been fully satisfactory, their price had been high. Therefore, she had finally persuaded marketing and production to let her go out for bids on Earl's Puffs, a highly popular line. Longmore Packaging's bid promised to save Earl's at least $30,000 a year over Imperial's.

Jim Shaw was Longmore's sales representative. He had joined Longmore recently after having worked for years for Domison Bag, a long-term reliable supplier of bags to Earl's. Louise knew Jim Shaw well and had worked on the Puff bid with him. She wondered if he was as technically proficient with boxes as he had been with bags, but Jim had indicated to her he had been pleased with the move to his new firm and was delighted to be able to continue doing business with her.

The first order for Puff's boxes totaled $15,600. Longmore was to get its films from Imperial. Louise had given Jim Shaw physical samples of the Puff boxes. However, Imperial had sent films of an earlier Puff design and Longmore had consequently misprinted the whole order.

The situation had not become apparent until the boxes were delivered to Earl's plant and the filling department foreman discovered the mistake. He had immediately phoned Louise, the plant manager, and the marketing manager because there were a number of Puff's orders outstanding that had to be filled immediately. In view of the necessity to supply Puff's orders, marketing and production agreed they could not wait but would have to put the Puffs into the old design boxes.

Louise had telephoned Jim Shaw to inform him of the error and asked him to come over immediately. She knew that Jim would be upset and had asked marketing and production not to discuss the situation with him. She believed Jim should not know the boxes would be used. It seemed to her that Longmore should shoulder the blame for this incident, even though she wondered if Imperial's action had been totally unintentional. Since she had submitted the correct samples to Jim Shaw, she believed Longmore should have checked the prints they received before running off the whole order. It was difficult for her, however, to establish what penalty, if any, Longmore should be asked to shoulder in this case.

Case 4–2

Ranek, Inc.

"Those WR93 castings you ordered from Roberts are no good, Marsha. They are all too short by a substantial margin, so I have no choice but to reject the whole batch. What do you want me to do with them?"

"Just hold on to them for awhile, Frank, till I find out what's going on here. I will get back to you shortly."

Marsha Dinsmore, buyer at Ranek, Inc. had just received the bad news from Frank Wild, head of quality assurance at Ranek regarding the 172 aluminum castings she had ordered for the first assembly run of the new PSW Model two weeks hence. She was not expecting any difficulties with this order, since she remembered buying the same castings for the earlier PSV Model. Marsha realized that a lack of castings could have a disastrous impact on the PSW assembly and introduction plans, for which extensive advance promotion had already begun. Therefore, she immediately tried to find out what went wrong with this order.

Engineering Information

A few hours later Marsha found out that the $150 casting did not meet specifications as shown on the engineering drawing sent to the supplier. All previous deliveries of the same casting had been identical in defects. However, the chief engineer, John Vickers, had made some adjustments for the PSV Model which made it possible to use the castings as supplied. According to John Vickers it was not possible to make the same adjustments for the PSW Model, nor was it possible to fix up the defective castings.

The PSV Model Plans

Current plans for the PSV Model called for continued assembly until the PSW Model had taken over the complete market. No one was quite certain how many more PSVs might be made. Sales estimates ranged from a minimum of 100 over the next year to 500 over the next three years. It was unlikely that repairs of old PSV Models would require more than 10 castings per year for the next 10 years.

Roberts Foundry

Steve Roberts, president and owner of Roberts Foundry, the supplier of the castings, claimed that the WR93 castings supplied were exactly the same as those of all earlier orders which had all been accepted by Ranek. He was very surprised to hear from Marsha that there were difficulties with the castings.

The normal lead time on aluminum castings with Roberts Foundry was about eight weeks. Marsha knew that Mr. Roberts was hungry for more business, even though his shop was very busy. He was currently working on a number of other Ranek orders. Roberts Foundry received about 40 percent of Ranek's $400,000 total aluminum casting business. Gaskell and Sons, a long-term reliable supplier, received the remaining 60 percent. The current lead time with Gaskell was about 10 weeks.

After assembling this information Marsha wondered what action to take next.

Case 4–3

Control Data Canada, Ltd.*

Shortly before Christmas, Mrs. Maxine Mist, fleet administrator of Control Data Canada, Ltd., was reviewing the executive automobile fleet policy of the company. The vice president of human resources had requested that she recommend for or against changing the current policy of providing Level I executives with North American-produced automobiles.

The Company

Control Data Canada, Ltd., of Mississauga, Ontario was incorporated in 1962 as a wholly owned subsidiary of Control Data Corporation in Minneapolis, Minnesota. The company shared several office locations with Commercial Credit Corporation, Ltd., another Control Data Corporation subsidiary, which was a multinational financial organization involved in large custom-tailored leasing and financing transactions. In December 1978, Control Data Canada, Ltd., had also assumed control of Ticket Reservation Systems of Canada, Ltd. (Ticketron), a firm offering computerized ticketing and subscription control systems for the sports and entertainment industry.

Since its establishment in 1962, Control Data Canada, Ltd., had increased revenues and profits through internal growth as well as the acquisition of existing companies. The major revenue producers were the CYBER line of computer systems and the sophisticated defense products of Computing Devices Company. Exhibit 1 shows the current organization chart.

In total, Control Data had over 2,000 employees in 27 facilities in eight cities across Canada. The major products and services offered by the company included the following: computing systems, professional services to computer users, data services, computer products, peripheral systems, educational services, and the defense and scientific electronic systems designed and manufactured by Computing Devices Company.

Fleet Administration

Maxine Mist joined Control Data, Ltd., in 1978 as fleet administrator, reporting to the vice president of human resources. She was responsible for 24 Level I executive automobiles, 91 Level II automobiles, and 3 service vehicles. In addition, she ad-

---

*This case was prepared under a grant from the Can-Nafa Fleet Foundation, Inc. by Douglas H. Clark, under the supervision of Professor Michiel R. Leenders.

EXHIBIT 1   Control Data Canada Ltd. Organization Chart

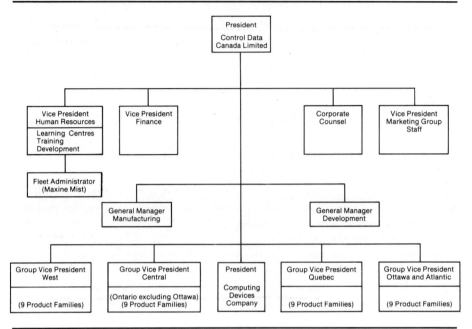

ministered the company's automobile reimbursement plans for approximately 97 sales and professional consulting staff, who were paid by Control Data for business miles driven in their personal automobiles.

Each of the executives in Exhibit 1 except Mrs. Mist were provided with a Level I automobile. Other executives, who had occupied Level I positions prior to a recent reorganization, were also provided with Level I automobiles.

Control Data Canada leased its automobiles from Commercial Credit Corporation, Ltd. Level I executives were charged $3,600 per year through payroll deductions for their personal use of company automobiles, while Level II executives paid $3,000 per year. Each automobile was tailored to the executive's wishes within the broad outlines of corporate automobile policy. It was a common practice for executives who were about to acquire a new automobile to visit Mrs. Mist's office where they could review brochures, compare color combinations and receive expert advice about available options. In addition, Mrs. Mist could arrange for them to test drive demonstrator cars. Executives usually requested and followed her professional advice regardless of their own corporate position.

Within some broad guidelines, Control Data's executive automobile policy was reasonably flexible. Level I executives were allowed to order any automobiles they wanted, subject to the following constraints:

The automobile had to be produced—not just assembled—in North America (for example, Volvo did not qualify in spite of having a Canadian assembly plant).
The automobile could not be a soft-top convertible or a station wagon.

If the automobile price exceeded a "basis" value, the excess over the basis would be charged back to the executive through payroll deductions.

In addition to these constraints, the executives were vigorously discouraged from ordering automobiles equipped with turbo chargers because of Control Data's unsatisfactory maintenance experience on cars with such options.

The Level II automobile policy was similar, but slightly more restrictive than for Level I executives. The major constraints were:

The automobiles had to be produced in North America.
The automobile could not be a soft-top convertible or a station wagon and could not have a sun roof.
The basis value was somewhat lower than for Level I autos.
The engine could not be larger than 6 cylinders.

In spite of these restrictions, it was not intended that Control Data executives should be required to drive substandard automobiles. It was hoped, rather, that the automobiles would project the appropriate image for both the company and the executives. For example, the automobile and options selected to establish the basis value of Level I automobiles for the current model year was a Regency Brougham Oldsmobile 4-door sedan equipped as follows: 8-cylinder, 5-liter engine, automatic transmission, power brakes, power steering, power windows, power trunk, power driver and passenger seats, power door locks, steel belted radial white wall tires, wire wheel covers, automatic air conditioning, tinted glass all around, rear window electric defroster, AM/FM stereo cassette radio, tilted telescopic steering wheel, cruise control, front and rear floor mats, custom light group, outside dual remote mirrors, vinyl roof, body side moulding, heavy-duty cooling, power antenna, and intermittent pulse windshield wipers. The executive could order any car up to the value of the above automobile (within the constraints) without triggering an excess value payroll deduction.

Level II automobiles were normally leased on a 45-month program, but disposed of after 24 months or 72,000 kilometers. Because of their tendency to depreciate less quickly, Level I automobiles could be placed on a 60-month lease program, and could be retained by Control Data for 36 months or 80,000 kilometers. The executive automobiles were usually "low mileage" vehicles.

Control Data paid for all maintenance and repair costs on executive automobiles. When they came up for disposal, they were offered to the driver at book value, leaving Control Data with no gain or loss on disposal. Approximately 85 to 90 percent of executive automobiles were disposed of in this manner. If the executive did not wish to purchase the company car, it was offered to other Control Data employees at wholesale price, in which case the company would realize a gain or loss on disposal. If the automobile had been abused or neglected by the driver, the loss on disposal could be charged back to the executive's department. On rare occasions, the automobile would be disposed of outside the company.

Policy Review

The vice president of human resources had asked Mrs. Mist for a recommendation either for or against altering the Level I automobile policy to include automobiles produced outside North America. The request was the indirect result of a

Level I executive asking if he could order a Jaguar the next time his automobile came up for renewal. Mrs. Mist expected that the president of Control Data Canada, Ltd., in consultation with Commercial Credit Corporation would make the final policy decision. She knew, however, that her recommendation would be given serious consideration, but that it would have to be accompanied by an appropriate rationale.

There were a number of considerations which Mrs. Mist felt would have some influence on her recommendation. In her opinion, executives viewed their company automobile as a real and important perk. As such, its prestige value was probably greater than its cost. She felt that it was important to the executives to be able to choose something noticeably different from the norm. She was aware that a number of other companies did supply their executives with "exotic" automobiles if requested. On the other hand, she thought that Commercial Credit Corporation would recommend against supplying foreign automobiles for a number of reasons, primarily difficulty and cost of maintenance and unreliable disposal values. Among the National Association of Fleet Administrators, reciprocity on a voluntary basis was commonplace. With respect to reciprocity, Mrs. Mist was aware of Control Data's position as a major supplier to the North American automobile industry. She was also aware, however, that Control Data exported a major portion of its products, particularly to NATO and SEATO countries.

Mrs. Mist felt that if she recommended in favor of offering foreign as well as domestic automobiles to Level I executives, she would also have to suggest some new method of calculating the basis value. In her opinion it would not be fair to allow an executive to order an expensive foreign automobile, and then penalize him or her with a large payroll deduction because of a choice significantly above the basis value calculated for domestic automobiles.

CHAPTER 5

Quantity Considerations

The last decade has seen a dramatic change in management attitudes to both quality and quantity, with profound impact on the acquisition process. The need to cut down on unnecessary inventory costs, and to increase productivity and competitiveness has led to a new perspective on quantity. The most telling evidence is the drive to increase frequency of deliveries, while decreasing the amount delivered at one time. Accompanying efforts in set-up time reduction, just-in-time (JIT) systems, order cost reduction, and electronic data interchange are all part of the same drive.

The decision of *how much* to acquire logically follows clarification of *what* is required. The natural response is to say "buy as much as you need." Such a simple answer is not sufficient, however. Many factors significantly complicate the quantity decision. First, managers must make purchase decisions before, often a long time before, actual requirements are known. Therefore, they must rely on forecasts, not only of future demand, but also of lead times, prices, and other costs. Such forecasts are rarely, if ever, perfect. Second, there are costs associated with placing orders, holding inventory, and running out of materials and goods. Third, materials may not be available in the desired quantities without paying a higher price or delivery charge. Fourth, suppliers may offer reduced prices for buying larger quantities. Lastly, shortages may cause serious consequences.

In many organizations the decision of how much to purchase is made more important by the close relationship of purchase quantity and scheduled use.

It is necessary to distinguish between how much to buy in an individual purchase or release and what portion to buy from an individual vendor. This chapter deals only with individual order quantities; the allotment to suppliers is discussed in Chapter 6.

CLASSIFICATION OF PURCHASES

A variety of classification systems is available to help in inventory control and in quantity decisions. One distinction is between types of requirement; for example, raw materials, parts and subassemblies, MRO items, resale items, or capital goods.

A second way to classify items is by the frequency with which they are purchased. Some items, often of a capital nature, are obtained infrequently whereas others may be bought on a repetitive basis. A number of purchase quantity rules are in use for repetitive purchases. These will be discussed later in this chapter. Quite different decision criteria are appropriate for infrequent purchases.

A third classification is whether or not purchases are for stock replenishment. Presumably most stock items are repetitive purchases and the risk of buying too much would be viewed quite differently from overbuying on nonrepetitive purchases.

A fourth classification is based on the physical nature of the purchased items. Solids, liquids, or gases might be purchased. Some might be quite unstable, volatile, or otherwise perishable (or even dangerous) and thus require quite different handling, storage conditions, and purchase quantity rules than more stable or safer materials. Similarly, the nature of the packaging material and the size and shape of the package will affect the purchaser's ability to store items and hence the desired purchase quantity.

A fifth classification is based on transport type. Items shipped a short distance by the purchaser's own truck might be purchased in much smaller quantities than those coming a long distance by common carriers or by ship.

A final classification is based on monetary value. The Italian Vilfredo Pareto observed that, regardless of the country studied, a small portion of the population controlled most of the wealth. The observation led to the Pareto curve whose general principles hold in a wide range of situations. In materials management, for example, the Pareto curve usually holds for items purchased, number of suppliers, items held in inventory and many other aspects. The Pareto curve is often called the 80–20 rule, or more usefully, ABC analysis which results in three classes, A, B, and C as follows:

Class	Percent of Total Items Purchased	Percent of Total Purchase Dollars
A items	10	70–80
B items	10–20	10–15
C items	70–80	10–20

These percentages may vary somewhat from organization to organization and some organizations may use more classes. The principle of separation is very powerful in materials management because it allows concentration of management efforts in the areas of highest payoff. For example, a manufacturer with total annual purchases of $30.4 million had the following breakdown:

Number of Items	Percent of Items	Annual Purchase Volume	Percent Annual Purchase Volume	Class
1095	10.0%	$21,600,000	71.1%	A
2168	19.9	5,900,000	19.4	B
7660	70.1	2,900,000	9.5	C
10,923	100.0%	$30,400,000	100.0%	

A similar analysis of the organization's suppliers or inventories would be expected to show a similarly high portion of total value from a relatively small number of suppliers and items respectively.

Purchase volume is a combination of unit price and number of units so it is not sufficient to classify either high-priced or high-unit volume items as As on that basis alone. Annual value must be calculated and a classification into three groups on this basis, as shown below, is a good starting point.

Category	Unit value	Annual volume
A	high	high
A	high	medium
A	medium	high
B	high	low
B	medium	medium
B	low	high
C	medium	low
C	low	medium
C	low	low

How can a purchasing or materials manager use such a classification? It pays to spend far more managerial time and effort on A and B items than on C items. Because supply assurance is usually equally important for all items (for want of a nail the kingdom was lost), it is common to manage C items by carrying large inventories, by having stockless buying agreements like systems contracting, and by reviewing the items infrequently. These techniques reduce paperwork and managerial effort (for most items) but maintain a high service coverage. A items are particularly critical in financial terms and are, therefore, barring other considerations, normally carried in small quantities and ordered and reviewed frequently. B items fall between the A and C categories and are well suited to a systematic approach with less frequent reviews than A items. It should be noted that some B or C items may require A care because of their special nature, perishability, or other considerations.

FORECASTING

Forecasting is very much a part of the materials management picture. Forecasts of usage, supply, market conditions, technology, price, and so on, are always necessary to make good decisions. The problem is how to plan to meet the needs of the future, which requires answers to questions, such as: Where should the responsibility for forecasting future usage lie? Should the materials management group be allowed to second-guess sales, production, or user forecasts? Should suppliers be held responsible for meeting forecasts or actual requirements? Should the procurement manager be held responsible for meeting actual needs or forecasts?

In most manufacturing organizations the need for raw materials, parts, and subassemblies is usually derived from a sales forecast which is the responsibility of marketing. In service organizations and public agencies, the materials function often must both make forecasts and acquire items. In resale, the buyer may have to assess the expected sales volume (including volumes at reduced prices for seasonal goods), as well as make purchase commitments recognizing seasons. Whatever the situation, missed forecasts are quickly forgotten but substantial overages or shortages are long remembered. Materials managers are often blamed for overages or shortages no matter who made the original forecast or how bad the forecast was.

The real problem with forecasts is their unreliability. Forecasts will usually be wrong, but will they exceed or fall short of actual requirements and by how much? In a chemical company the marketing group's demand forecast for a consumer product resulted in the following usage estimates for a basic petrochemical commodity:

Year	Barrels
1	70,000
2	120,000
3	190,000
4	280,000
5	390,000

At $60 per barrel (at the time of the decision) this was a significant purchase. Discussion with the marketing group revealed considerable uncertainty regarding this forecast (see Figure 5–1). In five years demand could be as low as 70,000 or as high as 600,000 barrels. This wide range of possible requirements made the procurement plan far more difficult because it had to be prepared to recognize all possible outcomes. For example, a take-or-pay commitment for 100,000 barrels per year after the first year was obviously not acceptable because actual needs might be well below that level. Simultaneously, provisions had to be found for substantial increases in requirements should actual needs greatly exceed the forecast.

To a supplier a substantial variation from forecast may appear as a procurement ploy. If demand falls below forecast, the supplier may suspect that the original forecast was an attempt to obtain a favorable price or other concessions. Should demand exceed forecast, supplier costs may well increase because of overtime, rush buying, and changed production schedules.

FIGURE 5–1   Forecasts Showing Uncertainty

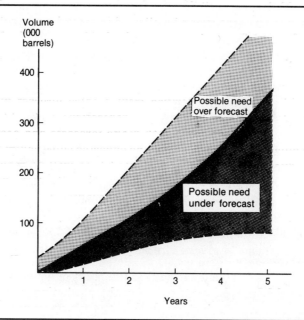

Purchasers need to share forecast uncertainty regularly with suppliers so that their quotations may take uncertainty into account. Such sharing is obviously impossible if buyers themselves are not aware of the uncertainty and its potential impact on the supplier. Forecasts should also be updated regularly. In the above chemical company example, quarterly updates for the next year and annual updates beyond that would be appropriate.

Forecasting Techniques

There are many forecasting techniques that have been developed and an extensive literature that describes them. This section will review some briefly but will not describe any technique in detail.

One of the most common classes is the qualitative approach of gathering opinions from a number of people and using these opinions with a degree of judgment to give a forecast. Market forecasts developed from the estimates of sales staff, district sales managers, and so on, are an example. Such forecast may also flow from the top down. The Delphi technique is a formal approach to such forecasting. Collective opinion forecasts lack the rigor of more quantitative techniques but are not necessarily any less accurate. Often, knowledgeable people with intimate market knowledge have a "feel" that is hard to define but which gives good forecasting results.

Quantitative forecasting attempts to use past data to predict the future. One class of quantitative forecasting techniques tries to identify leading indicators from which linear or multiple regression models are developed. A carpet manufacturer might use building permits issued, mortgage rates, apartment vacancy rates, and so on, to predict carpet sales. The model might take the form:

$$\begin{array}{l}\text{Carpet sales}\\ \text{next month}\end{array} = A + B \begin{array}{l}\text{Building permits}\\ \text{last month}\end{array} + C \begin{array}{l}\text{Building permits}\\ \text{two months ago}\end{array} +$$

$$D \begin{array}{l}\text{Mortgage}\\ \text{rate}\end{array} + E \begin{array}{l}\text{Vacancy}\\ \text{rate}\end{array} + F \begin{array}{l}\text{Carpet sales}\\ \text{last month}\end{array}$$

where $A-F$ are the derived regression constants. Standard computer programs are used to develop and test such models. Chosen indicators are usually believed to cause changes in sales although even good models do not prove a cause-and-effect relationship. Indicator figures must be available far enough ahead to give a forecast that allows time for managerial decisions.

The second quantitative forecasting class assumes that sales (or other items to be forecast) follow a repetitive pattern over time. The analyst's job in such time series forecasting is to identify the pattern and develop a forecast. The six relevant aspects of the pattern are constant value, trend, seasonal variations, other cyclical variations, random variations, and turning points. These features are illustrated in Figure 5–2.

INVENTORIES

Many purchases cover repetitive items often held in inventory. Thus, inventory policy has a great influence on the purchase quantity decisions. It is important in making inventory or purchase order size decisions to understand why inventories exist and what the relevant tradeoffs are in making different lot-sizing and inventory-quantity decisions.

Inventory management is complicated by the rapidly changing environment within which inventory and purchasing planning is carried out. Inventories always seem to be too big, too small, of the wrong type, or in the wrong place. With changing economic conditions, what is too little in one period may easily become too much in the next.

Because of the high cost of carrying inventory, many systems have been developed to reduce stocks. Japanese manufacturers have spearheaded such efforts in mass production industries. Suppliers, often located very near the plant, deliver items directly to the point of use in the plant at very frequent intervals. The use of Kanbans and a variety of other just-in-time inventory management schemes has revolutionized manufacturing thinking about all forms of inventories. Nevertheless, it is useful to understand the nature and

FIGURE 5–2   Illustration of Some Forecasting Terms

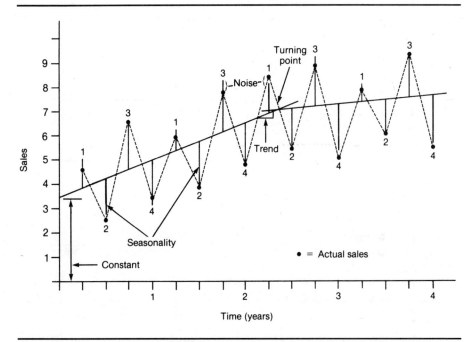

costs of inventories so that appropriate policies and procedures can be developed for specific organizational needs. North American manufacturers have begun to rely heavily on material requirements planning systems that have similar goals of reducing inventories wherever possible by having accurate, timely information on all aspects of the manufacturing system, thorough coordination of all departments, and rigorous adherence to the system.

Like purchases, inventories may be classified in a variety of ways including ABC analysis (see Figure 5–3), nature of the items carried, and frequency of use. Modern computer and word processing systems allow extensive automation of purchasing and inventory control. Control of all items is improved and managerial time is freed for the negotiations, value engineering, research and other managerial tasks necessary to deal effectively with A and B items.

Inventory Costs

Inventories exist for many purposes including:

To provide and maintain good customer service.

To smooth the flow of goods through the productive process.

FIGURE 5–3   ABC Classification of Inventory

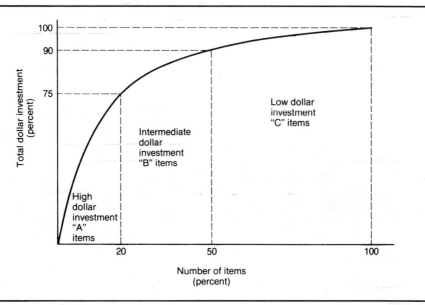

To provide protection against the uncertainties of supply and demand. To obtain a reasonable utilization of people and equipment.

For every item carried in inventory, the costs of having it must be less than the costs of not having it. Inventory exists for this reason alone. Inventory costs are real but are often not easy to quantify accurately. The relevance of cost elements in a given situation depends on the decisions to be made. Many costs remain fixed when the order size of only one item is doubled but the same costs may well become variable when 5,000 items are under consideration. The main types of inventory costs are described in the following sections.

Carrying, Holding, or Possession Costs.   These include handling charges; the cost of storage facilities or warehouse rentals; the cost of equipment to handle inventory; storage, labor, and operating costs; insurance premiums; breakage; pilferage; obsolescence; taxes; and investment or opportunity costs. In short, any cost associated with having, as opposed to not having, inventory is involved.

Ordering or Purchase Costs.   These include the managerial, clerical, material, telephone, mailing, accounting, transportation, inspection, and receiving costs associated with a purchase or production order. What costs would be saved by not ordering or by combining two orders? Header costs are those incurred by identifying and placing an order with a vendor. Line item costs refer to the cost of adding a line to a purchase order. Most orders will involve one header and several line item costs. Electronic data interchange, or direct vendor access systems try to reduce ordering of purchase costs significantly as well as reduce lead time at the same time.

Setup Costs.   These refer to all the costs of setting up a production run. Setup costs may be substantial. They include such learning-related factors as early spoilage and low production output until standard rates are achieved, as well as the more common considerations such as setup employees' wages and other costs, machine downtime, extra tool wear, parts (and equipment) damaged during setup, and so on. Both the purchaser's and vendors' setup costs are relevant.

It should be pointed out that the successful reduction of setup costs and times permits smaller production runs and hence smaller purchaser order quantities.

Stockout Costs.   These are the costs of not having the required parts or materials on hand when and where they are needed. They include lost contribution on lost sales (both present and future), change-over costs necessitated by the shortage, substitution of less suitable or more expensive parts or materials, rescheduling and expediting costs, labor and machine idle time, and so on. Often customer and user goodwill may be affected and occasionally penalties must be paid. The impact of stockouts on customers will vary. In a seller's market an unsatisfied customer may not be lost as easily as in a buyer's market. In addition, each individual customer will react differently to a shortage.

In many organizations stockout costs are very difficult to assess accurately. The general perception, however, is that in many cases, stockout costs may be substantial and much larger than carrying costs.

Price Variation Costs.   Vendors often offer items in larger quantities at price and transportation discounts. Purchase in small quantities may result in higher purchase and transportation costs but buying in larger quantities may result in significantly higher holding costs. This price discount problem will be discussed in Chapter 7.

Many inventory costs may be hard to identify, collect and measure. One can try to trace the individual costs attributable to individual items and use these in decision making. Usually such costs will be applicable to a broader class of items. A second approach is to forecast the impact of a major change in inventory systems on various cost centers. For example, what will be the impact on stores of a switch to systems contracting for half of the *C* items? Or, what would be the impact of a just-in-time system on price, carrying, ordering, and stockout costs? Because most inventory models are based on balancing carrying, order, and stockout costs to obtain an optimal order and inventory size, the quality and availability of cost data are important considerations.

The Functions of Inventory

The following classification of inventory function, suggested by Britney,[1] reveals the multipurpose roles played by inventories.

Transit or Pipeline Inventories.   These inventories are used to stock the supply and distribution pipelines linking an organization to its suppliers and customers as well as internal transportation points. They exist because of the need to move material from one point to another. Obviously transit inventories are dependent on location and mode of transportation. A decision to use a distant supplier with rail transport will probably create a far larger raw materials transit inventory than one to use a local supplier with truck delivery. Work-in-progress transit inventories are determined by process design and plant layout. Finished goods transit inventories are determined by marketing policies and distribution channels. The point at which ownership changes is one of the policies affecting both raw materials and finished goods inventories.

A decision affecting transit inventories may well have an impact on other functional inventory classes. If a rail strike is expected, anticipation stocks will be forced up. If lead time variations are high, buffer inventories may have to be enlarged. Organizations should recognize these tradeoffs and consider them in decision making. Once an organization's site is established, however, operational decisions must recognize this site as fixed. For example, a number of Great Lakes steel companies use water transport not available in the winter. They must build seasonal or anticipation raw materials to overcome this problem. As long as the cost of building and carrying this inventory is less than the cost of switching to an alternative means of winter transport, this practice will continue.

In *just-in-time* (JIT) production a variety of means are used to reduce transit inventories, including the use of local suppliers, small batches in special containers, and trucks specifically designed for side loading in small quantities.

Cycle Inventories.   These stocks arise because of management's decision to purchase, produce, or sell in lots rather than individual units or continuously. Cycle inventories accumulate at various points in operating systems. The size of the lot is a tradeoff between the cost of holding inventory

---

[1]R. R. Britney, "Inventories: Their Functions, Forms and Control", paper presented to the Canadian Association for Production and Inventory Control, May 1971.

and the cost of making more frequent orders and/or setups. A mathematical description of this relationship, the economic order quantity, will be discussed later. In JIT the need for cycle inventories is reduced by setup cost and time reduction.

Buffer Inventories. Buffer inventories, also called safety stocks, exist as a result of uncertainties in the demand or supply of units at various points in the production system. Raw material buffer stocks give some protection against the uncertainties of supplier performance due to shutdowns, strikes, lead time variations, late deliveries to and from the supplier, poor quality units that cannot be accepted, and so on. Work-in-process buffer inventories protect against machine breakdown, employee illness, and so on. Finished goods buffers protect against unforeseen demand or production failures.

Management efforts to reduce supply uncertainties may have substantial payoffs in reduced inventories. Options may include: using local sources, reducing demand uncertainty, reducing lead time, having excess capacity, or reducing stockout costs. Buffer inventory levels should be determined by balancing carrying cost against stockout cost.

Buying in expectation of major market shortages is a longer time-frame variation of buffer inventory. It may require large sums and top management strategic review. Chapter 7 discusses forward buying more fully.

Another class of buffer stock is that purchased in anticipation, but not certainty, of a price increase. In this case the trade-off is between extra carrying costs and avoidance of higher purchase cost. This trade-off can be structured as shown in Figure 5–4. Obviously intermediate levels of price increase and the timing of increases will also be identified. Other buffer stock trade-offs can be structured similarly.

Anticipation Inventories. Anticipation stocks are accumulated for a well-defined future need. They differ from buffer stocks in that they are committed in the face of more certainty and therefore have less risk attached to them. Seasonal inventories are an excellent example. The stocking of commodities at harvest time for further processing during the year is a typical example. Reasons for anticipation stocks may include strikes, weather, shortages, or announced price increases.

The managerial decision is considerably easier than with buffer stocks because the relative certainty of events makes probability estimates unnecessary. Unfortunately, in times of shortages and rapid price increases, organizations may not be able to commit enough funds to meet the clear need for more anticipation stocks. Public organizations working under pre-established budgets may not be able to obtain authorization and funds. Many private organizations short of working capital may be similarly frustrated.

Spare parts inventories are a special form of buffer and anticipation

FIGURE 5–4   Decision to Inventory in Anticipation of a Possible Price Increase

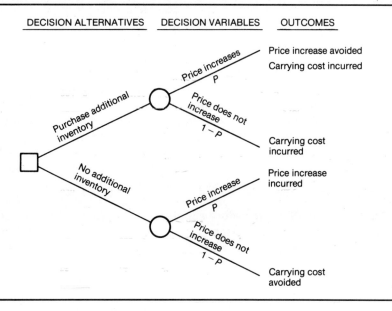

inventories related to the maintenance of capital assets. Consider this simple example. A factory has a large machine with two main $2,000 shafts. If either shaft wears out or breaks, the machine and the rest of the factory must be shut down. If new shafts are in stock, repairs can be made in four hours. If new shafts are not in stock, repairs will take an additional 44 hours, resulting in additional costs of $2,500 and $500 for expediting each shaft. The factory normally works eight months per year; maintenance and repairs are performed during the other four months. The manager must decide how many shafts to stock for the eight-month operating season.

The manager estimates that the probability that no shafts will be needed is 0.5, that one shaft will be needed is 0.3, and that a second will be needed at the same time as the first is 0.2. The manager further estimates the cost of carrying a shaft for a season at $500. The manager's decision is shown diagrammatically in Figure 5–5. Using the expected value criterion, it shows expected costs of $1,600 for stocking none, $850 for stocking one, and $650 for stocking two.

Decoupling Inventories.   The existence of decoupling inventories at major linkage points makes it possible to carry on activities on each side of the point relatively independently of each other. The amounts and locations of raw material, work-in-process, and finished goods decoupling inventories

FIGURE 5–5 Typical Maintenance Part Inventory Decision

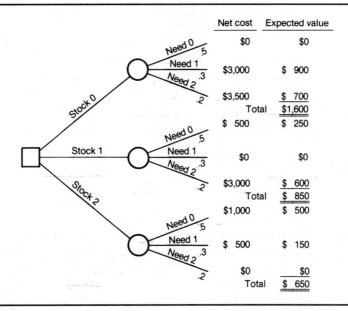

depend on the costs and increased operating flexibility benefits of having them.

The ability to plan a plant's operations independently of the short-run behavior of suppliers or customers is highly valued by most North American and European managers. It gives flexibility and independence to both parties and is an excellent area for negotiations. Many contracts specify that a supplier maintain a certain finished goods inventory. The appropriate size of such inventory depends on the situation.

Work-in-process decoupling inventory may be substantial if many operations are planned for a product, especially when the operations take very different times and different lot sizes, and where the necessary machines are simultaneously being used to produce other products. Such conditions typify job shops. Line flow operations can greatly reduce decoupling inventory but are less flexible. The degree of flexibility is clearly an important managerial decision, so decoupling inventories often play a wider role than may be evident at first glance.

By examining the functions of inventory it is clear that they are the result of many interrelated decisions and policies within an organization. At any time, any of the inventory functional types will be physically indistinguishable from the others. Frequently, a particular item may serve many of the functions simultaneously. Why, then, classify inventories by function? The answer lies in the degree of controllability of each class. Some inventories are essentially fixed and uncontrollable whereas others are controllable. (In the long term, of course, all inventories are controllable.) A management directive to reduce total inventories by 20 percent could, because of purchasing and marketing policies and prior commitments on cycle and seasonal inventories, reduce decoupling and buffer inventories to nearly zero with potentially disastrous results. Proper inventory management requires a thorough understanding of both the forms and the functions of inventory.

The Forms of Inventory

Inventories may be classified by form as well; indeed this classification is much more common. The five commonly recognized forms are raw materials, work-in-process, finished goods, MRO items, and resale items. Scrap or obsolete materials, although technically regarded as inventory, will not be considered here (see Chapter 9 dealing with disposal).

Raw materials for manufacturers are stocks of the basic material inputs into the organization's manufacturing process. As labor and other materials are added to these inputs, they are transformed into work-in-process inventories. When production is completed, they become finished goods. In general, the forms are distinguished by the amount of labor and materials added by the organization. The classification is relative in that a supplier's finished goods may become a purchaser's raw materials.

For resource industries, service organizations and public organizations, MRO inventories may be substantial. In resource industries a significant portion of such inventory may be maintenance or repair parts to support the heavy capital investment base.

In resale organizations the main categories are goods for resale and inventories to maintain building and equipment. Figure 5–6 focuses on the main inventories by forms and functions.

Inventory Function and Form Framework

Combining the five forms and five functions of manufacturing inventory gives the 25 types of inventory which make up the inventory profile of an organization. They are presented in Figure 5–6 along with some of the managerial decision variables affecting each type. Not all inventory types will be present to the same extent in each organization; indeed some may be completely absent. The 15 types make inventory control a more complex but a more easily focused task.

Controlling Inventory

The behavior of inventories is a direct result of diverse policies and decisions within an organization. User, finance, production, marketing, and purchasing decisions can all have crucial influences on stock levels. Long-

FIGURE 5–6 Inventory Forms and Functions

Inventory Function	Raw material 1	Work-in-process 2	Finished goods 3	MRO 4	Resale 5
1 Transit (pipeline)	Design of supply system, supplier location, transportation mode	Design of layout and materials handling system	*Logistics Decisions* — Design of plant location and product distribution system	Supplier location, transportation mode, small shipments	Warehouse location, distribution, transportation mode
2 Cycle (EOQ, lots)	Order size, order cost	Lot size, setup	*Product/Process Design Decisions* — Distribution costs, lot sizes	OEM or not and order size	Order size and order cost
3 Buffer (uncertainty)	Probability distributions of price, supply & stock-out & carrying costs	Probability distributions of machine and product capabilities	*Management Risk Level Decisions & Uncertainty* — Probability distributions of demand and associated carrying and stock-out cost	Probability distributions of breakdowns during use	Probability distributions of demand associated carrying and stock-out costs

FIGURE 5–6 (concluded)

Inventory Function

	Raw material 1	Work-in-process 2	Finished goods 3	MRO 4	Resale 5
	Price/Availability/Decisions & Uncertainty, Seasonality Capacity				
4 Anticipation (price) (shortage)	Know future supply & demand price levels	Capacity, production costs of hire, fire, transfer, overtime, idle time, etc.	Demand patterns (seasonal)	Maintenance planning projects	Supply and demand patterns and price levels
			Production Control Decisions		
5 Decoupling (interdependence)	Dependence/independence from supplier behavior	Dependence/independence of successive production operations	Dependence/independence from market behavior	Stock at vendor or at user	Stock at vendor, stock self or buyer stock

term fixed marketing or procurement policies may render finished goods transit, or raw materials transit and cycle inventories quite inflexible, whereas short-term production scheduling may provide a great amount of flexibility of work-in-process decoupling inventories. Long-term supply contracts coupled with falling demand may lead to raw materials accumulation. To be effective, managers must recognize the behavior and controllability of each type of inventory in both the short and long terms. For effective management they must also coordinate the policies and decisions of all functional areas.

Often managers use various informal rules of thumb in their decision making. A common one is that turnover should be four times per year (or some other number). Such a condition would hold for an organization with average inventories of $250,000 and cost of annual sales of $1 million. The rule of thumb would dictate that as the cost of sales rises to $2 million, inventories should be $500,000. However, a closer look at the components of that inventory must be taken.

Cycle inventories, produced in economic order lots (see the next section), increase proportionally to the square root of demand so, as demand doubles, cycle inventories should rise by a factor of only about 1.4. In addition, economic order quantity lots vary with the square roots of setup and carrying costs, and ordering raw materials or storing them may have quite different cost structures from setting up machines, issuing production orders, or storing finished goods.

Transit inventories depend on supply and distribution networks, not sales. A change in the distribution system to accommodate extra sales could more than double or even reduce finished goods transit inventory. Anticipation stocks vary with the pattern of demand, not demand itself. Decoupling inventories may remain unchanged. Buffer inventories may increase or decrease in response to demand and supply instabilities. Many of these effects will balance each other but the point remains: rules of thumb are crude ways of controlling inventory levels. Even if they seem to work, managers never know if they are the best available. Any set of rules must be interpreted intelligently and reevaluated periodically.

It is clear from the earlier discussion that the Japanese efforts to reduce all forms of inventories have addressed all of the functions described above. For example, transit times and inventory levels have been reduced by having vendors located nearby. Cycle inventories have been brought down by reducing setup times, buffer inventories by reducing uncertainty, improving quality, and decoupling inventories by better planning and better quality. It is a continuing challenge to search for better ways to control inventories.

Most appropriate Place to order in order to minimize ordering costs. (least expensive)

FIGURE 5–7   Material Carrying and Order Costs

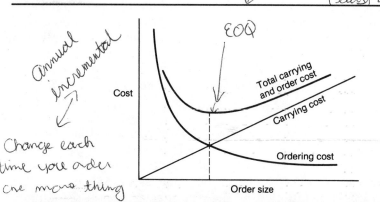

Annual incremental

Change each time you order one more thing

EOQ

Cost

Total carrying and order cost

Carrying cost

Ordering cost

Order size

Economic Order Quantity Models for Cycle Inventories

Fixed Quantity Models.   The classic trade-off in determining the lot sizes in which to make or buy cycle inventories is between the costs of carrying extra inventory and the costs of purchasing or making more frequently. The objective of the model is to minimize the total annual costs. In the very simplest form of this model, annual demand (R), lead time (L), price (C), variable order or setup cost (S), and holding cost percentage (K) are all constant now and in the future. When inventory drops to the reorder point (P), a fixed economic order quantity (Q) is ordered which arrives after lead time (L). Back orders and stockouts are not allowed.

Total cost is given as purchase cost, plus setup or order cost, plus holding cost, or:

$$TC = RC + \frac{RS}{Q} + \frac{QKC}{2}$$

Using differential calculus the minimum value of Q (also known as the EOQ or Q_{opt}) is found at:

$$Q_{opt} = \frac{2RS}{KC}$$

This is the value at which order cost and carrying cost are equal. Figures 5–7 and 5–8 show how costs vary with changes in order size and how

FIGURE 5-8 Simple Fixed Quantity Model

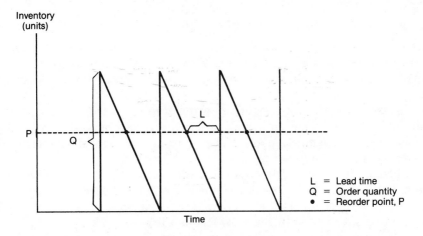

inventory levels change over time using this model. As an example of the use of the model, consider the following:

R = annual demand = 900 units
C = delivered purchase cost = \$45/unit
K = carrying cost percentage = 25 percent
S = order cost = \$50/order
L = lead time = 10 working days
$Q_{opt} = \dfrac{2RS}{KC}$ = 89 units

The reorder point, P, is the lead time, L, times daily demand.

$$P = \frac{LR}{250} = \frac{10 \times 900}{250} = 36 \text{ (assumes 250 working days)}$$

This model suggests an order of 89 units whenever the inventory drops to 36 units. The last unit will be used just as the next order arrives. Average inventory will be 89/2 = 44.5 units. In practice, it might be advisable to keep some safety stock which must be added to the average inventory. Also, the bottom of the cost curve (see Figure 5–7) is relatively flat (and asymmetric) so that there might be advantages in ordering eight dozen or 100 units instead. In this case these quantities would cost an additional \$2.52 and \$6.27 respectively out of a total annual cost of about \$41,500.

The assumptions behind the EOQ model place some rather severe restrictions on its general applicability. Numerous other models have been developed which take into account relaxation of one or more of the assumptions. The reader may wish to refer to books on inventory management for a more extensive discussion.

Fixed Period Models.   In many situations ordering every so often rather than whenever the stock reaches a certain level is desirable from an operations viewpoint. The scheduling of workload is easier when employees can be assigned to check certain classes of inventory every day, week, month, and so on.

In fixed quantity models, orders are placed when the reorder point is reached but in fixed period models orders are placed only at review time. The inventory level must, therefore, be adjusted to prevent stockouts during the review period and lead time.

Fixed period models attempt to determine the optimal order period. The minimum cost period can be determined as follows. There are R/Q cycles per year and therefore T (the fraction of the year) is Q/R. This value of Q can then be substituted in the EOQ formula to give:

$$T_{opt}R = \frac{2RS}{KC} \ or: T_{opt} = \frac{2S}{RKC}$$

For the example used above:

$$T_{opt} = \frac{2 \times 50}{900 \times 0.25 \times 45} = 0.1 \text{ or, 10 times per year}$$

For a year of 250 working days, this is 25 working days or once every five weeks. The optimum order quantity, Q, is RT_{opt} or 90 units. This is the same result as before. Company procedures may make a review every four weeks or monthly more attractive. In this case T would change to 0.08 and Q to 72 at an additional cost of $23.77 per year over the optimum value.

Probabilistic Models and Service Coverage.   The aforementioned models assume that all parameters are known absolutely. It is far more common to have some variation in forecast demands, lead times, and so on. Probabilistic lot size models take these variations into account. The models are more complex than the deterministic ones above but the probabilistic approach gives much more information on likely outcomes.

The major decision variable is how much buffer inventory to carry to give the desired service coverage. The service coverage can be defined as the portion of user requests served. If there are 400 requests for a particular item in a year and 372 were immediately satisfied, the service coverage would be 93 percent.

Service coverage can also be defined as the portion of demand serviced immediately. If the 372 orders in the above example were for one unit each and the 28 other, unserviced ones, for five units each, the service coverage could be defined as 372/(372 + (28 × 5)) or 73 percent. It is obviously important to understand exactly what is meant by service coverage in an organization.

Holding a large inventory to prevent stockouts, and thus to maintain a high service coverage, is expensive. Similarly, a high number of stockouts is costly. Stockout costs are often difficult and expensive to determine but nevertheless real. Setting service coverage requires managers to make explicit and implicit evaluations of these costs so that the appropriate balance between carrying and stockout can be achieved.

In independent demand situations the appropriate service coverage can be determined by the following ratio called the *critical fractile:*[2]

$$Critical\ fractile = \frac{C_u}{C_u + C_o}$$

C_u = cost of understocking

C_o = cost of overstocking

For illustrative purposes, assume that management has estimated the following costs and probabilities of customer action as a result of a stockout:

	Cost	Probability	Expected value
Back order placed	$ 10	0.50	$ 5.00
Order cancelled (lost contribution)	50	0.45	22.50
Customer's business lost forever	600	0.05	30.00
Miscellaneous costs (expediting, etc.)			25.00
		Total	$82.50

Management further estimates that holding a unit of this item for one time period costs $10. The desired service coverage is thus:

$$\frac{C_u}{C_u + C_o} = \frac{\$82.50}{\$82.50 + \$10.00} = 0.89\ or\ 89\%$$

Because of the expense and difficulty of obtaining these costs and probability estimates for individual items, managers often set service coverage arbitrarily, typically about 95 percent, implying a ratio of stockout to holding costs of about 19 to 1. In practice, setting and managing service coverage is difficult because of the complexity of item classification, function, and interdependence. Service coverage need not be as high on some items as on others but an item that may be relatively unimportant to one customer may be crucial to another. If the customer is an assembly line, a low service coverage on one component makes higher service coverage on others unnecessary. Also, some customers will tolerate much lower service coverage

---

[2]B. B. Jackson, "The Critical Fractile Model," case 9-175-058 available from Harvard Case Services.

FIGURE 5–9   Fixed Order Quantity Model with Buffer Inventory
               and Variation in Demand

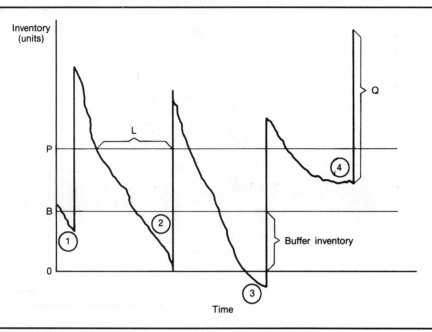

than will others. Within an organization customers are internal departments, and service coverage attained is one measure of materials management's effectiveness. It is useful to stress that service coverage and inventory
investment required are closely related. It becomes expensive to achieve
very high service coverage, and a high service coverage expectation without
the necessary financial backup can lead only to frustration. Procurement
is, of course, also interested in service coverage as it pertains to supplier
performance.

Service coverage can be used to determine the appropriate level of buffer
inventory. The situation is shown in Figures 5–9 and 5–10. Four situations
can arise as shown from left to right in Figure 5–9.

1. Only some of the buffer inventory was used.

2. No buffer inventory remained but there was no stockout.

3. There was a stockout.

4. All the buffer inventory remained.

Figure 5–10 is basically an EOQ model except that it is not certain how
many units will be used between placing and receipt of an order. Using the
desired service coverage, knowledge of the standard deviation of average

FIGURE 5-10 Determination of Buffer Inventory to Achieve
Desired Coverage

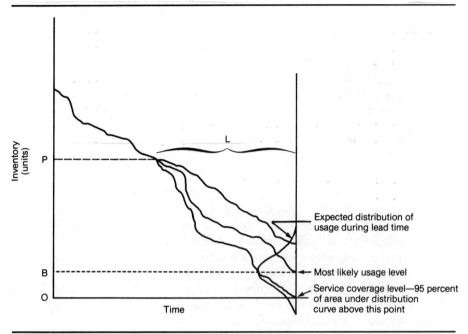

daily demand, an assumption of a normal demand distribution, and ele-
level. This level is shown in Figure 5-10 for a desired service coverage of
95 percent.

The complexity of probabilistic models increases greatly when lead
times, usable quantities received, inventory shrinkage rates, and so on, also
vary under conditions of uncertainty, when nonnormal distributions are
observed, and when the variations change with time. Simulation models
and other more advanced statistical techniques can be used to solve these
complex situations.

MATERIAL REQUIREMENTS PLANNING (MRP)

One of the assumptions behind the lot-sizing models just described is
that demand for the item being purchased or made is independent of all
other demands. This situation is true for most manufacturers' finished
goods. However, subassemblies, raw materials and parts do not exhibit
this independence. Demand for these items is dependent on the assembly
schedule for finished goods. Similarly, many MRO items depend on
maintenance schedules. Recognition of the existence of demand dependence lies behind the technique known as material requirements planning
(MRP).

MRP differs from the EOQ-type systems in a number of important dimensions. Tersine,[3] for example, summarized these differences as follows:

MRP system	EOQ-type system
product/component oriented	part oriented (every item)
dependent (derived) demand	independent demand
discrete/lumpy demand	continuous item demand
no lead time demand	continuous lead time demand
time-phased ordering signal	reorder point ordering signal
future production base	historical demand base
forecast end items only	forecast all items
quantity and time based system	quantity based system
safety stock for end items only	safety stock for all items

These are important differences in philosophy between the two inventory management systems. For example, in the traditional EOQ model when the stock of an item runs low enough to reach a reorder point, it is replenished. Under an MRP system, however, items are replenished only when they are needed as determined by the master production schedule. EOQ models, based on historical usage, attempt to provide high customer service coverage while optimizing the balance between order (setup) and carrying costs. MRP systems, in contrast, attempt to support the activities of manufacturing or maintenance by meeting the needs of the master production schedule which is based on forecasts and firm orders.

In order to determine needs, MRP systems need an accurate bill of materials for each final product. These bills can take many forms but it is conceptually advantageous to view them as structural trees. Several general types of structural tree can be identified. Process industries such as oil refiners and drug and food manufacturers generally take a few raw materials and make a much larger number of end products. Manufacturer/assemblers such as the automobile companies make a number of components, purchase others, and assemble them into end products. Assemblers, such as electronics companies, buy components and assemble them into finished goods. Schematic diagrams of these structural types are shown in Figure 5–11. Each type of firm can use MRP profitably but the greatest benefits usually accrue to the middle group because of the greater complexity of its operations.

The goals of MRP are to minimize inventory, to maintain a high service coverage, and to coordinate delivery schedules and manufacturing and purchasing activities. These aims often conflict in other systems, but under MRP are achievable simultaneously. This feature, and the ability of modern MRP systems to allow rapid replanning and rescheduling in response to the changes of a dynamic environment, are responsible for the attractiveness of MRP.

---

[3]R. J. Tersine, *Principles of Inventory and Materials Management,* 2nd ed. (New York: Elsevier Science Publishing, 1982), p. 311.

FIGURE 5–11   Structural Tree Types

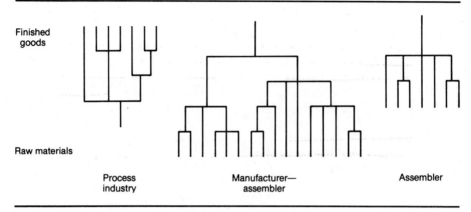

SOURCE: R. G. Schroeder, *Operations Management* (New York: McGraw-Hill, 1981), p. 420.

FIGURE 5–12   Structural Tree for the Manufacture of A

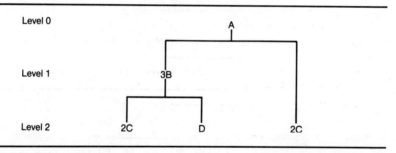

The Workings of MRP

Consider the manufacture of a final product A made up of three units of B and two of C. Each B is made up of two units of C and one of D. This structural relationship is shown in Figure 5–12. C and D might be raw materials, or purchased parts, or subassemblies. Components of any subassemblies made in-house should be included in the structural tree.

The structural tree is divided into levels and clearly shows the dependent demand feature. MRP systems calculate requirements for components in each level starting from the top down. C occurs twice, once as a component of B and once as a component of A. Consequently it could be placed in either (or both) level 1 or level 2. Demand for C cannot be calculated properly before demand for B is determined. Therefore, according to the MRP principle of low-level coding, C is placed only in level 2.

The top row of Figure 5–13 shows the master production schedule for A derived from the demand figures supplied by the marketing department.

FIGURE 5–13   MRP Plan for A

	week:	0	1	2	3	4	5	6	7	8	9	10
Level 0	demand		20	30	0	50	25	10	15	20	5	25
item A	scheduled receipts		25	0	0	30	25	10	15	20	5	25
lead time 1 week	on hand order	45	50	20	20	0	0	0	0	0	0	0
	release		0	0	30	25	10	15	20	5	25	—
Level 1 item B:	demand		0	0	90	75	30	45	60	15	75	—
3 per A lead time:	scheduled receipts		0	0	20	75	30	45	60	15	75	—
2 weeks	on hand order	70	70	70	0	0	0	0	0	0	0	—
	release		20	75	30	45	60	15	75	—	—	—
Level 2 item C:	demand		40	150	120	140	140	60	190	10+	50+	—
2 per A + 2 per B lead time:	scheduled receipts		30	75	105	140	140	60	190	10+	50+	—
2 weeks	on hand order	100	90	15	0	0	0	0	0	—	—	—
	release		105	140	140	60	190	10+	50+	—	—	—
Level 2 item D:	demand		20	75	30	45	60	15	75	—	—	—
1 per B lead time:	scheduled receipts		30	60	25	45	60	15	75	—	—	—
3 weeks	on hand order	10	20	5	0	0	0	0	0	—	—	—
	release		45	60	15	75	—	—	—	—	—	—

The schedule is divided into weekly periods and may result from firm orders or forecasts. Figure 5–13 also gives the current inventory status, the expected receipts from previous orders, and the required lead times to make or purchase A, B, C and D. Given this information, managers can derive a schedule for the release of shop orders for production of A. Using these derived numbers and similar logic, schedules for release of shop or purchase orders for B, and subsequently, C and D can be obtained. The schedules and their derivation are also shown in Figure 5–13.

The time periods (buckets) are typically weeks although in principle longer or shorter periods could be used. Use of very short periods makes the system effectively bucketless. The example makes a clear distinction between "0" and "—." The symbol "0" represents a conscious decision to require, make, or hold no items. The symbol "—" means that the appropriate values are not yet known because the demand figures that will generate a value lie beyond the current 10-week time horizon. Indeed, the values for D show that, to ensure continued supply of A, no inventories and no expediting, a time horizon of at least six weeks is required. A new set of forecasts and an updated master production schedule will be required within four weeks.

Negative inventory values, not found in this schedule, would indicate a stockout and signal management to take appropriate action.

This example illustrates the three basic principles and three inputs of MRP. Dependence of demand has been discussed. The second principle is the netting of inventory and the expected receipt of open orders to give the row labeled "on hand." The third principle is the time phasing which uses information on lead times and needs to put the shop or purchase orders in the right time bucket.

There are three basic MRP inputs. The whole system is driven by the requirements forecast by time period (the master production schedule) for the item in level 0. The structured bill of materials is the second input. The third input is the file that contains information on inventories and open orders so that the quantity and timing of orders can be calculated.

The logic of MRP allows simultaneous determination of how much and when to order. The calculations hinge on the assumptions that all information is accurate and known with certainty, that material will be ordered as required, that the plant has the capacity to produce infinite quantities, and that ordering or setup costs are not significant. These assumptions do not generally hold.

MRP Lot Sizing

Figure 5-13 assumes that shop or purchase orders will be released only in the exact quantities required. Although this lot-for-lot order size rule minimizes inventory, it may give high setup or order costs. If for A, the setup cost is $20 per order and the annual carrying cost is $26 per unit, the derived EOQ is 40 units (based on annualizing the 10-week demand of 200 units). The revised order release schedules for A and B are shown in Figure 5-14.

Because the demand for B, C, and D is dependent on the scheduled order release for A, changing the lot-sizing rule for A has a marked effect on the demand pattern for B and other dependent items. The above example used an EOQ lot-sizing rule. Is it the appropriate one? The EOQ approach assumes a steady demand but the demand for A is quite lumpy. Several algorithms and heuristics have been developed to deal with this problem. They make

FIGURE 5–14   MRP Order Release Plan for A and B Using EOQ Lot
Sizing for A

	week:	1	2	3	4	5	6	7	8	9	10
A	demand sched-uled		20	30	0	50	25	10	15	20	5	25
	re-ceipts		25	0	0	40	40	0	0	40	0	40
	on hand	45	50	20	20	10	25	15	0	20	15	0
	order release		0	0	40	40	0	0	40	0	40	—
B	demand sched-uled		0	0	120	120	0	0	120	0	120	—
	re-ceipts		0	0	50	120	0	0	120	0	120	—
	on hand	70	70	70	0	0	0	0	0	0	0	0
	order release		50	120	0	0	120	0	120	—	—	—

the same trade-off between carrying and setup or ordering cost as the EOQ
approach but typically identify the number of future periods' requirements
to make or buy each setup or order, a number which varies with fluctuating
demand. The algorithms and heuristics define rules on which the decision
is based.

For illustrative purposes the procedure for the incremental order quantity heuristic will be described using the demand pattern for A already
described, R_t as period demand, t as period number, S as setup cost, and H
as period holding cost. The first week with a net positive order requirement
is week three. Therefore, the first cycle will begin in week three and it will
be renumbered as period one. S has already been incurred but items made
and used in period one will incur no holding cost. The question is, should
the 25 units of A required for period two also be made in period one? The
heuristic uses the rule:

If $S \leq H (t - 1) R_t$ a new cycle will begin in period t;
if not, the existing cycle will continue.

For A with setup costs of \$20, holding costs of \$0.50 per week, and a
one-week lead time, the schedule shown above is calculated. Cycle 1 ends

FIGURE 5-14 *(concluded)*

Week:	1	2	3	4	5	6	7	8	9	10
Net requirement	0	0	0	30	25	10	15	20	5	25
Cycle number 1:										
Period numbers			1	2	3	4				
$H(t - 1)R_t$			0	12.5	10	22.5				
Cycle number 2:										
Period numbers						1	2	3	4	
$H(t - 1)R_t$						0	10	5	37.5	
Cycle number 3:										
Period numbers										1
Requirement schedule	0	0	0	65	0	0	40	0	0	25+
Order schedule	0	0	65	0	0	40	0	0	25+	—

in period 3 because, for period 4, $H(t - 1)R_t = (0.50)(4 - 1)(15) = 22.5$ which exceeds S. According to this schedule, 65 units of A would be ordered in week three, 40 units in week 6, and at least 25 units in week 9. The even spacing of these orders is a result of the demand pattern and costs, not of the heuristic itself.

The table below compares the costs over the 10-week period for A using six different lot-sizing rules. Even though 10 weeks is insufficient time to draw firm conclusions, it is clear that there are cost differences and that, for this example, the algorithms and heuristics seem to perform better than lot-for-lot or EOQ.

Lot-sizing rules remain an area of active research because the best (lowest cost) rule in any case depends on setup costs, order costs (and their ratio), the variability of demand, the length of the planning horizon, and the size of the planning period. As Orlicky[4] has pointed out, "if the requirements data are changed, *the example can be rigged so as to produce practically any results desired.*" Even the Wagner-Whitin algorithm, which is an optimizing one, has its drawbacks (complexity and computer requirements) so there is no one best model even for individual situations. Materials managers must evaluate several models and find one that seems to give acceptable, although perhaps not optimal, results over a long period.

---

[4]J. Orlicky, *Material Requirements Planning* (New York: McGraw-Hill, 1975), p. 136.

Lot-sizing rule	Set-ups	Inventory	Costs
Lot-for-lot	7	90	$185.00
EOQ	4	175	167.50
Incremental order quantity[5]	3	165	142.50
Silver and Meal[6]	3	165	142.50
Part-period balancing[7]	4	145	152.50
Wagner-Whitin algorithm[8]	3	165	142.50

This example examined the effect on item *A* only. The lower level items could be treated similarly. In the above example the extreme lumpiness for *B, C* and *D*, derived from the calculation for *A*, results in lot-for-lot order quantities being optimum in many cases. Again the appropriate lot sizes will depend on the specific features of *B, C,* and *D*. In a multi-product plant, with many common parts, demand for *B, C* or *D* may be affected by other end products. The complex and dynamic nature of this environment makes the lot-sizing decision a challenge.

Safety Stock

The calculations in Figure 5–13 show inventory at 0 after the starting stocks have been drawn down. Because lead times, forecasts, and so on, are known to be at least occasionally wrong, it makes sense to carry some safety stock to ensure that production can continue. Inventories can be kept low by carrying safety stock only at the finished goods level and expending extra effort to reduce lead time uncertainties. Proper planning for safety stock will ensure that it is accounted for at the master production schedule level so that balanced sets of components are produced.

One area of uncertainty that warrants special mention is that of a reject allowance. If a purchased or fabricated part is known to contain a certain portion of unacceptable units, the MRP generated order should be scaled up accordingly.

---

[5] J. R. Freeland and J. L. Colley, "A Simple Heuristic Method for Lot Sizing in a Time-Phased Reorder System," *Production and Inventory Management,* 1st Quarter 1982; W. J. Boe and C. Yilmaz, "The Incremental Order Quantity," *Production and Inventory Management,* 2nd Quarter, 1983.

[6] E. A. Silver and H. C. Meal, "A Heuristic for Selecting Lot Size Quantities for the Case of a Deterministic Time-Varying Demand Rate and Discrete Opportunities for Replenishment," *Production and Inventory Management,* 2nd Quarter 1973.

[7] See, for example, R. L. LaForge, "MRP and the Part-Period Algorithm," *Journal of Purchasing and Materials Management,* Winter 1982, and references therein.

[8] H. M. Wagner and T. M. Whitin, "Dynamic Version of the Economic Lot Size Model," *Management Science,* No. 1, 1958; R. A. Kaimann, "A Fallacy of 'E.O.Q.ing,'" *Production and Inventory Management,* 1st Quarter 1968.

Infinite Capacity

As presented earlier, MRP places no restrictions on the number of units of any item that the plant or a supplier can produce in a time bucket. Clearly, however, plants do have capacities. The situation is very complex in job shops making a constantly changing mix of many products, with many common subunits and with the same machines and workers making many different items. Even though MRP will give a time-phased output plan, it may not be a feasible one. The job of scheduling work on the shop floor, and of dealing with absenteeism, breakdowns, poor quality, and unexpected delays remains. A long time horizon and the use of anticipation inventories help but they have their own costs. Clearly, more is needed to overcome this basic flaw in MRP logic. Modern MRP systems have ways of doing so.

Modern MRP Systems

Modern MRP systems are more complex than the simple logic presented in Figure 5–13. The most significant advance has been the addition of capacity requirements planning (CRP). CRP performs a similar function for manufacturing resources that MRP performs for materials. When the MRP system has developed a materials plan, CRP translates the plan into the required human and machine resources by work station and time bucket. It then compares the required resources against a file of available resources. If insufficient capacity exists, the manager must adjust either the capacity or the master production schedule. This feedback loop to the master production schedule results in the term *closed-loop MRP* to describe this development. A closed-loop system is shown schematically in Figure 5–15.

The CRP module is often linked to a module that controls the manufacturing plan on the shop floor. The goal is to measure output by work center against the previously determined plan. This information allows identification of trouble spots and is necessary on an ongoing basis for capacity planning.

MRP systems must be updated frequently to ensure that decisions are made on the basis of consistent, complete, and accurate data. The updating can be either partial or complete. Complete regenerations of large systems are time consuming and expensive, so, typically, such updates are done infrequently (weekly), often at night. Reliance on such a regenerative system leads to slow response to environmental changes and to poor information and large deviations from plan late in the regenerative time period. In contrast, net change systems are updated partially to show the net effects of change whenever new data are entered. The nervousness and incompleteness of such systems can create suboptimal production plans. Insertion of dampeners to filter out relatively minor changes reduces the nervousness. Most systems offer a combination of net-change and regenerative modes.

FIGURE 5–15   Schematic of a Closed Loop MRP System

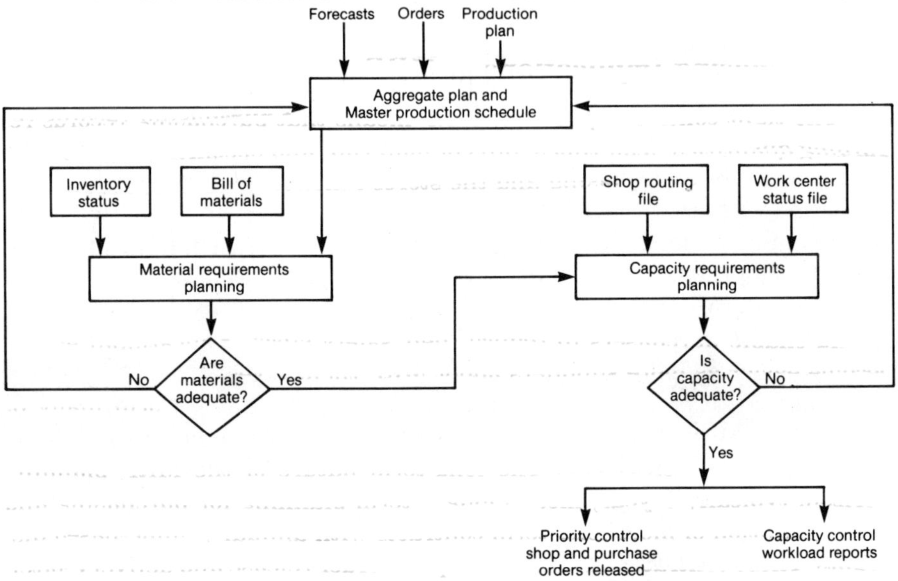

SOURCE: Adapted from J. G. Monks, *Operations Management,* 2nd ed. (New York: McGraw-Hill, 1982), p. 487, and R. J. Tersine, *Principles of Inventory and Materials Management,* 2nd ed. (New York: Elsevier Science Publishing, 1982), p. 288.

Many modern systems also have modules that connect to the accounting system and which help in developing product costs and in budgeting.

A modern MRP system is thus a lot more than simply a device to calculate how much material to obtain and when to do so. It is an information and communication system that encompasses all facets of the organization. It provides managers with performance measures, planned order releases (purchase orders, shop orders, and rescheduling notices), and the ability to simulate a master production schedule in response to proposed changes in production loading (by, for example, a new order, delayed materials, a broken machine, or an ill worker). The integration required of such systems forces organizations to maintain highly accurate information, abandon rules of thumb, and use common data in all departments. The results are reduced inventory levels, higher service coverage, ready access to high quality information, and, most importantly, the ability to replan quickly in response to unforeseen problems.

Not all organizations have been successful in implementing MRP systems. Implementation may take years and involve major investments in training, data preparation, and organizational adjustments as well as in software, computer time, and possibly hardware. However, most organizations with successfully implemented systems feel that the reduced inventory, lead times, split orders and expediting, and increased delivery promises met and discipline resulting from MRP make the investment worthwhile.

Purchasing Implications of MRP

The tight control required by MRP means that purchasing records regarding quantities, lead times, bills of material, and specifications must be impeccable. Also, purchasing and the stores function become more centralized and access to stores more tightly controlled.

The on-time delivery required of MRP needs cooperation from suppliers. Purchasers must, therefore, educate their suppliers to the importance of quantity, quality, and delivery promises to the purchaser. Such education should enable purchasers to reduce their safety stock. Educational efforts become easier as more suppliers adopt MRP themselves.

Many MRP systems have purchasing modules that perform many of the routine clerical purchasing tasks. The purchaser's job becomes more analytical and professional. The long-term nature of the MRP planning horizon, typically a year, means longer term planning for purchasing and the negotiation of more long-term contracts with annual volume-based discounts. These contracts have more frequent order release and delivery, often in nonstandard lot sizes. Quantity discounts on individual orders become much less relevant in favor of on-time delivery of high-quality product.

Purchasers must understand the production processes both of their own organizations and of their suppliers. The tighter nature of MRP-using organizations increases the responsibility on purchasing to be creative and flexible in providing assistance to minimize the inevitable problems that will occur in supply lines. The MRP system provides purchasers with an information window to production scheduling so they are better able to use judgment in dealing with suppliers. Because of the reduced resource slack that results from MRP, purchasers must incorporate de-expediting into their activities as well as the more usual expediting role. The integrating and forward-looking nature of MRP means an increase in specialization in the purchasing department. Also, specialization will be based on finished product line outputs rather than on raw material inputs.

In contrast to MRP, Japanese manufacturers have developed their own means of achieving many of the goals of MRP—reduced inventories, high service coverage, and so on—through just-in-time production methods.

JUST-IN-TIME (JIT)

The relative success of many Japanese companies across a wide range of industries in world markets has prompted many studies of Japanese manufacturing. Many successful Japanese companies use a radically different manufacturing philosophy popularly and descriptively termed *just-in-time (JIT)*. JIT production means that components and raw materials arrive at a work center exactly as they are needed. This feature greatly reduces queues of work-in-process inventory. The goals of JIT production are similar to those of MRP—providing the right part at the right place at the right time—but the ways of achieving these goals are radically different and the results impressive. Whereas MRP is computer based, JIT is industrial engineering based.

JIT is ideal for production systems with a relatively small product line produced repetitively with reasonably level loading. It is not a good technique for job shops with a lot of nonstandard products nor for manufacturers of wide product lines. In these environments EOQ and MRP are better techniques (see Figures 5–16 and 5–17), but there are many JIT features that are good practice in any operation.

In JIT, product design begins with two key questions—will it sell, and can it be made easily? These questions imply cooperation between marketing and operations. Once these questions have been answered positively, attention turns to design of the process itself. The emphasis is on laying out the machines so that production will follow a smooth flow. Automation (often simple) of both production and materials handling is incorporated wherever possible. Frequently, U-shaped lines are used which facilitate teamwork, worker flexibility, rework, passage through the plant, and material and tool handling. In process design the Japanese strive to standardize cycle times and to run a constant product mix, based on the monthly production plan, through the system. This practice makes the production process repetitive for at least a month. For example, a manufacturer of three products (or models) A, B, and C of equal cycle time and monthly demands of 1,000, 2,000, and 500 respectively might have a production schedule of BABABCB or BBBBAAC repeated 500 times in the month.

The ability to smooth production, as in the above example, implies very low setup and order costs to allow the very small lot sizes, ideally one. JIT treats setup and order costs as variable rather than as the fixed ones implied by the EOQ equation. By continuously seeking ways to reduce setup times, the Japanese have managed impressive gains. Setups, which traditionally required three to four hours, have been reduced to less than 15 minutes in some JIT facilities. These dramatic improvements have been achieved by managerial attention to detail on the shop floor, the development and modification of special jigs, fixtures, tools, and machines, and thorough methods training. Setup simplification in Japan is aided by their willingness to modify purchased machines, their acquisition of machines from only a few sources, and their frequent manufacture of machines in-house—often special purpose, light, simple, and inexpensive enough to become a dedicated part of the process. Order costs, conceptually similar to setup costs, have similarly been reduced.

One of the necessary corollaries of having components and materials arrive just as they are needed is that the arriving items must be perfect. In JIT a number of interrelated principles are used to ensure high-quality output from each step in the production process.

First, responsibility for quality rests with the maker of a part not with the quality control department. In addition, workers and managers habitually seek improvement of the status quo, striving for perfection. Quality improvements are often obtained from special projects with defined goals, measures of achievement, and endings. Also, workers are responsible for correcting their own errors, doing rework, and so on.

Second, the use of production workers instead of quality control inspectors builds quality in rather than inspecting it in. This feature and the small lot sizes allow every process to be controlled closely and permit inspection of every piece of output. Workers have authority to stop the production line when quality problems arise. This aspect signifies that quality is a more important goal of the production system than is output.

Third, JIT insists on compliance to quality standards. Purchasers reject marginally unacceptable items and visit supplier plants to check quality on the shop floor for themselves. Because such visits are frequent, JIT manufacturers document their quality in easily understood terms and post the results in prominent places. This process forces the manufacturer to define precisely what quality is.

JIT control of quality is helped by the small lot sizes that prevent the buildup of large lots of bad items. JIT tends to have excess production capacity so that the plants are not stressed to produce the required quantities. In the same vein, machines are maintained and checked regularly and run no faster than the recommended rates. Plant housekeeping is generally good. The quality control department acts as a quality facilitator for production personnel giving advice in problem solving. This department also does some testing but the tests tend to be on final products not easily assignable to a single production worker, or special tests requiring special equipment, facilities, knowledge, or long times not available to personnel on the shop floor. Automatic checking devices are used wherever possible. Where necessary, sample lots are chosen to consist of the first and last units produced rather than a larger, random sample. Analytical tools include the standard statistical techniques, often known by workers, and cause-and-effect diagrams to help solve problems.

JIT requires great dedication by both workers and managers to hard work and helping the organization. By Western standards JIT workers must be flexible. They are trained to do several different jobs and are moved around frequently. The workers are responsible for quality and output. Workers continuously seek ways to improve all facets of operations, and are rewarded for finding problems which can then be solved. The JIT plant has a high proportion of the line workers that add value in the production process and correspondingly fewer staff personnel. The environment is much like many quality-of-work-life programs—consensus decision making involves and commits everyone.

In summary, JIT is a mixture of high quality working environment, excellent industrial engineering practice, and a healthy focused factory attitude that operations are strategically important. The order and discipline

FIGURE 5–16   Comparison of Manufacturing Systems

	Lot-oriented inventory systems		
Degree of inventory control:	Loose ←		
System name:	ROP (Reorder point)	LRP (Lot requirements planning)	ROP/shortage list
Genesis:	Old as man	Industrial Revolution	Industrial Revolution
Explosion?	No	Yes	Yes
Backward Scheduled?	No	No	No
Hot list/ expediting	Yes	Yes	Yes
Role of computer:	Optional	Optional	Optional
Typical Inventory level	Months	Weeks-months	Days-weeks
Common applications:	Small manufacturers— and larger ones in monopolistic or protected environment	Design engineering oriented manufacturers	Job-lot manufacturing with large product variety—less competitive environment
Rationale:	Small manufacturers tend to lack management, technical, financial resources to upgrade their inventory system.	LRP is simple and satisfactory for the limited cases of design-oriented manufacturing.	A popular system that many firms have large investments in. Firm may lack financial resources and competitive motivation to upgrade.

SOURCE: R. J. Schonberger, "Selecting the Right Manufacturing Inventory System: Western and Japanese Approaches," *Production and Inventory Management Journal,* 2nd Quarter 1983, Journal of the American Production and Inventory Control Society, Inc., pp. 34 and 39.

Lotless inventory systems

→ Tight

MRP	Synchro-MRP	*Kanban*	Production line
1960s (U.S.)	1980s(Japan)	1970s(Japan)	Industrial Revolution
Yes	Yes	Yes	Yes
Yes	Yes	Yes	Yes
No	No	No	No
Essential	Essential	Peripheral	Peripheral
Days-weeks	Hours-days	Minutes-hours	Zero-minutes
Job-lot manufacturing with large product variety— highly competitive environment	Repetitive manufacturing with considerable product variety	Repetitive manufacturing with moderate product variety	Repetitive manufacturing with little product variety
Considerably improves customer service; also cuts excess inventories. Works even with diverse product lines and deep bills of materials.	Provides very tight planning and control of parts from large numbers of fabrication centers.	Drastically cuts inventories and simplifies planning and control.	Cuts inventories to zero and eliminates most "shop paper."

FIGURE 5–17   Matching Inventory System to Manufacturing Type

Type of manufacturer	Manufacturing Inventory Systems						
	ROP	LRP	ROP/ shortage list	MRP	Synchro- MRP	Kanban	Pro- duction line
Repetitive OEM few models	Poor ◄————————————————————————► Good						
Many models	Poor ◄——————————————————————► Good						
Many fabricated parts	Poor ◄——————————————► Good						
Job-lot fabrication	Poor ◄———► Transitory ◄——► Good						
Design engineering- oriented	Poor ◄——► Good						
Small or protected	Transitory						

SOURCE: R. J. Schonberger, "Selecting the Right Manufacturing Inventory System: Western and Japanese Approaches," *Production and Inventory Management Journal*, 2nd Quarter 1983, p. 43.

are achieved through management effort to develop streamlined plant configurations that remove variability. The JIT system has often been described as one that pulls material through the factory rather than pushing it through. The use of a kanban system as a control device illustrates this point well.

Kanban is a simple but effective control system that helps make JIT production work. Kanban is not synonymous with JIT although the term is often incorrectly so used and the two are closely related. *Kanban* is Japanese for *card;* the use of cards is central to many Japanese control systems including the one at Toyota whose kanban system has received much attention.

Kanban systems require the small lot size features of JIT and discrete production units. The systems are most useful for high volume parts used on a regular basis. They are much less useful for expensive or large items which cost a lot to store or carry, for infrequently or irregularly used items, or for process industries which don't produce in discrete units.

Two types of kanban systems exist—single card and double card. In double card systems two types of cards (kanban) exist—conveyance

(C-kanban) and production of (P-kanban). Single card systems use only the C-kanban. The two-card system's operation is shown in Figure 5–18 and uses the following rules.[9]

1. No parts may be made unless there is a P-kanban authorizing production. Workers may do maintenance, cleaning, or work on improvement projects until a P-kanban arrives rather than making parts not yet asked for. Similarly, C-kanban control the transport of parts between departments.

2. Only standard containers may be used and they are always filled with the prescribed small quantity.

3. There is precisely one C-kanban and one P-kanban per container.

The system is driven by the user department pulling material through the system by the use of kanban. The main managerial tools in this system are the container size and the number of containers (and therefore kanban) in the system. The control is very precise, flexible, and responsive. It prevents an unwanted buildup of inventory.

In JIT there is a close cooperation between vendor and purchaser to solve problems, and suppliers and customers have stable, long-term relationships. In keeping with the JIT philosophy, suppliers, usually few in number, are often located close to their customers to facilitate communication, on-time delivery of small lots of parts, low pipeline and safety stocks, and low purchasing costs. The situation in many JIT companies is much like extensive backward vertical integration. The organizations avoid formal ownership ties but achieve many of the same ends by close coordination and systems integration that smooth operations. The job of a purchaser in the JIT environment is one of a facilitator, negotiator, communicator, and developer rather than of an expediter.

QUESTIONS FOR REVIEW AND DISCUSSION

1. Why is it expensive to carry inventories?

2. What is the difference between JIT and MRP?

3. What problems do inaccurate usage forecasts create for buyers? For suppliers?

4. Why is it useful to make a distinction between dependent and independent demand?

5. In a typical department store identify various forms and functions of inventory. How could total investment in inventories be lowered? What might be the potential consequences?

---

[9]R. J. Schonberger, *Japanese Manufacturing Techniques: Nine Hidden Lessons in Simplicity* (New York: Free Press, 1982), p. 224.

FIGURE 5–18   The Operation of a Dual-Card *Kanban* System

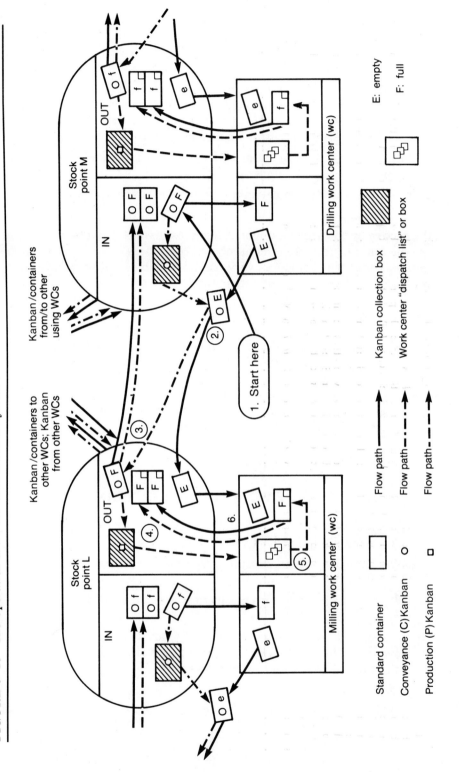

1. Find the note "Start here," pointing to a full parts container about to be moved into Drilling. Its C-kanban is detached and placed in a collection box for Stock Point M.
2. The container most recently emptied in drilling is taken to Stock Point M, where a C-kanban is attached to it.
3. The empty container and C-kanban are taken to Stock Point L (in another part of the plant or another building), where the C-kanban is detached and reattached to a full container, which is taken back to Stock Point M. The last act also triggers production activities through use of a production kanban (P-kanban) as follows.
4. The full container just taken had a P-kanban attached to it. Before it leaves Stock Point L, its P-kanban is detached and placed in a collection box.
5. P-kanban (that apply to Milling) are taken to Milling every hour or so, where they go into the dispatch box and become the dispatch list of jobs to be worked on next. They are worked on in the order of receipt from Stock Point L.
6. Parts for each completed job go into an empty containers taken from Stock Point L, the P-kanban is attached, and the full container is moved to Stock Point L.

SOURCE: R. J. Schonberger, *Japanese Manufacturing Techniques: Nine Hidden Lessons in Simplicity* (New York: Free Press, 1982), pp. 222–24.

6. Why would anyone prefer to use a fixed period reordering model over a fixed quantity one?

7. Of what interest is ABC analysis?

8. What is a kanban and why is it used?

9. What is a master production schedule and what role does it perform?

10. What is the relationship between lead times and inventory levels?

REFERENCES

Ansari, A. and Jim Heckel. "JIT Purchasing: Impact of Freight and Inventory Costs." *Journal of Purchasing and Materials Management,* Summer 1987.

Boe, Warren J. and Cengiz Yilmaz. "The Incremental Order Quantity." *Production and Inventory Management,* 2nd Quarter 1983.

Bragg, Daniel J. and Chan K. Hahn. "Material Requirements Planning and Purchasing." *Journal of Purchasing and Materials Management,* Summer 1982.

Benton, W.C. "Purchasing Quantity Discount Procedures and MRP." *Journal of Purchasing and Materials Management,* Spring 1983.

Hahn, Chan K.; Peter A. Pinto; and Daniel J. Bragg. "'Just-in-time' Production and Purchasing." *Journal of Purchasing and Materials Management,* Fall 1983.

Hall, Robert W. *Zero Inventories.* Homewood, Ill: Dow Jones-Irwin, 1983.

Hall, Robert W. *Attaining Manufacturing Excellence.* Homewood, Ill: Dow Jones-Irwin, 1987.

Krupp, James A. G. "MRP Failures and the Purchasing Interface." *Journal of Purchasing and Materials Management,* Summer 1984.

Manoochehri, G.H. "Suppliers and the Just-In-Time Concept." *Journal of Purchasing Materials Management,* Winter 1984.

Mayer, R.R. "Optimum Safety Stocks When Demands and Lead Times Vary." *Journal of Purchasing and Materials Management,* Spring 1984.

Monden, Yasuhiro. "What Makes the Toyota Production System Really Tick?" *Industrial Engineering.* January 1981.

Monks, Joseph G. *Operations Management: Theory and Problems.* 3rd ed. New York: McGraw-Hill, 1987.

O'Neal, Charles R. "The Buyer-Seller Linkage in a Just-in-time Environment" *Journal of Purchasing and Materials Management,* Spring 1987.

Schmenner, Roger W. *Production/Operations Management: Concepts and Situations.* 3rd ed. Chicago: Science Research Associates, 1987.

Schonberger, Richard J. *World Class Manufacturing: The Lessons of Simplicity Applied.* New York: Free Press, 1986.

Tersine, Richard J. *Production Operations Management: Concepts, Structure, and Analysis.* New York: North-Holland, 1985.

Case 5–1

F&P CUSTOMER SERVICES DIVISION (A)

On the first Thursday of December, Norm Holloway, Purchasing Officer at Fisher & Paykel's Customer Services Division in Auckland, New Zealand, received a telephone call from John Wardrop. John, Purchasing Manager, Laundry Division, wanted to borrow 500 automatic washer seals, because there was a critical shortage on the assembly line. Norm said he would check on the situation and call John right back.

Fisher & Paykel Limited, Customer Services Division

Fisher & Paykel, (F&P), was New Zealand's largest appliance manufacturer. It produced a full range of home appliances and also distributed a number of imported Japanese products under the Matsushita National brand name.

The Customer Services Division, formed ten years earlier, coordinated all aftersales service backup for all products sold by F&P to the end of their economic life. This function included not only parts service, but also aftersales service training for dealer personnel, a small service department to handle major repairs for which dealers were not qualified, and the marketing of accessories to the product line, such as do-it-yourself repair kits for owners, microwave oven cookware, and TV aerials. The division employed about 200 persons of which 12 worked in the purchasing and stock control section.

Currently the division's stock at cost amounted to about U.S. $2.2 million comprising about 28,000 line items. Total purchases were about $6 million. The purchasing and stock control functions were based on an on-line computer system which was currently being revised.

In the storage and packing area the following activities were carried out:

1. Receipt, inspection and storage location of inward goods.

2. Assembly and manufacture of certain parts.

3. Prepackaging of certain parts.

4. Bulk storage of lifetime stocks.

5. Picking and packing of customer orders.

6. Counter sales.

About 650 customer orders comprising an average of two or three line items each were sent out on a typical day. The division's service level was over 95 percent. An express delivery service was available at a premium on request, allowing door-to-door delivery within 24 hours anywhere in New Zealand.

A company manual stated that the Customer Services Division was a vital link between F&P and its customers. Customer requests for service were supposed to fall into F&P's highest priority category.

Acquisition of Parts for Customer Services Division

The acquisition of parts for the Customer Services Division (CSD) was looked after by its purchasing department, headed by Jim Cockburn. If a part was still used in the production of new appliances at F&P, the CSD requests were combined with production orders and actually purchased by the purchasing staff in the manufacturing divisions. For example, part number 400916, a lower face seal used in an automatic washing machine, was purchased by the laundry division's purchasing staff. CSD gave a firm commitment for all active parts three months out and estimated requirements for an additional six months. These commitments and estimates were updated monthly and sent to the appropriate manufacturing division's purchasing staff.

Once a manufacturing division discontinued an appliance line the CSD purchasing department started to purchase directly from the manufacturer of the item. If the part was made in-house a major buy was often made along with the last manufacturing order for the item.

Parts Lending Between Divisions

It was not unusual for CSD to receive requests from manufacturing divisions to assist in cases of shortages on the assembly line. Because F&P operated on an MRP basis, the manufacturing divisions ran tight on supply, and delayed deliveries from outside vendors or in-house departments could shut down production. In the past weeks such requests to CSD had averaged at about five or six per week. Especially during the last six months, an unusually high sales period for F&P, these requests had been common. Moreover, when CSD agreed to lend such parts, it often had difficulty getting them back on the dates promised by the manufacturing divisions. The quantities requested by the manufacturing divisions were invariably large by CSD standards. CSD staff believed that manufacturing division personnel did not see returning borrowed parts to CSD as a high priority.

It should be noted, however, that not all borrowing that took place was done by the manufacturing divisions. CSD also borrowed parts from the manufacturing divisions when it ran short. During the past year CSD's borrowing requests had been fewer than manufacturing's and, almost invariably, had involved smaller quantities. Moreover, when CSD borrowed parts, the manufacturing division just withheld the borrowed quantities from the next delivery to CSD. For example, if CSD borrowed 60 parts 10 days in advance of a 200-part monthly delivery, the manufacturing division would deliver 140 parts 10 days later and consider the matter closed.

CSD, however, had no similar way of getting back borrowed parts. Because CSD depended on the manufacturing division to return the parts along with outstanding orders, it could only request that borrowed parts be returned at the manufacturing division's earliest convenience.

All orders placed through manufacturing divisions were charged to CSD at a small markup for the procurement and handling services involved. Borrowed parts between divisions were charged back at the same cost.

Part 400916—Lower Face Seal

On the first Thursday in December, Norm Holloway, Purchasing Officer for laundry products in CSD, received a call from John Wardrop, requesting a loan of 500 pieces of part 400916. This assembly with brass metal inserts and a circular coil spring was used as a seal between the motor and the bowl. It fitted around the main spindle joining motor and bowl and it had a carbon phenolic face on a rubber boot. Part 400916 cost about $3.00 and was purchased from a U.K. supplier on a six-month lead time, in monthly lots of about 5,000 to 6,000 pieces. It was considered an A item in CSD. CSD packaged all seals arriving from laundry into individual cartons to protect the phenolic face. This operation normally required 4 to 5 days and meant part 400916 could not be sent to customers until it was packed.

Norm Holloway checked the CSD stock status and the usage of part 400916. He found the following:

Stock on Thursday	- 2510
Average monthly usage	- 1800
Orders outstanding:	1000 due 20/11 (overdue) current year
	2028 due 19/12 current year
	1618 due 24/01 next year
	1764 due 20/02 next year

John Wardrop indicated that the laundry manufacturing division was experiencing serious supply problems since a ship was late in arriving. He indicated that the borrowed order could be returned on the following Thursday.

Norm Holloway knew John Wardrop's purchasing group had borrowed parts before and that sometimes these were returned as promised and sometimes not. He knew of several instances where CSD had experienced serious stockouts because parts had been lent. When such stockouts occurred, dealers often reacted by ordering larger quantities to increase their safety stocks. Thus, a relatively small shortage could suddenly increase dramatically.

Part 400916 was normally ordered by dealers for stock. It was a frequently-replaced part on automatic washing machines; it was often replaced during repairs for other problems. Thus, it was normal for larger dealers to carry 400916 in stock to ensure rapid repairs.

It was CSD's normal policy to carry a safety stock of at least one month's supply on overseas parts like part 400916. Thus, normal stock positions should range from one to three months usage. Safety stock levels and order quantities were incorporated in CSD's computerized control system.

Norm Holloway knew that CSD normally tried to accommodate borrowing requests when it was reasonable to do so. He also remembered some instances where production personnel, when refused, tried to talk to others in the Customer Services Division including its General Manager. He had to phone John Wardrop back quickly to let John know whether the 500 pieces of part 400916 could be lent by CSD.

Case 5–2

DENVER GAMES

In early April, Paul Brock, materials manager for Denver Games, received a requisition to purchase the June production requirements for the "Trap" game. This would be the third time he had ordered Trap components in the current year and he wondered if current company ordering policies and procedures really made sense. Paul had joined Denver Games eight months previously and had spent a considerable amount of time familiarizing himself with the company. He believed the "Trap" requisition was typical and wondered whether improvements were possible.

Company Background

Denver Games was a family-owned business incorporated in 1897. Originally toys were the only products produced, but games and hobby kits were added to the line after 1920. Denver Games was a leader in the industry and had a well-known brand name and a reputation for quality and new product innovation.

Approximately 75 percent of sales were manufactured and assembled in-house and 25 percent of sales were finished product resale items imported from the Far East.

The organization at Denver Games consisted of a president, an executive committee, a middle management group, salaried support personnel, and approximately 150 hourly paid workers.

The manufacturing process for games usually involved equipment to make boxes and playing boards augmented by packing lines. Most of the printing requirements were met by an outside supplier under a long-term agreement.

During the past three years, the efficiency in manufacturing had been improved through capital expenditures for modern machinery and the intensive use of industrial engineering in order to reduce the hourly paid work force.

Last year, the company had changed to the product manager concept and added two managers. At the same time, a technical manager and a materials manager (Paul Brock) had also been hired. Part of Paul's mandate was to improve the efficiency of the materials department.

The company plant was at capacity and suffered from a shortage of space in spite of a new warehouse that had been recently built for finished goods inventory. The labor force was kept fairly stable throughout the year by building inventory during slack times.

New Program Development

Of prime importance to Denver Games was the need to develop a series of new programs annually; each program referred to a new game, hobby kit, or toy, introduced for distribution. The organization had to react quickly to determine (1) market desires, (2) the elements of competition, (3) concept development, (4) defined program requirements, and (5) goods and services required to manufacture these items. Failure to comply with this rigid schedule could result in the loss of sales and market position, especially in view of the seasonal buying pattern of the consumer. (See Exhibit 1 for an overview of new program introductions over the past four years.)

Sales Forecasting and Production Planning

An annual sales forecast was developed by the sales and marketing departments reflecting anticipated sales for a calendar year. This forecast was initially issued in October, prior to the start of a new calendar period which would commence the following January and run to December. This sales forecast was reviewed four to six times annually, with upward or downward revisions by program reflecting current sales and anticipated trends. Some programs could be revised upward as much as 300 percent of the initial forecast, or be decreased as much as 70 percent. Many toys and games were directly tied to current TV programs and might have very short lives. Generally, sales peaked at Christmas. Regular yearly demand came from sales

EXHIBIT 1   Program Category Totals by Year and Related Data

	Four years ago	Three years ago	Two years ago	Last year
Number of programs carried over from prior year	860	956	905	967
New program introductions	182	156	310	391
New program introductions as a percent of carryover	21	16	34	40
Total program (new and carryover)	1,042	1,112	1,215	1,357
Average number of hourly personnel employed	242	187	165	154

for birthdays and gifts as well as from special department store and chain promotions. For instance, a big discount store could decide to run a "special sale." There were penalty clauses for not keeping larger, regular customers supplied. The big retail sales month was December, and, if the goods were not produced by October 1, management figured the Christmas market would be missed.

The sales forecast was refined into a manufacturing plan by the production control department which scheduled manufacturing runs by program, balancing the needs of sales and plant loading capacity.

The manufacturing plan was then issued to the materials department for inventory control and procurement purposes.

The seven major considerations which guided Paul Brock's work were:

1. Company policy dictated that all components and materials required for production must be in house four weeks ahead of a scheduled run. This policy was developed to allow for flexibility in the scheduling and manufacturing process.

2. Company policy dictated that a safety stock of finished goods required at a given month end had to be 15 percent of the next month's sales forecast. This responsibility for setting the safety stock level rested with sales (that is, the corporate philosophy was to be in an "in-stock" position at all times on finished products).

3. Inventory carrying charges were calculated at 2 percent per month.

4. Normal lead time for printed components was four weeks after receipt of order on repeat programs; 8—12 weeks on new program introductions.

5. A computer printout was issued weekly indicating the following data *for finished or completed units only:*
   a. Sales forecast this year.
   b. Revised sales forecast this year.
   c. Last year sales by month (actual).
   d. This year sales by month (actual).

  e. Manufacturing schedule by month this year.
  f. Opening inventory as of January 1.
  g. Free balance by month: finished goods inventory left over after fulfilling booked orders during a given month.
  h. Commit quantity: the degree of confidence relative to the sales forecast indicated in units. For example, the sales forecast for a particular program might read 100,000 units; the commit quantity might read 70,000 units.
  i. Program category: defined the program as a No. 1, or No. 2, or No. 3 category. No. 1 referred to a program considered staple and sufficient materials had to be in stock at all times. No. 2 category was a program considered semi-staple; sufficient materials should be in stock at all times, but less significant than No. 1. No. 3 category referred to a sensitive product about which no automatic decisions should be made. An audit of current program categories indicated that 66 percent of the total product line of manufactured programs were classified in the No. 3 category.

  6. Production runs could not be smaller than 10,000 units, as setup costs were significant.

  7. Authority to purchase was limited to buying, or having on hand, that number of components and materials required to produce finished goods not exceeding the commit quantity indicated by program. From the materials department's point of view, the term used to denote this situation was the *net commit quantity*. This number was derived by taking the indicated *commit quantity* (that is, 50,000 units) less the "opening inventory" of finished units as of January 1, (that is, 10,000 units). This figure equalled the net commit quantity, or authority to purchase. In effect, for the example cited above, authority was limited to purchase, or have on hand, that number of components or materials to produce 40,000 finished units only.

The authority to purchase, and the development of commit quantities, had been recently initiated. Usually, the majority of purchases were made to meet the requirements of each scheduled production run only. This practice was a direct response to the wide fluctuations experienced with sales forecasts to avoid excessive obsolete and surplus inventories.

Purchasing performance in the materials department was evaluated by two major criteria. First was the ability to have the necessary components and materials in house four weeks ahead of the scheduled production run. The second was based on the ability to purchase components and materials at a cost less than, or not exceeding, the standard costs developed. This evaluation was provided by a purchase variance report issued monthly by the accounting department. Purchase prices were compared to standard cost levels to show positive or negative variances.

Standard costs were developed annually, usually in late September, for use in the following calendar year commencing January 1. The basis for setting standard costs for components and materials was to take the most recent invoice price and add on the appropriate duty, exchange, freight, and royalty factor. In addition, the accounting department (based on historical trends) factored in any anticipated increases or decreases.

Paul Brock realized that the materials department did not provide any input into developing standard costs. Furthermore, he had no opportunity to examine standard costs prior to issue. He also recognized that no consideration was given during the setting of standards to the size of purchase indicated on the base invoice price.

The "Trap" Situation

Paul took another look at the "Trap" requisition order and decided to calculate the total cost for the August and June requirements under current company policy. He gathered the following information from the computer:

Program: "Trap"   *Sales forecast* = 65,000 Units
Commit quantity: 50,000 Units   *Category 1   Open Inv:* 10,000
Manufacturing schedule: 10,000 units February   (Complete)
                                          10,000 units April   (Complete)
                                          10,000 units June
                                          10,000 units August
                                          10,000 units October
Net authority to purchase: Confidence level 50,000 less opening inventory of
                                          10,000 units = 40,000 units (less individual components and materials on hand or on order).

The on-hand inventory of unique components as of April 1, was as follows: (a) lid wrap—10,000, (b) face label—6,000, (c) box wrap—11,000, (d) rules—8,000, (e) printed deck—7,000, (f) playing cards—20,000 sets, (g) trays c/w lid—9,000 sets (h) triangles and stars—9,000 sets.

Then he made the following summary of the purchases that would have to be made:

a. Purchase 4,000 face labels for delivery May 1. Cost is $62.30/M + $384.00 set up cost + $35.00 to issue purchase order* and carrying costs of 2% = $681.56.

   (i) Purchase 10,000 face labels for delivery July 1. Cost is $62.30/M + $384.00 set up cost + $35.00 to issue purchase order and carrying costs @ 2% = $1,062.84.
   Total cost incurred: $1,744.40 or $124.60/M.

b. Purchase 2,000 rules for delivery May 1. Cost is 2,000 × $88.90/M + $148.00 set up + $35.00 to issue purchase order and carrying costs 2% = $368.02.

   (i) Purchase 10,000 rules for delivery July 1. Cost is 10,000 × $88.90/M + $148.00 set up + $35.00 to issue purchase order and carrying costs @ 2% = $1,093.44.
   Total cost incurred: $1,461.46 or $121.79/M.

c. Purchase 3,000 printed decks for delivery May 1. Cost is $96.50/M + $124.00 set up + $35.00 to issue purchase order and carrying charges @ 2% = $457.47.

   (i) Purchase 10,000 printed decks for delivery July 1. Cost is $96.50/M + $124.00 set up + $35.00 to issue purchase order and carrying charges @ 2% = $1,146.48.

---

*Purchase order cost of $35 was determined by dividing the total budget for the materials department by the total number of purchase orders.

Total cost incurred: $1,603.95 or $123.38/M.

d. Purchase 1,000 sets of trays c/w lids for delivery May 1. Cost is $39.20/ M + 100.00 set up + $35.00 to issue purchase order and carrying charges @ 2% = $177.68.

  (i) Purchase 10,000 sets of trays c/w lid for delivery July 1. Cost is $39.20/ M + $100.00 set up + $35.00 to issue purchase order and carrying charges @ 2% = $537.54.

  Total cost incurred: $715.22 or $65.02/M.

e. Purchase 1,000 sets of triangles/stars for delivery May 1. Cost is $139.88/ M + $100.00 set up cost + $35.00 to issue purchase order and cost of carrying inventory @ 2% = $280.38.

  (i) Purchase 10,000 sets of triangles and stars for delivery July 1. Cost is $139.88/M + $100.00 set up cost + $35.00 to issue purchase order and cost of carrying inventory @ 2% = $1,564.48.

  Total cost incurred: $1,844.86 or $167.71/M.

f. Purchase 9,000 box wraps for delivery July 1. Cost is $52.30/M + $74.00 set up + $35.00 to issue purchase order and carrying costs @ 2% = $591.29.

  Total cost incurred: $591.29 or $65.69/M.

g. Purchase 10,000 lid wraps for delivery July 1. Cost is $78.10/M + $434.00 set up cost + $35.00 to issue purchase order and carrying cost @ 2% = $1,275.00.

  Total cost incurred: $1,275.00 or $127.50/M.

Thus, the total costs incurred would come to $9,236.18.

Conclusion

Paul was concerned that this would be the third time this year he would be purchasing parts for "Trap" and wondered what he could do to improve the situation.

Case 5–3

Joan Baker

Joan Baker, purchasing manager at Stanton, Inc., was very concerned about the company's stockroom operations. Faulty records, a rash of last-minute rush orders, and interference with production were troubles she had become aware of since becoming manager nine months earlier.

Company Background

Stanton, Inc., located near Buffalo, New York, manufactured concrete mixers and heavy material moving equipment, including dump truck and plowing accessories. Current sales totaled about $23 million. The company was privately held and the owner-president had been personally involved in management from his initial purchase of the company in 1968. At the time of purchase the company was in receivership, but effective management subsequently turned the company around. Currently, the company enjoyed an excellent reputation in the trade for a well-engineered, high-quality, sturdy product line.

Over the years the president had aggressively pursued sales opportunities in the Northeastern United States and Canada. He also believed in keeping overhead down and all aspects of operations as simple as possible. He did not like computers, and all of the corporate record systems, including purchasing's, were manual. Concrete mixers were the major product line and sales of these were highly seasonal and cyclical, closely tied to the construction industry. The high manufacturing period started in February and ended by September. During this time the company operated two 10½ hour shifts for four days a week from Monday to Thursday. Each production worker was paid for·10 hours' work, including a half-hour lunch or snack break. The two 15-minute coffee breaks in each shift were not paid and stretched the total shift time to 10½ hours.

All concrete mixer sales were to customer order with six to eight weeks lead time. Normally, with the exception of the hydrostatics, this was sufficient time to order the necessary materials and parts. About 60 percent of all concrete mixers were sold through distributors located in Chicago, Detroit, Toronto, Montreal, and New Jersey. Normally, these distributors or their customers performed final assembly themselves. Thus, all mixer parts were sent on a flat bed to the distributor who mounted them on the chassis. The remaining 40 percent of the mixers produced were sold as fully assembled units and driven from Stanton's plant to the customer.

Plant Organization

Major departments in the plant included the following. In the machine shop various forgings and parts were machined. These included, for example, axle and drum roll forgings and the rod for the drum track. There were three welding areas. The first was primarily devoted to drums; the second, to welding the tracks to drums in a special 12-foot-high fixture; and the third, to smaller parts and water tanks. The steel fabrication area had breaks and shears and was used for cutting and shaping sheet metal, angle iron, brackets, and so on. In the first assembly area all of those parts which had to be assembled to mixers prior to painting were attached. Then the mixers were painted and in final assembly the hydraulics, lights, water hoses and water tanks and mud flaps were put on. The service area in the plant provided maintenance and repair facilities and also contained the repair parts store room.

The company was nonunionized and in the high season employed 166 people including 140 hourly paid production and maintenance workers. Managers reported directly to the president, but enjoyed a high degree of autonomy within their functional areas.

Purchasing and Stores

As purchasing manager, Joan supervised six employees (see Exhibit 1) and was responsible for annual purchases of $13.75 million. These purchases were received into inventory in one of two ways. Large expensive items, such as transmissions, chassis, hydrostatics, forgings, and mild steel, which represented 83 percent of pur-

EXHIBIT 1   Partial Organization Chart

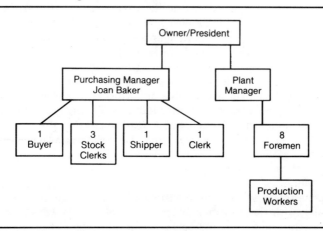

chases in dollar value, were individually cataloged and allocated by job number as they were received.

Chassis were stored in an unclosed yard until required for assembly. Transmissions and hydrostatics were kept in storage areas inside the plant near assembly, mild steel was stored in fabrication and welding, and forgings in the machine shop. The stockroom clerks took inventory counts of all high value items every Friday.

The remaining items, which comprised 17 percent of annual purchases, were sent from the receiving dock to the stockroom. This locked area contained about 13,000 different parts, including all kinds of nuts and bolts, rubberized parts, gaskets, hoses, lights, solenoids, and welding and machine shop supplies. It was staffed by three clerks. Normally, one clerk worked days from 8:30 A.M. to 5:00 P.M. and another from 5:00 P.M. to 1:30 A.M. The third clerk would work either the first or second shift, depending on how busy it was.

Stores operated on a form of min/max system with total inventory ranging from a low of $600 thousand to a high of $1.5 million. Order quantities varied depending on the time of year. In February, March, and April, purchasing paid particular attention to total season requirements and the possibility of quantity discounts and price breaks. Near the end of the season, however, Joan was anxious to avoid carrying excess stock and would try to order only in sufficient quantities to meet requirements until September.

Joan would purchase total annual requirements for the company for both repair and production using past usage of repair parts as a guide. As orders for parts were received the repair portion was directly sent to repair stores by the stockroom clerks.

A Typical Day's Operation

The first production shift in the plant arrived at 7:00 A.M. Those workers needing parts at this time requested their foreman (all of whom had keys to the stockroom) to open the stockroom so that they could take out the trays prepared the previous evening with their parts requirements. If no tray had been prepared, the worker or the foreman usually took the necessary items, often without bothering to record the removal. At 8:00 A.M. the stockroom clerk opened the stores area, handled stock requisitions as they arose and in slower periods started to put away the return trays from the previous night shift and assemble new trays of parts for the coming second shift. In addition, store clerks were required to assemble kits of stores parts for mixers leaving the plant to be assembled by customers or distributors. Normally, these kits were requested for shipping in the 3:00 P.M. to 6:00 P.M. time slot. As shortages were noted in bins, or as bin minimums were reached, stores clerks filled out requisitions for replenishment and sent these to purchasing.

All workers were required to return their trays of parts before shift end to the stockroom. This way any unused parts were returned to the bins and each worker was responsible for his or her own parts used. Workers were also expected to order their parts requirements for the following day by the end of the shift. Since it sometimes was not exactly clear what such parts requirements might be, because the progress of work on the next shift could only be guessed at, it was not unusual for workers to over or under order parts requirements.

At 5:00 P.M. the second shift in the stockroom started and at 5:30 P.M. the second production shift. Trays were handed out to incoming workers and the stockroom continued the same routine as on the first shift. At 2:00 A.M. the stockroom clerk went off duty, while the plant continued working until 4:00 A.M. The foremen on the night shift opened the stockroom as required during the absence of the stock clerk and also locked up after the second shift trays were returned along with parts lists requirements for the next evening shift.

Problems with the Current System

Joan Baker had observed a variety of problems with the existing stores setup. An unusually large number of rush orders at the last minute forced purchasing to buy at high prices in small quantities and to upset vendor relations. Stock clerks complained about being overworked. There were frequent discrepancies between stores records and actual bin counts. Since stores bins were only counted once a year at audit time, these discrepancies were normally caught when a bin showed empty while the record indicated otherwise. The repair stores clerk, who did not report to Joan, but was part of the service department's complement, occasionally "borrowed" parts for emergency requirements, without informing the stores clerks of his actions. The foremen complained about the amount of time they and their workers were wasting on stores items. Harried stores clerks at times did not have the chance to record removals or requests for replenishment. On Fridays, when no production took place, stores clerks worked their normal 8½-hour shifts and were supposed to catch up in addition to the stock taking for the high value items. However, discovering shortages on Fridays accomplished little for the following week's production.

Joan Baker realized that the stockroom problem was of overall company concern. Therefore, she discussed the situation with the factory manager and both agreed to do some more investigation. A methods and time study specialist from the engineering department was requested to assist. He found out that the average production worker spent two 10-minute periods, normally at the beginning and at the end of each shift, waiting at the stockroom. He also found that the stores clerks had no spare time. In purchasing, Joan Baker did a special study on rush orders which showed the company was losing about $4,000 a month on stores parts prices alone, not counting extra purchasing and stores time and tie-up of capital in concrete mixers awaiting missing parts before shipment.

Joan knew that the average rate of pay for the 140 production workers was about $14.50 per hour. Wages of stock clerks averaged $15,600 per year. Fringe benefits were about 30 percent. She realized that hiring more stock clerks was one potential solution, but she was already concerned about the high cost of inventories and inventory control. She wondered if other ideas might be more sensible under the circumstances. Unfortunately, she did not know what to suggest. She knew the existing store system had been in operation for at least 30 years and that significant changes might well be difficult to implement.

At a recent management meeting, the president had announced that a substantial increase in production level was contemplated which would raise the total number of production employees from 140 to at least 160 people. Joan Baker was anxious to resolve the stockroom issue before this increase in production took place.

Case 5–4

LAMSON CORPORATION

In this game you will have the chance to try your skill at inventory and operations planning using information similar in type to that available to Mr. Marino, the operations manager of Lamson Corporation, a large multiplant manufacturer of sewer pipes. Every two weeks in the summer sales period Mr. Marino had to decide how many tiles of each type and size should be produced during the coming two weeks. In doing this, he took into account sales trends, the time of the year, the capacity of Lamson's tile-making machinery, the stock of the various size tiles on hand, the cost of overtime production and the cost of missed deliveries. In this game you will be able to make similar decisions although the game will be a simplified version of the actual situation. The most important feature of this simplification is that you will be dealing with only two sizes of sewer tile—the 18″ diameter size and the 36″ diameter size. Mr. Marino, in contrast, had to decide on production levels for 13 different sizes of tiles and which plants would produce what mix.

Sales Patterns

Company sales, and industry sales in general, were very much influenced by general economic as well as seasonal factors. Since weather affected tile laying conditions and the number of construction starts, sewer tiles exhibited a yearly sales trend of the following general shape (see Exhibit 1). Sales were low for six months from October 1 to April 1 and rose rapidly in the spring to a summer peak and then tapered off again. About one third of all annual sales were made in the two middle months of the year while about three fourths were made in the summer sales season. However, there was not necessarily a smooth rise and fall in sales in any particular year. The curve shown is only the average of the experience of many years. In any given year, biweekly sales might vary ±25 percent from levels they would assume if a smooth sales curve existed. The maximum number of 18″ tiles sold in any two-week period between April and October of last year was 4,550. The similar figure for 36″ tiles was 2,000. Major fluctuations in annual levels of sales and mix were caused by economic conditions.

EXHIBIT 1

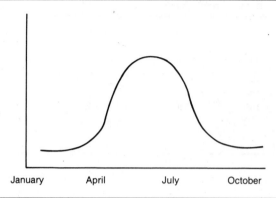

In the game you are about to play, Period 1 refers to the first two weeks in April. Thus, company sales are just leaving the low part of the annual swing. The game culminates in Period 12, the last two weeks in September. At this point sales are reentering the low winter period. Between Periods 1 and 12, sales follow the general shape of the curve shown in Exhibit 1.

All sales made by Lamson are booked for delivery within the period being considered. That is, there is no advance ordering. Mr. Marino has no idea what the sales for any coming period will be other than from judgment of the sales level of prior periods and from consideration of the general shape of the sales trend curve.

Production Constraints

The most popular sizes of concrete tile sold by Lamson were the 18″ diameter and the 36″ diameter sizes. Mr. Marino had found that together these tiles accounted for a large part of tile sales; in fact, roughly one half of each period's production was devoted to one or other of these sizes. The other half of each period's production was used for the other sizes of tiles produced by Lamson. In order to simplify the game, it has been assumed that Mr. Marino will continue to schedule the production of the less popular eleven tile sizes and that he will use half the production time each period for these sizes. Each participating group will be asked to schedule the numbers of 18″ and 36″ tile to be produced during each period. Thus, each group will in fact schedule the production of a summer season's supply of 18″ and 36″-diameter tile.

There are nine possible volume combinations of 18″ and 36″ tile for the output of the tile-making machines. Four of these output values involved the normal capacity output of the plants. The other five values called for 50 percent overtime production (50 percent overtime represented maximum output possible for Lamson).

The nine production levels possible for 18″ and 36″ tile in each two-week period are shown in Exhibit 2.

Please notice that tradeoffs are involved in choosing a production level for a period. If the number of 18″ tiles to be produced is increased, the number of 36″ tiles that can be produced will necessarily decrease unless overtime is used.

EXHIBIT 2   The Nine Possible Production Choices Open to Mr. Marino
Each Two-Week Period

Normal Capacity		50% Overtime	
18" Tiles	*36" Tiles*	*18" Tiles*	*36" Tiles*
6,000	0	9,000	0
4,000	600	7,000	600
2,000	1,200	5,000	1,200
0	1,800	3,000	1,800
		1,000	2,400

Costs Involved

Inventory Costs.   In deciding on production alternatives, Mr. Marino bore in mind several costs which he knew to be fairly accurate. For instance, storage costs of 18" tile for one period were an average of $2.00. This amount took into account interest on tied-up capital, insurance against breakage, and direct handling expense. The inventory carrying costs on each 36" tile were higher and averaged $6.00 per tile per period. Mr. Marino had found that over the period of a season, inventory carrying charges could reasonably be calculated on the basis of inventory on hand at the end of each period.

Stockout Costs.   Stockout costs also had to be considered by Mr. Marino. A stockout occurred whenever a sale in a particular period could not be filled because there were insufficient tiles of the required diameter on hand or in production during that period. For instance, if 100 tiles were on hand at the beginning of a period, 2,000 tiles were produced during the period, and sales during the period totaled 2,200, then a stockout of 100 tiles would occur. When such a stockout occurred, there was a chance that a future customer of Lamson would be lost. Furthermore, Lamson lost the profit potential on the missed order. Mr. Marino had assessed the risks and costs involved and thought that a stockout cost Lamson $20 for each 18" tile and $60 for each 36" tile. This figure took into account the fact that the larger the number of tiles that could not be delivered, the more apt the customer was to take future business elsewhere. Stockouts could not be made up in subsequent periods. If a stockout occurred, the sale was lost forever to the firm and the above costs were incurred.

Overtime Costs.   If overtime was used in any period, a fixed charge of $20,000 was incurred. This charge was used mainly to pay extra wages to the employees. The amount was fixed because the employees had been guaranteed a minimum amount each period overtime was used.

How to Play the Game

In the actual conduct of this game, teams will be used to make the production decisions normally made by Mr. Marino regarding the 18" and 36" diameter tile.

Before each period, each team will be required to decide on the production level that will be used in the plant. This decision will be made by the team by whatever means it chooses. Thus, a prediction from a plot of past period sales might be used by some teams, a pure guess by others. In making the decision, teams will want to consider both the possibilities of future sales and the inventories of tiles now on hand.

After each team has decided on the production level it desires for the coming period, the instructor will announce what sales have been for this period. Given this information, teams will then be able to calculate inventory on hand, inventory, stockout, and overtime costs. These add up to a total period cost which is added to a cumulative total of costs.

The object of the game is to keep the total costs incurred over 12 periods to a minimum. This means that teams will have to decide whether it would be cheaper in the long run to incur overtime costs, inventory carrying costs, or stock-out costs. It is impossible to avoid all three. At the end of the 12th period the game will be stopped and final costs figured. Your team's results will be compared to those of other teams. During subsequent discussions the merits of various inventory and production policies can be evaluated. Teams will probably find it advantageous to split the work of making sales estimates, calculating costs and keeping records among the various members.

Result Form Used.   To make the keeping of results easier for all teams, Exhibit 3 will be used. The exact steps in using this form are:

1. Decide on the production level to be used in the forthcoming period.

2. Enter number of tiles to be produced in Columns A (18″) and J (36″).

3. Fill in stock on hand at start of period in Columns B (18″) and K (36″). These figures come from Columns E (18″) and N (36″) of the previous period.

4. Enter total stock available for sale in the period in Columns C and L.
   Entry in Column C (18″ tiles) = Entry in Column A +
   Entry in Column B.
   Entry in Column L (36″ tiles) = Entry in Column J +
   Entry in Column K.

5. Obtain actual sales in period from Instructor. Enter in Columns D (18″) and M (36″).

6. Compute inventory remaining at the end of the period. Enter in Columns E and N.
   Entry in Column E (18″ tiles) = Entry in Column C −
   Entry in Column D.
   Entry in Column N (36″ tiles) = Entry in Column L −
   Entry in Column M.
   Enter zero if an entry is calculated as negative. There can be no negative inventory on hand.

7. Compute inventory carrying costs and enter in Columns F and O.
   Entry in Column F (18″ tiles) = $2.00 × No. in Column E.
   Entry in Column O (36″ tiles) = $6.00 × No. in Column N.

8. Computer stockouts incurred in period, enter in Columns G and P if zero or a positive number. Enter zero if an entry is calculated as negative; there can be no negative stockouts.

Entry in Column G (18″ tiles) = Entry in Column D −
Entry in Column C.
Entry in Column P (36″ tiles) = Entry in Column M −
Entry in Column L.

9. Compute stockout costs, enter in Columns H and Q.

10. Compute total period inventory cost, enter in Column R.
Entry in Column R = Entry in Column F (18″ tiles) + Entry in Column O (36″ tiles).

11. Compute total period stockout costs, enter in Column S.
Entry in Column S = Entry in Column H (18″ tiles) + Entry in Column Q (36″ tiles).

12. If overtime was used, enter $20,000 in Column T. If no overtime used, enter zero.

13. Compute total period cost and enter in Column U. Entry in Column U = Entry in Column R (total period inventory cost) + Entry in Column S (total period stockout cost) + Entry in Column T (overtime cost).

14. Compute cumulative total to date, enter in Column V. Entry in Column V = Entry in Column U for current period + Entry in Column V for last period.

Example.   Each team member should carefully trace the proceedings as outlined in the following example to understand fully all of the steps involved in playing and recording the game.

Mr. Marino has already used the form to record the operating results of the two periods prior to the first period for which you will be required to decide the production level (Period 1). Lamson started Period 1 with 400 18″ tiles (Column B) and 100 36″ tiles on hand (Column K). Because he knew that a special, large order for 18″ tiles would be placed in Period 1 (a most unusual size of order at this time of year), Mr. Marino decided to go to overtime and to produce 7,000 18″ tiles (Column A) and 600 36″ tiles (Column J). Thus 7,400 18″ tiles (Column C) and 700 36″ tiles (Column L) were available for sales during Period 1.

In actual fact, the special order was smaller than Mr. Marino had anticipated and total sales turned out to be 6,000 for the 18″ tiles (Column D) and 800 for the 36″ tiles (Column M). Because 18″ inventory available for sale exceeded sales, Mr. Marino entered 1,400 in Column E to show there was inventory remaining at the end of the period, and then entered zero in Column G to show that there had been no stockout of 18″ tiles. Column F then shows the inventory cost incurred by having 1,400 18″ tiles on hand at the end of the period ($2.00 × 1400 = $2800.00). Column H shows that no stockout cost was incurred. Because demand for the 36″ tiles (800) exceeded the total available for sale (700), a stockout of 100 occurred and no tiles were left in inventory at the end of Period 1. To show this, zero was entered in Column N and 100 was entered in Column P. There was a zero inventory carrying cost entered in Column O while a stockout cost of $6,000 was entered in Column Q ($60 × 100 = $6,000).

The total inventory carrying cost ($2,800 + 0 = $2,800) was entered in Column R and the total stockout cost (0 + $6,000 = $6,000) was entered in Column S. A sum of $20,000 was entered in Column T because overtime was used. The total

EXHIBIT 3

Number	MONTH	(A) Number produced	(B) Stock on hand at start of period	(C) Total available for sale (C=A+B)	(D) Sales in period	(E) Inventory remaining at end of period (E=C−D) (Minimum=0)	(F) Inventory carrying cost ($2 × E)	(G) Number of stock-outs (G=D−C if greater than 0)	(H) Stock-out cost (H=$20 × G)	(J) Number produced	(K) Stock on hand at start of period	(L) Total available for sale (L=J+K)	(M) Sales in period	(N) Inventory remaining at end of period (N=L−M) (Minimum=0)	(O) Inventory carrying cost ($6 × N)	(P) Number of stock-outs (P=M−L if greater than 0)	(Q) Stock-out cost (Q=$60 × P)	(R) Total inventory cost (R=F+O)	(S) Total stock-out cost (S=H+Q)	(T) Overtime cost $20,000 (if used)	(U) Total period cost (U=R+S+T)	(V) Cumulative total to date
						18″ Tiles								**36″ Tiles**						**TOTALS**		
−1	March	7,000	400	7,400	6,000	1,400	$2,800	0	0	600	100	700	800	0	0	100	6,000	$2,800	$6,000	$20,000	$28,800	(28,800)
0	August	2,000	1,400	3,400	1,400	2,000	$4,000	0	0	1,200	0	1,200	500	700	4,200	0	0	$8,200	0	0	$ 8,200	(37,000)
1	April	1000	2000	3000	2250	750	1500	0	0	2400	700	3100	750	2350	5700		0	7200	0			
2	April	100	1750	2750	2300	450	900	0	0	2350	2350	4700	1500		6700							
3	May				3200					1800			1450									
4	May	3000			4500								1850									
5	June				4200								1700									
6	June				5850								2100									
7	July				4500								1700									
8	July				3200								2000									
9	August				4550								2050									
10	August				460								1830									
11	September																					
12	September				1900								900									
	Total																					

period cost was calculated to be $2,800 + $6,000 + $20,000 = $28,800. This amount was then entered in Column U and also Column V.

Lamson began Period O with 1,400 18″ tiles (Column B) and zero 36″ tiles on hand (Column K). These totals had been brought down from Columns E and N respectively of Period 1. At the beginning of Period O, Mr. Marino elected to produce 2,000 18″ tiles (Column A) and 1,200 36″ tiles (Column J). No overtime was called for. Thus there were 3,400 18″ tiles (Column C) and 1,200 36″ tiles (Column L) available for sale in Period O.

In Period O, sales totaled 1,400 18″ tiles (Column D) and 500 36″ tiles (Column M). Thus the inventory remaining at the end of the period was 2,000 18″ tiles (Column E) and 700 36″ tiles (Column N). There were zero stockouts (Columns G and P). Inventory carrying costs were computed to be $2.00 × 2,000 = $4,000 (Column F) and $6.00 × 700 = $4,200 (Column O). There were no stockout costs (Column H and Q) because stockouts equalled zero in this period.

The total inventory carrying cost for Period O was $8,200 ($4,000 + $4,200). This amount was entered in column R, while zero was entered in Column S since there had been no stockouts in the period. There was no overtime used, consequently a zero was entered in Column T. The Column U entry shows that the total period costs incurred were $8,200. The Column V entry was $28,800 + $8,200 = $37,000. Since your team did not incur these costs, we will wipe them off the slate and have you start with a zero cost at the beginning of Period 1 in Column V.

A Few Operating Rules During the Game

1. The only production combinations your team may choose are those given in Exhibit 2.

2. If your team makes a calculation mistake, a penalty of $25,000 will be assessed and all figures will be corrected.

3. If your team is unable to reach a decision by the time called for by the instructor, it will be automatically be decided that you produce 2,000 18″ tiles and 1,200 36″ tiles.

4. Normally, at the beginning of the game, each team will have approximately 10 minutes to make a decision. This time will decrease as the game progresses.

Start of Game.   The game proper starts in Period 1. At the beginning of the game there are 2,000 18″ tiles on hand (brought down from Column E of Period O) and 700 36″ tiles on hand (brought down from Column N of Period O). It is now up to each team to pick the production level most appropriate for Period 1 and thus start the playing of the game.

CHAPTER 6

Supplier Selection and Supplier Relations

The key decision in supply management centers on supplier selection. Supplier performance has a greater impact on the productivity, quality, and competitiveness of the purchasing organization than most managers realize. Recent trends to buy instead of make, to improve quality, lower inventories, and to integrate supplier and purchaser systems have underlined the need for outstanding supplier performance. Therefore, the supplier selection decision is the single most important decision that can be made in purchasing. Depending on the nature of the purchase, whether it is a repeat, modified repeat, or a new requirement, the size of the dollar amount involved, the market conditions, the criticality or impact of the decision may vary and the selection process and final decision may change. Whereas in the past most buyers felt that the supplier selection decision should be purchasing's domain, today's trend to team purchasing recognizes the necessity to bring key organizational resources outside and inside of the purchasing department together to achieve sound supplier selection decisions. Moreover, the trend to fewer vendors, longer term contracts, electronic data interchange (EDI) and continuing improvement in quality, price, and service requires much closer coordination and communication between various people in both the buying and selling organizations. Therefore, improving buyer-seller relationships is one of the key concerns in the overall area of supplier selection.

Outstanding supplier performance normally requires extensive communication and cooperation between various representatives of the buying organization and the selling organization over a long period of time. In full recognition of this, progressive procurement organizations are pursuing ways and means of limiting their total number of suppliers and maximizing the results from fewer key vendors. Bringing new vendors onstream is expensive and is often accompanied by a period of learning and aggravation for both sides. Frequent supplier switching for the sake of a seemingly lower price may not result in obtaining best long-term value. As quality improvement programs and just-in-time production efforts take hold, proximity of the vendor's premises to those of the purchaser becomes a significant consideration. An imaginative and aggressive supplier development effort, both with existing and new sources, holds high promise as a review of existing vendors discloses gaps and as new technology evolves into new requirements. System compatibility, also, between purchaser and vendor has become more vital as ways and means are found to speed up the time taken from requisition to actual receipt of order.

These exciting new approaches to supplier selection and relationships between vendors and purchasers are in stark contrast to the old-fashioned hard-nosed way of procurement. It used to be reasonably common that suppliers were dropped with little notice when they failed to provide the lowest quote on an annual contract. The ideas of sharing information and assisting vendors to improve quality, quantity, delivery, price, and service performance were rather novel in the past two decades. Nevertheless, the supplier selection decision (and the decision to stay with an existing source, rather than try an untested new vendor) remains the focal point in the procurement process.

Make or Buy

A critical strategic decision for any organization centers on the issue of make or buy. The whole character of the organization may be colored by the organization's stance on this decision. It is one of vital importance to an organization's productivity and competitiveness. Also, it appears that current managerial thinking on this issue is starting to change. Traditionally, the make option tended to be favored by many large organizations, resulting in backward integration, and ownership of a large range of manufacturing and subassembly facilities. Purchases were largely confined to raw materials, which were then processed in-house. New management trends favoring flexibility and focus on corporate strengths, closeness to the customer, and increased emphasis on productivity and competitiveness, reinforce the idea of buying outside. It would be very unusual if any one organization was superior to competition in all aspects of manufacturing. By buying outside from capable suppliers those requirements for which the buying organization has no special manufacturing advantage, the management of the buying organization can concentrate better on its main mission. This philosophy has already resulted in the divestiture of many divisions in large multinational firms and has created an expanded scope for purchasing in the process. With the world as a marketplace, it is the purchaser's responsibility to search for or develop world class suppliers suitable for the strategic needs of the buying organization. For example, Japanese automobile manufacturers purchase up to 40 percent more outside than their North American or Western European counterparts. They also expend extensive development efforts to ensure their suppliers meet stringent quality, delivery, and price objectives.

A recent North American phenomenon has been the tendency to purchase services outside that were traditionally in-house. These include some of the more traditional services such as security, food services, and maintenance, but also computer programming, training, engineering, accounting, legal, research, and personnel. Thus, a new class of purchases involving services has evolved. (For a full description of the purchase of services, see Chapter 15.)

The make-or-buy decision is an interesting one because of its many dimensions. Almost every organization is faced with it continually. For manufacturing companies the make alternative may be a natural extension of activities already present or an opportunity for diversification. For non-manufacturing concerns it is normally a question of services rather than products. Should a hospital have its own laundry, operate its own dietary, security, and maintenance services, or should it purchase these outside? Becoming one's own supplier is an alternative that has not received much attention in this text so far, and yet it is a vital point in every organization's procurement strategy.

What should be the attitude of an organization toward this make-or-buy issue? Many organizations do not have a consciously expressed policy with reference to this issue but prefer to decide each issue as it arises. Moreover, it can be difficult to gather clean accounting data for economic analysis to support such decisions.

If it were possible to discuss the question in the aggregate for the individual firm, the problem should be formulated in terms of: "What should our organization's objective be in terms of how much value added as a percentage of final product or service cost and in what form?" A strong purchasing group, capable of assuring supply at reasonable prices, would favor a buy tendency when other factors are not of overriding importance. For example, one corporation found its purchasing ability in foreign markets such a competitive asset that it deliberately divested itself of certain manufacturing facilities common to every competitor in the industry.

The North American and European steel industries have moved towards divesting themselves of old blast furnaces and steel-making equipment. By purchasing steel slabs from Third World countries at attractive prices, they have been able to concentrate on the high value-added portion of steel finishing and making their organizations more competitive.

Reasons for Make Instead of Buy

There are many reasons that may lead an organization to produce in-house rather than purchase. These include:

1. Occasionally, such small quantities of a special item may be required to make production of it by a vendor prohibitive because of the cost.

2. Manufacture may be undertaken to secure the desired quality.

The quality requirements may be so exacting or so unusual as to require special processing methods that vendors cannot be expected to provide.

3. Manufacture may be undertaken as a means of greater assurance of supply. Under some circumstances, a closer coordination of the supply with the demand is possible when the item is manufactured by the user.

4. In some industries, manufacturers find it essential to make their own equipment because no suitable suppliers exist or because they wish to preserve technological secrets. One large chemical firm owns its own equipment-making plant where about 60 percent of all corporate requirements are manufactured. Experimentation in recent years showed it was possible to subcontract certain parts of equipment to various vendors leaving final assembly and manufacture of particularly sensitive components to the corporation's own shop.

5. It may be cheaper to manufacture than to buy. There are conditions under which a company may temporarily or even permanently produce certain items more cheaply than they can be bought, due consideration being given to transportation and other costs. The volume of certain items used may be so large that it is possible to manufacture them at a production cost as low as that of any accessible supplier and thus to save an amount equivalent to the latter's marketing expense and profit.

6. Particularly in depression or recession, the manufacturer with idle equipment and labor may undertake production, rather than buy, to use surplus production capacity. Even in more normal times, when items of satisfactory quality can be obtained from reliable suppliers, manufacture by the company itself may be undertaken as a means of increasing the total volume of production over which the overhead burden can be distributed.

7. The make-or-buy decision can be an integral part of the overall production plan of a company. Any organization wishing to smooth production or employment can use make or buy as one alternative. If a significant portion of total requirements is purchased, it may be possible to ensure steady running of the corporation's own facilities, leaving the suppliers to bear the burden of fluctuations in demand.

8. Occasionally, although the cost of manufacturing an item may not be any lower for a user than that of vendors from whom it could buy, yet those vendors, through collusion, legislative protection, or unwise pricing policy, may be asking an exorbitant price. A company that is manufacturing even a small part of its requirements is in a strategic position to bargain with such suppliers.

9. The organization may wish to protect the personnel of the company and to maintain the organization. This same contention is used

as an argument against abandoning manufacture, once undertaken, in favor of buying outside. In organizations where hold-the-line policies are in effect with regard to hiring and which simultaneously are seeking to reduce the number of employees by better systems and technological change, normal attrition may not be fast enough to reduce the number of employees. Shifting employees to products or services formerly purchased may be one way to avoid direct firing or layoff costs.

10. Competitive, political, social, or environmental reasons may force a company to make even when it might have preferred to buy. When a competitor acquires ownership of a key source or raw material, it may force similar action. Many countries insist that a certain amount of processing of raw materials be done within national boundaries. A company located in a high unemployment area may decide to make certain items to help alleviate this situation. A company may have to process further certain by-products to make them environmentally acceptable. In each of these instances, cost may not be of overriding concern.

11. Finally, there is a purely emotional reason. The management of some organizations appears to take pride in size.

Dangers Involved in Decision to Manufacture

Thus, there is an imposing list of reasons for undertaking, under the proper circumstances, to manufacture certain items rather than to purchase them. However, dangers involved in this decision include:

1. The organization may lack administrative or technical experience in the production of the items in question, which are often substantially unlike those which the company is manufacturing for sale. What is now proposed assumes that the purchaser can produce this item as a sideline and can do a better job than the original manufacturer.

2. A marketing problem may develop. If the company's requirements for the particular item in question subsequently become less than originally planned for, auxiliary facilities have been built up to meet the larger demand expected; it naturally follows that the company has the option of producing a volume beyond its own requirements and disposing of the surplus in the general market. Under these circumstances the company may actually be confronted by a marketing problem as well as by a technical and an administrative one.

3. There may be a loss of goodwill. To sever business relations with former suppliers may arouse their actual resentment. This may prove particularly serious if the displaced supplier is one through whom the manufacturer's finished product was sold as well as one from whom the manufacturer had bought. Such action is likely to raise the question

in the minds of those companies from which other items are still bought as to how long it will be before they, in turn, are dropped.

4. Frequently, certain suppliers have built such a reputation for themselves that they have been able to build a real preference for their component as part of the finished product. Normally, these are branded items which can be used to make the total piece of equipment more acceptable to the final user. For example, most diesel engine manufacturers buy Bosch or Simms injection pumps, not because they are cheap, or difficult to manufacture, but because the ultimate consumers want them. The manufacturers of road grading equipment and other construction or mining equipment frequently let the customer specify the power plant brand and see this option as advantageous in selling their equipment.

5. Companies wishing to maintain a leading position in their industry must be constantly engaged in some form of research so their product may be continually improved and production costs reduced. A concern that specializes in manufacturing a major line can do this. A company in which that product is merely a sideline can rarely afford to devote the same attention to it; consequently, no matter how great an advantage existed originally, it is likely to be only a matter of time before the company in which such an item is a sideline finds itself outclassed both as to product and as to cost.

6. Closer coordination of inventory with requirements is one of the arguments advanced for manufacturing rather than buying. Actually, this result is not as easy to obtain as might at first appear.

7. A decision to make, once made, is often difficult to reverse. Union pressures and management inertia combine to preserve the status quo.

8. It is difficult to determine the true long-term costs of the make decision. Experience has made it amply clear that once management has definitely committed itself to a policy of procurement by manufacture, it is not difficult for costs to be figured to justify both the original decision and a continuance of the practice.

9. A lack of flexibility in selecting possible sources and substitute items is likely to result.

Thus, it becomes increasingly evident that the make-or-buy decision is often a difficult one and that the decision to manufacture, once made, is likely to place the organization in a position from which it is difficult to withdraw. It is purchasing's responsibility to ensure that the buy alternative is seriously investigated before a make decision is ever made.

The Grey Zone in Make or Buy

Research by Nollet and Leenders[1] suggests that a "grey zone" may exist in make-or-buy situations. There may be a range of options between 100 percent make or 100 percent buy. This middle ground may be particularly useful for testing and learning without having to make the full commitment to make or buy. Particularly, in the purchase of services where no equipment investment is involved, it may be that substantial economies accrue to the organization that can substitute low cost internal labor for expensive outside help or low cost external labor for expensive inside help.

Further research into the role of manufacturing engineering by Paul Coughlan of Ireland suggests an interesting make-or-buy implication. To what extent should the purchasing company's engineering group get involved in specifying processes and work layouts for a subcontractor or a supplier? Thus, the purchaser's own manufacturing engineering group can combine its efforts with an outside supplier who basically supplies space, equipment, and labor. Whether a lack of manufacturing engineering strength on the part of the supplier is a desirable longer term situation is open to debate. Moreover, overspecification of processes and equipment by the buyer's manufacturing engineers may prevent innovative process or product solutions by the vendor.

Given the changing emphasis towards buying outside or outsourcing, the middle ground or grey zone in make-or-buy may offer valuable opportunities or superior options for both purchaser and supplier.

SUBCONTRACTING

In its simplest form a subcontract is a purchase order written with more explicit terms and conditions. Its complexity and management varies in direct proportion to the value and size of the program to be managed. The management of a subcontract may require unique skills and abilities because of the amount and type of correspondence, charts, program reviews and management reporting which are necessary. Additionally, payment may be handled differently and is usually negotiated along with the actual pricing and terms and conditions of the subcontract.

The use of a subcontract is appropriate when placing orders for work which is difficult to define, will take a long period of time and will be extremely costly. For example, aerospace companies subcontract many of the larger structural components and avionics. Wings, landing gears, and radar systems are examples of high cost items which might be purchased on a subcontract. A similar form of subcontracting is often used in the

---

[1]M. R. Leenders and J. Nollet. "The Grey Zone in Make or Buy," *Journal of Purchasing and Materials Management,* Fall, 1984, pp. 10-15.

construction industry where a building contractor might subcontract the electrical or plumbing of a building or project.

In the aerospace industry the subcontract is normally administered by a team which might include:

Subcontract Administrator (SCA).   Provides the business management skills for the team. The SCA is responsible for all matters which affect cost or schedule. Contractual matters are controlled by the SCA as is all correspondence to the supplier.

Equipment Engineer.   Provides technical guidance to the supplier through the SCA; turns requirements into specifications and drawings, and assists in the preparation and maintenance of the Statement of Work; chairs design reviews and is involved in all technical interfaces with the supplier.

Quality Assurance Representative.   Assures that the supplier has an acceptable quality plan, provides on-site inspection and acceptance of goods; coordinates quality problems and waivers with the Equipment Engineer.

Reliability Engineer.   Ensures that reliability requirements are suitable for the procurement at hand and that the supplier complies; establishes the level of reliability for the hardware being purchased; generates reliability documents and approves supplier-generated documents.

Material Price/Cost Analyst.   Assists the SCA in preparation of the cost proposal; analyzes and evaluates supplier submittals and assists the Subcontract Administrator in the negotiation.

Program Office Representative.   Provides direction and assistance to the supplier concerning schedule preparation, reporting, and control through the SCA; maintains internal schedule and cost control for the program; is the normal customer contact between the purchasing organization and the ultimate customer.

On-Site Representative.   Attends supplier status meetings and provides on-site assistance for quality, engineering, shortage, and cost problems.

Managing the subcontract is a complex activity which requires knowledge about performance to date as well as the ability to anticipate actions needed to ensure the desired end results. The SCA must maintain cost, schedule, technical, and configuration control from the beginning to the completion of the task.

Cost control of the subcontract begins with the negotiation of a fair and reasonable cost, proper choice of the contract type, and thoughtfully imposed incentives. Schedule control requires the development of a good master schedule which covers all necessary contract activities realistically. Well designed written reports and recovery programs, where necessary, are essential. Technical control must be instigated to ensure that the end product conforms to all the performance parameters of the specifications which were established at the award of the contract. Configuration control assures that all changes are documented. Good configuration control is essential to "aftermarket" and spares considerations for the product.

Unlike a normal purchase order of minimal complexity where final closeout may be accomplished by delivery and payment, a major subcontract involves more definite actions to close. These actions vary with the contract type and difficulty of the item/task being procured. Quite often large and complex procurements require a number of changes during the period of performance. These changes result in cost claims which must be settled prior to contract closure. Additionally, any tooling or data supplied to the contractor to support the effort must be returned. All deliverable material, data, and reports must be received and inspected. Each subcontract's requirements will vary in the complexity of the closure requirements; however, in all cases a subcontract performance summary should be written to provide a basis for evaluation of the supplier for future bidder or supplier selection. Such a report also is necessary in providing information for subsequent claims or renegotiation.

THE SUPPLIER SELECTION DECISION

For the remainder of this chapter, the assumption will be made that the decision to place a certain volume of business with a supplier should always be based on a reasonable set of criteria. The art of good purchasing is to make the reasoning behind this decision as sound as possible. Normally, the purchaser's perception of the vendor's ability to meet satisfactory quality, quantity, delivery, price, and service objectives will govern this decision. Some of the more important vendor attributes related to these prime purchasing objectives may include past history, facilities and technical strength, financial status, organization and management, reputation, systems, procedural compliance, communications, labor relations, and location. Obviously, the nature and the amount of the purchase will influence the weighting attached to each objective and hence the evidence that needs to be provided to support the selection decision. For example, for a small order of new circuit boards to be used by engineers in a new product design, the quality and rapid delivery are of greater significance than price. The vendor should probably be local for ease of communication with the design engineers and have good technical credentials. On the other hand, a large printed circuit board order for a production run would have price as one of the key factors, and delivery should be on time, but not necessarily unusually fast.

FIGURE 6–1 A Simple One-Stage Supplier Selection Decision

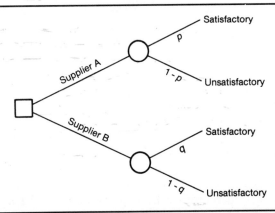

Thus, even on requirements with identical technical specifications, the weighting attached to the vendor selection criteria may vary. It is this sensitivity to organizational needs that separates the good buyer from the average. The one result every buyer wishes to avoid is unacceptable vendor performance. This may create costs far out of proportion to the size of the original purchase, it upsets interdepartmental relations, and it strains vendor goodwill.

Research into the risk assessment behavior of buyers shows that the perceived risk of placing business with an untried and unknown supplier is high. A distinction between routine, repetitive purchases, and less standard acquisitions needs to be made. The risk is seen to be higher with unknown materials, parts, or equipment, and with increased dollar amounts. Buyers attempt to share this risk with others by asking for advice, such as engineering judgment, and by seeking additional information, which includes the placing of a trial order.

The vendor selection decision can be seen as decision making under uncertainty and can be represented by a decision tree. Figure 6–1 shows a very simple, one-stage situation with only two suppliers seriously considered and two possible outcomes. It illustrates, however, the uncertain environment present in almost every supplier choice and the risk inherent in the decision. To use decision trees effectively, the buyer needs to identify the options, the criteria for evaluation, and assess the probabilities of success and failure. This simple tree could apply to a special one-time purchase without expectation of follow-on business for some time to come.

The more normal situation for repetitive purchases is shown in Figure 6–2. Whether the chosen source performs well or not for the current purchase under consideration, the future decision about which supplier to deal with next time around may well affect the present decision. For example, if the business is placed with supplier C and C fails, then this may mean that only A could be considered a reasonable source at the next stage. If

FIGURE 6–2   Simplified Three-Stage Decision Tree for Supplier Selection

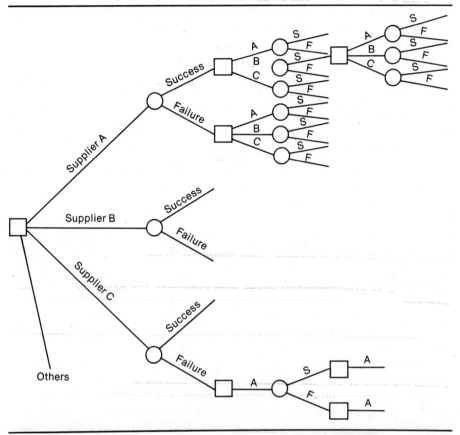

having A as a sole source, without alternatives, is not acceptable, choosing C as the supplier at the first stage does not make any sense.

It is necessary to consider the selection decision as part of a chain of events, rather than as an isolated instance. This addition of a time frame—past, present, and future—makes the sourcing decision even more complex. However, as long as the objective of finding and keeping good sources is clearly kept in mind, the decision can be evaluated in a reasonable business context. It is useful, therefore, at this point to examine the attributes of a good supplier before raising the question as to where good sources may be found.

Good or Preferred Suppliers

A good or preferred supplier should be one that provides the quality specified and delivers on time as promised; has an acceptable price; and reacts to unforeseen needs such as: suddenly accelerated or decelerated volumes of business, changes in specifications, service problems, and any other legitimate requests. The good supplier takes the initiative in suggesting better ways of serving customers and attempts to find new ways of developing products and services which will allow customers to perform their operations more economically. The good supplier will warn ahead of time of material shortages, strikes, and anything else that may affect the purchaser's operations. It will provide technological and other expertise when requested by customers or when the supplier believes it could assist the purchaser. It will remain competitive on a continuing basis. Suppliers like this are hard to find. In many industries there may only be one, two, or three that fit this bill. The art of a good purchasing department is to find and keep top suppliers over time. In fact, purchasing could be defined as the fight for good suppliers.

Many of the qualities listed in the earlier mentioned requirements create additional cost for the supplier in the short run. To make it worthwhile for the supplier to incur these costs, there must be assurance that special care will be rewarded with additional future business. The greatest reward a customer can give is assurance of future business in response to satisfactory performance. It is important to avoid a very high and rapid supplier turnover. Occasionally, preferred suppliers have been given the axe on the basis of incomplete information. The reactions of suppliers are understandable if they lose the next order after they have gone to great lengths to please a customer's special demands in terms of overtime, quick delivery, or unusual quality because someone else bids a few hundred dollars lower. Every supplier switch costs the customer something. Quality assurance needs to inspect the new premises, new contacts need to be established with supplier personnel, and new data inputs are required for the various computer systems. A supplier switch may well have substantial costs attached, depending on the commodity and supplier. If a supplier does not have the expectation of getting a contract renewal it may well choose not to make long-term raw material commitments so necessary to the continued running of the business. If purchasing is late in terms of contract renewal, even continuing with the same source may result in a period of stockouts. Although uncertainty regarding future business is certainly one of purchasing's powerful tools to keep suppliers on their toes, it does have its drawbacks. Should some of the current predictions regarding shortages of basic raw materials hold up, some customers may well be in a very difficult position when suppliers establish priorities of customers on vital requirements.

Suppose that the earlier premise is granted. The real danger clearly lies in becoming puppets of suppliers. Suppliers know that customers depend on them, and they may charge excessively or let quality or delivery slip, or slow down or stop continuing improvement programs. As an aside, it is ironic that many purchasers who buy from other divisions within a multidivisional organization find that these divisions give their captive in-house customers low priority. This is where careful supplier management becomes important. In the first place, it requires an understanding and identification of value. Value is the ultimate long-term cost to the user of the product or service acquired. It does not mean lowest purchase price, or lowest investment in inventory, or fastest delivery time, or lowest delivery cost, or longest life, or highest disposal value, or even the highest attainable quality; it is an optimal amount cutting across all of these. The purchase price frequently is one important part of this total. Second, it is the duty of the purchasing department to make sure that the price quoted is reasonable in view of the total set of circumstances surrounding the purchase and represents good long-term value.

Supplier Goodwill

Good sources of supply are one assurance of good quality production today, and progressive thinking and planning is a further assurance of improved quality tomorrow. Superior sources of supply, therefore, are an important asset to any organization.

It has long been considered sound marketing policy to develop goodwill on the part of customers toward the seller. This goodwill has been cultivated through the development of trademarks and brands, through extensive advertising, through missionary efforts as well as through regular calls by sales personnel, and through the many other devices which have appealed to the imaginations of marketing managers. Sellers are jealous of this goodwill, considering it one of their major assets. It has real commercial value and is so recognized by courts of law.

Goodwill between a company and its suppliers needs to be just as carefully cultivated and just as jealously guarded. When purchasing directors and the management behind such directors are as aggressive in their attempts to maintain proper and friendly relations with suppliers as sales managers are in their relations with customers, many a costly error will be avoided. Failure to maintain these relations is often more serious than is sometimes believed. Companies have even been forced to engage in the manufacture of their own supplies because of an unwise attitude toward former sources of supply. Since strategic plans are so often based on the assumption that supply sources will be cooperative, it makes sense to assure that such cooperation will be forthcoming.

No matter how carefully a purchasing, using, or production department may plan, it is inevitable that emergencies will arise and that actual needs will be different from anticipated requirements. In these circumstances the purchaser will receive a more favorable response from vendors who perceive the purchaser as a valuable customer. The shortages of many basic materials in recent years had the most serious effects on companies which had ignored developing good vendor relations during past periods of buyers' markets. The purchasing manual from a large corporation states:

The purchasing department has more contacts with other companies than any other department except sales. An opinion of a company is formed by contacts with its employees. The buyer has it in his or her hands to enhance or detract from the company's good name in his or her relations with vendors and their sales representatives and has a major responsibility to form a good reputation for the company and for the goodwill it commands.

Another manual states:

Friendship can be cultivated even through the very manner in which a sales representative is told that he or she has lost, or cannot have, an order. These may seem small things, but courtesy, square dealing, honesty, and straightforwardness beget friendship and respect. They are appreciated by sellers, and the buyer benefits largely from them.

Mindful of the characteristics of a good supplier, and the necessity for supplier goodwill, it is now appropriate to turn to the problem of locating sources.

Sources of Information about Suppliers

Knowledge of sources is a primary qualification for any effective buyer. Some buyers rely solely on their experience and memory for their knowledge of sources. Perhaps in a very limited number of instances, this practice may be satisfactory; when the requirements are exceedingly simple or obtainable from a limited number of suppliers, it may not be worthwhile to maintain elaborate supplier records. These cases, however, are so few as to be almost negligible. The normal principal sources consist of catalogs (both printed and microfilm), trade journals, advertisements of various sorts, vendor and commodity directories, salespeoples' interviews, and the purchasing department's own records.

Catalogs.   Catalogs of the commonly known sources of supply, covering the most important materials in which a company is interested, are properly considered essential in any well-managed purchasing office. The value of such catalogs depends largely on the form in which they are presented (a matter for the most part beyond the control of the buyer), the readiness with which the material contained in them is available, and the use which is made of such information.

Jobbers' catalogs contain many items from a variety of manufacturing sources and offer, to a certain extent, a directory of available commodities within the jobbers' fields. Equipment and machinery catalogs provide information as to the specifications of, and the location of a source of supply for, replacement parts as well as new equipment.

Catalogs frequently provide price information. Many supplies and materials are sold from standard list prices, and quotations are made by quoting discounts only. Catalogs are also reference books called for by department heads and engineers.

The availability of the material in the catalogs is largely a matter of the manner in which they are indexed and filed, a not-so-simple task. Catalogs are issued in all sorts of sizes and in binders which make them difficult to handle.

In some cases all catalogs, regardless of size, thickness, or specification are filed together. In other cases catalogs are grouped and filed in comparable sizes, as nearly as can be. The identification of individual catalogs is commonly achieved by numbering them consecutively, frequently with the number pasted on the back of the catalog. A number of influential associations have endorsed a standard size of $7\frac{3}{4} \times 10\frac{5}{8}$, among them the National Association of Purchasing Management, American Society of Mechanical Engineers, Southern Supply and Machinery Dealers Association, and Automotive Jobbers Association. The general use of a standard size would simplify the filing problem.

Proper indexing of catalogs is essential. Some firms use loose-leaf ledgers with sheets especially printed for catalog filing; others use a form of card index. Indexing should be according to suppliers' names as well as products listed. It should be specific, definite, and easily understandable.

A proper catalog has the advantage of being a permanent record, always in the office of the buyer. Salespeople are not always available; advertisements are frequently forgotten; but the catalog is an ever-present reminder of the existence of the vendor issuing it.

Microfilm Files. Several companies have issued catalogs of suppliers with all information recorded on microfilm. An example of this service is that provided by VSMF (Visual Search Microfilm File). Information about more than 3,100 suppliers and their products serving the aerospace and electronics industries has been recorded on over 100,000 frames of 16 mm. microfilm. A comprehensive indexing system, a reader for the films, and a printer which permits a full-size sheet reproduction of the information on the film are included in the service.

Trade Journals. Trade journals also are a valuable source of information as to potential suppliers. The list of such publications is, of course, very long, and the individual items in it vary tremendously in value. Yet, in every field there are worthwhile trade magazines, and buyers read extensively those dealing with their own industry and with those industries to which they sell and from which they buy. These journals are utilized in two ways. The first use is a study of the text, which not only adds to buyer's general information but suggests new products and substitute materials. The trade gossip provides information about suppliers and their personnel. The second use has to do with advertising. A consistent perusal of the advertisements in such publications is a worthwhile habit cultivated by all keen buyers.

Industrial Advertising. As a general source of information to the purchasing officer, the exact value of industrial advertising is a matter of dispute. Advertising people generally, even professional teachers of the subject, are definite in their opinion that in spite of many weaknesses, industrial advertising has value; buyers generally read it and are, perhaps unconsciously, influenced by it.

Trade Directories. Trade directories are another useful source of information. They vary widely in their accuracy and usefulness, and care must be exercised in their use.

Trade registers, or trade directories, are volumes which list leading manufacturers, their addresses, number of branches, affiliations, products, and, in some instances, their financial standing or their position in the trade. They also contain listings of the trade names of articles on the market with names of the manufacturers, and classified lists of materials, supplies, equipment, and other items offered for sale, under each of which is given the name and location of available manufacturing sources of supply.

These registers, then, are so arranged that they may be consulted either by way of the commodity, the manufacturer, or the trade name.

Such standard directories as, for example, *Thomas' Register of American Manufacturers* and *MacRae's Blue Book* and the Kompass publications in Europe, not to mention the more specialized directories, serve a useful purpose. The yellow pages of telephone directories provide lists of local suppliers.

Sales Representation and Ethical Conduct. Sales representation may constitute one of the most valuable sources of information available, with references to sources of supply, types of products, and trade information generally. An alert buyer makes it a point to see as many sales representatives as possible without neglecting other duties. It is essential to develop good supplier relations which begin with a friendly, courteous, sympathetic, and frank attitude toward the vendor salesperson. The buyer should endeavor not to waste any time. After the visit, a record is made of the call together with new information obtained. Some purchasers make it a point to see personally every sales representative who calls at the office; others, because of lack of time and the pressure of other duties, are unable to follow such a rule, but they do make sure that someone interviews every visitor in order that no one may go away feeling rebuffed. The representative who receives brusque treatment is less likely to make extra effort to render special services or to offer new ideas readily.

Most organizations have policies and procedures guidelines concerning the relations between the purchasing office and vendors' representatives. Purchasing and materials management associations in many countries around the world have adopted their own codes of ethics governing the relationship between vendor and purchaser. All of them are based on the requirement that both vendor and purchaser need to deal ethically with one another to assure a sound basis for business dealings. Thus, courtesy, honesty, and fairness are stressed and buyers are urged to behave in such a fashion as to reflect the organization's wishes. Normally, this includes seeing vendors without delay, to be truthful in all statements, to cover all elements of procurement in order that the final understanding may be complete, to not ask vendors to quote unless they have a reasonable chance at the business, to keep specifications fair and clear and competition open and fair, to respect the confidence of vendors with regard to all confidential information, not to take advantage improperly of sellers' errors, to cooperate with vendors in solving their difficulties and to negotiate prompt and fair adjustment in cases of dispute. It is also expected that a buyer be courteous in stating rejection of bids with explanations that are reasonable, but not to betray confidential information, to answer letters promptly and to handle samples, tests, and reports with prompt, complete, and truthful information. Lastly, all codes of ethics stress a need to avoid all obligations to sellers except strict business obligations.

Occasionally, sales representatives attempt to bypass purchasing because they believe it may be to their advantage to do so. Such attempts are unfortunate from everyone's point of view. If the vendor secures an order without the knowledge and agreement of purchasing, internal dissension may be created, as well as resentment against the sales representative. The short-term gain may turn into a long-term loss. Although purchasing personnel are expected to be well acquainted with the organization's operation, equipment, materials, and its varied requirements, and to be qualified to pass on the practicality of suggestions and proposals that may be made by sales representatives and technical people, the purchaser does not, as a rule, have the background that constitutes the basis for the technical person's special knowledge. Therefore, it is often necessary to refer such proposals to others better qualified to handle them. However, the best way to reach the right people in any organization is through purchasing.

Vendor Files.   Information from any source, if of value, should be recorded. One such record has already been mentioned, the index accompanying the catalog file. Another common record is the vendor file, commonly on small cards or simple computer file, classified by names of vendors. Such files contain information concerning the address of the vendor, past orders placed with the company, data concerning its general fitness and reliability and the vendor's willingness to meet the particular requirements of the purchaser, and other pertinent information of any sort that might be of value to the buyer. A third record is a commodity file, in which material is classified on the basis of the product. The information in such files relates to the sources from which the product has been purchased in the past, perhaps the price paid, the point of shipment, and a cross-reference to the vendor file. Miscellaneous information is also given, such as whether specifications are called for, whether a contract already exists covering the item, whether competitive bids are commonly asked for, and such other data as may be of importance. Accompanying such files as those dealing with sources are, of course, those relating to price and other records. Some of these have already been discussed in earlier chapters, and others will be discussed later.

Visits to Suppliers.   Some purchasing executives feel that visits to suppliers are particularly useful when there are no difficulties to discuss. By such friendly visits the purchasing officer frequently can talk with higher executives rather than confining themselves to someone who happens to be directly responsible for handling a specific complaint. This helps to cement good relations at all levels of management and may reveal much about a supplier's future plans that might not otherwise come to attention. Such a visitation policy does raise certain problems not found in the more routine types of visits, such as who should make the visits, how best to get worthwhile information, and the best use to put the data to, once obtained. Experience has indicated that in order to get the best results from such trips, it is desirable (1) to draw up in advance a general outline of the kinds of information to be sought; (2) to gather all reasonably available information, both general and specific, about the company in advance of the trip; and (3) to prepare a detailed report of the findings, once the visit is completed. When the visits are carefully planned, the direct expense incurred is small compared with the returns.

Samples.   In addition to the usual inquiries concerning the potential supplier and to a plant visit, samples of the vendor's product can be tested. Some thought may well be devoted, therefore, to the problem of how to handle what may be called the "sample problem." Frequently a sales representative for a new product urges the buyer to accept a sample for test purposes. This raises questions as to what samples to accept, how to ensure a fair test of those accepted, who should bear the expense of testing, and whether or not the vendor should be given the results of the test.[2]

Narrowing the List

From any or all of these various sources of information, the buyer is able to make up a list of available vendors from whom the items required can be acquired. The next step is to reduce this list to workable length, retaining only the most likely sources of supply. From this short list, the best source (or sources, if more than one are to be used) must be selected. Obviously, the extent to which the investigation and analysis of sources are carried will depend on the cost and the importance of the item involved. A

---

[2]For a discussion of the use of samples, see Chapter 4.

large number of items which the purchasing department is called on to buy are so inexpensive and are consumed in such small quantities as to render any studied investigation unwise.

In reducing the number of potential suppliers to a practical list or in passing on the desirability of a new supplier (either for a new product or for one already being used), it is obvious that an adequate study must be made of each vendor's qualifications. The investigation required may be drawn out and extensive. It may well require joint inquiry by the buyer, cooperating with representatives of using and technical departments such as engineering, quality control, systems, maintenance, and so on.

SUPPLIER EVALUATION

Existing and Potential Sources

The evaluation of suppliers is a continuing purchasing task. Current suppliers have to be monitored to see if expected performance materializes. New sources need to be screened to see if their potential warrants serious future consideration. Since most organizations tend to place a significant portion of repetitive business with the same suppliers, evaluation of current sources will be discussed first.

Informal and Formal Evaluation of Current Suppliers

A current supplier is one which has passed through earlier supplier screening efforts and subsequently received, at a minimum, one order. Most buyers would tend to separate current suppliers into at least two categories. Some vendors are still so new to the supplier force that it is not clear just how good they are. The second group constitutes "established suppliers" who over the past have proven to be reliable, good sources. Both groups are evaluated continuously, formally and informally. Nevertheless, it is common practice to pay extra special attention to those new sources who have not yet established a proven track record of satisfactory performance over time under a variety of market conditions.

Informal Evaluation. Informal evaluation includes assessments of personal contacts between vendor and personnel in the purchaser's organization in all functions where such contact takes place. "How are things going with vendor X?" is a typical question that can and should be asked by purchasing personnel when in contact with others in their own organization. Similarly, street talk obtained at professional meetings, conferences, and from the media can be useful in checking out and comparing such personal impressions. A knowledgeable buyer will have accumulated a wealth of such information on suppliers and will always be on the alert for signs that new information may affect the overall assessment of a vendor. In fact, in most small organizations almost all evaluation of current sources is carried out informally. When users and buyers are in daily personal contact and feedback on both satisfactory and unsatisfactory supplier performance is quick, such informality makes a lot of sense.

In larger organizations, however, communication lines are stretched, purchasers and users may be in totally different locations and large contracts may be agreed to by a head office purchasing group, while daily vendor contact is handled by materials departments at various locations. If vendors are also large, requirements in different locations of the country or the world may be met with varying degrees of success by different plants belonging to the same vendor. As the buying organization grows larger, therefore, the need for formality in evaluating current sources also increases.

Executive Round Table Discussions. One simple semi-formal supplier evaluation tool available is the regular, annual eyeball-to-eyeball discussion between top managers in the purchaser's organization and those of the vendor. Normally, these top-level discussions are confined to major suppliers of major requirements. The presence of top executives of both sides lends weight to the occasion and permits discussion of past performance, future expectations, economic, social, and technological trends, long-term plans, and so on, in a high-level context. The person in charge of the materials function normally makes the arrangements for such sessions and invites the appropriate executives to take part. These round table discussions can help cement relationships between the purchaser and vendor at a high level, and when repeated over time can provide invaluable information for both sides. They would normally, but not exclusively, take place on the purchaser's premises.

Obviously, the number of such high-level sessions must be limited. Equivalent lower-level sessions for vendors further down on the priority list also have considerable merit and permit a regular update in a broader context than the normal vendor-purchaser contacts geared to specific current orders.

Formal Vendor Evaluation and Rating. In evaluating current sources, the obvious question is, "How well did the supplier do?" As orders are delivered, it should be possible to keep track of whether quality, quantity, price, delivery, and service objectives and other terms and conditions were met. Most formal vendor rating schemes attempt to track actual performance over time. Thus, corrective action can be taken as needed. Also, when the time for placing another order arrives, the past record can be used to assess whether the same vendor should again be seriously considered or not.

Most formal vendor rating schemes track vendor performance on quality, price, delivery, and service. A very simple scheme for smaller organizations might include a notation only as to whether these factors were acceptable or not for specific orders received. A somewhat more detailed evaluation might include a summary of supplier performance over time. For example, delivery performance can be summarized as follows:

Top rating:	*a.* Meets delivery dates without expediting.
	b. Requested delivery dates are usually accepted.
Good:	*c.* Usually meets shipping dates without substantial follow-up.
	d. Often is able to accept requested delivery dates.
Fair:	*e.* Shipments sometimes late, substantial amount of follow-up required.
Unsatisfactory:	*f.* Shipments usually late, delivery promises seldom met, constant expediting required.

Actual price performance of a vendor is easily tracked, as discrepancies between agreed-to prices and those actually invoiced by vendors should normally be brought to purchasing's attention anyway. Price ratings of vendors are, therefore, often of a comparison type, actual price versus target, or actual price versus lowest price received from other vendors supplying the same requirement.

It is in the service area that perhaps most judgment is called for. Opinions need to be collected on the quality of technical assistance, vendor attitude and response time to requests for assistance, support staff qualifications, and so on. It is normal, therefore, to have a relatively simple rating scheme for service such as outstanding, acceptable, and poor along with explanations regarding specific incidents to explain these ratings.

Some organizations handicap vendors by assigning points and scales to each factor and each rating. Particularly in cases where several sources supply the same goods or services, such schemes permit cross comparisons. Outstanding performance of a vendor can then be rewarded with additional business, while poor performance will, at the least, result in less business, or possibly dropping a supplier altogether. For example, a relatively simple point system used by a medium-size manufacturer of packaging equipment for its castings and machine parts requirements was as shown in Figure 6–3.

Obviously, the selection of the factors, weights, and form of measurement will require considerable thought to ensure congruence between the organization's priorities for this product class and the rating scheme's ability to identify superior vendors correctly. For different product classes different factors, weights, and measures should probably be used to reflect varying impact on the organization.

FIGURE 6–3 Example of a Vendor Point Rating System

Factor	Weight	How Measured	Vendor Performance Past 12 Months	Rating
Quality	40	1% defective subtracts 5%	0.8% defective	$\dfrac{40(100 - (0.8 \times 5))}{100} = 38.4$
Delivery	30	1 day late subtracts 1%	average 3 days late	$\dfrac{30(100 - (3 \times 1))}{100} = 29.1$
Price	20	$\dfrac{\text{lowest price paid}}{\text{price charged}}$	$\dfrac{\$46}{\$50}$	$\dfrac{20 \, \dfrac{46}{50} \times 100}{100} = 18.4$
Service	10	good = 100% fair = 70% poor = 40%	fair = 70%	$\dfrac{10(70)}{(100)} = 7.0$
Total Points	100			Vendor Rating $\quad$ 92.9

Clearly, most organizations track major suppliers much more closely than those sources deemed to have less impact on organizational performance. Some organizations use annual dollar volume as a guide towards such categorization, for example, identifying A, B, and C sources, much the same as inventories can be classified using the Pareto distribution (see Chapter 5). Some organizations add a special category of "critical" goods or services regardless of dollar volume, where unsatisfactory performance by a vendor might result in serious problems for the purchasing organization. The purpose of such categorization is to fit each category with an appropriate vendor rating scheme. In a fully computerized system, all vendor performance data would be entered as orders were received, and the buyer should have on-line access so as to be able to discuss a particular vendor's performance at any time.

Vendors need to be informed periodically as to how they stand on the rating scale. Improved performance on the part of the supplier often results from the knowledge that its rating is lower than some competitor's.

PURCHASER–SUPPLIER RELATIONS

Certainly one of the major assessments a purchaser must make is whether the current relationship with a supplier is a satisfactory one or not. This relationship is highly complex and different people inside the purchasing organization may have different perceptions of it. In the simplest form, with a new supplier just after a relatively small order has been placed but no deliveries have yet been made, it may consist only of an assessment of the agreement just reached and the buyer's quick impression of the sales representative. For a long-term supplier of major needs the assessment will be based on past and current performance, personal relationships with a number of personnel in both organizations, and even future expectations. Such assessments may well change as a result of competitive action in the marketplace. What may look like a good price deal today may not look so attractive when information comes to light that a fully competent competitor could have supplied the same materials or items for substantially less.

The following model (see Figure 6–4) attempts to provide a simple framework for clarifying the current purchaser-supplier relationship in terms of satisfaction and stability. The assumptions behind it are:

1. That satisfaction with a current supplier relationship can be assessed, however crudely, at least in macro-terms, whether it is satisfactory or not.

2. That an unsatisfied party (seller or purchaser or both) will attempt to move to a more satisfactory situation.

3. That attempts to move may affect the stability of the relationship.

Not important

FIGURE 6–4   A Simple Purchaser-Supplier Satisfaction Model

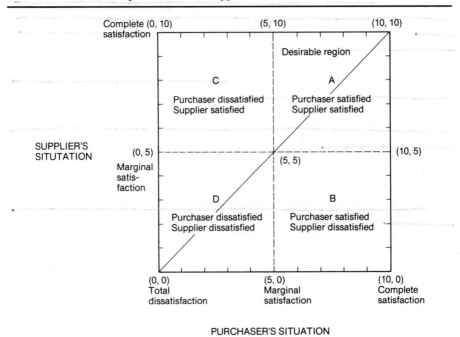

PURCHASER'S SITUATION

4. That attempts to move may fall in the win-lose, as well as the lose-lose, lose-win, and win-win categories.

5. That purchaser and seller may well have different perceptions of the same relationship.

6. That many tools and techniques and approaches exist which will assist either party in moving positions and improving stability.

A. The Upper Right-Hand Quadrant.   (5,5–10,5–10,10–5,10) Region. Considerable satisfaction exists on both sides and stability is likely. Long-term relationships may be built on this kind of foundation. Considerable room for improvement is still possible within this quadrant in moving from a (5,5) situation toward a (10,10) objective.

B. The Lower Right-Hand Quadrant.   (5,0–10,0–10,5–5,5) Region. In this region the buyer is at least marginally satisfied, but the seller is not. This is the mirror image of the C region, and the seller is likely to initiate action for change which may end up subsequently in any of the four regions. Stability is not likely over the long run.

   The above comments are, of course, general in nature. It is entirely possible for a powerful purchaser or a powerful supplier to maintain a B or C region position respectively for a long time with a weak counterpart.

C. **The Upper Left-Hand Quadrant.** (0,5–5,5–5,10–1,10) Region. The supplier is at least marginally satisfied, but the purchaser is not. The purchaser will attempt to improve the buying situation. If this is done at the expense of the seller, a see-saw may be created whereby the purchaser's efforts result in the supplier's moving down the satisfaction scale into the D region. The assumption is that the most dissatisfied party is the most likely instigator of change. It is also possible that such instigations may reduce satisfaction for both parties so that both end up in the D region. Hopefully, changes might result in both parties moving into the A region.

D. **The Lower Left-Hand Quadrant.** (0,0–5,0–5,5–0,5) Region. Both parties agree that significant dissatisfaction exists on both sides. This kind of situation is not likely to be stable for any length of time, since each side will be striving to improve at least its own satisfaction.

The Diagonal Line. The diagonal in the diagram may be seen as a "fairness or stability" line. As long as positions move along this line both purchaser and supplier are at least equally well off. Its end points of (0,0) and (10,10) represent two extremes. The (0,0) position is completely undesirable from either standpoint and is a "total war" picture which is extremely unstable. It represents an unlikely starting point for any long-term stable position since memories of this unhappy state of affairs are likely to prevent substantial improvements. The obvious solution is disassociation and the seeking of a new source by the purchaser.

The (10,10) position represents a utopian view rarely found in reality. It requires a degree of mutual trust and sharing and respect that is difficult to achieve in our society of "buyer beware" and where competition and the price mechanism are supposed to work freely. In some systems contracting and just-in-time production situations, a relationship close to the (10,10) state has been developed. Buyers are willing to share risks and information with the seller, and the seller is willing to open the books for buyer inspection. Problems are ironed out in an amicable and mutually acceptable manner and both parties benefit from the relationship.

The middle position of (5,5) should really be considered as a minimum acceptable goal for both sides, and few agreements should be reached by the purchaser without achieving at least this place. Adjustments in positions should, hopefully, travel along the diagonal and towards the (10,10) corner. Substantial departures from the diagonal raise the difficulty that the agreement may be seen as less beneficial to one party than the other, with the possibility of jealousy and the attempt by the less-satisfied party to bring the other down to a more common denominator. The region of greatest

Not important

FIGURE 6–5   Purchaser-Supplier Satisfaction Model Showing (1) Congruent (2) Noncongruent Perceptions

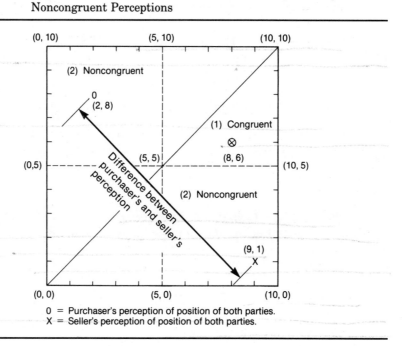

0 = Purchaser's perception of position of both parties.
X = Seller's perception of position of both parties.

stability will, therefore, lie close to the (5,5)–(10,10) portion of the diagonal line.

Perceptions

This model becomes more complex when the perceptions of both parties are considered, both with respect to their own position, as well as the other side's. For example, the purchaser's perception may be that the relationship is in the A region. The supplier's perception may or may not match this view. Let us look at the congruent side first.

Congruent Situations

Where both buyer's and supplier's perceptions agree, congruence exists and both parties would record their own and the other side's satisfaction on the same place on the chart. This does not necessarily mean that both parties are satisfied with the situation. Both at least have the same starting point, and mutual agreement on this is useful. For example, take a (8,6) situation, and both buyer and seller agree that the buyer is better satisfied with the current arrangement than the seller. Chances that both will be willing to work towards a corrective solution are reasonable (see Figure 6–5).

Noncongruent Perceptions

Lack of congruence in perceptions of relative positions will present a problem in itself. Take, for example, the situation where the buyer's perceptions of the situation is (2,8), but the seller's perception is (9,1) (see Figure 6–5). The buyer thinks the supplier has a pretty good deal but is quite dissatisfied with the purchaser's situation. The seller's opinion is the exact opposite. So both parties are dissatisfied, but their actions are likely to lead to even further dissatisfaction on the other side. This would normally be a highly unstable situation. It may be possible to settle differences of perception through discussion among the managers involved. Such resolution will be necessary before any attempts can be undertaken to improve the position of either side.

Using the Framework

The model is based on the assumption that both purchaser and seller are capable of expressing a view on the degree of satisfaction that exists with a relationship. Essential elements of this relationship would include perceptions on prices paid, service, delivery, and quality performance, and whether the demands and cooperation of the other party are reasonable in view of the circumstances. Personality factors are also a likely component. These measures are, of course, difficult to quantify, but ranking of relative positions compared to other suppliers (or customers) may well be possible. Even though absolute quantification is difficult, this model may be useful in a number of ways.

From a purchasing point of view, it is possible to assess the total package of current supplier relationships and to determine how many fall inside the desirable region and how many outside. A significant percentage of unsatisfactory or marginal situations will mean a substantial amount of work to restructure current arrangements. The purchasing perception of a relationship may be shared with a supplier to check on congruence and as a starting point for mutual diagnosis and plan for change. Even the process of attempting to assess contracts and suppliers against the model's framework may be useful in establishing the key variables which are relevant for the particular commodity under study. Finally, the severity of the situation is a good indicator of the need for action and the tools and techniques which might be applied. For example, a purchaser may wish to work harder at a (1,5) than a (5,5) situation of equal dollar value and corporate impact.

Tools and Techniques for Moving Positions

A number of purchasing and marketing means may be used to shift positions on the satisfaction chart. The use of some of these will adversely affect the perceptions of the other party, and these might be called "crunch" tools or negative measures. Others are likely to be viewed in less severe terms and might be considered "stroking" methods or positive approaches. For example, crunch tools for the purchaser include:

1. Complete severance of purchases without advance notice.
2. Refusal to pay bills.
3. Refusal to accept shipments.
4. Use or threat of legal action.

For the supplier examples would include:

1. Refusal to send shipments as promised.
2. Unilateral substantial price increase without notice.
3. Insistence on unreasonable length of contract, take or pay commitments, onerous escalation clauses, or other unreasonable terms and conditions and use of take it or leave it propositions.

"Stroking" techniques by the purchaser would include:

1. Granting of substantial volumes of business, long-run commitments, or 100 percent requirements contracts.
2. Sharing of internal information on forecasts, problems, and opportunities to invite a mutual search of alternatives.
3. Evidence of willingness and ability to work towards changed behavior in the purchasing organization to improve the seller's position.
4. Rapid positive response to requests from suppliers for discussions and adjustments in price, quality, delivery, and service.

On the marketing side examples could be:

1. Willingness and ability to make rapid price, delivery, and quality adjustments in response to purchasing requests without a major hassle.
2. Invitation to the purchaser to discuss mutual problems and opportunities.
3. The giving of notice substantially in advance of pending changes in price, lead times, and availability to allow the purchaser maximum time to plan ahead.

It is interesting that "stroking" techniques are more likely to be used in the A region, further strengthening the stability of the relationship, whereas the use of crunch tools may well accomplish short-term objectives but may impair future chances of a desirable stable relationship.

The perception of a relationship is based on both the results obtained as well as the process by which they have been achieved. For example, a price concession extremely grudgingly granted by a supplier and continually negatively referred to by supplier's personnel may create less satisfaction for the purchaser than one more amicably reached. Crunch methods pleasantly applied may be far more palatable than the same tool used in a hard-nosed way. For example, an unavoidable price increase can be explained in person by a supplier's sales manager well in advance more palatably than by circular letter after the increase has been put into effect. A purchasing manager can visit a supplier's plant to determine ways and means of solving a quality problem and explain that no deliveries can be accepted until the problem is solved, instead of sending back shipment after shipment as unacceptable. The results-process combination puts a heavy emphasis on managerial judgment and capability to accomplish change effectively.

Supplier Management

The foregoing discussion on the satisfaction-stability framework underlines the need for extensive communications and communication skills for both parties in the buying-selling relationship. The whole art of supplier management from a purchasing perspective is to bring both sides into an effective working relationship. This will require substantial coordination work inside the purchaser's organization to ensure that the people most vitally concerned with a particular vendor's performance are fully involved in the planning and execution of a program leading to the desired long-term relationship. Therefore, the team approach to long-term vendor relations is probably the only reasonable option. In such team purchasing, the buyer, purchasing agent, or supply manager will probably be required to play the coordination and project manager role.

Without internal cooperation and a congruent strategic internal approach to the improvement of vendor relations, the whole idea of supplier management is impossible. The members of the internal team are the ones who have to deal directly with their appropriate counterparts on the supplier side. The necessity for good management of this interface is obvious. Immediate and concerted action needs to be taken when either side detects problems or sees problems. Awareness of the full details of each side's situation, aspirations, strengths, and weaknesses is necessary for any team member to be able to assess the impact of changes, problems, or opportunities on the other side. In simple words, the seller's and purchaser's personnel need to understand their own organization and the other very well so that both sides can work on continuing improvement for mutual benefit. Such understanding can only come through exposure, discussion, mutual problem solving, and willingness to investigate every aspect of a meaningful relationship frankly. Given that in many organizations it is difficult for individual employees and different functional areas to work well together towards a common goal, it is easy to appreciate the challenge posed by adding the supplier's organization to this set. It may well be that the development of superior supplier relations will be the most critical challenge for supply managers in the decades ahead.

Moreover, the ability to develop effective working relationships with vendors will be dependent on purchasing's ability to develop effective working relationships internally. Thus, purchasing's status within the organization and the availability of qualified purchasing personnel will be key determinants of the organization's ability to get the most out of its supplier force.

THE EVALUATION OF POTENTIAL SOURCES

Obviously, the evaluation of an existing supplier is substantially easier than the evaluation of a potential source. Since checking out a potential supplier often requires an extensive amount of time and resources, it should only be done for those vendors on the short list who stand a serious chance of receiving an order of significance. Where such a potential vendor competes with an existing supplier, the expected performance of the new source should, hopefully, better that of the existing one.

In evaluating potential sources, the most common major factors are technical or engineering capability, manufacturing or distribution strengths, financial strengths, and management capability.

The use of trial orders has been mentioned as a popular means of testing a supplier's capability, but popular as this may be, it still begs the question as to whether the trial order should have been placed with a particular source at all. Even though a supplier may complete a trial order successfully, it may not be an acceptable source in the long run.

The evaluation of potential sources, therefore, attempts to answer two key questions:

1. Is this vendor capable of supplying the purchaser's requirements satisfactorily in both the short and long term?

2. Is this vendor motivated to supply these requirements in the way the purchaser expects in the short and long term?

The first question can be largely answered on a technical basis. The second probes the human side. Why should vendor personnel give special attention to this purchaser's requirements?

Technical, Engineering, and Manufacturing Strengths

Technical and engineering capability along with manufacturing strengths impinge on a number of concerns for the purchaser. The most obvious first factor is the quality capability of the vendor. Chapter 4 has already discussed a variety of means of evaluating potential vendors, including the quality capability survey. It is possible, however, that a company capable of meeting current quality standards may still lack the engineering and technical strengths to stay with new technological advances. Similarly, manufacturing may lack capacity, or the space to expand, or the flexibility to meet a variety of requirements. Presumably, the reason for selecting one vendor over another is because of greater strengths in areas of importance to the purchaser. The evaluation of the vendor, therefore, should focus not only on current capability, but also on the vendor's future strengths. Only in very large organizations might the procurement or materials group have sufficient technical strength to conduct such vendor evaluations on its own. It is normal that other functions such as engineering, manufacturing, using departments, or quality control provide expert assistance to assess a potential vendor on technical and manufacturing strengths.

Should the vendor be a distributor, the stress might be more on distribution capability. The nature of the agreement with supplying manufacturers, its inventory policies, and ability to respond to special requirements would all be assessed, along with such technical strengths of the personnel as might be necessary to assist the purchasing organization to make the right choices among a series of different acceptable options.

Management and Financial Evaluation

As the tendency towards greater reliance on single sources for a longer period of time continues, along with greater interest in materials requirements and just-in-time production, a potential supplier's management strengths take on added significance. From the procurement point of view, the key question is: "Is the management of this supplier a corporate strength or a weakness?" This will require a detailed examination of the organization structure, qualifications of managers, management controls, the reward-punishment system, training and development, corporate strategies, and policies and procedures. It is also useful to have an explanation as to why the vendor's management believes it is managing well and an indication of its most notable successes and failures. A functional assessment of strengths and weaknesses in areas like marketing, procurement, systems, and so on, will substantiate the overall picture. For example, consider a contract where the vendor spends a substantial percentage of total contract volume on raw materials and parts with outside suppliers or subcontractors. An evaluation of this vendor's procurement system, organization, procedures, and personnel is vital and can best be carried out by competent procurement staff in the organization which is letting the contract.

An assessment of this sort will require submission of documentation by the vendor as well as personal visits by qualified personnel from the buying organization. In some very large organizations considering the letting of large contracts, a task force or a special new vendor committee is required to submit a formal report detailing the management strengths and weaknesses of potential vendors and this evaluation may well carry the project.

The financial strengths and weaknesses of a supplier obviously affect its capability to respond to the needs of customers. There are often substantial opportunities for negotiation if the purchaser is fully familiar with the financial status of a supplier. For example, the offer of advance payment or cash discounts will have no appeal to a cash rich source but may be highly attractive to a firm short of working capital. A supplier with substantial inventories may be able to offer supply assurance and a degree of price protection at times of shortages which cannot be matched by others without the materials or the funds to acquire them.

Individual financial measures which may be examined include, but are not limited to, credit rating, capital structure, profitability, ability to meet interest and dividend obligations, working capital, inventory turnover, current ratio, and return on investment. Presumably, financial stability and strength are indicators of good management and competitive ability. Financial statements, therefore, are a reasonable source of information about a supplier's past performance. Whether the vendor will continue to perform in the same manner in the future is an assessment the purchaser must make, taking all available information, including the financial side, into account.

There is general agreement among procurement executives that a supplier's management capability and financial strength are vital factors in source evaluation and selection. Even after a satisfactory evaluation of management, financial, and technical strengths of a supplier has been completed, the question remains as to what weight should be accorded to each of the various dimensions. Also, should the purchaser take the initiative in insisting that the vendor correct certain deficiencies, particularly on the management or financial side?

Many examples exist illustrating the need for supplier strength. These are normally related to the long-term survival of the company. Small suppliers are frequently dependent on the health, age, and abilities of the owner-manager. Every time this individual steps into an automobile the fate of the company rides along. The attitudes of this individual to certain customers may be very important in supply assurance.

Most long-term and significant supplier-purchaser relationships are highly dependent on the relationships and communication channels built by the respective managers in each organization. Unless each side is willing and able to listen and react to information supplied by the other side, problems are not likely to be resolved to mutual satisfaction.

Additional Source Selection Considerations

One might think that after a vendor had been found who could meet all the requirements, the search would be over. Such is not the case. Shall the buyer, in buying a given item, rely on a single supplier, or utilize several? Shall the buyer buy directly from manufacturers or through distributors? Shall the buyer give preference to local sources, consider minority groups, and environmental and political concerns? How should the buyer react to commercial bribery in any of its various forms? Should a buyer take an active role in developing new sources or even try to have the requirements made in-house? To understand the difficulties involved in making a final selection of source, it may be necessary to consider some or all of these options. In doing so, it shall be assumed that adequate investigation has been made of the vendor's financial standing, general reputation for fairness, and capacity to meet the requirements as to quality, quantity, delivery, and service and that prices are not unreasonable.

Concentration of Purchases with One Source

Shall the buyer rely upon a single supplier, or utilize several? The answer to this question must be the very unsatisfactory one, "It all depends."

Briefly, the arguments for placing all orders for a given item with one supplier are as follows:

1. Prior commitments, a successful past relationship, or an ongoing long-term contract with a preferred vendor might prevent even the possibility of splitting the order.

2. The supplier may be the exclusive owner of certain essential patents or processes and, therefore, be the only possible source. Under such circumstances the purchaser has no choice, provided that no satisfactory substitute item is available.

3. A given supplier may be so outstanding in the quality of product or in the service provided as to preclude serious consideration of buying elsewhere.

4. The order may be so small as to make it not worthwhile, if only because of added clerical expense, to divide it.

5. Concentrating purchases may make possible certain discounts or lower freight rates that could not be had otherwise.

6. The supplier is more cooperative, more interested, and more willing to please having all the buyer's business. This argument, of course, loses much of its weight if even the total order amounts to but little or, although fairly large, represents but a very small proportion of the seller's total sales.

7. A special case arises when the purchase of an item involves a die, tool, mold charge, or costly setup. The expense of duplicating this equipment or setup is likely to be substantial. Under such circumstances, probably most buyers confine their business to the possessor of the die, tool, or mold.

8. When all orders are placed with one supplier, deliveries may be more easily scheduled.

9. The use of just-in-time production or stockless buying or systems contracting provides many advantages which are not possible to obtain unless business is concentrated with one or at best a very few suppliers.

10. Effective supplier management requires considerable resources and time. Therefore, the fewer vendors the better.

11. The Japanese have been particularly successful in using single sources.

On the other hand, there are arguments for diversification—provided, of course, that the sacrifice is not too great:

1. It has been common practice among the majority of buyers to use more than one source, especially on the important items.

2. Knowing that competitors are getting some of the business may tend to keep the supplier more alert to the need for giving good prices and service.

3. Assurance of supply is increased. Should fire, strikes, breakdowns, or accidents occur to any one supplier, deliveries can still be obtained from the others.

4. Even should floods, railway strikes, or other widespread occurrences develop which may affect all suppliers to some extent, the chances of securing at least a part of the goods are increased.

5. Some companies diversify their purchases because they do not want to become the sole support of one company, with the responsibility that such a position entails.

6. Assigning orders to several suppliers gives a company a greater degree of flexibility, because it can call on the unused capacity of all the suppliers instead of only one.

7. Even in situations involving close and cooperative vendor relationships, it is possible to make backup arrangements so that vendor X specializes in product Q and backs up vendor Y, who specializes in product R and backs up vendor X.

8. Strategic reasons, such as military preparedness and supply security may require multiple sourcing.

9. Government regulations may insist that multiple vendors, or small or minority sources be used. Because of the high risk associated with a small or single minority source, multiple sourcing may be necessary.

10. Sufficient capacity may not be available to accommodate the purchaser's current or future needs.

11. Potential new or future vendors may have to be tested with trial orders, while other sources receive the bulk of the current business.

Numerous examples exist showing the advantages of one approach over another. A typical example favoring sole sourcing was as follows:

A very high-quality custom printer found that none of the company's ink suppliers could satisfactorily meet the exacting requirements of the unusual jobs the firm was called on to perform. A special arrangement with one supplier which involved extensive research and development resulted in a satisfactory, but expensive, product. Since the printer was in a position to pass ink costs to its customers who were more interested in quality and delivery than price, the printer found working with this one source advantageous in several ways. To protect against shortages, strikes, and other interference, the supplier agreed to maintain a special inventory in both the supplier's and customer's plants. When market shortages developed, the suppliers put all customers except this printer on quotas.

A typical example favoring multiple sourcing was the purchaser of recreational equipment. One supplier, a sole source for a large segment of equipment, was strongly favored by engineering and production and had provided excellent service over the years. However, prices had increased substantially despite large volume increases. Only when a second source was brought in by the purchasing agent, over strong initial engineering and production objections, did the first supplier become concerned over price performance. Both suppliers performed well and competed strongly with the result that savings over the following five years ran into millions of dollars.

Genuine concern exists among purchasing executives as to how much business should be placed with one supplier, particularly if the supplier is small. It is feared that sudden discontinuance of purchases may put the supplier's survival in jeopardy, and, yet, the purchaser does not wish to reduce flexibility by being tied to dependent sources. One simple rule of thumb traditionally used was that no more than a certain percentage, say 20 or 30 percent, of the total supplier's business should be with one customer.

If a decision is made to divide an order among several vendors, there is then the question of the basis on which the division is to be made. The actual practice varies widely. One method is to divide the business equally. Another is to place the large share with a favored supplier and give the rest to one or more alternates. In the chemical industry, as in several others, it is common practice to place business with various vendors on a percentage of total requirements basis. Total requirements may be estimated, not necessarily guaranteed, and there may not even be a minimum volume requirement. Each supplier knows what their own percentage of the business amounts to, but may not be aware who the competition is or how much business each competitor received if the number of sources exceeds two. There is, and can be, no common practice or "best" method or procedure, although renewed interest in single sourcing is consistent with a number of current trends.

Purchase from Manufacturer or Distributor

The question sometimes arises whether to purchase from the manufacturer directly or from some trade channel such as a wholesaler, distributor, or even a retailer. Occasionally, pressure is brought to bear by various types of trade associations particularly to induce the purchaser to patronize the wholesaler, jobber, or mill supply house. The real issue involved here is often closely related to buying from local sources. The question is not primarily one of proximity to the user's plant but rather one of buying channels.

The justification for using trade channels is found in the services which they render. If wholesalers are carrying the products of various manufacturers and spreading marketing costs over a variety of items, they may be able to lay down the product at the buyer's plant at a lower cost, particularly when the unit of sale is small and customers are widely scattered or when the demand is irregular. Furthermore, they may carry a stock of goods greater than a manufacturer could afford to carry in its own branch warehouse and therefore be in a better position to make prompt deliveries and to fill emergency orders. Again, they may be able to buy in car or truckload lots, with a saving in transportation charges, and a consequent lower cost to the buyer.

Local sentiment may be strongly in favor of a certain jobber. Public agencies are particularly susceptible to such influence. Sometimes, concerns that sell through jobbers tend, as a matter of policy, to buy whenever possible through jobbers.

On the other hand, some large organizations often seek ways of going around the supply house, particularly where the buyer's requirements of supply items are large, where the shipments are made directly from the original manufacturer, and where no selling effort or service is rendered by the wholesaler. Some manufacturers operate their own supply houses to get the large discount. Others have attempted to persuade the original manufacturers to establish quantity discounts—a practice not unlike that in the steel trade.

Still others have sought to develop sources among small manufacturers not having a widespread distributive organization. Some attempts have been made to secure a special service from a chosen distributor, such as an agreement whereby the latter would add to its staff "two people exclusively for the purpose of locating and expediting nuisance items in other lines." A similar arrangement might place a travel agency employee directly on the purchaser's premises to improve service.

Geographical Location of Sources

Shall purchases be confined as largely as possible to local sources, or shall geographical location be largely disregarded? Most buyers *prefer* to buy from local sources, and a substantial percentage of these indicate that they are willing to pay more or accept less satisfactory quality or service to do so. This is particularly true of the larger companies.

This policy rests on two bases. The first is that a local source can frequently offer more dependable service than one located at a distance. For example, deliveries may be more prompt both because the distance is shorter and because the dangers of interruption in transportation service are reduced. Knowledge of the buyer's peculiar requirements, as well as of the seller's special qualifications, may be based on an intimacy of knowledge not possessed by others. There may be greater flexibility in meeting the purchaser's requirements; and local suppliers may be just as well equipped as to facilities, know-how, and financial strength as any of those located at more distant points. Thus, there may well be sound economic reasons for preferring a local source to a more distant one. In just-in-time production systems, proximity of the vendor's plant to that of the purchaser is vital. Organizations such as the automotive companies, for example, have thus found themselves encouraging vendors to relocate plants closer to automobile assembly operations.

A second basis for selecting local sources rests on equally sound, although somewhat less tangible, grounds. The organization owes much to the local community. The facility is located there, from it is drawn the bulk of the employees, and often a substantial part of its financial support, as well as a notable part of its sales, is local in character. The local community provides the company's personnel with their housing, schools, churches, and social life. Executives are constantly asked by local business owners or managers at local professional and social gatherings why they are not receiving any business. To recognize these facts is good public relations.

Therefore, if a local source of supply can be found that can render a buyer as good a value as can be located elsewhere, it should be supported. Moreover, buyers should attempt to develop local sources when potential exists.

This policy has two complicating elements. One is that the purchasing agent's primary responsibility is to buy well. Emotion should rarely supplant good business judgment, for to do so, in the long run, is to render the local community a poor service indeed. A second complication arises through the difficulty of defining "local." Technological changes have affected not only the size and distribution of the centers of population but also the commercial and business structure, resulting, among other things, in a widening of market areas and hence the sources from which suppliers can be obtained.

Therefore, what once might properly have been called local has, for many areas and many items, become state or federal. There is no easy rule by which a buyer can decide the economic boundaries of the local community.

Trade Relations

Under what circumstances, if at all, shall trade relations or reciprocity be practiced? A workable, though none too exact, definition of *reciprocity* is as follows: "Reciprocity is the practice of giving preference in buying to those vendors who are customers of the buying company as opposed to vendors who do not buy from the company." This broad statement, however, is scarcely the form in which the problem arises. Much fruitless criticism has been advanced on the part of those who apparently do not fully realize that so far as purchasing departments, at least, are concerned, reciprocity is not a debatable policy to the extent that it involves purchasing requirements under conditions which will result in higher prices or inferior service. Purchasing directors do debate the issue as to how far it can be practiced, *assuming that conditions of price, service, and quality are substantially the same.*

The case against any general use of reciprocity rests on the belief that the practice is at variance with the sound principles of either buying or selling. The sale of a product must be based on the qualities of the product sold and of the service attending the transaction. There is only one permanent basis for a continuing customer-supplier relationship: the conviction on the part of the buyer that the product of a particular seller is the one best adapted to the need and is the best all-around value available. As long as the sales department concentrates its attention on this appeal, it will find and retain permanent customers.

Few purchasing officers would object to reciprocal buying on the basis that quality, service, and price must be equal. In practice, abuse is practically certain to creep in. For instance, buyers are urged to buy from X not because X is a customer but because X is Y's customer and Y is our customer, and Y wants to sell to X.

The normal expectation of a seller using reciprocity as an argument is that the purchaser is willing to grant price, quality, or delivery concessions. In North America reciprocity is on shaky legal grounds, and the U.S. Supreme Court has upheld the Clayton Act under Section 7 that reciprocity may be restrictive to trade and create unfair competition.[3]

On an international scale, a form of reciprocity is practiced widely by governments. For example, a foreign company may receive a government contract on the condition that it meets stringent local content requirements. Thus, the supplier is forced to develop new sources, often at substantial cost,

---

[3]The case is *FTC v. Consolidated Foods* (1965) 380 U.S. 592.

to secure the business. Furthermore, such foreign contracts often involve barter as the purchaser insists on paying with raw materials or locally manufactured goods.

Attitude toward Gratuities

How shall the purchasing manager deal with the problem of excessive entertainment and gifts in any one of their varied and subtle forms? Here is a practice that seeks, through gifts, entertainment, and even open bribery, to influence the decision of persons responsible for making a choice between suppliers.

Such attempts to influence decisions unfairly are directed not only toward purchasing personnel. Work managers, supervisors, and others in production or engineering who are directly responsible for, or largely influence, decisions regarding types of materials to be procured are also approached. In such cases, even though the purchasing officer is not directly influenced, the buyer's task is affected. So serious do some organizations consider this whole problem that they forbid any employee to receive any gift, no matter how trivial, from any supplier, actual or potential.

It is, of course, difficult always to distinguish between legitimate expenditures by suppliers in the interest of goodwill, and illegitimate expenditures made in an attempt to place the buyer under some obligation to the vendor. In these borderline cases, only ordinary common sense can provide the answer.

The National Association of Purchasing Management (NAPM) and the Purchasing Management Association of Canada (PMAC) in their codes of ethics strongly condemn gratuities. It is true, however, that every year a small number of cases are uncovered of individuals who do not abide by this code, thereby placing the whole profession under suspicion. Part of the blame must clearly lie with those who use illegal enticements to secure business. For example, a salesperson calls on a purchaser and invites him or her out to lunch so they may discuss a transaction without losing time or as a matter of courtesy. Such action is presumed to be in the interests of goodwill, although the cost of the lunch must be added to the selling price. An attractive but inexpensive gift may be given by the vendor's company to adorn the desk of the buyer. The vendor's name appears on the gift, and therefore it is construed as advertising. The sales representative may send a bottle of wine or sporting event tickets after a deal has been completed.

It is but a step from this type of effort to entertaining a prospective buyer at a dinner, followed perhaps by a theater party. The custom of giving simple gifts may develop into the granting of much larger ones. It is difficult to draw the line between these different situations. In some organizations the purchasing manager or buyer not infrequently refuses to allow sales personnel to pay for luncheons or at least insists on paying for as many luncheons as do prospective sellers.

Aside from its economic aspects, the practice of commercial bribery is involved in many legal cases. Fundamentally, the rulings on commercial bribery rest on the doctrine of agency. Any breach of faith on the part of the agent, who has always been recognized by law as keeping a fiduciary position, is not permitted; therefore, the agent's acceptance of a bribe to do anything in conflict with the interests of its principal is not permitted by law.

The evils of commercial bribery are more far-reaching than would at first appear. Although originating with only one concern, bribery is rapidly likely to become a practice of the entire industry. A producer, no matter how superior the quality of goods or how low its price, is likely to find it extremely difficult to sell in competition with concerns practicing bribery. The prices paid by the buyer who accepts bribes are almost certain to be higher than they would be under other circumstances. Defects in workmanship or quality are likely to be smoothed over by the buyer who accepts bribes hidden from his or her employer. Materials may be deliberately damaged or destroyed to make products of some manufacturers who do not offer bribes appear unsatisfactory. There is no occasion for going further into an analysis of this practice. It takes many forms, but regardless of the guise in which it appears, there is nothing to be said for it.

Even though bribery is outlawed in North America, it may flourish in other parts of the world, legally or not. The spectacular revelations about the bribed sales of U.S. aircraft to other countries during the mid-1970s were a sad reminder of the pervasiveness of such practices in our world.

Joint Purchasing with Supplier

Sometimes a purchasing department becomes involved with buying certain items for suppliers, believing it can purchase more efficiently than they. Since the suppliers would realize substantial savings, some of these might be passed along to the purchaser. Although the purchasing department will incur some additional expense, there would be a net gain to both parties in the transaction. The close relationship that would exist between the suppliers and purchasers, furthermore, would enable purchasers to know more about the production costs of those companies and to ascertain whether or not it was paying a fair price for the products. The purchaser would, moreover, be sure of the quality of the materials used and would increase buying power. Nevertheless, the vendor may claim that quality difficulties stem from the poor quality of material supplied. With a reduction in the number of buyers in the market of the raw materials, there would be less false activity and thus greater price stability. This last reason is rather important. Not infrequently, when a large company requests bids from individual suppliers, they in turn enter the material markets to make inquiries about prices and quantities available. If six suppliers are bidding on an offer, their preliminary inquiries for material required to fill the prospective order will be multiplied six times.

Purchasing for Company Personnel

Still another problem faced by most purchasing departments is that of the extent to which it is justified in using its facilities to obtain merchandise for employees of the organization or for its executives at better terms than they could individually obtain through their own efforts. Many companies not only sell their own merchandise to their employees at a substantial discount and also allow them to buy at cost any of the merchandise bought by the company for its own use but go even further and make it possible for employees to obtain merchandise which the company itself neither makes nor uses.

There are many reasons why a company should pursue a policy of employee purchasing. Under certain circumstances, of course, it is imperative that a company make some provision for supplying its employees with at least the necessities of life, a condition particularly true in mining and lumbering towns. A policy of employee purchasing, it is also argued, provides the means for increasing real wages at little or no cost to the company. It may increase the loyalty of the employees to the organization and thus form a part of the fringe benefits. Many times, employees feel they are entitled to any considerations or advantages the company can obtain for them. Furthermore, whatever the procurement manager may think about the general practice, it is often somewhat difficult to refuse a request from a top executive to "see what can be done about a discount."

Many companies, on the other hand, have steadfastly refused to adopt such a policy. There is some question of just how much prices are really reduced compared with the prices of the chain store, the supermarket, the discount store, and other low-cost distributive outlets. Some ill will toward the company may be aroused, since the ordinary retailer is likely to feel that the manufacturer is entering into direct competition or at least is bringing pressure to grant discounts to the manufacturer's employees.

Unfortunately, few people realize how difficult it is for a purchasing department to handle numerous small requests of a personal nature. It is a time-consuming and unrewarding task, since a complete market search is almost impossible, and any quality, price, or service troubles arising from the purchase are always brought back to those involved.

Social, Political, and Environmental Concerns

Recognition has come, rather belatedly, that certain noneconomic factors may have a significant bearing on procurement sourcing decisions. These fall into the social, political, and environmental areas.

Social. Most organizations recognize that their existence may affect the social concerns of society. Some social problems can be addressed through purchasing policy and actions. For example, it is possible to purchase from social agencies employing addicts, former prisoners, or the physically and mentally handicapped certain items or services which assist in the employment of these people. It is possible to purchase from suppliers located in low-income or certain geographical areas of high unemployment. The U.S. government has tried in a variety of ways to encourage purchasing from small or minority suppliers by requiring that on public contracts a certain percentage of total value be placed with such vendors.

Most larger organizations recognize the problems and opportunities present through the exercise of purchasing power in the social area. It is not easy for a hard-nosed purchasing manager, used to standard low-risk, reputable sources, and extensive competition, to consider dealing with the high-risk sources often represented by this class. Most purchasing managers agree that the "deal" must make good business sense and that an arrangement based on charity will sooner or later collapse. Without purchasing initiative to seek out those suppliers who might have reasonable potential, it is unlikely that much can or will be accomplished. Too many of the potential sources are small, have few resources, and low marketing skills. Recognition of supplier weaknesses and the willingness to be of assistance are, therefore, necessary ingredients. Normally, sources like these will be local allowing for personal contact, watchfulness, and support through the development stage.

Political. The basic question in the political area is: Should the acquisition area be seen as a means of furthering political objectives? Public agencies have long been under pressure of this sort. "Buy local" is a common requirement for city and state purchasing officials. "Buy American" is a normal corollary requirement. The attempt by the Canadian government to direct the Department of Supply and Services to spread purchases across the country, approximately in line with population distribution, is another example. For military purposes, the U.S. government has a long-standing tradition of support and development of a national supply base to afford protection in the case of conflict.

The question always arises as to how much of a premium should be paid to conform with political directives. Should a city purchasing agent buy buses from the local manufacturer at a 12 percent premium over those obtainable from another state or other country?

For private industry political questions are also present. Should the corporation support the political and economic aims of the governing body? Governments have little hesitation on large business deals to specify that a minimum percentage should have domestic content. In the aerospace industry, for example, foreign plane orders are often contingent on the ability to arrange for suitable subcontracting in the customer's home country. It is interesting that governments have no fear to tread where private industry is forbidden to walk. Multinationals often find themselves caught in countries with different political views. American companies for many years had not been allowed to trade with China and Cuba. American subsidiaries in other countries face strong national pressure to export to Cuba or the USSR the same products that the American parent is not allowed to sell from American soil. The same holds for purchasing from countries with whom trade is not encouraged by the government. American subsidiaries frequently find themselves caught between the desire of the local government to encourage local purchases and the U.S. government which encourages exports from the parent or the parent's suppliers. The growing role of government in all business affairs is likely to increase difficulties of this kind in the future. Their resolution is far from easy and will require a great deal of tact and understanding.

Environmental.   Although environmental concerns are not new to our society, genuine purchasing concern as a potential area of influence is. The first problem is: Should our organization purchase materials, products, or equipment which may directly or indirectly increase environmental concerns? Should the purchasing group raise the environmental questions when others in the organization fail to do so?

The second problem is: Should we purchase from sources, domestic or international, that we know are not following sound environmental practices? These are not easy questions answered glibly out of context. It is possible to evade the issue by putting government in the control seat, saying, "as long as government allows it, it must be all right." A practical purchasing consideration is that government may shut down a polluting supplier with little notice, endangering supply assurance.

Overall Vendor Selection Consideration

Before a purchaser can make a final vendor choice, a decision on all the important questions of policy just discussed must be reached: whether to patronize a single or several sources of supply; whether to buy directly from the manufacturer or through a distributor; whether to buy wholly from local sources; to what extent, if at all, to practice reciprocity; what weight to give social, political, and environmental concerns; and how to deal with the problem of commercial bribery. Having formulated a policy with reference to these matters the basis has been laid for settling the specific issues as they arise later on. Most purchasing managers are compelled sooner or later to take a position on these issues and, having done so, have gone a long way toward selecting their sources.

FIGURE 6–6   Supplier Development Initiative with the Purchaser

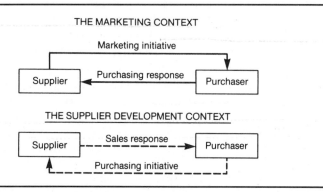

Reverse Marketing/Supplier Development

In supplier selection the assumption has so far been made that at least one suitable and willing supplier already exists and that the purchaser's problem is primarily one of determining who is the best vendor. It is possible, however, that no suitable source is available and that the purchaser may have to create a source. Reverse marketing or supplier development implies a degree of aggressive procurement involvement not normally encountered in supplier selection. For example, it frequently places a purchasing manager in a position where a prospective supplier must be persuaded to accept an order. In this no-choice context the purchaser does not initiate supplier development as an appropriate technique or tool; it is the only alternative other than making the part in-house.

Reverse marketing/supplier development should take a broader point of view. It defines the need for developing new or existing suppliers as follows: the purchaser is aware that benefits will accrue to both the supplier and the purchaser, benefits of which the supplier may not be aware. These benefits may be limited to the particular order at hand, or they may include more far-reaching results, such as technical, financial, and management processes, skills, or quality levels; reduction of marketing effort; use of long-term forecasts or permitting smoother manufacturing levels and a minimum of inventory; and so on.

It is the aggressiveness and initiative by the purchaser that makes the difference (see Figure 6-6). In the normal market context the purchaser responds to marketing efforts. In reverse marketing, the purchaser, not the marketer, has the initiative and may quote prices, terms, and conditions as part of the aggressive role. This is why the term *reverse marketing* has been chosen as a synonym for supplier development. Numerous examples show that high payoffs are possible from the purchasing initiative and that suppliers of all sizes may be approached in this fashion.

A further reason for reverse marketing is that there are bound to be deficiencies in the normal industrial marketing-purchasing process in which the marketer traditionally takes the initiative. Even when a supplier and a purchaser have entered into a regular vendor-vendee relationship, often neither party is fully aware of all the opportunities for additional business which may exist between them. This might arise because of salesperson and buyer specialization, a lack of aggressiveness by the salesperson, or a lack of inquisitiveness by the purchaser.

If gaps are evident even where an established vendor-vendee relationship exists, there must be even greater shortcomings where no such relationship has yet been established. For example, a vendor may be unable to cover its full market because of geography, limited advertising, or lack of coverage by its sales force, distributors, or agents. Most suppliers have lines of products which receive more management attention and sales push than other products also made or sold by the same company. It is always difficult to keep entirely up to date. A time lag may exist between the time of product introduction and the time the purchaser finds out about it. By filling these gaps through aggressiveness, the purchaser effectively strengthens this whole process.

One of the most important arguments in favor of reverse marketing not yet mentioned arises from future considerations. If the procurement role is envisaged as encompassing not only the need to fill current requirements but also the need to prepare for the future, supplier development can be valuable in assuring future sources of supply

There are at least three outside forces which would suggest the increasing necessity for purchaser initiative in the creation of future sources of supply. One of these forces is technological. The increasing rate of development of new products, materials, and processes will tend to make the industrial marketing task even more complex and more open to shortcomings. In addition to this, the stepping-up of international trade will tend to widen supplier horizons and may create a need for purchaser aggressiveness in the development of foreign sources of supply. One of the most demanding and important tasks of management of a subsidiary in an underdeveloped country is the problem of supplier development. Lastly, new management concerns dealing with quality, delivery, inventories, continuing improvement, and systems require purchasers to be more aggressive with vendors and to develop sources to their expectations.

In their *Reverse Marketing* text, Leenders and Blenkhorn identify the challenges and opportunities inherent in the process of reverse marketing.[4] The role of aggressor forces the purchaser to prepare carefully and to identify needs and options, probably with greater precision and detail than under

---

[4]Michiel R. Leenders and David L. Blenkhorn, *Reverse Marketing: The New Buyer-Supplier Relationship* (New York: The Free Press, 1988).

the traditional, more passive, seller-buyer approach. This extra preparation and homework tends to pay off handsomely in large improvements in quality, delivery, price, service, or other objectives the purchaser may be pursuing.

Reverse marketing need not be limited to the creation of new sources, but can be applied to existing vendors where the gap between purchaser expectations and vendor reality is large. In view of the excellent results obtained by those practicing reverse marketing, it is easy to predict increased use of reverse marketing/supplier development in the future.

QUESTIONS FOR REVIEW AND DISCUSSION

1. Why should any organization switch from making to buying?

2. What are the advantages of single sourcing?

3. Where does the borderline fall between gratuities and bribery?

4. What are the advantages of purchasing from small local sources?

5. What constitutes a preferred supplier?

6. What is the relationship between satisfaction and stability in buyer-supplier relations?

7. What is reverse marketing and why is it used?

8. Why should a purchasing department not buy for personal use of employees of the organization?

9. What are typical sources of information about potential suppliers?

10. Why might purchasing from distributors or wholesalers be preferable over buying directly from the manufacturer?

REFERENCES

Buffa, Frank P. and Wade M. Jackson. "A Goal Programming Model for Purchasing Planning." *Journal of Purchasing and Materials Management*, Fall 1983.

Dale, Barrie G. and Malcolm T. Cunningham. "The Purchasing/Manufacturing Interface in the Make-or-Buy Decision." *Journal of Purchasing and Materials Management*, Spring 1983.

Dubinsky, Alan J. and Thomas N. Ingram. "Salespeople View Buyer Behavior." *Journal of Purchasing and Materials Management*, Fall 1982.

Felch, Robert I. "Standards of Conduct: The Key to Supplier Relationships." *Journal of Purchasing and Materials Management*, Fall 1985.

Gambino, Anthony J. *The Make-or-Buy Decision*. Hamilton, Ontario, and New York: Society of Management Accountants of Canada and National Association of Accountants, 1980.

Giunipero, Larry C. "Differences between Minority and Non-Minority Suppliers." *Journal of Purchasing and Materials Management*, Spring 1980.

Leenders, Michiel R. and David L. Blenkhorn. *Reverse Marketing: The New Buyer-Supplier Relationship*. New York: Free Press, 1988.

Lehmann, Donald R. and John O'Shaughnessy. "Decision Criteria Used in Buying Different Categories of Products." *Journal of Purchasing and Materials Management*, Spring 1982.

Monczka, Robert M.; Larry C. Guinipero; and Robert F. Reck. "Perceived Importance of Supplier Information." *Journal of Purchasing and Materials Management*, Spring 1981.

Narasimhan, Ram. "An Analytical Approach to Supplier Selection." *Journal of Purchasing and Materials Management*, Winter 1983.

Pilfold, David, "Requesting Proposals for Development and Innovation." *Purchasing and Supply Management*, May 1982.

Soukup, William R. "Supplier Selection Strategies." *Journal of Purchasing and Materials Management*, Summer 1987.

Case 6–1

UNIFOOD INC.

In August, Charijean Watanabe, the Hawaiian Area Director for Unifood Inc., with local headquarters in Honolulu, had just received another complaint from the Sheraton Waikiki Hotel's storeroom manager about a late and incomplete grocery delivery. Incidents of poor service from their major grocery product vendor, Johnson Foods, had increased dramatically in the last six months, and Charijean was wondering what action she should take.

Unifood Inc. (U.I.) was a wholly owned food and beverage purchasing subsidiary of the Sheraton Hotel worldwide headquarters. U.I. offices were located from Hawaii to London, England. There were 19 U.S. regional purchasing centers, three international centers and an export center in Boston. Purchases made by U.I. had reached $130 million. Although not all Sheraton hotels used U.I., the company operated hotels in areas where U.I. had purchasing centers and many of the franchised Sheraton hotels did use U.I. services. In addition, other hotel and food service operators

This case was prepared by Associate Professor John Patterson, University of Guelph, and Assistant Professor Morton Fox, University of Hawaii, under grants from the Canadian Hospitality Industry and the Statler Foundation and with support from the University of Hawaii. It was developed for use by the Advanced Management Program for the Hospitality Industry (AMPHI) as the basis for class discussion rather than to illustrate either effective or ineffective handling of an administrative situation.

also used U.I.'s services. Currently, 40 percent of the food service purchasing volume was done for non-Sheraton properties.

U.I. services included food purchasing, quality control, one-call shopping, food commodity market research, local and regional market information, purchasing analysis and consultation, and seminars and training. Two new services, recently incorporated into U.I., were kitchen design and operational consulting.

U.I.'s services were described by the company as having several distinct advantages. They fell into the following categories:

1. *Lower Prices.* Unifood consolidated orders from many individual units into huge quantity purchases, taking advantage of economies of scale to obtain quantity discounts. Unifood's national and regional price agreements with major manufacturers, packers, and suppliers assured customers of continuously favorable food costs in a constantly fluctuating market.

2. *Quality Control.* Professional Unifood buyers ensured that purchases consistently met customers' standards of quality. Unifood buyers were in the markets selecting top quality products weekly. A growing list of products bearing the Unifood private label were an added guarantee of quality.

3. *Market Information.* Unifood provided its customers with a monthly Food Purchase Price Index and 30-Day Forecast, unique in the industry. The regional buyers kept customers informed of the newest products, prices, and trends.

4. *One-call Shopping.* Meat, produce, grocery, poultry, dairy, seafood and frozen food items were ordered in one telephone call to the Unifood buyer. This time-saving convenience was provided without sacrificing the advantage of competitive buying.

5. *Food Purchasing Analysis.* Savings achieved through Unifood varied, depending on individual requirements and customary purchasing methods. Unifood provided a survey that compared actual quantities and prices to Unifood's prices for similar or better quality items, and estimated annual dollar savings.

6. *Purchasing Systems.* Unifood personnel tailored a complete food purchasing system to fit a customer's hotel, motor inn, restaurant, club, or school feeding operation and trained the customer's personnel in its proper use.

In the final analysis, U.I.'s major benefits to user organizations were product cost reduction and time savings achieved through one-call shopping.

Using their larger purchasing volumes, U.I. was generally able to negotiate a discount of 8-10 percent better than that given individual operators from suppliers. U.I., in turn, charged their clients a 2-3 percent commission on their purchasing dollar volumes.

U.I. Hawaii

U.I.'s Hawaii purchasing center was responsible for servicing the state of Hawaii. Its only clients were the twelve Sheraton hotels in Hawaii, which had over 6500 rooms. Of these hotels, six were located on Oahu, two on Kauai, two on Hawaii, one each on Molokai and Maui — each one with a full complement of food and beverage operations ranging from snack stands to gourmet restaurants. As a result, the purchasing volume for U.I. Hawaii was approximately $30 million. A general breakdown of purchases by product grouping was 46.3 percent meat, including poultry and fish; 11.0 percent dairy; 15.8 percent produce; 13.9 percent grocery; and 13.0 percent alcoholic beverage.

U.I.'s Hawaiian office was in the basement of the Sheraton Waikiki. The 1900-room hotel also housed the Sheraton Pacific Divisional headquarters. Having a location in Honolulu, which contained 80 percent of Hawaii's population, gave U.I. access to all the major food and beverage vendors and importing support services in Hawaii.

U.I. was responsible for purchasing food and beverage products but not for receiving them, so that staff was small in comparison to the purchasing volume and geographic spread of the operation. Besides Charijean Watanabe, the Area Director who was responsible for purchasing the meat, dry goods and produce, there was one assistant buyer who handled purchases of alcoholic beverages and dairy products. This person also provided a back-up to Charijean in the operation of the office since she was visiting each hotel property four times per year. Charijean and her assistant worked very closely with the individual hotel purchasing agents, storeroom managers and executive chefs. In addition, she consulted regularly with the Food and Beverage Vice President for the Pacific Division of Sheraton. Her direct reporting responsibility was to the U.S. West Coast Regional Director of U.I.

Charijean described the food and beverage purchasing market in Hawaii as being dependent upon volume of purchases, since the vast majority of food and beverage items were imported. The field of competition for the food and beverage wholesale market in Hawaii consisted of the retail grocery business, which was the largest in terms of purchasing volumes, the military's over 100,000 active duty personnel and their dependents stationed in Hawaii, and, finally, the food service establishments. U.I. Hawaii was the largest single buyer in this last segment, and normally did command a real advantage when negotiating purchases and obtaining good service for their accounts.

Unifood Operations

Each Sheraton hotel in Hawaii contracted with U.I. for their food and beverage requirements. U.I., in turn, used a weekly bid process with the local purveyors for all of the food groupings in Chart 1 except dairy products which were contracted on an annual basis. In providing the various services to customers, U.I. prescribed a regular routine of general procedures. The unit purchasing agent or senior storekeeper was responsible for coordinating the unit's food and beverage requirements and phoned through to Unifood two to six times per week, using the guidelines shown in Chart 1.

The U.I. purchasing agent in turn combined all unit requirements and ordered products by telephone for direct delivery to the appropriate unit. (Most Hawaiian Sheraton hotels did have a purchasing agent, but two of the smaller properties had only a senior storekeeper.)

Unifood Inc. Hawaii required that vendor invoices accompany the shipment to each unit. On Oahu goods delivered without an invoice were refused. On neighbor islands, a Goods Received Without Invoice form was completed and forwarded to the U.I. office. Back order or product substitution was not allowed without prior

CHART 1   Unifood Inc. Order Guidelines

Product	Hotel Orders per Week	Hotel Delivery per Week
Meat	3x	3x
Fish	3x	3x
Poultry	3x	3x
Dairy	5x	5x
Produce	6x	6x
Alcoholic Beverages	1x	1x
Dry Goods	2x	2x

approval from U.I. Hawaii. Stockouts and back orders had to be reported to U.I. as soon as the vendor realized that the product was not in stock. If there were substitution suggestions, the vendor was expected to call U.I. in advance to present them.

U.I. expected that purveyors would provide sales support. This included salesmen who regularly visited the U.I. offices to discuss account problems such as product quality, order delivery accuracy, delivery scheduling, and invoice discrepancies. In addition, new product samples or product substitution samples would be examined and discussed.

Unifood Inc. Dry Goods

U.I. major dry good (grocery) items for Hawaii were canned fruits, fruit and vegetable juices, table condiments, oils and salad dressings, canned meats, staples such as sugar and flour, spices, crackers, packaged cookies, nuts, and dried grains, such as rice.

These items were not purchased on a long-term contract arrangement, but checked frequently by comparative pricing done on a monthly basis. Products were normally ordered once or twice per week for delivery on the same schedule. Product substitutions for dry goods had not been common in the Hawaiian market, and U.I. would not accept them without direct authorization.

Charijean Watanabe

Charijean Watanabe was a graduate of the Travel Industry Management program at the University of Hawaii. She also obtained an associate science degree in food service management from a local community college. Born and raised on Oahu, she was familiar with the state's history and ethnic background, as well as the importance of tourism and its supporting facilities to the state's economy.

After graduation, Charijean worked in various skill level and junior management food service positions. Seven years ago, she became the assistant buyer for U.I. in Hawaii, and was promoted to area manager two years later upon the retirement of her supervisor. Since assuming her present position, she succeeded in enhancing the visibility of U.I. among both the Sheraton hotels and purveyors, and spent a

CHART 2   Typical Daily Schedule

Time	Activity	Comments
8:00 a.m.-9:00 a.m.	Special Projects	Specification Design
9:00 a.m.-10:00 a.m.	Receipt of orders	
10:00 a.m.-11:00 a.m.	Determining who to purchase from	
11:00 a.m.-12:00 p.m.	Placing the order	
12:00 p.m.-1:00 p.m.	Lunch	
1:00 p.m.-2:00 p.m.	Special Projects	Stockout/substitution negotiation
2:00 p.m.-4:00 p.m.	Visit vendors Product tests Typing memos See Salesmen	

great deal of time in improving communication and interaction with appropriate personnel at the individual hotels. Currently, she spent about 60 percent of her time performing purchasing duties and 40 percent of her time visiting hotels and purveyors or engaging in product testing. She had also become active in several professional and trade organizations associated with the hospitality industry. A typical daily schedule for Charijean Watanabe is shown in Chart 2.

The Dry Goods Issue

Currently, U.I. used five purveyors for their purchases of dry goods. Two of these five, Johnson Foods and Crafton Inc., were very large mainland U.S.-based manufacturers and distributors. Two, Chun Grocery Products and Hiroshi Inc., were locally owned and operated. The fifth, Newton Wholesalers, was a new food purveying arm of a locally operated general merchandise wholesaler.

As Charijean described them, these purveyors each had a specific character, and U.I.'s relations with them varied. Johnson Food was a national company with headquarters in Los Angeles and a strong West Coast market share. They dealt in paper goods and a full range of dry goods. They had good quality products, and fairly high prices to match. Locally, they leased all of their delivery vehicles and had a weak sales support team. U.I. spent about 10 percent of their dry good purchasing dollar with Johnson Foods. Another national firm was Crafton Inc., which had headquarters in Chicago and a very strong presence and market share on the east coast of the U.S. In Hawaii, they had a good sales support team. Their products were of good quality and offered at a reasonable price. Currently, 50 percent of U.I.'s dry goods purchasing was through Crafton Inc.

Chun Grocery Products, the largest of the locally-owned and operated purveyors, had a good variety of products. There was no sales support team whatsoever, but prices were relatively inexpensive. The quality varied, however, and buyers had to be fully acquainted with each product purchased in order to be sure about the item.

As well, a close monitoring of delivered products was required. Up to 30 percent of U.I. dry goods purchases was directed to Chun Grocery Products. Also locally-owned was Hiroshi Inc., a small purveyor that specialized in Japanese food products. Again, there was no sales support function but the prices were good. The product line was narrow, and they had previously shown no willingness to expand their product lines or their business. U.I. spent 10 percent of their dry goods purchasing dollar with Hiroshi Inc.

Newton Wholesalers was a thirty-year-old general wholesaling company that had recently established a food service division to market paper products, dry goods, meat, fish and poultry. Newton recently negotiated a cost-plus contract to supply 100 percent of a major chain department store's food service business in Hawaii. Recently, U.I. had started buying 10 percent of their products from Newton. Newton had attempted to support their sales, even though their resources were stretched. Product quality was only fair but they had indicated that they were attempting to improve in this area while maintaining their competitive pricing. The recent use of Newton wholesalers as a product source for 10 percent of U.I.'s dry goods business had been at the direct expense of Johnson/Crafton.

Merger

In the summer, Johnson Foods and Crafton Inc. merged. This was completed without informing buying organizations, even after the fact. One of the outcomes of this merger was the elimination of one or the other's local support organization depending upon recent sales strengths in local markets. In Hawaii, although the invoicing was now titled Johnson/Crafton, the Crafton organization was basically eliminated for various economies-of-scale reasons.

The merger had caused a great deal of confusion to U.I. in Hawaii. Exhibits 1 and 2 describe some of the initial confusion. Charijean reviewed a list of recurring problems with the Johnson/Crafton account (shown in Exhibit 3). She had continually over the last two months brought these issues to the attention of the Johnson sales agent, the manager for national accounts, and the company's general manager. It appeared, however, as if little corrective action was taken. Although Sheraton purchasing agents and the divisional food and beverage vice-president were cognizant of the situation and were supportive, they left corrective action up to Unifoods. Their only stipulations had been that product quality must be maintained and a complete line of products must be available for Sheraton's use in Hawaii.

Alternatives

Charijean had identified some alternative courses of action to resolve, or at least reduce, the severity of the problem with dry goods purchases.

1. Attempting to bring even greater pressure upon Johnson/Crafton to improve their service came to mind first. But recent attempts had proven futile, and she felt that continued requests to the point of begging were not the responsibility of nor an appropriate action for U.I.

2. Increasing the proportion of U.I. dry goods purchases to Chung Grocery and/or Hiroshi was possible, but presented some problems. Hiroshi did not want to expand, nor did they provide the needed sales support. Chung Grocery, on the other hand, did not have any sales support and did not have as extensive a product

EXHIBIT 1   Food and Beverage Controllers

July 16

To: All Food and Beverage Controllers

From: Charijean Watanabe—Unifood Hawaii

Subject: Johnson/Crafton Merger

The recent Johnson/Crafton company merger has caused some confusion with deliveries, product labels, invoicing and prices. They have officially merged as one company as of July 9. You will note that the invoice has changed to Johnson/Crafton.

Unifood was not informed of the merger period and has shipped and priced merchandise under the previous separate structure, where Johnson and Crafton were independent companies. You will thus see price discrepancies on your shipments for the week of July 9.

Please bear with this situation until the complete reorganization takes place and proper pricing can be established between Johnson/Crafton and Unifood. Call us if you have any further questions. Thank you.

**For the interim period, there will be a 9 percent upcharge on the quoted prices for all *neighbor island shipments*. This will be in effect until a neighbor island price list is submitted to Unifood.

cc: All Purchasing Agents

---

line and support facilities as Johnson/Crafton. Also, product quality had been suspect in the recent past, and any weakness in this area was unacceptable to Sheraton.

3. A large expansion of business with Newton Wholesalers was also considered. The obvious drawbacks, according to Charijean, were their lack of experience in this type of business, their current small size and their already stretched resources. In addition, more work on quality needed to be demonstrated. Another consideration that concerned Charijean was the effect a firm such as U.I. would have on a small company such as Newton Wholesalers. If current business were expanded to 50 percent of U.I. dry good purchases, that amount would essentially account for over 75 percent of Newton Wholesalers' sales.

Charijean had searched the Hawaii market for other dry goods purveyors but had been unsuccessful in identifying any. The possibility of dealing directly with any firm on the West Coast of the United States did not appear to be possible; distance, service difficulties, shipping costs, and logistics almost automatically ruled out such a move.

Conclusion

The situation did not appear to be improving, and Sheraton hotel management was getting anxious for a decision. They wanted action so that what they considered a serious ongoing problem would be rectified.

EXHIBIT 2 Letter to Purchasing Agents

August 2

To: All Purchasing Agents
From: Chari Watanabe, Unifood Hawaii
Subject: Johnson Foods and Crafton Inc.

After an absolutely chaotic beginning, finally Johnson/Crafton may be getting part of their act together.

First, let us address their delivery schedule. Deliveries will be made for the next day delivery provided that we are able to call in orders before 12:00 noon. All delivery days will remain the same, with the exception of the Sheraton Makaha, which has changed from Thursday to Wednesday.

Neighbor Island hotels will be billed at Oahu prices, and orders will be sent to you freight collect. There is no minimum order. Previously, there had been an eleven case minimum and the pricing structure was different for Oahu and Neighbor Island Hotels.

The Johnson volume discount program with Sheraton has been discontinued. In the past, had you ordered 75 cases or more, a 1 percent discount was awarded to you.

I have noticed that many of our deliveries are being short-shipped, that is, Johnson/Crafton is charging you for items but not sending them. Please be extra carefully sure to check in their merchandise. I am also not being informed by that company about out-of-stocks and short orders, so please excuse us if we do not call you on a timely basis.

I have been informed that Johnson/Crafton will be carrying both Johnson and Crafton labels, however, Crafton labels will be limited to about 300 items, still to be named. When I call in the order, I do specify Johnson or Crafton labels, but they may not be able to accommodate us.

In short, things remain quite a mess. We are in the process of looking for another grocery purveyor to complement the number of purveyors that we do business with, but this may take a few weeks.

cc: V.P. Food and Beverage Sheraton Pacific
     All Executive Chefs
     Noda
     Seitz

EXHIBIT 3 Continual Service Problems with Johnson/Crafton

---

1. Requests for product prices from the order desk are not being followed through. This delays completion of our purchase orders and prevents us from giving the hotels quotations on a timely basis. Recent orders via the telephone have required a long waiting time to get through to the order desks.

EXHIBIT 3   *(concluded)*

2. We were not informed of the merger until after the fact. In addition, their regular salesperson was on vacation the first two weeks after the merger was completed. An interim salesperson was assigned to our account but was unfamiliar with our product lines and usage statistics. The general manager of the newly merged firm has not initiated any direct communication with U.I. since the merger. This is a complete departure from past practice and creates much ill will.

3. There have been a number of ongoing errors in invoicing. Orders are being delivered without invoices, which is contrary to past custom. Invoices for an entire order are being sent without Johnson/Crafton's filling the entire order or notifying Unifood of any back orders or shortfills. Price discrepancies, almost always above quoted figures, are a common occurrence. Price lists are not being submitted to U.I. on a timely basis (usually once per month).

4. Substitution of lower-quality goods has occurred without price adjustment and/or informing U.I. prior to delivery to the hotels.

5. The usual procedure for all hotels is to have both the vendor's driver and the hotel shopkeeper put deliveries into their storage area. The vendor has now refused to follow this procedure and will only unload the merchandise at the loading dock.

6. Product testing by U.I. and the hotels has been suspended because the vendor has not indicated which items in their line of products will be carried and which products will be discontinued. In addition, no new items have been introduced to Unifood since the merger two months ago.

Case 6–2

DAVIDSON EQUIPMENT

Tom Dennison, purchasing manager at Davidson Equipment, was concerned about his British supplier of engine parts. Some recent warranty claims had upset relations and Tom wondered what action he should take.

Davidson Equipment sold replacement parts for heavy equipment and also serviced equipment in its own 28-bay shop. About 70 percent of Davidson's $75 million annual parts sales were for Truro equipment. Truro had an excellent reputation in the trade for quality equipment and was one of the most popular brands available. Since Davidson was not an official Truro dealer, but an independent, it had to purchase parts from dealers or other sources. A number of suppliers could provide substitutes for official Truro parts. British Pistons supplied both pistons and piston liners to Davidson for an annual volume of about $1 million. Although British Pistons had a local firm acting as its American manufacturer's representative, Davidson had always ordered parts directly from Britain.

Recently, two machines which had piston liners installed in the shop were returned under warranty and found to have cracked liners. The warranty on one machine came to $50,000, the other $30,000. Tom knew that of dozens of installations this was the first instance of two quick warranty claims. British Pistons had agreed to pay Davidson its cost on these two warranties, but warned Davidson at the same time that if any further warranty claims were submitted it would stop supplying Davidson. No actual transfer of funds had yet taken place from British Pistons to Davidson Equipment, however. Tom Dennison was concerned about losing British Pistons as a supplier because good engine parts suppliers were very difficult to find. Moreover, he knew that Davidson was getting good prices from British Pistons because Truro, aware of its competitive position in the repair business, had started to price much more aggressively than in the past. Since the British pound had risen at the same time and since British Pistons continuously had the best prices laid down at Davidson, Tom figured their margins must have shrunk substantially. Further-more, Tom was not at all sure that the piston liners had been fully tested before installation.

A procedure used years earlier was to tap liners lightly with a hammer. If a resonant sound was produced, there were no cracks in the liner. In the past, liners had also been numbered and inspected individually on receipt. Tom also wondered whether recommended installation procedures as outlined in the service manual had been followed to the letter in the two warranty claim cases. Finally, Tom won-dered what costs should be charged under these circumstances and whether a reduced rate might not be more appropriate.

Tom considered the possibility of purchasing British Pistons parts through their local manufacturer's representative and then holding the local firm responsible for warranties. It might also be possible to reduce the price of engine parts and sell them without warranty.

When a genuine Truro liner cracked, it was normal that Truro replaced the faulty liner and the dealer decided whether the customer was entitled to full war-ranty or not. Claims had to be submitted to Truro within a set period of time or else they would not be recognized.

Tom believed that if Davidson were to rely on Truro alone for parts, Davidson would always be at a disadvantage to Truro dealers who would be able to purchase parts at lower prices. Thus, having competitive outside sources was, in Tom's opinion, a key objective for purchasing.

Tom knew that the counteroffer from British Pistons needed a reaction from Davidson, but he was not sure he fully understood the implications of accepting their offer in its existing form.

Case 6–3

STEVENS CONSTRUCTION, INC.

Eric Busch, purchasing agent for Stevens Construction, Inc., faced a supplier selection decision on the bending of reinforcing rod for a major construction project. Should he select a local supplier or one more distant at a lower price?

Company Background

Stevens Construction, located in the western part of the country was one of the largest construction companies in the region. The company was not involved in residential units, but built high-rise office towers, plants, government buildings, and roads. It had a reputation for high-quality, on-time work and the company had grown rapidly in the past 20 years, keeping pace with the general expansion of the region.

Reinforcing Steel

Reinforcing steel, used in almost all of the projects in which Stevens was involved, was purchased by Eric Busch from several steel mills. During the past 18 months all of the bending required in preparation for the job site had been done by Adams & Adams, a small local steel fabricator. In the last year, total bending requirements had amounted to 4,000 tons. Adams & Adams had charged identical prices per ton for small and large jobs during this period. When a new construction job was undertaken and the steel requirements known, Eric Busch would request a quotation from Adams & Adams over the telephone, and invariably, the price per ton quoted was the same as for a previous job. Adams & Adams was also a supplier of reinforcing steel itself. Therefore, Eric Busch had worked out an arrangement of mutual help during periods of shortages or problems caused by the steel mills in not supplying certain sizes on time. Adams & Adams would use Stevens steel and Stevens would use Adams & Adams steel to satisfy all projects. This arrangement had worked very well with the result that no reinforcing rod shortages had occurred in any construction projects during the last 18 months. Adams & Adams also owned a major share in a detailing firm which did approximately 70 percent of the reinforcing detailing work required by Stevens. In the opinion of Eric Busch, Adams & Adams had done an excellent job on delivery and quality during the time it had been sole supplier of bending requirements for Stevens.

Recently, Stevens had successfully quoted on a large, two-year contract which would require about 3,000 tons of reinforcing steel. Because of the size of the job, Eric Busch decided to look for another quote for the bending of the steel once it became clear that Stevens would receive the contract. The contract price had included a bending estimate using the current prices of Adams & Adams. The closest reasonable other supplier Eric Busch could find was Blackstone Steel, a major fabricator in a city 200 miles away. Blackstone quoted a price $7 per ton, FOB the Stevens plant, lower than the one submitted by Adams & Adams. This quote was made on the condition that all transport would be in full loads, with no emergency short shipment transport charges. Eric Busch had checked Blackstone out very carefully and knew them to be a reputable firm, capable of doing good-quality work. He now wondered if he should place the contract with them or whether he should stay with Adams & Adams.

Case 6–4

PLASTIC CABLE CLIPS

In mid-September Robyn Pemberton, purchasing officer in the laundry division of Fisher & Paykel Limited, located in Auckland, New Zealand, was wondering which procurement option made most sense for the plastic cable clips requirements for the new line of washing machines.

The Laundry Division

Fisher & Paykel Limited was the largest home appliance manufacturer in New Zealand with sales of its major appliances amounting to $135,000,000 and total sales of $270,000,000 for the fiscal year ending March 31, including $36,000,000 of export sales and royalty income. It comprised eight operating divisions, one of which was the laundry division employing over 500 people to produce washing machines and dryers. Currently, the laundry division produced about 50,000 washing machines, solely for the domestic market.

The New Washing Machine

For the last two years, the laundry division had been developing a new line of automatic washing machines scheduled for market introduction in late 1985. The planning and development of the new machine was conducted by a seven-person committee of engineers, production, and marketing people as well as a purchasing coordinator.

The new machine, designed entirely by F&P, used electronic controls. It was believed to be technologically advanced by world standards. Its manufacturing process would be highly automated, featuring considerable part rationalization and cost reduction over the old production line. In fact, maintaining costs at the lowest possible level was one of the key priorities of the planning committee.

With good opportunities for export and royalty income, the Laundry Division hoped to produce between 75,000 and 100,000 new washing machines a year. However, 50,000 machines were planned for the first full year of production. The first production run was scheduled for the beginning of next April.

Plastic Cable Clips

The old washing machine used about twenty different plastic cable ties for a total of about 250 ties in each machine. At the moment, the laundry division bought nearly $1,250,000 a year worth of plastic cable ties: about $500,000 from Olson Plastics, a New Zealand manufacturer; $500,000 from Barry Cleaver and Sons, a local agent importing mostly from Japan; $200,000 from G. T. Rollman, another local agent importing from Australia; and at most $50,000 from Plastic Distributing, a relatively new and smaller multisource New Zealand agent.

The ties to be used in the new machine required new specifications because of the automated production process. None of the existing ties suppliers actually had in stock the kind of parts required.

A year earlier, Robyn Pemberton, who was the purchasing coordinator for the new washing machine, managed to convince the planning committee to draw on the technical expertise of Barry Cleaver, the New Zealand agent currently supplying some of the plastic ties. As a result of Barry Cleaver's input, the number of ties required was reduced to half a dozen new parts for a total of about 45 plastic clips to be used in each new machine. Robyn Pemberton made it very clear to Barry Cleaver that all current plastic ties suppliers would be asked to submit quotations as soon as all the specifications on the new clips would be finalized and that his involvement would not give him any preferential treatment over the others.

Vendor Selection

Because of design changes, the specifications for the new cable clips were not confirmed until early July. Robyn promptly sent letters asking for quotations to the four existing plastic ties suppliers (see Exhibit 1).

Olson Plastics

Olson Plastics, the only New Zealand manufacturer of plastic ties, clips, and rivets, had been supplying F&P for many years. Robyn Pemberton believed that F&P would be among its top five customers. With occasional quality and service problems, Robyn felt the quality of Olson's products was not as high as of the other ties suppliers. Olson's prices for certain parts were twice as high as prices for imported parts. But deliveries were Robyn's major area of concern with this supplier. Even with a six- to eight-month lead time, deliveries were unreliable and Robyn had to chase every order. She believed Olson had capacity problems although they did not wish to admit it.

However, Olson enjoyed government protection in the sense that, under normal circumstances, a New Zealand agent could not import products which could be made domestically.

Barry Cleaver and Sons

Barry Cleaver and Sons, a New Zealand agent for three generations with an excellent reputation, was receiving about $2 million a year worth of orders from F&P. Its prices and service were normally excellent. Delivery was good providing adequate lead time of six to eight months was given. Barry Cleaver was getting F&P plastic parts from Japan and, during sellers' markets, would have difficulty obtaining supply because of the relative low importance of its orders.

However, Robyn was concerned about the long-term availability of the imported parts as the agent's license could be revoked if it was proven that a domestic supply

EXHIBIT 1   Quotation Request Letter Sample

5 July

Dear Sir,

The following new parts are required, commencing next March, 1985. Please advise price, minimum quantity, and delivery details.

Part	Description	Qty/Annum
816549	Clip snap .125M × .5	30,000
816553	Clip snap .250M × .75	30,000
817709	Clip-tie HM FT	60,000
817803	Clip-lock HBX	165,000
817923	Clip-tie HM FT (SS)	650,000
817975	Clip-tie HM RS.2	135,000

Samples would be appreciated when possible.

Awaiting your reply with interest.

Yours faithfully,
FISHER & PAYKEL LIMITED

R. H. Pemberton (Mrs)
PURCHASING OFFICER
LAUNDRY DIVISION

---

alternative existed. F&P was legally free to buy from any agent in New Zealand. It was up to the agent to justify its stance with the Department of Trade and Industry. However, Robyn was well aware of the Department's licensing policy (see Exhibit 2), as she remembered vividly a problem encountered with plastic rivets and a few cable ties in May.

Barry Cleaver had been supplying F&P with Japanese rivets and cable ties until Olson complained to Trade and Industry. As a result, Barry Cleaver not only had to stop importing and start purchasing from Olson at three times the former price, but he was also having a terrible time meeting F&P volume requirements and had to deliver some of the parts on a daily basis. After F&P started noticing that the rivets purchased from Barry Cleaver came in Olson's boxes, Robyn asked Olson for quotes on the rivets, but was subsequently surprised to discover that Olson's prices were dearer than Barry Cleaver's.

G. T. Rollman

G. T. Rollman was a large New Zealand agent importing from Australia. Although the prices were high, the service was excellent and the delivery was good. The average lead time was three to four months but, in urgent situations, it could supply within six weeks by airfreighting the stock.

Robyn Pemberton was also conscious of the advantage of Australian sourcing due to the Closer Economic Relations Agreement between New Zealand and Aus-

EXHIBIT 2   New Zealand Government Standard Licensing Policy[1]

The following policy applies to all item codes except those for which specific policies are set on the following pages.

1. Goods of Types Not Produced in New Zealand

    Licenses will generally be granted to meet reasonable requirements for goods of types not produced in New Zealand.

    Licenses will not be issued under this provision unless it is quite clear that the goods to be imported are not substitutable for domestic alternatives.

    The applicants will need to provide adequate evidence that suitable alternatives are not available from New Zealand manufacturers.

    In considering applications Trade and Industry will assess the extent to which established licensing provisions have been and are being used to import the goods concerned. The aim of this is to ensure that domestic production is not detrimentally affected by the consequential availability of license to import directly competitive goods.

2. All Other Goods
    Licenses may be granted in special circumstances such as:

    * Established trading patterns arising from continuing special licensing provision.
    * Shortfalls in normal domestic supply.
    * Special provision for the requirements of new manufacturers.
    * Applications under general policies and provisions set out in Annex III.

Note: Item Codes which fall under Industry Development Plans are subject to any special import licensing provisions of those plans.

---

[1]This policy does not apply to Australian-made products.

tralia. She knew that a higher New Zealand and Australian content in the new washing machine would permit F&P free or minimum duty access to the Australian market. Although she had to inform the costing department of the country of origin of each part purchased, she did not know at what level some price reduction on a part would offset a duty increase. She had tried to find out more information on this subject but no one had been very explicit. With the labor government in July 1984, a considerable amount of uncertainty existed. All she knew was that the group purchasing department of F&P was pushing for as much New Zealand and Australian content as possible.

Plastic Distributing

Plastic Distributing was a local agent with annual sales under $1 million that imported plastic products from a number of countries. This young company was eager to obtain orders but offered little technical backup.

In the past, Robyn had given it the odd order, especially when supply was tight.

EXHIBIT 3   Summary of Quotes/Prices per 1,000

Part No.	Description	Barry Cleaver	Olson	Plastic Dist.	Rollman
816549	Clip snap 1.25M × .5	76.00	54.00	99.95	—
816553	Clip snap .250M × .75	76.00	119.80	99.95	—
817709	Clip-tie HM FT	25.20	36.80	28.26	—
817803	Clip-lock HBX	39.20	61.82	—	134.40
817923	Clip-tie HM FT (SS)	23.06	20.40	28.12	—
817975	Clip-tie HM RS.2	38.40	50.00	63.22	—

She had asked this agent to quote on the new plastic clips mostly for comparison purposes.

Selection Decision

Quotes started arriving on July 10, with Barry Cleaver's response. But it was not until September 12 that she obtained Olson's prices (see Exhibit 3 for a summary of quotes). In mid-September Robyn called Barry Cleaver and asked for a meeting. Barry Cleaver came with a technical expert to meet with Robyn and her supervisor, John Wardrop. Barry made clear that the recent problem encountered with the supply of rivets and cable ties was in the process of being solved, as they had been able to regain their importing license from Trade and Industry by proving that Olson did not have sufficient capacity to meet the demand. Barry Cleaver assured Robyn and John that he felt there would be no problem to import all the new plastic clips required for the new washing machines.

Robyn was wondering what to do. In light of Deming's philosophy adopted by Fisher & Paykel as a whole, she felt some pressure toward single sourcing. However, she was not convinced of the soundness of single sourcing in the context of this purchase. She was also wondering to what extent Olson Plastics realized what their situation would be once the old washing machine would be phased out, should she choose to go with Barry Cleaver. She was debating whether she should call on Olson for further consultation. In any event, she knew a decision had to be reached quickly in view of the lead time involved with the first production run scheduled for next April.

CHAPTER 7

Price Determination

Determination of the price to be paid is a major purchasing decision. The ability to get a "good price" is sometimes held to be the prime test of a good buyer. If by "good price" is meant greatest value, broadly defined, this is true.

While price is only one aspect of the overall purchasing job, it is extremely important. Basically, the purchasing department exists to satisfy the firm's purchase requirements at a lower overall cost than could be accomplished through decentralized purchasing. The purchasing department must be alert to different pricing methods, know when each is appropriate, and use skill in arriving at the price to be paid. There is no reason to apologize for emphasizing price or for giving it a place of importance among the factors to be considered. The purchaser rightly is expected to get the best value possible for the organization whose funds are spent. Any price quoted should be analyzed, irrespective of who the supplier is or what the item may be. The price paid by the purchaser is as much a factor in the final decision on what is the "best buy" as are the technical properties of the product.

RELATION OF COST TO PRICE

Every purchasing manager believes the vendor should be paid a fair price. But what does "fair price" mean? A fair price is the lowest price that ensures a continuous supply of the proper quality where and when needed.

A "continuous supply" is possible in the long run only from a vendor who is making a reasonable profit. The vendor's total costs, including a reasonable profit, must be covered by total sales in the long run. Any one item in the line, however, may never contribute "its full share" over any given period, but even for such an item the price paid should at least cover the direct costs incurred.

A fair price to one seller for any one item may be higher than a fair price to another or for an equally satisfactory substitute item. Both may be "fair prices" as far as the buyer is concerned, and the buyer may pay both prices at the same time.

Merely because a price is set by a monopolist or is established through collusion among the sellers does not, in and of itself, make that price unfair or excessive. Likewise, the prevailing price need not necessarily be a fair price, as, for example, when such price is a "black" or "gray" market price or when it is depressed or raised through monopolistic or coercive action.

The purchasing manager is called on continuously to exercise judgment as to what the "fair price" should be under a variety of circumstances. To determine this fair price, he or she must have experience (data) and common sense. In part, of course, accuracy in weighing the various factors which culminate in a "fair and just price" is a matter of capitalizing on past experience.

Meaning of Cost

Assuming this concept of a fair price is sound, what are the relationships between cost and price? Clearly, to stay in business over the long run a supplier must cover total costs, including overhead, and receive a profit. Unless costs, including profit, are covered, eventually the vendor will be forced out of business. This reduces the number of sources available to the buyer and may cause scarcity, higher prices, less satisfactory service, and lower quality.

But what is to be included in the term cost? At times it is defined to mean only direct labor and material costs, and in a period of depressed business conditions, a seller may be willing merely to recover this amount rather than not make a sale at all. Or cost may mean direct labor and material costs with some contribution toward overhead. If the cost for a particular item includes overhead, is the latter charged at the actual rate (provided it can be determined) or is it charged at an average rate? The average rate may be far from the actual.

Most knowledgeable business people realize that determination of the cost of a particular article is not a precise process. However, it is common practice to refer to the cost of an article very precisely. In manufacturing industries there are two basic classifications of costs—direct and indirect.

Direct costs usually are defined as those which can be specifically and accurately assigned to a given unit of production; that is, materials, such as 10 pounds of steel; or labor, such as 30 minutes of a person's time on a machine or assembly line. However, under accepted accounting practices, the actual price of the specific material used may not be the cost that is included in figuring direct material costs. Because the price paid for material may fluctuate up or down over a period of time, it is common practice to use a so-called standard cost. Some companies use as a standard cost for materials the last price paid in the immediately prior fiscal period. Other companies use an average price for a specific period.

Indirect costs are those incurred in the operation of a production plant or process but which normally cannot be related directly to any given unit of production. Some examples of indirect costs are rent, property taxes, machine depreciation, expenses of general supervisors, data processing, power, heat, and light.

Classification of costs into variable, semivariable, and fixed categories is a common accounting practice and a necessity for any meaningful analysis of price/cost relationships. Most direct costs are variable, because they vary with the units produced. For example, a product which requires 10 pounds of steel for one unit will require 100 pounds for 10 units. Semivariable costs may vary with the number of units produced but are partly variable and partly fixed. For example, more heat, light, and power will be used when a plant is operating at 90 percent of capacity than when operating at a 50 percent rate, but the difference is not directly proportional to the number of units produced. In fact, there would be some costs (fixed) for heat, light, and power if production were stopped completely for a period of time.

Fixed costs generally remain the same regardless of the number of units produced. For example, real estate taxes will be the same for a given period of time regardless of whether one unit or 100,000 units are produced. Several accounting methods can be used to allocate fixed costs. A common method is to apply a percentage of direct costs in order to allocate the cost of factory overhead. Full allocation of fixed expenses will depend on an accurate forecast of production and the percentage used. Obviously as full production capacity is reached, the percentage rate will decline.

We can now define costs as so many dollars and cents per unit based on an average cost for raw material over a period of time, direct labor costs, and an estimated volume of production over a period of time on which the distribution of overhead is based.

If this definition of cost is acceptable, then a logical question is, whose cost? Some manufacturers are more efficient than others. Usually all sell the same item at about the same price. But should this price be high enough to cover only the most efficient supplier's costs, or should it cover the costs of all vendors?

Furthermore, cost does not necessarily determine market price. When a seller insists that the price must be a given amount because of costs, this position is not really justified. In the final analysis, goods are worth and will sell for what the market will pay.

Moreover, no seller is entitled to a price that yields a profit merely because the vendor is in business or assumes risk. If such were the case, every business automatically would be entitled to a profit regardless of costs, quality, or service. Unless a seller can supply a market with goods that are needed and desired by users and can supply them with reasonable efficiency, that seller is not entitled to get a price that even covers costs.

How Vendors Establish Price

Depending on the commodity and industry, the market may vary from almost pure competition to oligopoly and monopoly. Pricing will vary accordingly. Most firms are not anxious to disclose just how prices are set for competitive reasons, but the two traditional approaches are the cost and the market approach.

The Cost Approach

The cost approach to pricing says that the price should be a certain amount over direct costs, allowing for sufficient contribution to cover indirect costs and overhead and leaving a certain margin for profit. For the purchaser, the cost approach offers a number of opportunities to seek low-cost suppliers, to suggest lower cost manufacturing alternatives, and to question the size of the margin over direct costs. Negotiation, used with cost-analysis techniques, is a particularly useful tool.

The Market Approach

The market approach implies that prices are set in the marketplace and may not be directly related to cost. If demand is high relative to supply, prices are expected to rise; when demand is low relative to supply, prices should decline. This, too, is an oversimplification. Some economists hold that large multinational, multiproduct firms have such a grip on the marketplace that pure competition does not exist and that prices will not drop even though supply exceeds demand. In the market approach, the purchaser must either live with prevailing market prices or find ways around them. If nothing can be done to attack the price structure directly, it may still be possible to select those suppliers who are willing to offer nonprice incentives, such as holding inventory, technical service, good quality, excellent delivery, transportation concessions, and early warning of impending price and new product changes. Negotiation, therefore, may center on items other than price.

Many economists hold that substitution of like but not identical materials or products is one of the most powerful forces preventing a completely monopolistic or oligopolistic grip on a market. For example, aluminum and copper may be interchanged in a number of applications. The aluminum and copper markets, therefore, are not independent of one another. The purchaser's ability to recognize these trade-offs and to effect design and use changes to take advantage of substitution is one determinant of flexibility. Make or buy is another question. If access to the raw materials, technological process, and labor skills is not severely restricted, one alternative may be for an organization to make its own requirements to avoid excess market prices.

Sometimes purchasers use long-term contracts as an inducement for the supplier to ignore market conditions. This approach may be successful in certain instances, but it is normal for suppliers to find ways and means around such commitments once it becomes obvious that the prevailing market price is substantially above that paid by their long-term customers.

Government Influence on Pricing

The government's role in establishing price has changed dramatically. The role of government has been twofold. Not only has the government taken an active role in determining prices by establishing production quotas and instituting (from time to time) various forms of wage/price controls, but it also regulates the ways that buyer and seller are allowed to behave in agreeing on prices. Since other governments are active in price control and have in a number of situations created dual pricing for domestic use and exports, it is difficult to see how the U.S. and Canadian governments will be able to ignore their position. Prices may be determined by review or control boards or by strong moral suasion. They are likely to be augmented by governmental controls like quotas, tariffs, and export permits.

Legislation Affecting Price Determination

United States.   The federal government has taken an active interest in how a buyer and seller agree on a price. The government's position largely has been a protective role to prevent the stronger party from imposing too onerous conditions on the weaker one or preventing collusion so that competition will be maintained.

The two most important federal laws affecting competition and pricing practices are the Sherman and Robinson-Patman Acts. The Sherman Antitrust Act of 1890 states that any combination, conspiracy, or collusion with the intent of restricting trade in interstate commerce is illegal. This means that it is illegal for vendors to get together to set prices (price fixing) or determine the terms and conditions under which they will sell. It also means that buyers cannot get together to set the prices they will pay.[1] The Robinson-Patman Act (Federal Antiprice Discrimination Act of 1936) says that a vendor must sell the same item, in the same quantity, to all customers at the same price. It is known as the "one-price law." Some exceptions are

---

[1]Even with federal legislation prohibiting price fixing, there are frequent instances where the Justice Department has charged firms with violations. See, for example, Andy Pasztor, "U.S. Files First Bid-Rigging Charges in Its Investigation of Piping Industry," *The Wall Street Journal*, August 31, 1987, p. 40 and Andy Pasztor, "Big Moving Firms Subpoenaed in Inquiry into Bid-Rigging on Military Contracts," *The Wall Street Journal*, November 3, 1987, p. 12.

permitted, such as a lower price (1) for a larger purchase quantity, providing the seller can cost justify the lower price through cost accounting data, (2) to move distress or obsolete merchandise, or (3) to meet the lower price of local competition in a particular geographic area. The act also goes on to state that it shall be illegal for a buyer knowingly to induce or accept a discriminatory price. However, the courts have been realistic in their interpretation of the law, holding that it is the job of the buyer to get the best possible price for his or her company, and that as long as he or she does not intentionally mislead the seller into giving a more favorable price than is available to other buyers of the same item, the law is not being violated.

If the buyer feels a seller is violating either the Sherman Act or the Robinson-Patman Act, a charge detailing the violation can be made to the Federal Trade Commission, which was set up to investigate alleged improprieties. From a buyer's standpoint, bringing a seller's actions to the government's attention has few advantages. Since most of the time government's reaction is relatively slow, the need for the item may be gone and conditions may be substantially changed by the time the complaint is decided. Most sellers would view the lodging of a complaint as a particularly unfriendly act, making it difficult for the organization to maintain a reasonable future relationship with the particular vendor. For this reason, complaints are not common, and most are lodged by governmental buying agencies rather than corporations.

Canada.   Canadian federal pricing legislation differs from U.S. legislation, but it has essentially the same intent. The Competition Investigation Act prohibits certain pricing practices in an attempt to maintain competition in the marketplace and applies to both buyers and sellers. Violation of the statute is a criminal offense. Section 31(1) states that suppliers or buyers may not "conspire, combine, agree, or arrange with another person" to raise prices unreasonably or to otherwise restrain competition. It does not prevent the exchange of data within a trade or professional association, providing it does not lessen price competition. Section 32 makes bid rigging a per se violation, which means that the prosecution needs only to establish the existence of an agreement to gain a conviction; there is no requirement to prove that the agreement unduly affected competition. Section 34 makes it illegal for a supplier to grant a price concession to one buyer that is not available to all other buyers (similar to the U.S. Robinson-Patman Act).

Quantity discounts are permitted, as are one-time price cuts to clear out inventory. As in the United States, the Canadian buyer who knowingly is on the receiving end of price discrimination also has violated the law. Section 38 covers price maintenance and applies to the purchase of goods for resale. Essentially it says that a supplier should not, by threat or promise, attempt to influence how the firms that buy from it then price their products for resale.

TYPES OF PURCHASES AND METHODS OF PRICE DETERMINATION

Analysis of suppliers' costs is by no means the only basis for price determination. What other means can be used? Much depends on the type of product being bought. There are four general classes:

1. *Raw materials.* This group is made up of the so-called *sensitive commodities,* such as copper, wheat, and crude petroleum.

2. *Special items.* This group includes items and materials which are special to the organization's product line and, therefore, are custom ordered, as well as purchases of equipment and items of a nonrepetitive nature.

3. *Standard production items.* This group includes such items as bolts and nuts, many forms of commercial steel, valves, and tubing, whose prices are fairly stable and are quoted on a basis of "list price with some discount."

4. *Items of small value.* This group includes items of such small comparative value that the expenditure of any particular effort to check price prior to purchase is not justified.

Sensitive Commodities. For the sensitive commodities, the price at any particular moment probably is less important than the trend of the price movement. The price can be determined readily in most instances because many of these commodities are bought and sold on well-organized markets. Prices are reported regularly in many of the trade and business journals, such as *Iron Age* and *The Wall Street Journal.*

These quoted market prices also can be useful in developing (1) prices-paid evaluation systems and (2) price indexes for use in price escalator clauses.

To the extent that such quoted prices are a fair reflection of market conditions, the current cash price is known and is substantially uniform for a given grade. Yet, it is common knowledge among buyers that such published market quotations usually are on the high side, and the astute buyer probably can get a lower price. With commodities of this sort a company's requirements usually are sufficiently adjustable, so that an immediate order is seldom a necessity and purchase can be postponed if the trend of prices is downward.

The price trend is a matter of importance in the purchase of any type of commodity, but it is particularly important with this group. Insofar as "careful and studious timing" is essential to getting the right price, both the type of information required as a basis for such timing and the sources from which the information can be obtained differ from those necessary in dealing with other groups of items. Commodity study research, discussed in Chapter 11, is particularly useful in buying these items.

Special Items.   Special items include a large variety of purchased parts or special materials peculiar to the organization's end product or service. Make or buy is always a significant consideration on these items because of their proprietary nature. Prices normally are obtained by quotation because no published price lists are available. Subcontracts are common, and the availability of compatible or special equipment, skilled labor, and capacity may be significant factors in determining price. Since large differences may exist between suppliers in terms of these factors and their desire for business, prices may vary substantially between bidders. Each product in this group is unique and may need special attention. A diligent search for suppliers willing and able to handle such special requirements, including an advantageous price, may pay off handsomely.

Equipment and nonrepetitive purchases also normally are handled with extensive use of quotations.

Standard Production Items.   The third group of items includes those standard production items whose prices are comparatively stable and are likely to be quoted on a basis of list less certain discounts. This group includes a wide range of items commonly obtainable from a substantial list of sources. The inventory problems related to this class of requirements are largely routine. Changes in price do occur, but they are far less frequent than with raw materials and are likely to be moderate. Prices usually are obtained from catalogs or similar publications of vendors, supplemented by periodic discount sheets.

It should not be concluded from this that such purchases are unimportant or that the prices quoted should not be examined with care. Quite the contrary is true. The items are important in themselves; the annual dollar volume of purchases is often impressive; and real attention needs to be paid to the unit price. When a requisition is received by the purchasing department, the first step commonly would be to refer to past purchase records as the first source of information. If the material in question has been regularly purchased or orders have been placed for it recently, an up-to-date price record and catalog file will give all the information pertaining to the transaction, such as the various firms able to supply the commodity, the firms from which purchases have been made, and the prices paid. This information will be sufficiently recent and reliable to enable the buyer to place the order without extended investigation. However, if the buyer does not feel justified in proceeding on the basis of this information, a list of available suppliers from vendor files, catalogs, and other sources can be assembled and quotation requests can be sent to selected sources.

One of the best sources for current prices and discounts is sales representatives. Few manufacturers rely wholly on catalogs for sales but follow up such material by visits from their salespersons. Much useful data can be obtained from such visits. The buyer learns of price revisions, which should be noted in the appropriate catalog, ascertains the probable date of publication of new editions, and is assured that the corporation is on the proper mailing lists. In some lines confidential discounts, usually based on quantity, are uncovered. Advance notice of intended price changes sometimes is given. It is the buyer's duty to be alert to the possibilities of such information in order that full advantage may be taken of them.

A sales representative may quote the buyer a price while in the buyer's office, and the buyer may accept by issuing a PO. There likely will be no problem, although legally the salesperson probably doesn't have agency authority, and the offer made by the salesperson does not legally commit the selling company *until* it has been accepted by an officer of the selling company. If the buyer wishes to accept such an offer, and to know that the offer is legally binding, he or she should ask the salesperson to furnish a letter, signed by an officer of the selling company, stating that the salesperson possesses the authority of a sales agent.

Items of Small Value.   The fourth group of commodities for the purpose of price determination includes items of such small value, comparatively speaking, that they do not justify any particular effort to analyze the price in detail. Every purchasing department must buy numerous items of this sort from time to time; yet these items do not in themselves justify a catalog file, even when such catalogs are available, nor do they represent enough money to warrant sending out for individual quotations. Actually, the pricing problem on such items is handled in a variety of ways; the following constitutes an excellent summary of these procedures:

It is common practice to send out unpriced orders for such items. Another common practice is to indicate on the order the last price paid, this price being taken from the record of purchases or past purchases if the last purchase was not too far back. Other buyers make a practice of grouping these small items under some contract arrangement or on a cost-plus basis with suppliers who undertake to have the materials on hand when needed, and who are willing to submit to periodical checking as to the fairness of the prices they charge.

In most cases, sources of supply for these items are local and current prices often are obtained by telephone and then placed on the face of the purchase order so they become a part of the agreement of purchase. The most common practice of all, however, is perhaps to depend on the integrity of the suppliers and to omit any detailed checking of the proper price on items of small value. Many purchasing managers believe that their best assurance is the confidence they have in carefully selected sources of supply and they feel secure in relying on the vendors to give them the best available price without requiring them to name the price in advance, and without checking it when the invoice is received.

Another and final method for controlling prices for these small dollar items consists of the practice of spot-checking. This means the selection of an occasional item which then is carefully investigated to develop the exact basis on which the supplier is pricing. Discovery of unfair or improper prices by such spot checks is considered a reason for discontinuing the source of supply who is discovered to be taking advantage of the nature of the transaction in pricing.

Perhaps a more effective way to buy items of small value, such as those included in the MRO group, is to use the systems-contracting techniques described in Chapter 3.

Somewhat similar to the small value purchase problem is the emergency requirement. Here, as for example with equipment breakdown, time may be of much greater value than money and the buyer may wish to get the vendor started immediately, even though price has not been determined. The buyer may decide merely to say "start" or "ship" and issue an unpriced purchase order. If the price charged on the invoice is out of line, it can be challenged before payment.

The Use of Quotations and Competitive Bidding

Quotations normally are secured when the size of the proposed commitment exceeds some minimum dollar amount: for example, $1,000. Governmental purchases commonly must be on a bid basis; here the law requires that the award shall be made to the lowest responsible bidder. In industrial practice, proposals may be solicited with a view to selecting those firms with whom negotiations as to the final price will be carried on.

The extent to which competitive bidding is relied on to secure an acceptable price varies widely. On the one hand, it is a common practice for buyers of routine supplies, purchased from the same sources time after time, to issue unpriced orders. The same thing occasionally happens in a very strong seller's market for some critical item when prices are rising so rapidly that the vendor refuses to quote a fixed price. Whenever possible, however, price should be indicated on the purchase order. In fact, from a legal point of view, a purchase order *must* either contain a price or a method of its determination for the contract to be binding.

When it is decided to ask for competitive bids, certain essential steps are called for. These are a careful initial selection of dependable, potential sources; an accurate wording of the request to bid; submission of bid requests to a sufficient number of suppliers to assure a truly competitive price; proper treatment of such quotations, once received; and a careful analysis of them prior to making the award.

The first step is to select possible vendors from whom quotations are to be solicited; this amounts, in fact, to a preliminary screening of the sources of supply. It is assumed that the bidders must (1) be qualified to make the item in question in accordance with the buyer's specifications and to deliver it within the desired date, (2) be sufficiently reliable in other respects to warrant serious consideration as suppliers, (3) be numerous enough to ensure a truly competitive price, but (4) not be more numerous than necessary.

The first two of these qualifications have been considered in our discussion of sources. The *number* of suppliers to whom inquiries are sent is largely a matter of the buyer's judgment. Ordinarily, at least two vendors are invited to bid. More often, three or four are invited to submit bids. A multiplicity of bidders does not ensure a truly competitive price, although under ordinary circumstances it is an important factor, provided that the bidders are comparable in every major respect and provided that each is sufficiently reliable so that the buyer would be willing to purchase from that vendor.

The buyer normally will exclude from the bid list those firms with whom it is unlikely that an order would be placed, even though their prices were low. Sometimes bids are solicited solely for the purpose of checking the prices of regular suppliers or for inventory-pricing purposes. It should be remembered, however, that a company is put to some expense—at times, a very considerable one—when it submits a bid. It should not be asked to bear this cost without good reason. Moreover, the receipt of a request to bid is an encouragement to the vendor and implies that an order is possible. Therefore, purchasers should not solicit quotations unless placement of a purchase order is a possibility.

Having decided on the companies that are to be invited to bid, a general inquiry is addressed to them, in which all the necessary information is set forth. A complete description of the item or items, the date on which these items are wanted, and the date by which the bid is to be returned are included. In many instances, a telephone inquiry is substituted for a formal request to bid.

Subsequent to the mailing of an inquiry but prior to the announcement of the purchase award, bidders naturally are anxious to know how their quotations compare with those of their competitors. Since sealed bids, used in governmental purchasing, are not commonly used in private industry, the purchaser is in a position to know how the bids, as they are received, compare with one another. However, if the bids are examined on receipt, it is important that this information be treated in strictest confidence. Indeed, some buyers deliberately keep themselves in ignorance of the quotations until such time as they are ready to analyze the bids; thus they are in a position truthfully to tell any inquiring bidder that they do not know how the bid prices compare. Even after the award is made, it probably is the better policy not to reveal to unsuccessful bidders the amount by which they failed to meet the successful bid.

Firm Bidding

The reason for the confidential treatment of bid price information is its connection with a problem practically all buyers have to face, namely, that of "firm bidding." Most firms have a policy of notifying suppliers that original bids must be final and that revisions will not be permitted under any circumstances. Exceptions are made only in case of obvious error.

Particularly in times of falling prices, suppliers, extremely anxious to get business, try by various devices to assure that their bids will be the lowest. Not infrequently they have been encouraged in this procedure by those purchasers who have acceded to requests that revisions be allowed. Unfortunately, it is also true that there are buyers who deliberately play one bidder against another and who even seek to secure lower prices by relating imaginary bids to prospective suppliers. The responsibility for deviations from a policy of firm bidding must be laid at the door of the purchaser as well as of the supplier.

A policy of firm bidding is sound and should be deviated from only under the most unusual circumstances. To those who contend that it is impossible to adopt such a policy, the answer is that it actually is the practice followed in many concerns. The advantage of firm bidding as a general policy, however, need no particular explanation. If rigidly adhered to, it is the fairest possible means of treating all suppliers alike. It tends to stress the quality and service elements in the transaction instead of the price factor. Assuming that bids are solicited only from honest and dependable suppliers and that the buyer is not obligated to place the order with the lowest bidder, it removes from suppliers the temptation to try to use inferior materials or workmanship once their bid has been accepted. It saves the purchaser time by removing the necessity of constant bargaining with suppliers over price.

Occasionally the buyer may, after reviewing the bids submitted, notify the bidders that all bids are being rejected, and that another bid request is being issued or that the item will be bought through a means other than competitive bidding. This may be done if it is obvious that the bidders did not fully understand the specifications, if collusion on the part of the bidders is suspected, or if it is felt that all prices quoted are unrealistically high.

Determination of Most Advantageous Bid

Typically, a bid analysis sheet is used to array the bids of all vendors and the particulars of each bid (see Chapter 3 for example). But after the bids have been submitted and compared, which should be selected? The lowest bid customarily is accepted.[2] The objective of securing bids from various sources is to obtain the lowest price, and the purpose of supplying detailed specifications and statements of requirements is to assure that the buyer receives the same items or services irrespective of whom the supplier may be. Governmental contracts must be awarded to the lowest bidder unless very special reasons can be shown for not doing so.

However, there are several cases in which the lowest bidder may not receive the order. Information received by the buyer subsequent to the re-

---

[2]This statement is made on the assumption that the lowest bid comes from a reliable supplier; presumably, of course, only reliable firms have been invited to bid.

quest for bids may indicate that the firm submitting the lowest bid is not reliable. Even the lowest bid may be higher than the buyer believes justifiable. Or there may be reason to believe that collusion existed among the bidders.

There are other reasons why the lowest bid is not always accepted: plant management, engineering, or using departments may express a preference for a certain manufacturer's product. Possibly a slight difference in price may not be considered enough to compensate for the confidence insured by a particular supplier's product. A small difference in price may not seem to justify changing from a source of supply that has been satisfactory over a long period; yet the bid process may have been considered essential in assuring that the company was receiving the proper price treatment.

Selecting the supplier, once the quotations are received, is not a simple matter of listing the bidders and picking out the one whose price is apparently low, because the obvious price comparisons may be misleading. Of two apparently identical bids, one actually may be higher than the other. One supplier's installation costs may be lower than another's. If prices quoted are FOB origin, the transportation charges may be markedly different. One supplier's price may be much lower because it is trying to break into a new market or is trying to force its only real competitor out of business. One vendor's product may require tooling which must be amortized. One supplier may quote a fixed price; another may insist on an escalator clause that could push the price above a competitor's firm bid. These and other similar factors are likely to render a snap judgment on comparative price a mistake.

Collusive Bidding

A buyer also may reject all bids if it is suspected that the suppliers are acting in collusion with one another. In such cases the proper policy to pursue is often difficult to determine but there are various possibilities. Legal action is possible but seldom is feasible because of the expense, delay, and uncertainty of the outcome. Often, unfortunately, the only apparent solution is simply to accept the situation with the feeling that there is nothing the buyer can do about it anyway. Another possibility is to seek new sources of supply either inside or outside the area within which the buyer customarily has purchased materials or services. Resorting to substitute materials, temporarily or even permanently, may be an effective means of meeting the situation. Another possibility is to reject all the bids and then to attempt, by a process of negotiation or bargaining with one or another of the suppliers, to reduce the price. If circumstances make the last alternative the most feasible, a question of ethics is involved. Some purchasing officers feel that when collusion among the vendors exists it is ethical for them to attempt to force down suppliers' prices by means which ordinarily would not be adopted.

The Problem of Identical Prices

It is not unusual for the buyer to receive identical bids from various sources. Since such bids may indicate intensive competition on the one hand, and discrimination or collusion on the other, the purchaser must take care in handling such situations. Some of the factors which tend to make identical or parallel prices suspect are when:

1. Identical pricing marks a novel break in the historical pattern of price behavior.
2. There is evidence of communication between sellers or buyers regarding prices.
3. There is an "artificial" standardization of the product.
4. Identical prices are submitted in bids to buyers on complex, detailed, or novel specifications.
5. Deviations from uniform prices become the matter of industrywide concern—the subject of meetings, and even organized sanctions.

The purchaser can take four different types of action to discourage identical pricing. The first is the encouragement of small sellers who form the nonconformist group in an industry and are anxious to grow. The second is to allow bidders to bid on parts of large contracts if they feel the total contract may be too large. The third is the encouragement of firm bidding without revision. And the fourth is to choose criteria in making the award, so as to discourage future identical bids.

If identical bids have been received, the buyer can reject all bids, and then either call for new bids or negotiate directly with one or more specific vendors. In these circumstances, it might be appropriate in the letter to vendors notifying them that all bids have been rejected to make a polite reference to the illegality of all forms of price fixing. However, if it is decided that the contract should be awarded at this time, various alternatives are available. It may be given to:

1. The smallest supplier.
2. The one with the largest domestic content.
3. The most distant firm, forcing it to absorb the largest freight portion.
4. The firm with the smallest market share.
5. The firm most likely to grant nonprice concessions.
6. The firm whose past performance has been best.

Executive Order 10936, dated April 24, 1961, directed the reporting by all federal procurement agencies to the U.S. Department of Justice of all identical bids over $10,000 per line item. State and local purchasing departments also were asked to report identical bids. However this program was judged ineffective, relative to the administrative resources required, and it was revoked on July 6, 1983, by Executive Order 12430, entitled "Reports of Identical Bids," although it was emphasized that there is a continuing need to aggressively pursue "all cases of suspected criminal conduct, noncompetitive practices, kickbacks, and other procurement irregularities." Although the annual report entitled "Identical Bidding in Public Procurement" no longer will be available, the National Association of Attorneys General does publish an "Antitrust Report," summarizing state antitrust cases, their current status or the final outcome.[3]

Negotiation as a Method of Price Determination

Competitive bidding is the most efficient means of obtaining a fair price for items bought, for the forces of competition are used to bring the price down to a level at which the efficient vendor will only be able to cover production and distribution costs, plus make a minimum profit. If a vendor wants the order, that vendor will "sharpen the pencil" and give the buyer an attractive quote. This places a good deal of pressure on the vendor, and competitive bidding should be used whenever possible.

However, for the bid process to work efficiently, several conditions are necessary: (1) There must be at least two, and preferably several, qualified vendors; (2) The vendors must want the business; competitive bidding works best in a buyer's market; (3) The specifications must be clear, so that each bidder knows precisely what is being bid on, and so the buyer easily can compare the quotes received from various bidders; and (4) There must be honest bidding and the absence of any collusion between the bidders. When any of these conditions is absent—that is, a sole source situation, a seller's market, specifications not complete or subject to varying interpretations, or suspected vendor collusion—then negotiation is the preferred method of price determination.

Negotiation is the most sophisticated and most expensive means of price determination. It is used on large dollar purchases where competitive bidding is not appropriate. Negotiation requires that the buyer sit down across a table with a vendor, and through discussion they arrive at a common understanding on the essentials of a purchase/sale contract, such as delivery, specifications, warranty, prices, and terms. Because of the interrelation of these factors and many others, it is a difficult art and requires the exercise of judgment and tact. Negotiation is an attempt to find an agreement which allows both parties to realize their objectives. It is used most often when the buyer is in a sole-source situation; in that case, both parties know that a purchase contract will be issued and their task is to define a set of terms and conditions acceptable to both. Because of the expense and time involved,

---

[3]*State and Local Government Purchasing,* 2nd ed. (Lexington, Ky.: Council of State Governments, 1983), p. 35.

true negotiation normally will not be used unless the dollar amount is quite large; $50,000 or more is the general minimum set by some organizations.

Reasonable negotiation is expected by buyer and seller alike. It is within reasonable bounds of negotiation to insist that a supplier:

1. Operate in an efficient manner.
2. Keep prices in line with costs.
3. Not take advantage of a privileged position.
4. Make proper and reasonable adjustment of claims.
5. Be prepared to consider the special needs of the buyer's organization.

While negotiation normally is thought of as a means of establishing price to be paid, and this is the main focus, many other areas or conditions can be negotiated. In fact, *any* aspect of the purchase/sale agreement is subject to negotiation. A few of these areas are:

1. Quality.
   a. Specification compliance.
   b. Performance compliance.
   c. Test criteria.
   d. Rejection procedures.
   e. Liability.
   f. Reliability.
   g. Design changes.
2. Support.
   a. Technical assistance.
   b. Product research and development.
   c. Warranty.
   d. Spare parts.
   e. Training.
   f. Tooling.
   g. Packaging.
   h. Data sharing, including technical data.
3. Supply.
   a. Lead times.
   b. Delivery schedule.
   c. Consignment stocks.
   d. Expansion options.
   e. Vendor inventories
   f. Cancellation options.
4. Transportation.
   a. FOB terms.
   b. Carrier.
   c. Commodity classification.
   d. Freight allowance/equalization.
   e. Multiple delivery points.

5. Price.
    a. Purchase order price.
    b. Discounts (cash, quantity, and trade).
    c. Escalation provisions.
    d. Exchange terms (monetary rate fluctuation).
    e. Import duties.
    f. Payment of taxes.

Price Haggling. Negotiating a fair price should not be confused with *price haggling*. Purchasing managers generally frown on haggling, and properly so, for in the long run the cost to the buyer far outweighs any temporary advantage. For a purchaser to tell a sales representative that he or she has received a quotation that was not, in fact, received or that is not comparable; to fake telephone calls in the sales representative's presence; to leave real or fictitious bids of competitors in open sight for a sales representative to see; to mislead as to the quantity needed—these and similar practices are illustrations of that "sharp practice" so properly condemned by the Code of Ethics of the National Association of Purchasing Management.

Revision of Price Upward. Negotiation need not result in a lower price. Occasionally, there may be revision upward of the price paid, compared to the vendor's initial proposal. If in the negotiation it becomes clear that the vendor has either misinterpreted the specifications or underestimated the resources needed to perform the work, the buyer will bring this to the vendor's attention so the proposal may be adjusted accordingly. A good contract is one that both parties can live with, and the vendor should not lose money, providing the operation is efficient. When a purchaser cooperates in granting increases not required by the original vendor proposal, the buyer is in a position to request decreases in prices if unforeseen events occur which result in the vendor's being able to produce the material or product at a substantial saving.

Cost/Price Analysis

The party in the strongest position in a negotiation session is the one which has the best data. Recognizing the importance of cost, it is common practice for the purchasing manager to make the best estimate possible of the supplier's costs as one means of judging the reasonableness of the price proposed. When the supplier is given a request for proposal (RFP), which is an invitation to make an offer which both parties agree will be subject to further negotiation, it is normal for the buyer to also request that the proposal be accompanied by a cost breakdown. If the vendor has nothing to hide and is confident in the work of its estimating department it should be willing to supply the requested cost breakdown. But, if a cost breakdown cannot be obtained, then the buyer must do a cost buildup, which is far more time consuming and difficult to do.

Many larger firms have within the purchasing department cost analysts to assist the buyer in analyzing vendor costs in preparation for negotiation (see also Chapter 11 on purchasing research). These cost estimates must be based on such data as are available. The prices of raw material entering into the product are commonly accessible and the amounts required are also fairly well known. For component parts, catalog prices often offer a clue. Transportation costs are easily determined. The buyer's own engineers should provide data on processing costs. Burden and general overhead rates can be approximated.

Overhead costs generally consist of indirect costs incurred in the manufacturing, research, or engineering facilities of the company. Equipment depreciation typically is the largest single element in manufacturing burden. It is important to know how these burden costs are distributed to a given product. If overhead is allocated as a fixed percentage of direct labor costs and there is an increase in labor costs, overhead costs can be unduly inflated unless the allocation percentage is changed.

The growing tendency for industry to become more capital intensive has increased the relative percentage of overhead versus direct labor and materials. Since some items in the overhead such as local real estate taxes are attributable to the location of the supplier and others are properly seen as depreciation or investment at varying technological and economic risk levels, the analysis and allocation of these costs to individual products are particularly difficult.

Both tooling costs and engineering costs often are included as a part of general manufacturing burden, but it probably is wisest to pull them out for analysis as separate items, since each may account for a relatively large amount of cost. The buyer wants to know what it should cost a reasonably efficient vendor to build the tooling, ownership of completed tooling, life expectancy (number of units), and whether the tooling can be used with other equipment than that owned by the vendor. Only with such information can the buyer guard against being charged twice for the same tooling. In the case of engineering labor, it usually is quite expensive on an hourly basis and the buyer does not want to pay the vendor for engineering work which really isn't necessary.

General and administrative expense includes items such as selling, promotion, advertising, executive salaries, and legal expense. Frequently there is no justification for the supplier to charge an advertising allocation in the price of a product manufactured to the buyer's specifications.

Material costs can be estimated from a bill of material, a drawing, or a sample of the product. The buyer can arrive at material costs by multiplying material quantities per unit by raw material prices. Sometimes a material usage curve will be helpful. The purpose of the curve is to chart what improvement should occur from buying economies and lower scrap rates as experience is gained in the manufacturing process. Use of price indexes and maintenance of price trend records is standard practice.

Direct labor estimates are not made as easily as material estimates. Even though labor costs are normally labeled direct for machine operators and assembly line workers, in reality they tend to be more fixed than most managers care to admit. Most organizations prefer not to lay off personnel and there are strong pressures to keep the so-called direct labor force reasonably stable and employed. This means that inventories and overtime often are used to smooth fluctuations in demand and also that labor cost becomes at least semivariable and subject to allocation.

Product mix, run sizes, and labor turnover may affect labor costs substantially. The greater the mix, the shorter the lot size produced, and the higher the turnover, the greater direct labor costs will be. These three factors alone may create substantial cost differences between suppliers of an identical end product. Geographical considerations also play a large part since differences in labor rates do exist between plant locations. Such differences may change dramatically over time, as the rapid increases in direct labor rates in Japan and Germany have demonstrated. The astute cost analyst will estimate the supplier's real labor costs, taking the above considerations into account.

The Learning Curve

The learning curve[4] provides an analytical framework for quantifying the commonly recognized principle that one becomes more proficient with experience. Its origins lie in the aircraft industry in World War II when it was empirically determined that labor time per plane declined dramatically as volume increased. Subsequent studies showed that the same phenomenon occurred in a variety of industries and situations. Although conceptually most closely identified with direct labor, most experts believe the learning curve is actually brought about by a combination of a large number of factors which include:

1. The learning rate of labor.
2. The motivation of labor and management to increase output.
3. The development of improved methods, procedures, and support systems.
4. The substitution of better materials, tools, and equipment or more effective use of materials, tools, and equipment.
5. The flexibility of the job and the people associated with it.

---

[4]Also called the *time reduction curve* or *progress curve*. When used to analyze overall management efficiency and effectiveness changes in a business strategy context, the term *improvement curve* is used also.

TABLE 7–1   Learning Curve Example

Units Produced	Cumulative Labor Hours	Average Labor Hours per Unit
100	100,000	1,000
200	180,000	900
400	324,000	810
800	583,200	729

6. The ratio of labor versus machine time in the task.

7. The amount of preplanning done in advance of the task.

8. The turnover of labor in the unit.

We know the learning curve happens; its presence has been empirically determined a sufficient number of times that its existence is no longer in doubt. The reasons for it sound plausible enough; yet it is still not possible to determine in advance just what the learning rate should be for a brand new product or a novel task.

The learning curve has tremendous implications for cost determination, management by objectives, and negotiation. For example, take a 90 percent learning curve. Suppose we wish to purchase 800 units of a highly labor-intensive, expensive product which will be produced by a group of workers over a two-year period. The first 100 units have been produced at an average labor time of 1,000 hours. With a 90 percent learning curve, the average labor time for the first 200 units would drop to 900 hours. Table 7–1 shows the figures.[5]

These figures may be plotted on rectangular coordinates as shown in Figure 7–1. Using logarithmic coordinates this curve is a straight line, as shown in Figure 7–2.

It is important to recognize that the choice of learning curve, be it 95, 90, 85, or 80 percent or any other figure, is not an exact science. Normally the buyer, lacking past experience with a particular purchased item, will start with an 80 percent curve and then adjust it up or down to fit the particular situation. The new product situation can be compared to other situations where the same or similar circumstances were present. It can be readily established afterwards what really happened and what the actual curve was. It also is possible to wait for some preliminary production data,

---

[5]The figures in Table 7–1 use the cumulative average curve technique. As the quantity doubles, the rate of learning is constant. This is known as the *Boeing Curve*. An alternative approach, which produces a unit curve, is referred to as the *Wright Curve*. Further exposition of the two approaches, which produce somewhat different results, is presented in Charles H. Adams, "The Improvement Curve Technique," Section 1.13 in the *Guide to Purchasing* (New York: The National Association of Purchasing Management, 1980).

FIGURE 7–1   Ninety Percent Learning Curve Plotted on Standard Graph Paper

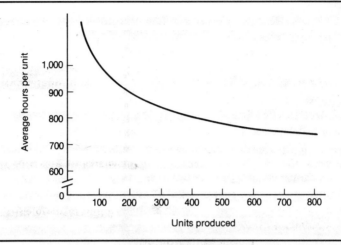

FIGURE 7–2   Ninety Percent Learning Curve Plotted on Log-Log Paper

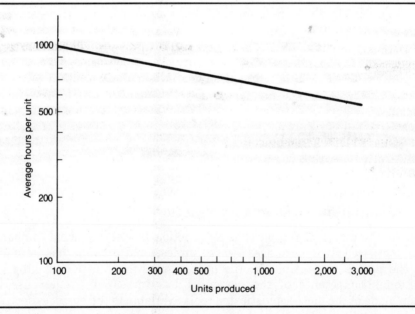

which can then be used to plot the curve since, theoretically, only two points are required to fix the curve's location (using log-log paper). Thus, for new products and relatively short runs, actual production information may be requested on the first significant run and renegotiation requested on the basis of actual data if uncertainty exists as to which learning curve is appropriate.

The learning curve or improvement function implies that improvement never stops, no matter how large the volume becomes. The potential of the learning curve in materials management has not yet been fully explored. It is a powerful concept and of great use to the buyer. Progressive discounts, shortened lead times, and better value should be planned and obtained through its use.

Some purchasing managers believe they are not justified in going very far into suppliers' costs. They take this position for several reasons: (1) In many cases suppliers do not know their costs, and it would be useless to inquire into them. (2) The interpretation of cost calls for an exercise of judgment, and differences of opinion would arise even if all the figures were available. (3) Some suppliers will not divulge this information. (4) The seller's costs do not determine market prices. (5) The buyer is not interested in the supplier's costs anyway; the primary concern is getting the best price consistent with quality, service, and quantity. If a seller offers a price which does not cover costs, either in ignorance or with full recognition of what he or she is doing, the matter is the seller's problem and not the buyer's.

To a considerable extent, much of this reasoning is true. However, there are some limitations. In the first place, unless a buyer has some idea of a supplier's costs, at least in a general way, it is difficult to judge the reasonableness of the supplier's prices. Furthermore, the position that the buyer is neither concerned with nor responsible for vendors who offer merchandise below cost must recognize two things: first, that the buyer cannot complain if ruinous, vicious price cutting eliminates or handicaps efficient suppliers, and, second, that the buyer cannot maintain an attitude of indifference when the sellers offer merchandise below cost and then become intensely concerned when prices rise materially above cost as vendors fight for financial survival.

Negotiation Strategy and Practice

As the status of the purchasing function in well-managed companies has increased in importance, a more professional attitude has developed in the people responsible for the operation of the function. As the professional competence of the personnel has increased, greater use has been made of the more sophisticated tools available to the business decision-making executive. Negotiation is a prime example of this developing professionalism.

The discussion of some of the elements and considerations which affect the price of an item makes it obvious that negotiation can be a valuable technique to use in reaching an agreement with a supplier on the many variables affecting a specific price. This is not to say that all buying-selling transactions require the use of negotiations. Nor is the intention to indicate that negotiation is used only in determining price. Reaching a clear understanding of time schedules for deliveries, factors affecting quality, and methods of packaging may require negotiations of equal or greater importance than those applying to price.

A list of some of the various kinds of purchasing situations in which the use of negotiations should prove of value follows:

1. Any written contract covering price, specifications, terms of delivery, and quality standards.

2. The purchase of items made to the buyer's specifications. Special importance should be attached to "first buys," since thorough exploration of the needs of the buyer and the supplier often will result in a better product at a lower price.

3. When changes are made in drawings or specifications after a purchase order has been issued.

4. When quotations have been solicited from responsible bidders and no acceptable bids have been received.

5. When problems of tooling or packaging occur.

6. When changing economic or market conditions require changes in quantities or prices.

7. When problems of termination of a contract involve disposal of facilities, materials, or tooling.

8. When there are problems of accepting any of the various elements entering into cost type contracts.

9. Problems arising under the various type of contracts used in defense and governmental contracting.

Success in negotiation largely is a function of the quality and amount of planning which has been done. Figure 7–3 presents a model of the negotiation process. The basic steps in developing a strategy for negotiation are:

1. Develop the specific objectives (outcomes) desired from the negotiation.

2. Analyze the vendor's bargaining position. What is the vendor's capacity, backlog, and profitability? How confident is the vendor of getting the contract? Is there any time urgency?

3. Gather pertinent data. Here is where cost analysis comes into play.

4. Attempt to recognize the vendor's needs. In a successful negotiation, both parties must win.

5. Determine the facts of the situation. A fact is defined as an item of information about which agreement is expected. For example, if the

FIGURE 7–3   Model of the Negotiation Process

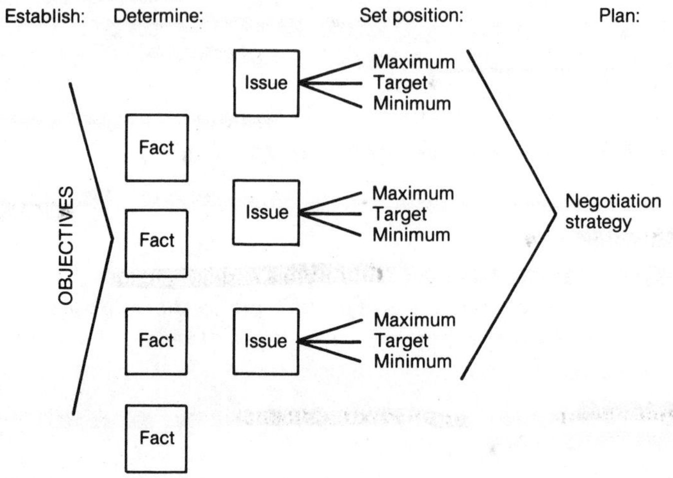

vendor's cost breakdown states that the direct labor rate is $8.10 per hour, and you agree, that is a fact.

6. Determine the issues. An issue is something over which disagreement is expected. The purpose of negotiation is to resolve issues so that a mutually satisfactory contract can be signed. For example, if the vendor claims the manufacturing burden rate is 300 percent of direct labor costs, but your analysis indicates a 240 percent burden rate is realistic, this becomes an issue to be settled through negotiation.

7. Set the buyer's position on each issue. What data will be used to support the buyer's position?

8. Plan the negotiation strategy. Which issues should be discussed first? Where is the buyer willing to compromise? Who will make up the negotiation team (it frequently is composed of someone from both engineering and quality control, headed by the buyer)?

9. Brief all persons on your team who are going to participate in the negotiations.

10. Conduct a dress rehearsal for your people who are going to participate in the negotiations.

11. Conduct the actual negotiations with an impersonal calmness.

Ground Rules for Successful Negotiation

While negotiation skill is more of an art than a science (although cost analysis techniques will provide the buyer a sound technical basis for setting the buying organization's position on key issues and planning and executing a strategy), the experience of many organizations and purchasing managers has resulted in some general negotiation ground rules. If the buyer is not following each of these ground rules, it is likely that, from a buying point of view, negotiation outcomes probably could be improved. These ground rules are broken down into three time phases—before, during, and after the negotiation sessions:

I. Before the Session:
    A. Preparation
        1. Establish possible sources.
        2. Analyze the vendor's position.
        3. Make a facilities survey.
        4. Make a financial analysis of the vendor.
        5. Analyze the vendor's proposal.
        6. Organize the negotiation team.
        7. Get a clear understanding of the work statement.
        8. Determine negotiation objectives.
        9. Prepare alternative action courses.
        10. Know your own authority.
        11. Provide adequate conference facilities.
        12. Set up the meeting room in advance.
    B. Basic Ideas
        1. Be prepared to compromise.
        2. You will have to "sell" your position.
        3. Keep a poker face.
        4. Don't ever underestimate the seller.
        5. Never let your guard down.
        6. Take your time and do the job right.
        7. Alcohol and negotiation don't mix.
        8. Be reasonable; don't push too far.
        9. Regardless of your offer, the seller will want more.
        10. Nervousness on your part will be interpreted as a sign of weakness.
II. During the Session:
    A. Size Up the Seller
        1. Watch for roving eyeballs—and your opponent can read upside down.
        2. Spot their leader—who really can make concessions?
        3. If they're hesitant to discuss an issue, it indicates a weakness.
        4. If the seller has no data on a key issue, it shows vulnerability.
        5. Be intense; concentrate; look the other party right in the eye and listen to what he or she has to say.
    B. Strategy
        1. Take command—sit at the head of the table.

    2. Know names and pronunciation of vendor personnel.
    3. Establish extent of vendor representatives' authority.
    4. Assess supplier's minimum position.
    5. Talk positive.
    6. Phrase your questions to encourage a positive answer.
    7. Compromise on minor points when advantageous.
    8. If you compromise early in the session, you set the stage for the vendor to reciprocate.
    9. Start with the easy issues first.
    10. Avoid taking an either-or-position. The vendor may get up and leave.
    11. Never give anything away.
    12. Don't go beyond your mental and physical endurance.

C. Tactics
    1. Don't reveal maximum position.
    2. Don't argue without reason.
    3. Don't lose your cool.
    4. Don't commit beyond your authority.
    5. Remember, the supplier has to "win" too.
    6. Don't interrupt; it is disrespectful and may "turn the other party off."
    7. The best reply to a totally unacceptable offer is complete silence.
    8. Don't go off on tangents—keep the discussion on track—time is valuable.

D. Resolving Negotiation Deadlocks
    1. Go on to another point.
    2. "I see your position—now try to understand mine."
    3. "You suggest a solution."
    4. "We've come too far to get bogged down now."

III. After the Session:
    1. Make sure all items are covered in the final agreement.
    2. Know how and when to terminate a session.
    3. Keep complete notes on all points of agreement—both parties should initial or sign.
    4. Analyze what happened and why.

Provision for Price Changes

Guarantee against Price Decline.   For goods bought on a recurring basis and for raw materials, the contract may be written at the price in effect at the time the contract is negotiated. The contract then provides for a reduction during a subsequent period if there is a downward price movement in the marketplace. The contract normally will specify that price movement will be determined by the list price reported in a specific business or trade journal. The buyer is more likely to be influenced by such guarantees when they are offered in an effort to overcome reluctance to buy, induced by a fear that prices are likely to drop still further.

Price Protection Clause.   When a buyer enters into a long-term contract for raw materials or other key purchased items with one or more vendors, the buyer may want to keep open the option of taking advantage of a lower price offered by a different vendor. This might be done by either (1) buying from the noncontract vendor, or (2) forcing the contract vendor(s) to meet the lower price now available from the noncontract suppliers. Therefore, a price protection clause may be incorporated into the contract specifying that "if the buyer is offered material of equal quality in similar quantities under like terms from a responsible vendor, at a lower delivered cost to the buyer than specified in this contract, the seller on being furnished written evidence of this offer shall either meet the lower delivered price or allow the buyer to purchase from the other vendor at the lower delivered price and deduct the quantity purchased from the quantity specified in this contract."

Escalator Clauses.   The actual wording of many escalator clauses provides for either increase or decrease in price if costs change. Clauses providing for escalation came into common use during World War II when suppliers believed that their future costs were so uncertain as to make a firm quotation either impossible or, if covering all probable risks, so high as to make it unattractive, and perhaps unfair, to the buyer. They also were used extensively during many of the hyperinflation years during the 1970s.

In designing any particular escalator contract, several general and many specific problems—such as the proportion of the total price subject to adjustment; the particular measures of prices and wage rates to be used in making the adjustment; the methods to be followed in applying these averages to the base price; the limitations, if any, on the amount of adjustment; and the methods for making payment—will be encountered. In times of price stability, escalation usually is reserved for long-term contracts, on the principle that certain costs may rise and that the seller has no appreciable control over this rise. In times of inflation, shortages, and sellers' markets, escalation becomes common on even short-term contracts as sellers attempt to assure themselves the opportunity to raise prices and preserve contribution margins. Changes in material and direct labor costs generally are tied to one of the published price and cost indexes, such as those of the Bureau of Labor Statistics or one of the trade publications such as *Iron Age* or the *Chemical Marketing Reporter*. Finding a meaningful index to which escalation may be tied is a real problem in many instances. Since most escalation is automatic once the index, the portion of the contract subject to escalation, the frequency of revision, and the length of contract have been agreed to, the need for care in deciding on these factors is obvious.

The following is an illustrative escalator clause:

Labor

Adjustment with respect to labor costs shall be made on the basis of monthly average hourly earnings for the (Durable Goods Industry, subclass Machinery), as furnished by the Bureau of Labor Statistics (hereafter called the Labor Index). Adjustments shall be calculated with respect to each calendar quarter up to the completion date specified in contract. The percentage increase or decrease in the quarterly index (obtained by averaging the Labor Index for each month of the calendar quarter) shall be obtained by comparison with the Labor Index for the basic month. The basic month shall be — —, 198—. The labor adjustment for each calendar quarter as thus determined shall be obtained by applying such percentage of increase or decrease to the total amount expended by the contractor for direct labor during such quarter.

Materials

Adjustment with respect to materials shall be made on the basis of the materials index for Group VI (Metals and Metal Products), as furnished by the Bureau of Labor Statistics (hereafter called the Materials Index). Adjustments shall be determined with respect to each calendar quarter up to the completion date specified in the contract. The percentage of increase or decrease in the quarterly index (obtained by averaging the Materials Index for each month of the calendar quarter) shall be obtained by comparison with the Materials Index for the basic month. The basic month shall be — —, 198—. The material adjustment for each calendar quarter shall be obtained by applying to the contract material cost the percentage of increase or decrease shown by the Materials Index for that quarter.

A buyer who uses escalator clauses must remember that one legal essential to any enforceable purchase contract is that it contain either a definite price or the means of arriving at one. No contract for future delivery can be enforced if the price of the item is conditioned entirely on the will of one of the parties. The clauses cited earlier would appear to be adequate. So too are those clauses authorizing the seller to change price as costs of production change, provided that these costs can be reasonably determined from the vendor's accounting records.

Most-Favored-Customer Clause. Another commonly used price protection clause (sometimes referred to as a "most-favored nation clause") specifies that the vendor, over the duration of the contract, will not offer a lower price to other buyers, or if a lower price is offered to others, it will apply to this contract also.

Discounts

Discounts fall into two classes. The first class consists of inside prices and various other forms of price concessions that are not always defensible either legally or commercially. The second class consists of ordinary cash, trade, and quantity discounts which are thoroughly legitimate and fair.

The line of distinction between these two classes is difficult to draw for it is not always easy to define what is legitimate and what is not. Clearly there are certain types of apparent price concessions, such as *inside prices*, which no responsible purchasing agent should even request and which under most circumstances should be refused if offered. A vendor who offers an inside price to one buyer will offer a similar or lower price to another. A seller who is not open and honest in pricing policy is not one with whom a purchaser can afford to do business.

The second class of discounts warrants more attention.

Cash Discounts.   Cash discounts are granted by virtually every seller of industrial goods, although the actual discount terms are a matter of individual trade custom and vary considerably from one industry to another. The purpose of a cash discount is to secure the prompt payment of an account.

Most sellers expect buyers to take the cash discount. The net price is commonly fixed at a point which will yield a fair profit to the vendor and is the price the vendor expects most customers to pay. Those who do not pay within the time limit are penalized and are expected to pay the gross price. However, variations in cash discount amounts frequently are made without due regard for the real purpose for which such discounts should be granted and are used, instead, merely as another means of varying prices. If a buyer secures a cash discount not commonly granted in the past, he or she may be sure that the net result is merely a reduction in the price, regardless of the name used. On the other hand, a reduction in the size of the cash discount is, in effect, an increase in the price.

Cash discounts, therefore, sometimes raise rather difficult questions of price policy, but if they are granted on the same terms to all buyers and if postdating and other similar practices are not granted to some buyers and denied to others, then the purchasing office's major interest in cash discounts is confined largely to being sure they are called to the attention of the proper financial managers. The purchaser ordinarily cannot be held responsible for a failure to take cash discounts, since this depends on the financial resources of the company and is, therefore, a matter of financial rather than purchasing policy. The purchaser should, however, be very careful to secure such cash discounts as customarily are granted. It is a part of the buyer's responsibility to see that inspection is promptly made, that goods are accepted without unnecessary loss of time, and that all documents are handled expeditiously so all discounts quoted may be taken. A discount of 2 percent if payment is made within 10 days, with the gross amount due in 30 days, is the equivalent of earning an annual interest rate of approximately 36 percent. If the buying company does not pay within the 10-day discount period but instead pays 20 days later, the effective cost for the use of that money for the 20 days is 2 percent (the lost discount). Since there are approximately 18 20-day periods in a year, $2\% \times 18 = 36\%$, the effective annual interest rate.

To establish the exact date by which payment must be mailed to deduct the cash discount from the payment amount, and to avoid the confusion which often results from handling incorrectly prepared vendor invoices, some firms include a clause in their purchase order specifying that "determination of the cash discount payment period will be calculated from either the date of delivery of acceptable goods, or the receipt of a properly prepared invoice, whichever date is later."

Trade Discounts.   Trade discounts are granted by a manufacturer to a buyer because the purchasing firm is a particular type of distributor or user. In general, they aim to protect the distributor by making it more profitable for a purchaser to buy from the distributor than directly from the manufacturer. When manufacturers have found that various types of distributors can sell their merchandise in a given territory more cheaply than they can, they usually rely on the distributors' services. To ensure that goods will move through the channels selected, the distributor is granted a trade discount approximating the cost of doing business.

However, trade discounts are not always used properly. Protection is sometimes granted distributors not entitled to it, since the services which they render manufacturers, and presumably customers, are not commensurate with the discount they obtain. Generally speaking, buyers dealing in small quantities who secure a great variety of items from a single source or who depend on frequent and very prompt deliveries are more likely to obtain their supplies from wholesalers and other distributors receiving trade discounts. With the larger accounts, manufacturers are more likely to sell directly, even though they may reserve the smaller accounts in the same territory for the wholesalers. Some manufacturers refuse to sell to accounts purchasing below a stipulated minimum.

Discounts often are available to a buyer who also purchases aftermarket requirements (replacement parts for units already sold). The supplier may put the buyer who wishes to buy items which will be sold to the aftermarket into one of several price classifications: (1) an OEM (original equipment manufacturer) class, (2) a class with its distributors, or (3) a separate OEM aftermarket class. Aftermarket suppliers often do special packaging, part numbering, or stocking, which may justify a special price schedule. The buyer needs to know what price classifications the vendor uses and the qualifications for placing the buyer in a particular classification.[6]

---

[6]Mark S. Miller, "Purchasing for the Aftermarket: What To Consider," *Purchasing World*, November 1984, p. 110.

Multiple Discounts.   In some industries and trades, prices are quoted on a multiple discount basis. For example, 10, 10 and 10 means that, for an item listed at $100, the actual price to be paid by the purchaser is ($100 − 10%) − 10%(100 − 10%) − 10%[(100 − 10%) − 10%(100 − 10%)] = $90 − $9 − $8.10 = $72.90. The 10, 10 and 10 is, therefore, equivalent to a discount of 0.271. Tables are available listing the most common multiple discount combinations and their equivalent discount.

Quantity Discounts.   Quantity discounts may be granted for buying in particular quantities and vary roughly in proportion to the amount purchased. From the seller's standpoint, the justification for granting such discounts is usually that quantity purchasing results in savings to the seller, enabling a lower price to the buyer who has made such savings possible. These savings may be of two classes: first, savings in marketing expense and, second, savings in production expense.[7]

In the late 1940s, the Federal Trade Commission, in administering the Robinson-Patman Act from time to time, proceeded against buyers who were alleged to have knowingly received lower prices from sellers than their competitors. It is obvious that in most cases it would be extremely difficult for the buyer to prove the seller had cost savings which could justify the lower price.

In 1953, the U.S. Supreme Court ruled in the case of the Automatic Canteen Company of America that:

1. The mere inducement of receipt of a lower price is not unlawful.

2. It is lawful for a buyer to accept anything which it is lawful for a seller to give.

3. It is only the prohibited discrimination a buyer may not induce or receive.

4. It is not unlawful for a buyer to receive a prohibited discrimination unless he knows or, as a reasonably prudent buyer, should know that the differential is prohibited.

The court concluded that to prove cost justification according to the Federal Trade Commission's accounting standards would place a heavy burden on a buyer — it would require a study of the seller's business and "would almost inevitably," to quote the court, "require a degree of cooperation between buyer and seller, as against other buyers, that may offend other

---

[7]The U.S. Supreme Court in May 1948, ruled in the case of the Morton Salt Company (68 S. Ct.) that no wholesaler, retailer, or manufacturer whose product is sold to the public through these channels may grant quantity discounts unless they can be justified by (a) lower costs "due to quantity manufacture, delivery, or sale" or (b) "the seller's good-faith effort to meet a competitor's equally low price." Furthermore, it ruled that the Federal Trade Commission need not prove that discounts are discriminatory. The burden of proof is on the seller to prove the law is not being violated.

antitrust policies, and it might also expose the seller's cost secrets to the prejudice of arm's-length bargaining in the future." The court added: "Finally, not one, but as here, approximately 80 different sellers' costs may be in issue." The court dismissed the case against Automatic Canteen.

The savings in marketing expense arise because it may be no more costly to sell a large order than a small one; the billing expense is the same; and the increased cost of packing, crating, and shipping is not proportional. When these circumstances exist, a direct quantity discount not exceeding the difference in cost of handling the small and the large order is justified.

There are substantial savings in production costs as a result of securing a large order instead of a small one. For instance, placing orders in advance of the time when actual production begins is an aid in production planning.

From the buyer's viewpoint, the question of quantity discounts is intimately connected with that of inventory policy. While it is true that the larger the size of a given order, the lower the unit price likely will be, the carrying charges on the buyer's larger inventory are more costly. Hence, the savings on the size of order must be compared against the increased inventory costs.

The Price-Discount Problem

A normal situation in purchasing occurs when a price discount is offered if purchases are made in larger quantities. Acceptance of a larger quantity provides a form of anticipation inventory. The problem may be solved in several ways. Marginally, the question is: should we increase the size of our inventory so that we obtain the benefits of the lower price? Put this way, it can be analyzed as a return on investment decision. The simple EOQ model is not of much assistance here since it cannot account for the purchase price differential directly. It is possible to use the EOQ model to eliminate some alternatives, however, and to check the final solution. Total cost calculations are required to find the optimal point.

The following problem is illustrative of the calculation.

Sample Price-Discount Problem

R = 900 units (annual demand)
S = $50 (order cost)
K = .25 (carrying cost) or 25 percent
C = $45 for 0–199 units per order
$43 for 200–399 units per order
$41.50 for 400–799 units per order
$40.00 for 800 and over units per order

Sample Calculations for the Price-Discount Problem

	100	200	400	800
Total annual price paid	$40,500	$38,700	$37,350	$36,000
Carrying cost	562	1,075	2,075	4,000
Order cost	450	225	112	56
Total cost	41,512	40,000	39,537	40,056
Average inventory	$2,250	$4,300	$8,300	$16,000
EOQ	Units 89	92*	93*	94*

*Not feasible

A simple marginal analysis shows that in moving from 100 per order to 200 the additional average investment is $4,300 − $2,250 = $2,050. The saving in price is $40,500 − $38,700 = $1,800, and the order cost saving is $450 − $225 = $225. For an additional investment of $2,050 the savings are $2,025 which is almost a 100 percent return and is well in excess of the 25 percent carrying cost. In going from 400 to 800 the additional investment is $7,700 for a total price and order savings of $1,406.25. This falls below the 25 percent carrying cost and would not be a desirable result. The total cost figures show that the optimal purchase quantity is at the 400 level. The largest single saving occurs at the first price break at the 200 level.

The EOQs with an asterisk are not feasible because the price range and the volume do not match. For example, the price for the second EOQ of 92 is $45. Yet, for the 200—400 range, the actual price is $43.00. The EOQ may be used, however, in the following way. In going from right to left on the table (from the lowest unit price to the highest price) proceed until the first valid EOQ is obtained. This is 89 for the 0 to 199 price range. Then the order quantity at each price discount about this EOQ is checked to see whether total costs at the higher order quantity are lower or higher than at the EOQ. Doing this for the example shown gives us a total cost at the valid EOQ level of 89 of:

Total annual price paid	$40,500
Carrying cost	500
Order cost	500
Total cost	$41,500

Since this total cost at the feasible EOQ of 89 units is above the total cost at the 200 order quantity level and the 400 and 800 order levels as well, the proper order quantity is 400, which gives the lowest total cost of all options.

The discussion so far has assumed that the quantity discount offered is based on orders of the full amount, forcing the purchaser to carry substantial inventories. It is preferable, of course, from the purchaser's standpoint to take delivery in smaller quantities but to still get the lower discount price. This could well be negotiated through annual contracts, cumulative discounts or blanket orders. This type of analysis can also identify what extra price differential the purchaser might be willing to pay to avoid carrying substantial stocks.

Quantity Discounts and Source Selection

The quantity discount question is of interest to many buyers for a second reason: all quantity discounts, and especially those of the cumulative type, tend to restrict the number of suppliers thereby affecting the choice of source.

Since there is real justification for quantity discounts when properly used, the buyer should obtain such discounts whenever possible. Ordinarily they come through the pressure of competition among sellers. Furthermore, an argument may be advanced that such discounts are a matter of right. The buyer is purchasing goods or merchandise, not crating, or packing materials, or transportation. The seller presumably should expect to earn a profit not from those wholly auxiliary services but rather from manufacturing and selling the merchandise processed. These auxiliary services are necessary; they must be performed; they must be paid for; and it is natural to expect the buyer to pay for them. But the buyer should not be expected to pay more than the actual cost of these auxiliary services.

When an attempt is made to justify quantity discounts on the basis that they contribute to reduced production costs through providing a volume of business large enough to reduce the overhead expenses, somewhat more cautious reasoning is necessary. It is true that in some lines of business the larger the output, the lower the overhead cost per unit of product. It also may be true that without the volume from the large customers, the average cost of production would be higher. However, the small buyers may place a greater total proportion of the seller's business than do the large ones. So far as production costs are concerned therefore, the small buyers contribute even more toward that volume so essential to the per unit production cost than does the larger buyer.

Another contention is that large customers ordering early in the season, or even prior to the time actual production of a season's supply begins, should be granted higher discounts because their orders keep the mill in production. Such a buyer probably may be entitled to a lower price than one who waits until later in the season to order. However, such a discount, since it is justified by the early placement of an order and therefore should be granted to every buyer placing an early order regardless of its size, is not properly a quantity discount but is a time discount.

Cumulative Discounts.   Another type of quantity discount is cumulative and varies in proportion to the quantity purchased; however, instead of being computed on the size of the order placed at any one time, it is based on the quantity purchased over a period of time. Such discounts are commonly granted as an incentive to a company for continued patronage. It is hoped they will induce a purchaser to concentrate purchases largely with a single source rather than distributing them over many sources, thus benefiting the company offering the discount. Generally speaking, the purchaser should not scatter orders over too large a number of sources, for distributing one's orders over many sources is uneconomical and costly. No supplier, under such circumstances, is likely to give the same careful attention to the buyer's requirements as he would if he felt he were getting the larger portion of the purchaser's business.

The use of cumulative discounts must meet the same cost justification rules under the Robinson-Patman Act as other quantity discounts. However, as long as the buyer is not knowingly accepting or inducing discriminatory quantity discounts, then the responsibility for justification rests solely with the seller.

Reference has been made to the legitimate and illegitimate use of discounts. There is a reason for cash discounts. Trade discounts, as far as they are necessary to the well-being of a desirable source of supply, have their proper place. Quantity discounts may be earned and justified. However, discounts also may be used illegitimately. They may be used to grant price concessions, to pursue a policy of price cutting under a guise of legitimate business practice, or to play certain types of buyers against others. Indeed, under the Robinson-Patman Act, the buyer as well as the seller may be found guilty of the discriminatory use of quantity discounts.

Contract Cancellation

In practice, cancellations usually occur during a period of falling prices. At such times, if the price has declined since the placing of the order, some buyers may try to take advantage of all sorts of loopholes in the purchase order or sales agreement to reject merchandise. To avoid completion of the transaction, they take advantage of technicalities which under other circumstances would be of no concern to them whatever. One can have sympathy for the buyer with a contract at a price higher than the market. There is little justification, however, for the purchaser who follows a cancellation policy under this situation. A contract should be considered a binding obligation. The practice referred to is an instance of "sharp practice," which hopefully is becoming less and less prevalent as the years go by. There may be occasions when a buyer justifiably seeks to cancel the contract, but to do so merely because the market price has fallen is not one of them.

In some instances, the buyer knows when the purchase order is placed that the customer for whose job the materials are being bought may unexpectedly cancel the order, thus forcing cancellation of purchase orders for materials planned for the job. This is a common risk when purchasing materials for use on a government contract, for appropriation changes often force the government to cancel its order, and results then in cancellation of a great many purchase orders by firms who were to have been suppliers to the government under the now-cancelled government contract. Or, severe changes in the business cycle may trigger purchase order cancellations. If cancellation is a possibility, the basis and terms of cancellation should be agreed on in advance and made part of the terms and conditions of the purchase order. Problems such as how to value, and what is an appropriate payment for, partially completed work on a now-cancelled purchase order are best settled before the situation arises.

FORWARD BUYING AND COMMODITIES

Forward buying is the commitment of purchases in anticipation of future requirements beyond current lead times. Thus, an organization may buy ahead because of anticipated shortages, strikes, or price increases. As the time between procurement commitment and actual use of the requirement grows, uncertainties also increase. One common uncertainty is whether the actual need will be realized. A second concern is with price. How can the purchaser ascertain that the price currently committed is reasonable compared to the actual price which would have been paid had the forward buy not been made?

Commodities represent a special class of purchases frequently associated with forward buying. Almost all organizations purchase commodities in a variety of processed forms. For example, an electrical equipment manufacturer may buy a substantial amount of wire, the cost of which is significantly affected by the price of copper. Many organizations buy commodities for further processing or for resale. For them the way they buy and the prices they pay for commodities may be the single most important factor in success. Cash prices for selected commodities are reported daily in *The Wall Street Journal*.

Forward Buying versus Speculation

All forward buying involves some risk. In ordinary forward buying, purchases are largely confined to actually known requirements or to carefully estimated requirements for a limited period of time in advance. The essential controlling factor is need. Even when the organization uses order points and order quantities, the amount to be bought may be increased or decreased in accordance both with probable use and with the price trend, rather than automatically reordering a given amount. Temporarily, no order may be placed at all.

This may be true even where purchases have to be made many months in advance, as in the case of seasonal products, such as wheat, or those that must be obtained abroad, such as jute or carpet wools. Obviously, the price risk increases as the lead time grows longer, but the basic reason for these forward commitments is assurance of supply to meet requirements and, only secondarily, price.

Speculation seeks to take advantage of price movements with need for supply as a secondary concern. At times of rising prices commitments for quantities beyond anticipated needs would be called speculation. At times of falling prices, speculation would consist of withholding purchases or reducing quantities purchased below the safety limits, and risking stockouts, as well as rush orders at high prices, if the anticipated price decline did not materialize.

At best, any speculation, in the accepted meaning of the term, is a risky business, but speculation with other people's money has been cataloged as a crime. It is purchasing's responsibility to provide for the known needs to the best advantage possible at the time, and to keep the investment in unused materials at the lowest point consistent with safety of operation.

Speculation versus Gambling

Just where the line of distinction between speculation and gambling is to be drawn is a matter of individual judgment. There are certain practices, however, which can only be classified as gambling. If a person undertakes a venture in which there is an unknown chance to win, it is clear that venture is not speculation. If a purchaser tries to guess what the market trend is likely to be for some commodity with which he or she has had no experience and practically no knowledge, he or she is a gambler. Others in the same category are those who, regardless of their experience with a particular commodity, lack adequate data on which to forecast probable price movements.

The distinction between ordinary forward buying, speculative purchasing, and gambling should be reasonably clear. It is important to note that the three policies are quite different. The first policy is, in most cases, unavoidable. The second is debatable. If an organization deliberately undertakes a policy of speculative buying, it is adopting a policy which it may feel is profitable, but which cannot be harmonized with the purpose for which it is organized. Gambling is never to be condoned.

Organizing for Forward Buying

The organization for determination and execution of policy with regard to long-term commitments on commodities whose prices fluctuate varies widely depending on the organization's size, the extent to which it desires to speculate, and the percentage of total cost represented by those volatile commodities. In some instances, the top executive exercises complete control, based almost wholly on personal judgment. In other cases, although the top executive assumes direct responsibility, an informal committee provides assistance.

Some organizations have a person other than the purchasing manager, whose sole responsibility is over speculative materials and who reports directly to top management. In a large number of firms the purchasing manager controls the inventory of such commodities. In a few companies almost complete reliance for policy execution is placed in the hands of an outside agency that specializes in speculative commodities.

The soundest practice for most organizations would appear to be to place responsibility for policy in the hands of a committee consisting of the top executive or general manager, an economist, and the purchasing manager. Actual execution of the broad policy as laid down should rest with the purchasing department.

Control of Forward Buying

Safeguards should be set up to ensure that the administration of a speculation will be kept within proper bounds. The following checks set up by one leather company are given merely as an illustration: (1) Speculative buying must be confined to those hides which are used in the production either of several different leathers or of the leathers for which there is a stable demand. (2) Daily conferences are held among the president, treasurer, sales manager, and hide buyer. (3) Orders for future delivery of leather are varied in some measure in accordance with the company's need for protection on hide holdings. Since the leather buyer is willing to place orders for future delivery of leather when prices are satisfactory, this company follows the practice of using unfilled orders as a partial hedge of its hide holdings. In general, the policy is to have approximately 50 percent of the total hides which a company owns covered by sales contracts for future production of leather. (4) A further check is provided by an operating budget which controls the physical volume of hides rather than the financial expenditures and which is brought up for reconsideration whenever it is felt necessary. (5) There is a final check which consists of the use of adequate and reliable information, statistical and otherwise, as a basis for judging price and market trends.

This particular company does not follow the practice of hedging on an organized commodity exchange as a means of avoiding undue risk, though many companies, including some leather companies, do. Nor does this company use any of the special accounting procedures, such as last-in, first-out, or reproduction-cost-of-sales, in connection with its forward purchases.

These various control devices, regarded as a unit rather than as unrelated checks, should prove effective. They are obviously not foolproof, nor do they ensure absolutely against the dangers inherent in buying well in advance. However, elasticity in the administration of any policy is essential, and, for this one company at least, the procedure outlined combines reasonable protection with such elasticity.

In organizations requiring large quantities of commodities whose prices fluctuate widely, the risks involved in buying ahead may under some circumstances be substantially minimized through the use of the commodity exchanges.

THE COMMODITY EXCHANGES

The prime function of an organized commodity exchange is to furnish an established marketplace where the forces of supply and demand may operate freely as buyers and sellers carry on their trading. An exchange which has facilities for both cash and futures trading can also be used for hedging operations. The rules governing the operation of an exchange are concerned primarily with procedures for the orderly handling of the transactions negotiated on the exchange, providing, among other things, terms and time of payment, time of delivery, grades of products traded, and methods of settling disputes.

In general, the purposes of a commodity exchange will be served best if the following conditions are present:

1. The products traded are capable of reasonably accurate grading.
2. There is a large enough number of sellers and buyers and a large enough volume of business so that no one buyer or seller can significantly influence the market.

In order for a commodity exchange to be useful for hedging operations, the following conditions should also be present:

1. Trading in "futures"—the buying or selling of the commodity for delivery at a specified future date.
2. A fairly close correlation between "basis" and other grades.
3. A reasonable but not necessarily consistent correlation between "spot" and "future" prices.

All of these conditions usually are present on the major grain and cotton exchanges, and in varying degrees on the minor exchanges, such as those on which hides, silk, metals, rubber, coffee, and sugar are traded. Financial futures also permit a firm to hedge against interest rate fluctuations, which are one of the strongest factors affecting exchange rate fluctuations.[8]

---

[8]Martin Mayer, "Suddenly, It's Chicago: In Trading Pits Once Dominated by Pork Bellies and Wheat, Financial Futures Have Been Setting World Prices," *The New York Times Magazine*, March 27, 1988, p. 23.

In most cases, the prices quoted on the exchanges and the record of transactions completed furnish some clue, at least, to the current market price and to the extent of the trading in those commodities. They offer an opportunity, some to a greater extent than others, of protecting the buyer against basic price risks through hedging.

Limitations of the Exchanges

There are limitations to these exchanges as a source of physical supply for the buyer. In spite of a reasonable attempt to define the market grades, the grading is often not sufficiently accurate for manufacturing purposes. The cotton requirements of a textile manufacturer are likely to be so exacting that even the comparatively narrow limits of any specific exchange grade are too broad. Moreover, the rules of the exchange are such that the actual deliveries of cotton do not have to be of a specific grade but may be of any grade above or below basic cotton, provided, of course, that the essential financial adjustment is made. This also holds true for wheat. Millers who sell patented, blended flours must have specific types and grades of wheat most satisfactorily procured only by purchase through sample.

There are other reasons why these exchanges are not satisfactory for the buyer endeavoring to meet actual physical commodity requirements. On some of the exchanges, no spot market exists. On others there is a certain lack of confidence in the validity of the prices quoted. Crude rubber, for example, is purchased primarily by tire manufacturers, a small group of very large buyers. On the hide exchange, on the other hand, a majority of hides sold are by-products of the packing industry, offered by a limited number of sellers. An increase or a decrease in the price of hides, however, does not have the same effect on supply that such changes might have on some other commodities.

It is not asserted that these sellers use their position to manipulate the market artificially any more than it is asserted that the buyers of rubber manipulate the market to their advantage. In these two cases, however, the prices quoted might not properly reflect supply and demand conditions.

Hedging

Perhaps the greatest advantage of the commodity exchanges to a manufacturer is that they provide an opportunity to offset transactions and thus to protect to some extent against price risks. This is commonly done by *hedging*.

A hedging contract involves a simultaneous purchase and sale in two different markets, which are assumed to operate so that a loss in one will be offset by an equal gain in the other. Normally this is done by a purchase and sale of the same amount of the same commodity simultaneously in the spot and future markets.

Hedging can occur only when trading in futures is possible. A simple example of hedging to illustrate the above statement follows:

In the cash market	*In the futures market*
On September 1:	
Processor buys	Processor sells
5,000 bushels of wheat shipped from country elevator at $4 per bushel (delivered Chicago)	5,000 bushels of December wheat futures at $4.10 per bushel
On October 20:	
Processor sells	Processor buys
flour based on wheat equivalent of 5,000 bushels priced at $3.85 per bushel (delivered at Chicago)	5,000 bushels of December wheat futures at $3.95 per bushel
Loss of 15¢ per bushel	Gain of 15¢ per bushel

In the foregoing example it is assumed that the cash or spot price and the futures price maintained a direct correlation, but this is not always the case. Thus, there may be some gain or loss from a hedging operation when the spread between the spot price and the futures price does not remain constant. *Hedging can be looked on as a form of insurance, and like insurance, it is seldom possible to obtain 100 percent protection against all loss, except at prohibitive costs.* As the time between the spot and future declines, the premium or discount on the future declines toward zero (which it reaches when spot = future). On seasonal commodities, this decline in price differential usually begins six to eight months in advance. Under certain circumstances this phenomenon can make "risk-free" speculation possible. For example, when the speculator has access to a large amount of money, at least three times the value of the contract, and when a six- to eight-month future premium exceeds the sum of contract carrying cost and inventory and commission cost, the "speculator" can buy spot and short the future with a precalculated profit. Volume on the exchange should be heavy for this kind of operation.

While there are other variations to the techniques used in hedging, the one simple example is sufficient for the present discussion of forward and speculative buying.

Successful hedging on an exchange requires skill and experience and capital resources. This suggests certain limitations imposed on small organizations. It also explains why organizations using large amounts of a certain commodity often own seats on the exchange which deals in that commodity. A representative of the firm may then be constantly on the watch for advantageous opportunities for placing, withdrawing, or switching hedges between months and can translate this judgment into action immediately. To be successful, the actual procedure of hedging calls for the close observation of accumulating stocks of the commodity, the consequent widening or narrowing of the spreads between prices quoted on futures contracts, and the resulting opportunities for advance opening and closing of trades. These factors are momentarily shifting on the exchanges. The skill of the hedger is reflected in the ability to recognize and grasp these momentary opportunities.

Hedging may not always be helpful or advantageous to the purchaser. One obstacle to a wider use of the exchanges is the lack of understanding by potential users as to when and how to use them. Another limitation is the vacuum effect when one of the relatively few large commodity brokers goes bankrupt, pulling some clients along.

Moreover, most brokers have not shown extensive interest in the industrial market. Most brokers probably will admit that they can barely afford to service a straight hedger, because they may have to send out six monthly position statements and four or more margin calls for a single round turn commission while their faithful "traders" will often maintain a substantial cash account and net them several round turn commissions per month with a minimum of bookkeeping.

Many managers still view futures trading with suspicion and tend to blame past mistakes on the system rather than managerial errors of judgment. The large variations in commodity prices in recent years may well have sensitized a number of managers to the opportunities in futures trading, where before there seemed little need to be involved.

Sources of Information regarding Price Trends

On what is the buyer's judgment as to price trends based? Roughly speaking, there are three general sources of information, all subject to marked limitations with respect to their value and dependability.

One source of information consists of the services of specialized forecasting agencies, such as the Babson Statistical Organization, and Moody's Investors Service.

The second includes a wide variety of governmental and other published data. These include the *Federal Reserve System Bulletin,* the *Survey of Current Business,* the *Journal of Commerce, Business Week, Barron's,* and *The Wall Street Journal.* Trade magazines are also helpful in particular industries and are typified by such publications as *Iron Age* and *Chemical Marketing Reporter.*

The third comprises the highly unscientific—but nevertheless valuable, if properly weighted—information derived from sales representatives, other buyers, and others with whom the buyer comes in daily contact.

One of the most valuable publications is the "Report on Business" published as a part of *N.A.P.M. Insight,* released monthly by the National Association of Purchasing Management. The Business Survey Committee of N.A.P.M. provides a useful service by presenting a composite reading by purchasing managers from 250 organizations across the United States on prices, inventory levels, lead times, new orders, production, and employment. Information is presented on specific commodity changes, as well as summary commodity reports by the various N.A.P.M. commodity committees.

QUESTIONS FOR REVIEW AND DISCUSSION

1. What are the significance of the Sherman Antitrust and the Robinson-Patman Acts to the industrial buyer?
2. What advantages does the competitive bid process have as a method of price determination?
3. What are cash discounts, quantity discounts, trade discounts, and cumulative discounts? Should the buyer attempt to use these discounts? How?
4. When, and how, is negotiation used, and what can be negotiated?
5. What is a *learning curve* and how can it be used?
6. How is vendor cost related to vendor price?
7. What are the various ways by which prices are determined?
8. What methods can the buyer use to establish price for (1) sensitive commodities, (2) special items, (3) standard production items, and (4) items of small value?
9. Distinguish between direct and indirect costs. How can the buyer analyze these costs?
10. What can the buyer do if he or she suspects collusion on the part of vendors?
11. Why might a buyer wish to hedge a commodity purchase?
12. Does hedging remove all risk?
13. What is the difference between forward buying, speculation, and gambling? In what situation would a buyer use each technique?
14. What is a commodity exchange?

REFERENCES

Adams, Charles H. "The Improvement Curve Technique," Section 1.13 of the N.A.P.M. *Guide to Purchasing*. New York: National Association of Purchasing Management, 1980.

Caltrider, James M. "Price Adjustment Clauses Based on Cost Indices." *Journal of Purchasing and Materials Management,* Spring 1987.

Commodity Year Book. New York: Commodity Research Bureau, Inc., 1984.

Farris, Martin T. "Purchasing Reciprocity and Antitrust Revisited." *Journal of Purchasing and Materials Management,* Summer 1981.

Fartuch, Nicholas; Paul J. Kuzdrall; and Robert R. Britney. "A Taxonomy of Price-Quantity Discount Practices and Lot-Sizing Approaches." Working Paper Series No. 84-06, Research and Publications Division, School of Business Administration, The University of Western Ontario, January 1984.

French, Warren; Jan Henkel; and James Cox, III. "When the Buyer is the Object of Price Discrimination." *Journal of Purchasing and Materials Management,* Spring 1979.

Holmes, George. "Commercial Negotiation—Ancient Practice, Modern Philosophy." *Journal of Purchasing and Materials Management,* Fall 1982.

Mayer, Martin. "Suddenly, It's Chicago: In Trading Pits Once Dominated by Pork Bellies and Wheat, Financial Futures Have Been Setting World Prices." *The New York Times Magazine.* March 27, 1988.

McFillen, James M.; Ross R. Reck; and W.C. Benton. "An Experiment in Purchasing Negotiations." *Journal of Purchasing and Materials Management,* Summer 1983.

Roman, Jay. "Control of Contract Escalation." *Journal of Purchasing and Materials Management,* Fall 1982.

Tersine, Richard J., and Michele Gengler. "Simplified Forward Buying with Price Changes." *Journal of Purchasing and Materials Management,* Winter 1982.

Yelle, Louis E. "Common Flaws in Learning Curve Analysis." *Journal of Purchasing and Materials Management,* Fall 1985.

Case 7–1

SEATIDE CRAFTS, INC. (A)

Donna Jackson had recently been hired as a buyer at Seatide Crafts, a reputable producer of high-quality gifts located on the Maine coast. Donna reported directly to the president, who until recently had looked after all purchases personally. She was a business school graduate and had worked in the purchasing office of an automotive parts manufacturer before moving to Seatide. In her previous job she had been well aware of economical order quantities and had done a special study which had resulted in alterations in the computer program and some substantially different buying patterns. Donna wondered about the possibility of using a microcomputer for purchasing, scheduling, and inventory control at Seatide. However, it was still too early for such a move since she had been on the job for only eight months and was still becoming better acquainted with the organization and its requirements.

During the last two weeks, Donna had conducted an informal study to get some feel for the marginal cost of a typical purchase order and she estimated it to be about $60. She also believed carrying costs to be about 2 percent per month since Seatide was still expanding rapidly and projects were available which would return at least that amount. Since the president had always bought hand to mouth, only as required,

Donna found herself ordering the same items frequently and she wondered if this really was the most economical way to proceed.

A typical example were the cheese knives which were part of every cutting board sold. These polished stainless steel knives cost $3.00 each FOB Seatide. Seatide produced cutting boards twice a month in order quantities ranging from 200 to 300 per manufacturing order. Donna suspected the current order quantity and frequency were not optimal and decided to see if she could determine what they should be.

Case 7–2

SEATIDE CRAFTS, INC. (B)

Donna Jackson, buyer at Seatide Crafts, was examining the purchase of cheese knives for the company's cutting board line [see Seatide Crafts (A) for further details]. In discussing this item with the supplier's sales representative, she found out that the supplier incurred significant setup costs for this specialty item, amounting to about $200 for every run. The sales representative also explained that they currently produced these knives once per month in average quantities of about 500 per run. Seatide was the only customer for this type of knife. Since the supplier was in a tight working capital position, it was this company's policy not to carry any excess inventories. Donna tried to find out how much direct labor and material costs were per knife, but she could not get the sales representative to disclose this. Seatide's production superintendent guessed that direct labor and material cost per knife would amount to about $1.25, but he said he could be off by 25¢ either way. Knives were currently delivered twice per month to Seatide in average quantities of 250 knives per order. Donna estimated current delivery charges to be about $20 per order, but she did not know what the impact of larger or smaller order sizes would be on delivery charges.

Donna wondered if she could not use the above information to obtain a quantity discount from her supplier, recognizing that Seatide's own carrying costs were about 2 percent per month.

Case 7–3

SEATIDE CRAFTS, INC. (C)

Donna Jackson, buyer at Seatide Crafts had recently investigated the company's purchases of cheese knives [see Seatide Crafts (A) and (B) for further background]. She had located an alternate source for knives which gave her the following quotation:

Order quantities	Price
500– 999	$3.00 ea. FOB Seatide
1000–2999	2.75 ea. FOB Seatide

3000–5999	2.50 ea. FOB Seatide
6000–9999	2.25 ea. FOB Seatide

Donna was satisfied the quality of these knives was equivalent to that from the current supplier. She wondered about three specific aspects of this offer:

1. Were the discounts offered interesting enough to be seriously considered by Seatide?

2. Compared to her calculations in Seatide (B) were the prices attractive enough to switch from her current source?

3. Should she have two suppliers for knives, and if so, in what quantity should she buy from each?

Case 7–4

THE MORRISON INSTITUTE

"Gord, this is Bill Sykes at the computer center. What's going on with the price of the computer forms this year? At the rate we're spending, my budget's never going to last the year."

"Look, Bill, we got an excellent price on multipart forms, but we had to accept a higher price on single-part forms in the bid. Overall, the institute saves quite a bit."

"That's not much help to me, Gord; you know we use nothing but singles. Why, I can get these forms cheaper downtown. I thought purchasing was supposed to save us money by buying in bulk."

"So we do, Bill, but you have to look at the overall budget, not just your own."

"Well, I know what I'm going to do with my next budget, I can tell you. I'm fighting for a big increase, 'cause I can't afford your prices!"

Gord Martin, purchasing manager for the Morrison Institute was upset. This was the fourth such call in the week since the last budget statement. All the major big single-part users were annoyed, apparently, and Gord couldn't seem to make them understand that the institute was saving money on the current contract.

The Morrison Institute was a large, well-known, and highly respected educational and research and development center. There were over 40 different units within the institute, many of which contained scientists and researchers with worldwide reputations. The institute, headed by a director, was centrally administered for such functions as accounting, finance, personnel, physical plant, security, and purchasing. The total budget exceeded $150 million per year and total purchases amounted to about $30 million per year, including utilities. In the past decade funding for the various programs at the institute had become more difficult to obtain, so that extensive efforts had taken place to control budgets and find opportunities for savings. Normally, each budget unit had an administrative assistant who looked after a variety of business matters on behalf of the unit head.

The Forms Order

Gord Martin, purchasing manager at the institute, had been instrumental in an extensive purchasing drive to achieve better value. Whereas in the past many purchasing decisions were made by the administrative assistants in individual research units, most of these were now handled by central purchasing. Instead of individual orders for requirements as needed, annual contracts for forecast requirements were now in place for repetitive and common items and services. Each unit was charged in the budget for requirements at cost. Institute policy did not permit unit heads to go shopping for better prices.

The forms contract covered two main types. Single-part forms were standard and were used extensively in the computer center and three other units. Total annual consumption of single-part forms amounted to $130,000 in the past year. Multicopy forms were normally custom forms designed for specific applications. The multicopy form manufacturer provided a free systems analysis with the design of new forms as part of the whole contract. The institute required about 12 such new forms a year. The remaining multicopy forms were carryovers from previous years. Multicopy forms usually ranged from two to seven copies per form. Total annual usage of multicopy forms amounted to about $140,000 the previous year. Central administration was one of the main users of multipart forms, although each unit usually had at least several multicopy forms specifically devoted to its own requirements. The multicopy form supplier, Wallace, Inc., had been selected by a special committee three years earlier after extensive presentations from a variety of suppliers.

Gord Martin had in the past year awarded the single-part forms to Jones Forms and the multicopy forms to Wallace, Inc. For the current year's requirements Gord Martin had decided to go for quotes for each contract separately, but also gave each supplier the option of quoting for a combined total. Jones Forms and Wallace, Inc., were the two lowest bidders as follows:

	Single-part forms	Multicopy forms	Combined total
Jones Forms	$125,000	$170,000	$283,100
Wallace, Inc.	135,000	150,000	270,750

[handwritten annotations: "save more if bought from one supplier.", "one from each 275", "+", "+", "×40% =", "413,537.50", "× 5%"]

Since the current year's requirements of both forms were about 6 percent higher than last year's and the price of paper had risen about 3 percent, Gord Martin was delighted with the result of the quotes. The fact that both suppliers were willing to discount further for the combined total meant to Gord that the strategy of combining the two forms types made sense. The combined total discount was in the form of a rebate at year end. Jones offered 4 percent and Wallace, Inc., a 5 percent rebate. It was institute policy that such rebates went into a general fund, rather than being redistributed to individual user units.

Gord Martin had, therefore, awarded the current contract for both forms to Wallace, Inc. The angry phone calls from the units which were heavy users of single-part forms were a surprise to him. He suspected that the Jones Forms sales representative had discussed his quote with several unit heads and had informed them that the institute was paying a substantial premium for single-part forms.

Gord Martin was concerned about this user reaction since he felt that close purchasing-unit head ties were essential for the well-being of the institute. Moreover, he was aware that changing technology was affecting the whole forms area. Multicopy forms had traditionally been typed. Errors required laborious corrections on copies. Gord had noticed an increasing tendency to type one form and then make Xerox copies as required. In other areas, with the advent of word processing capability, the preference was to make copies on the printer. He was not sure at what rate these changes would proceed and wondered how they might affect his purchasing stance regarding forms in the future.

Case 7–5

CLAREBROOK HOSPITAL

In early April, Don Jameson, Director of the Materials Management Division at the Clarebrook Hospital (CH) received a telephone call from the hospital's Controller, Mr. S. Durham. Mr. Durham told Don about a letter that the hospital's accounts payable section had received from a major contract vendor, Medical Products Group Ltd, (MPG). In the letter, MPG claimed that the hospital had taken discounts late, without legal authority, and was not fulfilling contract terms. MPG asked for prompt payment of $20,000. Mr. Durham asked Don to convince the vendor to overlook the late payments and allow the discounts to be taken.

CLAREBROOK HOSPITAL

Clarebrook Hospital was a 700-bed facility with an excellent long-term reputation for high quality community service.

MATERIALS MANAGEMENT DEPARTMENT
1. Organization

Don Jameson became manager of the Materials Management Department at CH six years ago. He had extensive experience in materials management and computer systems analysis, and had been stores manager at CH for three years.

Top management's increasing awareness of the potential cost control benefits of centralized materials management had led to several organizational changes. Last year, Don was made director of the Materials Management Division (MMD). One month ago responsibility for the hospital's Linen and Transportation (busing, portering) Service Departments was transferred to the MMD. At the same time, Don became a member of the executive team, reporting to the senior vice president— administration (see Exhibit 1).

2. Computerization Program

Five years ago, the administration decided to install an in-house computer system to handle inventory, purchasing, payables, payroll, human resources, budgeting, and control. At that time the inventory, purchasing, and payables systems were run manually, and the hospital purchased computer time from a service bureau for other tasks.

Four years ago, following a detailed assessment of needs, and writing of specifications, bids were called. A systems contractor, Health Care Systems Ltd., was
chosen to do a detailed computer capacity assessment, select hardware, and write
systems software.

Three years ago, the formal switchover of operations to the internal Hewlett
Packard system occurred, although development work on several modules in the
Inventory, Purchasing, and Payables System (IPPS) continued.

Rapid expansion of computer usage, and contractor under estimation of storage
requirements soon led to storage capacity constraints, which delayed complete implementation. Four months ago, the situation had become so acute that the decision
was made to "twin" the existing system and install a separate HP dedicated to the
IPPS. Start-up of the twin system was scheduled for this September. The contractor's
personnel were splitting their time between completing overall software development
and working on twin system installation.

Don was responsible for coordinating IPPS installation and testing. The only
non-MMD hospital personnel involved in this project were in the accounts payable
section of the General Accounting Department (see Exhibit 1).

3. Contract Purchasing Process

The hospital dealt with 600 to 800 vendors. Seven to ten large suppliers
had long-term contracts, typically renegotiated at three- to five-year intervals.

The computer system monitored inventory on a perpetual basis. Inventory
records were used to forecast future demand. Order lead time assumptions were
stored in memory, and combined with the demand forecasts to calculate two
reorder points, the reorder quantity, and minimum balance (safety stock) for
each inventory item.

To even out purchasing agent workload, a "vendor day" system was used.
Each vendor was assigned one or two designated order days in the week.
Each working day the computer scanned the perpetual inventory records. It
then produced a list of the products of each designated vendor with inventory levels less than the calculated first reorder points. This list was displayed on the agent's computer terminal and included the applicable reorder
quantities, in vendor units, and purchase order numbers. Any item in the
inventory which was drawn down below the second reorder point was ordered
immediately, regardless of the designated vendor day. The agent then released
the orders by telephone. The computer generated a receiving report for each
order and two copies were printed in the receiving section's office. The purchasing
system worked on an exception basis, and the receiving report described the
original, computer-generated order unless modified by agent input after the
release.

The vendor was expected to deliver the order within ten days. The goods
arrived at receiving, were inspected for external damage, and were checked for
type and quantity. One day after arrival, one copy of the completed receiving
report was sent to the accounts payable section for processing. The other copy
was retained for stores records. Accounts payable held the receiving report until
the vendor's invoice arrived in the mail. The invoice and receiving report were

EXHIBIT 1   Organization Chart

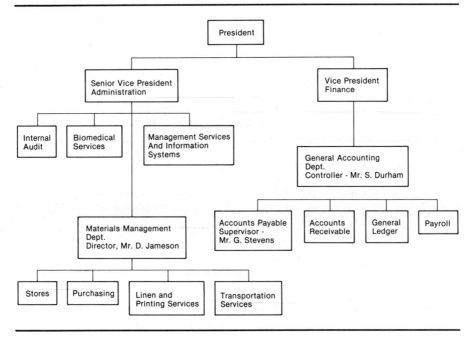

then manually matched, a process which typically took one to two days from invoice receipt. If there were no problems, an input was made into a computerized check writing program.

Due to computer capacity limitations, accounts payable made a check printing run only when there was sufficient volume to justify it. Checks were typically printed three to ten days after input. Completed checks were processed by the internal mail system (one to two days) and sent by post to the vendor. A diagram of the process is shown in Exhibit 2.

An accounts payable enhancement module was part of the original IPPS package. This module was designed to automatically match invoices with receiving reports, sort incoming invoices for discount terms, and set up a check printing run for discounted invoices as often as necessary. At the time of the switchover to the in-house computer a year ago, the enhancement module had been scheduled to be in service by this April. However, the schedule had slipped to a July implementation target.

Don had significant doubts whether even this target would be met. The enhancement module could be run on the existing system, but 'twin' system installation and system software development were competing demands on contractor personnel time.

EXHIBIT 2 Purchase Order Processing

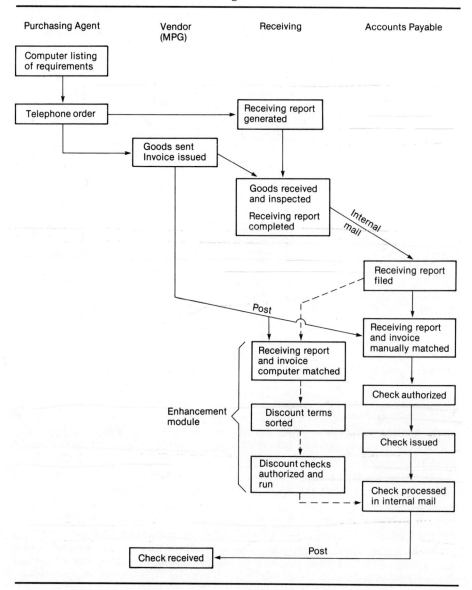

MEDICAL PRODUCTS GROUP CONTRACT

Medical Products Group (MPG) was a division of a large U.S. multinational. It marketed a broad line of medical and surgical supplies, including intravenous solutions and catheters. During the past year CH had total purchases of $1.5 million with MPG.

MPG had supplied CH for almost twenty years. At the start, MPG had offered certain plastic products which were unavailable from other suppliers. For the first eighteen years, long-term contracts of three to five years were negotiated or extended. The contract terms guaranteed prices for the first year, with negotiated escalations in subsequent years. In the past, the vendor had been willing to reduce desired price increases when the hospital was faced with budget restrictions. Vendor relations had been good, with a vendor sales representative contacting the hospital purchasing agent once a week.

At the last contract negotiation two years ago, MPG asked for a five-year term. However, two new factors impacted on the negotiations. Competition had increased, with one of MPG's competitors offering the desired plastic supplies at competitive prices. In addition, MMD had agreed to enter into a cooperative purchasing agreement with other local hospitals at the termination of their supply contracts two years from now. These hospitals also dealt with MPG. However, the group contract would be let on a bid basis. As the representative of the largest user, Don expected to have considerable input into the tendering and evaluation process.

A contract was signed with MPG for the interim period. Prices for most of the product line were guaranteed for the duration. Invoice terms were 2 percent off invoice if paid within 15 days of issue.

CURRENT SITUATION

In late February, the accounts payable supervisor, Mr. Gene Stevens, mentioned to Don that MPG was unhappy with the length of time that it was taking the hospital to make payments.

In early April, the hospital controller, Mr. S. Durham, contacted Don. He indicated that the accounts payable section had received a letter from MPG claiming that the hospital had taken discounts late, without legal authority. MPG asked for payment of $20,000 in lost discounts, consistent with contract terms. They stated that unless prompt payment was made, interest would be charged on the owed balance. Mr. Durham asked Don to contact the vendor and ask them to overlook the late payments, since the hospital was a major customer of MPG.

Accounts payable received copies of all vendor contracts. However, Don knew that the controller had directed accounts payable to take all discounts, regardless of contract terms, and that contracts were filed and forgotten. This was not a written or authorized policy, and MMD had not been consulted or formally told about the practice. The controller's rationale for taking all discounts was "that if the vendor did not complain, it is to our advantage and besides we do a lot of business with most of these vendors and we should get back as much as we can."

The manual payables system, previously in use, had handled discount invoices reasonably well. There had been one incident the previous year in which an invoice had been paid, less a discount of $202.00, to a small vendor after the discount period. The vendor had responded immediately by withholding services and shortly after that their contract was terminated.

MMD had received little or no warning of a problem from MPG's sales representatives. MPG's accounts receivable department had not informed their sales department of the late payments until early April. Discussions with MPG representatives revealed that discount periods were measured from the date of invoice issue to the date the payments were received. Mailing time was from two to four days each way. Typically, MPG was receiving a check from the hospital 17 to 18 days after they issued an invoice.

Discussions with Mr. Stevens, the accounts payable supervisor, revealed that they were receiving complaints from other vendors. Don estimated that if discounts were not taken on all contracts, it would represent a loss of $75,000 to $100,000 per annum, an amount which could adversely affect the hospital's cash flow capability.

Start-up of the accounts payable enhancement module, now scheduled for July, would eliminate the problem. Thus, one option would be to do nothing and let the problem solve itself. Another alternative would be to implement a manual invoice sorting system. This would involve little cost for MPG invoices only, but four full-time clerks would be required in accounts payable to sort and categorize all the incoming invoices. Use of a manual sorting and check writing system would reduce the invoice matching and check writing time to one to two days.

Discussions with the systems contractor revealed that a stopgap discount sorting routine could be programmed and implemented within 20 days, at a cost of $15,000 to $20,000. Another alternative was to 'crash' the implementation of the enhancement module. This would cost $10,000, since the contractor would have to take resources away from other clients.

Don knew that he had to act quickly to head off more serious vendor relations problems.

Case 7–6

PRICE FORECASTING EXERCISE*

You and _____other members of the class have been asked to forecast the price of a commodity on _____ . So that your organization may take the most advantageous procurement action possible, your organization needs $500,000 worth of this commodity for delivery between _____ and _____ .
The amount—$500,000 worth—is based on the spot price of this commodity on _____ . Your report must address the following four questions:

---

*Your instructor will supply the missing information, dates, etc.

Question 1

What is the current _____ spot price of this commodity, based on what quotation? What is the specification of the commodity and what is the minimum amount of purchase required for the quoted price to hold? How much in weight or volume does $500,000 represent?

Question 2

What is the current futures for _____ ?

Question 3

What spot price do you forecast for this commodity on _____ ? Why?

Question 4

In view of your forecast, what recommendation would you make to the executive committee of your organization with regard to the purchase of this commodity? Would you advise buying now and taking delivery now or later? Would you hedge? Would you delay purchase? Anything else? What savings do you forecast from your recommendation?

QUALIFICATIONS

1. The commodity selected may not be a pegged price in the market in which you are purchasing. It must be a freely fluctuating price and it must be traded on a recognized commodity exchange. Prices must be reported daily in an accessible news source.

2. Approval for a selected commodity must come from the instructor. No two teams may select the same commodity. Commodity selection is on a first-come, first-served basis.

3. Foreign exchange rates may be an important consideration in your decision.

4. This report has four parts:
   a. A written report (of at least two copies) to be handed in on _____ before 4:30 P.M.
   b. A five minute class report to be presented orally during class on _____ .
   c. A written evaluation report (of at least two copies) to be handed in before 4:30 P.M., _____ , including the _____ actual spot price. The evaluation should compare a savings (loss) estimate in view of the recommended action for the weight calculated in the report.
   d. A one-minute report on _____ , highlighting the evaluation.

5. Group names and commodity selections to be submitted no later than 4:30 P.M., _____ .

Special Remarks

1. The amount of $500,000 is in U.S. dollars. Exchange rates with foreign currencies have to be considered as part of this problem.

2. There is a commission charge for every commodity. Please determine what this is for your commodity and include it in your calculations.

3. In the case of purchase and storage ahead, the carrying cost is 2 percent per month.

4. If the market has a daily variation and quotes high and low closing for the day, please be consistent and use the same type of quotation throughout.

5. Use the same source (publication) for your future price and your spot price.

Case 7–7

COMMODITY PURCHASING GAME

In this game you will have the chance to try your skill as a commodity purchaser. You will be using information similar in type to that available to Mrs. Martin, the purchasing manager of a well-known chocolate bar corporation.

Because raw material accounts for 50 percent of the cost of producing a chocolate bar, the purchasers in the chocolate bar business have a great deal of responsibility on their shoulders.

Among other functions, Mrs. Martin, at the beginning of each month has to decide how many pounds of cocoa should be purchased during the coming weeks of that month. When doing this, she takes into account the expected need of the production department, the time of the year, the inventory on hand, the cost of short supply, the cost of carrying inventory and, finally, the commodity market trends, more specifically, cocoa.

You will be able in this game to make similar decisions, although the game will be a simplified version of the actual situation. The most important features of this simplification are first, it will not be possible for you to buy cocoa after the first day of the month (you are allowed to purchase cocoa only once a month—on the first day); and, second, it will not be possible for you to buy cocoa on the futures market.

Cocoa Need

Company sales, and industry sales in general, are very much influenced by seasonal factors. Because the chocolate has a tendency to melt in the warm months of the year, sales usually slow down during the summer months and rebuild very quickly in the fall when the manufacturers start their promotion again. For the last six years, July has been the slowest month for sales and September the biggest.

Because chocolate bars have a limited shelf life, and because it is company policy to supply freshly made chocolate bars to the retailers, it is company practice not to stockpile finished goods. Actually, chocolate bars sold in one month have to be produced in the same month.

In the last five years, the company's cocoa need has grown almost constantly. Cocoa requirements have increased 200 percent in this five-year period. Last year's cocoa purchases were 4.76 million pounds. An average of the cocoa requirements for the last three years, broken down per month, is shown in Exhibit 1. The curve shown is only the average of the experience of many years. In any given year, the monthly percentage of total need might vary ± three percentage points from what is given by the curve. For example, January's figure of 10 percent is really the mid-point of a possible low of 7 percent and a possible high of 13 percent.

From past experience, Mrs. Martin knows that the production department uses approximately 60 percent of the total yearly cocoa purchases in the last six months of the year. And, moreover, 55 percent of this last six months' need is used in September and October.

Production scheduling is done on a weekly basis. Mrs. Martin has no precise idea of what the actual total monthly production need for cocoa will be on the first day of that month, other than from her judgment of need level of prior periods and from consideration of the general shape of the need curve shown in Exhibit 1.

Raw Material

Cocoa, the basic raw material in chocolate, has an especially volatile price, and there is no way to hedge completely against the wide price swings. Chocolate comes from cocoa beans, a crop subject to wide production fluctuations with a stable and generally rising demand. Furthermore, it takes 7 years for new cocoa trees to come into production (15 years to reach full production), and drought and disease can sharply reduce supply in a matter of months or even weeks.

Using the company's expected sales and expenses for the year, Mrs. Martin estimates that when she pays 24 cents a pound for cocoa, the contribution per pound purchased to profit is 6.5 cents, and any increase in the price paid for cocoa has a direct reverse effect on the amount of contribution and vice versa. (If she pays 25 cents per pound, then the contribution would be one cent less or 5.5 cents, etc.)

In order to be as efficient as possible in her predictions of future cocoa prices, Mrs. Martin keeps informed by means of trade journals; she follows the futures market closely and studies the past performance of cocoa prices.

As of October 1, Mrs. Martin has assembled the information given in Exhibits 2, 3 and 4. Company policy does not allow her to carry an inventory of more than 1.2 million pounds of raw cocoa in her monthly ending inventory. The company is short of funds, and the president is not anxious to exceed borrowing limits set by the bank.

Costs Involved

In deciding on purchasing alternatives, Mrs. Martin bears in mind several costs which she knows to be fairly accurate. These costs are inventory costs and stockout costs.

Inventory Costs.   Storage cost for one pound of raw material is 0.2 cents per month. This amount takes into account interest on tied-up capital, insurance,

EXHIBIT 1   Cocoa Need per Month by the Production Department

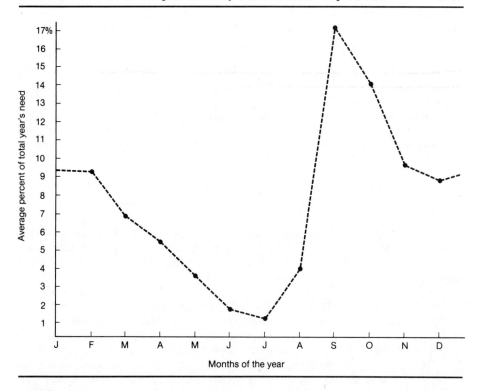

EXHIBIT 2   Size of Upcoming Crops Hold Key to Cocoa Prices (October 1)

Prices of cocoa beans have risen 8 percent since September 22. The increase follows a roller-coaster ride which took the market from a long-time low in July of last year to a 39-month peak in mid-July of this year, then down again by some 21 percent.

Harvesting of the main crop in Ghana, the world's largest cocoa producer, reportedly has been delayed by adverse weather. In addition, recent rains may have reduced yields in several African-producing areas. Black pod disease reportedly has hit the Brazilian crop, and Russia has told Ghana it wants early deliveries of the 100,000 long tons of cocoa pledged for this season and of cocoa on which Accra defaulted last season. Ghana, in turn, has requested an extension of one month or more for deliveries on sales contracts with the United States and Europe that were originally scheduled for the current quarter.

Future Boost

Renewed buying interest by large manufacturers, coupled with trade and speculative purchases, helped boost cocoa futures. However, the extent to which supplies tighten in the next month or two will depend greatly on the size of invisible stocks and of future government purchases from African growers, who have been given an incentive through purchase price increases by the Cocoa Marketing Boards.

EXHIBIT 2   *(continued)*

The current New York spot prices of Accra (Ghanaian) cocoa beans, at 24 cents per pound compares with quotes of 22.25 cents on September 22, 16.75 cents a year ago, and a peak 28.25 cents on July 14 of the current year. During the 10-week price slump, the open interest in New York cocoa futures shrank from a record 38,054 contracts (30,000 pounds each) on August 10 to fewer than 28,700 contracts; it now aggregates 29,500 contracts.

On the New York Cocoa Exchange, the December future currently is selling at around 22.52 cents, up from 20.22 cents on December 22. The March option is quoted at around 23.11 cents, against 20.92 cents on September 22. The May future is selling at 23.54 cents. The distant December option is at 24.72 cents.

British Bean Experts

According to London's Gill and Duffus, Ltd., unfavorable weather held this year's world cocoa bean crop to 1,214,000 long tons, 20 percent below a year earlier. In the face of this dip, relatively attractive prices and rising incomes are expected to push the current year's world cocoa bean grindings (not to be confused with actual consumption) to a record 1,414,000 long tons. This is 83,000 long tons (6.2 percent) above that of last year.

Allowing 1 percent for loss in weight, output seems to be lagging anticipated grindings by a record 212,000 long tons. This being the case, the October 1 world carry-over of cocoa beans, which is estimated at around 366,000 long tons, is barely a three-month supply. Nine years ago, a similar drop to a three-month supply saw prices averaging 34 cents, far above the current market.

On the eve of the coming season, the trade lacks accurate information on the size of the major new African crops. During recent months, African governments have sold ahead a large portion of the prospective new main crop at prices well above those of a year ago. Ghana's advance sales are placed above 275,000 long tons, some 100,000 more than last year, at prices ranging between 23 cents and 26 cents a pound.

Prior to the recent reports of adverse weather, the trade generally estimated the coming season's world cocoa output at around 1,300,000 long tons, some 60,000 to 86,000 tons above last season. This includes this year's prospective main and mid crops in Ghana of between 435,000 and 475,000 long tons versus 410,000 tons last year, and a record 572,000 long tons two years ago. Guess estimates for Nigeria range between 200,000 and 210,000 tons, against 182,000 last season, and a record 294,000 tons two years ago but may fail to account fully for losses due to the country's tribal unrest. Output from the Ivory Coast is tentatively forecast at between 120,000 and 150,000 tons, up from 112,00 tons last season, and close to its record of 145,000 tons.

Bad weather and pod rot, a fungus that causes seed to rot, have caused the experts to drop their estimates on the Brazilian crop to 130,000 or 135,000 long tons, down from 158,000 tons of last season. Recent reports indicate that the crops in other Latin American countries also will lag last season's levels, which may drop next season's yields for our southern neighbors some 60,000 to 75,000 tons below the 283,000 tons of last year. Adding everything together, the coming season's cocoa bean harvest is

EXHIBIT 2 *(concluded)*

likely to range between 1,250,000 and 1,350,000 long tons, which would be a good deal smaller than the current year's anticipated world cocoa bean grindings.

How closely output matches next year's consumption is the key to the cocoa market. Bulls on cocoa believe that prices have not been high enough to discourage the steady rise in usage. They attribute the July to September slump mainly to forecasts of increased crops, tight money, and the large open interest which invited volatile prices.

EXHIBIT 3   Cocoa Spot Price and Cocoa Futures Market (October 1)

	Futures Market
December	22.52
March	23.11
May	23.54
July	23.92
September	24.31
December (next year)	24.72

Spot Price: 24.0 cents per pound.

---

deterioration, and direct handling expense. Mrs. Martin knows that over the period of a season, inventory carrying charges can reasonably be calculated on the basis of inventory on hand at the end of each month.

Stockout Costs.   Mrs. Martin also considers stockout costs. A stockout cost occurs whenever the production demand for raw cocoa in a particular month is greater than the available raw cocoa in inventory. For example, if 50,000 pounds of raw cocoa are on hand at the beginning of the month, 50,000 pounds are purchased, and the need during the month totals 110,000 pounds, then a stockout of 10,000 pounds occurs. The company then has to place rush orders for raw cocoa and, consequently, is forced to pay a three-cent per pound premium.

Mrs. Martin's Commission

The president of the company was convinced that incentives for executives were important. Therefore, part of Mrs. Martin's salary was based on her performance as a cocoa purchaser. She received a 5 percent commission on the monthly net contribution to profits.

> Net Monthly Contribution = Monthly contribution less
> monthly stock-out costs
> (or monthly inventory carrying costs)

EXHIBIT 4   Past Performance of Cocoa on the Commodity Market

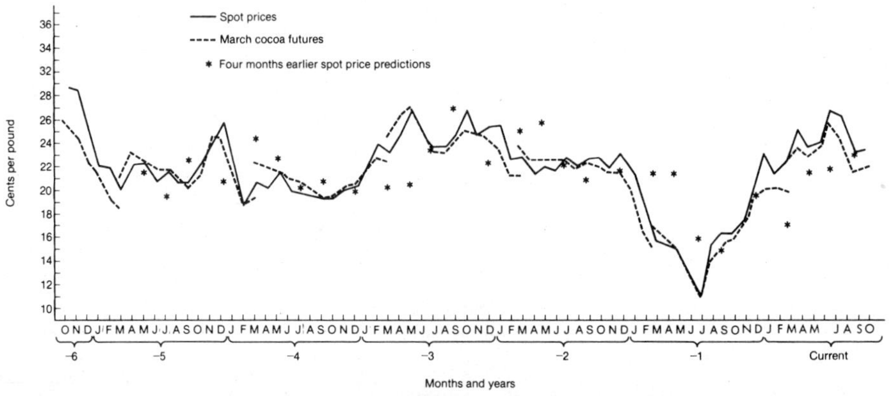

Closing Inventory Target

At the end of the game, each group is expected to have a closing inventory of 200,000 pounds of raw cocoa. Every group who fails to reach this 200,000 pound target will be penalized in the following way.

1. For every pound in excess of the aforementioned target:

As in every other month, the company will have to pay an inventory carrying cost, and, moreover, there will be an extra charge of 2.8 cents per pound over the 200,000 pound target.

2. For every pound short in relation to the aforementioned target:

The company will have to pay 3.0 cents per pound and will have to buy sufficient cocoa at the September 1 spot price to bring the inventory level to 200,000 pounds.

How to Play the Game

In the actual conduct of this game, teams will be used to make the purchasing decisions normally made by Mrs. Martin. On the first day of each month, each team will be required to decide on the quantity of cocoa to be purchased. This decision will be made by the team by whatever means it chooses. Thus, a prediction from a plot of past months' performance might be used by some teams, a pure guess by others. In making the decision, teams will want to consider both the possibilities of future needs and the inventories now on hand as well as their forecast of cocoa spot prices behavior.

After each team has made its purchasing decision for the coming month, the instructor will announce the next month's spot price and actual consumption during the past month. Given this information, teams will then be able to calculate, using Exhibit 5, all of the necessary costs and, finally, the "net commission of the purchaser." They can then decide how much cocoa, if any, to purchase for the next month.

EXHIBIT 5 Result Form

	Stock on hand at start of month in lbs. = ending inventory of previous month	Purchases in lbs.	Total available for production in lbs. (3 = 1 + 2)	Production requirements in lbs.	Ending inventory in lbs. (5 = 3 − 4) Cannot be less than 0 or greater than 1,200,000 lbs. Penalty for any excess of $1,000 in commission	Stock-out in lbs. (6 = 4 − 3 if greater than 0)	Stock-out costs (7 = 6 × $.03)	Inventory carrying costs (8 = 5 × $.002)	Contribution per lbs. purchased ($.065 − ($SPOT − $.24)	Total monthly contribution (10 = 2 × 9)	Total monthly costs (11 = 7 + 8)	Net monthly contribution (12 = 10 − 11)	Monthly commission on contribution (13 = 5% × 12)	Cumulative commission (14 = 13 + 14 previous month)
	1	2	3	4	5	6	7	8	9	10	11	12	13	14
August	50M	350M	400M	450M	0	50M	$1.500	0	3.5¢	$12.250	$1.500	$10.750	$537	($537
September	0	1,100M	1,100M	900M	200M	0	0	$400	6.5¢	$70.400	$400	$70.000	$3.500	($4.037
October	200M													
November														
December														
January														
February														
March														
April														
May														
June														
July														
August														
September														

15. Stock at end of September
(15 = 5 of September)   _____

If (15) is less than 200,000 lbs.

16. Purchases in quantity   _____

17. September contribution per pounds purchased ($.065 − ($SPOT − $.24))   _____

18. Final added contribution
(18 = 16 × 17)   _____

19. Extra cost
(19 = line 16 × $.03)   _____

20. Net September contribution
(20 = 18 − 19)   _____

21. September commission
(21 = (.05 × 20) − 13 of September)   _____

22. Total cumulative commission
(22 = 21 + 14 of August)   _____

If (15) is greater than 200,000 lbs.

23. Extra cost
(23 = (15 − 200,000) × $.028)   _____

24. Net September contribution
(24 = 12 of September − 23)   _____

25. September commission
(25 = .05 × 24)   _____

26. Total cumulative commission
(26 = 25 + 14 of August)   _____

The object of the game is to increase as much as possible the purchaser's cumulative commission over 12 months. This means that teams will have to decide whether it would be cheaper in the long run to incur some inventory or stockout costs, depending on their predictions of the cocoa price behavior on the commodity market. At the end of each month, every team's results will be shown on the screen in front of the class and, at the end of the 12th month, the class will discuss each team's method of predicting sales and cocoa prices. Teams will probably find it advantageous to split the work of making sales estimates, calculating costs and profit, and estimating the next period cocoa spot price.

Summary of Important Points to Remember When Playing the Game

1. Purchases can be made only on the first day of the month.
2. You cannot buy cocoa on the futures market.
3. It is a company practice to purchase cocoa on the first day of each month.
4. It is not possible to carry an inventory of more than 1.2 million pounds of raw cocoa. Penalty for excess of $1,000 in commission and excess stock will be returned to the vendor with a 3.0¢ penalty per pound on top of the $1,000 penalty.
5. At a purchase price of 24 cents per pound, the cocoa will bring a contribution to profit of 6.5 cents. This contribution is directly related to the purchased price. (A one-cent increase in the cost results in a one-cent decrease in the contribution, and vice versa.)
6. There is an inventory carrying cost and a stockout cost which are directly deducted from the contribution amount to give the net contribution.
7. There is a closing inventory target of 200,000 pounds.

Result Form Used

To make the keeping of results easier for each team, a form has been distributed (see Exhibit 5). The exact steps in using this form are shown on the form itself.

Concluding Result Form

Because there is a closing inventory target of 200,000 pounds, you will be required to fill the concluding result form (see Exhibit 5) at the end of September. The steps in filling this form are as shown on the form itself.

Example

Each team member should carefully trace the proceedings as outlined in the following example to understand all of the steps involved in playing and recording the game.

Mrs. Martin has already used the "Result Form" to record the operating results of the two months prior to October. On August 1, Mrs. Martin had to decide how many pounds of cocoa should be purchased. Knowing the spot price on August 1 was

27 cents a pound, she thought, after consulting the trade journals and studying the futures market, that the prices would go down; therefore, she decided to purchase cocoa to supply the need of the current month only. She then consulted the production need curve and came to the conclusion that the need of that month would be approximately 300,000 pounds. Knowing that she had 50,000 pounds of cocoa in inventory, and wanting to keep a safe margin, she purchased 350,000 pounds of cocoa at the price of 27 cents per pound. She then entered the following figures on the "Result Form."

Column (1) = 50,000 pounds (from column (5) previous month)
Column (2) = 350,000 pounds
Column (3) = 400,000 pounds

Column (9) = $.035 = $.065 − ($.27 − $.24)
Column (10) = $12,250

At the end of the month of August, Mrs. Martin received from the production department the exact figure of the month's requirements, 450,000 pounds. Since there were only 400,000 pounds of cocoa in inventory, the company had had to make a last minute order to another user of cocoa at a premium of $.03/lb. With this information, Mrs. Martin could now calculate her net commission according to the company's norms. She entered the following figures on the "Result Form."

Column (4) =   450,000 pounds
Column (5) =   0 pounds
Column (6) =   50,000 pounds
Column (7) = $ 1,500
Column (8) = $ 0

Column (11) = $ 1,500
Column (12) = $ 10,750
Column (13) = $ 537
Column (14) = $ 537

Start of the Game

The game proper starts on October 1. At the beginning of the game, there are 200,000 pounds of cocoa on hand. It is now up to each team at this time to decide on the coming year's purchases and, thus, start playing the game. We will assume that the cumulative commission of $4,037 to the end of September has been paid to Mrs. Martin and that each team will start again from zero. Please use Exhibit 6 as the sample for your group's reporting form which should be handed in to the instructor each period.

EXHIBIT 6 Report Form

Decision Report	Result Report	
Month i .... Group #	Last month's results net commission	Cumulative commission to date
Purchases .... pounds of cocoa	$	$ ....

CHAPTER 8

Purchasing Transportation Services

Purchased goods must be transported from the point they are grown, mined, or manufactured to the place needed. The purchase of transportation services demands a high degree of skill and knowledge, if the costs of movement are to be minimized while at the same time meeting service needs. Due to the complexity of the transportation industry, the multitude of rules and regulations, and the significantly larger number of alternatives available as a result of deregulation, getting the best value for an organization's transportation dollar involves much more than simply "getting the best transportation rate."

The total transportation costs in the United States for movement of goods is estimated at nearly seven percent of gross national product, or about $279 billion. This breaks down into the following dollar amounts for 1986 by type of freight as:[1]

Highway	$213.3 billion
Railroads	27.8 billion
Water	18.9 billion
Pipelines	8.5 billion
Air	7.6 billion
Freight forwarders	.3 billion
Loading and unloading	3.1 billion
Total	$279.5 billion

A large share of that total (about half, or about $140 billion) is for the movement of goods from the vendor's facility to the point where the industrial buyer needs them. Depending on the type of goods being moved, transportation may account for as much as 40 percent of the total cost of the item, particularly if it is of relatively low value and bulky, such as con-

---

[1]Transportation Policy Associates, *Transportation in America* (Washington, D.C., 5th edition, July 1987 supplement).

struction materials. But in the case of very high value, low weight and bulk electronics goods, transport costs may be less than 1 percent of total purchase costs. It is not unusual in many firms to find that an average of 10 percent of their purchase expenditures go for incoming transportation costs. While target savings vary from firm to firm, many have found that only a modest effort to manage incoming transportation services more efficiently will result in substantial savings, often from 10 to 15 percent of the freight bill.

If minimization of costs were the only objective in buying transportation services, the task would be easy. However, the transportation buyer must look not only at cost but also at service provided. For example, items are purchased to meet a production schedule, and the available modes of transport require different amounts of transport time. If items are shipped by a method requiring a long shipment time, inventory may be exhausted and a plant or process shut down before the items arrive. Also, reliability may differ substantially among various transportation companies, and service levels, lost shipments, and damage may vary greatly between two different carriers. The buyer should use the same skill and attention in selecting carriers as used in selecting vendors. The effects of transportation deregulation have made the carrier selection and pricing decision far more important today than in the period before 1980.

In addition, as organizations move into the implementation of just-in-time (JIT) purchasing systems, transportation buying decisions become crucial. With JIT, deliveries must be on time, with no damage to the items in transit. Also, in global sourcing (Chapter 12) because of extended lead times and movement distances the transport decisions assume greater significance.

ORGANIZATION FOR TRANSPORTATION DECISIONS

Due to the large number of dollars involved in the movement of goods into and out of an organization and the potential effect on profits, large firms have a separate traffic department with specialists in areas such as selection of carriers and routing, determination of freight classification and rates, tracing shipments, and handling claims in the case of loss or damage to goods during shipment. In the very large firm, the transportation function may be specialized even further, based on the purpose of shipment. For example, an automobile producer may have three separate transportation departments, one concerned with incoming materials shipments, one making the decisions on in-plant and interplant materials movement, and the third concerned with the shipment of finished goods through the distribution channels to customers. In an organization operating under the materials management concept, the traffic manager may have responsibility for all types of materials movement. A 1988 study by the Center for Advanced Purchasing Studies found that in 204 relatively large organizations using materials management about two thirds of them (67 percent) assigned responsibility for inbound traffic to the materials manager.[2] The traffic manager must recognize that handling and shipping of raw materials and finished goods does not add value to the product itself. Instead, it is a key cost element in the operation of the firm and should be managed to minimize costs, within the parameters of needed service.

In the medium-size and smaller organization, the number of traffic decisions may not be large enough to warrant a full-time traffic specialist. Here the transport decisions are handled by the buyer or purchasing manager. This means that the buyer must have enough knowledge to make decisions on preferred free on board (FOB) terms, classification of freight, selection of carriers and routing, determination of freight rates, preparation of necessary documentation, expediting and tracing of freight shipments, filing and settlement of claims for loss or damage in transit, and payment procedures for transport services received.

The involvement of the purchasing department in transportation decisions is significant and growing, as a result of the added alternatives opened up by deregulation. A *Purchasing World* survey of 1,300 firms done in 1983 found that in 86 percent of the firms the purchasing department was responsible for specifying the mode or carrier for inbound shipments. In 52 percent of the firms it also did the same on outbound freight.[3]

A 1988 study by the Center for Advanced Purchasing Studies found that in the 297 relatively large organizations reporting, 41 percent had the inbound traffic function report to purchasing; 31 percent had purchasing responsible for *both* inbound and outbound traffic. This study also found that since 1980 personnel travel has been newly assigned to purchasing in 14 percent of the organizations and traffic/transportation in 13 percent. Purchasing assumed an increased role or responsibility (since 1980) for traffic/transportation in 23 percent of the organizations and for personnel travel in 16 percent.[4]

Regulation of Carriers

For about 90 years, from 1887 to 1977, the transportation industry was closely regulated under laws passed by Congress and regulations promulgated by various regulatory agencies. These laws generally were passed to assure that transport services were available in all geographic areas and without discrimination. Figure 8–1 presents a brief summary of the applicable transport laws.

Department of Transportation (DOT).   This is an arm of the exec-

---

[2]Harold E. Fearon, *Purchasing Organizational Relationships* (Tempe, Ariz.: Center for Advanced Purchasing Studies/National Association of Purchasing Management, 1988), p. 36.

[3]"Profile of the Purchasing Professional—1983," *Purchasing World*, November 1983, p. 55.

[4]Fearon, pp. 14–16.

FIGURE 8–1   Laws Regulating Transportation

Year Enacted	Law	Purpose of Law
1887	Interstate Commerce Act	Federal regulation of railroads.
1903	Elkins Act	Prohibited RR from giving rebates or reductions from published rates.
1906	Hepburn Act	ICC directives made binding without court action. RR can appeal, but burden of proof is on the RR.
1910	Mann-Elkins Act	ICC given authority to act in rate matters in absence of a shipper complaint.
1920	Transportation Act	ICC given authority to act on RR entry and abandonment of service.
1926	Air Commerce Act	Air safety standards became responsibility of Commerce Department.
1934	Air Mail Act	Competitive bidding required for air mail contracts. Prohibited airframe manufacturers from controlling airlines.
1935	Motor Carrier Act	ICC given authority to regulate trucking industry.
1938	Civil Aeronautics Act	Civil Aeronautics Authority established to regulate airlines.
1940	Transportation Act	ICC must consider impact of rate regulations on all modes of transport.
1940	Presidential Order	Civil Aeronautics Authority became Civil Aeronautics Board (CAB). Civil Aeronautics Administration (CAA) established within Commerce Department to promote air service and enforce safety standards.
1948	Reed-Bulwinkle Act	Rate bureaus in railroad and trucking industry exempt from antitrust laws.
1956	Federal Highway Act	Established Federal Highway Trust Fund.
1958	Transportation Act	ICC cannot increase rates of one mode to protect another. ICC can order abandonment of passenger service.

FIGURE 8–1   *(concluded)*

Year Enacted	Law	Purpose of Law
1966	Department of Transportation Act	Cabinet-level department (DOT) established.
1970	Rail Passenger Service Act	National Railroad Passenger Corporation (Amtrak) set up.
1973	Regional Rail Reorganization Act	U.S. Railway Association set up to reorganize bankrupt Northeast RRs.
1976	Railroad Revitalization and Regulatory Reform Act	Gave RR greater freedom in setting rates.
1977	Air Cargo Act	Air cargo industry deregulated.
1978	Airline Deregulation Act	Began the deregulation of passenger air transportation.
1980	Motor Carrier Act	Relaxed ICC regulation of trucking, allowing easier entry of new firms and flexibility in setting rates.
1980	Staggers Rail Act	Gave RR greater freedom to set rates and to enter into long-term contracts with shippers; piggyback service completely deregulated.
1982	Bus Regulatory Reform Act	Removes all regulation of bus package express service after November 1985.
1984	Shipping Act of 1984	Puts ocean carriers in the U.S. foreign trades on an equal footing with non-U.S. carriers.

utive branch of the government and is headed by a secretary, who has cabinet status. It was established by Congress in 1966 with responsibility for safety, systems, technology, and mass transit development. The intent of Congress was "to concentrate and allocate federal resources in order to attain an integrated national transportation system, to identify significant transportation problems, to provide executive leadership in transportation, and to provide policy guidance. . . ."[5]

There are two major independent regulatory commissions, whose members are appointed by the president of the United States, with the consent

---

[5]Grant M. Davis, *The Department of Transportation* (Lexington, Mass.: Heath Lexington Books, 1970), p. 2.

of the Senate. These commissions administer transportation policy as established by Congress:

1. Federal Maritime Commission (FMC).

2. Interstate Commerce Commission (ICC).

Federal Maritime Commission (FMC).   The FMC was organized in 1961, although it has regulatory powers similar to those of its predecessor agencies. Three areas are of concern: (1) regulation of U.S. common carriers by water in foreign trade; (2) regulation of U.S. water carriers in domestic, offshore service, such as between U.S. mainland ports and Alaska, Hawaii, or Puerto Rico; and (3) control of freight rates of common ocean carriers in domestic offshore service. The FMC has much less regulatory power over oceanborne foreign commerce, due to the freedom of the seas principle.

Interstate Commerce Commission (ICC).   The ICC is the oldest of the regulatory agencies, dating from 1887. The original act has been amended several times and now is known simply as the Interstate Commerce Act. The ICC regulates, in varying degrees, all surface carrier modes of transport, including (1) establishment of operating rights, routes, and freight rates; (2) mergers, expansions, and abandonments; (3) award of damages and administration of railroad bankruptcies; (4) development of uniform systems of accounts and records for carriers; (5) investigation and authorization of the issuance of securities or the assumption of financial obligations by railroads and certain motor vehicle common or contract carriers; and (6) development of emergency preparedness programs for rail, motor, and inland waterway transportation. The specific aspects of the ICC Act of interest to freight movers are (1) Part I, which covers railroads and pipelines; (2) Part II, added in 1935, on motor carriers; (3) Part III, added in 1940, covering water carriers; and (4) Part IV, added in 1942, covering freight forwarders.

Under ICC jurisdiction, common carriers are required to:

1. Furnish adequate freight transportation on reasonable request.

2. Cooperate with other carriers in establishing reasonable through rates so that adequate service is available over the entire transportation system.

3. Establish fair and reasonable freight classifications and rates.

To accomplish the above three objectives, the ICC is divided into three divisions: Division I handles operating rights; Division II handles rates, tariffs, and valuation; and Division III handles finance and service. In addition, there are five bureaus within the ICC which do most of the data gathering and analysis as needed by any of the three divisions. These bureaus also handle many of the matters which do not need the attention and review of the full commission. These bureaus are:

1. *Bureau of Accounts:* Does the necessary accounting and cost collection data so that financial data on specific carriers' operating results are complete, uniform, and accurate.

2. *Bureau of Economics:* Generates statistical data and analyzes results to provide inputs for decisions necessary to assure the economic health of the nation's transport system.

3. *Bureau of Enforcement:* Conducts investigations into cases where persons or carriers are charged with violating specific provisons of the ICC Act; cooperates with U.S. Justice Department in prosecuting violators.

4. *Bureau of Operations:* Monitors carriers' operations to assure they are in conformity with the act; informs carriers of violations in rates and other operating assets.

5. *Bureau of Traffic:* Reviews the filing of tariffs, observance of tariffs, and renders opinions on the applicability of tariffs in specific situations.

The ICC has a field staff that makes periodic visits to carriers to check on observance of ICC regulations and investigates complaints which may be made by shippers, carriers, and the general public.

Transportation Deregulation

Over the last 10 years or so, there has been much interest and discussion on the feasibilty and advisability of removing all, or a significant amount, of the regulation of the transportation industry. The proponents of deregulation argue that our present regulatory system is grossly inefficient; that it protects the inefficiently operated carrier and encourages poor carrier management; that it discourages competition; that it denies shippers the frequent and efficient service needed from carriers; and that it results in shippers paying substantially higher prices for freight movement than would be the case with free competition. They argue that unnecessarily high transport rates have fueled the inflationary trend and by raising a firm's cost of goods sold have made it more difficult for U.S. firms to compete in world markets.

The proponents of our current regulatory system argue that it is working well; that the United States has the lowest cost and most efficient transport system in the world; and that, as a result, it is still the only major transport system that is privately, and not governmentally, owned. They further argue that regulation is needed to protect the public interest, and that, in its absence, large segments of the business community would not receive the transport service they need and at a price enabling them to compete with other firms.[6]

Air Cargo Industry.   The air cargo industry was deregulated in late 1977, giving air cargo carriers the right to begin serving additional markets, revise schedules, and adjust rates. In addition, deregulation also eliminated barriers to air cargo carriers owning a motor carrier. Under the 1977 Air Cargo Act, any firm now can apply for an all-cargo certificate, regardless of prior experience. Since March 1979 air cargo carriers are free to establish their tariffs at whatever levels they wish.

Air Passenger Industry.   The law deregulating the air passenger traffic industry was passed in 1978 (Public Law 95-504, the Airline Deregulation Act), culminating a four-year effort. Under this law, the Civil Aeronautics Board was phased out in 1985. Basically, the law allowed existing airlines to pick one new, additional domestic or international route in each of the next three years after the act was passed. Now there is totally free entry into and exit from the airline business, and airline management has had to cope with a world of competition from new, low-cost entrants. Some of the major, old-line air carriers have experienced a flow of red ink and some—for example, Braniff and Continental— declared bankruptcy. Some economists predict that by 1990 there will be four or five giant airlines in the United States and several specialized, smaller airlines, as mergers take place to gain advantages of scale.[7] By 1986, the six largest air carriers had 84 percent of the market, up from 73 percent in 1978.[8]

Motor Freight Industry.   Trucking has undergone many changes since passage of the Motor Carrier Act of 1980, which became effective July 1, 1980. Adherents of deregulation claimed it would result in major benefits to the buyer through a wider variety of price/service options and greater competition in pricing.[9] Those opposing deregulation, which included many carriers, claimed that it would not help shippers, stating that " . . . shippers have much to lose with deregulation . . . rates would go up, some routes would be dropped, decisions on plant locations would be affected—shippers

[6]Roger E. Jerman, Donald D. Anderson, and James A. Constantin. "Shipper Carrier Perspectives on Transportation Regulation," *Journal of Purchasing and Materials Management.* Spring 1977, pp. 23–28.

[7]"A Painful Transition for the Transport Industry." *Business Week.* November 28. 1983. p. 83.

[8]"Is Deregulation Working?" *Business Week.* December 22. 1986. p. 52.

[9]Thomas F. Dillon, "What Will Deregulation Mean to Purchasing?" *Purchasing.* March 7. 1979, pp. 48–52.

would simply not be able to depend on the trucking industry as they now do."[10]

It was the intent of Congress in passing the Motor Carrier Act that this ambitious law would conserve energy and provide more cost effective service to benefit the buyer. The "Declaration of National Transportation Policy" was amended to state that the goal is "to promote competitive and efficient motor transportation" and "to allow a variety of quality and price options to meet the changing market demands and diverse requirements of the shipping public."

Several portions of the law were designed to conserve energy. First, it eliminates rules requiring carriers to take circuitous routes or to stop at intermediate points. Formerly, some firms were given authority to provide service from point *A*, Denver, to point *B*, for example, Albuquerque, but only through point *C*, for example, Salt Lake City. Such a requirement now has been eliminated, and the carrier now can go directly from point *A* to point *B*. Second, trucks are allowed to make pickups and deliveries at intermediate stops along their routes, and are not limited to only certain cities. The law also allows certain carriers of agricultural and other exempt goods (exempt in that carriers of these goods do not need ICC licenses) such as private carriers and agricultural cooperatives to backhaul certain portions of their annual tonnage in nonexempt goods. An example of this would be a truck carrying corn from Nebraska to Illinois being able to pick up a farm tractor (nonexempt) and bring it back (backhaul) to the agricultural area.

Several sections of the Motor Carrier Act of 1980 are designed to increase competition. First, there is greater ease of entry into the industry. Less documentation is needed for certification and in cases where objections are raised against certification, the burden of proof is shifted from the applicant to those raising the objections. The new law requires that the ICC grant a certificate to anyone who can supply a useful service, unless it finds that the service would be inconsistent with present or future public convenience. Diversion of traffic or revenue from an existing carrier(s) is not by itself sufficient evidence to warrant denial of an application; second, the law permits the ICC to require through routes and joint rates between motor and water carriers where it is needed; third, the restrictions on categories of commodities that could be hauled were relaxed. A motor carrier now may provide service as a general common carrier and at the same time provide specialized contract carriage to specific shippers. Previous to this act, such dual operations were not permitted. Also, the limitation that a contract carrier could serve not more than eight shippers was eliminated. Thus the advantages of contract carriage—specific scheduling, volume movement and discounts, and specialized equipment—are now more feasible for the shipper. Last, and probably most significant, Section 11 of the act makes it

---

[10]"ACT Plans to Battle Deregulation of Trucking," *Purchasing* , April 11, 1979, p. 13.

possible for the shipper to negotiate rates with motor carriers by allowing a "zone of freedom," which provides that rates can increase or decrease up to 10 percent per year without ICC approval for each of two years only. If it deems it advisable, the ICC also can authorize an additional five percent per year, for two years. Tied to this flexibility of rates is the provision which eliminates the antitrust immunity for some rates in the regulated sector of the industry.

The law also requires that a carrier must file a bond, insurance policy, or other security in an amount not less than $750,000 for a single occurrence to cover public liability, property damage, and cargo. The ICC may set a higher amount if it deems necessary.

As a result of the Motor Carrier Act of 1980, there will be more trucks and trucking firms competing for the same freight, but there will not be enough freight to be profitable for everyone. Some firms will be eliminated as time goes on.

Since deregulation began in 1978, 17,000 new firms entered the trucking industry and 6,470 went out of business.[11] Several well-known firms, such as Cooper-Jarrett, T.I.M.E.-D.C., and Wilson Freight exited the market. Heavy price discounting has occurred; for example, discounts in the Northeast have ranged from 25 to 35 percent. The impact has been primarily on the full-truckload carriers—to begin business requires only a truck and ICC authority; much of the full-load business has shifted to the new carriers. The impact on the small shipment carriers has been less, since to go into that business requires more capital to set up terminals and billing and communications systems.

Railroad Industry. The Staggers Rail Act of 1980 was intended to enable the railroads, which had been heavily regulated since 1887, to compete more fully with one another and with trucks and barge lines. Pricing procedures were relaxed, allowing railroads to raise or lower their rates up to 1984 by specified percentages. Many of the contract rate agreements negotiated did contain price reductions. For the first time in history, railroads are now entitled to enter into long-term rate and service contracts with shippers. Abandonment and merger procedures also were expedited. Piggyback service was completely deregulated.

Deregulation has caused many changes in the railroad industry. Mergers have reduced the number of large rail-freight carriers; there were 13 in 1978, but now there are six regional rail systems—three in the east and three in the west. These six systems carry 86 percent of the rail freight.[12] With deregulation, rate changes can be made faster, and railroads now are free to combine several modes of transport into one system. The words used

---

[11]"Is Deregulation Working?" *Business Week.*
[12]*Ibid.*

to describe the new services are *multimodal* or *fully integrated,* also referred to as *total transportation.*

The bottom line is that this new, partially deregulated transportation environment provides a substantially larger number of alternatives for the buyer. Entry of new carriers is markedly easier; rate making is facilitated; and price competition now exists. The buyer can negotiate special rates and services directly with the carrier. Freight movement by joint methods (intermodal movement) is now made more simple and economical.

BASIC PRINCIPLES OF THE COMMON CARRIER SYSTEM

Over the past several decades, various laws, regulations, and interpretations have established the basic framework within which the common carrier system operates (see Figure 8-1). While this umbrella is constantly changing as we move into an era of less regulation, and possibly to total deregulation, the buyer should be aware of the basic principles.

No Discrimination

Common carriers enjoy the status of a public utility, in the sense that they are granted the right to service shippers at various geographical points and have some protection against competition from new entrants into the market; in effect, they are in a partial monopoly position. Therefore, they may not discriminate among customers and are obligated to offer the same services to both small and large shippers, and at consistent rates. Of course, lower rates for volume shipments are permissible, much the same as quantity discounts may be justified for larger buyers. With deregulation, the buyer has some flexibility to negotiate rates and services provided directly with the carrier. In addition, to begin service, a common carrier must make application to the appropriate regulatory agency and show that it is responsible and able to provide adequate service. It cannot begin service until approval has been granted. Basically, when a carrier receives permission to engage in interstate transportation, it agrees to serve both large and small shippers, wherever they are located on the routes granted, and to give them equal treatment and at equal rates.

Inherent Advantages of Different Transport Modes

Each form of common carrier transportation, for example, rail, truck, or air, has its own distinct advantages for shippers in respect to speed, available capacity, flexibility, and cost. By the same token, each mode has inherent disadvantages. For example, comparing air with truck transport, air has the advantage in terms of speed and time; truck transport can accommodate greater volume and has lower rates and greater flexibility in terms of delivery points. The astute buyer must recognize these advantages/ limitations and arrive at the best overall balance, considering the needs of the organization.

FOB TERMS

The term FOB stands for *free on board,* meaning that goods are delivered to a specified point with all transport charges paid. The specific responsibilities of the seller and buyer under FOB and FAS, *free alongside ship,* terms are covered in Articles 2–319 and 2–323 of the *Uniform Commercial Code.* The selection of the FOB point is important to the purchaser, for it determines three things:

1. Who pays the carrier.
2. When legal title to goods being shipped passes to the buyer.
3. Who is responsible for preparing and pursuing claims with the carrier in the event goods are lost or damaged during shipment.

The claim that FOB destination is always preferable because the seller pays the transportation charges is incorrect. While the seller may pay the transportation charges, in the final analysis the charges are borne by the buyer, since transportation costs will be included in the delivered price charged by the vendor. In effect, if the buyer lets the vendor make the transportation decisions, then the buyer is allowing the vendor to spend the buyer's money.

There are several variations in FOB terms, as Figure 8–2 shows. In purchases from foreign suppliers, the ocean carrier typically does not provide any insurance on goods in transit; therefore, it is important when goods are bought FOB origin for the buyer to assure that adequate insurance coverage is provided. The two marine freight terms commonly used are *C&F* and *CIF*. C&F, *cost and freight,* is similar to FOB origin, with freight charges paid by the seller. However, under C&F the buyer assumes all risk and should provide for insurance. CIF, *cost, insurance, and freight,* means that the seller will pay the freight charges and provide appropriate insurance coverage. This is similar to FOB destination, freight prepaid.

In some instances, the buyer may wish to obtain equalization of freight charges with the nearest shipping point of the seller, or some competitive shipping point. In that case, the following clause can be used: "Freight charges to be equalized with those applicable from seller's shipping point producing lowest transportation cost to buyer's destination."

FIGURE 8–2 FOB Terms and Responsibilities

FOB Term	Payment of Freight Charges	Bears Freight Charges	Owns Goods in Transit	Files Claims (if any)	Explanation
FOB origin, or FOB freight collect	Buyer	Buyer	Buyer	Buyer	Title and control of goods passes to buyer when carrier signs for goods at point of origin
FOB origin, freight prepaid	Seller	Seller	Buyer	Buyer	Seller pays freight charges and adds to invoice
FOB origin, freight prepaid and charged back	Seller	Buyer	Buyer	Buyer	
FOB destination, freight collect	Buyer	Buyer	Seller	Seller	Title remains with seller until goods are delivered.
FOB destination, freight prepaid	Seller	Seller	Seller	Seller	
FOB destination, freight prepaid and charged back	Seller	Buyer	Seller	Seller	Seller pays freight charges and adds to invoice
FOB destination, freight collect and allowed	Buyer	Seller	Seller	Seller	Buyer pays freight charges and deducts from seller's invoice

Freight Classification

Proper classification of freight shipments is of primary importance in the purchase of transportation services. Shippers are responsible for knowing the specific description of the merchandise being moved, and this classification determines the applicable tariff, or freight rate. For example, the gauge of steel being shipped determines the appropriate freight classification; if the wrong classification is indicated it literally can make a difference of thousands of dollars in freight charges on a large shipment. These commodity word descriptions must be used in shipping orders and bills of lading and must conform to those in the applicable tariff, including packing specifications where different rates are provided for the same article according to the manner in which it is packed for shipment. Failure to use the correct classification description will result in the carrier assessing an incorrect rate and possibly result in a charge that the shipper is fraudulently classifying shipments to get unwarranted low rates.

Classifications for rate-making purposes are based on many factors, such as weight per cubic foot, value per pound, and risk of damage or pilferage. Since shipments moving a long distance may move on several different railroads, the ICC has the responsibility of assuring that a uniform classification system is used. This is done through the Uniform Freight Classification, which became effective May 30, 1952, and is updated as needed. When motor carriers were brought under regulation in 1935, a National Motor Freight Classification was established and is in use today, although the New England states have their own classification system, the Coordinated Motor Freight Classification.

Most articles are shipped under a "class rating," which is the normal freight classification, which then determines the applicable freight rate. However, the ICC can authorize special "commodity rates," which normally are lower than the class rates and are granted to meet a particularly competitive situation and depend in part on volume moved. A shipper and a carrier normally will work together in petitioning the ICC for this special commodity rate. For example, if a firm requires steel scrap as a principal raw material and an economic imbalance develops which causes a local shortage of steel scrap, the alternative is to transport scrap from some distance to meet production requirements. But the class rate on steel scrap may be so high that it is uneconomic to buy and transport the distant scrap by rail. The buyer and carrier may decide to petition the ICC for a commodity rate on scrap, between these two points, on economic grounds of necessity to keep the industry in operation. The ICC may grant this special lower rate on an economic necessity basis, either permanently or temporarily.

Selection of Carrier and Routing

Normally, the buyer will wish to specify how purchased items are to be shipped; this is the buyer's legal right if the purchase has been made under any of the FOB origin terms. If the purchaser has received superior past service from a particular carrier, it then becomes the preferable means of shipment. Or, a carrier may have been particularly helpful in assisting the shipper in petitioning the ICC for favorable rates on certain items of merchandise.

As one would expect, buyers are most concerned that the vendor (carrier) meet its delivery promises (deliver on schedule) and provide the movement service without damaging the goods. Recent surveys conducted by *Purchasing World* indicate that the following 15 factors are considered important by the buyer, in descending order of priority: (1) on-time deliveries, (2) care in handling, (3) time in transit, (4) rates, (5) shipment tracing, (6) insurance coverage, (7) door-to-door deliveries, (8) claims record, (9) regular schedules, (10) shipment security, (11) through routing, (12) geographic coverage, (13) types of equipment, (14) consolidating/breaking capabilities, and (15) intermodal capabilities.[13]

On the other hand, if the buyer has relatively little expertise in the traffic area and the vendor has a skilled traffic department, it might be wise to rely on the vendor's judgment in carrier selection and routing. Also, in a time of shortage of transport equipment (RR cars or trucks), the vendor may have better information about the local situation and what arrangements will get best results. And, if the item to be shipped has special dimensional characteristics, requiring special rail cars, the vendor may be in a better position to know what's available and the clearances needed for proper shipment.

The first step is to determine the mode of transport, for example, rail, truck, air, water, and so on, which will best meet the transport requirement. Next, a decision must be made on a specific carrier and the specific routing of the shipment. This information should be a part of the purchase order. The buyer then may wish to keep track of the freight movement to assure that it is going as planned.

The factors to be considered in selection of mode of shipment, carrier, and routing include:

Required Delivery Time.   The required date for material receipt may make the selection of mode of shipment quite simple. If two-day delivery from a distant point is needed, the only viable alternative probably is air shipment. If a longer time is available, other modes can be considered. Most carriers can supply estimates of normal delivery times and the purchasing department also can rely on past experience with particular modes and carriers.

Reliability and Service Quality.   While two carriers may offer

---

[13]Richard L. Dunn, "A Basic Guide to Choosing Transportation Services," *Purchasing World,* September 1982, p. 47.

freight service between the same points, the reliability and dependability may differ greatly. One carrier may: (1) be more attentive to customer needs; (2) be more dependable in living up to its commitments; (3) incur less damage, overall, to merchandise shipped; and (4) in general be the best freight vendor. The buyer's past experience is the best indicator of service quality.

Available Services. If the item to be shipped is large and bulky, this may dictate a particular mode of transportation. Special container requirements may indicate only certain carriers who have the unique equipment to handle the job.

Type of Item Being Shipped. Bulk liquids, for example, may indicate RR tank car, barge, or pipeline. Also, safety requirements in the case of potentially explosive items may make certain carriers and routings impractical.

Shipment Size. Items of small size and bulk can be moved by U.S. mail, United Parcel Service, or air freight forwarders. Larger shipments probably can be more economically moved by rail or truck.

Possibility of Damage. Certain items, such as fine china or electronics equipment, by their nature have a high risk of damage in shipment. In this case, the buyer may select a mode and carrier by which the shipment can come straight through to its destination, with no transfers at distribution points to another carrier. It is part of the buyer's responsibility to insure that the packaging of goods is appropriate for both the contents and mode of transport.

Cost of the Transport Service. The buyer should select the mode, carrier, and routing that will provide for the safe movement of goods, within the required time, at lowest total transport cost. This requires a thorough knowledge of freight classifications and tariffs. Also, the buyer may make certain tradeoffs in purchasing transportation, just as are made in selection of vendors for other purchases.

Carrier Financial Situation. If any volume of freight is moved, some damages will be incurred, resulting in claims against the carrier. Should the carrier get into financial difficulty, or even become insolvent, collection on claims becomes a problem. Therefore, the buyer should avoid those carriers who are on the margin financially.

Handling of Claims. Inevitably, some damage claims will arise in the shipment of quantities of merchandise. Prompt and efficient investigation and settlement of claims is another key factor in carrier selection.

In the case of motor freight carriers, there is a wide mixture of types available:

1. Private motor carriers, not regulated by the ICC, which move freight between units of the same firm.
2. For-hire carriers, who transport freight for a fee, and may be either common, contract, or exempt, which include the following:
   a. Regulated carriers, subject to ICC regulation, who move freight in interstate commerce.
   b. Exempt carriers, not subject to ICC regulation because of the type freight carried, for example, livestock or newspapers.
   c. Common carriers, regulated by the ICC who hold themselves out to the general public.
   d. Contract carriers, who move freight only by agreement with specific firms.
   e. Regular route carriers, who transport only between specific points.
   f. Irregular route carriers, who serve communities within a defined area, over irregular routes.
   g. General freight carriers, who transport a variety of commodities, using terminal facilities for consolidation and distribution of goods.
   h. Specialized carriers, who have special equipment for movement of specific types of commodities, for example, chemicals.

Four types of terminals are in common use: (1) pickup and delivery, (2) break-bulk, (3) relay, and (4) interlining. The person who selects motor carriers and routes needs to be familiar with the various types of carriers and systems for movement in order to choose the best combination(s).[14]

Since with deregulation more carriers are available, the buyer now can use a variety of transportation directories, similar to the standard vendor selection directories, to develop an initial list of alternatives. For example, the *Inbound Traffic Guide* (published by the same firm which does *Thomas Register of American Manufacturers,* probably the most used vendor selection directory) publishes an annual directory of approximately 400 pages which simplifies the identification of firms in the transportation area: air courier, air express, air forwarding, air freight, barges, customs house brokers, expedited package service, export packing, freight consolidation, freight forwarding, foreign freight forwarding, hazardous waste carriers, ports, public warehouses, railroads, shippers associations, special equipment carriers, steamships, truck leasing, local haul trucking, long haul trucking, short haul trucking, and bulk transfer facilities.[15] A similar directory is published by Chilton in its *Distribution* magazine, listing motor carriers, ocean carriers, airport facilities, North American ports, air freight and small package express services, rail services, and commercial warehousing.[16]

---

[14]National Association of Purchasing Management, "Guide to Trucking," Section 3.15 of the *Guide to Purchasing* (undated).

[15]*1987 Inbound Traffic Guide* (New York: Thomas Publishing Company), 1987.

[16]*Distribution,* July 1988.

FIGURE 8–3 Carrier Rating Form

Carrier name: _____ Date: _____

Business allocation decision (circle one)

              Decline   Status quo   Growth

Areas rated:

1. Branch/plant
   a. Tracing, expediting (0–5): responds quickly, accurately.
   b. Pickup and delivery service (0–10): reliable, on schedule, customer service-oriented.
   c. Loss and damage (0–5): incidence, reconciles discrepancies quickly, good controls.
   d. Transit time reliability (0–10): service performance, customer satisfaction.
   e. Equipment condition (0–10): in proper repair, placards available.
   f. Special service and innovativeness (0–10): provides trailer spotting when requested, trailer pools, provides special pickups and deliveries.

2. Corporate
   a. Billing (0–5): accuracy, submits original freight bills.
   b. Financial (0–15): quick debt/worth, operating ratios, trends, mergers, ownership.
   c. Service (0–10): interface tracing, expediting, general carrier cooperation.
   d. Claims ratio, payment or claim resolution history, loss and damage control program.
   e. Data inquiry (0–15): automated systems, agreeable interface.
   f. Innovativeness (0–5): industry leader, new ideas, distribution-oriented.
   g. Pricing (0–5): willingness to negotiate, independent action, alerts shipper.

Carrier Rating Systems. Also, since now the buyer is not "locked in" to only certain carriers, but can elect to change carriers or split business among competing carriers, it is important, at least for those 20 percent of the carriers with which the firm does 80 percent of its transport volume, that some formal system for rating carrier performance be developed and used. An example of a simple form developed by one company to assist plants and the corporate office to evaluate experience with each carrier is shown in Figure 8–3.

Private or Leased Carriers. One possibility is the use of private or leased equipment. A private carrier or a leased carrier does not offer service to the general public. Many companies have elected to contract for exclusive use of equipment; and some have established their own trucking fleet, through use of either company-owned or leased tractors and vans.

Leasing gives the firm much greater flexibility in scheduling freight services. It can be economically advantageous, but unless the equipment can be fully utilized, through planned backhauls of either semifinished or finished goods, it may turn out to be more costly than use of the common carrier system. Also, it is important that the firm recognize and provide adequate protection against the very substantial dollar liability that may result in the case of accident.

Under deregulation, the use of private or leased vehicles is a much more viable alternative, and is a type of make-buy decision. The regulations covering use of private or leased equipment have been relaxed to permit firms with wholly-owned subsidiaries to engage in intercorporate hauling and to backhaul product, which may provide the volume needed to make this alternative economically worthwhile.

Freight Rates

The charges for freight movement are determined by the classification of the item transported and the appropriate rate tariff. The tariffs of common carriers are publicly available to any interested party, although they are voluminous and difficult to read and interpret except by someone skilled in rate analysis. With deregulation, rate changes occur more frequently, and many carriers have their own, separate tariffs. Even the ICC finds it difficult to keep up with the changes.

The basic charge is determined by the class rate, although lower commodity rates can be arranged for some items. Additional variations are available, providing the shipper is knowledgeable and innovative enough to obtain them.

Quantity Breaks.   As with other purchases, carriers (vendors) offer lower rates if the quantity of an individual shipment is large enough. Both rail and motor carriers offer discounts for full carload (CL) or truckload (TL) shipments. These will be substantially less per pound than less-than-carload (LCL) or less-than-truckload (LTL) quantities. If the shipper can consolidate smaller shipments to the same destination, a lower rate may be available (called a *pool car*). In some instances, shippers may band together through a shippers' association to get pool car transport rates.

The unit train is another innovation in which the shipper gets a quantity discount. By special arrangement with a railroad, a utility company is provided one or more complete trains, consisting of 100 + coal cars, which run shuttle between the coal mines and the utility's place of use. This speeds up the movement, and the materials are moved at an advantageous commodity rate. Also, under the Staggers Rail Act of 1980, shippers now can enter into long-term price and service contracts directly with a railroad.

Under the pricing flexibility granted by the Motor Carrier Act of 1980, four basic types of rate discounts have developed; the buyer in some instances can take advantage of one or more of them and possibly enjoy substantial savings:

Aggregate Tender Rates.   This provides a discount if the shipper will group multiple small shipments for pickup or delivery at one point.

Flat Percentage Discount.   This provides a discount to the shipper if a specified total minimum weight of less-than-truckload shipments is moved per month. This encourages the shipper to group volume with one carrier.

Increased Volume–Increased Discount Percentage.   Discount (often up to 25 percent) is applied if a firm increases its volume of LTL shipments by a certain amount over the previous month's volume.

Specific Origin and Destination Points.   This provides a specified discount if volume from a specified point to a specified delivery point reaches a given level.[17]

Through Rates.   Basically, the longer the distance over which materials are transported, the lower is the per mile transport cost. For example, the tariff for transport from A to B may be $1.00, and from B to C also $1.00, but the through rate, A to C, may be only $1.80. Three ways in which the through rate might be used for inbound freight are:

Diversion and Reconsignment.   Here the shipper may change the destination of a rail car to a different location, or change the party to which the shipment is destined, and still pay the long-haul freight rate, providing the railroad is notified before the car passes a predetermined point. There is a charge for this service, but the freight bill still may be less than a combination of the two short-haul rates. For example, a shipper starts a carload of apples from the state of Washington, with Pittsburgh as the destination. Under the diversion privilege, the shipper can change the destination to another city, for example, Atlanta or Miami, and still pay the long-haul rate providing the railroad is notified of the new destination *before* the car passes an agreed-on point, such as, the Mississippi River. This privilege is particularly useful in movement of perishable items or items in which the allowable transit time is short and a determination of final destination has not yet been made.

Stop-Off Privilege.   This permits a shipper to ship a full carload from point A to D, at the long-haul rate, but to stop the shipment at intermediate points B and C and drop off or pick up quantities. While the freight rate is

---

[17]J. L. Cavinato and A. J. Stenger, "Purchasing Transportation in the Changing Trucking Industry," *Journal of Purchasing and Materials Management,* Spring, 1983, p. 4.

calculated at the full carload weight even though the total shipment does not go to point D, it still may be cheaper than the LCL rates on shipments to points B, C, and D.

Fabrication or Storage-in-Transit.   By special arrangement with a railroad, and approved by the ICC, a buyer of raw materials can ship from point A, stop the shipment at intermediate point B, fabricate the raw material, reload it within a specified number of days, such as 60 days, and ship it to final destination C, all at the long-haul rate from A to C. In general, the movement must be on a straight line, but this shouldn't be interpreted literally. For example, a buyer of steel can purchase it in Chicago, have it shipped to Milwaukee under the fabrication-in-transit privilege, fabricate it, and reload it for rail shipment to Lansing, Michigan, all at the long haul, Chicago to Lansing rate. While an extra charge is paid for the in-transit privilege, it still is cheaper in total than paying two separate short-haul charges. Items can be unloaded for storage for several months under the same arrangement. The in-transit privilege is available with motor freight also. The economic rationale for this privilege is that, without it, manufacture would be done at either the point of raw material production or at the final use point, and intermediate points (Milwaukee, in the above example) would not be able to compete for manufacturing or storage functions.

RELEASED RATES

The common carrier assumes liability for the full value of the goods shipped, unless damage occurs due to acts of God or shipper negligence. However, the shipper may negotiate a released rate, which is a lower than normal rate, if it is willing to accept a lower than full liability for damage on the part of the carrier. The shipper must assess the relationship between the lower rate and the risk of damage. It may decide to carry a separate insurance policy to protect against the increased risk of damage.

Intermodal Shipments.   To be competitive with other shipping modes, the railroads have developed special equipment and services. Piggyback service, where truck trailers are loaded on special rail cars for long distance shipment, and containerization, where specially designed containers are loaded, delivered by rail or truck to a wharf, hoisted on board a ship, and then offloaded onto rail or truck carriers for shipments to their final destination, are examples of current innovations in shipping methods. Since under the Staggers Rail Act of 1980 piggyback service has been completely deregulated, attractive arrangements often are possible using this intermodal method. Growth in piggybacking has been substantial.

Small Shipments.   Under deregulation, competition for small shipment services (normally defined as 70 lbs. or less) has become intense.

Buyers now can use some of the standard purchasing techniques, such as systems contracts, aggressive negotiation, multiple sourcing, quotation analysis, target pricing, and vendor evaluation, to get better financial arrangements with carriers. One company, for example, compiled records on all shipments made or received in one metropolitan area and then asked carriers (vendors) to quote on a blanket contract basis for providing small shipment service to all its plants in that area.[18]

Documentation in Freight Shipments

The bill of lading (B/L) is the key document in the movement of goods. The bill has been standardized by the ICC, and carriers are responsible to issue proper bills, although in practice they normally are prepared by the shipper. Figure 8–4 shows a bill of lading.

While the bill of lading may be prepared in whatever number of copies is convenient, the following three copies are required:

1. *Copy 1, Original:* Describes shipment and is a receipt by the carrier for the goods. Signed by both shipper's and carrier's agents, it is proof that shipment was made and is evidence of ownership. It is a contract and fixes carrier liability; normally it will be kept by the party who has title to goods in transit, for it must be provided to support any damage claims.

2. *Copy 2, Shipping Order:* Retained by carrier; used as shipping instructions and as a basis for billing.

3. *Copy 3, Memorandum:* Simply acknowledges that B/L has been issued.

There are several variations on the B/L:

1. *Uniform Straight Bill of Lading:* This is the complete B/L and contains the complete contract terms and conditions. Separate form is needed for motor and rail shipments.

2. *Straight Bill of Lading—Short Form:* Contains those provisions uniform to both motor and rail. Short bills are not furnished by carriers, but instead are preprinted by shippers.

3. *Unit Bill of Lading:* This is prepared in four copies; the extra copy is the railroad's waybill. This waybill moves with the shipment and may be of assistance in expediting freight movement.

4. *Uniform Order Bill of Lading:* Printed on yellow paper (the other B/Ls must be on white paper), this also is called a sight draft bill of lading. It is a negotiable instrument and must be surrendered to the carrier at destination before goods can be obtained. Its primary use is to prevent

---

[18]Thomas F. Dillon, "Small Shipments: Target for Better Buying," *Purchasing World,* August 1983, p. 42.

FIGURE 8–4

STRAIGHT BILL OF LADING—SHORT FORM

ORIGINAL — NOT NEGOTIABLE
(To be printed on white paper)

Shipper's No. 9523.

Carrier's No. ....

Southern Pacific Transportation Co.
(Name of Carrier)

RECEIVED, subject to the classifications and tariffs in effect on the date of the issue of this Bill of Lading,

At ....Guadalupe, Calif. .... February 23, , 1988

From........ DORFLER OIL CO OF CALIF ....

the property described below, in apparent good order, except as noted (contents and condition of contents of packages unknown), marked, consigned, and destined as indicated below, which said carrier (the word carrier being understood throughout this contract as meaning any person or corporation in possession of the property under the contract) agrees to carry to its usual place of delivery at said destination, if on its route, otherwise to deliver to another carrier on the route to said destination. It is mutually agreed, as to each carrier of all or any of said property over all or any portion of said route to destination, and as to each party at any time interested in all or any of said property, that every service to be performed hereunder shall be subject to all the terms and conditions of the Uniform Domestic Straight Bill of Lading set forth (1) in Uniform Freight Classification in effect on the date hereof, if this is a rail or a rail-water shipment, or (2) in the applicable motor carrier classification or tariff if this is a motor carrier shipment.

Shipper hereby certifies that he is familiar with all the terms and conditions of the said bill of lading, including those on the back thereof, set forth in the classification or tariff which governs the transportation of this shipment, and the said terms and conditions are hereby agreed to by the shipper and accepted for himself and his assigns

Consigned to .. CLETRON ASPHALT   1584 Parkway Road
(Mail or street address of consignee—For purposes of notification only.)
Destination .. Phoenix .... State Ariz .. County .... Delivery Address★ ....
(★To be filled in only when shipper desires and governing tariffs provide for delivery thereat.)
Route .. SP
Delivering Carrier .. ATSF Dlvy .... Length .... Car or Vehicle Initials .. SP .. No. 726805
Trailer Initials Number .... Length .... Plan ....
Container Initials Number .... Length .... Plan ....

No. Packages	Kind of Package, Description of Articles, Special Marks, and Exceptions	*Weight (Subject to Correction)	Class or Rate	Check Column	Subject to Section 7 of Conditions of applicable bill of lading, if this shipment is to be delivered to the consignee without recourse on the consignor, the consignor shall sign the following statement:
20725	Gals.Liquid Asphalt AR16000	178234			The carrier shall not make delivery of this shipment without payment of freight and all other lawful charges
	If delayed for any reason				(Signature of consignor)
	notify Traffic Manager,				If charges are to be prepaid, write or stamp here, "To be Prepaid"
	Dorfler Oil Co., PO Box 2900,				
	Costa Mesa, CA 92626				To be Prepaid
	State cause of delay and				
	date car will go forward				Received $ ...... to apply in prepayment of the charges on the property described hereon
	TCFB Wt. Agmt. #2888				
					Agent or Cashier

*If the shipment moves between two ports by a carrier by water, the law requires that the bill of lading shall state whether it is carrier's or shipper's weight.

Note.—Where the rate is dependent on value, shippers are required to state specifically in writing the agreed or declared value of the property.

The agreed or declared value of the property is hereby specifically stated by the shipper to be not exceeding .... per ....

Per ....
(The signature here acknowledges only the amount prepaid.)
Charges advanced

$ ....

DORFLER OIL CO. .... Shipper. .... _Lee Smith_ .... Agent.

Per .. _Jack Jones_ .... Per .... 2/23/88 .. 11 AM

Permanent post office address of shipper .. PO Box 2900, Costa Mesa, CA 92626 delivery until payment is made for the goods. To obtain payment, the shipper must provide a sight draft, along with the original copy of the B/L, to his bank; when the draft clears, the bank gives the B/L to the shipper, who then can obtain delivery of the merchandise.

Each shipment must have a bill of lading, which is the contract, spelling out the legal liabilities of all parties. No changes to the original B/L can be made unless approved by the carrier's agent, in writing on the B/L.

Expediting and Tracing Shipments

As with the normal purchase of goods and services, expediting means applying pressure to the carrier (vendor) in an attempt to encourage faster than normal delivery service. The carrier often can and will provide faster service to assist the shipper in meeting an emergency requirement, provided such requests are made sparingly. Expediting should be done through the carrier's general agent and, if at all possible, the carrier should be notified of the need for speed as far in advance of the shipment as possible.

Tracing is similar to follow-up, for it attempts to determine the status (location) of items that have been shipped, have not yet been received, and thus are somewhere within the transportation system. Tracing also is done through the carrier's agent, although the shipper may work right along with the carrier's agent in attempting to locate the shipment. If tracing locates a shipment and indicates it will not be delivered by the due date, then expediting is needed.

Getting results in tracing is a function of the kinds of movement records maintained by the carrier and the type of information available to the person doing the tracing. For example, in attempting to trace a CL rail shipment, the tracer should have (1) date material shipped, (2) description of material, (3) car number, (4) carrier, (5) origin, (6) destination, and (7) route.

While the ease with which various shipments can be traced will vary among carriers and various modes of transportation and may change from time to time as carriers and modes change their policies and record-keeping systems, the current traceability is:

CL rail: If one has the car initial and number, date of shipment, and routing, the railroad quickly can locate a car. Most have computerized locator systems.

LCL rail: Ability to locate a given shipment varies greatly among carriers. Some maintain detailed records; others maintain minimum records, making tracing almost impossible.

TL motor: If the shipper has the trailer number, most carriers can quickly tell the approximate current location, since it is kept track of through a series of movement points.

LTL motor: Normally, motor carriers can give complete and accurate information, since they account for LTL shipments as they move through the various checkpoints.

Air shipment: Information on exact location normally can be obtained with little difficulty.

Parcel Post: No records are maintained; tracing is impossible.

United Parcel Service: Shipment status can be supplied quickly and accurately.

Freight forwarders: Since they use the service of common carriers, it is possible to trace these shipments in the same way that other shipments can be traced.

Water carriers: Shipment can be located easily, for material is receipted for when put aboard, and it normally doesn't change carriers.

Loss or Damage Claims

The carrier is responsible for the full, actual damage to or loss of merchandise while in its possession. To collect on proper claims, the owner of the merchandise must file properly supported claims. If the merchandise is being shipped under any of the FOB origin terms, the buyer will have to pursue the claim. If the shipment is FOB destination, the vendor must process the claim, but since the merchandise is in the buyer's hands, the buyer will have to supply much of the information to support the claim.

Section 20(1) of the Interstate Commerce Act specifies that shippers must have at least nine months to file claims in writing with a carrier and that if a claim is disallowed by a carrier, the shipper must have two years to bring court suit. The Straight Bill of Lading Condition 2(B) provides: ". . . Claims must be filed in writing with the receiving or delivering carrier, or carrier issuing this bill of lading; or carrier on whose line the loss, damage, injury, or delay occurred, within nine months after delivery of the property or, in case of failure to make delivery, then within nine months after a reasonable time for delivery has elapsed; and suits shall be instituted against any carrier only within two years and one day from the day when notice in writing is given by the carrier to the claimant that the carrier has disallowed the claim. . . ."

Under this provision, carriers generally have established nine months as the claim filing period, and two years and one day for the filing of court suits in the case of disallowed claims.

Unconcealed Loss or Damage.   When it is evident on delivery that loss or damage has occurred, this must be noted on the carrier's delivery receipt, and signed by the carrier's delivering agent. If this is not done, the carrier may maintain that he received a "clear receipt" and not admit any liability. It is a good idea for the receiving department to have an instant camera available, take one or more photos of the damaged items and have them signed by the carrier's representative. Then, the local freight agent should be notified and an inspection report requested. This telephone request should be followed up in writing.

If it can be proven that the loss or damage occurred while the goods were in the carrier's possession, and if the cost of the damage can be established, prompt carrier payment should be expected. However, with the entry into the market of many new motor carriers, and an increasing number of bankruptcies, some shippers have had difficulty in collecting amounts due them. This points up the need on the buyer's part to do a careful job of financial analysis in selecting motor carriers.

Concealed Loss or Damage.   Merchandise found short or damaged only after the container is opened is known as *concealed loss or damage.* The unpacking should be discontinued, photos taken, and the carrier's local agent should be requested to inspect the items and prepare an inspection report.

Concealed loss or damage claims often are difficult to collect, because it is hard to determine whether the loss or damage took place while the shipment was in the carrier's possession or whether it occurred before the shipment was delivered to the carrier.

Payment of Freight Bills

ICC rules provide that all common carrier freight bills must be paid within a set number of days. Current regulations require common carrier rail bills to be paid within five days, and common carrier motor bills within seven days, of receipt. Obviously, if the vendor pays the bills and includes them in its invoice for goods submitted to the buyer, the buyer may not be paying the charges for, say, 30 to 60 days, depending on the payment arrangements covered by the purchase order. If a maximum payment period was not specified and standardized, some large shippers, by virtue of their volume, might insist on very long payment terms, which would discriminate against the smaller shippers.

If, due to the short-payment terms, the shipper pays an overcharge as a result of (1) an error in classification, (2) an error in rate charged, (3) an error in weight, (4) duplicate payment of the same freight bill, or (5) calculation error(s), there is a three-year period to file an overcharge claim with the carrier. If the claim is substantiated by evidence, there should be no problem in recovering from the carrier, assuming the carrier is not in financial difficulty. By the same token, the carrier has three years to bill shippers for any undercharges. Procedures for filing of loss or damage and overcharge claims for air shipments vary with individual airlines.

Demurrage charges often are incurred by shippers or receivers of merchandise. This simply is a daily penalty charge for a rail car or a motor van that is tied up beyond the normal time for loading or unloading. Typically, the period before which the "clock" begins to run on the demurrage penalties starts from 7 A.M. of the first regular working day by which the carrier has spotted the car or van ready for unloading. The free period on the loading of outbound rail cars is 24 hours; for the unloading of inbound cars it is 48 hours. For motor carrier vans, the free period is much shorter.

If demurrage were not charged, some firms would use the carrier's equipment as a free storage facility. The daily demurrage rate becomes progressively higher the longer the car or trailer is tied up, until it gets almost prohibitive. A shipper can enter into an averaging agreement with a carrier, whereby cars or vans unloaded one day early may be used to offset cars which are unloaded a day late. In an averaging agreement, settlement is made monthly. If the shipper owes the carrier, payment must be made; if the carrier owes the shipper, no payment is made, but instead the net car balance starts at zero in the new month. The purchasing department should be aware of the normal number of rail cars or vans which can be unloaded each day, and attempt to schedule shipments in so that they do not "back up" and result in payment of demurrage penalties.

Freight Audits

Because of the complex regulations under which carriers operate, and the increased number of alternatives available under deregulation, a careful audit of paid freight bills often will uncover instances of overpayment to the carrier. Since the shipper has three years to file claims for overpayment, this audit can be done on a yearly basis without jeopardizing the shipper's ability to collect.

In the larger firm, in-house freight bill audit capability often is available. In the smaller firm, the use of an outside freight audit consultant, referred to as a *traffic consultant* or *rate shark,* should be used. The rate shark will examine all paid freight bills in an attempt to spot overpayment due to wrong classification, wrong rate, duplicate payment, or calculation errors. When overpayments are found, the rate shark will process a claim with the carrier. The agreement with the shipper typically is that the rate shark retains 50 percent of the dollars recovered, although occasionally the outside auditor will work for a smaller percentage. Due to the complexity of the freight purchase area, even a company with a sophisticated, well-trained traffic staff probably pays some overcharges, and with the advice of an outside auditor could generate substantial recoveries. And with the rate shark, if nothing is recovered, no payment is made.

DEVELOPING A TRANSPORTATION STRATEGY

The changes in the transportation system and alternatives have been dramatic over the past several years. From a rather mundane, routine type of buying, it has moved into an era where the same principles of effective purchasing can and should be applied. Development of a transportation strategy should include:

Value analysis of alternatives: A service requirement value analysis may turn up totally adequate, lower cost transport arrangements.

Price analysis: Rates vary substantially and decisions should be made only after consideration of all possibilities. Competitive quotes should be obtained. Negotiation of big-ticket transportation now is possible.

Consolidate freight, where possible: Volume discounts may reduce transport costs substantially. Systems contracts and blanket orders may be advantageous.

Analyze and evaluate vendors: Carrier selection and evaluation systems can provide data needed for better decision making.

Reassess the possibilities of using different transport modes. This would include transport modes, such as private trucking and intermodal transportation, for example, piggybacking. The savings often are substantial.

Develop closer relationship with selected carriers: Data which enable better planning of transport requirements should be interchanged, to take advantage of the specialized knowledge of both buyer and carrier.

QUESTIONS FOR REVIEW AND DISCUSSION

1. How has transportation deregulation affected the purchase of transportation services?
2. What factors should be considered in selecting a carrier?
3. How do firms organize to handle the traffic function?
4. How should a buyer of motor freight services evaluate the advisability of using a "released rate"?
5. What types of traffic damage might occur, and how should each be handled?
6. Why is classification so important in buying transportation services?
7. What is the use and significance of the bill of lading?
8. What does FOB mean? What variations are there in FOB terms?
9. When might a buyer want to use one of the "through rate" provisions?
10. What strategies should be developed to effectively manage the transportation function?

REFERENCES

Augello, William J. *Freight Claims in Plain English.* Rev. ed. Huntington, New York: Shippers National Freight Claims Council, 1983.

Cavinato, J. L., and A. J. Stenger. "Purchasing Transportation in the Changing Trucking Industry." *Journal of Purchasing and Materials Management,* Spring 1983.

Cavinato, J. L. "Transportation Contracts: Pointers and Pitfalls for Buyers." *Journal of Purchasing and Materials Management,* Winter 1984.

Dunn, Richard L. "A Basic Guide to Choosing Transportation Services." *Purchasing World,* September 1982.

"Is Deregulation Working?" *Business Week,* December 22, 1986.

Sampson, Roy J.; Martin T. Farris; and David L. Shrock. *Domestic Transportation: Practice, Theory and Policy.* 5th ed. Boston: Houghton Mifflin, 1985.

Tyworth, J. E.; J. L. Cavinato; and C.J. Langley, Jr. *Traffic Management: Planning, Operations, and Control.* Reading, Mass.: Addison-Wesley, 1987.

Case 8–1

AIRFREIGHT COST RECOVERY

Lionel Flashman, Purchasing Officer in the laundry division of Fisher & Paykel Limited located in Auckland, New Zealand, was wondering what he could do to recover the excess airfreight costs incurred because Smaldon Industries, of Brisbane, Australia, was repeatedly late in its deliveries.

The Laundry Division

The laundry division, one of eight wholly-owned operating divisions of Fisher & Paykel Limited, employed over 500 people to produce washing machines and dryers. With New Zealand's economic recovery, the sales and profit results of the division had exceeded expectations.

The laundry division was currently developing a new line of washing machines for introduction within eight months. It was planning to phase out its current line after new model introduction. However, the discussions about the phasing out had been going on for the last three years and had been delayed several times already. In fact, demand was such that the division could not produce enough washing machines and thus the priority of purchasing was to ensure parts availability. Demand was expected to remain strong for laundry products throughout the coming year.

National and international suppliers, who had also experienced an upturn in their own markets, had had to adjust to meet the division's increased orders, tightening their available capacity.

At the same time however, the continuing strength of the Japanese yen and

Australian dollar[1] was putting increasing pressures on costs for the imported content of the appliances, which varied between 50 and 55 percent of the costs of material used, depending on the product.

With charges also increased for petrol and transport, the division's purchasing staff was under pressure to control procurement costs as tightly as possible. Purchases of materials and services accounted for nearly 60 percent of all sales revenue.

Similar to the rest of the company, the division was also strongly encouraged to apply Deming's management philosophy, as part of the company-wide commitment to the "pursuit of excellence" plan.

Like everyone else in the company, Lionel Flashman was well aware that the first two points of Deming's "14 obligations" for improving quality and productivity were:

1. Create constancy of purpose towards improvement of product and service.

2. Adopt the new philosophy that we no longer need to live with commonly accepted delays, mistakes, defective materials, and workmanship.

Smaldon Industries

Smaldon Industries was a manufacturer of powder metal products[2] located in Brisbane, Australia, with sales of about $5 million. Smaldon was the sole supplier of a dozen very specialized parts used for the gear box of F&P's current line of washing machines. These parts varied in price between NZ$0.12 to NZ$3.40 per unit. Fisher & Paykel owned the tooling for all of these parts.

Lionel was aware that there were at least three other Australian companies and, of course, many Japanese and other foreign firms that produced powder metal products.

While other F&P divisions used Smaldon as a supplier, the laundry division accounted for 95 percent of Smaldon's business with F&P. Lionel was aware that other divisions were currently investigating the adoption of Smaldon's products. However, no powder metal parts would be required for the new line of washing machines.

The laundry division had been dealing with Smaldon for at least 15 years. F&P was their largest New Zealand customer, totaling over one-half million NZ dollars of business. The relationship between F&P and Smaldon had always been extremely cordial over the years, with Dennis Smaldon, the managing director, often looking after F&P orders or intervening personally, when in some instances, their products were not meeting F&P tolerance requirements. On a few occasions in the last year Dennis Smaldon had pushed some urgent F&P orders and given F&P priority over other customers.

However, Lionel was aware that Smaldon had experienced some problem with his staff and production planning, with a high turnover of key management personnel

---

[1]The exchange rate was NZ$1 for A$0.60

[2]Powder metallurgy is a method of forming metal powder into solid blocks or finished molded products by applying heat and pressure to the powder. It provides an economical way of forming metals into products of intricate shape. It can also incorporate nonmetallic materials like graphite for the production of self-lubricating bearings.

over the last few years. A new general manager, Matthew Lee, who had been hired recently, seemed highly competent. As a result of some recosting by Matthew Lee, last October Smaldon had increased its prices to 20 percent on the average, the first increase in the last three years.

S-417

The most expensive and intricate part supplied by Smaldon Industries was the S-417, a self-lubricating bearing and key part that was used at the beginning of the production line and which could not possibly be installed later on in the process. Each piece cost NZ$3.40 and Smaldon supplied about 50,000 of these annually.

Delivery

Dennis Smaldon received quarterly orders as well as four-week delivery requirements on a constant basis. A five-month lead time was the norm from the time of order to the time of use on the production line. Typically, Lionel would ask for an early December shipment for an early January entry into stock. One month was required from Australia to be on the safe side, although the sailing was only three to four days, to allow sufficient time for loading and unloading as well as customs clearance. F&P policy for overseas parts was to receive the parts in stock four weeks before needed on the production line. In accordance with MRP, the company had no safety stock. F&P was buying from the factory, which meant it paid all transport costs.

Smaldon had been sending regular shipments of parts and although there had been some delivery problems at various intervals in the past, no serious ones had occurred over the past few years. Last August, however, Dennis Smaldon called Lionel and warned that there could be delivery problems with the S-417. Some of the raw materials for this part came from England and had been held up in the United Kingdom dockers' strike. He had had to fly some stock from England. However, he thought he would have enough stock to fill F&P requirements until his next shipment arrived.

If all went well, it was possible to receive stock from Australia via seafreight within 14 days, but that meant making special arrangements for quick customs clearance and wharfies' compensation. However, the company strongly discouraged dealing directly with customs to "hurry things along," as it could jeopardize customs treatment for all divisions.

The sole shipping alternative was airfreight, which could be delayed if there was a ship sailing shortly after required ship date. For the supplier, it meant being able to drop the shipment the night before flight departure. There were five flights a week from Brisbane to Auckland as opposed to two ships a month. However, it was felt that risks of stock-out increased with airfreight as airport customs were slower and far stricter. It was estimated that one out of five times airport customs would hold up the merchandise and F&P would have to go through a great deal of trouble and documentation to clear up the shipment. In addition, air freight increased the volume of paperwork and processing, with much smaller shipments received at more frequent intervals. Trucking costs would also increase substantially.

Smaldon had been flying the S-417 parts since September, while shipments for other Smaldon parts continued by sea. Although the washer assembly line had never been stopped, on several occasions the margin had been very close. "We have been living from hand to mouth," said Lionel. A dozen times he had had to borrow supply from spare parts in the customer services division, which had lent two days production at a time. Lionel knew it was difficult to return these parts and the customer services division did not appreciate this borrowing practice.

Lionel was especially concerned with the increased costs incurred by airfreighting. The last 4.8 metric ton shipment coming by seafreight had cost 41.9 cents per kilo. Airfreight varied depending on the size of the shipment. A month ago, he had received 900 S-417 parts weighing 126 kilos at a cost of NZ$214.32. Last week, a shipment of 1,390 kilos had cost NZ$1,751.98.

Fisher & Paykel had no established policy for recovering extra airfreight costs. Lionel said the prevailing attitude was "get the stuff here and worry about it later." Although most suppliers occasionally missed a shipping date and had to airfreight, Lionel felt that Smaldon was by far the worst. "I have to watch him like a hawk," he stressed. He knew that on occasion F&P had negotiated recovery payment with late suppliers and had received credit notes for 50 to 100 percent of the excess freight cost.

Lionel was wondering how to approach Dennis Smaldon with this issue. He wished the company had a uniform way of dealing with such matters. Although he had not compiled exact data, he estimated that his division had incurred between $20,000 to $30,000 extra shipping costs on the S-417 alone in the last five months. He was aware also that Smaldon had had to airfreight U.K. raw material himself on at least one occasion and had not passed this cost on to F&P. He was also concerned about not antagonizing Smaldon and curtailing future willingness to supply at all.

Lionel's supervisor, John Wardrop, had asked him to address the issue immediately and come up with some recommendations.

Case 8–2

I.XL* INDUSTRIES LIMITED

Wilf Schafer, Purchasing Agent for I.XL Industries Limited, Medicine Hat, Alberta, realized that the local recession had significantly reduced the demand for construction, and hence the requirement for their clay brick, their primary product, to about 55 percent of previous production levels, and that management meetings had dealt with the challenge of managing I.XL under the new low demand condition. Wilf felt that purchasing could make a significant contribution by avoiding unnecessary costs and stocks, since improving cash flow was the company's main objective during this

---

*Registered trademark of I.XL Industries Ltd.

critical period. One product in particular, a chemical coloring agent for brick, came immediately to mind. Current purchase quantities created six to eight months stock, which Wilf believed should be cut substantially, even if new transportation arrangements would have to be made.

I.XL Industries Limited

I.XL products included sewer pipe and other clay products, but the company's primary output was brick. The clay to make their products was mined locally by I.XL in some 20 to 30 varieties. Natural brick colors came in white, buff and red, depending on the clays used; however, brown color ranges could not be achieved with clay mixes alone. This required importing a coloring agent to provide the proper color. I.XL's supplier of record, most competitive in the marketplace, was located in Newcastle, Delaware, U.S.A., on the Atlantic coast. This company had been selected because of quality of product and competitive price.

I.XL purchases had been in 100-lb. bags, by rail car lots of either 35 or 55 tons, arranged through a Canadian distributor shipped FOB Medicine Hat. Current demand was estimated at 60 tons per year.

Wilf wished to investigate possible opportunities for savings. First, he wondered why he would not be able to buy directly from the American supplier, FOB, the supplier's plant in Delaware. Upon contacting the supplier, he found out the Canadian representative had exclusive rights to sales in Canada, but purchase could be made FOB Newcastle, Delaware, at more attractive prices. The purchase order and payment in Canadian funds could be made via the Canadian representative. This would allow I.XL to proceed to investigate transportation savings, if any. Wilf believed that the agent made a commission on the transportation costs, which certainly could produce a saving for I.XL.

In his investigations, Wilf had determined, with the assistance of the comptroller, that inventory carrying costs for I.XL were about 20 percent per annum. The comptroller also informed Wilf that for practical purposes, he could consider one U.S. dollar to be 1.29 Canadian dollars, when comparing quotations given in these respective currencies. Wilf was curious whether or not it would be more economical in the long term to continue to buy in carload lots and store the raw materials, or reduce inventory and resulting storing costs by purchasing in smaller, more frequent lots.

Wilf, in drafting his ideas, noted that the chemical coloring agent was federal sales tax exempt, and also was duty free under the appropriate tariff item. He recognized that the coloring agent was the only chemical purchased from this supplier. He had just received a new quote from the Canadian representative, which for the first time included a truckload quantity. The following prices quoted are in Canadian dollars.

700 bag railcar $67.50/100 Kg

1100 bag railcar 64.40/100 Kg

455 bag truckload 62.60/100 Kg

All above prices FOB Medicine Hat.

If purchased FOB Newcastle, Delaware, the price was $34.72/100 Kg in U.S. funds, provided a minimum of 10 tons was purchased at a time.

While perusing these figures, Wilf received a phone call in response to his request the day before, informing him that the estimated haulage charges for a 45-foot trailer of 24 tons would be $2,600 Canadian, from Newcastle to Medicine Hat. A 10-ton shipment would cost at least 25 percent more for transportation.

CHAPTER 9

Disposal of Scrap, Surplus, or Obsolete Material

Managers are concerned with the effective, efficient, and profitable disposal of scrap, surplus, obsolete, and waste materials generated within the firm. In recent years, disposal problems have become more complex and important, as companies have become larger, more diversified in product lines, and more decentralized in management. More recently, a new dimension has been added to the overall disposal problem: the need to develop and use new methods to avoid the generation of solid waste products and better means of disposing of other wastes which are discharged into the air and waterways, causing pollution.

While this chapter will analyze and discuss the purchasing department's role in disposition of surplus and waste, the alert purchasing executive must also keep abreast of new technology concerned with avoiding and eliminating causes of pollution.

The salvage of all types of materials in U.S. industry is big business. It is estimated that sales of scrap and waste materials of all types are in excess of $15 billion per year.[1] Not only does the proper sale of scrap, surplus, and waste result in additional income for the seller, it also prevents pollution and serves to conserve raw material resources and energy. For example, every ton of iron and steel scrap recycled saves one-and-one-half tons of iron ore, one ton of coke and one-half ton of limestone, plus the energy required to convert the raw materials into virgin product. The energy savings in the recycling of metals such as zinc, iron/steel, and aluminum is estimated to run from 60 to 95 percent, with 75 percent a good average.

An increasingly complex and stringent set of federal and state regulations has been enacted over the last decade to protect the environment. This has complicated the scrap recovery process and increased the potential

---

[1] The Institute of Scrap Iron and Steel, Inc., 1627 K Street, N.W., Suite 700, Washington, D.C. 20006, is a national association of firms who are predominantly processors and brokers of scrap. The institute publishes several reports on the scrap industry and provides much data.

liability risks for both the generators and processors of scrap. For example, with metalworking turnings, oil and chemical residues present a risk; plated, coated, or painted scrap may contain cadmium, lead, or zinc; pipe, insulated or coated wire and cable often have asbestos, lead, or chemical residues; and closed containers present a risk of explosions and chemical residues. The purchasing department must be aware of these risks, as they affect its ability to profitably dispose of scrap and surplus.

Three pieces of federal legislation impact the scrap disposal market and procedures used:

1. Resource Conservation and Recovery Act (RCRA), passed in 1976. This was the cornerstone hazardous waste control law, although it was not implemented by the Environmental Protection Agency (EPA) until 1980. The RCRA identifies which industrial wastes are corrosive, toxic, ignitable, or chemically reactive. The EPA has promulgated regulations prescribing how these potentially dangerous items are to be treated, disposed of, or stored. In some instances RCRA permits are needed.

2. Toxic Substances Control Act, passed in 1976. This regulates procedures used in the manufacture, use, and distribution of chemicals. Included are polychlorinated Biphenyls (PCBs), which the 1979 EPA regulations specify must be disposed of in chemical waste landfills.

3. Comprehensive Environmental Response, Compensation, and Liability Act, passed in 1980. This is known as Superfund, for it gives the EPA authority to order the cleanup of solid waste sites and to recover the costs, if necessary, from those responsible for the pollution damage. This potential liability has made it more costly to process certain types of scrap and will reduce the amounts of secondary (reprocessed) materials available.[2] About 10 states have passed tougher cleanup laws since 1983, requiring that companies which own or sell industrial property foot the cleanup bill on properties on which pollution of the site through improper disposal of hazardous waste has caused health risks to the community.[3]

SAVINGS POTENTIAL

It is surprising that more attention has not been given by companies to the whole problem of disposal. The reasons are probably several. One of the most important is that scrap is suggestive of something which has no

---

[2]Tom Stundza, "Scrap Scrapes Against the Environment," *Purchasing*, April 9, 1987, p. 64A7.

[3]"Making Firms Liable for Cleaning Toxic Sites," *The Wall Street Journal*, March 9, 1988, p. 27.

value and which the junkman can take away—in other words, something which a company is willing to sell if it can get anything for it, but which, if not, it is willing even to pay somebody to haul away. Another reason is that many concerns are not large enough to maintain disposal departments, since the amounts of scrap and surplus they have do not appear great enough to warrant particular attention. Yet, these items may be a source of potential profit.

At times of raw material shortages, scrap is likely to command very high prices. England found in the 1970s that its domestically controlled price of waste rags of about $60 per ton was well below that of the European market, resulting in an exodus of this material for which a special domestic collection program had been set up to encourage local manufacture of toilet tissue. The result was a shortage of raw materials for the English mills, and a tissue shortage forcing imports of an item that could well have been manufactured locally.

The disposition of all kinds of scrap and surplus materials should always be handled to reduce the net loss to the lowest possible figure or, if possible, achieve the highest potential gain. The first thought, therefore, should be to balance against each other the net returns obtained from each one of several methods of disposition. Thus, excess material can frequently be transferred from one plant of a company to another of the same company. Such a procedure involves little outlay except for packing, handling, and shipping. At other times, by reprocessing or reconditioning, the material can be salvaged for use within the plant. Such cases clearly involve a somewhat larger outlay, and there may be some question as to whether, once the material has been so treated, its value, either for the purpose originally intended or for some substitute use, is great enough to warrant the expense. Since the decision whether to undertake the reclamation of any particular lot of material is essentially one of production costs and of the resultant quality, it should be—and commonly is—made by the production or engineering departments instead of by the scrap department. The most the purchasing manager can do is to suggest that this treatment be considered before the material is disposed of in other ways.

In some companies there is, within the manufacturing department, a separate salvage or "utilization" division to pass on questions about possible reclamation. Indeed, the place of the "salvage engineer" is well established among many larger firms. This salvage division is primarily a manufacturing rather than a sales division and is concerned with such duties as the development of salvage processes, the actual reclamation of waste, scrap, or excess material, and the reduction of the volume of such material.

CATEGORIES OF MATERIAL FOR DISPOSAL

No matter how well a company may be managed, some excess, waste, scrap, surplus, and obsolete material is bound to develop. Every organization tries, of course, to keep such material at a minimum. But try as it may, this never will be wholly successful. The existence of this class of material is the result of a wide variety of causes, among which are overoptimism in the sales forecast; changes in design and specifications; errors in estimating mill usage; inevitable losses in processing; careless use of material by factory personnel; and overbuying resulting from attempts to avoid the threat of rising prices or to secure quantity discounts on large purchases.

We are not presently concerned at this time with the methods by which excess, waste, scrap, or obsolete material may be kept at a minimum, for these already have been discussed in connection with proper inventory and stores control, standardization, quality determination, and forward buying. The immediate problem has to do with the disposition of these materials when they do appear. We first need to distinguish among the five categories of material for disposal.

EXCESS OR SURPLUS MATERIAL

Excess (or surplus) material is that stock which is in excess of a reasonable requirement of the organization. It arises because of errors in the amount bought or because anticipated production did not materialize. Such material may be handled in various ways. In some cases it may be desirable merely to store it until required, particularly if the material is of a non-perishable character, if storage costs are not excessive, and if there is a reasonable expectation that the material will be required in the future. Occasionally it may be substituted for more active material. Or, if the company operates a number of plants, it may be possible to transfer the excess to another plant. There are times, however, when these conditions do not exist and when fairly prompt sale is desirable. The chances for change in the style or design may be so great as to diminish considerably the probability that this particular material may be required. Or, it may be perishable. Factory requirements may be such as to postpone the demand for large amounts of this material so far into the future that the most economical action is to dispose of it and repurchase at a later date.

Many companies set some rough rule of thumb by which to determine when a stock item is to be classed as surplus. Thus, according to one manufacturing organization:

> Generally speaking, the question of excess material should be decided on a six-month basis. Customarily, the excess would be that amount of material on hand which represents more than a six-months' supply. There are exceptions, however. Some material deteriorates so rapidly that any quantity on hand greater than two or three months' supply be treated as excess material. In other cases, where it takes six months or longer to buy new material, more-lengthy supply periods are frequently essential.

This rule suggests that all material should be grouped into rough classifications, and normal requirement and supply periods established for each. Mere classification in itself is not sufficient. As with all classes of material, systematic, physical stock taking, continuous review of inventory records, and occasional cleanup campaigns are also necessary.

Another source of excess material usually appears on the completion of a construction project. The company just referred to covers this situation as follows:

> All new material for a specific property on order and not used on the project in question constitutes an inventory and must be treated as such. As soon as the work is completed, all new, unused material should be transferred immediately to the custody of the stores department. The original cost of the material should be charged to "Reclamation Stores" which is an unclassified segment of the Stores Account and credited to the property order or authorization.

Provision is also made for the proper accounting of used material created or resulting from demolition work carried on in conjunction with construction projects.

In the case of one large manufacturing company, if the sales department has definitely obligated the company to make a certain quantity of an item, or has set up a sales budget for that quantity subsequently accepted by the management, and later finds itself unable to dispose of its quota, the losses sustained on the excess material are charged to that particular item or sales classification. The same practice is followed if the sales department, by virtue of recommending a change in design, creates an excess of material. This company feels that the loss should not be absorbed generally or distributed over other departments.

Obsolete Material or Equipment

Obsolete material differs from excess stock in that whereas the latter presumably could be consumed at some future date, the former is unlikely ever to be used inside the organization which purchased it. For example, typewriter ribbons in a stockroom become obsolete when the machines they fit are replaced by word processing equipment. Material becomes obsolete as a result of a change in the production process or when some better material is substituted for that originally used.

Once material has been declared obsolete, it is wise to dispose of it for the best price that can be obtained.

Although material or equipment may be obsolete to one user, this need not mean that it is obsolete for others. An airline may decide to discontinue using a certain type of airplane. This action makes not only the plane but also the repair and maintenance parts inventory obsolete. But both may have substantial value to other airlines or users of planes.

Rejected End Products

Because of the uncertainties of the production process, or because of complex end-product quality specifications, a certain percentage of completed products may be rejected by outgoing quality control as unsatisfactory. In some instances these finished products can be repaired or reworked to bring them up to standard, but in other instances it is not economic to do so. The semiconductor industry is a good example, for because of the technological complexities of the process, the "yield" on a particular production line may be such that only 70 percent of the finished devices measure up to end-product specifications.

The rejected products may then be sold to users who do not require the normal quality in purchased items. These might be classified as factory seconds. One problem is that if the end product is identified with a name or trademark, unscrupulous buyers may then turn around and market the item as one which measures up to the stated quality requirements for the original item. To avoid this, the sale contract may include a statement that "the buyer agrees and warrants that the product will not be resold in its present form or for its original usage application." If the seller does not feel this contract clause provides adequate protection, then the firm may find it necessary to destroy the rejected items (as is done in the pharmaceutical industry), remove the distinguishing mark or identification, or melt the product down to recover any valuable metal content.

Scrap Material

Scrap material differs from excess or obsolete stock since it cannot properly be classified as new or unused. *Scrap* is a term which may be applied to material or equipment which is no longer serviceable and has been discarded. It includes such items as worn machinery and old tools. In such cases, scrap arises because the company is replacing old machines with others which are more modern and more productive. A concern buying new machines, tools, and other equipment normally maintains a depreciation charge intended to cover the original cost of such items, so that the value of a machine has been written off by the time it is finally discarded. Such a depreciation charge normally covers an obsolescence factor as well as ordinary wear and tear. Actually, however, a discarded or scrapped machine may still have a value for some other manufacturer in the same type of business or in some other industry. It consequently may be disposed of at a price which will show a profit in many instances. This replacement of old or obsolete machines by others capable of larger production at the same or lower cost provides a real profit-making opportunity.

Another form of scrap is represented by the many by-products of the production process, such as fly from cotton spinning, warp ends from weaving, and ferrous and nonferrous metal scrap from boring, planing, and stamping machines; flash metal from the foundry process; or paper cuttings from the binding process, as when this book was bound. Startup adjustment scrap is frequently significant, and in industries like paper making, paper converting, printing, polyethylene pellet manufacture, and many others it is one major reason for a significant price increase for small custom orders. The faster and the more automated the equipment, the higher the start-up scrap will be as a percentage of the total material used in small orders. Commonly, items of this class, which are a normal part of the production process, are considered a form of scrap; such material may frequently be salvaged. In the metal industries, the importance of scrap in this form has a definite bearing on costs and prices. For instance, a selection from among forgings, stampings, or castings may depend on the waste weight. The waste weight to be removed in finishing plus labor costs of removing it may make a higher priced article the better value. In turning brass parts, the cost of the material (brass rod) may be greater than the price of the finished parts, because the recovered brass scrap is such an important element in the cost. Indeed, scrap is so valuable as an element in cost that it is not unusual for the purchase contract on nonferrous metals to include a price at which the scrap will be repurchased by the supplier.

Scrap metals normally are separated into ferrous and nonferrous categories. Ferrous includes those products conceived from iron and generally are attracted by the scrap man's geiger counter (an ordinary magnet). The ferrous group consists of scrap steel, cast iron, white iron, and so on. The nonferrous group includes four broad families: (1) red metals, which are copper based, (2) white metals, which are aluminum, tin, lead, or zinc based, (3) nickel alloys, and (4) precious metals—for example, gold, silver, palladium—known as exotics.

There are some 1,000 scrap dealers and brokers in the United States who buy, broker, and/or process scrap, acting as intermediaries between the seller (normally the purchasing department) and the final buyer (such as a steel mill). These scrap buyers are represented by the Institute of Scrap Iron and Steel (ISIS), which has about 900 member firms, and the National Association of Recycling Industries (NARI), with about 500 members. These two, key scrap buyers/processors trade associations are in the process of merging the following four divisions into one: ferrous metals processors; nonferrous metals processors; paper and nonmetallic scrap processors; and buyers of scrap metals, paper, and other recyclable materials.[4]

These trade associations have developed detailed, extensive specifications governing the grading and shipping of scrap materials. The ISIS deals basically with ferrous materials; the NARI is basically concerned with nonferrous materials; and the National Association of Secondary Material and Industries provides specifications for recyclable paper items. The specifi-

---

[4]"Scrap Industry Trade Groups Are Merged," *Purchasing*, July 16, 1987, p. 25.

cations provide guidance regarding such things as cleanness, residual alloys, presence of off-grade material, packaging, and delivery. Examples of both ISIS and NARI specifications are:

ISIS Code 200: No. 1 heavy melting steel. Wrought iron and/or steel scrap ¼ inch and over in thickness. Individual pieces are not over 60 × 24 inches (charging box size) prepared in a manner to insure compact charging.[5]

NARI Code "Birch" 4.—No. 2 Copper Wire. Shall consist of miscellaneous, unalloyed copper wire having a nominal 96 percent copper content (minimum 94 percent) as determined by electrolytic assay. Should be free of the following: "Excessively leaded, tinned, soldered copper wire; brass and bronze wire; excessive oil content, iron, and nonmetallics; copper wire from burning, containing insulation; hair wire; burnt wire which is brittle; and should be reasonably free of ash. Hydraulically briquetted copper wire subject to agreement.[6]

These specifications are used primarily by industrial scrap merchants when they describe lots for sale to the industrial buyer. They also could be used by the purchasing department in the sale of scrap generated in the firm, but if there are impurities (not allowed for by the specification) in the lot, then there is a risk that the sale might be voided.

Waste

Waste has been defined as material or supplies which have been changed during the production process and which "through carelessness, faulty production methods, poor handling, or other causes have been spoiled, broken, or otherwise rendered unfit for further use or reclamation." This definition is not entirely adequate. There is a form of waste not due to obsolescence and yet not a result of carelessness or poor handling. Waste, for example, may occur by the fact that the material is not up to specifications because of faulty machinery or breakdowns or because of chemical action not foreseen. In some instances, waste can be defined simply as the residue of materials which results from the normal manufacturing process and which has no economic (resale) value. An example is the smoke produced by burning fuel or in the smelting process, or the cutting oil which has become so badly contaminated as a result of the normal manufacturing process that it cannot be reclaimed. However, what is waste today and has no current economic value may change tomorrow. For example, years ago the natural gas pro-

---

[5]"Specifications for Iron and Steel Scrap, 1975," Institute of Scrap Iron and Steel, Inc., Washington, D.C. 20006, p. 3.

[6]NARI Circular NF–85: Standard Specifications for Nonferrous Scrap Metals and Guidelines for Metals Transactions," effective April 1, 1985, p. 6. The address of the new ISIS/NARI group is 1627 K Street, N.W., Suite 700, Washington, D.C. 20006.

duced in crude oil production was waste and was flared off in the oilfields because it had no sales value; today it has substantial economic value.

Theoretically, waste should not exist. However, there probably will never be a time when some waste will not exist in every plant. Every effort should be made to reduce the waste factor to the lowest possible point. Its reduction can be brought about in many ways, such as the installation of new processes and by improved production layout.

Some differences of opinion may exist as to the exact definitions of scrap, excess, and waste. From the standpoint of the purchasing manager who has to dispose of the material, these differences are secondary. The objective is to realize as large a return as possible from disposal of these items.

RESPONSIBILITY FOR MATERIAL DISPOSAL?

The question of the responsibility for the management of material disposal in an organization is rather difficult to answer. In large companies where substantial amounts of scrap, obsolete, surplus, and waste materials are generated, a separate department may be justified. The manager of such a department may report to the general manager or the production manager. The limited surveys which have been made to determine the location of disposal responsibility have indicated that most of the companies depend on the purchasing department to handle disposal sales. A recent study of purchasing organizational relationships, conducted in 1988 by the Center for Advanced Purchasing Studies, covered the practices of 297 major organizations in the United States. That study found that purchasing was responsible for scrap/surplus disposal in 57 percent of the firms.[7]

Some very legitimate reasons for assigning disposal of materials to the purchasing/materials management function include: (1) knowledge of probable price trend, (2) contact with salespeople is a good source of information as to possible users of the material, (3) familiarity with the company's own needs may suggest possible uses for, and transfer of, the material within the organization, and (4) unless a specific department is established within the firm to handle this function, purchasing is probably the only logical choice.

In conglomerate and highly diversified and decentralized types of organizations, there is a great need for the coordination of salvage disposal if the best possible results are to be obtained. Where a corporate purchasing department is included in the home office organization structure, even if

---

[7]Harold E. Fearon, *Purchasing Organizational Relationships* (Tempe, Ariz.: Center for Advanced Purchasing Studies/National Association of Purchasing Management, 1988), p. 14.

only in a consulting relationship with the various divisions of the company, available information and records and established channels of communication should help to ensure that salvage materials generated in any part of the company are considered for use in all parts of the company before being offered for sale outside the company.

The general conclusion is that, except in the cases of companies with separate salvage departments, management has found the purchasing department, because of its knowledge of materials, markets, prices, and possible uses, in a better position than other departments of the company to salvage what can be used and to dispose of what cannot.

Keys to Profitable Disposal

Obviously, the optimum solution would be not to generate materials that need disposal. While this is not totally possible, every effort should be made, through good planning and taking advantage of modern technology, to *minimize* the quantity of material generated.

If scrap results as a normal, unavoidable part of the operation, it is essential that it be *segregated* by type, alloy, grade, size, and weight. This should be done at the point where scrap is generated. If two types of scrap, for example steel and copper scrap, are mixed, the return per pound on sale likely will be less than the lowest priced scrap, since any buyer must go to the expense of separating the scrap before processing.

Also, every effort should be made to obtain *maximum competition* from sources available to buy scrap or surplus material. Unfortunately, the number of potential users and buyers of scrap in a particular area may be small, resulting in a noncompetitive disposal situation. Purchasing should actively attempt to find new buyers and encourage them to compete in terms of price paid and service provided.

Disposal Channels

There are several possible means of materials disposal. In general, the options are, in order of maximum return to the selling company:

Use Elsewhere within the Firm on an "As Is" Basis. An attempt should be made to use the material "as is," or with economical modification, for a purpose other than that for which it was purchased: for example, substitution for similar grades and nearby sizes, and shearing or stripping sheet metals to obtain narrower widths. In the case of a multidivision operation, periodically each division should circulate to all other divisions a list of scrap/surplus/obsolete material and equipment; arrangements then may be made for interplant transfer of some of the items.

Reclaim for Use within the Plant. For example, can the material be reclaimed or modified for use by welding? Welding has become a very important factor in disposing of materials to advantage. Defective and spoiled castings and fabricated metal parts can be reclaimed at little expense; short ends of bar stock, pipe, and so on, can be welded into working lengths; and worn or broken jigs, fixtures, and machine parts can be built up or patched. Furthermore, castings and fabricated metal parts can be reduced in size by either the arc or acetylene cutting process. Or, perhaps a steel washer(s) could be stamped out of a piece of scrap (referred to as *off-fall*) which is a normal output of the production process. Precious metal scrap often is shipped to a precious metal refiner, who processes it into its original form and returns it for use as a raw material, charging the purchasing department a tolling charge for its services. As a result of the materials shortages of the early 1970s, many firms have become interested in the possibilities of recycling of materials, such as paper, copper, zinc, tin, aluminum cans, and precious metals. In addition to economic advantages, this may provide a partial solution to some of our environmental problems.

Sell to Another Firm for Use on an "As Is" Basis.   Can any other manufacturer use the material either "as is," or with economical modification? It should be noted that sales can often be made direct to other users who may be able to use a disposal item in lieu of a raw material they currently are buying. Or, one firm's surplus or obsolete equipment may solve another firm's equipment requirements nicely. A good example of this is the market which has existed for years for DC–3 aircraft which are obsolete for one air carrier and are bought for use by supplemental or commuter airlines. In some cases, and particularly prevalent in public agencies, surplus or obsolete equipment and vehicles are sold at public auction. Some companies permit employees to buy, as part of their employee relations program, used equipment or surplus materials at preset price. If this is done, adequate controls should be established to assure that the return to the firm is at a reasonable level.

Return to the Vendor.   Can it be returned to the manufacturer or supplier from whom it was purchased, either for cash or for credit on other later purchases? A great deal of steel scrap is sold by large-quantity purchasers directly back to the mills, who use it as a raw material in the steel production process. Normally, the firm using this disposal avenue must be a large consumer. In the case of surplus (new) inventory items, the original vendor may be willing to allow full credit on returned items.

Sale through a Broker.   Brokers can handle the sale of scrap. Their role is to bring buyer and seller together, for which they take a commission. Much metal scrap is disposed of through this channel. Brokers also exist to handle the purchase and sale of obsolete, surplus, used, and rebuilt equipment and typically specialize by either industry—for example, bakery, or type of equipment—for example, computers. This medium often is used by the selling organization and may present interesting alternatives for the buyer in the equipment acquisition process.[8]

Sale to a Local Scrap or Surplus Dealer.   All communities of any size will have one or more scrap dealers. The return from sale through this channel likely will be low, for four reasons: (1) There may be only one dealer, a noncompetitive, sole buying source; (2) The dealer assumes the risk of investment, holding, and attempting to find a buyer. The profit margin for assuming this risk may be quite high; (3) Extra movement and handling, which is costly, is involved; and (4) The seller usually doesn't become an expert in the scrap market, due to the relatively small volumes involved; the scrap or surplus dealer is an expert. However, the industrial scrap merchant may provide several valuable services, for example, recommendations on handling, sorting, and processing methods; supply collection containers; and provide pickup of materials.

Discard, Destroy, or Donate the Material or Item.   If no buyer or user can be found for the item, the firm may have to destroy or bury the item. This can be quite costly and caution should be taken to protect the environment and to assure that disposal methods for dangerous materials do not create a safety hazard to the public.[9] In some instances a firm may decide to donate used equipment to an educational or charitable organization, taking a tax deduction. Since the tax aspects of such contributions are complex, the advice of tax counsel should be obtained as part of the decision process.

Disposal Procedures

When scrap is sold, careful attention should be given to the selection of a buyer and to the procedure for handling the sale. The yellow pages of the telephone directory provide lists of dealers who buy scrap and waste products. The *American Metal Market,* a daily paper, provides price information for most waste and scrap products for the major markets in the United States and *Iron Age* (weekly) also provides current price quotations.

In connection with the selling and delivery of material, a system should be set up which will be consistently followed and will afford the company

---

[8]The Machinery Dealers National Association, P.O. Box 19128, Washington, D.C. 20036 may be a useful source of information for locating equipment brokers.

[9]"Finding Waste Disposal Sites Is a Major Sourcing Headache," *Purchasing,* July 23, 1981, pp. 14-15.

protection against all possible loss through slipshod methods, dishonest employees, and irregular practice on the part of the purchaser. All sales should be approved by a department head and cash sales should be handled through the cashier and never by the individual whose duty it is to negotiate the sale. All delivery of by-products sold should be effected through the issuing of an order form and sufficient number of copies made to provide a complete record for all departments involved in the transaction. The shipping department should determine the weight, count, and so on, and this figure should go to the billing department without going through the hands of those who negotiate the sale.

Any department responsible for the performance of this function should maintain a list of reputable dealers in the particular line of material or equipment to be disposed of and should periodically review this list. At frequent intervals, the proper plant official should be instructed to clean up the stock and report on the weights and quantities of the different items or classes of items ready for disposal.

A common procedure is to send out invitations to four or five dealers to call and inspect the lots at the factory and quote their prices FOB factory yard. Such transactions usually are subject to the accepted bidders check of weights and quantities and are paid for in cash before removal. Not infrequently, acceptable and dependable purchasers with whom satisfactory connections have already been established are relied on as desirable purchasers and no bids are called for from others.

If a firm generates large amounts of scrap materials consistently, the bidders may be asked to bid on the purchase of this scrap over a time period of six months to a year. However, it is advisable to rebid or renegotiate such contracts at least annually, to encourage competition. Often the disposal agreement will have an escalator clause in it, tying the price to changes in the overall market, as reported in a specifically designated issue, such as, the first Tuesday of each month, of the *American Metal Market*. The market prices of many grades of scrap materials can vary widely over a relatively short time period, which is the reason for the use of escalator clauses. For example, over a one-year period, the scrap price for steel, No. 1, heavy, ton increased from $71 to $80 (13 percent); zinc, old, East, pound went from 15 to 20 cents (33 percent); lead, clean solids, East, pound rose from 10.8 to 21.5 cents (99 percent); and paper, old corrugated box, ton surged from $12 to $40 (a 233 percent jump). Scrap prices are just as volatile on the downside during certain time periods.[10]

The contract for sale of scrap items should include price and how determined, quantities involved (all or a percentage), time of delivery, FOB point, cancellation privileges, how weights are determined, and payment terms.

---

[10] "Business Datatrack," *Purchasing World*, June 1987, p. 26.

A Disposal Example

Disposal is still a managerial attitudinal problem, since most items can be disposed of profitably by use of imagination. The following examples are from a large forest products company which acquired a logging-lumber-veneer-flooring operation that was on the verge of bankruptcy. The new manager called a meeting of all salaried personnel, at which he stressed two major points:

1. "We don't have any problems—only opportunities to solve a few difficulties."

2. "There is no such thing as junk or waste, because there is a buyer for everything at the right price."

He concluded by telling the staff he expected them to provide him with the means of profitably disposing of all by-products within two months. The following is a partial list of the accomplishments within three months of this meeting:

1. Two years before the takeover, the state Department of Lands and Forests had insisted that some areas be "clean cut" and reseeded to birch. Balsam fir and spruce were just being cut and left to rot. A visit to a newsprint company resulted in an offer of $26 per cord for this pulpwood delivered to their plant. Contractors were hired to cut and deliver it for $22, resulting in a profit of $4 per cord to the company, plus a 100 percent saving of the former cost of cutting the spruce and balsam fir.

2. A trucker had been hired to carry away veneer "cores." A gang saw was installed to cut them into boards which were automatically the right length for crating veneer, saving the veneer mill from having to buy crating material from the saw mill. Surplus cores were treated and sold as ornamental fence posts at $1 each.

3. A plant visit to a fine paper manufacturer resulted in an offer of $28 per ton for hardwood chips from the veneer and flooring mills which had previously been dumped in the sawdust pit.

4. Cutoffs from the flooring mill which had formerly been thrown into the sawdust pile were shipped some distance for $40 per ton (delivered) to a manufacturer of hardwood floor tiles.

5. Slabs from the sawmill which had formerly been chipped and dumped in the sawdust pit were end-cut and sold to a distributor who stored them for a year (to air dry) and then resold them to campers for firewood over a radius of about 50 miles. He bought them for $4 per "estimated" cord (and made a killing by reselling them for about $32 per cord). This distributor initiated negotiations to cut up the "slash"

in the bush at the same price for the same purpose. This would be pure windfall profit—and would leave less debris in the logging areas.

QUESTIONS FOR REVIEW AND DISCUSSION

1. Why is scrap disposal often a responsibility of the purchasing department?
2. How can the firm obtain maximum return from disposal of unneeded items?
3. What specific procedures should purchasing use to dispose of unneeded items?
4. What are the channels used in disposing of items? What are the advantages of each?
5. What is the difference between surplus material, obsolete material, rejects, scrap, and waste?
6. What are the four categories of scrap metals? Give an example of an item in each category. What formal specifications are available for use in buying and selling these metals?

REFERENCES

Bird, Monroe M., and Stephen W. Clopton. "A New Look at Scrap Management." *Journal of Purchasing and Materials Management,* Winter 1977.

Farrell, Paul V., coordinating ed. *Aljian's Purchasing Handbook.* 4th ed. New York: McGraw-Hill, 1982, Section 24.

"In Lean Times, Scrap Sales Take on New Importance." *Purchasing,* January 13, 1983.

"NARI Circular NF–82: Standard Classifications for Nonferrous Scrap Metals." New York: National Association of Recycling Industries, 1982.

"Specifications for Iron and Steel Scrap." Washington, D.C.: Institute of Scrap Iron and Steel, 1975.

Stundza, Tom. "Scrap Scrapes Against the Environment." *Purchasing,* April 9, 1987, pp. 64A4–64A11.

Case 9–1

MEREDITH OLSON

Meredith Olson, manager of purchases for the Greater Davenport School District, received a telephone call in early May from Watson Educational Supply. Apparently, Watson was closing its local warehouse and introducing a new distribution system whereby Greater Davenport would be served from Chicago, about 200 miles away.

Since the new owner of the warehouse was anxious to move in quickly, the Watson representative asked Meredith to come to the warehouse the following day at 2 p.m. to discuss the possibility of purchasing all stock in the warehouse at an advantageous price.

Meredith was surprised not to have heard earlier of Watson's plans. The district had purchased a variety of its requirements from Watson in the past. Since school budgets were extremely tight, she felt she should not pass up an opportunity at genuine savings and decided she should at least go and have a look. However, she wanted to be able to cope with all eventualities and wondered how she might best prepare herself.

Case 9–2

XEROX CANADA, INC. [B]

For the 1982 model year the Ford Motor Company announced that it would offer a limited number of automobiles modified to operate exclusively on propane. At that time Mr. Frank Attard, fleet administrator for Xerox Canada, Inc., began to urge most of the company's service branch managers to supply such vehicles to their service technicians. By January 1984, the company had 220 propane automobiles among its total fleet of 1,400. A number of these units would soon approach normal retirement age of 33 to 36 months. While their performance had been quite satisfactory, Mr. Attard was concerned about the possibility that they might be more difficult to dispose of profitably than gasoline-powered models.

Xerox Fleet Administration

Frank Attard joined the Haloid Company of Canada Limited (predecessor to Xerox Canada, Inc.) late in 1955 as an electronics specialist. During nearly 30 years with the company, he had served as service technician, service branch manager, Toronto area service manager, national service manager, and Toronto office manager. By January 1984, he had nearly 20 years' experience as fleet administrator. Mr. Attard essentially controlled fleet policy while the clerical administration was decentralized at the service branch level.

Each year, Mr. Attard negotiated an umbrella agreement with a single multinational leasing company, which would be used as the standard of reference for subsequent individual open finance leases for all new company automobiles. He then negotiated individually with Ford, Chrysler, and General Motors to give each of the manufacturers an opportunity to have specific models appear on his annual selector list. In these negotiations, the principal considerations of Mr. Attard, and hence the primary areas of competition among the manufacturers were:

Parts carrying capacity (usually 800 pounds minimum).

Optimal vehicle size.

Purchase (lease) cost.

Ongoing operating costs.

Reliability/durability over three-year average life.

The car as a company-provided benefit.

The car as a taxable benefit.

Level of service from the manufacturer.

Resale values.

The manufacturers competed strenuously to get their models on Mr. Attard's selector list, and even after its publication they occasionally offered additional volume incentives. The selector list, sent to each service branch manager, specifically named the makes and models of automobile which could be leased for the service technicians. Any automobile not on the list could be ordered only with Mr. Attard's personal approval. Also made available to the service branch managers were the (specially negotiated) prices of options which service technicians were permitted to order at their personal expense.

According to Mr. Attard, Xerox had pioneered the concept of allowing drivers of company vehicles to make a significant investment in options at dealer cost, financed by the driver. He felt that permitting drivers to customize their automobiles gave the drivers a personal stake in the company vehicle. He thought the drivers would then treat the cars like their own and would be more likely to buy them at the end of the lease. Recently, the majority of service technicians were buying $500 to $2,000 worth of options for their company automobiles, 85 to 90 percent of which were purchased by their drivers at the end of their lease.

When the driver did not purchase the company automobile at the end of the lease, they were offered first to other Xerox employees, then to the general public by private treaty, to wholesalers, or were disposed of by auction. Some even went back to the dealer, although Mr. Attard felt this was one of the least profitable ways of disposing of a car.

Propane Automobiles

Because of the energy crisis which gained worldwide attention beginning in 1973, propane began to attract attention as an alternate transportation fuel in North America in the late 1970s. It was particularly attractive in Canada because 40 to 50 percent of annual propane production was exported while Canada imported large volumes of crude oil from which gasoline and diesel fuel were derived. In 1983 enough propane was exported from Canada to fuel 300,000 automobiles each traveling an average 20,000 miles.

By the early 1980s the propane industry was actively promoting the conversion of gasoline cars to propane. The major advantages quoted were:

1. In Ontario—7 percent provincial sales tax exemption on new or used automobiles converted to propane, and on the conversion kit components.

2. In Ontario—elimination of the (20 percent) road tax applied to other fuels used in licensed vehicles.

3. A $400 federal government grant for farm and commercial vehicles converted to burn propane exclusively.

4. An average 40 percent savings on fuel cost per mile.

5. An average 50 percent savings on motor oil, oil filters, and spark plugs.

6. A 100 to 300 percent extension of engine life.

7. Elimination of smoke and smell.

8. Substantial reduction in air pollution.

Xerox employed between 1,100 and 1,200 service technicians who required company automobiles (in addition to over 100 automobiles in the executive fleet). Depending on the number of lines of Xerox equipment a technician actually serviced, his automobile had to be capable of carrying between 200 and 800 pounds of spare parts, supplies, and tools. Although conversion kits had been available for some time to either convert gasoline-powered automobiles to use propane, or to use propane and gasoline interchangeably (dual use), Mr. Attard had never given prolonged consideration to converting Xerox automobiles. Among his reasons for rejecting such an option were the following:

Propane performed better in engines with higher compression and a more advanced ignition curve than gasoline, which tended to be associated with "modification" rather than "conversion."

There were reports of dual fuel conversions which had not performed satisfactorily on either fuel.

Dual fuel automobiles would probably have neither the necessary space nor weight-carrying capacity for Xerox service technicians.

Mr. Attard felt that propane could cause engine damage if conversions were not performed properly and he did not want to have a small conversion firm responsible for causing damage to a large number of Xerox cars.

Beginning with the 1982 model year, the Ford Motor Company offered factory propane automobiles powered by its new 2.3 liter (140 CID) 4-cylinder motor. The option was offered on Ford Granada and Mercury Cougar models. Beginning with the 1983 model year, propane was offered on the Ford LTD and Mercury Marquis models. Mr. Attard viewed the propane introduction by Ford as an opportunity for Xerox to realize substantial fuel savings while avoiding the major risks which had previously prevented him from seriously considering propane conversions. He was reasonably certain that Ford would not introduce a vehicle to the marketplace until it had been thoroughly tested. He was even more certain that when Ford offered propane vehicles to such an important customer as Xerox, Ford would do everything possible to maintain customer satisfaction, even if it meant going well beyond the terms of the warranty.

The Ford modification to its 2.3 liter engine for use with propane was significant but not extreme. The cylinder head was planed to raise the compression ratio from 9.0:1 to 10.0:1. Valve rotators were added to try to delay valve and valve seat wear. The ignition spark timing was advanced from about 8° before center to about 12° before center at idle. Finally, a number of seals and fittings were replaced with tighter-fitting ones.

Mr. Attard tried to persuade all service branch managers where propane was available to order the propane-equipped 1982 Ford products. For the 1983 model year it was almost mandatory west of the Ontario-Quebec border where propane

EXHIBIT 1 Xerox Canada Incorporated (customer service personal mileage reimbursement rates effective November 1, 1982)

	Cents per Mile	*Cents per Kilometer*
Propane vehicles	8	5
Subcompacts	12	7.5
All other vehicles	14	8.75

was considered to be both conveniently available and attractively priced. The only cars on the selector list that year were the Ford LTD 4-door sedan powered by propane, the Chrysler K wagon, and the Chrysler K 4-door sedan. To order the Chrysler models, a service branch manager was required to cite legitimate unavailability of propane. By the 1984 model year it was assumed that service branch managers in areas of convenient propane supply would have become aware of the significant fuel cost savings offered by propane. The Ford propane models still appeared on the selector list, but no coercion was used to promote them. The personal mileage charges, however, still favored propane (see Exhibit 1), reflecting its lower operating cost. Since about 45 percent of total car mileage was personal driving, the charge rates were considered a significant incentive.

It should be noted that while the Ford LTD propane automobile was the preferred car on the selector list, the LTD gasoline model was not a substitute. U.S. Environmental Protection Agency ratings had placed the 1983 Ford LTD 140 C.I.D. (2.3 litre) 4-cylinder automatic at 21 miles per (U.S.) gallon combined city and country, versus 29 miles per (U.S.) gallon for the Chrysler K cars' 135 C.I.D. (2.2 litre) 4-cylinder automatic.

By December 1983, the Xerox Canada service fleet included 220 propane-powered automobiles, of which 57 were 1982 models, 116 were 1983 models, and 47 were 1984 models. Most of the 1982 models would be due for replacement before the end of 1984.

Performance of the Propane Automobiles

Xerox Canada, Inc., had experienced normal performance from the propane-powered automobiles. Although the propane could generally be purchased for half the price of gasoline, it was only about 85 percent as efficient. As a result, Xerox realized fuel cost savings of approximately 40 percent attributable to propane.

Mechanical performance of the propane vehicles had been quite satisfactory, with only a few minor problems which were corrected by Ford. There had been one major recall of the 1982 models to replace a defective propane valve, but no other serious problems had been encountered.

In January 1984, Mr. Attard received word which he felt justified his earlier decision to acquire propane vehicles only from a major manufacturer. Some of the Ford's factory propane vehicles had been run hot with resultant damage to the valves and cylinder heads. Rather than deal with the problem on an ad hoc warranty basis, Ford had decided to recall all the propane vehicles it had manufactured to date for a factory rebuild, which would include replacement of the exhaust valves with hardened ones that could stand more heat, and the cylinder heads with new ones containing high-nickel valve seat and valve guide inserts which could stand more heat with less wear. The total cost of the recall, beginning in February 1984 was to be borne by the Ford Motor Company, which also had volunteered to supply the Xerox service technicians with replacement vehicles during the recall period.

The Disposal Question

While the savings associated with using propane were apparent, Mr. Attard was somewhat concerned about the value of the propane automobiles at the time of disposal. Propane was readily available in the locations where the cars were currently being driven—at a fuel saving of nearly 50 percent per liter, or 40 percent per mile compared to gasoline. Nearly 90 percent of Xerox vehicles were purchased by the service technicians when they reached the normal retirement age of 33 to 36 months, or 50,000 to 55,000 miles, but Mr. Attard did not know if such a percentage would apply to the propane automobiles.

Mr. Attard knew that the drivers would be aware of the fuel cost savings associated with propane after having driven the vehicles for almost three years. However, he did not have any indication of their interest as potential buyers when the Xerox autos became due for disposal. He assumed that the recall could influence drivers either positively or negatively. On the positive side, it would indicate to the drivers that Ford was standing behind its propane vehicles regardless of cost. On the negative side, the drivers would be aware that Ford was fitting the automobiles with a number of nonstandard parts, which could result in maintenance and disposal problems in the future.

When Xerox acquired propane automobiles, the cost to the leasing company was approximately $900 to $1,000 greater than the identical model with gasoline power—minus the $400 federal government incentive rebate. However, in Ontario, the lease payments were actually less because in spite of the $500 to $600 greater capitalization for the propane unit, the leasing company was not required to charge the 7 percent provincial sales tax on top of the monthly lease payment. In other provinces the lease payments were marginally higher. On disposal, the propane autos would not be subject to the 7 percent provincial sales tax in Ontario (although the relevant taxes would be the same as for gasoline-powered cars in other provinces). Mr. Attard felt that if the drivers of the propane-powered automobiles wished to purchase them when they reached disposal age, it would be fair for Xerox to price them the same as an equivalent gasoline car plus a premium of $200 to $300 for the book value of the propane modification. However, he was aware that at a recent propane seminar, the president of Toronto Auto Auctions had indicated that in his company's very limited experience, propane-powered automobiles generally brought somewhat less than equivalent gasoline autos, primarily because the concept was still new and most dealers at the auctions lacked experience with propane.

CHAPTER 10

Legal Aspects of Purchasing

The competent professional purchaser does not require the training of a lawyer but should understand the basic principles of commercial law. Such understanding should enable recognition of problems and situations which require professional legal counsel and also provide the knowledge to avoid legal pitfalls in day-to-day operations.

Seldom will either buyer or seller resort to the courts to enforce a purchase contract or assess financial damages. In those infrequent situations where formal legal action is the last resort, the legal costs can be high and the outcome uncertain. *The competent purchaser wishes to avoid such situations and will take legal action only as a last resort.* A knowledge of the law of contracts will help the purchaser avoid such legal involvements and position the organization to successfully pursue, or defend itself against, such lawsuits.

LEGAL AUTHORITY OF THE PURCHASING OFFICER

What is the purchasing officer's legal status? Briefly, he or she has the authority to attend to the business of purchasing in accordance with the instructions given by his or her employer. These instructions are usually broad in character. In general, there should be, and in all progressive organizations there is, a clear understanding as to what the purchasing officer is expected to do. This normally is covered by a job description (see Figure 2–3). Attention already has been called to the necessity for a clear understanding of duties simply as a matter of good business policy. The reasons for this clear understanding, important as they are from other points of view, are strengthened by the fact that the law assumes an agreement between the agent and the employer as to the scope of the authority. Presumably, the purchasing officer performs these assigned duties to the full extent of his or her capacity. In other words, the purchasing officer has a right to expect from the employer a clear understanding as to duties and responsibilities; the purchasing officer, in turn, is expected to perform these duties in a loyal, honest, and careful manner. So long as he or she does this, the obligations to the employer, from a legal point of view, are fulfilled. In agreeing to render service to an employer, there is no implied agreement that no errors will be made, for some errors are incidental to all vocations.

By special stipulation, the purchasing manager may even assume responsibility to the principal for the risks from honest error, but such arrangements are rare. Nevertheless, when a person accepts an appointment to serve as an agent for the principal, there does exist the implication that the person possesses the necessary skill to carry on the work. In some cases, a very high degree of skill is demanded and accepting an appointment under such circumstances implies the necessary skill. There are, of course, many possible modifications of this general statement. The purchasing officer becomes liable to the employer when damage occurs through active fault or through negligence. Many difficulties arise in attempting to define what negligence is, although in general it may be said to constitute an "omission of due care under given circumstances."

The buyer also has an obligation to keep his or her employer informed about specific actions taken to perform the purchasing function, and report resultant outcomes from same. In addition, records must be kept and an accounting made for any funds or property handled. If the purchaser does not fulfill these obligations, his or her employer may sue for damages.[1]

Since the purchasing officer is acting as an agent for the company he or she represents, it follows that the officer is in a position to bind the company within limits. Actually, of course, the power of an agent to bind the principal may greatly exceed the right to do so. This right is confined by the limits assigned, that is, in accordance with the actual authorization; power to bind the principal, however, is defined by the *apparent* scope of authority, which in the case of most purchasing officers is rather broad. Furthermore, to avoid personal liability, it must be made clear to the person with whom the buyer deals that he or she is acting as an agent. In fact, the law requires even more if buyers are not to be held personally liable; not only must they indicate the fact that they are acting as agents but also the person with whom they are dealing must agree to hold the principal responsible, even though the latter is at the moment unknown.

The actual authority delegated to an agent is not limited to those acts which, by words, the agent is expressly and directly authorized to perform. Every actual authorization, whether general or special, includes by implication all such authority as is necessary, usual, and proper to carry through to completion the main authority conferred. The extent of the agent's implied authority must be determined from the nature of the business to be transacted. These powers will be broad in the case of one acting as a general agent or manager. It is the duty of the third party dealing with the agent to ascertain the scope of the agent's authority. Statements of the agent as

---

[1]Russell Decker, "It's Your Duty to Be a 'Company' Man or Woman," *Purchasing*, May 8, 1986, pp. 63–64.

to the extent of powers cannot be relied on by the third party. Any limitation on the agent's power which is known to the third person is binding on the third person.

PERSONAL LIABILITY OF THE PURCHASING OFFICER

The purchasing officer may be held personally liable under certain conditions when signing contracts. These conditions include: (1) when he or she makes a false statement concerning authority *with intent to deceive* or when the misrepresentation has the natural and probable consequence of misleading; (2) when agents perform a damaging act without authority, even though believing they have such authority; (3) when performing an act which is itself illegal, even on authority from the employer; (4) when willfully performing an act which results in damage to anyone; (5) when they perform damaging acts outside the scope of authority, even though the act is performed with the intention of rendering the employer a valuable service. In each of these cases, the vendor ordinarily has no recourse to the company employing the agent, since there existed no valid contract between the seller and the purchasing firm. Since such a contract does not exist, the only recourse which the vendor commonly has is to the agent personally.

Should the question arise as to who may be sued on contracts made within the apparent scope of the agent's authority but beyond the actual scope, because of the fact that there were limitations on the latter unknown to the seller, it may still follow that the principal can be held liable. Under these circumstances, the agent probably is in the wrong and is, of course, answerable to the principal. Buyers may also be answerable to the seller, on the ground of deceit, or the charge that they are the real contracting parties, or for breach of the warranty that they were authorized to make the precise contract they attempted to make for the principal.

Moreover, suits have been brought by sellers against purchasing managers when it was discovered that the latter's principal was for some reason unable to pay the account. For example, such conditions have arisen when (1) the employer became insolvent or bankrupt; (2) the employer endeavored to avoid the legal obligations to accept and pay for merchandise purchased by the purchasing manager; or (3) the employer became involved in litigation with the seller, whose lawyers decided that the contract price could be readily collected personally from the purchasing manager.

Although a purchasing officer should never attempt to perform the duties of a competent lawyer, the alert buyer and purchasing manager should keep informed about court decisions and changes in laws which affect his or her actions. Purchasing trade publications normally report court decisions and major changes in laws which have an impact on the performance of the buying function.

As previously stated, purchasing officers are personally liable for the commission of any illegal act, and this liability holds even though they are unconscious of the illegality of the act and though it is done under the direction of the employer. A buyer is not likely to commit an illegal act consciously; but under stress of severe competition, in an effort to secure as favorable terms as possible for his company, the buyer may run afoul of the law unintentionally. It is well to remember that the antitrust acts apply to buyers as much as to sellers. The U.S. Supreme Court has held that these acts are applicable to all attempts to restrain trade, even though the restraint is exercised on those not engaged in the same line of business and is based on purchasing activities rather than selling activities—provided that the net result of the act is to restrain competition.

THE PURCHASE ORDER CONTRACT

Many federal, state, and local statutes govern purchasing practice, but the Uniform Commercial Code (UCC) covers most of the transactions involving purchase and sale of goods and services. The UCC resulted from the joint efforts of the American Law Institute and the National Conference of Commissioners on Uniform State Laws. Since the first publication of the Uniform Commercial Code in 1952, with subsequent revisions and refinements in 1958, 1962, 1966, 1972, and 1977, all of the states except Louisiana have enacted the code into law.[2] Article 2, *Sales* governs purchase/sale transactions and applies to transactions by *Merchants,* defined as "a person who deals in goods of the kind or otherwise by his occupation holds himself out as having knowledge or skill peculiar to the practices or goods involved in the transaction or to whom such knowledge or skill may be attributed by his employment of an agent or broker or other intermediary who by his occupation holds himself out as having such knowledge or skill."[3]

The UCC applies only to legal situations arising in the United States (and then only to 49 of the states—not to Louisiana. Since Louisiana has a legal system based on the Napoleonic Code, there would be no need to adopt the UCC, which clarifies and updates English common law). If the buyer feels that legal problems may arise in dealing with a vendor outside the United States, the purchase contract then should specify under which country's laws the dispute would be adjudicated. Canada, for example, does not have anything which approximates a standardized set of commercial laws for the entire country; each province has developed its own set of laws dealing with property and civil rights within its boundaries, and there are major differences between the laws of each province.

---

[2]The American Law Institute and National Conference of Commissioners on Uniform State Laws, *Uniform Commercial Code,* 1978 Official Text (Philadelphia, PA: The American Law Institute, 1978).

[3]Ibid., 2–104.

A valid contract is based on four factors:

1. Competent parties—either principals or qualified agents.
2. Legal subject matter or purpose.
3. An offer and an acceptance.
4. Consideration.

The purchase order generally is regarded as containing the buyer's offer and becomes a legal contract when accepted by the vendor. Many purchase order forms have a copy that includes provision for acknowledgement or acceptance. There has never been universal agreement on how detailed the terms and conditions which are printed on the purchase order should be. Some companies' forms use the reverse side to spell out the complete terms and conditions which apply to any transaction. Some companies may include a separate printed sheet detailing terms and conditions applying to that specific order. Other companies provide only for the very basic items necessary for a valid offer and depend on the provisions of the UCC for proper legal coverage. The purchasing officer should depend on the legal counsel responsible for handling legal matters for the company in determining the policy to be followed.

An *offer* can be equally valid if made by a vendor, either in writing or verbally. Such an offer becomes a legal contract when accepted by the buyer.

Regardless of whether an offer is made by the buyer or the vendor, it can be modified or revoked before it is accepted. However, an offer in writing that includes an assurance that the price will remain firm for a specified period may not be revoked prior to the expiration of the period. Under the UCC, if a vendor makes a firm offer to sell, it generally must be held open for a "reasonable" time period. This reasonable time period generally has been held to be three months, unless a shorter period is stated by the vendor at the time the offer was made.[4]

The courts have generally held that advertisements and price lists do not constitute legal offers unless specifically directed to the buyer or unless an order placed on the basis of the advertisement or price list is specifically accepted by the vendor.

Acceptance of Orders

Since the purchase order form or the sales contract is intended to include all the essential conditions surrounding the transactions, it is customary to include in the agreement a statement such as, "Acceptance of this order implies the acceptance of conditions contained thereon." The purpose of such

---

[4]Ibid., 2–205.

a provision is to make all the conditions legally binding on the seller and to avoid cases in which the seller advances the defense that he or she was not aware of certain conditions. Statements similar to that indicated are found in practically all purchase agreements, to give warning that there are conditions attached, either on the front or on the reverse side of the contract.

Having placed an order with a vendor, the purchasing officer wishes to assure that the order has been accepted. To obtain such assurance, it is customary to insist on a definite vendor acknowledgement usually in written form. It is not uncommon to incorporate as a part of the contract a clause requiring that the acceptance be made in a particular manner, in which case a form is enclosed with the order, and the purchase order contains a clause which stipulates: "This order must be acknowledged on the enclosed form."

The question may arise as to when an offer either of sale or of purchase has been accepted. As a matter of law, the person making an offer may demand, as one of the conditions, that acceptance be indicated in a specific manner. Ordinarily, however, when an offer is made, the offeror either expressly or by implication requires the offeree to send the answer by mail or telegraph. When the answer is duly posted or telegraphed, the acceptance is communicated, and the contract is completed from the moment the letter is mailed or the telegram is sent. Former technical rules on acceptance that a mailed offer must be accepted by a mailed acceptance no longer apply; any reasonable manner of acceptance is satisfactory, unless the offeror makes it quite clear that acceptance must be made in a particular manner.[5]

Sometimes the vendor may use an acknowledgement form of its own, which may conflict with some of the conditions stated in the purchase order. Often in such situations, a careful comparison is not made of *all* conditions stated in the offer with *all* conditions stated in the acceptance. If litigation subsequently occurs between buyer and seller, application of the UCC may resolve the question:

(1) A definite and reasonable expression of acceptance or a written confirmation which is sent within a reasonable time operates as an acceptance even though it states terms additional to or different from those offered or agreed upon unless acceptance is expressly made conditional on assent to the additional or different terms.

(2) The additional terms are to be construed as proposals for addition to the contract. Between merchants such terms become part of the contract unless:

    a. the offer expressly limits acceptance to the terms of the offer;

---

[5]Ibid., 2–206.

   b. they materially alter it; or

   c. notification of objection to them has already been given or is given
     within a reasonable time after notice of them is received.[6]

Thus, if the buyer does not wish to get into a dispute as to whether the vendor's acceptance materially alters any of the provisions of the original offer, on the face of the purchase order (PO) should be typed a statement that "Absolutely no deviations from the terms and conditions as contained in this offer will be permitted."

Purchases Made Orally

Most professional buyers have occasion to place orders over the telephone or orally in person. However, the UCC specifies that:

1. Normally there must be some written notation if the value of the order for the sale of goods is $500 or more.

2. If the seller supplies a memorandum which is not in accordance with the buyer's understanding of the oral order, he or she must give a notice of objection to the supplier within 10 days of receipt of the memorandum to preserve his legal rights.[7]

AUTHORITY OF VENDOR'S REPRESENTATIVES

Another important consideration relates to the authority of the salesperson representing a company with which the purchasing officer is transacting business. Subject to the many exceptions arising out of varying circumstances, the courts have consistently held that although an employer is bound by all the acts of an agent acting within the scope of the employment, a salesperson's ordinary authority is simply to solicit orders and to send them to his or her employer for ratification and acceptance. It therefore behooves the purchasing officer to know definitely whether or not salespeople have the authority to conclude a contract without referring it to the company which they represent.

Even if a vendor does not authorize its salespeople to enter into binding contracts, and although the company may do nothing to lead others to believe that its representative has such power, yet if the salesperson does enter into a contract with a buyer, that contract is likely to be held valid unless the seller notifies the buyer within a reasonable time that the salesperson has exceeded his or her authority. In other words, a contract results because the conduct of the employer is interpreted as acceptance. If the purchasing officer wishes assurance that the salesperson does have authority to sign the con-

---

[6]Ibid., 2–207.
[7]Ibid., 2–201.

tract for the vendor, it is a simple matter to request a letter, signed by an officer of the vendor firm, specifying that the salesperson has the authority of a sales agent.

False statements on the part of the seller or its representative regarding the character of the merchandise being purchased cause the contract to become voidable at the option of the other party. It is true that this "undoubted right" to rely on vendors' statements is at best a highly qualified right, the value of which depends on the circumstances surrounding the transaction. However, aside from any legal question which is involved under ordinary circumstances, the seller is likely to be sufficiently jealous of its reputation and goodwill to make substantial concessions.

INSPECTION

One important right of the buyer is that of inspecting the goods before acceptance. The purpose of this rule is to give the buyer an opportunity to determine whether or not the goods tendered comply with the contract description. It is well established that buyers who inspect goods *before* entering into a contract of sale are put on guard and are expected to use their own judgment with respect to quality, quantity, and other characteristics of the merchandise. The UCC states that "when the buyer before entering into the contract has examined the goods or the sample or model as fully as he desired or has refused to examine the goods there is no implied warranty with regard to defects which an examination ought in the circumstances to have revealed to him."[8]

Where a purchaser accepts merchandise after inspection, either as to quality or quantity, the buyer ordinarily is prevented from raising an issue with respect to these points. Also, a vendor cannot be held responsible for the failure of equipment to perform the work which the buyer expected of it, if the latter merely provides material specifications without indicating to the seller the purpose to which the equipment or goods are to be put. In some purchase contracts, payment may be required before the buyer has had an opportunity to inspect the goods; for example, payment may be made before the vendor actually ships the goods. Payment in this case does not constitute an acceptance of the goods or impair the buyer's right to inspect or any of the buyer's remedies on breach of contract.[9]

The courts generally have held that if a purchaser is not sufficiently experienced to be able to judge adequately the goods inspected, or if he or she relies on a fraudulent statement made by a seller and purchases in consequence of that fraudulent statement, the buyer then may rescind the contract or hold the vendor liable for damages.

---

[8]Ibid., 2–316 (3).
[9]Ibid., 2–512.

CANCELLATION OF ORDERS AND
BREACH OF CONTRACT

Once a contract is made, it is expected that both parties will adhere to the agreement. Occasionally one or the other seeks to cancel the contract after it has been made. Ordinarily this is a more serious problem for the seller than it is for the buyer, although occasionally a seller may wish to avoid complying with the terms of an agreement, in which event he merely may refuse to manufacture the goods or delay the delivery beyond the period stipulated in the agreement. The rights of the purchaser under these circumstances depend on the conditions surrounding the transaction. The seller is likely to be able, without liability, to delay delivering purchased goods when the buyer orders a change in the original agreement which may delay the seller in making delivery.

If the seller fails to make delivery by the agreed time, the purchaser may without obligation refuse to accept delivery at a later date. However, the attempt to secure what the buyer might consider reasonable damages resulting from a breached sales contract is likely to be difficult, since the courts experience a good deal of trouble in laying down rules for the guidance of the jury in estimating the amount of damages justly allowed a buyer who sustains financial losses resulting from a seller's failure to fulfill a contract of sale. If there is a general rule, it is that the damages allowable to a purchaser if a seller fails to deliver goods according to contract are measured by the difference between the original contract price and the market value of the merchandise at the time when the buyer learned of the breach of contract and at the place where the goods should have been delivered.[10]

The seller is sometimes confronted by an attempted cancellation on the part of the buyer. It is not unusual, therefore, to find in the sales contract the following clause: "This contract is not subject to cancellation." As a matter of fact, the inclusion of such a clause has little practical effect, unless, indeed, it is intended merely to indicate to purchasers that if they attempt to cancel, a suit for breach of contract may be expected.

However, in a very strong seller's market, where the breach of contract by the seller is related to failure to deliver on a promised date or even to abide by the agreed price, the practical alternatives open to the buyer are almost nil. The latter still wants the goods and may be unable to acquire them from any other supplier on time or at any better price. Much the same restriction, in fact, exists even where the contract provides for the option of cancellation by the buyer. The purchaser wants goods, not damages or the right to cancel. Since the chances of getting them as promptly from any other supplier are slight, the buyer is likely to do the best he can with the

---

[10]Ibid., 2–713.

original vendor provided, of course, that bad faith as to either price or delivery is not involved.

WARRANTIES

Over time the rules governing warranty arrangements between buyer and seller have advanced from *caveat emptor* (let the buyer beware) to the legal provisions of the UCC which recognize three types of warranties:

1. Express warranty.
2. Implied warranty of merchantability.
3. Implied warranty of fitness for a particular purpose.[11]

Essentially, express warranties include promises, specifications, samples, and descriptions pertaining to the goods which are the subject of the negotiation.

Implied warranty of merchantability has to do with the merchantable quality of goods, and the UCC statutes applying have developed out of mercantile practices. Accepted trade standards of quality, fitness for the intended uses, and conformance to promises or specified fact made on the container or label are all used as measures of marketable quality.

Implied warranty of fitness for a purpose usually results from a buyer's request for material or equipment to meet a particular need or accomplish a specific purpose. The UCC provides that "where the seller at the time of contracting has reason to know any particular purpose for which the goods are required and that the buyer is relying on the seller's skill or judgment to select or furnish suitable goods, there is . . . an implied warranty that the goods shall be fit for such purpose."[12] If the buyer provides detailed specifications for the item requested, the seller is relieved of any warranty of fitness for a purpose.

ACCEPTANCE AND REJECTION OF GOODS

The acceptance of goods is an assent by the buyer to become the owner of the goods tendered by the seller. No unusual formalities are necessary to indicate that the buyer has accepted the goods. Any words or acts which indicate the buyer's intention to become the owner of the goods are sufficient. If the buyer keeps the goods and exercises rights of ownership over them, acceptance has taken place, even though the buyer may have expressly stated that the goods are rejected. If the goods tendered do not comply with

---

[11]Ibid., 2–313, 2–314, and 2–315.
[12]Ibid., 2–315.

the sales contract, the buyer is under no duty to accept them; but if the buyer does accept the goods, he or she does not thereby waive the right to damages for the seller's breach of contract. If the buyer accepts goods which do not comply with the sales contract, the seller must be notified of the breach within a reasonable time. What is a "reasonable time" is determined by normal commercial standards.[13]

In the event the vendor delivers goods or the tender of delivery fails in any way to conform to the contract, the buyer has the option to (1) reject the whole shipment, (2) accept the whole shipment, or (3) accept part of the shipment and reject the balance. Rejection, of course, must be within a reasonable time after delivery and the vendor must be notified promptly. The buyer must hold the goods, using reasonable care, until the seller has had sufficient time to remove them.[14] The question of whether to reject goods delivered under a particular order may arise from various causes and may be dealt with in a variety of ways. For instance, the goods may be late, may have been delivered in the wrong amount, or may fail to meet the specifications. The important thing to keep in mind is that the purchaser wants the goods. A lawsuit, therefore, is not desirable, even though the buyer is granted any one of the commonly recognized judicial remedies for breach of contract, such as money damages or insistence on performance. Aside from the fact that it is goods the buyer wants, legal action is uncertain and often costly; it may take a great deal of time; and it may cause the loss of a friendly supplier.

The purchasing officer, therefore, usually seeks other means of adjustment. Several courses are open. The first question is the seriousness of the breach. If not too serious, a simple warning to the vendor may be quite adequate. If somewhat more stringent action is called for and if the goods received are usable for some purpose, even though not quite up to specifications, a price adjustment frequently can be worked out to the mutual satisfaction of the buyer and the seller. Sometimes the goods, though not usable in the form received, may be reprocessed or otherwise made usable by the vendor, or by the purchaser at the vendor's expense. If the goods are component parts, they may be replaced by the supplier. If equipment is involved, or even processed material that is incapable of being efficiently used in its present form, the vendor may correct the defects at the user's plant. Or, as a last resort, the goods may be rejected and shipped back to the supplier, usually at the vendor's expense.

Protection against Price Fluctuations

Cancellations can be the direct result of action by the buyer. They arise in two ways, the first of which is not recommended. It comes about because

---

13Ibid., 2–607.
14Ibid., 2–601 and 2–602.

the buyer, if compelled to live up to the agreement, would lose money. Conditions may have changed or sales may have fallen off. Therefore, the buyer no longer wants the goods. The market price may have dropped and the buyer could now buy the goods for less money. Faced with these conditions, the buyer seeks some form of relief. He or she becomes extremely watchful of deliveries and rejects goods which arrive even a day late. Inspection is tightened up, and failure to meet any detail in the specifications is seized on as an excuse for rejection. Such methods should never be followed by a good purchasing officer.

The second form of cancellation may arise in a perfectly legal and ethical manner, through evoking a clause—occasionally inserted in purchase contracts—which seeks to guarantee against price decline. In purchasing goods subject to price fluctuations, it is in the interest of the buyer to be protected against unreasonable price increases. Occasionally a long-term contract is drawn up which leaves the determination of the exact price open until deliveries are called for. To meet these conditions, a clause such as the following may be incorporated in purchase contracts:

> Seller warrants that the prices stated herein are as low as any net prices now given by you to any customer for like materials, and seller agrees that if at any time during the life of this order seller quotes or sells at lower prices similar materials under similar conditions, such lower prices shall be substituted for the prices stated herein.

These stipulations against price decline are not confined to purchase agreements; under some circumstances the buyer may receive price reductions on the seller's initiative. An example of this type of clause is the following:

> Should the purchaser at the time of any delivery, on account of this contract, be offered a lower price on goods of equal quality and in like quantity by a reputable manufacturer, he will furnish the seller satisfactory proof of same, in which event the seller will either supply such shipment at the lower price or permit the buyer to purchase such quantity elsewhere, and the quantity so purchased elsewhere will be deducted from the total quantity of this contract. Should the seller reduce his prices during the terms of this contract, the buyer shall receive the benefit of such lower prices.

Such clauses are legally enforceable and frequently work to the buyer's advantage. However, the administrative problems in seeing to it that these clauses are lived up to are substantial. The moral effect doubtlessly is greater than the legal.

Title to Purchased Goods

The professional buyer should have a clear understanding of when the title of goods passes from the seller to the buyer. Normally, there will be an agreement on the FOB (free on board) point, and the buyer receives title at that point (see Chapter 13). Sections 2–319 and 2–320 of the UCC cover the legal obligations under the various shipping terms (FOB, FAS, CIF, and C & F). On capital goods it is particularly important for tax and depreciation reasons to establish title before the tax year ends.

If the buyer specifies a particular carrier for transportation of goods, the seller is responsible for following the buyer's instructions, which are part of the contractual agreement, subject to any substitution necessary because of the failure of the specified carrier to provide adequate transportation services. Of course, the seller must promptly notify the buyer of any substitutions made. If the buyer elects not to specify a particular carrier, the seller then may choose any reasonable carrier, routing, and other arrangements. Whether or not the shipment is at the buyer's expense, as determined by the FOB term used, the seller must see to any arrangements, reasonable in the circumstances, such as refrigeration, watering of livestock, protection against cold, and selection of specialized cars.[15]

In some instances, the buyer is given possession of the goods prior to the passing of a legal title. This is known as a *conditional sales contract* and the full title passes to the buyer only when final payment is made. This procedure permits a buyer to obtain needed material or equipment now and to pay at some future time.

PATENTS AND PRODUCT LIABILITY

Patents are granted by the U.S. Patent Office (or a similar agency in other countries) to provide the inventor/developer the sole rights of making, using, and selling the item in question—and denying others the right to also do so, unless the inventor decides to sell his patent rights.

Unless otherwise agreed between buyer and seller, if a vendor regularly deals in a particular line of goods, that vendor implicitly warrants that the goods delivered do not infringe against the patent rights of any third party. However, when the buyer orders goods to be assembled, prepared, or manufactured to his own specifications, and if this results in an infringement of patent or trademark, then the buyer may be liable to legal action. There is, under such circumstances, a tacit representation on the part of the buyer that the seller will be safe in manufacturing according to the specifications, and the buyer then is obliged to indemnify the seller for any loss suffered.[16] If a charge of patent infringement is made against the buyer, he must notify the vendor promptly so that the charge can be defended, or settlement made, in a timely manner. Also, if a seller attempts to include a patent disclaimer clause in the sales contract, the buyer should be extremely cautious in

---

[15]Ibid., 2–504.
[16]Ibid., 2–312 (3).

accepting such a clause, since he may find himself in costly litigation if patent infringement has occurred.

An even more delicate matter may arise when a buyer requests a vendor to manufacture an item, to the buyer's specifications, which includes a new idea, process, or product which has not yet been awarded patent protection. This often happens in the high-technology industries.

The buyer does not want to lose the right to the new development and possible subsequent financial rewards. The buyer's purchase contract should address this matter with an appropriate protection clause, formulated with advice of legal counsel.

Product safety and product liability considerations have become much more important over the last two decades, due to increased government regulations and judicial interpretations of the existing laws. This has magnified the involvement and responsibility of purchasing managers, as firms attempt to reduce the financial threat arising from product liability problems.

The strict liability concept is based on the idea that manufacturers warrant that their products are not unreasonably hazardous, but if they are, the manufacturer is responsible to persons injured through use of the product. Under strict liability, the burden of proof was on the injured party to prove that the product was defective, that the defect was present when the product left the manufacturer, and that the defect did cause the injury. The law focused on showing that there was a design defect, and the plaintiff (injured party) had to prove fault on the part of the manufacturer.

In the 1960s, the trend has been toward application of the concept of absolute liability on the part of the manufacturer or seller for all accidents involving the use of its products. The courts have begun to hold that the manufacturer or seller is responsible to the consuming public when it markets a product causing personal injury, and that the financial burden of accidental injury is the responsibility of the manufacturer and is considered to be a cost of production.[17] The plaintiff (injured party) does not even have to prove that the product was unreasonably dangerous. The key issue is whether the manufacturer should have expected misuse or abnormal use by the consumer; if so, the manufacturer is liable. Since this interpretation, a large number of damage awards have gone against producers and sellers.

The purchasing department now must take a more active role in confirming that potentially hazardous purchased items incorporated into an end product or service are properly inspected to make sure they are not defective. This requires a close working relationship with other departments of the firm, such as design, engineering, quality control, manufacturing,

---

[17]*Greenman* v. *Yuba Power Products, California* (1963).

and marketing, to assure that the organization is not being unreasonably exposed to product liability lawsuits.

Commercial Arbitration

Regardless of the type of contract, disputes sooner or later will arise. These disagreements are annoying, but, for reasons that have been given, it usually is not advantageous to go to the court over them. In the majority of cases they are settled by some compromise. Occasions do arise when such compromises cannot be effected. To meet these situations and yet to avoid the necessity of resorting to a court of law, arbitration clauses frequently are included in commercial contracts. These provide that an impartial arbitrator, or panel of arbitrators, will listen to the evidence and then render a judgment, to which both parties have agreed in advance to accept, without appeal. This is much less costly and time consuming than court action.

However, merely because the contract includes a provision calling for arbitration, the purchasing officer may not be as fully covered as many have believed. There are prepared arbitration clauses which are valid, irrevocable, and enforceable under the arbitration laws[18] of certain states, notably: New York, New Jersey, Pennsylvania, Massachusetts, California, Louisiana, Connecticut, Rhode Island, New Hampshire, Arizona, Oregon, Ohio, and Wisconsin. For matters under jurisdiction of the federal courts, there is the Federal Arbitration Law. Even in states which do not have such laws, it is possible to demand arbitration if provision is made for the necessary procedure in the contract, and if there is a statute making *"future* disputes" the subject of binding arbitration agreements.

The use of arbitration clauses in contracts is a reasonable measure of protection against costly litigation. To ensure this protection, the following queries should be made with reference to arbitration clauses which are to be incorporated in commercial agreements:

1. Is your clause in proper form under the appropriate arbitration laws? Unless properly drawn, it may not be legally valid, irrevocable, and enforceable.

2. Does your clause fully express the will of the parties or is it ambiguous? If it is uncertain in its terms, the time and expense involved in determining the scope of the clause and the powers of the arbitrators under it may destroy its value or increase costs.

3. Does your clause assure the appointment of impartial arbitrators? If a person serving as arbitrator is an agent, advocate, relative, or representative of a party, or has a personal interest in the matter

---

[18]The *Code of Arbitration Practice and Procedure* of the American Arbitration Association contains full information on the arbitration laws of the various states.

being arbitrated, the award rendered may be vacated by the court on the ground of evident corruption or partiality on the part of an arbitrator.

4. Does your clause provide adequately, by reference to the rules of an association or otherwise, for a method of naming arbitrators, thus safeguarding against deadlocks or defaults in the proceedings? If not, the actual hearing of the dispute may be unduly delayed, and the practical value of the arbitration may be defeated.

QUESTIONS FOR REVIEW AND DISCUSSION

1. Under what conditions is it realistic for a buyer to cancel a contract? For a seller to cancel a contract?
2. Does a vendor have to accept a PO exactly as offered by the buyer to create a legally binding contract? Explain.
3. How much knowledge of the legal aspects of purchasing should a buyer have?
4. What is commercial arbitration? When and how should it be used?
5. Does a salesperson have basically the same legal authority as a buyer? If not, how do they differ?
6. What are the legal rights of the buyer if goods delivered by a vendor do not measure up to the specifications?
7. Under what conditions might purchasing agents be held personally liable for contracts they enter into?
8. Is an oral contract legally enforceable? Under what conditions?
9. What authority does a purchasing agent have to make decisions which are binding on the principal? What responsibility do purchasing agents have for the consequences of their decisions?
10. What actions can the purchasing agent take to protect patent rights and avoid legal action for patent infringement?

REFERENCES

Barlow, C. Wayne. *The Buyer and the Law.* Boston, Mass.: CBI Publishing Co., Inc., 1982.

Decker, Russell. "It's Your Duty to be a 'Company' Man or Woman." *Purchasing,* May 8, 1986, pp. 63–64.

Decker, Russell. "Keep Contract Terms the Way You Want Them." *Purchasing,* April 30, 1981, pp. 51–59.

Decker, Russell. "Major Purchases Must Be in Writing." *Purchasing,* February 12, 1981, pp. 91–92.

Hayes, H. Michael, and James L. Porter. "The Battle of the Forms: Present Practices and Future Directions." *Journal of Purchasing and Materials Management,* Spring 1980, pp. 13–18.

McGonagle, John J., Jr. *Business Agreements: Complete Guide to Oral and Written Contracts.* Radnor, Pa.: Chilton Book Co., 1982.

Murray, John E., Jr. *Purchasing and the Law.* Pittsburgh, Pa.: Purchasing Management Association of Pittsburgh, 1980.

Ritterskamp, James J. *Purchasing Manager's Desk Book of Purchasing Law.* Englewood Cliffs, N.J.: Prentice Hall, 1987.

Staples, William A. "Product Liability and the Purchasing Manager." *Journal of Purchasing and Materials Management,* Winter 1980, pp. 13–16.

Uniform Commercial Code, 1978 official text. Philadelphia, Pa.: American Law Institute and National Conference of Commissioners on Uniform State Laws, 1978.

Wiesner, Donald A. "Don't Let Inaction Rob You of Your Rights." *Purchasing,* April 30, 1981, pp. 59–65.

Case 10–1

MOFFAT, INC.

Anita Valdez, purchasing manager for Moffat, Inc., had just heard that a label problem had developed on the company's prime product line. After a meeting with the president, marketing, engineering, production, and quality control managers, Anita was left to formulate the negotiation strategy with the equipment supplier.

Moffat, Inc., had started in the 1960s as one of many small companies catering to the needs of a more health conscious public demanding more natural foods. The company had been particularly successful with its premium line of jams packaged in a distinctive design earthenware jar. Moffat had grown substantially over the past 20 years and broadened its product line to include a full range of cereals, herbal teas, pickles, sauces, and condiments, in addition to the traditional food preserves and jams that had given the company its initial success.

Over the past few years, the plant manager and engineering had worked on a significant expansion and equipment renovation program. Plans for a new high speed jam jar filling machine had involved substantial development work with Anderson Engineering. The unusual shape of the earthenware jar and the high speed of filling required a custom-designed machine costing about $400,000. Anderson Engineering had been selected as the designer and manufacturer of this equipment because of their reputation for quality and innovative engineering. Progress payments were made by Moffat with a final $100,000 payment due four weeks after successful testing of the equipment. Since Moffat had no prior experience with Anderson's equipment,

who contract w/ & why;
type of warranties; if they have bee altered to or not.
who should mottet sue;
who would win?

Cases 421

Moffat's engineering manager had requested Anderson to specify the label glue which would be compatible with the equipment and Moffat's special jar. Anderson had recommended Wilson's glue type FJ 443, a relatively expensive, fully synthetic glue. Based on this recommendation, Anita Valdez had placed an order for this glue and found that Wilson insisted it could only be ordered in lots of a substantial size. Wilson claimed that it did not carry type FJ 443 in stock and their minimum order quantity represented about four months' estimated use for Moffat's at a $28,000 cost. After consulting with engineering and production managers, Anita placed an order with Wilson for a four-month supply. Glue delivery coincided with the installation of the Anderson machine.

Both the Anderson machine and glue were delivered as planned and test runs proved highly successful. Thus, earlier than originally expected, the new packaging machine was put into full production.

Six weeks later, however, the marketing manager started to receive complaints from retailers that labels were falling off the jars. An immediate investigation by quality control, engineering, and production came to the conclusion that the glue was at fault and that rework of existing stock in the warehouse and in the retail trade would cost $120,000.

Anita Valdez was asked by Moffat's angry president "to go after Anderson and make sure they pick up the tab for this whole mess." She was not sure how to proceed. A quick check with accounts payable revealed that both Anderson and Wilson had been paid in full two weeks earlier.

W

Case 10–2

JONES & BOND

Mr. Carter, director of purchases for Suffolk Power Corporation, had just received a legal opinion from Jones & Bond regarding the cross arm failure on a new power line. Suffolk had run into major problems during the erection phase of the new ornamental tubular poles, and Mr. Carter was anxious to assure early safe operation of the line. He was not sure on how to proceed with respect to repairs and recovery of additional costs since three different suppliers had participated in the project.

At the time of the cross arm failure, it was not clear what caused the problem. Only after extensive engineering tests which lasted almost three months was the prime cause found. Had the conductors been strung immediately or had the insulators been installed, as had been normal practice in all other tubular steel pole erections in this country, failure of the arms within a month of installation would not have occurred.

Mr. Carter had advised all three suppliers involved of the difficulties as soon as they arose. All three expressed concern and all claimed their part of the job could not have been responsible and that all work had been done to specifications. All

EXHIBIT 1   Suffolk Power Corporation
              System Engineering Department

Memorandum: (Excerpt)

Re: Replacement of Henry Nelson Company—345KV Cross Arms—Addison-
   Smithfield-Mesa Valley

It is required that all the groundwire and conductor cross arms on the line be removed and replaced by modified or new cross arms. It is the purpose of this correspondence to review the problems that have occurred and to outline a specific specification for the handling of these damaged cross arms. We will also continue the procedures for the installation of new cross arms on poles already erected and on new poles which have not been erected.

Through an extensive engineering research program, it was determined that the existing Nelson Company cross arms have low fatigue properties. First, the existing cross arm will fail by low velocity wind induced (aeolian) vibration which can cause a fatigue failure in less than a month. Second, the cross arm can fail by fatigue over a period of approximately 15 years by the continuing reversal of stresses due to the galloping of the conductors.

The problem of aeolian vibration can be resolved by the use of dampening devices mounted on the ends of the cross arms. Examples would be the use of insulator strings on the conductor cross arms and stockbridge dampers on the groundwire cross arms. The problem of designing for galloping requires the reduction of the stress level at the weld of the cross arm shaft to the cross arm baseplate. This can be accomplished by the use of stiffener bars on existing cross arms which have been fabricated but not erected. It can be accomplished on the damaged arms by the use of new thicker baseplates for the conductor cross arms. On new cross arms to be fabricated, there will be some of both of the types previously described.

Summary of Estimates:

Damaged arm repair:	
1,310–Structures Canadian	$ 746,252.60
Nondamaged arm repair:	
1,245–Structures Canadian	464,588.44
3,007–Henry Nelson	628,430.40
Contractor–remove and replace	640,000.00
Research costs	200,000.00
Total	$2,679,271.44

---

offered to be of any assistance they could and gave a number of suggestions throughout the research phase. All of the work on the line was halted until the reason for the failure was clear. Once the real cause was found, engineering was able to make recommendations for repair and strengthening which would prevent recurrence of the same difficulties (see Exhibit 1). Purchasing had obtained preliminary estimates showing an additional cost of about $2.6 million. Mr. Carter had written a letter to

Suffolk Power's legal firm, Jones & Bond, summarizing the situation to date (see Exhibit 2).

Jones & Bone had met with Mr. Carter five days later and confirmed their statements in this meeting by letter the following day (see Exhibit 3).

Twenty-six months had now passed since the beginning of the three-year project (see Exhibit 4). Suffolk Power Corporation was facing tremendous demand pressures for more power and simultaneously had not received particularly favorable treatment with rate increase requests. Mr. Carter was not sure where the extra funds to repair the cross arms would come from. The very high demand for capital in the corporation made it imperative that every avenue be explored to recover the extra costs to be incurred on the line. Workers had expressed fear about working near and with the poles. Since on-time completion and safety were also both of the highest priority, Mr. Carter wondered what action to take next.

EXHIBIT 2   Suffolk Power Corporation
                Director of Purchases

Memorandum to: T. R. Bond

Subject: Ornamental Poles and Arms

The company has experienced a most unfortunate failure of the eight arms of each of its first 345KV ornamental tubular steel pole transmission lines. The failure results in our believing that we should try to recover our losses from two or all of the three contractors involved in (1) engineering, (2) designing and fabricating, and (3) erecting these poles and arms.

We purchased the engineering assistance from Pettigrew Associates of New York, N.Y. This contract issued two years ago covered the technical assistance we needed to lay out the line circling our service area from Addison to Smithfield to Mesa Valley substations; the drawing up of specifications for our use in obtaining bids on the poles, arms and appurtenances; and their assistance to us in the evaluation of the bids on poles and arms when received.

Pettigrew Associates performed the services required by this contract according to the original schedule, and we had no idea that there was any difficulty with any of their performance until failure of the arms occurred. An analysis of the failure of the arms proved that failure was occasioned by what is known as the aeolian effect of wind on these free-standing poles and arms. Had the insulators and cables been installed immediately as the poles and arms were constructed, there apparently would have been no failures; but our erection contractor chose to erect the poles and arms and then return months later to install the insulators and cables. It is well proven now that neither McTaggart Construction Company (our erector), the Nelson Company (the pole and arm fabricator), nor Pettigrew Associates (the engineer), or Suffolk knew of the possible low velocity wind induced vibration (aeolian) that could cause arm fatigue and failure. Pettigrew contends they did not draw up a detailed specification for poles and arms but rather a "performance" type specification.

EXHIBIT 2 *(concluded)*

Suffolk contends that the performance specifications should have included sufficient performance description to permit the poles to be erected without arm failure, and, if the aeolian effect existed and was a construction parameter that should have been avoided, they should have known it and so specified.

Suffolk awarded its contract for the designing, furnishing, and fabricating of poles and arms to the H. Nelson Company of Dallas, Texas. Our testing has proven that the poles and arms that Nelson Company designed and furnished to Suffolk would have withstood all of the performance requirements had we installed the insulators or some type of dampeners on the arms and not subjected them to the wind induced vibration in the freestanding condition. H. Nelson Company claims no knowledge of the aeolian effect. All arms need to be reworked and given more strength through the use of heavier materials; but this is not because of the aeolian effect but rather to strengthen the arms to withstand "galloping" conditions of the cables that develop in certain wind situations. Perhaps Pettigrew Associates were derelict in not protecting us from this possible hazard also.

The McTaggart Construction Company in Indianapolis was awarded our contract for unloading of the poles and arms, installation of the foundations, erection of the poles and arms, and the stringing of the wire and cables. In our discussion of the arm failure with McTaggart, we attempted to point out their contributing to the failure by not installing insulators or dampeners and/or the cables and wires immediately on erection of the poles and arms. They claimed they have erected lattice steel towers and ornamental poles for many years without any concern or knowledge of the aeolian effect of wind-induced vibration and, therefore, could not know they had such an erection hazard to contend with. They have put insulators on while erecting on other tubular pole jobs, but they did it because of other erection problems—not the wind vibration.

We have attempted to have each of these companies assume obligation for our losses but to no avail yet. The costs likely to be incurred are as follows:

a. Rework of arms at Nelson Co. .... $ 628,430.40
b. Rework of a portion of the arms at Structures Canadian 1,210,841.04
c. Installation costs to be paid to McTaggart Construction 640,000.00
d. Suffolk's cost (study and processing) 200,000.00
    Total cost $2,679,271.44

Your immediate attention to this matter would be very much appreciated.

John Carter

EXHIBIT 3   Jones & Bond
Attorneys and Counselors
Chicago, Illinois

Mr. John Carter,
Director of Purchases,
Suffolk Power Corporation.

Dear Mr. Carter:

RE: 345KV Transmission Pole Failures

This will confirm our opinion as expressed at the meeting held in your office on Monday. As you will recall, two basic legal matters were discussed, to wit the possible bases of liability of the three parties involved and whether the company would jeopardize its rights by proceeding to repair the poles without first consulting any of those parties.

Concerning the latter, if the company is entitled to recover from anyone, it can reasonably expect to recover the cost of correcting the problem. The cost of doing so must be reasonable, and the repair must also be reasonably likely to correct the problem. In other words you cannot recover for a "gold plating" job, nor can you recover the cost of a repair which does not correct the problem. This right to recover is not affected by a failure to negotiate in advance with any party against which a claim might be made. If, however, any such party is consulted in advance of the commencement of a repair program and is given a chance to participate in determining the repair to be used, the chances of later being required to defend either the necessity of that repair or its cost would be greatly reduced.

With respect to the liabilities of each party, the contracts and related documents have been reviewed in detail on the basis of the company's findings that the cause of the damage to the pole arm was wind vibration, which can be substantially avoided by dampening the arms with conductors, rather than letting the bare arms stand. As stated at the meeting, the bases for potential liability of each party can be set out, and the Company can then assess the value of each on the basis of the known facts.

McTaggart Construction Company performed its services pursuant to a detailed contract which covered the work to be done but which did not provide any specific rights or remedies for a situation like the one now faced. In order to recover from McTaggart, whether on a theory of breach of contract or of negligence, it will be necessary to show that in erecting the poles, McTaggart did not exercise the degree of care, skill, and diligence that a reasonably competent contractor, purporting to be able to erect poles and lines, would have exercised. The McTaggart contract does not, in our opinion, impose any burden on McTaggart for engineering or design adequacy.

1. *Faulty design:* this would require that Nelson be shown to have had general design responsibility and that the current problem is a result of faulty design. The principal problem in this area is that the contract appears to give Nelson the burden of designing to Pettigrew Associates' specifications only.

EXHIBIT 3 *(continued)*

___

As for Henry Nelson Company, their contract consists of a purchase order with detailed specifications attached thereto. There are no commercial terms, such as warranties, in the contract which relate directly to the arm failure problem. There are, however, four (4) possible bases of liability which are:

2. *Breach of warranty:* if Nelson had reason to know the use to which the poles would be put and to know that Suffolk was relying on Nelson's skills and ability to produce a product fit for that purpose, then there would be in the contract an implied warranty that the poles would be fit for the purpose for which they were intended to be used. The primary weakness here is that the poles may well be fit for their ultimate intended use, and it would be necessary to show that Nelson knew or had reason to know that the poles would be erected and left standing without conductors.

3. *Failure to detail assembly procedures:* Section 14 of the Pettigrew Specification indicates in part that "the Vendor shall provide sketches indicating assembly procedures and the most desirable attachment points for raising the structures." With the benefit of hindsight, it can be argued that this includes the responsibility to direct that the arms be hung with conductors, although there seems to be general agreement that this is not necessarily what 14 was intended to cover.

4. *Failure to comply with the National Electrical Safety Code:* Item 24 of the Pettigrew specification requires compliance with the NESC, and it appears that there may be some basis for asserting that Nelson did not comply. This depends, as I understand it, largely upon whether the relevant section of the NESC can be construed as covering poles erected without conductors.

Finally, as regards Pettigrew Associates, the company has a contract pursuant to which Pettigrew is selected ". . . to perform the engineering and design services in connection with (the) Addison-Smithfield-Mesa Valley 345KV Transmission Line Project." Article I provides that Pettigrew will ". . . furnish complete project administration for coordinating and expediting the work" and is to perform services ". . . of the highest professional character . . ." with Pettigrew being ". . . fully responsible to Suffolk for the correctness of the engineering design and related data . . . ," which included pole design. In addition, Pettigrew evaluated all bids, including designs offered, and recommended the award to H. Nelson. If it can be shown either that the engineering design and related data were not correct or were not of the highest professional quality, then the company should have a sound cause of action against Pettigrew. I might add that the term "incorrect" can readily be construed to include omissions. As for the professional quality ground, it would be necessary to introduce expert testimony or evidence, or both, to establish that a top quality engineer would have at least considered the wind vibration problem.

___

EXHIBIT 3 *(concluded)*

Depending on the facts which you are able to establish, the company may have a cause of action against one or more of the parties involved. We would be pleased to assist you further, should you so request, in progressing any claim the company may wish to make.

Yours very truly,
T. R. Bond

EXHIBIT 4   Suffolk Power Corporation
          Timetable for the New Addison-Smithfield-Mesa Valley Power Line

Year 1:
March	Management approves use of ornamental tubular steel poles for the 140-mile line
April–July	Preliminary work and search for engineering consultant.
August	Pettigrew Associates selected as consulting engineers to prepare pole specifications, line layout, and assist in selection of manufacturer and erection.

Year 2:
March	Pettigrew Associates submit pole specifications and line layout
April–July	Engineering and purchasing evaluation of manufacturing of poles for the first half of the line.
July	H. Nelson selected as the pole manufacturer.
June–September	Engineering and purchasing evaluation of foundation and erection contractors.
September	McTaggart Construction chosen for both foundation and erection of the new line.
October	Delivery of test poles by H. Nelson. Tests prove poles meet specifications.
January	Installation starts. New poles draw favorable employee and public attention.
February 20	H. Nelson completes manufacture of poles for Addison-Smithfield section.
February 24	First cross arm failure noted. Purchasing notifies all three suppliers. All deny blame.
February 26	All project work halted.

EXHIBIT 4   *(concluded)*

Year 3:

March–April	Continuing pole cross arm failures. Engineering search for causes.
May 11	Engineering determines reason for failure.
May 25	Purchasing determines repair costs.
May 25	Mr. Carter sends memo to Jones & Bond for a legal opinion.
May 30	Jones & Bond representatives meet with Mr. Carter.
May 31	Letter from T. R. Bond confirming legal opinion.

Year 4:

April 30	Project deadline.

CHAPTER 11

Research, Budgets, Evaluation and Reporting

In a rapidly changing environment such as we have experienced recently, innovation and improvements in productivity can best be managed if we look at what might be possible, develop comprehensive plans, evaluate accomplishments and shortfalls, and report outcomes. This chapter will cover purchasing research, purchasing budgets, evaluation of purchasing performance, and reports to management.

PURCHASING RESEARCH

Purchasing research is the systematic collection, classification, and analysis of data as the basis for better purchasing decisions. The first complete study on purchasing research, published in 1963, reported that at that time approximately one-third of the 304 firms participating in the study had a purchasing research staff.[1] Fig. 11–1 shows some of the data (information) which might be required for effective buying decisions. The studies conducted in purchasing research include projects under the major research headings of:

1. Purchased materials, products, or services (value analysis).
2. Commodities.
3. Vendors.
4. Purchasing system.

Considerable attention has been given to a similar activity in the counterpart function of marketing research. Marketing research generally is well accepted in all medium- to large-size firms as a necessary ingredient in decision making, and it has produced significant results for those firms that practice marketing research systematically.

---

[1]Harold E. Fearon and John H. Hoagland, *Purchasing Research in American Industry*, Research Study 58 (New York: American Management Association, 1963).

FIGURE 11–1   Ingredients of Effective Buying

Purchasing research, if approached in an organized manner, also has the potential for generating major improvements in purchasing decision making, although it has been overlooked by many firms in the past.

Organization for Purchasing Research

A firm could conduct purchasing research in one of two ways: (1) the assignment of full-time staff personnel to the task, or (2) the use of regularly assigned buying and administrative personnel to conduct purchasing research as a secondary assignment.

As with its counterpart function, marketing research, there are some persuasive arguments for the establishment of full-time staff personnel to perform the purchasing research task. (These positions typically are titled purchase researcher, purchase analyst, value analyst, purchase economist, or commodity specialist.)

Time.   A thorough job of collecting and analyzing data requires blocks of time, and in many purchasing departments the buyers and administrators just do not have this time. They are fully occupied finding workable solutions to immediate problems.

Specialized Skill.   Many areas of purchasing research (for example, economic studies and system analysis) require in-depth knowledge of research techniques. These research techniques call for a level of skill not possessed by the typical buyer, primarily because research skill is not one of the criteria used in selecting persons for buying positions. Administrative assignments in purchasing also typically do not require this as a primary skill.

Perspective.   The purchase researcher often must take a broad view of the overall effects of purchasing decisions on operating results. The buyer, on the other hand, may be so engrossed in his or her own narrow responsibility area that the big picture goes unrecognized.

There are arguments for placing the responsibility for purchasing research with the buyer and/or the purchasing administrator.

Immediate Knowledge.   The buyer is intimately familiar with the items he or she buys. A staff person does not have such information, initially, and may overlook important data. A system that requires a staff person to spend a good deal of time in going to the buyer or administrator for data may be inefficient.

Locus of Decision Making.   In the final analysis, purchasing decisions are made by the buyer or administrator; the staff member merely presents data and advises. In some instances, conflict may develop between the staff person and the decision maker; thus the recommendations of the staff may not receive fair consideration and the value of the researcher's efforts will be negated.

Cost.   The salary and related organizational expense of a full-time staff member adds to the administrative costs of operating the purchasing department. If the results of staff analysis do not add appreciably to the improvement of purchasing decisions, the expense is unwarranted.

One possibility—somewhat of a compromise between the use of a full-time purchase researcher and the spreading out of research responsibility to individual buyers—is the formation of a committee to pursue various projects. Such committees have various titles such as task force, tiger team, or value analysis committee.

The difficulty with the committee approach is that it is hard to pinpoint responsibility for results when it is diffused over a number of individuals. However, the committee approach can work satisfactorily, provided

FIGURE 11-2   Organization for Purchasing Research in a Large Food Producer

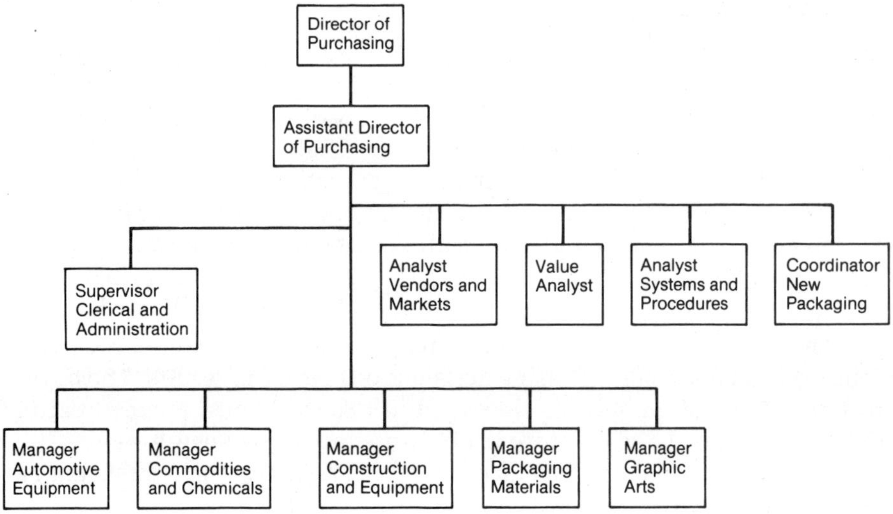

that (1) committee members are carefully selected to ensure that each really has something to contribute; (2) the committee has strong leadership (from a functional point of view, it probably should be someone from the materials area); (3) a specific set of objectives and expectations of results is formulated and communicated to each member and the committee as a whole; and (4) each committee member's normal job responsibilities are rearranged to give that person the time and the resources necessary to ensure results. If any of these four conditions is not present, less than optimum outcomes are almost certain.

Current evidence indicates that research efforts normally will be most productive when persons are assigned to this activity on a full-time basis.[2] Logic dictates that if a full-time researcher or analyst is the primary vehicle through which purchasing research is done, that individual will produce more and better research results. He or she has the primary assignment and time to do the research, and since the person presumably was selected, in part, on the basis of research ability and willingness and desire to do research, the results should be of higher quality.

Figure 11-2, presents an example of the organization structure for purchasing research in a large food-producing company. A capsule view of how this purchase research effort fits into the overall purchasing organization and where this firm places its major emphasis follows:

---

[2]Ibid, pp. 31, 37, and 40.

Company A processes a wide variety of consumer food products and related lines of consumer goods. Annual sales are over a billion dollars.

Purchases, which account for over 70 percent of the sales dollar, are handled centrally; individual divisions and plants do, however, make the commitments for the raw agricultural materials, with guidance from the central office purchasing department. Packaging, equipment, and chemicals are purchased by the central office.

Four full-time purchase research personnel aid the director and assistant director of purchasing and the five purchasing managers by doing special purchasing projects and providing information and advice on purchase alternatives. Supervision of the researchers is handled primarily by the assistant director of purchasing. The work of the four analysts has been specialized, as follows:

The analyst, vendors and markets, does work in (1) locating and assisting in the analysis of the capabilities and reliability of new and continuing vendors; (2) acting as the program coordinator to ensure that the individual plant purchasing departments each has its own purchase cost reduction program in place and operating; (3) assisting individual plants in coping with material shortages, by better planning of requirements, by assisting in expediting effort, and by locating alternate sources; and (4) monitoring the status of vendor labor agreements and problems to avoid unanticipated supply interruptions due to strikes.

The value analyst handles special projects relating to ways the purchase requirements could be met at lower cost. Included are make/lease/buy studies on specific items, standardization of purchases, substitution of materials, cost analysis of purchased items to establish negotiation targets, and price forecasting of key purchased items.

The analyst, systems and procedures, conducts continuing studies to improve the administrative methods used in processing purchase transactions. Utilization of computer services is a key activity area.

The coordinator, new packaging, works with the marketing and industrial engineering departments in determining the design and purchase of new packages. Interface with vendor personnel is a key element of the coordinator's assignment. After design decisions are reached, the actual purchase of production quantities is handled by the manager, packaging materials. Much of the work of the coordinator is in the value-engineering area (ensuring that the design selected will perform the function at the lowest cost possible).

Figure 11–3 presents a job description for a purchasing research manager in another large firm, in which the research staff consists of three professional research people.

Since the types of data which bear on a major purchasing decision are numerous and since many different items are bought, the number of possible purchase-research projects is almost infinite. However, even if a company has full-time purchase analysts, it has limited resources and must use some

FIGURE 11–3   Job Description, Manager of Purchasing Research

Objectives
1. Investigate and implement, and may initiate, programs and procedures involving the cost reduction of purchased goods and services and the storing, accounting, and disbursing of stores.
2. Develop, recommend, and implement cost reductions in operating the purchasing department.
3. Develop, recommend, and implement growth and educational programs for purchasing personnel.
4. Research and communicate trends and statistical data.
5. Direct special projects.

Method of Operation
   This position conducts, coordinates, and administers work that by nature would be too expensive and specialized to be conducted by purchasing management, purchasing agents, or other officers who have primary responsibility. The purchasing research group's concerns and activities fall into five basic categories:
1. Commodity-review program.
2. Purchasing policies and procedures to implement the commodity-review program.
3. Preparation of reports and summaries of data.
4. Departmental training and orientation.
5. Special projects.

Work in these categories covers areas such as market analysis, price analysis, cost analysis, make-or-buy studies, methods of procurement, and the economic areas associated with standardization.
   The total value of the purchased goods and services from which the manager may select or be assigned subjects for analysis is $300 million per year. The manager works closely with buying and administrative personnel to study, direct, coordinate, implement, and administer various studies, programs, systems, and procedures of purchasing activity.
   The manager assists in the administration of short- and long-range planning programs of the purchasing department. He or she studies purchasing procedures and recommends, implements, and administers changes to improve administrative control of purchasing activity, to provide better control, more comprehensive information, simplified procurement procedures, more effective purchase agreements and contract negotiations, and to reduce costs associated with procurement, through data processing applications.
   The principal challenge of the manager, purchasing research, is to research, initiate, develop, and coordinate procedures and programs for reducing the cost of purchased materials and services.

Principal Contacts
   Internal: all levels of management throughout the company.
   External: vendor personnel, government agencies, publishers of trade and technical papers, professional societies, economic consultants, government and private economists.

method of deciding which purchase-research projects should have top priority.

Following is a list of criteria that are used by firms in deciding where they will direct their research effort. This is not intended to be in priority order (although by far the most used is the "top dollar" criterion).

1. *Value of product or service.*
   Top dollar (current or projected).

2. *Product profitability.*
   Red dollar (unprofitable end product).

3. *Price/cost characteristics.*
   Infrequent price changes.
   Frequent or seasonal price fluctuations.
   End-product cost not competitive.
   Raw materials costs rising at a greater rate then selling price of product, resulting in reduced profit margin.

4. *Availability.*
   Limited number of suppliers.
   New suppliers adding to available supply.
   Possibility of imports.
   Possibility of in-house manufacture.

5. *Quality.*
   Have had quality or specification problem.

6. *Data Flows.*
   Information for decisions often inaccurate, late, or unavailable.
   Cost of data is excessive.
   Buyer doesn't have time to do analysis work.

Research on Purchased Materials, Products, or Services (Value Analysis)

The research topics in this area are principally concerned with the specific products being purchased. Most of them fall under the generally understood category of *value analysis*, which historically is the area of purchasing research that first received attention, publicity, and acceptance.[3] Value analysis (VA) originally was developed by Lawrence D. Miles of the General Electric purchasing organization. The technique received wide acceptance in U.S. industry, and it has been exported to Japan, where it is cited as a cornerstone of Japan's cost-effective manufacturing system. Japan

---

[3]The best, most comprehensive treatment of value analysis is by Lawrence D. Miles, *Techniques of Value Analysis and Engineering*, 2nd ed. (New York: McGraw-Hill, 1972).

even gives the Miles Award to those firms making most effective use of value analysis.[4]

Value analysis compares the *function* performed by a purchased item with the *cost*, in an attempt to find a lower cost alternative. Since purchasing decisions often are made under a good deal of time pressure, and since technology and manufacturing methods change fairly rapidly, in many instances a higher priced item is purchased than is necessary. Some people make the distinction that value analysis is done on purchased items used in the ongoing production process, while value engineering looks at cost savings possibilities in the design stage, where items are being specified, and before production purchases actually are made. Obviously, value engineering at the design stage to arrive at the lowest cost material specification and design that will adequately perform the function is the most efficient way to do the job, but unfortunately this analysis, due to time pressures, often is not done. Therefore, value analysis presents a fruitful area for purchase cost reduction. Detailed information on various aspects of the item to be purchased will enable a more intelligent choice from alternatives, thus providing better utilization of the purchasing dollar. Included as research topics are:

Lease or Buy.   Collection of data on the advantages and disadvantages of each alternative so that the most attractive decision can be identified.

Make or Buy.   Comparison of economic and managerial outcomes from each alternative in order that an informed choice can be made.

Packaging.   Investigation of processes and materials to determine the lowest cost method of meeting requirements.

Scrap Disposal.   Analysis of disposal methods, channels, and techniques to isolate those that will provide greatest net return to the firm.

Specification.   Analysis of current specs to be sure they outline the required level of performance, do not result in purchase of unneeded attributes or unnecessarily high levels of performance, and enable competitive purchasing.

Standardization.   Review of uses to which specific products are put and consideration of the possibility of using one item to fill the needs for which multiple items currently are purchased. For example, one large, multiplant company reviewed its entire purchase of work gloves and found that its annual buyout amounted to over $1 million and included some 400 different types and vendors. As a result of the value analysis, they were able to standardize on 46 different models, write blanket orders with vendors, negotiate lower prices, and save over $70,000 per year.

Substitution.   Analysis of the technical and economic ramifications of using a different item than the one presently purchased.

---

[4] "Japan Industry's U.S. Teacher," *New York Times*, December 5, 1983, p. 33

Transportation.   Investigation of movement requirements and alternative methods and costs. One firm found that by operating its own over-the-road vehicles, it would not only save in total transport cost but also would reduce congestion in and around its receiving area. The deregulation of freight transportation has opened up many value analysis savings possibilities.

The standard approach to value analysis, which encompasses most of the topics listed earlier, is to pose and provide detailed answers to a series of questions about the item currently being bought. Figure 11–4 details this approach and lists the standard value-analysis questions.

While value analysis is a relatively old concept from the 1950s and is where today's purchasing research started, it is every bit as applicable today. According to a 1986 study by *Purchasing* magazine,[5] the purposes of VA were (percent indicating): reduce costs (92 percent), improve quality (80 percent), encourage supplier involvement (49 percent), encourage creative teamwork within company (40 percent), better satisfy users' needs (33 percent), and meet new marketing objectives (26 percent).

Commodity Studies

These purchase research studies are directed at providing predictions, or answers to questions, about the short- and long-term future purchasing environment for a major purchased commodity or item. Such information should provide the basis for making sound decisions and presenting purchasing management and top management with relatively complete information concerning future supply and price of these items.

Typically, the focus of such research is on items that represent a major amount of purchase dollars, but it could be done on items of smaller dollar magnitude that are thought to be in critically short supply. Major raw materials, such as steel, copper, or zinc, normally would be studied, but manufactured items, such as motors or semiconductor devices, also might be researched. This area probably is the most sophisticated in terms of difficulty and skills needed to do a good job.

A comprehensive commodity study should include analyses of these major areas: (1) current status of our company, as a buyer, (2) production process alternatives, (3) uses of the item, (4) demand, (5) supply, (6) price, and (7) strategy to reduce cost and/or ensure supply. Figure 11–5 provides a set of guidelines that might be used to make a commodity study.

Some companies do very sophisticated commodity research, resulting in a well-documented strategic purchase plan. While a planning horizon of from 5 to 10 years is the norm, some firms make a 15-year rolling forecast,

---

[5]Somerby Dowst, "VA '86: Buyers Say VA is More Important Than Ever," *Purchasing*, June 26, 1986, p. 67.

FIGURE 11-4   The Value Analysis Approach: Comparison of Function to Cost

1. Select a relatively high-cost or high-volume purchased item to value analyze. This can be a part, material, or service. Select an item you suspect is costing more than it should.
2. Find out completely how the item is used and what is expected of it—its *function*.
3. Ask questions:
   a. Does its use contribute value?
   b. Is its cost proportionate to usefulness?
   c. Does it need all its features?
   d. Is there anything better, at a more favorable purchase price, for the intended use?
   e. Can the item be eliminated?
   f. If the item is not standard, can a standard item be used?
   g. If it is a standard item, does it completely fit your application or is it a misfit?
   h. Does the item have greater capacity than required?
   i. Is there a similar item in inventory that could be used?
   j. Can the weight be reduced?
   k. Are closer tolerances specified than are necessary?
   l. Is unnecessary machining performed on the item?
   m. Are unnecessarily fine finishes specified?
   n. Is commercial quality specified?
   o. Can you make the item cheaper yourself?
   p. If you are making it now, can you buy it for less?
   q. Is the item properly classified for shipping purposes to obtain lowest transportation rates?
   r. Can cost of packaging be reduced?
   s. Are your suppliers being asked by you for suggestions to reduce cost?
   t. Do material, reasonable labor, overhead, and profit total its cost?
   u. Will another dependable supplier provide it for less?
   v. Is anyone buying it for less?
4. Now:
   a. Pursue those suggestions that appear practical.
   b. Get samples of the proposed item(s).
   c. Select the best possibilities and propose changes.

---

updated each year. If a firm makes a 15-year strategic marketing plan, it makes sense to couple this with a strategic supply forecast and plan, for in the long term the acquisition of an adequate supply of critical materials may be the crucial determinant in the organization's success in meeting its market goals. Firms need to make realistic estimates of price trends so that they can plan their strategy of adjusting material inputs to counter this trend. Also, the availability of supply of many items is questionable, due to dependence of U.S. firms on foreign supply sources, whose stability due to international politics and depletion of reserves is doubtful. Table 11-1 presents some rough estimates of U.S. dependence on foreign supply sources.

FIGURE 11-5 Commodity Study Guidelines

The information resulting from a commodity study should:

1. Provide a basis for making sound procurement decisions.
2. Present purchasing management and top management with information concerning future supply and price of purchased items.

The completed commodity study should provide data and/or answers for each of the following points or questions. (The investigation should not be limited to these items; depending on the particular commodity under consideration, additional items may be very pertinent, and some of the listed items may not be important.)

I. *Current Status*
   1. Description of commodity.
   2. How and where commodity is used.
   3. Requirements.
   4. Suppliers.
   5. How commodity is purchased.
   6. How commodity is transported.
   7. Current contracts and expiration dates.
   8. Current price, terms, and annual expenditure.
   9. Scheduling.
  10. Receiving.
  11. Inspection.
  12. Expediting.
  13. Packaging.
  14. Storage capacity.

II. *Production Process*
   1. How is the item made?
   2. What materials are used in its manufacture? Supply/price status of these materials.
   3. What labor is required? Current and future labor situation.
   4. Are there alternative production processes?
   5. What changes are likely in the future?
   6. Possibility of making the item?
     a. Costs.
     b. Time factor.
     c. Problems.

III. *Uses of the item*
   1. Primary use(s).
   2. Secondary use(s).
   3. Possible substitutes: Economics of substitution.

IV. *Demand*
   1. Our requirements.
     a. Current.
     b. Projected into the future.
     c. Inventory status.
     d. Sources of forecast information.
     e. Lead times.

FIGURE 11–5   *(continued)*

  2. Competing demand, current and projected.
     a. By industry.
     b. By end-product use.
     c. By individual firms.
 V. *Supply*
  1. Current producers.
     a. Location.
     b. Reliability as a source.
     c. Quality levels.
     d. Labor situation.
     e. Ownership.
     f. Capacity.
     g. Distribution channels used.
     h. Sales strategy.
     i. Expansion plans.
     j. Warranties and guarantees.
     k. Strengths and weaknesses of each supplier.
  2. Total (aggregate) supply situation.
     a. Current.
     b. Projected.
  3. Import potential and problems.
  4. Pertinent government regulations and controls.
  5. Potential new suppliers.
  6. Technological change forecast.
  7. Political trends.
  8. Ecological problems.
  9. Weather.
 10. Capital investment per unit of output.
VI. *Price*
  1. Economic structure of producing industry.
  2. Price history and explanation of significant changes.
  3. Factors determining price.
  4. Cost to produce and deliver.
  5. Incremental costs.
  6. Co-products or by-products.
  7. Effect of materials and labor cost changes on prices.
  8. Transportation cost element.
  9. Tariff and import regulations.
 10. Effect of changes in the business cycle.
 11. Effect of quantity on price.
 12. Seasonal trends.
 13. Estimated profit margins of various vendors.
 14. Price objective(s) of vendors.
 15. Potential rock-bottom price.
 16. Do prices vary among various industries using the item?

FIGURE 11–5 *(concluded)*

17. Forecast of future price trend.
18. Specific pricing system used by various vendors.
19. Influence of actions of specific vendors on prices of others; that is, a price leader?
20. Relation to prices of other products.
21. Foreign exchange problems.

VII. *Strategy to Reduce Cost*

Considering forecast supply, usage, price, profitability, strengths and weaknesses of suppliers, and our position in the market, what is our plan to lower cost?

1. Make the item in our facility.
2. Short-term contract.
3. Long-term contract.
4. Acquire a producer.
5. Find a substitute.
6. Develop a new producer.
7. Import.
8. Exploit all methods to make maximum use of our purchasing power.
9. Detailed preplanning of negotiations.
10. Use of agents.
11. Hedging.
12. Toll contract.
13. Value engineering/analysis.
14. Handling of scrap.

VIII. *Appendix*

1. General information
   a. Specifications.
   b. Quality control requirements and methods.
   c. Freight rates and transportation costs.
   d. Storage capacity.
   e. Handling facilities.
   f. Weather problems.
   g. Raw material reserves.
2. Statistics
   a. Price trends.
   b. Production trends.
   c. Purchase trends.

The five specific research topics in this subject area are:

Demand Forecast.   Investigation of the firm's demand for the item, to include current and projected demand, inventory status, and lead times. Also considered are competing demands, current and projected, by industry and end-product use.

Supply Forecast.   Collection of data about current producers and sup-

TABLE 11–1   U.S. Dependence on Foreign Sources of Materials

Commodity	Percent of Current Need Imported
Natural rubber	100%
Sheet mica	100
Industrial diamonds	100
Manganese ore	98
Bauxite, alumina	94
Cobalt	91
Chromium, ferrochromium	90
Strontium	90
Bismuth	85
Tantalum	85
Platinum group	85
Asbestos	80
Tin	80
Titanium	78
Mercury	73
Nickel	72
Gold	69
Silver	68
Zinc	67
Cadmium	65
Tungsten	60
Potassium	60
Crude oil	37
Iron ore	30

SOURCES: U.S. Bureau of Mines, U.S. Department of Commerce, U.S. Geological Survey, A.D. Little, Inc.

pliers, the aggregate current and projected supply situation, and technological and political trends that might affect supply.

Price Forecast.   Based on information gathered and analyzed about demand and supply, this forecast provides a prediction of short- and long-term prices and the underlying reasons for those trends.

An example of a comprehensive supply-demand-price commodity study was the one done by several of the integrated petroleum companies in 1980 when a major steel company came to them with this proposal: (1) We will build a major, new facility in Alabama to make seamless pipe for the petroleum industry; (2) This new mill will assure you, the oil company buyer, the needed supply of oil country tubular goods (OCTG) for several years into the future. Also, the OCTG from the new mill will be of a more reliable quality than currently available from U.S. mills; (3) In order that we (the steel company) can obtain needed financing for this $650 million capital investment, you (the oil company) must sign a take-or-pay contract, committing a specified, substantial volume of purchases of OCTG for each of the next several years. Before a given petroleum company purchasing department could make a decision on the advisability of signing the take-or-pay commitment contract, a complete commodity study on the supply-demand-price of OCTG over the next several years was required.[6]

Purchase of Supply Source.   Consideration of the economic and legal ramifications of actually buying out a supply source to protect supply and/or costs.

Exchange Rate Fluctuation.   Consideration of methods for predicting changes in monetary exchange rates when buying from foreign sources and developing strategies to protect the buying firm against major fluctuations in the foreign exchange market.

As a review of Figure 11–5 will show, a well-done, comprehensive commodity study is a major undertaking, and if a thorough job of analysis is to be done, this requires the service of personnel who have both the technical expertise and the time. It would be the unusual situation where the buyer or purchasing administrator would have both; therefore, this tends to be a major activity area for the staff purchase researcher.

Vendor Research

While the two research areas discussed earlier were directed primarily at the item being purchased, research in this category has its principal emphasis on the source of the purchase. In short, the previous two areas were the *what*; this one concerns *from whom*. Obviously, the more knowledge a buyer has about present and potential vendors, their method of operation and market position, the better is his or her ability to select adequate, appropriate supply sources and to prepare for and successfully conduct vendor negotiations. The specific topic areas in this category are:

Analysis of Financial Capacity.   Investigation of the financial health of present or potential vendors so that the risk of the vendor's running into financial trouble and its effects on the buying firm can be assessed. While this type of analysis often is done within the financial department of a firm, in some cases it has been pulled into purchasing and made a responsibility of purchasing research, to ensure that it is done with requisite thoroughness, considering the potential dollar value of the risk involved. For example, several purchasers of computer systems and equipment from very substantial U.S. manufacturers have been surprised suddenly to find

---

[6]"U.S. Steel's Oil-Pipe Gamble," *New York Times*, November 14, 1983, p. 23.

that their supplier "has gone bankrupt" in the computer business. With proper analysis, such a situation could have been anticipated well in advance.

Analysis of Production Facilities. Collection of data on the vendor's physical facilities, emphasizing capacities and limitations.

Finding New Supply Source. Search to uncover new vendors for a purchase need. During the supply shortages of the 1970s, research on this topic consumed a great deal of the time of the purchase researcher, for many firms were totally unprepared. Through the information from the commodity studies currently underway, firms hope to avoid similar surprises down the road.

Estimate of Distribution Costs. Analysis of the steps performed in the process of moving items from their source to the point at which the firm takes possession, and calculation of the costs that the vendor should incur if the firm is reasonably efficient. This provides an input into what is a fair price and an evaluation of whether the most efficient distribution channels are being used.

Estimate of Manufacturing Costs. Analysis of what it should cost a vendor (direct material, direct labor, engineering, tooling, manufacturing overhead, general and administrative expense, and profit) to make an item, assuming reasonable efficiency. These data provide the basis for establishing a target price in negotiation planning. This is the most common research topic in this subject area, probably because it is productive of very large and immediate savings. Much cooperation between purchasing and the firm's industrial engineering personnel is needed for this research to produce maximum results. Many firms are experimenting with putting standard assumptions about the cost factors (for example, material prices and direct labor rates) into the computer and then writing a simple program that will permit the computer to produce a cost analysis for whatever set of specifications is fed into it. One company uses such a model to supply cost analysis data to its buyers on any purchase of corrugated. The computer is in the central office location, but it can be accessed through the telephone from any plant in the continental United States, thus giving the buyers immediate cost analysis capability.

Single Sourcing. Analyzing the vendor's management and capabilities as the basis for negotiating a complete contractual agreement, in which all contingencies are anticipated. The buyer may gain significant advantages from volume leverage. However, the potential costs from supply interruption caused by problems in the single-source supplier's plant or in the transportation system can be great.

Vendor Purchased Material Quality Assurance. Developing a system with vendors which will reach agreement on quality standards, arrive at quality yields, determine training needs of vendor production and quality personnel, establish a system for mutual tracking of quality performance, and determine needed corrective action. Starting in early 1980, firms became aware of the need to raise end-product/service quality performance, and that one of the elements is to work with key vendors in a mutual attempt to assure delivery of materials/parts which meet or exceed specifications.[7] This cooperation reduces the earlier, often present adversarial supplier relationship.

Supplier Attitude Survey.   Determination, through systematic survey techniques, of what vendors really think of the buying firm and its purchasing practices. This information is used in reviewing and modifying purchasing organization and policy. One firm developed a survey questionnaire through its purchase research group and then had an independent public accounting firm administer the questionnaire and summarize the results. The firm found, to its surprise, general vendor sentiment to the effect that (1) it as a buyer was very unappreciative of superior vendor efforts, (2) buying decisions often were made on a personal-favoritism basis, and (3) if vendors could sell their output to someone else, no sales would be made to this firm. Such sentiments would have drastic effects on this firm's material supply situation in the event of another general shortage situation such as occurred in 1973 and 1974. Obviously, purchasing management in this firm made some major changes to remedy the situation.

Vendor Performance Evaluation.   Collection and analysis of data as the basis for determining how good a job is being done by a given vendor so that decisions on sources for rebuys can be made more intelligently and present vendors can be advised where improvement is needed.

Vendor Sales Strategy.   Development of a better understanding of a vendor's objectives and the means it is using to achieve these goals, so that the buyer can anticipate the vendor's actions and design a purchasing strategy to provide for the continued supply of needed items at lowest cost.

Countertrade.   Locating vendors in foreign countries, analyzing their capabilities, and negotiating counterbalancing purchase agreements with them. Many foreign countries, and particularly the Peoples' Republic of China and those in the Soviet bloc, are short of U.S. currency. Therefore, when they buy goods from a U.S. firm, they insist that all, or a specified part, of the purchase price be paid for in raw materials or finished products exported from their country. This essentially is a barter agreement, and in some companies purchase-research specialists are responsible for gathering and analyzing the data that form the basis for such agreements.

It might be assumed that the buyer, because of close, continuing relationships with vendors, is in the best position to do meaningful vendor research. However, since much of this research is technical in nature, it may be advisable to use staff personnel who have the requisite skills if maximum decision-making data are to be obtained.

---

[7]"The Push for Quality," *Business Week*, June 8, 1987, pp. 131-144.

Purchasing System Research

Adequate knowledge about items to be purchased and the vendor from whom the purchase might be made, while important in attaining maximum value from the purchasing dollar, does not assure that the purchasing function will be discharged in the most efficient manner. Equally important is how the purchase is made. Efficient administrative procedures not only will reduce the expense of departmental operations but also will facilitate wise decisions on items purchased and their source. Research topics in the purchasing system area are directed at improving administration of the purchasing system. These might be described as systems and procedures studies with a special focus on materials administration. Specific topic areas usually researched include:

Blanket Orders.   Investigation of the ways in which umbrella-type contracts might be used to provide greater purchasing leverage and reduce administrative expense. With the prospect of recurring materials shortages, the use of long-term agreements as an inducement to ensure constant supply may be particularly attractive.

Formulation of Price Index.   Development of a procedure whereby an index or indexes can be prepared to show either the mix of prices actually paid for purchases or a mix of market prices against which actual prices paid can be compared, as one element in evaluating how well the purchasing department is performing. Typically more than one price index is used, covering (1) raw materials, (2) components, and (3) MRO items.

Price Discount Analysis.   Development of a computer model to facilitate decisions on when it is economically advisable to take advantage of available quantity/payment discounts.

Quotation Analysis.   Development of a computer model which can take line-item price quotations on a multitude of individual items from several vendors and determine the combination(s) which will result in minimum total cost to the buying firm.

Inventory Control.   Establishment of systems and procedures for the efficient and timely control of inventory so as to maximize inventory service levels for a given amount of dollar investment. Reorder points and quantities, stock objectives, and safety stocks would be recommended.

Materials Requirements Planning (MRP).   Planning and implementing an MRP system, which requires computerized bills of materials, inventory files, and the MRP scheduling logic. The successful introduction of such a system requires, in most firms, at least a two-year planning and implementation horizon. When properly established, the MRP system provides purchasing with accurate and timely ordering and expediting information, enabling purchasing to maximize buying leverage with vendors, improve vendor service levels, and reduce inventory investment and write-offs.

Learning Curve. Application of the time-reduction curve as a basis for establishing a target price in negotiation.

Payment or Cash-Discount Procedures. Investigation and improvement of the system for making payment on vendor accounts and taking advantage of cash discounts, where advantageous. For example, some firms have investigated the use of vendor invoices as part of their payment system and decided to discontinue them, thus eliminating one piece of paper, and resultant handling costs, from their system. They simply close the purchase order (PO) by matching the PO file copy with the receiving report and the incoming inspection report. If they agree, a check for the previously agreed-on amount is written to the vendor at the end of the cash discount period. The only major disadvantage is that purchases must be made FOB destination, for there is no way to add in transport charges.

Vendor Tracking Systems. Establishment of a system which routinely calls for and collects information from vendors on the status of material/work on an order which is under vendor control. Such information enables follow-up/expediting of business placed with a vendor to be done more accurately and in a more timely manner.

Receiving Systems. Review of the methods currently used to verify quantities delivered by vendors, for payment purposes, in an attempt to simplify the system. Some firms have looked at the use of the receiving report on a cost/benefit basis and concluded that the cost of completing and processing the receiving paperwork is substantially greater than the value of the protection provided; they now simply pay based on a comparison of the PO file copy with the vendor invoice on all noninventory purchases of under a certain dollar amount, for example, $200 or under. In the event the item or material really never was received, they depend on the requisitioner to call that to their attention, and then they go back to the vendor and ask for either proof of shipment or a replacement. If the purchase has been made from a reliable vendor, there should be no problem.

Small or Rush Order Procedures. Design of innovative methods for processing small or rush orders so that purchase needs are satisfied at lowest administrative cost. The blank check buying system (also called the check-with-purchase-order system) is an example of the kind of innovation that can result when someone takes a thorough look at present practices in an attempt to effect improvement—and when the "that's the way we've always done it" syndrome is avoided.

Systems Contracting. Investigation and establishment of arrangements with a single vendor, or a small group of vendors, for the supply of the buying firm's total annual requirement of a specific group of items.

Vendor Data Sharing. Determination of areas where the transfer of materials information—for example, usage, forecast requirements, production rates, schedule revision, quotations, and inventory on hand—between vendor and buyer would be to the mutual benefit of both parties. Establishment of the system, normally a buyer-supplier computer information exchange, for the routine transfer of this information.

Method for Evaluating Buyer Performance. Establishment of a system by which the job performance of buyers can be measured.

Method for Evaluating Purchasing Department Performance. Establishment of a system by which the actual performance of the total purchasing effort can be compared against predetermined criteria. On the basis of this evaluation, action to correct deficiencies can be taken.

Method for Evaluating Supplier Performance. Establishment of a system for rating how well vendors are meeting the requirements of the purchase orders and contracts they receive. Resultant data are essential for rebuy decisions and as a basis for providing feedback to the vendor on where improvement is needed.

Computer Applications. Determination of areas in which computer usage could provide more accurate and timely manipulation of data and improved purchase decision making. The actual design of the computer software system could be an output of these studies, although purchasing research typically is applications oriented and normally depends on the computer or management information systems people to develop the software to support needed applications. Electronic data interchange (EDI) system applications have assumed an increased importance in the past few years.

Study and development of computerized decision-making models also is under way by some purchase research groups. Computer decision-assisting systems process data used to assist management in selecting among alternatives; these systems typically select an alternative, using techniques such as mathematical relationships, simulations, or other algorithms. The outcome is definitive in nature and presents the results in either a deterministic or probabilistic fashion. Computer decision models are being developed in the areas of price-discount analysis, factory simulation as it affects materials usage, materials budgeting, quotation analysis, synthetic pricing, the negotiation process between opposing parties, and forward buying and futures trading.

While each of the research topics in this subject area is in the systems and procedures area and could be handled by personnel from that department of the firm, the results probably will be more useful if the research is done by people in purchasing who are aware of the problems and subtleties in day-to-day administrative activities and who have to live with, and make work, the changes that are made. The potential saving from research in this area is great, particularly in a large firm with many thousands of transactions and complex data flows.

An Assessment of Purchase Research Results

Managers who use purchasing research are satisfied that it has paid off for their firm. Those with organized purchase research efforts feel it would be impossible for purchasing to continue making the current level of contribution to corporate success and profits without an aggressive program. Purchasing research has arrived on the corporate scene, but most managers contend that its potential really has been only partially tapped.

Purchasing research can contribute substantially to the ability of the purchasing department to cope successfully with future materials uncertainties and the demands for greater purchasing efficiency. Astute, aggressive purchasing executives will explore carefully the opportunities for maximizing purchasing profit potential through this approach.

PURCHASE PLANNING

The actual planning process starts with information derived from the annual sales forecast, production forecasts, and general economic forecasts. The sales forecast will provide a total measure of the requirements of materials, products, and services to be acquired by purchasing; production forecasts will provide information on the location at which the materials, products, and services will be required; and the economic forecast will provide information useful in estimating general trends for prices, wages, and other costs.

In most purchasing operations, less than 20 percent of the items purchased account for over 80 percent of the dollars spent. In breaking down the broad forecast into specific plans, the next step is to make price and supply availability forecasts for each of the major items (the 20 percent of all items which account for 80 percent of total purchase expenditures).

The estimates of material consumption are broken down into time periods, monthly and quarterly. These quantities are checked against inventory control data which take into account lead times and safety stocks. These estimates then are related to the price trend and availability forecasts for the material under consideration and a buying plan is developed. If the forecasts predict ample supplies of the material and a possible weakening in prices, a probable buying policy will be to reduce inventories to the lowest level which is economically feasible. On the other hand, if the forecasts predict a short supply and increasing price trend, prudence indicates a buying policy which will ensure that adequate stocks are on hand or are covered by contract, and the possibility of forward buying is considered.

The procedure outlined earlier is used for both raw materials and component parts. In forecasting trends which will affect the availability and price of component parts, consideration has to be given to the conditions expected to be present for the period being forecasted in the industries in which the parts' suppliers operate.

The 80 percent of the items purchased which account for 20 percent of the dollars spent in the average purchasing function can be classified into related product groups. The pattern of analysis followed in forecasting for the major items can be used for the related product groups.

After the monthly and quarterly unit quantities and estimated dollar costs for each item or related product group are tabulated and modifications made as a result of developing a buying plan, individual buyers make an analysis of the items for which they are responsible to determine if further modifications in prices should be made because of the objectives which they have established to guide their activities for the period of the forecast.

Special projects, such as the construction of new facilities or the planning for the manufacture of new major products not previously produced, may create uncertainty as to the time periods when new equipment or products will be needed, making planning difficult.

PERT AND CPM

Within the past 20 years, new planning techniques have been developed which are useful in complex situations in which many variables and inter-relationships are present. The Critical Path Method (CPM) provides for determining the sequence of all tasks required from the start to the completion of a project. An arrow diagram is used to show graphically the interrelationship between tasks for any project and hence determine the longest or critical path required to complete a project. An estimated time requirement is assigned to each task.

The Program Evaluation Review Techniques (PERT) was developed by the U.S. Navy in cooperation with others for the purpose of reducing the development time for the Polaris Ballistic Missile System. PERT is similar to CPM in that each technique uses a network to diagram graphically the sequence of tasks, which in PERT terminology are called events. Events are also defined as being "highly identifiable points in time." The network lines connecting events are known as activities and represent the elapsed time required to complete an event. Unless stated otherwise, activities are stated in seven-day calendar weeks with an assumed 40-hour work week. Figure 11–6 shows a simple PERT network diagram.

When the time interval activity to accomplish an event is uncertain, an estimate of the shortest time and the longest time expected is shown on the activity line by number, that is, 5, 8, where five weeks is the shortest time and eight weeks the longest time that may be required to complete an event.

In Figure 11–6, phases 1 and 2 were related to internal data gathering for the purchasing plan, and phase 3 involved external information seeking from three different sources. This technique allows the purchasing manager to anticipate problems far enough in advance so that there is an opportunity to do something about them.

PURCHASING BUDGETS

When the purchasing manager prepares a budget, he or she is performing one of the key managerial functions—that of *planning*. The budgeting

FIGURE 11–6   Simple PERT Network

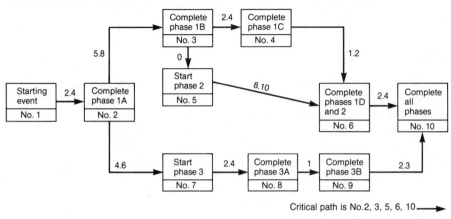

Critical path is No. 2, 3, 5, 6, 10 ——➤

process should start with a review of purchasing goals and objectives, followed by a forecast of action and resource needs to meet the goals, and then the development of a plan or budget. The development of purchase budgets fits in closely with purchasing research, for the manager must look into the future and then select that alternative (plan or budget) which will allow the goal(s) to be achieved most efficiently.

Four separate budgets should be developed:

Materials (Production) Purchase Budget

This budgeting process begins with an estimate of expected production, based on sales forecasts and plans. From the production schedule, which states the number of units to be completed in some coming time period, the plan for quantities to be purchased is developed. Purchasing then multiplies the purchase quantities times the anticipated purchase price to arrive at the total dollar budget for material purchases, subdivided by production time period. The purchase quantities, of course, are adjusted by planned changes in inventory levels. Much of the information on supply availability, which will impact inventory plans, and unit prices which will be paid, should come out of various purchase research studies in the commodity and vendor areas.

The primary advantage of going through this budget-planning process is that it isolates problems well in advance of their occurrence, for example, a total material cost that would result in a cost-of-goods-sold figure so high that profit would be reduced to an unacceptably low level, and gives purchasing an opportunity to explore and/or develop other alternatives. Typically the materials purchase budget has a planning horizon of one year or

less, except in the case of high-dollar, complex, long-production-cycle products, such as aircraft or nuclear power plants where a multiyear budget is
needed.

MRO BUDGET

This is a purchase plan, typically for a 12-month period, for all the
maintenance, repair, and operating supplies which will be needed and thus
purchased. Since the number of individual line items likely will be so large
that it is not feasible to budget for each item, this purchase plan normally
is arrived at by the use of past ratios, for example, MRO cost, adjusted by
anticipated changes in inventory and general price levels.

Capital Budget

The capital expenditure plan often has a several year horizon, based
on the firm's strategic plan for product lines, market shares, and new ven-
tures. Based on production needs, obsolescence of present equipment, equipment replacement needs, and expansion plans, decisions can be made on
projected capital purchases. In making the capital budget, such things as
vendor lead times (which may be quite long), cost of money, anticipated
price escalation, and the need for progress payments to equipment vendors
must be considered.

PURCHASING ADMINISTRATIVE BUDGET

This annual budget, based on anticipated operating workloads, should
be prepared for all of the expenses incurred in the operation of the purchasing
function. Such expenses include salaries and wages; space costs, including
heat and electricity; equipment costs for desks, office machines, files,
and typewriters; data processing costs, including computer usage or time-
sharing charges; travel and entertainment expense; educational expenditures for personnel who attend seminars and professional meetings; postage,
telephone, and telegraph charges; office supplies; subscription to trade publications; and additions to the purchasing library.

A good starting point is to review the actual operating expenditures for
the previous fiscal period. If a budget was in effect for the previous fiscal
period, a comparison between budget and actual expenditures may point up
problem areas. An attempt should be made to reconcile any substantial
differences. Expenditures should be compared with budget estimates on a
monthly basis. This procedure is one means of controlling operating expenses
and detecting problem areas promptly.

After reviewing the past department operating expense history, a
budget should be prepared for the next fiscal period. The new estimates
should include provision for salary increases and personnel additions or

deletions as anticipated by the requirements of the purchasing plan. New estimates of all other expenses required in the efficient operation of the department should be made in keeping with the requirements of the purchasing plan. The final budget should be coordinated with the total budget for the organization.

OPERATIONS REPORTS

The importance of good communications in achieving optimum results in the operations of a business is being given increasing attention by top management. As the tempo of business activity has quickened and companies have become larger, more diversified, and more decentralized in operations, information and its proper communication have become essential in the development of managerial controls.

Chapter 3 explored many of the information flows which directly affect the decision-making activities of purchasing personnel. These information flows can be broadly classified as originating from the interface relationships with other functional areas within the firm and contacts with the outside worldwide marketplace. When the materials plan and the budget are submitted to top company management executives for approval, they provide the basic reports about expected activity for the forecast period. The accuracy of the projected plans and strategies is checked when reports on the actual performance of the materials function are made.

Emphasis on what information should be reported will vary with the type of industry. Too many purchasing executives limit their reports to a tabulation of the figures showing:

1. Total dollar volume of purchases.
2. Total dollars spent for department operating expenses.
3. Total number of purchase orders issued.

In some instances these figures are related to each other by calculating average figures and percentages to show:

1. Average dollar cost of the purchase orders written as:

$$\frac{\text{Dollar cost of operating department}}{\text{Number of POs written}}$$

2. Operating costs as a percentage of total dollar volume of purchases.
3. Operating costs as a percentage of total dollar volume of sales.

Comparing the above figures and ratios with similar figures for previous time periods provides some perspective on what is happening in the purchasing function. However, these reports are of little use in providing a basis for evaluation of how effectively the purchasing function is providing the materials and equipment needed at the lowest net cost, considering quality, service, and the needs of the user. Note that the lowest price is not necessarily the lowest net cost.

Data processing equipment, properly programmed, is capable of providing information promptly and in a form that facilitates analysis of most purchasing activities.

What to report, the frequency of reporting, and how to report are decisions which require careful analysis. In some situations top management specifies the type of report, the frequency, and whether the report is to be written or presented orally. The personalities of major executives, the type of organization structure, and the nature of the industry have an influence on decisions affecting reporting procedures. Good reporting is important to the status and effective operation of the purchasing function because of the insights obtained from the analysis required in preparing reports, the information presented, and the opportunity to broaden management's understanding of the results to be obtained by effective purchasing.

In general, purchasing operating reports which are prepared on a regular basis, monthly, quarterly, semiannually, or annually, can be classified under the following headings and include:

1. *Market and economic conditions and price performance.*
   a. Price trends and changes for the major materials and commodities purchased. Comparisons with (1) standard costs where such accounting methods are used, (2) quoted market prices, and/or (3) target costs, as determined by cost analysis.[8]
   b. Changes in demand-supply conditions for the major items purchased. Effects of labor strikes or threatened strikes.
   c. Lead time expectations for major items.
2. *Inventory investment changes.*
   a. Dollar investment in inventories, classified by major commodity and materials groups.
   b. Days' or months' supply, and on order, for major commodity and materials groups.
   c. Ratio of inventory dollar investment to sales dollar volume.
   d. Rates of inventory turnover for major items.
3. *Purchasing operations and effectiveness.*
   a. Cost reductions resulting from purchase research and value analysis studies.

---

[8]One useful means of evaluating the reasonableness of prices actually paid is to compare actual price to an index of market prices. This can provide a good reading on whether the trend of purchasing's prices paid performance is better or worse than that being experienced by the overall market. A useful article on this approach is Patrick L. Hanafee, "Use of Price Indexes in MRO Buying," *Journal of Purchasing and Materials Management,* Spring 1981, pp. 2–9.

　　b. Quality rejection rates for major items.

　　c. Percentage of on-time deliveries.

　　d. Number of out-of-stock situations which caused interruption of scheduled production.

　　e. Number of change orders issued, classified by cause.

　　f. Number of requisitions received and processed.

　　g. Number of purchase orders issued.

　　h. Employee work load and productivity.

　　i. Transportation costs.

4. *Operations affecting administration and financial activities.*

　　a. Comparison of actual departmental operating costs to budget.

　　b. Cash discounts earned and cash discounts lost.

　　c. Commitments to purchase, classified by types of formal contracts and by purchase orders, aged by expected delivery dates.

　　d. Changes in cash discounts allowed by suppliers.

Special Project Reports

From time to time, there is a need to prepare special reports to bring to the attention of top management or to various functional managers matters which concern the interests of the firm. The alert purchasing executive who has an appreciation for the key position he or she occupies in the flow of information may have the opportunity to detect changes in trends of market practices or long-term supply situations. Purchasing departments having purchasing research staffs are in a good position to prepare such special reports.

Effective Report Presentation

Reports which are not read are a wasted effort. Reports consisting solely of a tabulation of figures often have little meaning to anyone except the compiler of the report.

A good starting point in preparing any report is for the writer to take the position of the person who is expected to read the report—what information is important in performing the job? Some of the fundamentals common to all reports are the need for clarity of presentation, simple and concise statements, and carefully checked information to ensure accuracy. A title should be used which clearly describes the nature of the report.

Most busy executives prefer to see a brief summary of the important information, and, if appropriate, conclusions at the beginning of the report. This procedure alerts the reader to what follows in the main body of the report. Recommendations, when appropriate, appear at the end of the report. Short statistical tabulations are usually included in the body of the report or may be shown graphically by pie charts, bar charts, or graphs. Most computer systems contain a computer graphics module which facilitates preparation of such visuals. Lengthy statistical tabulations should be provided in an appendix and identified and analyzed in the body of the report.

Provisions should be made in any system which issues regular reports to check from time to time to learn if the reports are useful to the recipients. All too frequently, reports continue to be issued because of habit rather than because they serve a useful purpose.

APPRAISING DEPARTMENT PERFORMANCE

Few organizations operate at full effectiveness. The company which is successful over time recognizes this fact of life and strives constantly to improve all aspects of its operation. In a highly competitive environment, only the efficient survive.

Why Is Appraisal Needed?

The benefits from a careful appraisal of purchasing department performance are many: (1) It focuses attention on the priority areas, making it more likely that objectives will be realized; (2) It provides data for taking corrective action, if needed, to improve performance; (3) By isolating problem areas, it should help to develop better relationships with other functional areas; (4) It spotlights training needs of personnel; (5) The possible need for additional resources, for example, personnel or computer support, is documented; (6) It provides the information to keep top management informed of purchasing progress; (7) Changes needed to improve the organization structure are recognized; (8) Those people performing at a better than normal level can be identified and rewarded, which should improve motivation in the organization.

An increasing number of managers have recognized that a properly organized purchasing function, staffed by competent employees, is capable of contributing significantly. Along with this recognition has come an awareness of the desirability of periodic appraisals of the performance of the function. Savings made flow directly to profit. In a free economy, profits are the lifeblood of business operation and a necessity for continued progress.

Problems in Appraising Efficiency

It is one thing to recognize the need for performance appraisal and quite a different situation to develop meaningful methods for measuring performance. For several years prior to 1950, various committees of the National Association of Purchasing Agents worked diligently to develop a uniform statistical method of evaluation which would apply generally to purchasing activities. It finally was concluded that no one method would fit all situations, and in 1947, after studying the problem for 15 years, a committee of the then National Association of Purchasing Agents (now NAPM) concluded that "It is impossible to establish an absolute yardstick for measuring the efficiency of all purchasing operations."[9] Later studies confirm this view.

During the 1950s, increasing attention was given to developing new methods for the evaluation of the purchasing function. Many large corporations developed methods which met their specific needs. The accounting profession also expressed its interest and published results of research projects.[10]

Continued interest in the subject of evaluation into the 1960s is evidenced by the publication of a comprehensive report by the American Management Association.[11] Over 200 companies cooperated in the study, and 75 percent indicated that some method of evaluation was used.

Research in organization theory and human behavior in organizations has produced greater understanding of how to organize for effective results. We have learned about the importance of clearly defining the purpose and the objectives or goals we expect a function and the employees in that function to achieve. A major problem in many organizations has been the lack of clearly defined objectives for the purchasing department and its personnel. Unless it can be determined what is to be evaluated, the question of how to make an evaluation has little meaning.

Purchasing Objectives

Much has been written in recent years about "management by objectives." Companies which have used the concept to improve operations have learned that it usually requires a substantial period of time, often several years, to develop the climate of managerial philosophy which is essential to full implementation.

The chief purchasing executive or materials manager has the basic responsibility for determining general objectives for the function and the coordination of such objectives with the strategic objectives of the company as a whole. Once the overall objectives or targets are outlined, they are provided to subordinates, not as a directive but as general guidelines for those who have decision-making authority, to use in establishing the objectives which will govern their activities for some period of time. When properly administered, the individual's objectives act as a motivating force to give direction to work and subsequently a basis for appraising performance. The more responsibility the individual exercises in establishing and

---

[9]As quoted in Paul Farrell, "Is There a Measure of Purchasing Productivity?" *Purchasing World,* February 1982, p. 49.

[10]*Purchasing* (New York: Arthur Andersen and Company, 1960). This publication was revised in 1975.

[11]F. Albert Hayes and George A. Renard, *Evaluating Purchasing Performance,* AMA Research Study 66 (New York: American Management Association, 1964).

implementing objectives, the greater the opportunity for the motivation of that employee and the individual's satisfaction which comes from a sense of accomplishment and achievement.

The establishment of objectives for a purchasing department is a procedure which is specific to a given organization at a particular period in time. The services of a competent purchasing research analyst or a purchasing research staff can be of great assistance in selecting objectives which will provide the greatest payback for the efforts expended.

Management by Objectives

Careful research and planning will provide a better understanding of the job which has to be done. The use of the "management by objectives" concept should provide a means to implement the planning process, motivate the personnel responsible for operating any plan developed, and provide a mechanism for appraising results. In the final analysis a good plan should help personnel to do a better job, but it is the attitude and ability of the people on the job which will obtain maximum results.

BUDGETS AND STANDARD COSTS

One of the key evaluation tools used in most organizations is the budgetary process. If the materials purchase, MRO, capital, and purchasing administrative budgets are carefully prepared, based on realistic assumptions about the future, they do provide a reasonable standard against which actual expenditures can be compared. If significant variances between budget (standard) and actual have occurred, in the absence of documented evidence that the assumptions on which the budget was based have changed, then a judgment can be made that performance was either superior or less than satisfactory, depending on whether the variance was positive or negative.

Standard costs also are used in many organizations to evaluate the purchasing department's pricing performance. Certainly the standard costs should be set based on anticipations of future overall market price movements; to do this with any degree of realism, purchasing must have a major input in setting such price/cost standards. If the standards are set solely by cost accounting, based almost completely on historical cost performance, then they lose much of their utility as a standard for judging performance. But if realistic standards, taking into account overall economic/market trends, are set, then they do provide a practical and useful type of standard for measuring purchasing's price effectiveness.

Procedures to Be Used in Evaluation

Two approaches can be taken in evaluating the performance of the purchasing function:

1. The continuing evaluation which compares the operating results with the plan, budget, and objectives established for the department and personnel.
2. The audit made by someone outside the department or the company.

While these two approaches are not mutually exclusive, in general practice in the company that has been progressive in its concepts of organization and has recognized the need to staff the purchasing department with highly competent people, there is less need to call on consultants from outside the company to participate in the evaluation process. Managements of organizations having well-established internal auditing departments obtain substantial help in evaluating various functional operations when internal auditors use a broader approach than just checking for integrity. Working cooperatively with the chief purchasing executive and staff, the auditors can help in making objective appraisals in areas such as:

1. Workload allocations.
2. Purchasing department relationships with other departments, and problem areas.
3. Relationships with vendors—vendors' attitudes toward the organization and toward the buyers.
4. Adherence to policies and procedures as detailed in policy statements and manuals.

Procedure to Be Used by an Outside Consultant

When an outside consultant is used for evaluation purposes, careful inquiry should be made to assure that the consultant has the specific expertise and breadth of experience needed for the job to be done. After a selection is made, a conference should be arranged between the consultant, the chief purchasing executive, and the executive to whom purchasing reports. A broad outline of the areas to be investigated should be agreed to by those attending the conference.

Contact with Top Management.   Clearly, for an outside consultant, the place to begin is with whoever represents top management, presumably the chief operating executive, president, or in some cases the general manager. The consultant probably will want to talk to the other top executives sooner or later, but this is not the starting point. Quite aside from assuring the complete cooperation of the president, there are various things to be learned at the outset:

1. What is the scope and responsibility of the department *as the president understands it?* This is important, because there are many instances in which confusion exists between the various levels of administration concerning just who is responsible for what. Often, too, it will be found that

the authority is not in fact exercised by those who are thought to be exercising it.

2. Who is responsible for determining purchasing policy concerning such important matters as inventory control and speculative buying? Are these policies set by the president or by some inner council of which the purchasing officer is not a member, or does the latter participate at all times?

3. Do purchasing officers hold their own on those occasions when called on to sit in the top councils, or, on the contrary, do they contribute little? Do they have a broad understanding of business problems, exercise responsible judgment when called on to do so, and command the respect of other top executives?

4. If the purchasing officer is not rated a top executive, on what occasion is advice called for, and is the advice worthwhile when given?

5. Is there more than one purchasing department in the organization, and, if there are several, what are their respective responsibilities?

6. Does the president keep in touch with purchasing policy and its administration and, if so, to what extent?

What is learned from the president (and other top executives) will give an indication of the attitude toward the importance of purchasing and of the degree to which there is confidence in the purchasing organization and personnel. In addition to this information, partly in the form of facts and partly in the form of impressions, there will be some very useful clues to be followed as the evaluation proceeds.

Interview with Head of Purchasing.   The second step would be a preliminary interview with the head of the purchasing department. There are several obvious reasons for such an interview, including the desirability of explaining why the consultant has been called in at all and making it clear that the whole attitude is one of cooperation and constructive assistance rather than seeking to find fault.

The main purpose of the interview, of course, is to make at least a tentative evaluation of the character and ability of the person who is presumably responsible for the policy, personnel, organization, and procedures of the department. What sort of a person is this? (1) Thoroughly familiar with, and a student of, materials and manufacturing processes and business problems and practices beyond those directly related to materials? (2) Managing the department singlehandedly, or delegating authority wherever possible? (3) Tactful, yet able to come to a decision with firmness? (4) Of a receptive mind and an ability to gather information wherever it may be found and to screen out the useful from the worthless? (5) Belonging to what professional associations? (6) Reading what magazines of a trade, general business, or broad cultural nature, either regularly or occasionally? (7) Giving the impression of being honest, fair, vigorous, and pleasant?

It is inevitable that, as a result of such conversations, certain definite impressions will be formed. Although the final result will be a matter of judgment in any case, there is need to be most careful in crystallizing impressions too early and without adequate information. Preliminary opinions must be treated *as preliminary*—to be checked and rechecked later on. The importance of all this cannot be overestimated, for, with the possible exception of the size-up of the president of the company, the qualifications of the head of the department constitute the most important single element in the whole analysis.

Remaining Steps in Evaluation.   From this point on, the exact order of the evaluation is not important. What the next step will be should depend on what is learned at the previous step. The significant thing is that a wide range of points should be checked, and not the order in which this is done. Sooner or later, judgments must be formed on several points.

Points for Judgment in Appraisal

Have Appropriate Objectives Been Established?   Is a well thought out statement of objectives and goals available for use in directing the efforts of the personnel in the purchasing department? Since a comprehensive listing of objectives to be achieved, in priority order, is the starting point for effective and efficient performance and is crucial in effective management, this should be the place to begin. Are these goals consistent with the overall goals of the organization? Has a goal been established for each of the major areas that impact overall purchasing performance? Are they stated in measurable terms? Do they cover both the short and long term? Are they well known and understood by purchasing personnel? Were inputs from all levels within the purchasing organization sought in the establishment of goals? Are they reviewed and updated periodically?

Is the Organization of the Department Based on Sound Principles?   Is the organization as it appears on paper the real, working organization? Are the lines of responsibility drawn with reasonable appreciation for the nature of the tasks and of the personnel available? Much of the required data on these points will be gained from the president or from the head of the department. But the information as to how well the organization works and whether it actually functions in the way that either the president or the head of the department *thinks* it does will be disclosed only by further study at the lower echelons within the department. One of the key evaluation points is how purchasing people really spend their time—is it in managing the function, or is there too much expediting and paper shuffling?

Is purchasing policy reasonably well defined? Are there purchasing policies that are accepted by the president, as well as by other top executives, such as the sales, production, and engineering managers, and that actually are followed? Policies are often extremely hard to define, frequently still harder to follow, and bound to change from time to time. None of these facts provides an excuse for the department's not having established policies.

The statement of policy should be written and widely distributed, not only among the members of the department itself but throughout the entire company and even among the suppliers. All of these groups should actually have a permanent copy of the statement in their possession. They not only should know and understand it but also should have immediate access to it for reference purposes. In no other way can the best results of full cooperation be expected. Furthermore, such general familiarity with the policies makes close integration with the policies of other departments more probable and necessary modifications easier to effect. The mere writing of such statements helps to define policy in the minds of those responsible for carrying it out and keeps them "on their toes" in the observance thereof. Moreover, to reduce a company's policies and procedures to writing is one of the best means of ensuring that the department head has carefully, critically, and constructively thought out the objectives, policies, and administrative problems confronting the organization. A listing of subjects appropriate for coverage by purchasing policy is contained in Chapter 3.

Are the Procedures Reasonable?   There are two good reasons for checking the procedures in some detail. One reason is to be able to judge their adequacy. The other is that there is *no surer way of locating clues to departmental problems* than going over the procedures with the greatest of care. There, if anywhere, general weaknesses will be disclosed.

The number of small orders and the volume of rush orders, for instance, are revealing types of information. An analysis of the purchase orders and a comparison of them with the corresponding requisitions will indicate both the completeness of the latter and the independence exercised in placing the former. It will be revealing, too, to learn something of the extent of carload orders as against less-than-carload orders, of the distribution of suppliers as between local suppliers and those from out-of-town, of the degree of reliance on supply houses as against manufacturers, and the total number of suppliers used. Are blanket orders used, and is there a system of controlling releases against them? Is there a separation of the purchasing, receiving, and accounts payable steps? The very forms themselves are clues to the familiarity of the personnel with the "tools of the trade." So, too, is the filing system: how promptly can documents be located and inquiries, both those originating within and those originating from outside the department, be answered? What system of document control is used? What records—vendor, purchase order, contract, quotation, price, or other—are kept? To what extent are the records that are kept used?

Procedures and forms are, as a rule, very dull things; to most people they are, indeed, very elementary and routine. But for an evaluator of efficiency there is no greater source of leads than a study of procedures. Here, too, it would be well to find out whether the department has a formal written description or manual of procedure. The preparation of a manual leads to exactness in thinking, to certainty of responsibility, and to smoothness of operation, although, of course, it can also have undesirable effects if it becomes too much of a "bible" and serves to cut down flexibility and initiative.

Is the Physical Layout of the Department Well Planned?   Is office space planned for the efficient performance of the work? Are there adequate reception room facilities to handle the salespeople and other callers? Do buyers have facilities where they can talk with salespeople without unnecessary interruptions? Proper office working facilities are not only important in building employee morale but also in obtaining the best possible attitude from the outsiders calling on the buyers and others in the department.

What Is the Record of the Department with Respect to Prices Paid and Delivery?   By a reasonable amount of the right kind of spot-checking, it is quite possible to determine whether the prices paid have been consistently at, below, or above the market. Particular attention should be devoted to the purchases of materials that are most important dollarwise. Are requirements combined to get purchasing clout? What has been the department's performance in getting deliveries on time? Has material arrived by the dates requested by the stores and production departments, or at least by the dates promised by the buyers to those departments? Have the buyers secured promised shipping dates from suppliers, and have the materials gone forward on those dates? Both of these—prices paid and deliveries—are obviously important points to check, and a reasonable effort should be made to learn whether or not all is being done that could be expected.

How Is Inventory Controlled?   Insofar as the department is responsible for inventory control, the following points must be looked into with great care: What evidences are there of dead stock? Have operating departments been handicapped by lack of material through the purchasing department's fault? Are there adequate controls on forward purchases? Are inventory and purchasing policies closely integrated administratively? An examination into these possibilities involves a study of the inventory policy itself, including the standards that are set, the devices for controlling the inventory, and the soundness of the judgment of those responsible.

What Is the Attitude of Other Departments?   Another checkpoint of great importance relates to the attitude of the other departments of the company toward the purchasing department and their feeling concerning its efficiency. Does the department have a reputation for being capable, alert to its opportunities, and helpful? Evidence on this score is one of the things which is often better obtained by an outside consultant than by an insider.

Attitude of Suppliers.   Related to this factor is the evidence of supplier goodwill. This, like intracompany goodwill, should be a factor of real concern. The fact that these attributes are difficult to measure statistically is not important. Fortunately, considering its significance, it can be gauged by an intelligent person who is sensitive to the reactions of others.

By following checkpoints of the type outlined in the foregoing, by gaining clues from cost and other statistical data, and by the proper use of reports, an appraisal of the efficiency of a department can be made.

Quite obviously the department administrator also must continually appraise his or her own work as well as that of the organization. True, judgments on these matters may not coincide with those of the executive head of the company, and they may not be wholly unbiased. Yet, provided that the administrator is competent, much can be accomplished. If too busy with other matters (though evaluation is part of good administration), handicapped by inertia, deficient in the ability to judge these things, or lacking in knowledge of good management, then a new administrator is needed.

There is much to be said, at the same time, in favor of an occasional outside check on the department. The much abused internal auditor and the outside consultant can bring a point of view which is very difficult for one who is continually "on the job" to get, and this is of value both to top management and to the department head. The latter gains because the independent critic can judge even better the degree of cooperation and the confidence in the department expressed by other departments of the business. Inefficient methods, otherwise easily overlooked, are spotted. The psychological effect of knowing an examination is to be made is excellent. The fact that the personnel in the department are forced to review and justify what they do helps considerably. At the same time, constructive and helpful suggestions should be forthcoming from the examiner and full credit should be given for what is commendable. And the consultant or internal auditor frequently makes it possible for the department head to secure the approval of the management group for desired changes, simply because recommendations have the support of a representative of the management from "outside."

The performance of any department might be improved by such analysis. Yet management probably has the most to gain from the independent appraisal of a department like purchasing, whose efficiency is inherently difficult to evaluate and whose real function is not always well understood. Any assistance that management can get which will enable it to specify the contributions it has a right to expect from such a department, to segregate the particular function from the other major activities of the business, and to evaluate more adequately the company policies in that area should profoundly better the individual company concerned and, by and large, the complete structure of the economy as a whole.

Review of Personnel Policy

One of the keys to the success of any organization is the people who make it up and are responsible for making it "go." Investigation of the personnel program should start with an analysis of the work to be done, including the size of the total workload and the way in which various tasks with similar characteristics can be combined. From this analysis it should be possible to make estimates of how many people are required and the educational and experience qualifications such people should have. A comparison of these findings with the actual members of the department and their job assignments should provide a basis on which to begin an evaluation of personnel policy.

Selection of Personnel.   The next query is whether the people on the various jobs are personally qualified for the work they are doing. This, in turn, calls for several other lines of inquiry. One concerns the *manner of selection*. Is there a fairly definite understanding of the qualifications? What are the personal characteristics wanted? What academic training is expected? What experience background is called for? From what sources are new personnel recruited? The answers to each of these and similar questions will, of course, vary with the particular circumstances. Thus, if a potential buyer is being sought, most managers will look for a person with analytical ability and good judgment, honesty, and of course, pleasing personality. Most likely the person will be a college graduate who has specialized, preferably, in business. Specialized coursework in purchasing or a major field of study in purchasing and materials management would be the ideal background.

Personnel Planning.   All too often personnel within a purchasing department are not reasonably distributed among the various age groups. As a result all the buyers are older persons who will retire at about the same time with no trained personnel coming along behind them. The well-managed organization is aware of such problems and to correct or avoid them has developed a specific personnel plan, indicating lines of succession and training/professional development needs of existing personnel.

In-House Training.   Another significant check point in the personnel program is the *training after employment*. Newcomers to the department have much to learn about purchasing, particularly since purchasing calls for specialized training. Under such circumstances, the new person is likely to have a good deal of difficulty in learning a new job in any office where no particular help is given, but instead information must be picked up by trial and error or from office mates, all of whom are busy with their own work. This means that the head of the department should actively encourage and take a continuing interest in the training of new employees. Professional development can be provided through an in-house training program or through the evening classes or short seminars conducted by many colleges and universities and the various professional purchasing associations. There are very few people nowadays who do not have ready geographical access to such professional development opportunities.

Is there an on-the-job training program? Many purchasing departments lack one. This is a most serious omission. Such a program may be built around the policy and procedure manuals. Study of the principal items purchased should be undertaken, perhaps with the aid of motion pictures. Likewise, study of the products and processes of the particular company will fill in gaps. Reading assignments, films, regular written reports, group discussions, and even occasional outside lectures will all serve, in proper proportions, to keep up interest and provide learning opportunities.

Senior members of the department also should be encouraged to remember that one's education is never completed, and that experience is by no means always the best teacher.

Compensation Plan.   A personnel program must cover more than selection and training. What is the *compensation plan?* Are people adequately paid? Is there a definite system for advancement, and, specifically, what are the young person's chances for advancement in rank and responsibility? Does the department have enough people to do the work properly and still keep everyone reasonably busy? What is the general morale of the personnel, including the attitude of each toward the others, toward the head of the department, and, of course, toward the company itself?

Extent and Areas of Current Performance Measurement

A recent study was conducted among 18 U.S. organizations to determine how these firms actually attempted to measure purchasing performance. The size of the purchasing organizations ranged from 10 to 650 people, and annual dollar purchases ranged from $35 million to $4 billion. This study concluded, among other things, that (1) each organization should pick those measures that best fit its operating situation, (2) several measures, rather than just one, are needed to provide a valid indicator of overall accomplishment, (3) a good data base is needed for measurement, and (4) since measurement is very costly, management should be very selective in deciding what and how much measurement should be attempted.

This study found that the following 13 categories were used by these organizations for purchasing performance measurement (the first seven measures appeared to be the key ones):

Price Effectiveness.   This is the actual price paid versus the planned purchase price or quoted market price. In multidepartment buying organizations, price differentials may be found between buying groups or locations.

Cost Savings.   This refers to the cost reduction (present price paid compared to previous price) and/or cost avoidance (if, for example, price paid is lower than the initial pricing that was obtained).

Administration and Control.   Actual expenditures are compared to budget. Time standards are used for work performance. It is used for planning and evaluation of work-force needs and management of the department.

Inventory Efficiency.   If part of purchasing department responsibility, measures include stock turnover by commodity group, dollars invested, and consigned inventory dollars.

Material Flow Control.   This refers to whether there was a smooth flow of materials from vendors. Some of the measures are open purchase orders, open orders past due, and performance in meeting delivery due dates.

Vendor Quality and Delivery.   How vendors perform, measured by on-time delivery percentages and material rejection rates, fits in this category.

Workload.   This category includes workload in (new work coming into the department), workload current (backlog in the department), and workload completed. Some of the factors measured are purchase requisitions received, pricing requests received, requisitions waiting action, purchase orders placed, and contracts written.

Efficiency.   Related outputs, such as number of line items placed on purchase orders, is compared with inputs, such as buyer time expended. Among the more common input measures are purchase orders per buyer, line items per buyer, dollars committed per buyer, and contracts written per buyer.

Regulatory/Societal/Environmental.   This category determines whether certain social goals, such as dollars placed with small business or minority-owned businesses, or percentage of dollar purchases made in labor-surplus areas, were met.

Procurement Planning and Research.   The techniques of purchase research and planning are measured to determine what was achieved in greater efficiency and effectiveness.

Competition.   Information is provided on the extent to which the purchasing organization attempts to develop competition among suppliers, and the effect of that effort on purchase prices. Measures include the percentage of purchase dollars placed through bidding, the number of second sources developed, and the amount of sole source purchases.

Transportation.   This category measures the effectiveness in maintaining shipment service levels at minimum costs. Some of the items looked at are cost of premium transportation, carrier delivery performance, in-transit shipment damage, and collection of damage claims.

Purchasing Procedure Audits.   This category measures progress made in the completion of purchase contracts and the extent to which established purchasing policies and procedures are being followed.[12]

A 1981 survey by *Purchasing* magazine of 1,000 industry executives who oversee the purchasing function, that is, the individual to whom purchasing directly reports, compared the evaluation criteria used in 1981 with those found in a similar survey in 1977. These surveys found that the evaluation criteria judged most important also focused primarily on cost/price and supplier quality/delivery performance. The 1981 survey found that, compared to 1977, more emphasis was being placed on total cost reduction, and management increasingly recognized that purchasing's role must include negotiation as well as supplier selection. Table 11–2 presents the top evaluation criteria used in both 1977 and 1981.[13]

A similar update survey was done by *Purchasing* magazine in 1984, again using "1,000 of your colleagues" to determine how purchasing managers rate the various indicators for measuring purchasing performance. The top-rated factors in order were:

1. Cost reduction or avoidance

2. Suppliers' quality performance

3. Supply availability (few stock-outs)

4. Suppliers' delivery performance

5. Product improvement

---

[12]Robert M. Monczka, Phillip L. Carter, and John H. Hoagland, *Purchasing Performance: Measurement and Control* (East Lansing, Mich.: Division of Research, Graduate School of Business Administration, Michigan State University, 1979), pp. 283–91. This study was sponsored by the National Science Foundation.

[13]"Management Adopts New Yardstick to Rate Buying," *Purchasing*, June 11, 1981, p. 14.

TABLE 11–2 Managements' Ranking of Top Criteria for Evaluating
Purchasing Performance

Rank	1981	1977
1	Cost reduction/avoidance	Suppliers' delivery performance
2	Suppliers' quality performance	Cost reduction/avoidance
3	Suppliers' delivery performance	Cost to spend a dollar
4	Negotiation results against target prices	Product improvement
5	Supply availability (few stockouts)	Accuracy in price forecasts

6. Negotiation against target prices[14]

The ratings in 1981 and 1984 were very similar, with cost reduction/ avoidance and quality the highest and next-to-highest ranked in both years. Delivery was third in 1981, but it dropped to fourth in 1984. Obviously price paid, quality received, and delivery performance are key to the evaluation of purchasing performance.

While there have been several studies of purchasing performance measurement in the last few years,[15] and it remains a high-interest topic in the minds of both purchasing professionals and academics, development of a universal performance standard remains as elusive as it was in the 1940s and 1950s when people began looking at the problem in depth.

A somewhat different approach grew out of a 1986 study based on interviews with CEOs and department heads in more than 50 firms and surveys of their counterparts in nearly 200 other companies.

It found that the traditional, formal reporting systems, which are based on hard data, do not always "do the job" in really telling the story of what purchasing has accomplished and in changing the perceptions that nonpurchasing managers have of purchasing. Instead, it found that five factors were key in shaping the perceptions which nonpurchasing managers have of purchasing. These were the major components of purchasing's image:

1. Output of purchasing: The tangible experiences personnel have with the routine and special services provided by purchasing.

---

[14]Somerby Dowst, "Updating the Numbers on Performance Measurement," *Purchasing,* August 1, 1984, p. 50.

[15]Alan R. Raedels, "Measuring the Productivity of Materials Management," *Journal of Purchasing and Materials Management,* Summer 1983, pp. 12–18; Arjan J. van Weele, "Purchasing Performance Measurement and Evaluation," *Journal of Purchasing and Materials Management,* Fall 1984, pp. 16–22.; and Fred P. Adams and Robert E. Niebuhr, "Improving Individual Productivity in Purchasing," *Journal of Purchasing and Materials Management,* Winter 1985, pp. 2–7.

2. Interactions with purchasing: This people-oriented dimension includes roles and role conflicts, personalities, and impressions.

3. Observations of purchasing: Auditors' findings and perceptions of purchasing's ethical behavior.

4. Reputation of purchasing: The esteem in which a department is held by others, based on both objective and subjective perceptions.

5. Expectations of purchasing: These are based on what nonpurchasing managers perceive purchasing to be doing in the areas of contributing to the missions of the firm, contributing to the budget process, and the development of purchasing skills which will support the activities of others in the organization.[16]

This study serves to again indicate both the importance and complexity of the purchasing measurement and communication activity in giving purchasing the stature needed to effectively contribute to the overall goals of the organization.

QUESTIONS FOR REVIEW AND DISCUSSION

1. How does value analysis differ from value engineering? What are the steps in performing value analysis on a purchased item?

2. What are the various subject areas of purchasing research? Which area do you think would be most productive in (a) the short run, and (b) the long run?

3. In what ways might a firm organize to do purchasing research? What are the advantages and disadvantages of each? Which would you recommend in a (a) small organization, (b) medium-size organization, and (c) a large organization?

4. On which basis would an organization decide where to direct its purchasing research efforts?

5. What questions would be asked in making a commodity study; where would you obtain the information?

6. What is the difference between a purchasing plan and a purchasing budget? In which areas should a purchasing budget be prepared? How would these budgets be established?

7. Why isn't there a standard system for evaluating purchasing performance that could be used by all types of firms and not-for-profit organizations? How difficult would it be to develop such a standard system?

8. What kinds of information on purchasing performance should be main-

---

[16]Joseph L. Cavinato, "Purchasing Performance: What Makes the Magic?" *Journal of Purchasing and Materials Management,* Fall 1987, pp. 10–16.

tained in the purchasing department? How can this information be used?

9. What are the key measures of purchasing performance? What will the purchasing manager learn from each?

10. When should purchasing performance be evaluated by an outside evaluator? How would that person go about making the evaluation?

11. Are standard costs and budgets useful in the appraisal process? Under what conditions?

12. How can management by objectives (MBO) fit into the management of the purchasing and materials management functions?

REFERENCES

Adams, Fred P., and Robert E. Niebuhr. "Improving Individual Productivity in Purchasing." *Journal of Purchasing and Materials Management,* Winter 1985.

Browning, J. M.; N. B. Zabriskie; and A. B. Huellmantel. "Strategic Purchasing Planning." *Journal of Purchasing and Materials Management,* Spring 1983.

Carusone, Peter S. "Buying Extractive Products: Criteria and Influences." *Journal of Purchasing and Materials Management,* Winter 1985.

Cavinato, Joseph L. "Purchasing Performance: What Makes the Magic?" *Journal of Purchasing and Materials Management,* Fall 1987.

Dowst, Somerby. "VA '86: Buyers Say VA is More Important Than Ever." *Purchasing,* June 26, 1986.

Farrell, Paul V., coordinating ed. *Aljian's Purchasing Handbook.* 4th ed. New York: McGraw-Hill, 1982, Sections 25 and 27.

Fearon, Harold. *Purchasing Research: Concepts and Current Practice.* New York: AMACOM, 1976.

Hanafee, Patrick L. "Use of Price Indexes in MRO Buying." *Journal of Purchasing and Materials Management,* Summer 1983.

Miles, L. D. *Techniques of Value Analysis and Engineering.* 2nd ed. New York: McGraw-Hill, 1972.

Monczka, Robert M.; Phillip L. Carter; and John H. Hoagland. *Purchasing Performance: Measurement and Control.* East Lansing, Mich.: Division of Research, Graduate School of Business Administration, Michigan State University, 1979.

Raedels, Alan R. "Measuring the Productivity of Materials Management." *Journal of Purchasing and Materials Management,* Summer 1983.

van Weele, Arjan J. "Purchasing Performance Measurement and Evaluation." *Journal of Purchasing and Materials Management,* Fall 1984.

Case 11–1

Arden Foods, Inc.

Bill Jones, purchase analyst in the corporate purchasing office at Arden Foods, was in the process of reviewing corrugated cartons purchases. He had gathered statistics on purchases from each plant and it was apparent that one supplier, Sartex, Inc., had managed to increase its share of total carton business dramatically over the past 20 years.

Company Background

Primarily a meat packer and producer of quality foods, Arden Foods operated 13 major plants across the country, each of which was a profit center and autonomous within general corporate policy. Each plant had its own production, sales, and administrative staff and did almost all of its own purchasing. Total sales last year were close to $2.5 billion.

Corporate Purchasing

The corporate purchasing staff had traditionally been very small at Arden Foods, consisting of a manager, a buyer, and two secretaries. This staff was largely occupied with statistical work and did some contract purchasing, only of branded items common to all plants. The corporate manager of purchasing reported to the vice president of finance. When the former manager retired a year ago, the new manager who took over believed a more aggressive stance for corporate purchasing was appropriate. One of his first moves was to visit all plant purchasing offices and this was followed by the first common meeting of all plant purchasing agents for a duration of two days. The plant purchasing agents pointed out that the statistics traditionally kept at head office were primarily of interest to the finance people, but were not particularly useful to them. As a result, Bill Jones, a recent college graduate who had specialized in purchasing and materials management, was "borrowed" by corporate purchasing from the largest plant's purchasing office. His job was to see if he could not only help develop more meaningful statistics, but also to investigate if corporate purchasing could provide better services to the plant locations.

Corrugated Carton Purchases

Bill Jones believed, and his manager agreed, that corrugated cartons represented a good sample area for him to start working on. Every plant purchased them and last year's total volume of purchases had been about $8.5 million.

From the statistics and in talking with buyers and purchasing agents, Bill Jones found out that historically a large share of the carton business had always gone to Sartex, Inc. Sartex was a large, well-known packaging producer with plants from coast to coast. There was no obligation on the part of any plant purchasing agent to favor Sartex. Actually, most plants had at least two suppliers and in some cases three or four. It was simply that over the years Sartex had demonstrated they were tops in service, quality, and competitiveness.

The purchasing agent in Arden's largest plant who had hired Bill originally, explained the situation this way:

> As the Sartex share of Arden business grew, a special relationship between us developed. Increases in the cost of liner board, wages, or other expenses were not automatically passed on, but justifiable increases were negotiated between us on an annual basis. There is a very good reason why Sartex has so much of my business. They deserve it!

In the last four years Sartex's share had increased 5 percent each year and was about 80 percent of the total current corrugated business available from all Arden plants. Bill Jones forecast that if this trend continued, Sartex might become a single source.

Bill Jones knew that each plant purchasing agent believed strongly in having full control over his corrugated purchases. As one explained:

> Corrugated is one product we have to have flexibility in and we must be able to deal directly with the local Sartex plant producing it. It is short notice business and sometimes they have to turn cartwheels to accommodate the last minute changes so common in our product line. Moreover, every plant has its own special products and requirements. The fact that all large corrugated producers are themselves decentralized with plants all over the country reinforces the need to be able to do corrugated business locally.

When Bill Jones had started this assignment, he had hoped that something obvious would present itself, allowing him to make some useful suggestions for improvements. Now it appeared that all plant purchasing agents were quite satisfied with the status quo, and that Arden Foods was lucky to have such a good source in Sartex. He, therefore, wondered how this information could be useful to corporate purchasing in the plants. Was there an opportunity here for Arden Foods, or was his first assignment a bust and should he turn to something else?

Case 11–2

Maral Pharmaceuticals

Hal Winger, packaging buyer for Maral Pharmaceuticals, was working on an import substitution project involving a local minority supplier. He was concerned, however, that his efforts would be fruitless since his original proposal had been flatly rejected by the plant manager as too expensive.

Maral Pharmaceuticals, a medium-size company, had over the years specialized in prescription skin care products, a market niche in which it had developed an excellent reputation. About three years ago, Maral had, after extensive testing, introduced a new facial cream in a special package which allowed for precise measurement of the quantity dispersed. The container, manufactured by a French firm for a different application, was fairly expensive at an FOB Maral's factory cost of

$0.27. What concerned Hal Winger even more, however, were the quality and delivery problems encountered. Communications with the manufacturer were difficult and Hal had the impression the manufacturer did not seem to care much about Maral's business, which, as Hal knew, was only a small proportion of the total volume produced.

With the cooperation of Maral's marketing, engineering, production, and quality control personnel, Hal had found a local minority supplier who appeared capable of meeting Maral's requirements. This custom molding firm, Precision Molding, Inc., (PMI) was owned by Al Jones, a bright engineer, who had purchased the firm several years earlier when the previous owner wished to retire. Precision Molding, Inc., had its own tool and die manufacturing operation as well as its own molding shop. It depended heavily on automotive contracts, a situation Al Jones wished to correct by acquiring more nonautomotive business. In conjunction with Maral's engineers, Al Jones had worked out a mold design for the cream dispenser and included several suggestions for minor improvements. The cost of the mold was $42,000, an investment Al Jones was in no position to make and which Maral would have to absorb up front. Al Jones quoted a unit price of $0.20 based on purchase quantities of 30,000 units at a time and an annual volume estimated at 300,000 units. Al Jones had submitted a cost breakdown of this quote as follows:

Resin	12¢
Labor	2
Overhead*	6
	20¢
*Overhead breakdown:	
Power	1¢
Depreciation	1
Interest	2
Space, Insurance, Light and Heat, Taxes, Supervision	2

When Hal submitted this quote along with the request for a $42,000 mold investment up front, the plant manager and treasurer both turned it down, arguing the 24-month payback on the mold was far too long and that the company had better investment opportunities with a 12-month payback.

Hal was disappointed, because he had hoped this project would assist in helping him meet his savings target for the year. When he talked the idea over with his manager, Doris Steenman, she suggested he give it another try. She said: "I am sure that if you can get the mold payback down to 15 months, you will get a warmer reception. There are not that many deals around this company that pay for themselves in one year." She also suggested Hal talk to marketing to see if some other products could use the same packaging and to the production scheduling group to check if different production quantities could be ordered.

When Hal talked to the marketing people, he found out that the package was ideal for another product to be introduced shortly and with an annual demand estimated at 100,000 units. Marketing had been uneasy about using the French package because of the difficulties encountered with it, and assured Hal that if he could get a reliable domestic source, this option would be highly attractive.

The scheduling group had for a number of years used a modified MRP system. When Hal discussed the new package idea with them, they told him that if the new product and the older one were to be packaged in the same package, a total package requirement of about 40,000 units would make sense and that the master production schedule could easily be adjusted to run the two products in conjunction.

Hal also discussed the situation with the resin supplier who indicated that his quote to Al Jones had been based on the lot size of 30,000 packages, but that a 40,000 unit lot would fall into a new price bracket 5 percent lower than the originally quoted price.

Hal wondered just what effect all of this new information would have on his original proposal. He knew that Al Jones had been adamant about his $0.20 quote. Al Jones had said: "I know I am classified as a minority supplier. But I don't want to hide behind that fact. I want no special favors from any of my customers. Nor am I in a position to make special gifts to anyone else. I have had to borrow at what I considered to be ridiculously high interest rates to buy this company. Now I have to make it pay off. My $0.20 price is as low as I can go, as far as I can see."

Case 11–3

MEC Corporation

In early March, Jack Allison, assistant manager of the purchasing and traffic department, was made responsible for administering the purchasing savings program for the following year by Robert Cochrane, the department manager, who was due to retire in the near future. The savings program had been in effect for a number of years without change, and Jack Allison wondered if the previous year's savings of some $300,000 on an eligible outlay of $24 million could not be considerably improved. Therefore, he instituted a review of methods, procedures, and attitudes to determine what course to adopt for the coming year.

MEC Corporation was part of a large conglomerate which had been formed in 1966. MEC produced a wide range of electrical products for the measurement and control of industrial processes. MEC had started in 1926 and had been privately owned until 1966. It had an excellent reputation for quality in the trade. MEC operated with a high degree of autonomy. The conglomerate's corporate headquarters was primarily concerned with financial planning. MEC's sales totaled about $60 million last year and were expected to reach $100 million within the next five years. MEC was divided into two sales divisions—industrial and utilities. Each accounted for about half of total sales.

Purchasing at MEC

Total purchases at MEC were about 40 percent of sales and were the responsibility of Robert Cochrane, director of purchases, who had been in his post for 22 years. He planned to retire next year and had recently brought in Jack Allison, an

EXHIBIT 1

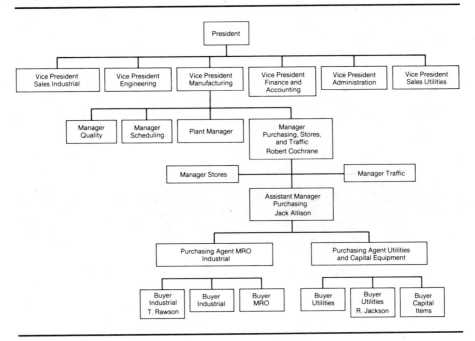

engineer, who had previously worked in quality control and design at MEC. There were two purchasing agents and six buyers. For production purchases the department was organized into the same divisions as corporate sales: industrial and utilities (see Exhibit 1 for organization chart). Production purchases included raw materials, such as copper, steel, aluminum, and purchased parts such as castings, stampings, and a wide variety of electrical and electronic items.

In April of last year, the vice president of manufacturing took over responsibility for purchasing from the vice president of administration who claimed that personnel and industrial relations matters prevented him from giving the purchasing function the necessary time.

Robert Cochrane told his assistant that when he responded to the vice president of administration his reports of total savings realized used to elicit little interest.

"I think they do some cash flow projections up top," said the department manager casually, "but I guess our small savings are not that important. At any rate, they've never asked for savings forecasts. However, I think that the vice president of manufacturing will show more practical enthusiasm."

Savings in Purchasing

Jack Allison had been given complete freedom to become acquainted with all facets of the purchasing operation. Robert Cochrane had thought it useful to give a few specific projects to Jack to work on during his familiarization phase, and the savings program was one area he asked Jack to take a good look at. Jack Allison

EXHIBIT 2   Rules for Reporting Purchasing Savings

1. The material must have been purchased before.
2. Savings apply to orders placed within the calendar year under consideration.
3. Savings due to mixed contribution by purchasing and the personnel of other departments may not be claimed by the buying staff.
4. Savings are: *a.* The improvement over the old unit price multiplied by the projected annual usage at the time the first new order is placed, less tooling investment, if any.

   b. On indirect material where no forecast is available, utilize the one-time saving and any reorders in the same calendar year.
5. Savings may not be carried beyond one year. If a one-time, several-year commitment is made, credit may be claimed for the first year's estimated consumption.
6. Savings reports for the current calendar year must be submitted to me prior to January 31 of the next year.*

R. Cochrane,
Manager, Purchasing, Stores,
and Traffic

*MEC Corporation's financial year-end was at the end of February.

---

went through the files to study past savings reports and talked to the buyers and purchasing agents about savings.

Rules for Reporting Purchasing Savings

Robert Cochrane had 10 years previously established rules about how savings should be calculated (see Exhibit 2). Jack Allison found that while nearly all of the senior personnel had seen the rules some of the juniors had not, and Jack experienced some trouble in digging them out. One of the older men expressed some discontent at not being able to claim savings for more than one year ("They're still real enough after 12 months," he growled), but few held any strong opinions on them. One man said cynically that he doubted whether such reports were even read. "Has management heard of purchasing?" he inquired innocently. One of the purchasing agents thought that avoidance of cost increases through negotiation should also be included.

Savings Report Forms

Jack Allison studied the slender file of forms from previous years and discussed one of the cases (see Exhibit 3) with Mr. Cochrane. He mentioned that there were no supporting documents attached and wondered to what extent the claims were checked.

"Oh, the divisional buyers have a pretty good idea of what's what," said the manager, "so I never required them to clutter up their claims with a lot of docu-

EXHIBIT 3   Buyer's Savings Report

Division ___SERVO___   Date: ___August 21___

1. M.E.C. part number: ___15723_____

2. Description: ___9V Nickel Battery Enclosure_____

3. Yearly usage: ___240,000_____

4. Purchase order no. (if applicable) ___S54754-1010_____

5. Savings Accomplished:
   Previous price: ___$1.872_____
   New unit price: ___$1.44_____
   Savings per unit: ___$0.432_____
   Savings this order: ___$103,680_____
   Savings per year: ___$103,680_____

6. How Was Saving Accomplished?
   Through the efforts of Ralph Jackson and myself placing orders
   simultaneously to earn the next price break and going a little long
   (with Division's agreement) on inventory.

7. Comments: ___It is my opinion that without interdivisional exchange of___
   buying intelligence on common commodities this saving would not have
   come about.

                                   Submitted by: ___T. Rawson_____

                                   Approved: ___R. Cochrane_____

                                   Date: ___August 21_____

mentation. However, as you know, all savings must be due to their efforts only. It's purchasing skills I'm demonstrating."

Jack Allison discussed the same savings report with T. Rawson, the buyer who had submitted it. "Would we work closely with production scheduling in such instances?" he asked. "For example, where did the consumption forecast come from?"

Rawson assured him that previous orders gave him a good idea of standard usage as it was a repetitive item, and that was how they usually derived their annual consumption for calculating claims. Of course, scheduling had cleared the requisition, but he never encouraged the operations people to pry into what he considered was purchasing's business. "It's just as well not to get these production guys involved in our commercial dealings with suppliers," he said seriously, "or before you know it you have back-door selling on your hands."

Motivation

Jack Allison found that the savings program played a relatively small part in the buyer's plans. It was something to be reported when the situation arose. Furthermore, he noted that higher in the buying echelon interest was desultory, as large orders were automatically handled by the seniors. Even Mr. Cochrane used to take a hand in the negotiation of equipment until the last year or so. The seniors skimmed the cream off. Relatively little attention was given to value analysis techniques.

Organization

Some cases of the two divisions buying the same material or components at different times without one buyer being conscious of the other's efforts had come to light. Separate savings reports dealing with the same commodity brought this to Jack Allison's attention.

Jack Allison had noted the buyers' reluctance to talk about their savings expertise outside of the department and wondered how necessary this secrecy was. It made him recall his own ignorance of what purchasing was doing when he was a member of the design or quality groups at MEC. He also wondered what action, if any, he should take now that the savings program had become his responsibility.

CHAPTER 12

Foreign Purchasing

Only recently have industrial buyers been willing to seek suppliers outside North America for reasons other than a domestic shortage. However, since the end of World War II, many different events and forces have set in motion developments aimed at relaxing the barriers to, and expanding, world trade. In the efforts to rebuild the economies of Western Europe and Japan after the war's massive destruction, international agreements included provisions for encouraging trade between the free nations. In 1960 the United States, Canada, and countries of Western Europe (later joined by Japan, Australia, and New Zealand) created the Organization for Economic Cooperation and Development (OECD) to enable closer cooperation on economic problems. And in 1967 the Kennedy Round—the sixth postwar round of multilateral trade negotiations held under the General Agreement on Tariffs and Trade (GATT)—was completed. In this round, the United States, Canada, the European Economic Community (Belgium, France, Greece, Italy, Luxembourg, the Netherlands, West Germany, Denmark, Ireland, and Great Britain), Japan, and other major trading powers agreed to deep cuts in their tariffs on manufactured goods. After some five years of negotiations, a new GATT became effective in 1980, providing for additional, gradual tariff reductions starting in July 1980 and concluding in 1987. Another GATT agreement was concluded in 1982, in which the member nations again endorsed the principle of free trade and pledged not to impose any new trade restrictions. Although the problems of country-protectionism through both tariff and nontariff (for example, import quotas and licensing agreements, and embargoes) measures, are far from solved, foreign trade and foreign purchasing have grown markedly over the past 40 years. Foreign buying represents an important alternative for the astute purchasing department.

WHY THE CONCERN WITH FOREIGN PURCHASING?

Several factors are focusing attention on the foreign purchasing alternative, not the least of which is that the world has grown a good deal smaller, figuratively, in the last 40 years, with the increased speed of transportation and communication.

TABLE 12–1   U.S. Imports and Exports, 1950–1987 ($ Billions)

Year	Imports	Exports	Surplus or (Deficit)
1950	$ 8,984	$ 10,282	$ 1,298
1960	15,075	20,612	5,537
1970	39,756	42,590	2,834
1980	256,984	220,786	(36,198)
1981	273,352	233,739	(39,613)
1982	254,885	212,275	(42,610)
1983	269,878	200,538	(69,340)
1984	341,177	217,888	(123,289)
1985	361,626	213,146	(148,480)
1986	366,100	206,400	(159,700)
1987	405,900	243,900	(162,000)

SOURCES: 1950 through 1985: *1985 International Trade Statistics Yearbook,* Volume 1, Trade by Country (New York: United Nations, 1987), p. 1,005; 1986 and 1987: *Economic Indicators, February 1988* (Washington, D.C.: United States Government Printing Office, 1988), p. 35.

U.S. Imports

In 1971 the United States imported more dollar value of merchandise than it exported for the first time since 1888. This trade deficit was due in part to rising prices for U.S. manufactures, and increased foreign competition in fields the United States once had dominated. The deficits that occurred in the 1970s and 1980s (1971, 1972, 1974, 1976, and each year thereafter) were due in large part to the sharp increases in the price of imported petroleum products, which quadrupled in 1974 and doubled in 1979–80.[1]

U.S. imports hit a new dollar high in 1985, with over $361 billion, compared to total exports of only $213 billion (Table 12–1). The resulting trade deficit of close to $150 billion also was an all-time high. Table 12–2 shows that the leading country sources of imported goods and commodities were Japan (20.2 percent of imports), Canada (18.9 percent), West Germany (5.9 percent), and Mexico (5.4 percent). In each case, the value of imports was substantially larger than the value of exports. In the case of Japan, it was over three times greater, accounted for primarily by imported motor vehicles.

The breakdown of types of commodities imported into the United States in 1985 is shown in Table 12–3. Machinery and transportation equipment were by far the largest types of imports, over two-and-a-half times greater than the value of imported mineral fuels ($142 billion compared to $56

[1]Figures from the U.S. Department of Commerce, *International Economic Indicators,* June 1982.

TABLE 12–2   U.S. Imports and Exports, 1985, by Principal Country or Region ($ Billions)

	Imports	Percent of Total Imports	Exports
Canada	$68	18.9	$46
Japan	72	20.2	22
Mexico	19	5.4	13
West Germany	21	5.9	9
United Kingdom	15	4.3	7
Korea	11	3.0	6
France	10	2.8	6
Hong Kong	9	2.5	3
Italy	10	2.9	5
Saudi Arabia	2	.6	4
USSR	.4	.1	2
Africa	16	3.5	7

SOURCE: *1985 International Trade Statistics Yearbook*, Volume 1, *Trade by Country* (New York: United Nations, 1987), p. 1,006.

TABLE 12–3   U.S. Imports, 1985, by Commodity ($ Billions)

Food	$ 20
Beverages and tobacco	4
Crude material, excluding fuels	11
Mineral fuels	56
Chemicals	15
Basic manufactured goods	50
Machinery, transportation equipment	142
Miscellaneous manufactured goods	52
Other	11
Total	$361

SOURCE: *1985 International Trade Statistics Yearbook*, Volume 1, Trade by Country (New York: United Nations, 1987), pp. 1007–1008.

billion). Basic manufactured goods and miscellaneous manufactured goods each accounted for about the same total dollars ($50 and $52 billion).

Delivery/Supply Changes. As a result of the severe material shortages of the 1970s, in part caused by the Arab Oil Embargo of 1973, the western world became aware that the long-run outlook is for further shortages and of the need to find additional world suppliers as traditional supply sources are depleted. In addition to the $56 billion of mineral fuels imports in 1985, the United States relies on foreign sources to meet some or all of its needs for more than 20 of the 80 strategic and critical minerals included in the national defense stockpiles.[2] This is discussed more fully in Chapter 11, "Research, Budgets, Evaluation and Reporting."

Government/Marketing Pressures.   North American firms produce many goods which are sold (exported) around the world. The United States exported $213 billion in 1985, up from $10 billion in 1950; Canada exported $120 billion (Canadian dollar value) in 1985, compared to $3 billion in 1950. It makes sense to consider the alternatives of buying from suppliers in customer countries; also many multinational firms accept that they have a social responsibility to buy product from suppliers in nations in which they operate plants, as a means of developing those nations. Additionally, many nations insist as a condition of sale of product—for example, aircraft—to their country that the seller agree to buy a specified value of goods in that country.

Cost Factors.   Competitive pressures have grown more intense over the past 10 years. This has caused North American firms to seek out and evaluate alternatives for reducing cost. As one U.S. vice president of operations puts it, "As long as the economies of offshore sourcing are equally available to our competition, we must continue to expand sourcing for our 'noncore' products overseas." A vice president of purchasing and transportation commented that his firm "is facing increasing cost pressure on many products. This, coupled with our need to compete in a global market, requires a firm commitment to buy wherever in the world we must to meet changing client demands." A third purchasing manager said "Our responsibility is to buy the best product at the best price. Our marketplace must be global and the United States must be prepared to compete."[3] In short, cost/competitive pressures make foreign sourcing a necessity for survival for many firms.

REASONS FOR FOREIGN BUYING

The reasons for sourcing abroad are many and vary with the specific commodity needed. However, the underlying, summary reason for using a foreign vendor is that better value is perceived to be available from that source than from a domestic vendor.

While the specific factor which makes the foreign buy look attractive

---

[2]Harry F. Young, *Atlas of United States Foreign Relations* (Washington, D.C.: United States Department of State, Bureau of Public Affairs, Office of Public Communication, June 1983), p. 61.

[3] Somerby Dowst, C.P.M., "International Buying—The Facts and Foolishness," *Purchasing,* June 25, 1987, p. 53.

will vary from commodity to commodity, (technological know-how can shift from one country to another over time, the ability and willingness to control quality can change, and from time to time a stronger U.S. dollar makes the price of foreign goods more attractive), there are nine specific reasons which may cause a foreign vendor to be selected as the preferred source.

Price

Most studies show that the ability of a foreign vendor to deliver product in the United States or Canada at a lower overall cost than domestic vendors is a key reason to buy foreign.[4] While it may seem surprising that a foreign vendor can produce and ship an item several thousand miles at lower cost, there are several reasons why this may be the case for a specific commodity:

1. The labor costs in the producing country may be substantially lower than in North America. Certainly this has been the case for many of the producers in the Far East and is a key reason why many U.S. firms have set up manufacturing facilities there.

2. The exchange rate may favor buying foreign. As the U.S. dollar got progressively stronger in 1983 and 1984, due to lower inflation rates in the United States compared to most of the rest of the world, it effectively reduced the selling price of products bought from foreign vendors.

3. The equipment and processes used by the foreign vendor may be more efficient than those used by domestic vendors. This may be because their equipment is newer, having been installed after World War II as a part of the rebuilding after the war's destruction, or because they have been putting a greater share of their gross national product into capital investment. A good example of this is the steel industry in the Far East.

4. The foreign vendor may be concentrating on certain products and pricing export products at particularly attractive levels to gain volume. While

---

[4]Ibid., p. 54. This study surveyed 1,000 buyers and found that the reasons why they buy foreign were lower price (74 percent), better quality (46 percent), only source available (41 percent), more advanced technology (23 percent), more consistent attitude (12 percent), more cooperative delivery (9 percent), and countertrade requirements (5 percent). Another study, Robert M. Monczka and Larry C. Giunipero, "International Purchasing: Characteristics and Implementation," *Journal of Purchasing and Materials Management,* Fall 1984, p. 4, also found that the most common reason for initially buying internationally was lower price from foreign sources, followed by the fact that international firms had worldwide operation and attitude, availability of foreign products, improved quality of foreign products, technology available from foreign sources, to fulfill countertrade/offset/local content requirements, due to developing worldwide competition, and improved delivery of foreign products.

there are many attempts to prevent dumping practices, control of this is complex and has never been particularly effective.

Quality

While the quality level of the foreign sources generally is no higher than from domestic suppliers, on some items it is more consistent—for example, steel pipe for the petroleum industry. This is due to several factors, such as newer, better capital equipment; better quality control systems; and the foreign vendor's success in motivating its work force to accept responsibility for doing it right the first time (the zero defects concept). Also, some North American firms buy foreign to round out their product line, with domestic suppliers furnishing "top-of-the-line" items and foreign vendors filling in some of the "low-end" holes.[5]

Unavailability of Items Domestically

Certain raw materials, for example, chrome ore, are available largely only from foreign sources. And as the comparative economic advantage shifts, some manufactured products—for example, certain office equipment such as typewriters and desktop computer printers, and video equipment—also primarily are available only from foreign producers.

Faster Delivery and Continuity of Supply

Because of limited equipment availability and capacity bottlenecks, in some instances the foreign vendor can deliver faster than the domestic supplier. The foreign supplier may even maintain an inventory of products in North America, available for immediate shipment.

Better Technical Service

If the foreign vendor has a well-organized distribution network in North America, better supply of parts, warranty service, and technical advice may be available than from domestic suppliers.

Technology

Increasingly, as firms domestically and overseas specialize, technological know-how in specific lines varies. Particularly in the case of capital equipment, such as for the primary metals industry (steel and aluminum),

---

[5]"Strong Incentives for Foreign Buying," *Purchasing World,* June 1983, p. 97.

foreign vendors may be far advanced, technologically, over their American counterparts.

Marketing Tool

To sell domestically made products in certain foreign countries, it may be necessary to agree to purchase agreed-on dollar amounts from vendors in those countries. This is particularly true in aircraft sales to governmentally owned, foreign airlines. The subject of countertrade will be discussed later in this chapter.

Tie-In with Foreign Subsidiaries

Many American firms operate manufacturing and distribution facilities in foreign countries. A conscious decision may be made, particularly in the case of developing countries, to support the local, foreign economy by purchasing there for export to North America.

Competitive Clout

Competition tends to pressure the domestic supplier to become more efficient, to the long-term benefit of both that vendor and the buyer. Several respondents to a *Purchasing World* survey commented that they use imports or the threat of imports as a lever to pressure concessions from domestic suppliers. One steel buyer reflected that "I doubt whether we'd be getting current $50/ton-and-higher discounts were it not for the import situation."[6]

POTENTIAL PROBLEM AREAS

While it is not possible in this chapter to give a complete discussion of all the potential problem areas faced in foreign buying and methods for minimizing the impact of each, the major ones can be highlighted. The same principles of effective purchasing discussed throughout this book apply to foreign purchasing, but some unique problems arise when dealing across country boundaries. Fourteen potential problem areas will be highlighted.

Source Location and Evaluation

The key to effective purchasing is, of course, selecting responsive and responsible vendors. This sometimes is difficult to do, since obtaining needed

---

[6]"PMs Find Bargains in Foreign Markets," *Purchasing World,* May 1982, p. 8.

evaluation data is both expensive and time consuming. The problem is intensified when the potential vendors are located perhaps thousands of miles away. However, the methods of obtaining data on foreign vendors essentially are the same as for domestic vendors (discussed in Chapter 6). In addition to the background data obtained (discussed later in this chapter under "Information Sources"), certainly the best method of obtaining detailed data is an on-site vendor visit. Since a visit to a vendor(s) located in another country is expensive and time consuming, it must be planned in great detail. If the dollars and risk involved are great, the on-site visit is a necessity. Firms doing a great deal of foreign buying will make frequent visits to overseas sources, for example, in a firm buying millions of dollars worth of video electronics equipment, the responsible purchasing manager may spend 20 to 30 percent of his or her time in the Far East visiting and negotiating with potential or actual suppliers.

Lead/Delivery Time

High-value, low-weight electronics items may move by air freight, and delivery time may be almost as short as from domestic suppliers. But if the purchased item is costly to transport, it must move by ocean shipment, and the lead time may be several months. This means that for the foreign purchasing of high-bulk, high-weight, low-value commodities, such as steel, the buying firm must do a much longer range planning job (which is possible in most firms) and must notify the foreign vendor promptly of any schedule changes. Also, the selection of the transportation carrier must be done with great care. To compensate for transport uncertainty, the buyer may insist that the vendor maintain a safety-stock inventory in North America. Some type of performance bond also might be required.

Expediting

Because of distance, expediting a foreign firm's production/shipment is more difficult. This places a premium on knowing a supplier's personnel and assuring that they are responsive. Some firms also arrange to have an expeditor on contract in the foreign country or to use personnel from a company-owned subsidiary closer to the vendor to assist with expediting problems.

Political and Labor Problems

Depending on the country in which the vendor is located, the risk of supply interruption due to governmental problems—for example, change in government or labor strikes—may be quite high. The buyer must assess the risk, and if it is high, then the buyer must establish some system to monitor these concerns so that warning signs of impending problems are flashed in time to devise an alternative solution.

Currency Fluctuations

Should payment be made in the buyer's currency or that of the country in which the purchase is made? If payment is to be made in a short period of time, there likely will be no problem. However, if payment is not due for several months, the exchange rates could change appreciably, making the price substantially higher or lower than at the time the agreement was signed. Since 1973, world exchange rates have freely floated, and sometimes rather rapidly, due to economic, political, and psychological factors. This means that the buyer, when contracting, also must make a forecast of how the exchange rates likely will move between now and the time of payment. In addition, certain countries from time to time impose restrictions and controls on the use of their currency. This requires that the buyer have a good source of financial advice. Probably the most conservative approach is to price in dollars, for the buyer then knows exactly what the cost will be, but this denies the advantage of a lower price if the dollar increases in exchange value between the time the contract is written and the time when payment is made. Various approaches are possible, such as pricing in the foreign vendor's currency with a contractual limit to the amount of exchange rate fluctuation permitted, up or down. Or, the really knowledgeable buyer may protect against an unfavorable rate change by dealing in foreign currency options (trading in currency options began in 1983).[7] Judicious use of this technique can limit foreign exchange risk, but use of this approach moves the purchasing department into an area which requires expertise that is relatively new.

Payment Methods

The method of payment often differs substantially in foreign buying compared to domestic buying. In some instances the foreign vendor may insist on cash with the order or before shipment. Vendors with whom the buyer has established a long-term relationship may be willing to ship on open account. But the seller may insist that title to goods does not pass until payment is made. The instrument used in this case is a bill of exchange (draft) which the seller draws on the buyer and to which it attaches the shipping document before handing it to its bank for collection. The bank, in turn, sends the documents to a bank in the buyer's country, together with instructions covering when the documents are to be released to the buyer—

---

[7]"A Safer Hedge in Currencies," *Business Week,* January 17, 1983, p. 102.

normally at time of presentation—a sight draft. Or the vendor may insist on a letter of credit, which is drawn by the buyer's bank at the buyer's request, and guarantees that the bank will pay the agreed-on amount when the prescribed conditions, such as satisfactory delivery, have been completed.

Quality

It is extremely important that there be a clear understanding between buyer and seller of the quality specifications. Misunderstandings can be quite costly, due to distances involved. Also, there could be a problem in interpretation due to use of the metric system if the buyer's company is not used to working in metrics. In addition, it is important that both buyer and seller agree to what quality control/acceptance procedures are to be used.

Rejects

In the event of rejection for quality reasons, what are the responsibilities of both parties? Due to distances, return and replacement of items is complex and time consuming. Are there provisions for the buyer reworking the items? Who pays for rework, and how are the rework costs calculated? Obviously, these areas should be agreed to in advance of the purchase.

Tariffs and Duties

A tariff is a schedule of duties (charges) imposed on the value of the good imported (or, in some cases, exported) into a country. While, theoretically, the world is moving, through the General Agreement on Tariffs and Trade (GATT) to the elimination of tariffs, they still exist. The buyer must know which tariff schedule(s) applies and how the duties are computed. Additionally, the contract should make it clear who pays the duty—buyer or seller? A Certificate of Origin, issued by a proper authority in the exporting country, is the document used to certify the origin of materials or labor in the manufacture of the item. It is used to obtain preferential tariff rates, when available.

Paperwork Costs

The National Committee on International Trade Documentation, in cooperation with the U.S. Department of Transportation, did a worldwide study to measure the amount of paperwork involved in international transactions. The results showed how large the "Paper Tiger" has grown. In an American company on average:

1. There are 46 different documents, for example, application, invoice, freight bill, certificate of origin, import license, bill of lading. An

additional 360 copies are generated from these documents. At the current rate of international trade, that totals out to 7 billion copies per year.

2. The average shipment coming into the United States takes 27 paperwork man-hours and costs $320.

Thus, the paperwork costs in foreign buying pose a major problem, besides being frustrating and a drag on the speed of operations. Perhaps one of the hardest jobs in making a purchase from a foreign source is facilitating the shipment. The recommendation of the National Committee on International Trade Documentation is to (1) *eliminate* documents whenever possible, (2) *simplify* documents, (3) *standardize* paperwork, and (4) *computerize.*[8]

Legal Problems

If potential legal problems are a risk in domestic buying, they are several times greater in foreign buying. If delivery time is critical, a penalty or liquidated-damages clause tied to late delivery may be advisable. Also, the buyer should attempt to get a clause into the contract specifying that any legal disputes be subject to U.S. laws and heard in a U.S. court. The seller, of course, may be hesitant to accept such a clause. Also, a performance bond may be required; or, a bank guaranty providing for payment in case of specified nonperformance may be substituted for the performance bond. Since litigation is time consuming and expensive, agreements to settle international trade disputes by international arbitration are becoming increasingly common.

Transportation

The shipping terms and responsibilities are more complex than in domestic transportation. The governing convention is something called *Incoterms;* almost any foreign purchase or sale contains a reference to Incoterms. They were revised in 1980 by the International Chamber of Commerce and assist greatly in standardizing and simplifying international trading practices. The 14 Incoterms are:

1. EXW (ex works).
2. FRC (free carrier at named point).
3. FOR/FOT (free on rail/free on truck).
4. FOA (free on board airport).

---

[8]"The Documentation Dilemma: Paperwork v. International Trade." *Inbound Traffic Guide,* July/August 1983, pp. 50-55.

5. FAS (free alongside ship).

6. FOB (free on board).

7. C & F (cost and freight).

8. CIF (cost, insurance, and freight).

9. FCP (freight carriage paid to).

10. CIP (freight carriage and insurance paid to).

11. EXS (ex ship).

12. EXQ (ex quay).

13. DAF (delivered at frontier).

14. DDP (delivered, duty paid).

Certain of the Incoterms apply to only sea transport: FAS, FOB, C & F, CIF, EXS, and EXO; FOA applies only to air transport; FOR/FOT applies only to rail transport; and EXW, FRC, DDP, DAF, CIP, and FCP apply to all modes of transport.[9]

Since each of the 14 Incoterms has as many as 20 separate conditions specifying buyer, seller, and carrier responsibilities, the buyer of import transportation must be familiar with them (or obtain good advice) before the agreement is made. In addition, packing and insurance decisions in foreign purchasing are much more complex than in domestic buying.

Language

Words mean different things in different cultures. An American word (legitimate or slang) may have a much different connotation in the United Kingdom or in South Africa (both English-speaking countries). Consider then the difficulties of communicating with someone who doesn't speak English, when everything must go through a translator and the North American buyer doesn't even know what connotations the words used by the translator have. Because of these language difficulties, some firms insist that the purchasing manager who is going to have repeated dealings with non-English speaking suppliers take a crash language course preparatory to discussions with foreign suppliers. The buyer still will have to use an interpreter, but the buyer will be a bit more comfortable in the discussion situation.

---

[9]"The Incoterms Compared," *The International Federation of Purchasing and Materials Management Journal*, No. 22, 1982, pp. 23-26.

Cultural and Social Customs

Even in various parts of North America, business customs vary from area to area, for example, Boston or New York City compared to Houston or Birmingham. Certainly business/social customs vary even more widely in foreign countries, and the buyer must adjust to these customs if he or she is to be effective in communicating and negotiating with suppliers. As an example, the National Association of Purchasing Management suggests eight guides for negotiating with Japanese suppliers:

1. Use high-level introductions.
2. Keep surface harmony.
3. Don't embarrass anyone.
4. Maintain a businesslike appearance.
5. Be patient; progress will come slowly.
6. Have business cards in Japanese and distribute them freely.
7. Speak Japanese, if only a little; at least know how to say the common greetings, good-byes, and thank-yous.
8. Pass out little mementos and gifts.[10]

Because of perceived problems involving U.S. firms in dealing with foreign customers or suppliers, Congress passed the Foreign Corrupt Practices Act (FCPA) in 1977. Basically, this law prohibits U.S. firms from providing or even offering payments to officials of foreign governments to obtain special advantages. The FCPA does allow facilitating payments ("grease") to persuade foreign officials to perform their normal duties. Since this type of environment is one in which the purchasing professional normally has had little experience, it is essential that he or she become familiar with the FCPA and individual country customs.[11]

INFORMATION SOURCES FOR LOCATING AND EVALUATING FOREIGN VENDORS

Due to the distances involved, the task of locating potential vendors is more difficult than in domestic source selection. However, with some variation, similar types of information sources are available to the buyer, as follows:

1. The U.S. Department of Commerce can supply current lists of names and addresses of foreign suppliers, by general types of products

---

[10]"An Approach to International Purchasing," PAL 49 (New York: The National Association of Purchasing Management, 1976).

[11]Jeffrey A. Fadiman, "A Traveler's Guide to Gifts and Bribes," *Harvard Business Review*, July–August 1986, pp. 122–136.

produced. The district offices, located in most major U.S. cities, can be helpful in obtaining this information.

2. The chamber of commerce located in major cities in the United States and around the world will help U.S. buyers locate sources.

3. The International Chamber of Commerce, headquartered in Washington D.C.,[12] has contacts through its country branches around the world and will supply leads to possible sources.

4. Almost all countries of the world maintain an embassy in Washington, D.C. The major industrial nations (and many of the lesser-developed countries) maintain a trade consulate in the United States (typically in Washington, D.C., but many also have an office in other major cities, such as New York, Miami, New Orleans, Chicago, San Francisco, or Los Angeles). If requested, they will supply names of vendors and often much background information, for their role is to promote exports from their country.

5. Typically, the purchasing department of a company with experience in foreign buying is willing to share that information with other buyers, providing they are not direct competitors. The local associations of the National Association of Purchasing Management (NAPM) and the Purchasing Management Association of Canada (PMAC) often can facilitate such an information exchange.

6. Current domestic suppliers often are in a position to supply information and leads on noncompetitive suppliers.

7. Importers and foreign trade brokers make it their business to keep abreast of developments in the supply base of the foreign countries with which they deal, and they can give the buyer a great deal of useful information.

8. Almost all the major banks have a foreign trade department. In addition to supplying information on currency, payment, and documentation procedures, and governmental approval procedures, this department can assist in locating potential sources.

9. Every major industrial country has at least one vendor locator directory, similar to the commonly used *Thomas Register of American Manufacturers*. For example, Kompass Publishers, Ltd, publishes vendor locator directories for the countries of Australia, Belgium, Brazil, Denmark, Finland, France, Holland, Hong Kong, Italy, Japan, Morocco, Norway, Singapore, Spain, Switzerland, Sweden, Taiwan, Thailand,

---

[12]The address is 1615 H. Street N.W., Washington, D.C. 20062

United Kingdom, and West Germany.[13] The foreign trade consulate or embassy of any nation will refer you to the appropriate directory, for that probably is what they use when asked to provide a list of potential vendors.

10. The International Federation of Purchasing and Materials Management (IFPMM), made up of member nation associations, maintains a list of correspondents in many foreign countries. These are buyers and purchasing managers who have agreed to supply to buyers in other nations information on vendors in their own country. *Note:* Both NAPM & PMAC announced in June 1988 that they are withdrawing from IFPMM effective June 1989!

11. Dun and Bradstreet has offices in many foreign countries and can supply a D & B report on many firms.

With availability of these information sources, locating foreign vendors is no real problem. The evaluation of a specific vendor's capabilities is a bit more difficult. Two key sources of evaluation information are the shared experiences of other purchasing people, which usually can be obtained simply by asking, and the supplier visit, which was discussed earlier in this chapter. If a supplier visit is not made, the buyer at least should ask the potential supplier for information such as (1) list of present and past North American customers, (2) payment procedures required, (3) banking reference, (4) facilities list, (5) memberships in quality, specification-setting associations, and (6) basic business information, such as length of time in business, sales and assets, product lines, and ownership.

ORGANIZATION FOR FOREIGN PURCHASING

Should purchases be made direct from the supplier or through an intermediary? This depends on factors such as how much specialized foreign buying knowledge is available in the purchasing department and the volume and frequency of foreign purchasing expected. There are several alternatives.

Import Broker or Sales Agent

For a fee (usually a percent of purchase value—and it can be as high as 25 percent), the broker or agent will assist in locating vendors and handling required paperwork. Title passes directly to the buying organization.

---

[13]The address of Kompass is RAC House, Lansdowne Road, Croydon, CR9 2HE, United Kingdom.

The buyer, of course, must make sure the fee is reasonable in regard to the services performed.

Import Merchant

The import merchant makes a contract with the buyer and then buys the product in its name from the foreign vendor, takes title, delivers to the delivery point agreed on with the buyer, and then bills the buyer for the agreed-on price. Obviously, the buyer pays a fee (buried in the price paid) for the buying services provided.

Trading Company

This typically is a large firm which normally handles a wide spectrum of products from one or a limited number of countries. It is used extensively by Japanese firms to move products into North America. The NAPM *Guide to Purchasing* cites as the advantages to the buyer of using a trading company: (1) convenience, (2) efficiency, (3) often lower costs, due to volume, (4) reduced lead times, since it often maintains inventory in North America, and (5) greater assurance of the product meeting quality specifications, since the trading company inspects in the producing country before shipment.[14] But, as with any vendor, the buyer should check out the trading company carefully.

Assignment within the Purchasing Department

If the foreign buying volume is small, it can be handled by a buyer who primarily buys from domestic sources. Vendors are located, evaluated, and purchase orders then are written directly with the foreign vendor. However, if the volume is adequate, it probably is worthwhile to train or recruit a specialized buyer or buyers who can develop expertise in foreign markets and vendors; import, documentation, and payment procedures; and currency fluctuations.

Foreign Buying Office

Many major North American firms have established a separate foreign buying office reporting to the headquarters purchasing department. This department then buys all the foreign-purchased items, for all the company's operations, direct from the foreign suppliers. This ob-

---

[14]C. L. Scott and Eddie S. W. Wong, "An Operational Approach to International Purchasing," in *Guide to Purchasing* (New York: National Association of Purchasing Management, 1975), p. 22.

viously involves an extraorganizational expense, but it may be justified due to:

1. Selection of better vendors, facilitated by on-site appraisal.
2. Better prices, since no middleman is involved.
3. Better quality control, through on-site inspection and communication.
4. Expediting is facilitated.
5. Better information on local conditions (governmental actions and pressures, exchange rates) can be obtained.
6. Better communication, since it is face to face.

While in the past it was typical to assign a manager from the North American purchasing department to manage the foreign buying office, the trend now is to select a knowledgeable citizen of the host country and bring him or her to North America for orientation and training. If the individual selected is a purchasing professional, nationality is irrelevant to his or her ability to do the job, except that the foreign national should be able to deal more effectively with language and cultural problems.

COUNTERTRADE COOPERATIVE

The Trade Act of 1982 allows for the formation of countertrading co-ops, which permit the members to jointly absorb the countertrade requirements of foreign sales. When the small- or medium-size firm participates in the co-op, often led by a large firm, it can facilitate its arrangements to make two- or three-party trades.

COUNTRY CONSIDERATIONS

Based on past experience, buyers tend to favor, justifiably, certain countries as sources for foreign purchases. Admittedly, such country preferences will change in the future, as competitive pressures cause firms to upgrade their performance. But in a 1981 survey by *Purchasing* magazine, in which 70 percent of the respondents said they did some foreign purchasing, with imports accounting for 10.9 percent of their total purchasing dollars, foreign suppliers were ranked on a national basis as shown in Table 12–4.[15]

Another 1981 study attempted to determine buyers' preferred country sources for imported products. Based on 376 responses (a 35 percent usable response rate), it was concluded that:

---

[15]"Buyers Launch Worldwide Search for Materials," *Purchasing,* February 26, 1981, pp. 14-15.

TABLE 12–4   Rating of Vendors on a National Basis

Rank	Quality	Service	Pricing	Fast Availability
1.	Canada	United States	Korea	United States
2.	Japan	Canada	Mexico	Canada
3.	West Germany	Japan	Taiwan	Korea
4.	United States	Korea	Italy	France
5.	Italy	West Germany	India	West Germany

SOURCE: *Purchasing*, February 26, 1981, p. 14.

Industrial buyers' *willingness* to buy foreign products is significantly influenced not only by the individual country, but also by the existing levels of economic development and political freedom. Buyers expressed the strongest willingness to buy from the developed countries of the world. The level of political freedom also appears to be an important influence. The only developed country to receive a relatively low rating (21st) was South Africa, which is classified as being only partly free. Communist countries were the least preferred sources of imported products . . . . [16]

The ranking of U.S. buyers' willingness to buy products from 44 countries was as follows (highest to lowest): United Kingdom, Australia, Japan, West Germany, Sweden, New Zealand, Mexico, Taiwan, Italy, Israel, France and Spain [tie], South Korea, Egypt, Brazil, Singapore, Venezuela, Argentina, Saudi Arabia, Poland, South Africa, Indonesia, Haiti, Thailand, India, Ivory Coast, New Guinea, Turkey, Honduras, Rumania, Hungary, Nigeria, El Salvador, Ethiopia, Zaire, Sudan, Ghana, Communist China, Angola, Libya, USSR, North Korea, Cuba and North Vietnam [tie].[17]

The substantial increase in foreign purchasing has resulted in greater attention to and research into world geographical purchasing considerations. A study published in 1984 looked at the "worldmindedness" of U.S. purchasing professionals. It concluded that some buyers are extremely nationalistic and unwilling to use foreign supply sources. The worldminded buyer, who is more likely to try foreign suppliers, was found to be more active in the international area—to travel abroad and to correspond with a significantly larger number of people abroad.[18]

A study published in 1985 looked at attitudes of U.S. purchasing managers toward Japanese vendors. It found that the U.S. purchasing manager

---

[16]John C. Crawford and Charles W. Lamb, Jr., "Source Preferences for Imported Products," *Journal of Purchasing and Materials Management*, Winter 1981, pp. 30-31.

[17]Ibid., p. 33.

[18]John C. Crawford, "The Worldmindedness of U.S. Purchasing Professionals," *Journal of Purchasing and Materials Management*, Fall 1984, pp. 25–26.

has a very positive view of Japanese suppliers: (1) 65 percent had a favorable attitude toward the quality of Japanese products; (2) 85 percent felt that Japanese products are reasonably priced; (3) most purchasing managers felt that Japanese advertising assists U.S. managers; (4) 75 percent felt that Japanese companies are reliable suppliers; (5) 80 percent said that Japanese suppliers are knowledgeable about their customers' needs; and (6) 85 percent felt that Japanese workers had pride in their work. The only negative attitude found was that the Japanese do not appear to be very good communicators at the personal level.[19]

A study conducted in 1984 and 1985 looked at the purchasing practices in the European operation of the truck components group of an American-based multinational corporation regarding sourcing in six less developed countries: East Germany, India, Italy, Portugal, Spain, and Turkey. It concluded that: (1) Successful international sourcing should reduce purchased material prices; (2) The use of LDC suppliers will increase quality variability; (3) Lead times will increase; (4) Supplier service—closeness of contact and ease of problem solving—will be adversely affected by the longer communication lines; and (5) Countertrade activities with some of the LDCs is a distinct possibility. Based on these conclusions, a formalized research approach to sourcing from LDCs was proposed.[20]

COUNTERTRADE

Countertrade is a fancy term for a barter agreement, but with some new twists. Barter has been around for years and takes place when payment between buyer and seller is made by the exchange of goods rather than cash. U.S. firms, in times of shortage, often swap merchandise, for example, a utility trades fuel oil to another utility in exchange for copper cable, as a matter of expediency. However, the complexities of international trade, particularly with developing countries, have brought some new variations, with purchasing right in the middle of the action. There are four principal variations.

Pure Barter

This is the exchange of goods with equal value. Typically, this takes place when a country such as Communist China, which is short of hard currency, agrees to swap its product for another country's product, such as tungsten for stainless steel. This normally is a rather clean transac-

[19]Newell E. Chiesl and Larry L. Knight, "Attitudes Toward Japanese Supply Sources," *Journal of Purchasing and Materials Management,* Summer 1985, pp. 2–6.

[20]J. R. Caddick and B. G. Dale, "Sourcing from Less Developed Countries: A Case Study," *Journal of Purchasing and Materials Management,* Fall 1987, pp. 17–23.

tion, for the firms (countries) merely are exchanging equivalent dollar values.

Mixed Barter

Here the seller ships product of a certain value—for example, motors—and agrees to take payment in a combination of cash and product—for example, wheat. It then is up to purchasing to resell the product for cash or to barter it to someone else. A commodity which changes hands twice is referred to as a *two-corner trade.* If it changes hands three times, it is a *three-corner deal.* Purchasing often gets involved in situations where the working out of the swaps is both difficult and time consuming.

Offset Arrangements

Under these agreements, in order to make the sale the selling company agrees to purchase a given percentage of the sales price in the customer country. The negotiation usually starts at 50 percent and then goes up or down from there. Whatever the figure agreed to, it then is up to purchasing to figure out how it can spend the specified amount for worthwhile goods or products. In some instances, the goods purchased later are resold, putting the purchasing department largely in the role of a trading company. Such resale occurs when purchasing cannot locate a vendor of suitable, needed merchandise in the customer country and simply makes a purchase of goods (that hopefully later will be salable) to complete the deal. But the rationale stated by one marketing director is that "[while] the countertrade aspect of trading . . . is a difficult way of doing business . . . and except in very rare cases . . . is not very profitable . . . still we hope we will have a long-term, meaningful, and mutually advantageous relationship with China—both for the selling of our equipment and the marketing of their goods."[21]

Foreign countries, when they buy North American-produced merchandise, often push hard for offsets for three reasons:

1. *Technology:* Foreign countries want to maintain their manufacturing base and know-how.

2. *Economic:* A country which needs American dollars, or wants to increase employment, can do it through offsets, and

3. *Political:* Offsets protect domestic producers and jobs and help to keep the present party in power.[22]

---

[21]"Buying from China," *Purchasing World,* December 1982, p. 34.

[22]"Offset: International Negotiating Game," in *Practical Purchasing Management* (Barrington, Ill.: Purchasing World, 1984), p. 142.

Co-Production

In co-production, the buying country insists that the selling firm agree to set up a producing plant in the buying country to make some of the components needed to assemble the finished product. This means additional employment in the buying country and the purchase of items needed for the producing plant. Such arrangements have been fairly common in the airframe industry. The purchasing department plays a key role in making such arrangements work.

Countertrade is primarily used in situations where a country has a shortage of foreign exchange or a shortage of credit to finance their desired trade flows. Also, when a country wishes to expand its exports or to develop export markets for new products, countertrade may be the vehicle to accomplish this.

At least 61 countries, including Canada, Switzerland, and Israel, require countertrade arrangements for companies wishing to sell goods or services in their country. Total world countertrade runs to approximately $150 billion per year, or about 8 percent of total world trade. While there is no vehicle for accurately assessing the magnitude of countertrade, it appears to be growing rapidly. In 1987 it was estimated that some 100 U.S. firms are participating in countertrade and 45 have established their own internal countertrade companies in an effort to better manage the activity.[23]

Countertrade is very common in the sale by U.S. firms of armament to foreign nations. For example, when Boeing made a sale of Awacs aircraft to the United Kingdom for $1.85 billion, it agreed to offsets which added up to 130 percent of the contract price. To sell F-16 fighter aircraft to Turkey, General Dynamics agreed to invest $800 million in Turkey, including a power plant, four hotels, and a fruit exporting business. While precise data are not available, the International Trade Commission estimates that nearly half the $47.8 billion in international weapon sales by U.S. firms between 1980 and 1984 included offsets.[24]

While in many instances, countertrade arrangements may present very complex problems to the selling firm's purchasing department in discharging the countertrade obligations, it may provide the opportunity to develop lower cost sources of supply in the world marketplace. However, since it has become a "way of life" for many purchasing professionals, several guidelines are suggested: (1) Decide whether countertrade is a viable alternative. If a company does not have the organization to do the international sourcing required, it should refuse to participate, (2) Build the cost of countertrade

---

[23]Warren E. Norquist, "Countertrade: Another Horizon for Purchasing," *Journal of Purchasing and Materials Management,* Summer 1987, p. 3.

[24]Eileen White, "Tool of Trade: As Arms Makers Offer Foreign Buyers More, Opposition is Growing," *The Wall Street Journal,* September 10, 1987, p. 1.

into the selling price, (3) Know the country—its government, politics, regulations, (4) Know the products involved, and what's available, and (5) Know the countertrade negotiation process—offset percentage, penalties, and time period.[25]

FOREIGN TRADE ZONES

A *foreign trade zone (FTZ)* is defined as

An isolated, enclosed, and policed area, operated as a public utility, in or adjacent to a port of entry, furnished with facilities for loading, unloading, handling, sorting, manipulating, manufacturing, and exhibiting goods and for reshipping them by land, water or air. Any foreign and domestic merchandise, except such as prohibited by law or such as the Board may order to be excluded as detrimental to the public interest, health or safety may be brought into a zone without being subject to the customs laws of the United States governing the entry of goods or the payment thereon; and such merchandise permitted in a zone may be stored, exhibited, manufactured, mixed, or manipulated in any manner, except as provided in the Act or other applicable laws or regulations. The merchandise may be exported, destroyed or sent into customs territory from the zone, in the original package or otherwise. It is subject to customs duties if sent into customs territory, but not if reshipped to foreign ports.[26]

The Foreign Trade Zones Act was passed in 1934. Initially FTZs were used primarily as custom-bonded warehouses, but the 1950 Boggs Amendment permitted manufacture and exhibition in the FTZ. As a consequence of the continuing foreign trade deficits, Congress amended the FTZ Act in 1980 to permit the base price of duty computation to exclude labor, overhead, and gain (profit). In 1975 there were only 27 FTZs. By 1987, there was a total of 247 general purpose zones and subzones for individual plants. The value of goods moving through them was $39 billion in 1986, some 62 times the 1975 amount. They are used by many of the larger companies, including all three major U.S. auto producers. Some 50 applications for new zones and subzones are under consideration.[27]

Each FTZ differs in character depending upon the functions performed in serving the pattern of trade peculiar to that trading area. The major functions which may be conducted within a zone are:

Transshipment. Goods may be stored, repacked, assembled, or other-

---

[25]David B. Yoffie, "Profiting from Countertrade," *Harvard Business Review,* May–June, 1984, pp. 8–16.

[26]*Code of Federal Regulations,* Title 15, 1981.

[27]Ken Slocum, "Import Battle: Foreign Trade Zones Aid Many Companies but Stir Up Criticism," *The Wall Street Journal,* September 30, 1987, p. 1.

wise manipulated while waiting shipment to another port, without the payment of duty or posting a bond.

Storage.   Part or all of the goods may be stored at a zone indefinitely. This is especially important for goods being held for new import quotas or until demand and price increase.

Manipulation.   Imported goods may be manipulated, or combined with domestic goods, and then either imported or reexported. Duty is paid only on imported merchandise.

Refunding of Duties, Taxes, and Drawbacks.   When imported merchandise that has passed through customs is returned to the zone, the owner immediately may obtain a 99 percent drawback of duties paid. Likewise, when products are transferred from bonded warehouses to foreign trade zones, the bond is cancelled and all obligations in regard to duty payment and time limitations are terminated. Also, exporters of domestic goods subject to internal revenue taxes receive a tax refund as soon as such products move into a foreign trade zone.

Exhibition and Display.   Users of a zone may exhibit and display their wares to customers without bond or duty payments. They can quote firm prices (since they can determine definite duty and tax rates in advance) and provide immediate delivery. Duty and taxes are applicable only to those goods that enter customs territory.

Manufacturing.   Manufacturing involving foreign goods can be carried on in the zone area. Foreign goods can be mixed with domestic goods and, when imported, duties are payable only on that part of the product consisting of foreign goods. This activity, made possible by the 1950 amendment to the original Cellar Act, offers an excellent opportunity for use of foreign trade zones. Some of the automobile producers take advantage of the FTZ possibility by bringing in parts which would have had a duty rate of from 4 to 25 percent, finishing the car manufacture in the FTZ, and then importing the completed car at a much lower 3 percent rate. Besides the lower duty rate, there is a savings on interest cost, since duty payments are not due until the auto leaves the FTZ and enters the United States.

If the purchasing executive has large overseas suppliers or is contemplating importing substantial amounts of dutiable products, savings can be realized on duties or drawbacks, and on the cost of shipping both imported materials to plants in the hinterland and manufactured products back to the same port for export.

The functions actually performed in any zone, in the last analysis, depend on the inherent nature of the trading and commercial community and demands made by users of zone facilities.

The principal reason for using a FTZ is to avoid, postpone, or reduce the tariff on imported goods, making imported goods more competitive in the U.S. marketplace. The potential disadvantages of the FTZ are (1) the additional labor costs and operating and handling costs associated with its use, and (2) the uncertainty of its long-term use. Because of political pressures, Congress could pass legislation curtailing the cost advantages of the FTZ or eliminating it entirely.

Foreign Trade Zones Compared with Bonded Warehouses

The purpose of bonded warehousing is to exempt the importer from paying duty on foreign commerce that will be reexported. The bonded warehouse allows for delay of the payment of duties until the owner moves the merchandise into the host country. Goods can be stored for three years.[28] At the end of the period, if duty has not been paid, the government sells the goods at public auction.

All merchandise exported from bonded warehouses must be shipped in the original package unless special permission has been received from the collector of customs. Any manufacturing must be conducted under strict supervision and the resulting items must be reexported.

TIBs and Duty Drawbacks

Through use of a temporary importation bond (TIB), materials can be imported for manufacture, a bond posted for twice the duty, the materials used in the manufacturing process, the completed product exported, and the TIB cancelled. While there is a fee for the TIB, the net effect is that no duty was paid on the material. The TIB is valid for one year, with two one-year extensions possible. However, if the goods are not exported on time, the penalty can be twice the normal duty, which is why the TIB must be for twice the normal duty.

Duty drawback permits a refund of 99 percent of duties paid on imported materials which later are exported. The buyer enters into a duty drawback contract with the U.S. government, imports the material for manufacture, and pays the normal duty. If the final manufactured or processed product is exported within five years of import, the 99 percent duty drawback can be obtained. The firm has three years from date of export of the final manufactured product to apply for the drawback.

QUESTIONS FOR REVIEW AND DISCUSSION

1. What are the factors/forces that have caused the increase in international trade? What growth will occur between now and the end of the century?

---

[28]Extensions may be granted on application.

2. Why have North American firms become actively involved in foreign purchasing?

3. What do firms see as the principal advantages gained when they buy foreign?

4. How can the buying firm minimize the problem areas connected with foreign buying? Which do you feel are most serious?

5. How can the buyer best get a list of potential foreign sources? Evaluate potential suppliers?

6. Discuss the pros and cons of buying direct versus using some form of middleman.

7. What are the forms of countertrade, and what problems do they cause for the buyer? How can the buyer make countertrade work?

8. How can the buyer make effective use of foreign trade zones?

REFERENCES

Burt, David N. "The Nuances of Negotiating Overseas." *Journal of Purchasing and Materials Management,* Winter 1984.

Caddick, J. R. and B. G. Dale. "Sourcing from Less Developed Countries: A Case Study." *Journal of Purchasing and Materials Management,* Fall 1987.

Chiesl, Newell E. and Larry L. Knight. "Attitudes Toward Japanese Supply Sources." *Journal of Purchasing and Materials Management,* Summer 1985.

Crawford, John C. "The Worldmindedness of U.S. Purchasing Professionals." *Journal of Purchasing and Materials Management,* Fall 1984.

Dowst, Somerby. "International Buying—The Facts and Foolishness." *Purchasing,* June 25, 1987.

Elderkin, Kenton W. and Warren E. Norquist. *Creative Countertrade.* Cambridge, Mass.: Ballinger, 1987.

Fadiman, Jeffrey A. "A Traveler's Guide to Gifts and Bribes." *Harvard Business Review,* July–August, 1986.

Farrell, Paul V., coordinating ed. *Aljian's Purchasing Handbook.* 4th ed. New York: McGraw-Hill, 1982, Section 22.

Ferguson, Wade. "Foreign Trade Zones: A Resource for Materials Managers." *Journal of Purchasing and Materials Management,* Winter 1985.

Foreign Commerce Handbook. Washington, D.C.: Chamber of Commerce of the United States, published annually.

Hanafee, Patrick L. "The Role of Purchasing and Materials Management in International Trade." *Journal of Purchasing and Materials Management,* Summer 1984.

Monczka, Robert M. and Larry C. Giunipero. "International Purchasing: Characteristics and Implementation." *Journal of Purchasing and Materials Management,* Fall 1984.

Norquist, Warren E. "Countertrade: Another Horizon for Purchasing." *Journal of Purchasing and Materials Management,* Summer 1987.

Slocum, Ken. "Import Battle: Foreign Trade Zones Aid Many Companies but Stir Up Criticism." *The Wall Street Journal,* September 30, 1987.

Wessel, David. "Buying Foreign: Despite Fallen Dollar, Americans Continue to Snap Up Imports." *The Wall Street Journal,* February 9, 1988.

Yoffie, David B. "Profiting from Countertrade." *Harvard Business Review,* May–June, 1984.

Case 12–1

MIRROR STAINLESS STEEL

In February, John Bongard, group purchasing manager for Fisher & Paykel Limited, in Auckland, New Zealand, had to select a supplier for the special stainless steel to be used in the new line of dishwashers.

The Range and Dishwasher Division

The Range and Dishwasher Division, one of eight operating divisions of Fisher & Paykel Limited, manufactured mostly dishwashers and electric ranges, 40 percent of which were exported to Australia and 10 percent to the Pacific Islands. Although last year had been a difficult year for the division because of intense competition for electric ranges and low demand for dishwashers, substantial improvements were expected with the recent introduction of the 650 wall oven and 10 minute cycle dishwasher.

The 10 Minute Cycle Dishwasher

The new 10 minute cycle dishwasher incorporated innovative design and manufacturing techniques at a reasonable price. It had been developed over the last two years and introduced at the end of last year. Mass production was scheduled to start by this July. In view of the extremely warm response received from F&P dealers, strong demand was anticipated in both New Zealand and Australia and plans were made to expand manufacturing capacity.

Mirror Stainless Steel

The old dishwasher used an outdated grade of dull finish stainless steel in its inside and on its door. With the new dishwasher, F&P marketing people wanted to change to a special mirror finish, improved grade stainless steel. Upon investigation, it was discovered that a new high strength, heat and corrosion resistant alloy existed with the cosmetic attributes favored by marketing. Because of its physical characteristics, the thickness of the steel sheets would be reduced from at least 0.6mm to 0.5mm, with a possibility of further gauge reduction as well. The old dishwasher required between 600 to 700 metric tons of stainless steel per year at a cost of US$1,400 to US$1,500 per metric ton. It was estimated that only 500 to 600 tons of the new material would be required in the first 12 production months.

Watson Steel of America

Watson Steel of America had been the sole supplier of stainless steel for the dishwashers over the last 15 years. John Bongard was very pleased with the price and service offered by this vendor. However, Watson did not produce the special alloy requested and although it suggested another alloy alternative, it had to be rejected for technical as well as financial reasons.

The Purchasing of the New Stainless Steel

The purchase of the new stainless steel fell under the responsibility of the group purchasing department, as it represented a major purchase involving international sourcing. John Bongard, group purchasing manager, had formed a six-member special committee composed of technical and commercial F&P experts as well as purchasing staff from both the Range and Dishwasher Division and his department to look into the situation. John himself would have the responsibility for the vendor selection and price negotiations. The subsequent physical ordering and day-to-day purchasing operations were the responsibility of the division.

A year ago the committee identified three possible sources for the new stainless steel:

1. Kunder Steel, a large West German steel manufacturer which operated in New Zealand through J. T. Hunter, a local agent.
2. Kim Nik Steel, a Korean company dealing through Kiroko Corporation, a trading company, with Paul Dickie as the local agent.
3. The giant Pera Steel Works, which produced this grade of stainless steel in two subsidiaries located respectively in Taiwan and Australia.

In line with Deming's philosophy adopted by Fisher & Paykel as a whole and for technical production compatibility reasons, single sourcing was the only option considered.

Initially, at the development stage of the new dishwasher and for its market introduction, Kunder Steel had supplied the new stainless steel since J. T. Hunter, its New Zealand agent, happened to have it in stock and there was not time to import it. However, John Bongard had made it very clear to both J. T. Hunter and Kunder Steel that this was a short-term decision and that testing and evaluation for long-term commitment would involve all three identified vendors.

Material Suitability

Over the last two years, all three possible vendors had sent repeated delegations of technical experts, offered advice, checked compatibility of materials, and undergone extensive testing of samples of their stainless steel.

Quality and technical issues were all controlled by the overseas manufacturers as opposed to their local intermediaries.

Although in February the results of testing were not completely finalized, John felt confident that all three suppliers offered viable products, with Kunder Steel the first one in terms of technical preference. Pera's steel from Taiwan was almost equivalent to Kunder's but Pera preferred to supply the material from Australia, a heavier gauge not suitable at the present time. John felt he could not eliminate the Australian source as a possibility, however, as some technical adjustments could make Pera's steel suitable, and in view of New Zealand's Closer Economic Relations Agreement with Australia. The terms of the agreement allowed duty concessions for New Zealand products exported to Australia in relation to the Australian/New Zealand area content of the products. John was aware of the remote possibility of political pressures to choose the Australian supplier. Pera was also the only of the three producers that had previous experience with this grade of steel for dishwasher application.

Supply Stability

The long-term stability of supply was one of the factors that most preoccupied John, not only in terms of material availability but also in terms of length of the supply chain or consistency of shipment.

Although the lead time, that is, time from the placement of order to availability from the factory, was similar for all three suppliers, the transit time varied considerably: six to eight weeks from Europe with possibility of delay of two to four weeks; 18 to 20 days from Korea or Taiwan with delays rarely exceeding two or three days; and optimally five days from Australia but with enormous risks of delays due to the bad industrial record of the Australian wharfies. The water between New Zealand and Australia was known as the most expensive water in the world.

Both Korea and Taiwan had direct, regular, and reliable shipping service to New Zealand, their ships typically returning with full cargos of beef and lamb. Their shipping rates were also substantially lower than Australian ones because of Australian and New Zealand government regulations and high labor costs.

European shipments would make up to a dozen stops at different ports around the world before reaching their New Zealand destination. They also had to pass through the politically unstable Panama or Suez Canals to avoid going the long way around South America or South Africa. Occasionally, it even happened that some ship would only go as far as Australia and drop their cargo there, feeling it was "close enough."

John was aware that one way of circumventing the shipping instability problem was to increase the stock levels. But with current New Zealand interest rates fluctuating between 13 and 16 percent for short-term deposits, the costs of servicing inventory were estimated at 20 to 30 percent of the value of the stock.

Price

By February, the data regarding price and terms of payment were available for all three suppliers (see Exhibit 1). These prices included cost, insurance and freight. As the person responsible for the price negotiations of this purchase for various volumes over a fixed period of time (12 months most likely), John knew that these prices had required extensive bargaining, especially with Kim Nik Steel, the Korean producer, which had become more interested in its market share for this new steel in the New Zealand market than the actual sales volume.

EXHIBIT 1   Prices and Terms of Payment

Name	Terms	Price per Metric Ton
Kunder Steel	90 days BOL*	4,240 DM
Kim Nik Steel	90 days BOL	1,450 US$
Pera Steel–Taiwan	60 days BOL	1,540 US$
Pera Steel–Australia	60 days BOL	1,950 A$

Exchange Rates as of Early February

NZ$1.00 = US$ 0.4540
NZ$1.00 = DM 1.4764
NZ$1.00 = A$ 0.5926

*Payment due 90 days from the date the bill of lading is issued.

John felt that a decision could not be made without taking into account the long-term trends of the various currencies involved. Exhibit 2 presents a chart of the major international currency movements in relation to the New Zealand dollar. He felt that the long-term outlook for the New Zealand currency was not good, as he anticipated further relative strengthening of the U.S. dollar against the other currencies.

Relationships with Suppliers

All three vendors considered were financially stable firms of substantial size. Fisher & Paykel had a proven history of good relations with both Kim Nik Steel and Pera Steel Works, which supplied other grades of steel.

The relationship with Kunder was new and had been initiated with the trial purchase of the new stainless steel. John said he had to admit that so far Kunder had performed satisfactorily for F&P and there had been no shipping problems at all.

With these various considerations in mind, John Bongard was trying to assess which of these three vendors made the most sense for a long-term commitment on the part of Fisher & Paykel. With mass production scheduled for July, he knew there was no time to spare.

Case 12–2

Surpil, Inc.

In September 1983, Joan Fisher, purchasing manager at Surpil, Inc., Atlanta, was considering an attractive offer for surgical sponges from a Taiwan supplier. The quality of samples submitted was excellent and the prices low enough to permit

EXHIBIT 2 Major International Currency Movements Relative to NZ$ (value of the currencies as of June 1 two years ago)

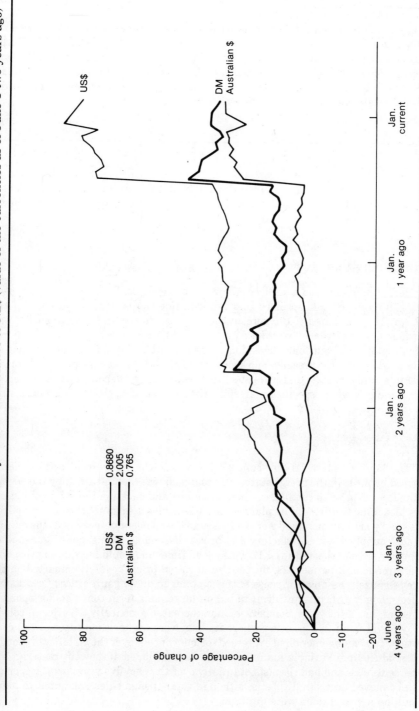

Surpil an acceptable return on a product which in recent years had seen a significant erosion because of strong competition.

Surpil, Inc., a major producer of surgical supplies, was a well-established organization with a reputation for high quality, reliability, and fast delivery. Surpil manufactured about 60 percent of its products and distributed the remainder, purchasing products which complemented and broadened the total line. The company had been conservatively managed over the years, was in sound financial condition, and had established a sound reputation in the trade.

Purchasing

John Fisher headed a department of 16 people, which included shipping, receiving, and stores. Purchases amounted to about 45 percent of total sales. Almost all purchases, with the exception of some plant equipment, were made from North American sources.

Laparotomy Sponges

Surpil manufactured a full line of laparotomy sponges. These sponges were used during surgery to soak up blood and liquid inside the patient in the area of the incision. They consisted of 100 percent cotton gauze, folded and sewn in such a way that four layers of gauze formed a square without loose ends or threads. A colored cotton tape loop, about four inches long, was sewn into the same corner so that an x-ray would reveal the presence of a sponge inadvertently left in the patient. Sponges came in a range of sizes and were sterilized before use. All sponges were subject to USP standards which specified materials, threads per inch, sizes, and so on.

Gauze and Sponges

The key raw material for sponges, the gauze, was 100 percent cotton, manufactured by mills in the greige state. This material was then bleached by the sponge manufacturer prior to cutting, sewing, assembly, and packing. Since Surpil did not have bleaching facilities in its plant, it purchased bleached gauze from a competitor. This supply arrangement had worked reasonably well over many years as the quality of gauze supplied was satisfactory and prices reasonable. The supplier guaranteed supply for six months, required 12 weeks lead time, but would guarantee price only for a three-month period. The fluctuation of cotton prices severely impacted on the price of gauze. The unwillingness of the supplier to quote gauze prices for a longer period made it difficult for Surpil to bid on large, long-term contracts for sponges. Moreover, in recent years, competition had increased drastically, and Surpil consistently found itself in a position where its bids were higher than those of the competition. Top management had expressed serious concern over the viability of sponges as a product line. Variable manufacturing costs included 40 percent material and 60 percent labor and had risen substantially over the past five years, whereas prices had not moved accordingly. Thus, although total sponge sales amounted to about $5 million a year, profits were minimal.

The Taiwan Offer

Early in July 1983, Joan Fisher received several samples of sponges from Otiwa Corporation, a manufacturer of health products in Taiwan. In May, Joan had noticed the availability of Otiwa's sponges through a general circular on business opportunities. Apparently, Otiwa Corporation wished to broaden its sales base beyond Taiwan and was looking for a North American customer. Joan had written for additional information and samples had been sent as requested. The samples appeared to be acceptable and the prices quoted were 20 percent below Surpil, Inc.'s, variable manufacturing costs. Joan passed the samples to the quality control group which reported that they were excellent and that USP specifications were clearly met. Joan then requested additional samples in all product sizes which were similarly tested and found to be fully satisfactory.

Manufacturing Response

Surpil's manufacturing manager had long been concerned about the sponge manufacturing area. He expressed a keen interest in discontinuing this operation as he had other uses in mind for the staff and the space. He, therefore, wanted Joan to go ahead with the foreign purchase as soon as possible.

Sales Response

The sales manager also was delighted with the prospect of having a lower cost source. One of Surpil's salesmen had just brought to his attention a substantial two-year contract, commencing February 1984, for a hospital purchasing group involving a total order exceeding $400,000. The sales manager knew that with sponges manufactured in Surpil's plant there was no hope of being competitive, both because of the high manufacturing cost and the uncertainty of gauze price. The Taiwan offer included a price guarantee for one year and an escalation for a second year not to exceed 5 percent. The sales manager believed Surpil could quote competitively with the Otiwa sponges and still receive a reasonable contribution. The hospital purchasing group's requirement did include a 5 percent escalation clause in the second year of the contract. It also had a provision that failure to supply would require the supplier to cover the difference between the price quoted in the original contract and prices paid to alternate sources.

Preliminary Negotiations

In early September 1983, Joan Fisher engaged in some preliminary negotiations with Otiwa by telex, which confirmed fixed prices for a year, USP specifications and Otiwa's willingness to accept the revocable letter of credit, with payment due 30 days after receipt of goods. Delivery would be 16 weeks.

Thus, by the third week of September 1983, Joan found herself wondering what action to recommend with respect to sponges. It was on the agenda for the weekly management meeting and she knew there was a high interest in resolving this matter quickly.

CHAPTER 13

Public Purchasing

Any coverage of the purchasing area should give due attention to the unique problems of purchasing by governmental agencies (federal, state, provincial, county, municipal, public school systems, public libraries, public colleges and universities, and various governmental commissions). The funds spent by public purchasing managers deserve the same serious attention as dollars spent for industrial purchases, since the source of these funds is the taxpayer. If public purchasing funds are spent effectively and efficiently, benefits will accrue to all those people who pay for, and obtain the benefits from the services provided by government.

If the total, annual tax-supported budget of a given governmental unit is $2 billion, purchased supplies, materials, services, and construction probably account for approximately $500 million, which is much less than the purchase/sales ratio of the average industrial firm, since government operations are very labor-intensive. Still, if an overall 10 percent reduction in purchasing costs could be effected through better management of the purchasing function, that would result in a savings to the taxpayer of some $50 million—a significant amount, to say the least. This translates into a higher level of service, lower tax rates, or some combination of both. The events which started in California in 1978 with the passage of Proposition 13, often referred to as the taxpayers' revolt, show that the public is interested in greater governmental efficiency and is mandating this through the ballot box. Passage by Congress in 1985 of the Gramm-Rudman-Hollings Act to provide automatic expenditure cuts in the event the federal budget deficit is not substantially reduced provides further evidence of this movement. Efficient and effective government purchasing can play a major role in making government both responsive and responsible to the needs of the people.

The figures in Table 13–1 indicate the magnitude of government spending. Government purchases, in total, have increased by about 71 percent from 1980 to 1987. The increase rate over that same period in federal government purchases (93 percent) was greater than that of state and local purchases (58 percent), due largely to stepped-up expenditures for national defense. Department of Defense (DOD) expenditures amount to approxi-

TABLE 13–1   Government Purchases of Goods and Services, 1929 to 1987
($ billions)

| | Purchases | | |
	Federal	State and Local	Total
1929	1.3	7.2	8.5
1933	2.0	6.0	8.0
1941	16.9	7.9	24.8
1950	18.4	19.5	37.9
1970	96.2	123.3	219.5
1975	123.1	215.4	338.4
1976	129.9	229.6	359.5
1977	144.4	251.8	396.2
1978	152.6	283.0	435.6
1979	166.6	309.8	476.4
1980	197.2	341.2	538.4
1981	229.0	368.0	596.9
1982	257.9	389.4	647.4
1983	283.5	391.5	675.0
1984	310.5	425.3	735.9
1985	353.9	464.7	818.6
1986	366.2	503.5	869.7
1987*	380.3	537.8	918.2

*Estimated, based on third quarter.

SOURCE: *Federal Reserve Bulletin,* December 1975, p. A54; November 1978, p. A52; December 1980, p. A50; January 1987, p. A51; October 1987, p. A51.

mately 80 percent of the total federal government purchases of goods and services.[1] Government purchasing is big business, deserving major attention from government administrators!

The most important message of this chapter is that government buying *basically does not differ* from industrial purchasing. The same concepts of good purchasing discussed in the previous chapters are applicable and should be followed to obtain maximum value for public dollars spent. The objectives of governmental purchasing are basically the same as for industrial purchasing, and include (1) assurance of continuity of supply to meet the service needs; (2) avoidance of duplication and waste through standardization; (3) maintenance of required quality standards in goods and services purchased; (4) development of a cooperative environment between purchasing and the agencies and departments served; (5) obtaining maximum savings through innovative buying and application of value analysis techniques; (6) admin-

[1]"Small Business Competition for Federal Procurement," Report 98–591, House Committee on Small Business, 98th Congress (1st Session), Washington, D.C., November 1983.

istering the purchase function with internal efficiency; and (7) purchase at the lowest price, consistent with quality, performance, and delivery requirements (or as the military puts it, "obtain the most bang for the buck").

The major focus of this chapter will be to point out those areas, or practices, of governmental purchasing which may differ, at least in part, from those of industrial buying. The differences largely are a matter of degree, often caused by the specific legislation and statutes under which public purchasing operates, and are not in direct conflict with industry practice.[2] The public purchasing manager, alert to these variations, will attempt to turn them into opportunities to maximize the utility obtained from public purchases. The major differences, or variations, between public and private purchasing practice apply to all types of public buying. The history, specific organization and practices of purchasing for the federal government, and for state and local government then will be discussed.

CHARACTERISTICS OF PUBLIC BUYING

Source of Authority

The authority of the public buyer is established by law, regulation, or statute, such as federal and state constitutions and laws and municipal ordinances. The public buyer must observe the appropriate legal structure under which purchasing operates; ultimate responsibility is to some legislative body and the voters who elect that body. The industrial buyer, on the other hand, is responsible to an administrative superior and, ultimately, to the owner(s) of the firm.

When questions of authority or the interpretation of the legal requirements arise, these will be referred to the legal officer of the governmental agency (ultimately the attorney general's office in the case of federal or state purchasing, or the county or city attorney). This relationship is synonymous with that of the legal counsel of a private firm. If legislative changes are needed to permit the public buyer to do a more effective buying job, the cooperation of the agency's legal advisor should be sought. While changing the law is difficult and may take a long time to accomplish, the public buyer continually must assess the situation and press for needed modifications. An example of one such change (legal authority to use blank check purchase orders) is discussed later in this chapter under the state and local government purchasing section.

Budgetary Restrictions/Limitations

The use of budgets as planning and control devices is well known to buyers in both private industry and in government. As with any planning

---

[2]W. Joseph Herrod, "Public Purchasing: Too Many Restrictions," *Purchasing World,* August 1987, p. 79.

mechanism, when the environment or assumptions under which the budget was made undergo change, then the plan (budget) should be revised. Often the final budget for purchasing is approved by a legislative body on a line item basis, and changes in the budget for each line item must be approved by that legislative body in advance of expenditure. Obtaining such approval may be a very time-consuming process, due to the series of steps and public hearings required.

As a result, if the needed funds are not already in the budget, the public buyer may find it impossible to take advantage of spot buys of larger quantities of materials at particularly advantageous prices. In the private firm, funds normally can be made available in a very short time if the purchasing department can present a convincing case for spending those funds. This puts a real premium in public buying on the long-term planning and budgeting needed to anticipate requirements and opportunities; this planning often must be done at least 18 months in advance. Additionally, careful planning is necessary to assure that last-minute, often unwise purchases are not made just to obligate funds by an end-of-the-year budget expiration date.

Outside Pressures

The public buyer realizes that the money spent comes from the taxpayer, and these taxpayers may become very vocal in their attempts to influence how this money is spent and with which vendors. It is not unusual for a given vendor firm to attempt to influence, through the political process, the placement of major dollar purchase contracts. In a sense, this is a type of reciprocity, with the taxpaying vendor firm feeling that since it is providing the tax dollars from which public purchases are made, it should be selected as the vendor from which government buys needed goods and services. It is the rare public buyer who does not, from time to time, receive a telephone call from a taxpayer who starts the conversation by saying, "You know, our firm pays a substantial amount of taxes, and we feel that we should receive better treatment, that is, be able to sell more, from governmental purchasing."

When the industrial buyer receives such a request, it can be countered by the response that "the supplier selected must be able to give us, in our judgment, the best ultimate value for dollars spent." However, the public buyer knows that such a statement may not satisfy the caller, and that public purchasing may have to supply facts and figures to back up its decision to buy from a particular vendor.

Greater Support of Public Service Programs

In the last decade, there has been much interest on the part of the public in providing increased government support to certain special interest segments of society. There may be minority member segments which are assumed to have been the victims of past unfair, discriminatory actions. Thus, the general public has deemed that, in the interests of equity, these special interest segments should receive special consideration in future actions. Through the legislative process, laws have been passed to encourage the redress of these past injustices, and purchasing is one natural area through which funds can be channeled to these special interest segments. Examples are programs to favor small business firms in the award of purchase contracts, or the support of minority-owned vendors through special consideration in evaluating vendor capability and the placement of purchases.[3]

While the long-term benefits to society may be worthwhile, in the short term, the governmental buyer may have to use a mix of vendors that meets the public's social demands but results in higher prices paid for items received. For example, a decision may be made that a specific percentage of total government purchasing dollars will be spent with minority-owned vendor firms. To meet that goal, a much greater amount of administrative time may be required to find and qualify vendors, and some purchases may be made from vendors which will not give maximum value for the purchase dollar. In the long run, this may be desirable to meet societal goals; in the short run, it's less than optimum purchasing. The public purchaser should make sure that the extra short-run costs from such actions are identified and agreed to by the legislative or administrative body setting such goals.

Absence of Interest Costs

One of the principal considerations in the industrial firm in determining inventory levels is the interest or opportunity cost of money tied up in inventory. An argument often is made that governmental agencies need not consider money costs in their decisions, since the funds are tax dollars that came into the governmental coffers at a specific date. This is spurious reasoning, for (1) government agencies today typically labor under a burden, large or small, of financial indebtedness, either short- or long-term, and interest cost is a very real cost of operation, and (2) when governmental funds are tied up in purchased inventories, these funds then are not available for employment in other productive uses. This effectively means that there is an opportunity cost of funds invested in inventory. The public buyer may have to take special care to educate other governmental administrators to the fact that inventory investment is expensive, and this cost should be considered in making inventory decisions. The very high (by historical standards) interest rates of the 1980s have substantially increased the costs of

---

[3]Whether such programs have been effective is debatable. See Claudia H. Deutsch, "Still on the Outside Looking In: For Minority Suppliers, Progress That Has Stalled," *The New York Times,* July 5, 1987, Section 3, pp. 1–7.

borrowing by governmental units and make these interest costs particularly important today.[4]

Absence of Inspection

Most industrial firms have a quality control or inspection department that handles decisions on both outgoing, finished products and incoming, raw materials or supplies. However, many governmental agencies (with the military as a notable exception) do not have any specialized inspection personnel. Yet, incoming inspection is needed in the case of many of the items bought.

Some steps need to be taken to assure that items delivered by vendors do meet the purchase specifications under which the purchase order was written. Then, some specific arrangement should be made to accomplish needed inspection. This could take several forms, depending on the specific item being bought: (1) The user can be advised to check delivered items immediately and report any quality variance; (2) The vendor may be asked to supply notarized copies of inspection reports which show the specific tests conducted and the raw test data which resulted and formed the basis for a decision to ship the items; (3) The buyer may send materials, or samples, out to an independent testing laboratory; (4) The buyer may employ someone to come into the organization to inspect purchased items, for example, the U.S. Department of Agriculture will inspect meat and produce items in most areas at a reasonable charge; (5) The buyer may decide to perform certain simple tests on selected items; or (6) A separate incoming quality control department can be established within the public agency, if a persuasive case can be made that this is needed to assure that fair value is received for dollars spent.

Lack of Traffic Expertise

Most industrial firms of any size have a traffic specialist or group who handles both inbound and outbound shipments. However, it is rare for public purchasing departments to have a traffic expert or access to such an individual. Yet, materials movement often accounts for a significant part of the total cost of items bought, and has increased in importance due to the widened alternatives resulting from transport deregulation (see Chapter 8). As a result of this lack of expertise, the public buyer normally specifies FOB destination as the shipping basis, which may not be most economical, since the buyer loses control over traffic decisions.

---

[4]Richard A. Reid, Carl Huth, and Donald N. Bryson, "Inventory Cost Determination: A Public Sector Challenge," *Journal of Purchasing and Materials Management*, Winter 1984, pp. 27–31.

A trained traffic person might make a major contribution in such areas as classification and routing of shipments, selection of carriers, determination of freight charges, and filing damage claims, generating savings that would be several times the salary received plus overhead. The Interstate Commerce Commission regulations permit a common carrier to offer preferential transport rates to political subdivisions for the movement of purchased items; if such rates are not being offered, the astute buyer often can negotiate such an arrangement.

Time Required to Modify the Organization

Changes in the organization structure of public purchasing—for example, the adding or deleting of positions, the changing of reporting relationships, or the redefinition of position duties and responsibilities—often take much longer to accomplish than would be required in an industrial firm. Frequently such changes require a public hearing and normally an investigation by someone from the personnel division. Also, the final approval may require action by some legislative body, such as a state legislature or a city council, and this may require several months. In one sense, this provides stability to public purchasing; on the other hand, the time required may be so long that managers get discouraged and don't bother pressing for needed change.

Procedures normally can be short circuited, when the need for speed is evident. And if the longer time to make organizational changes is recognized, this can be built into the planning horizon and action taken accordingly.

Salary Levels

It is easier to make salary level adjustments in the private sector than in public purchasing. However, contrary to popular opinion, the salary levels of public buyers, at least at the lower to medium job assignment levels, are equal to those in industrial purchasing. Thus, the public purchasing department is normally not at any salary disadvantage in recruiting personnel and should be able to attract good people. But at the top levels, government pays salaries that are far below those of industrial firms. A vice president of purchasing for a large manufacturing firm may be paid an annual salary of $85,000 or substantially more, while it is unusual for the top manager or director in a public purchasing department to make over $65,000. Some of the heads of state purchasing departments are paid a salary in the $40,000 range, which is low in relation to the responsibilities of the job. Hopefully, the legislative bodies who set public purchasing salaries now are beginning to recognize the need to pay more realistic salaries to attract top quality managers to public purchasing.

Information Cannot Be Kept Confidential

The public buyer lives in a "fishbowl." All information on prices submitted by vendors, and the price finally paid, must be made available to any taxpayer requesting it. Any special arrangements between the buyer and the successful vendor and the final purchase contract are public knowledge. Since vendors realize that all data are available to competitors, they naturally are hesitant to offer the public buyer any special deals in an attempt to gain business, for this quickly would become known and would be demanded immediately by all other customers also. The net effect is that the public buyer probably will pay, on the average, higher prices than paid by the buyer in the private firm.

Admittedly, there is an advantage in the buyer being able to compare prices with those that others are paying, and this is perfectly legal in public buying, for the buyer is free to talk and exchange vendor information and prices paid with other public buyers. This assures that one public buyer will not be paying a higher price than paid by other agencies. Yet, in the final analysis, this practice operates to the long-term disadvantage of the public buyer, for no vendor will be anxious to give a public buyer a particularly attractive price when that price immediately will be divulged to a number of other public buyers, who will demand equal treatment.

This requirement that data obtained by the public buyer be made available to all is the factor which creates the greatest obstacle to good purchasing by public agencies. It is an understandable requirement, since the funds are obtained from the collective taxpayer who has a right to know how and why tax dollars are spent. Yet, it puts the public buyer at a real disadvantage.

Importance of Specifications

Since a very large part of the purchasing actions of public buyers is based on the bidding process, it is vital that specifications for needed items be clear and accurate and written to assure that a maximum number of vendors can compete for the business. These specifications take the form of written descriptions, blueprints, drawings, performance requirements, industry standards, or commercial designation (trade or brand name). Unless all potential bidders can be furnished a complete and usable set of specifications, the bidding process will be imperfect and will not produce the competition necessary to provide best value. In addition, if a bidder can show that the specifications were not uniform, or were subject to varying interpretations, there is a good chance that legal action can be brought to overturn the purchasing department's contract award, which will result in lengthy and costly delays in contract performance.

The development of good, clean specifications requires considerable time and effort, and many governmental purchasing agencies have full-time personnel who work on the preparation and refinement of specifications. Considerable communication between the purchasing agency and the user is necessary to develop clear specifications, and the advantages of standard-ization between user agencies can be significant.

The public or private buyer can take advantage of the specification work done by governmental agencies at the local, county, state, or federal level. The federal government, through the General Services Administration (GSA), has developed a multitude of specifications for use in federal pur-chasing, and these are readily available to anyone wishing to use them. The *Index of Federal Specifications and Standards*[5] lists the available specifi-cations three ways: (1) alphabetically, (2) numerically, and (3) by federal supply class (FSC). Each specification or standard is described briefly and the price at which it can be purchased from the GSA is shown. A similar *Department of Defense Index of Specifications and Standards* lists the un-classified military specifications used by the Defense Department; it is a consolidation of separate indices formerly published by the individual mil-itary agencies. It also can be purchased from the Superintendent of Docu-ments.

While the work done in preparing these specifications can be of much use to other public buyers, it should be noted that some of them are more cumbersome than needed. The General Accounting Office has been partic-ularly critical of some of them and has advocated using simpler, commercial-type specifications where practical. An example of unneeded precision is the DOD 16-page specification for a whistle. The Pentagon says the whistle should "make an audible characteristic sound when blown by the mouth with medium or high pressure." Another example is the military specifi-cation for a DOD-approved taco shell.[6] A standard commercial specification normally would be only one page.

Emphasis on the Bid Process

Because the public buyer spends funds generated through the tax sys-tem, governmental statutes normally provide that the award of purchase contracts should be made on the basis of open, competitive bidding. This provision is supposed to assure that all qualified vendors, who are taxpayers or who employ personnel who are taxpayers, have an equal opportunity to compete for the sale of products or services needed in the operation of gov-ernment. Since the bids received are open to public inspection, it would be difficult for the public buyer to show favoritism to any one vendor. However, this system does tend to put a heavy weight on price as the basis for vendor

---

[5]The *Index* can be purchased from the Superintendent of Documents, U.S. Government Printing Office, Washington, D.C. 20402. It is also available at GSA regional offices, and the individual specifications may be purchased from the GSA, Specifications and Distribution Branch, Washington Navy Yard, Building 197, Washington, D.C. 20407.

[6]Tim Carrington, "In Wake of Foul-Ups, the Pentagon is Pressured to Shop Around for Bargains on Everyday Goods," *The Wall Street Journal*, October 3, 1986, p. 50.

selection, for it might be difficult for the buyer to defend selecting a vendor whose price is higher than that of the low bidder. Ideally, the buyer might choose to buy from other than the low bidder due to anticipated superior performance factors on the part of other than the low bidder, but this may be difficult to quantify and thus difficult to defend.

Competitive bidding is time consuming and requires administrative paperwork; for this reason, governmental statutes often will specify that informal bids may be used as the basis of award of purchase orders for requirements under a certain dollar amount, for example, $1,000. Also, in the case of items available from a sole source, purchase decisions may be made on the basis of formal negotiation; however, the sole source vendor situation should be avoided if at all possible, for this is a difficult situation and also costly, in terms of purchasing administrative costs.

When informal negotiations are used to buy requirements of relatively low value, all essential steps of formal bidding should be used, except that only a limited number of bids will be solicited, and this will be done by telephone requests to a limited number of vendors. The buyer needs accurate records of vendors requested to give a phone quote and the reason(s) why a particular vendor was selected, in the event that the decision later is challenged. Chapter 7 contains sections on "The Use of Quotations and Competitive Bidding," and "Negotiation as a Method of Price Determination."

Use of Bid Lists. On the purchase of those items which probably will require repeated purchase actions, a master bid list is compiled. This requires the buyer to specify the characteristics that should be present in any qualified vendor firm, such as size (which relates to ability to provide the needed quantities), financial stability, quality control procedures, finished goods inventory levels (which may determine how quickly items can be obtained), warranty policy, spare parts availability and accessibility of maintenance/repair personnel, and transportation facilities available. Then, the purchasing department will conduct whatever type of vendor survey or investigation is required to assure that a given vendor can meet the minimum level of each important characteristic. If a given vendor is checked out and found to be unsatisfactory, this information should be communicated directly to that vendor so the vendor will know the types of changes which will be necessary if it is to compete for future business.

Deletions from the bid list will be made in the case of vendors who receive purchase awards and then do not perform according to the terms of the purchasing agreement. This often is referred to as *blackballing* the vendor, and it is a perfectly legitimate practice, providing the decision to drop a vendor from the bid list can be substantiated with facts and figures from the purchasing department's vendor performance evaluation system. Obviously, a vendor who is being dropped from the bid list for cause should be notified of this action and the specific reasons for the action. One reason for deletion may be the unwillingness of a vendor to submit any bids over an extended period of time for specific requirements. If this is not done, the bid list may become too large and unwieldy, resulting in unneeded costs from sending out bid requests that will not be productive.

The public buyer generally must be willing to consider any vendor who requests to be put on the bid list, after, of course, an investigation of the vendor has been made. However, the competent public buyer is equally as aggressive as the private industry buyer in ferreting out new supply sources.

As part of the bidder qualification process, some type of vendor information form is used. However, even though this is a good initial starting point for the selection of qualified vendors, it will not contain enough information for a complete evaluation, and the public buyer probably will need to make an on-site vendor visit.

Advertising. The bid list, if properly developed and maintained, should provide a large enough group of qualified vendors to enable the public buyer to obtain competition in the bid process. However, many public purchasing agencies, as a matter of normal operating policy or because it specifically is required by statute or regulation, also advertise upcoming purchase needs in either the local newspaper or in the legal paper (normally a weekly). The advertisement says simply that if any given vendor firm wishes to receive a request for bid for a particular requirement, it should contact the purchasing department. The buyer then must determine whether the firm asking to bid meets the minimum vendor qualifications.

Advertising is simply a means of publicly announcing that a purchase will be made. In most instances, it will not produce any new vendors, but it assures that purchasing is not conducted under any veil of secrecy.

Bid Procedures. In a formal bid system, the bidder typically will be sent (1) a complete list of specifications which the item being supplied must meet (in complicated procurements, the specification package may consist of several pages—several hundred pages, in some instances—and may detail the kinds of quality control procedures the buyer will use to assure that the goods delivered do, in fact, meet specifications); (2) a list of instructions to the bidder, spelling out how, when, where, and in what form bids must be submitted; (3) general and special legal conditions which must be met by the successful bidder; and (4) a bid form on which the vendor will submit price, discounts, and other required information.

The bidder typically must submit any bid on or before a specified date and hour, as for example, 1 P.M. on March 15. No bids will be accepted after the bid closing; late bids are returned, unopened, to the bidder. No changes normally are permitted after the formal bid is received, although some agencies do permit the substitution of a new bid for the original, unopened bid, provided it is received before the bid opening date. The place where the bid must be delivered, usually the purchasing department, should be specified, and many public purchasing agencies use a locked container to maintain all sealed bids until the date and hour of the bid opening.

While these bid procedures may appear rather complicated, they do establish an environment in which the buying is conducted in such a way that all qualified vendors have an equal chance of consideration.

Use of Bid Bonds.   Often the bid package requires that any bidder submit a performance bond at the time of the bid. In some states, this is a legal requirement, particularly in the case of purchased items or construction contracts for large dollar amounts. As an alternative, some public purchasing agencies require that the bid be accompanied by a certified check or money order in a fixed percentage amount of the bid. In the event the bidder selected does not agree to sign the final purchase contract award, or does not perform according to the terms of the bid, this amount is retained by the purchasing agency as liquidated damages for nonperformance. Obviously, the bid bond or bid deposit is an attempt to discourage irresponsible bidders from competing. In high risk situations the extra cost of the bid bond, which in some way will be passed back as an extra cost to the buyer, is warranted; in the purchase of standard, stock items available from several sources, the use of a bond is questionable.

Technically, there are three general types of bonds available. The bidder purchases each, for a dollar premium, from an insurance company, thus effectively transferring some of the risk to the insurance carrier:

1. The *bid bond* guarantees that if the order is awarded to a specific bidder, it will accept the purchase contract. If the vendor refuses, the extra costs to the buyer of going to an alternative source are borne by the insurer.

2. The *performance bond* guarantees that the work done will be done according to specifications and in the time specified. If the buyer has to go to another vendor for rework or to get the order completed, purchasing is indemnified for these extra costs.

3. The *payment bond* protects the buyer against liens which might be granted to suppliers of material and labor to the bidder, in the event the bidder does not make proper payment to its vendors.

Bid Opening and Evaluation.   At the hour and date specified in the bid instructions, the buyer will open all bids and record the bids on some type of a bidder spread sheet. In some agencies, the buyer must call out the vendor name and bid, and a clerk records the information, checks the actual bid form for the amount, and then certifies that the information on the spread sheet is correct. Any citizen who wishes normally can attend the bid opening and examine any of the bids. Often vendors who have submitted bids, or ones who have chosen not to bid but who wish to see the bids of other vendors, will attend the opening. After the bids are recorded, the original bids should be retained for later inspection by any interested party for a specified time period (often 12 months).

The buyer then must make a selection of the successful bidder, based on the bid which will give the greatest value. Obviously, if all the specifications and conditions are met by a qualified vendor, the lowest bid will be selected. Otherwise, the bid process is destroyed. If other than the low bidder is selected, the buyer documents the decision very carefully, for it may be informally challenged later on in the courts.

In some public agencies, a purchase award cannot be made unless at least some minimum number of bids (often three) has been received. If the minimum number is not received, the requirement must be rebid, or the buyer must be able to justify that the nature of the requirement is such that it is impossible to obtain bids from any more vendors.

Bid Errors.   If the successful, low bidder notifies the buyer after the bid has been submitted, but before the award of the purchase order has been made, that an error has been made, the buyer normally will permit the bid to be withdrawn. However, the buyer makes some permanent note of this, since it reflects on the responsibility of the bidder.

A much more serious problem arises if the bidder, claiming a bid error, attempts to withdraw the bid *after* it has been awarded the order as the successful bidder. Of course, the use of a bid bond in the bid process is an attempt to protect the buyer if such a problem arises. If the bid bond wasn't used, the buyer must weigh the probability of having severe problems in court action to force performance or collect damages, against the problems and costs of now going to the closest other successful bidder (who now may not be interested) or going through the bid process again. Legal counsel is normally sought, but if the mistake was mechanical in nature, that is, the figures were added up incorrectly, the courts probably will side with the vendor. However, if it was an error in judgment, for example, the vendor misjudged the rate of escalation in material prices and used this figure in making the bid, then the courts generally will not permit relief to the vendor. Also, for the vendor to gain relief in the courts, the vendor must be able to show that once the error was discovered, the buying agency was notified promptly.

Obviously, if the buyer receives a bid which common sense and knowledge of the market would indicate is unrealistic, the bid should be rechecked and the bidder requested to reaffirm that it is a bona fide bid. In the long run, such action likely will be cheaper for the buying agency than if a long and involved legal action ensues, with an uncertain outcome.

Bid Awards.   As stated earlier, if two or more responsible bidders offer to meet the specifications and conditions, the low-price bidder is selected. If other than the low bidder is selected, the buyer must be prepared to justify the decision with additional information. If identical low bids are received, and the buyer has no evidence or indication of any collusion or other bid irregularities, then a public "flip of the coin" is a satisfactory means of resolving the deadlock. If the buyer suspects collusion, all bids should be rejected and the requirement rebid. Additionally, this should be reported to the appropriate legal counsel, for example, the Attorney General or federal Justice Department, for investigation and action.

The public buyer has no obligation to notify unsuccessful bidders of the award, since the bid opening was a public event and the bid and award documents are retained in the purchasing department and may be viewed, on request, by any interested individual. Courtesy suggests, however, that if an unsuccessful vendor makes a telephone or letter request for information, that information be provided promptly, and the requestor invited to come in and examine the file.

FEDERAL GOVERNMENT PURCHASING

There are some specific peculiarities in federal government purchasing, apart from those differences between public and private purchasing discussed earlier. While space does not permit an in-depth review of these items, a brief discussion is in order.

History

Congress passed a law in 1792 which gave the Treasury and War Departments the authority and responsibility to make purchases for the government. The position of purveyor of public supplies was established in the Treasury Department in 1795. Federal purchasing became more formalized with the Procurement Act of 1809, which required that formal advertising be used in purchasing to assure that all firms had a chance to bid on government requirements. Over the intervening years, federal legislation has been extended to require, in certain instances, such things as public bid openings and bid bonds, and has established extensive rules and procedures for military purchases.

In 1974 the Office of Federal Procurement Policy was set up to coordinate and improve the efficiency of government purchasing. This agency received much criticism for its failure to address major policy issues in federal purchasing; instead it was charged that it dealt primarily with procedural matters and made it difficult for the individual agencies, such as the Department of Defense, to meet their objectives. The OFPP sponsored the preparation of the Federal Acquisition Regulation (FAR). The new FAR became effective in 1984, replacing the Federal Procurement Regulations and the Defense Acquisition Regulations. Congress reauthorized the OFPP (P.L. 98–191) in 1983.

In an attempt to provide better systems, policies, methods, and criteria for the purchase of materials, equipment, and services by the federal government, the Federal Acquisition Reform Act was introduced in the U.S. Senate on January 5, 1979. The intent of this act was to establish that federal procurement actions should rely primarily on the private sector to (1) best meet public needs at lowest total cost, (2) substitute the incentives of competition for regulatory controls, (3) encourage innovation, (4) expand the supply base, (5) provide opportunities to minority-owned firms, (6) initiate large-scale production only after adequate operational testing, (7) allow contractors to make a profit commensurate with opportunities in other, comparable markets, and (8) promote effective competition by giving the government buyer concept, design, performance, price, total cost, service, and delivery alternatives.[7]

The Federal Acquisition Institute (FAI) was established in 1976 for the purpose of developing the knowledge and skills of federal procurement personnel through a program of determining training needs and then encouraging and/or providing seminars, courses, or other opportunities to meet these defined needs.

Probably the most significant piece of procurement legislation enacted by Congress this decade was the Competition in Contracting Act of 1984 (CICA). The intent of CICA was to eliminate some of the requirements for formal advertising; require more procurement planning and research; encourage greater use of commercial, as opposed to specially made, products; and foster the use of performance specifications. How effective CICA will be in cutting through the federal procurement bureaucracy remains to be determined.

Small Business Favoritism

Federal legislation in 1953 established the Small Business Administration (SBA), which was to provide aid, counsel, and assistance to small firms. In general, a small business is defined as one that is independently owned and operated, is not dominant in its field, and has dollar receipts below a certain number, depending on the particular industry. The SBA operates a Prime Contracts Program, which provides that on federal contracts above a certain dollar amount a percentage of the contract is set aside for small business firms. The SBA and the involved public buying agency then attempt to find and assist small firms in qualifying for and obtaining the amount of purchases set aside.

In 1961, Congress passed Public Law 87–305 which provides that "a fair proportion" of purchases of items from public funds be awarded to small business. If a large firm obtains a government contract over a certain amount, it must make a "best effort" to locate and place orders with small

---

[7]"Federal Acquisition Reform Act" introduced in the Senate of the United States, 96th Congress, 1st Session, on January 15, 1979, Section 2.

subcontractors for a specific percentage amount of the total contract. In many instances, this results in the payment of premium prices to place business with small firms, and increases the administrative expense of purchasing, but Congress justifies this action by arguing that small business must be supported if it is to survive. Within DOD (which accounts for about 80 percent of federal purchase dollars), small business got less than 20 percent of the dollars in FY 1982. DOD's purchases went to relatively few large firms; the top 25 got about 45 percent of the expenditures.[8]

Labor Surplus Area Favoritism

The Department of Labor classifies certain cities or areas as ones which have an unusually high unemployment rate or an unusually high number of hard-core disadvantaged persons. Certain government purchasing requirements then are set aside for placement of a given percentage of the total buy with firms in those areas. A small business in a labor surplus area is in a particularly advantageous position to compete for these purchases, although the net effect may be that the government (taxpayer) pays a premium price for purchased requirements.

Buy American Act

Congress passed the Buy American Act ostensibly to make sure that the United States maintains its production capability in several "essential" areas, even though foreign firms are able to produce more efficiently and thus undersell domestic firms on requirements for delivery in the United States. It provides that on certain government requirements the purchase order will be awarded to the domestic firm, providing that its price is not over a given percentage amount (normally 6 percent, or 12 percent if it is a labor surplus area) higher than that offered by the foreign vendor.

Renegotiation

Some of the items bought by the government, and particularly the military services, are so unique that only one supplier can be used; obviously competition cannot be depended on to give the public buyer a realistic price. Couple this with the delivery time pressures under which military purchasing operates in wartime, and you have the reason for the Renegotiation Law, first passed by Congress in World War II and later superceded during the Korean War by the Renegotiation Act of 1951. It was temporarily extended several times but expired in 1979. Government buyers then had to

---

[8]"Small Business Competition for Federal Procurement."

rely on the Vinson-Trammell Act, passed in the 1930s, which set allowable profit percentages which contractors can make on aircraft (12 percent), naval vessels (10 percent), and associated equipment. It was administered by the Internal Revenue Service.

Basically, these laws provided that if a firm has done over a certain total dollar annual amount of business with the government, its cost accounting records could be audited and any "excess profits" recovered by the government for deposit in the general treasury. Note that the renegotiation was done on a total business and not on a contract-by-contract basis, that is, losses on one contract were used to offset excess profits on other contracts.

However, the Vinson-Trammel Act was repealed in 1981 by the Department of Defense Authorization Act which gives the President the power to regulate contractor profit margins, but only during wartime. Thus there now is no way for the government buyer to legally recover any excess profits realized by a vendor. The Truth in Negotiations Act and the Cost Accounting Standards Act are the vehicles on which the government buyer must rely to assure that the data furnished by a vendor preparatory to negotiating a contract are current and factual.

General Services Administration (GSA)

As a result of a governmental committee (the Hoover Commission) report in 1949, Congress passed Public Law 152, the Federal Property and Administrative Services Act of 1949. The General Services Administration was set up under that act. GSA is responsible for all federal purchasing, except that done by Department of Defense (DOD), the National Aeronautics and Space Administration (NASA), and the Energy Research and Development Agency (ERDA). In fact, these agencies, as well as certain state, county, and local agencies, also can buy against GSA contracts. GSA is organized under a central office in Washington, and 10 regional offices. It sets standards for government purchases, buys and stores for later use (primarily through the Federal Supply Service, which is responsible for supplying common-use, commercial-type items to federal agencies), and issues long-term contracts at set prices. When an agency needs an item, it simply cites the appropriate GSA contract. In some instances, GSA actually operates retail-type stores, where any federal purchaser can go to obtain things such as office supplies and equipment. It also operates the GSA Interagency Motor Pool System.

GSA buying is, without question, big business. Total expenditures are approximately $5 billion per year, and the agency has close to 23,000 employees. Unfortunately, this governmental operation has not been free of scandal over the years, and during the 1970s more than 140 GSA employees and contractors were convicted of bribery or other wrongdoing. Starting in 1977, the GSA has been the subject of several investigations by the Internal Revenue Service and the U.S. Justice Department. However, in more recent years, the agency has operated under a strict code of ethics and its reputation for effective and efficient procurement has improved.[9]

Military Purchasing

Following the experience of World War II, and after several studies to review past experience, Congress passed the Armed Services Procurement Act of 1947 (Title 10 of the U.S. Code) which provides the authority for today's purchasing actions by the Department of Defense (DOD). In addition, it permits the use of negotiated procurements under certain conditions; it prohibits the use of cost plus profit-as-a-percentage-of-cost type contracts; and it establishes the policies under which purchasing for the Armed Forces is to be conducted. To meet the intent of the Armed Service Procurement Act, the Department of Defense originally adopted the Armed Service Procurement Regulations (ASPR) as the "bible" for military procurement personnel. Adoption of the Federal Acquisition Regulation (FAR) largely has superceded both the ASPR and the Defense Acquisition Regulation (DAR).

There are four types of contracts in common use by military buyers:

Firm-Fixed-Price (FFP) Contract. The price set is not subject to change, under any circumstances. This is the preferable type of contract, but if the delivery date is some months or years away and if there is substantial chance of price escalation, a vendor may feel that there is far too much risk of loss to agree to sell under a FFP contract.

Cost-Plus-Fixed-Fee (CPFF) Contract. In situations where it would be unreasonable to expect a vendor to agree to sell at a firm fixed price the CPFF contract can be used. This situation might occur if the item is experimental and the specifications are not firm, or if costs in the future cannot be predicted. The buyer agrees to reimburse the vendor for all reasonable costs incurred (under a set of definite policies under which "reasonable" is to be determined) in doing the job or producing the required item, plus a specified dollar amount of profit. A maximum amount may be specified for the cost. This contract type is far superior to the old "cost-plus-percentage" type, which encouraged the vendor to run the costs up as high as possible to increase the base on which the profit is figured. While the vendor bears little risk under the CPFF, since costs will be reimbursed, the vendor's profit percentage declines as the costs increase, giving some incentive to the vendor to control costs.

Cost-No-Fee (CNF) Contract. If the buyer can argue persuasively that there will be enough subsidiary benefits to the vendor from doing a

---

[9]Timothy D. Schellhardt, "Reagan's Head of the GSA Impresses Many by Streamlining and Cleaning Up Agency," *The Wall Street Journal*, December 21, 1982, p. 25.

particular job, then the vendor may be willing to do it provided only the costs are reimbursed. For example, the vendor may be willing to do the research and produce some new product if only the costs are returned, because doing the job may give the vendor some new technological or product knowledge, which then may be used to make large profits in some commercial market.

Cost-Plus-Incentive-Fee (CPIF) Contract.   In this type of contract, both buyer and seller agree on a target cost figure, a fixed fee, and a formula under which any cost over- or underruns are to be shared. For example, assume the agreed-on target cost is $100,000, the fixed fee is $10,000, and the incentive sharing formula is 50/50. If actual costs are $120,000, the $20,000 cost overrun would be shared equally between buyer and seller, based on the 50/50 sharing formula, and the vendor's profit would be reduced by $10,000, or to zero in this example. On the other hand, if total costs are only $90,000, then the vendor's share of the $10,000 cost underrun would be $5,000. Total profit then would be $10,000 + $5,000, or $15,000. This type of contract has the effect of motivating the vendor to be as efficient as possible, since the benefits of greater efficiency (or the penalties of inefficiency) accrue in part, based on the sharing formula, to the vendor.

With annual military expenditures comprising close to 80 percent of the total federal expenditure bill, it is obvious that very large dollar amounts can be saved or lost by the military's purchasing decision makers. For example, the 1983 purchase appropriation to build only 27 MX missiles was $2.5 billion.[10] Increasing attention is being given to searching out and correcting inefficient purchasing practices, since the aggregate purchase dollars are so large. A 1983 recommendation of the President's Private Sector Survey on Cost Control task force (made up primarily of unpaid business personnel—including leading executives from Fortune 500 companies) pointed out inefficiencies in spare parts procurement and the work done by defense vendors. For example, the task force estimated that $695 million could be saved over three years in the procurement of spare parts if adequate competition were encouraged. Congress has been increasingly concerned as to whether maximum value is being received from defense dollars paid to vendors; the Defense Department itself estimates that the shoddy work done by defense contractors adds anywhere from 10 to 50 percent to the cost of many weapons systems.[11] Spare parts procurement has come in for close review, based on reports from Air Force auditors. For example, the price of a turbine air seal used in maintenance of the F-111 fighter-bomber soared from $16 to $3,033.82 in one year. In a study of prices paid for nearly 15,000 engine parts, from 1980 to 1982, 65 percent of the part prices rose more

---

[10]"Hard Choices on the Hill," *Time,* August 1, 1983, p. 11.
[11]"Rooting out the Waste," *Time,* July 11, 1983, p. 20.

than 50 percent; 4,000 of the part prices rose more than 500 percent; some had risen by more than 1,000 percent. One gear-and-pinion assembly went from $31.59 each to $546, a 1,628 percent increase.[12]

The military is very sensitive to such criticism and is taking steps to make its purchasing practices more cost effective. For example, the Department of Defense is now making wider use of putting vendors on its "blacklist," if they are convicted of fraud or bribery or for repeated failure to perform properly on contracts received, thus denying them the opportunity of selling to the military.[13] The secretary of defense has ordered sweeping changes in its $13 billion yearly parts purchase. These include developing greater competition among vendors, identifying overpriced items and demanding refunds from their manufacturers. Also, the military buyer must attempt to obtain the rights to technical data and equipment designs when they contract with a vendor so it will be easier to obtain competition on later buys.[14] Evidently these changes are having some effect, for the Pentagon claims to have saved $1.5 billion in fiscal year 1987 through improvements in its system for buying spare parts. Increased competition, tighter cost controls, and longer vendor lead times were the factors cited for the savings.[15]

A strong recommendation of the Packard Commission, set up in 1986 to look at ways to improve efficiency in government, was that commercial, rather than made-to-order, items be bought wherever possible. In addition, it argued for greater standardization between the services in items purchased. However, the armed forces' purchasing bureaucracy employs 30–40,000 people to make some 15 million purchases per year, and change comes slowly.[16]

A recent concern among top procurement management in the Department of Defense is its dependence on foreign suppliers for key items which would be needed for a defense buildup. A small German plant 30 miles west of the Czechoslovakian border makes all the high-purity silicon the United States buys for chips used in thousands of missile guidance systems; ball bearings in U.S. submarines, aircraft, and tanks increasingly come from Europe and Asia; some Navy ships ride at anchor on Spanish-made chains. One estimate is that the Pentagon bought $9 billion of foreign parts and equipment in 1987, but some feel the total is much higher. The principal reasons for these large defense procurement dollars being spent with foreign

---

[12]"Cost Bombshells: Exploding Spare-Part Prices," *Time,* July 25, 1983, p. 16.

[13]Brooks Jackson, "Pentagon Blacklists More Suppliers in a Tougher Stance Toward Fraud," *The Wall Street Journal,* August 5, 1983, p. 21.

[14]Walter S. Mossberg and Edward T. Pound, "Weinberger Orders Military to Overhaul Pentagon System for Buying Spare Parts," *The Wall Street Journal,* September 6, 1983, p. 5.

[15]"Pentagon Logs $1.5 Billion in Parts-Buying Savings," *The Wall Street Journal,* March 22, 1988, p. 64.

[16]"A Rocket for the Pentagon," *The Economist,* May 30, 1987, pp. 67–68.

suppliers are the lower prices available overseas and the nonavailability of some items from domestic suppliers.[17]

The Pentagon is attempting to find the right balance between foreign and domestic vendors, between holding larger inventories and encouraging (and often financing) larger plant capacity, and between meeting defense needs and the needs and political pressures of the economy as a whole. Through a series of study initiatives and formation of a defense manufacturing board in 1988, the DOD hopes to "be instrumental in creating a heightened cultural environment that promotes a strong U.S. technology and manufacturing base."[18]

STATE AND LOCAL GOVERNMENT PURCHASING

While purchasing done by state, county, municipal, and other public agencies tends to follow all the basic guidelines of public purchasing, some of the unique aspects should be commented on briefly.

History

The state of Oklahoma was first to establish centralized purchasing in 1910. With that start, in the 1920s, along with budget reform, many additional states adopted central purchasing. By 1967, all the states, with the exception of Delaware, had adopted central purchasing.[19] However, in many states there is not total centralization of purchasing, for many state agencies often handle their purchasing separately from the central purchasing office. One good example of this is the state universities, which often do all the purchasing needed by their institutions using, where advantageous, existing state contracts.

Participation in GSA Contracts

Those political subdivisions (cities, counties, and states) which are the recipients of some type of federal grant or funding are eligible to use the GSA contracts. In some instances this will allow the agency to buy items at a lower price, and with substantially lower administrative cost, than could be accomplished otherwise. Certainly the public buyer should at least check out the GSA prices before making a decision.

---

[17]Tim Carrington, "Military's Dependence on Foreign Suppliers Causes Rising Concern," *The Wall Street Journal,* March 24, 1988, p. 1.

[18]"Debating U.S. Readiness for Making the Big Surge," *Insight,* March 28, 1988, p. 18.

[19]"Table 2: Estimated Volume of Purchases, Operating Costs, and Number of Employees, 1966–67," in George W. Jennings, ed., *State Purchasing* (Lexington, Kentucky: The Council of State Governments, 1969), p. 11.

Prison-Made Goods

Some states require that if one of the state's penal institutions produces items that also are required in the operation of state government, that penal institution must be given absolute preference in purchasing. The items produced might include foodstuffs, shoes, work clothing, and license plates. The public purchasing officer should know what kinds of items are available from the penal institutions and should communicate to the prison administrators the quality requirements which goods must meet.

Cooperative Purchasing

In the last decade or so, the cooperative purchasing approach has received much attention, interest, and use in public purchasing. Basically, it is a system whereby two or more public, or not-for-profit, purchasing departments pool their requirements so that they can talk with vendors about substantially larger purchase quantities than would be required by any one buyer. It has been used successfully by local government units, public school districts, and hospitals, and it has its primary advantage for the smaller purchasing unit. The savings from cooperative purchasing can be significant.

Two basic variations are used in cooperative purchasing: (1) joint buying, where two or more purchasing departments agree to pool their requirements for a particular item and let one of the purchasing departments commit the total purchase quantity to a specific vendor at a specific price, and (2) a formal, contractual arrangement where several individual purchasing departments agree to establish and fund a separate cooperative buying agency and to use the purchasing services of that agency. For example, several hospitals in a particular area could agree to pool their requirements for basic items and then hire a full-time buyer (manager) of a cooperative hospital purchasing agency. The administrative costs of the cooperative agency would be shared by all hospital members on some basis, such as size of hospital or total purchase dollars spent through the cooperative group. Such cooperative agencies exist in the health-care field in several states and many universities are affiliated with the cooperative buying arm of the National Association of Educational Buyers.

The Association of School Business Officials survey of a large group of local school agencies reported that about 61 percent of the 1,135 members reporting were participating in some type of cooperative purchasing arrangement. When asked to indicate the advantages of cooperative buying, some of the items they reported were (1) lower prices; (2) improved quality, through improved testing and vendor selection; (3) reduced administrative cost; (4) standardization; (5) better records; and (6) greater competition. Among the problems cited as arising from cooperative buying were (1) inferior products; (2) longer lead times; (3) limited items available; (4) more paperwork; and (5) inability of small vendors to compete, due to larger quantities required.[20]

Local-Bidder Preference Laws

In many governmental jurisdictions, the applicable law or statute states that, all other things being equal, local bidders must be granted a certain percentage price preference in bidding against nonlocal vendors. For example, if a local vendor submits a bid that is not over a given percent, for example, 5 percent, higher than nonlocal vendors, then the local vendor must be awarded the purchase order, assuming all other factors are equal. This is a form of protectionism, similar to that of the Buy American Act. The argument for this is that local vendors have employees in the local area, and the award of orders to local vendors provides support for the local economy.

This practice is opposed by most purchasing professionals as being noncompetitive, which means that higher prices are paid for purchases than are necessary. It negates the advantages of economic specialization, and local vendors, knowing that such a preference is to be applied, will have a tendency to submit a bid that is higher than they otherwise would present. If one believes in totally fair, open competition, then all vendors, regardless of location, should be permitted to compete solely on the basis of their ability to provide maximum value for the public funds expended. The National Association of State Purchasing Officials has gone on record as strongly opposing such a practice.

Innovations in Government Purchasing

The prevailing attitude of business people and the general public is that government purchasing systems and procedures are far less efficient and bound by substantially more "red tape" than the general practices of private industry. While that may be so, it need not be. Sound purchasing management applied to the governmental purchasing/materials management process can result in cost-saving innovations. For example, the Department of Materials Management of Maricopa County, Arizona (the largest county in the state in terms of both population and industry base, encompassing the metropolitan Phoenix area) has instituted a blank check (check with purchase order) system, as discussed in Chapter 3, as a means of reducing administrative payment cost and the aggravation of vendor back orders. Since the Arizona Revised Statutes (ARS) under which governmental units operate prohibited payment of public funds until materials or services ac-

---

[20]Richard E. Munsterman, *Purchasing and Supply Management Handbook for School Business Officials*. Research Bulletin No. 22 (Chicago: Association of School Business Officials of the United States and Canada, 1978, pp. 176–77.

tually were received, the legislature had to be persuaded to modify the appropriate ARS to permit use of this innovative system. With this legislative modification, the blank check buying system now can be used by many public purchasing units; for example, Arizona State University now makes the majority of its library purchases using this system.

The U.S. Treasury Department, which currently writes 22 million checks each year, has embarked on a program to pay its suppliers electronically. They call it "Vendor Express" and expect to have eliminated all checks to vendors by about 1991. This effort is similar to the Electronic Data Interchange (EDI) programs underway at firms such as General Motors.[21]

Health Care Purchasing

Many of the hospitals and clinics are operated by the public sector (federal, state, county, cities, and quasi-public not-for-profit corporations). The nation's approximately 6,000 hospitals constitute a $360 billion industry.[22] Approximately 20 percent of a hospital's revenue goes for the purchase of consumables (medical supplies, linens, food and so on) and construction and equipment. The largest hospital organization in the United States is Hospital Corporation of America (HCA), a for-profit corporation headquartered in Nashville, Tennessee. Founded in 1968 with one hospital, by 1987 HCA and its affiliates now own or manage hospitals and other medical facilities in more than 390 communities in the United States and throughout the world. Their efficiency and return-on-assets is directly affected by how the purchasing function is performed. To gain the needed economies of scale and expertise in purchasing, major contracts for equipment and common use items are negotiated and coordinated by their Materiel Management Department located at corporate headquarters. Similar type efficiencies are available when any hospital recognizes it must manage materials, instead of merely issuing purchase orders.

Because of the rapid rise of health care costs—in 1982 they increased 11.9 percent while the consumer price index rose less than 4 percent—it became clear that at that rate the Medicare Hospital Insurance Trust Fund would be depleted by 1990. Congress then instituted health-cost-containment procedures as part of the Tax Equity and Fiscal Responsibility Act (TEFRA) passed in 1982. Under TEFRA, illnesses are classified into over 400 so-called diagnosis-related groups (DRGs), and hospitals are reimbursed for Medicare patients at amounts based on the average cost of the specific DRG in each of nine regions of the country.[23] If a given hospital's costs for a particular procedure, such as a simple appendectomy, are greater than

---

[21]Robert Guenther, "U.S. Treasury Pays Suppliers Electronically," *The Wall Street Journal,* September 24, 1987, p. 25.
[22]"The Upheaval in Health Care," *Business Week,* July 25, 1983, p. 44.
[23]Ibid.

the average cost for that DRG in its area, it will lose money, for its actual costs will be only partially reimbursed. The DRG-based payment system has been adopted for reimbursements by state agencies and private businesses. Thus a real incentive for holding costs down has been applied. The DRG system encourages efficiency, and purchasing is one of the key areas where potentially large cost savings can be made.

Model Procurement Code

Starting in the late 1960s a committee of the American Bar Association began discussing the need for a model procurement code for state and local purchasing activities. The bar association felt such a code was needed for two reasons: first, the substantial increase in and amounts of money spent on state and local purchasing, and second, since the federal government supplies funds to state and local governments, the spending of these funds should comply with sound purchasing practices.

After going through several public hearings and drafts, the code was adopted in 1979. A number of states and cities served as pilot jurisdictions to provide feedback on the workability of the code; these included the states of Kentucky, Tennessee, New Mexico, Louisiana, and Utah, and the cities of Louisville, Kentucky; Knoxville, Tennessee; Baltimore, Maryland; and San Diego, California.[24]

The purpose of the code is to provide (1) policy guidance for managing and controlling the purchase of supplies, services, and construction for public purposes, (2) remedies for resolving controversies about public contracts, and (3) a set of ethical guides for public buyers. The Code itself is a 75-page document, divided into 12 parts or Articles, as follows:

Article 1: General provisions.

Article 2: Procurement organization.

Article 3: Source selection and contract formation.

Article 4: Specifications.

Article 5: Procurement of construction, architect-engineer and land surveying services.

Article 6: Modification and termination of contracts for supplies and services.

Article 7: Cost principles.

Article 8: Supply management.

Article 9: Legal and contractual remedies.

---

[24]*The Model Procurement Code for State and Local Governments* (Washington, D.C.: American Bar Association, February 1979), p. VI.

Article 10: Intergovernmental relations.

Article 11: Assistance to small and disadvantaged business; Federal assistance on contract procurement requirements.

Article 12: Ethics in public contracting.[25]

While certain of the individual sections and the wording of principles and policies therein are open to criticism and modification, the overall code has been helpful in assisting governmental units at all levels to improve their purchasing policies, procedures, and systems. Since the code was to provide a statute outlining the fundamentals of sound purchasing, the American Bar Association later presented a set of recommended, comprehensive, and integrated regulations which a governmental unit could use to implement the code. This 265-page document, published in 1980, gives the language which could be used in developing a comprehensive policy manual governing a public purchasing operation.[26]

As a follow-up to the full code, the American Bar Association approved and published in August 1982 a model procurement ordinance for use by smaller units of local government. This 26-page document generally is a condensation of the full code, with essentially the same articles, except that Articles 7, 8, 10, and 11 were not developed in condensed form.[27]

QUESTIONS FOR REVIEW AND DISCUSSION

1. What changes should be made in public purchasing to make it more effective?

2. Are there any differences between federal purchasing and state and local purchasing? Discuss.

3. How do the objectives of public purchasing differ from those of industrial buying?

4. Discuss the advantages and problems arising from local bidder preference laws in state and local purchasing.

5. What are performance bonds, and why are they used?

6. How does the bid process in public buying differ from that in industrial buying?

7. What are the major differences between public buying and industrial buying? Which would be easiest to do?

---

[25]Ibid., pp. XI–XXI.

[26]*The Model Procurement Code for State and Local Governments: Recommended Regulations* (Washington, D.C.: American Bar Association, August 1980).

[27]*The Model Procurement Ordinance for Local Governments* (Washington, D.C.: American Bar Association, August 1982).

8. Under what circumstances should each of the four common military contract types be used?

9. Considering the magnitude and complexity of military purchasing, can it ever really be efficient and cost effective? What changes should be made in current practices?

10. How can industrial buyers use federal government purchase specifications?

11. Does the Buy American Act promote efficient purchasing? Justify the continuation or repeal of the act.

12. Are there any major differences between purchasing for a health care organization and a manufacturing firm? What changes would be required?

REFERENCES

Cooperative Purchasing Guidelines. Park Ridge, Ill.: Association of School Business Officials of the United States and Canada, 1979.

Farrell, Paul V., coordinating ed. *Aljian's Purchasing Handbook*. 4th ed. New York: McGraw-Hill, 1982, Section 20.

Greisler, David S., and Sumer C. Aggarwal. "Hospital Materials Management: Potential for Improvement." *Journal of Purchasing and Materials Management,* Spring 1985.

The Model Procurement Code for State and Local Governments. Washington, D.C.: American Bar Association, February 1979.

The Model Procurement Code for State and Local Governments: Recommended Regulations. Washington, D.C.: American Bar Association, August 1980.

The Model Procurement Ordinance for Local Governments. Washington, D.C.: American Bar Association, August 1982.

Munsterman, Richard E. *Purchasing and Supply Management Handbook for School Business Officials,* Research Bulletin no. 22. Chicago: Association of School Business Officials of the United States and Canada, 1978.

Page, Harry R. *Public Purchasing and Materials Management*. Lexington, Mass.: Lexington Books, 1980.

Sherman, Stanley N. *Contract Management: Post Award*. Gaithersburg, Md: Wordcrafters Publications, 1987.

Sherman, Stanley N. *Government Procurement Management*. 2nd ed. Gaithersburg, Md: Wordcrafters Publications, 1985.

State and Local Government Purchasing. 2nd ed. Lexington, Ky.: Council of State Governments, 1983.

Suss, Warren H. "How to Sell to Uncle Sam." *Harvard Business Review*. November/December, 1984.

Case 13–1

FOLAN CITY

"I want you to know that I intend to fight this, and I am going to give the mayor a call right now!" shouted Bill Marsden as he hung up after talking with Andrea Sparton. They had been discussing the city's purchase of a compressor on which the Marsden firm had been low bidder but had not been awarded the contract. Andrea Sparton was director of purchases for Folan City, a West Coast municipality with about one million residents, well known for its natural attractions.

The compressor had been requested by the engineering shops and considerable care had been taken to draw up the appropriate specifications to reflect the variety of uses anticipated for this equipment. A Johnson, model TAR, was considered suitable, and bidders were invited to quote on this model or its equivalent.

Invitations to bid had been sent out and eight quotations were received, with Marsden, Inc., as the low bidder by $2,300. Since Marsden's bid was based on a make and model different from the one referred to in the invitation to bid, Andrea had asked the city engineering department to assess the model proposed by Marsden to see if it was equivalent. According to the city engineer, the Marsden model was inferior to the one requested. On the basis of that assessment, another firm which had quoted on the Johnson TAR model had been recommended by purchasing for this contract. This recommendation had gone to the city's finance committee, which had accepted purchasing's recommendation at its regular Tuesday night meeting. The following morning, Bill Marsden, president of Marsden, Inc., had telephoned Andrea to complain. Andrea realized that Bill Marsden was an influential local businessman whose aggressiveness was well known in local business and political circles. In his telephone call to Andrea, Bill maintained that the equipment he was offering was equivalent in quality and performance to the Johnson TAR model, and that, since he was the low bidder, he should receive the business. During his conversation with Andrea, he also managed to raise the point: "We, local suppliers, seem to have a difficult time with this city's purchasing office. If we quote high, we don't receive the business, and if we quote low, we aren't getting any business, either. What do we have to do to make an honest buck around here?"

Case 13–2

CITY OF HAMPTON "B2"

In early January John Cameron, director of purchasing and supply for the city of Hampton, Ontario, was evaluating bids on the Thorneton Home kitchen equipment. The bids were being evaluated on an item-by-item basis and, in most cases, identification of the lowest responsible bidder was relatively straightforward. However, evaluation of the bids on the dishwashing unit and accessories was more difficult. One vendor, Sheldon Food Equipment, offered what they claimed to be an equivalent unit for less than any bid for the brand originally specified.

City of Hampton Purchasing and Supply Division

The Purchasing and Supply Division (PSD) had purchasing, tendering, and disposal authority for the city of Hampton's engineering, fire, and landfill/sanitation departments and for the Social Services Division. The director of PSD also managed the central stores function. The mission of the PSD was to respond to the needs of the other departments and divisions, for goods and services at minimum cost, consistent with desired quality and delivery timing.

Purchasing agent authority was granted to the director of the PSD by a municipal bylaw. The director could call for quotations and make purchases of less than $30,000 on his own authority, provided that the funds were allocated in the current year's budget. Any purchase of greater than $30,000 required open public tender. PSD personnel evaluated the bids on tenders and made recommendations for contract awards. These recommendations were subject to the review and approval by the requisitioning department, the Board of Control, and the city council.

Purchases were initiated by submission of a purchase requisition, signed by the head of the user department. Preparation of the specifications for tendering was the responsibility of the requisitioning department. PSD personnel checked the specifications to ensure that competitive bidding would result.

John Cameron became Director of PSD two years ago at the age of 35. He reported to the city treasurer, Mr. P. Van Dyk, and dealt directly with other department and division heads on purchasing matters. John managed a staff of 15, in two sections, purchasing and clerical support/stores. The purchasing section consisted of three buyers, each assigned purchasing authority for a specified group of commodities. A partial organization chart is shown in Exhibit 1.

Thorneton Old Age Home

The Thorneton Old Age Home was a 470-bed residential and extended care institution, owned and operated by the city of Hampton. Operation of the home was the responsibility of the Thorneton home administrator, Mr. G. Willmot. He reported to the city's director of social services, Mr. D. Davis. The dietary department at Thorneton was managed by the head chef, Mr. A. Butson. A partial organization chart is shown in Exhibit 1.

EXHIBIT 1   City Administration—Partial Organization Chart

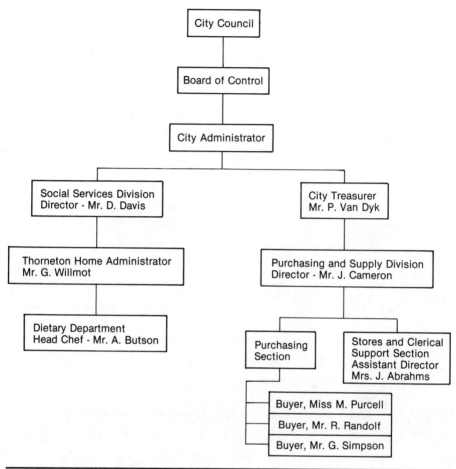

Kitchen Equipment Tender

The need for replacement of six pieces of kitchen equipment at Thorneton had been established as part of a kitchen renovation plan. An allowance of $35,000 was included in the city's capital budget. The budget year ended March 31.

In late November, the head chef at Thorneton, Mr. A. Butson, submitted a purchase requisition to the appropriate buyer, Miss M. Purcell. The requisition specified equipment from a well known manufacturer, Kitchen Systems Incorporated (KSI). The requisition was accompanied by a quotation for the requested equipment, from KSI's local branch manager, Mr. P. Orr. The quotation totaled $31,605, not including installation charges. The requisition is shown in Exhibit 2.

Miss Purcell discussed the order with Mr. Butson and found him to be quite adamant about wanting KSI equipment. She then briefed John on the situation and asked for his direction.

EXHIBIT 2　Purchase Requisition

Required by: A. Butson		Date Prepared:	Division Name: Thorneton Home	
Terms:		F.O.B.:	Carrier/Freight:	
Date goods required		Suppliers Shipping Date:	Ship to:	
Approvals			NO.: H0064820	
Dept. Head				
Purchasing Dept.			Special Instructions:	
Quantity	Unit		Description	
1			KSI XA-90 Dishwasher 208/3 phase-right to left C/W reg. steam 3/4″ injection, two extended vent connectors S/S panel, table limit switch	
1			Optional: Auto timer control package for above dishwasher	
1			3490 Booster	
1			KSI-SA-31 Food waste Group #2 electrical 208/3 using existing cone	
1			KSI FA-26 Potato Peeler C/W Base and Trap 208/3	
1			KSI GA-Z6 slicer 115/60/1 standard equipment	
1			KSI HA-Z6 Foodcutter 115/60/1	
1			KSI 12 qt. Mixer - Bench Model 115/60/1 12 qt. S/S Bowl Standard Beater and Whip	

Since the quotation exceeded $30,000, John could not purchase the equipment on his own authority. In addition, he had been told by a former Thorneton employee now working at city hall that the local branch manager of KSI and the head chef were personal friends and this concerned him. He wanted the purchase to be completely above board, so he directed Miss Purcell to prepare documents for open public bids of the equipment order.

John knew that PSD personnel did not have the time to write detailed specifications for orders of highly individual and specialized equipment. In addition, detailed specifications based on either design or performance would be costly to write for this relatively small order. End user departments were normally responsible for specifications, but John knew that the head chef had neither the technical ability nor the time to write specifications.

Aware of these limitations, John directed Miss Purcell to use brand specification in the tender documents, using the make and model numbers from the original purchase requisition and adding "or equivalent" to allow other manufacturers to compete. A bid list of 15 dealers was developed, using various directories, and the bid was publicly advertised. Documents were issued on December 5, with closing January 4. By closing, five companies had submitted bids. Excerpts from the tender documents are shown in Exhibit 3.

EXHIBIT 3   Summary of Bid Terms and Conditions

Section

4   *Specification Requirements*

The purpose is to obtain bids for various kitchen equipment in accordance with specifications as indicated below. Any vendor's trade name or catalog number mentioned in these specifications is for the sole purpose of designating a standard of quality and type and for no other reason. Note: The following items are supply and installation.

4–6   *One (1) Dishwasher*

208/3/60 right to left C/W regular steam ¾" injectors; two (2) extended vent connectors; stainless steel panel; table limit switch; Kitchen Systems Incorporated Model XA-90 or equivalent; installation and removal of old unit included.

Addendum No. 1 December 15

Please add the following to Section 4–6.

Installation to include the removal of the old unit. The contractor shall provide all necessary plumbing, electrical wiring, steam connections, ventilation, water connections, and all things necessary to have the new unit in working condition.

Addendum No. 2 December 19

Please revise Section 4–6 to read as follows:

One (1) Dishwasher

208/3/60—*LEFT TO RIGHT* c/w regular steam ¾" injectors, two (2) extended vent connectors; stainless steel panel, table limit switch; Kitchen Systems Incorporated Model XA-90 or equivalent.

EXHIBIT 3   *(concluded)*

4–7   *One (1) Automatic Control Package for above dishwasher*

4–8   *One (1) Steam Booster for above dishwasher; Kitchen System Incorporated*
        Model 36 or equivalent.

5   *Terms and Conditions*

5–7   *Disputes*
        In cases of disputes as to whether or not a product or service tendered or
           delivered meets the conditions in the accepted tender, the decision of the
           director of purchasing shall be final and binding on all parties.

5–10 *The City of Hampton reserves the right to award this on a lot, unit, or*
        item basis.

General Conditions, Instructions to Bidder, and Information to Bidder.

6   Brand Names—If and whenever in a specification a brand name, make,
           trade name, or name of manufacturer number is mentioned, it is for the
           sole purpose of establishing a grade or quality of material only, unless
           specified otherwise. Since the city does not wish to rule out other
           competition and equal brands or makes, the phrase "and approved
           equal" may be added. However, if a product other than the specified is
           bid, it is the vendor's responsibility . . . to prove to the city that said
           product is equal to the specifications . . .

Section

7   When required the city may request full demonstration of any unit(s) bid
           prior to the awarding of any contract.

7–9   The city reserves the right to accept or reject any or all bids or parts of
           bids, to waive irregularities and technicalities and to require rebids on
           the required materials. The city also reserves the right to waive minor
           variations in specifications (interpretation of minor variances will be
           made by the applicable city department personnel).

Each of the six pieces of equipment operated independently. Thus recommendations for purchase could be made on an item-by-item basis. In five of the six
decisions, the lowest responsible bidder was easily identified and the equivalence of
nonspecified brands was determined by examination of the specifications.

Evaluation of the dishwasher bids was more difficult since the equipment was
much more complex than the rest of the order. Of the five companies bidding, three
had bid on the specified KSI brand, one had offered both the specified brand and an
alternate, the Simplex SSL, and one had offered an alternate brand, the Food King
100 only. A summary of the dishwasher bids is shown in Exhibit 4.

The Simplex model SSL could be easily eliminated since its cost was greater
than the low bid for the KSI XA-90. However, the Food King 100, offered by Sheldon
Food Equipment, was considerably lower in price than the low bid for KSI equipment.
A summary of the specifications of the two models is shown in Exhibit 5.

John knew that Thorneton Home kitchen used two dishwashing units. One was
the old KSI XA-90 which was to be replaced. The other unit had been a KSI XA-90

EXHIBIT 4 Bid Summary

	White Ltd. "Alternate"	White Ltd.	Sheldon Food	Waverley Commercial Products	Reliable Food Services	KSI Canada
Dishwasher						
Make	Simplex	KSI	Food King	KSI	KSI	KSI
Model	SSL	XA-90	100	XA-90	XA-90	XA-90
Cost	$16,124.70	$14,040.00	$12,784.66	$14,100.24	$14,660.50	$15,804.00
Automatic Timer						
Make	Included in above	KSI	Food King	KSI	KSI	KSI
Model			100A			
Cost		$ 749.00	$ 586.18	$ 720.49	$ 675.80	$ 758.00 (installation not included)
Steam Booster						
Make	Included in above	KSI	Food King	KSI	KSI	KSI
Model		36	100X	36	36	36
Cost		$ 2,021.25	$ 1,619.68	$ 2,081.90	$ 2,031.34	$ 2,260.00
Installation Charge	$ 2,200.00	$ 2,550.00	$ 2,159.00	$ 1,552.00	$ 2,600.00	by others
Total	$18,324.70	$19,360.25	$17,149.52	$18,454.63	$19,967.64	$18,822.00

EXHIBIT 5 Dishwasher Specification Comparison

	KSI-XA-90	*Food King 100*
*Capacity (20″ × 20″ racks/hr)	194 (200–400 meals/sitting)	187 (200–400 meals/sitting)
Design	Fully automatic rack-type single tank with integral recirculating prewash.	Fully automatic rack-type single tank with integral recirculating prewash.
	Three chambers; two inspection doors.	Three chambers; two inspection doors.
Construction	Formed #18 stainless steel prewash and wash chambers; #16 stainless steel tank and hood; welded steel frame; stainless steel front panel.	#16 stainless steel hood and tank; heavy-gauge steel base; all internal sections in contact with spray are stainless steel or nickel-bronze.
Dimensions L × W × H	80″ × 25″ × 69″	68″ × 25″ × 64″
Pumps	Recirculating prewash 150 gpm; Power wash 195 gpm.	Recirculating prewash 95 gpm; Power wash 193 gpm.
Motors	Prewash 1 HP; Power wash 1½ HP.	Prewash ½ HP; Power wash 1½ HP; Conveyor ¼ HP.
Conveyor	Dual drive; driven by special reducer on Power-wash motor.	Single pawl driven by separate ¼ HP motor.
Functions: (1) Prewash	Stainless steel spray arms above and below; 36″ prewash section recirculating from prewash tank.	Spray distributed by 7 high-volume nozzles—3 above, 4 below; thermostatically controlled temperature; 22″ prewash section recirculating from prewash tank.
(2) Power wash	Fixed upper spray assembly; lower stationary centerfed spray assembly; thermometer included; wash tank heated by steam injectors.	Spray distributed by 7 stationary stand pipes—4 above, 3 below; thermometer included; wash tank heated by steam injectors.

EXHIBIT 5   *(concluded)*

	KSI-XA-90	*Food King 100*
(3) Final rinse	Double-acting rinse arms above and below, automatically activated; 50 percent of water then diverted to wash tank and 50 percent to prewash.	Spray distributed by 10 nozzles, 6 above and 4 below; 50 percent of water diverted to wash tank.
Electrical	Magnetic motor controllers; automatic overload protection and reset; low voltage protection.	NEMA type 3 cabinet switch; magnetic motor starters; auto overload protection; low voltage protection.
Water/electricity consumption	No data in specifications.	No data in specifications.
Option	2 HP prewash motor; 2 HP power wash motor; various materials options, e.g., stainless steel and chrome frame and legs.	Various materials options, e.g., stainless steel frame and legs.

*Not a constraint at Thorneton Home.

replaced six years ago with a Food King 100. The Food King 100 and the KSI XA-90 were used for the same dishwashing tasks and there had been no complaints about the performance of the Food King unit. A check of service records for the Food King unit had revealed no unusual maintenance problems in six years of operation.

End user acceptance of nonspecified brands was required prior to making recommendations to the Board of Control. John was concerned about the head chef's reaction since he had recommended only one piece of KSI equipment for the five nondishwasher items already evaluated.

Case 13–3

THE EASTERN COUNTIES REGION (R)

In February Hugh Carson joined the Eastern Counties Region Purchasing Department as senior buyer. Art Simpson, the purchasing agent who hired him, said: "Hugh, why don't you work with us for the next six months, become familiar with the work, and then we will sit down together and discuss your impressions. By August we will have to start work on our plans for next year and that will be an excellent time to incorporate any suggestions you may have. As you know, we are really just getting started here and you are likely to encounter all sorts of things that can stand improvement. I am interested in tackling the most important things first, so you will have to give some indication of your priorities."

As a busy first six months on the job neared their end in mid-July, Hugh received a reminder from Art who said: "Let's get together for half a day on August 3 to discuss what's going on. Just so that we may have as useful a session as possible, please put your key ideas down in memo form and have these to me by the end of July. Then we will make your memo the starting point of our discussion."

The Eastern Counties Region

The Eastern Counties Region was established the previous year to consolidate a number of counties, previously independently governed. One of the many objectives of the state in establishing regional government was to provide integrated region-wide services. Regional responsibilities included planning, the production and distribution of water, bulk sewage collection and treatment, roads, traffic, police, social services including day-care and senior citizen centers. The area encompassed about 800 square miles and employed approximately 1,200 full-time employees.

Purchasing Organization and Responsibilities

The purchasing agent reported to the director of finance. The purchasing department was responsible for the procurement of all supplies and services for the counties with the exception of major construction contracts (roadways, bridges, new buildings, and so on). Annual purchases were estimated at $38-$50 million.

Personnel in the purchasing department included a purchasing agent, a senior buyer, a buyer/expediter and two clerk/stenos. Art Simpson believed that because of the large variety and types of products and services required, it was not practical to organize buyers' responsibilities by product type or classification. Therefore, buyers' responsibilities were divided among the different using departments which included: 19 water treatment plants, 14 pollution control plants, 5 senior citizen homes, 5 day-care centers, 3 police detachments, totaling approximately 600 personnel, 3 road yards, 10 administration departments, 1 fleet maintenance center, 1 traffic department, 1 in-plant print shop, and 3 social services departments.

Hugh Carson's Impressions

Hugh Carson had previously worked as a buyer in the purchasing department of a large city in a nearby state. The regional job represented a promotion and an opportunity to help build a new department, a challenge he wished to experience. Several times during his first six months on the job he wondered why he had been so anxious to seek this new experience, because he found the present purchasing situation hectic. In his opinion, there were a large number of contributing factors. The more important of these follow.

The Paper Flow.   The paper flow in purchasing was massive in Hugh's opinion and could best be illustrated by the following annual figures. The department:

1. Processed between 12,000 and 14,000 purchase requisitions.

2. Issued between 10,000 and 11,000 purchase orders and written releases against blanket orders and contracts.

3. Prepared written specifications and issued 250–300 formal requests for quotation. Each request was prepared individually starting with a blank sheet of paper. This required a great deal of typing, use of colored letterhead, collation, and assembly.

4. Summarized all appropriate quotations and prepared reports to the regional board with recommendation of awards.

5. Issued normal day-to-day correspondence.

In Hugh's opinion, this paperwork kept him chained to his desk, always behind, and made it difficult to do other necessary tasks.

Interdepartmental Communication.   Hugh quickly found out that there was no coordination of purchases between similar departments. For example, the 19 different water treatment plants did their own requisitioning of supplies with no communication between them, as was the case with the pollution control plants and other units. This resulted in multiple orders for identical or similar products.

The Lack of Standardization.   Because of the poor communication between all departments, there was no standardization of materials. Every plant used different cleaning waxes, had preferences in tools different from the others, used different bearings for identical equipment, and so on. Hugh understood this was logical, given the evolution of the current governmental structure, but he believed it created many problems for both purchasers and users.

Storage Facilities.   Hugh believed there was a general shortage of storage area in the system. There was no central warehouse for inventory of general supplies and materials and none of the using departments had sufficient storage space to stock large quantities of supplies. This hindered economical volume purchasing.

Delays in Purchasing.   To Hugh, the time period from issue of requisition to the placement of the purchase order was too long. Requisitions from all using departments had to go first to each using department's supervisor who approved them before forwarding them to purchasing. This in itself created a delay. Since all the regional mail was handled by the region's own delivery service, this created a further delay. Finally, the backlog of orders in the purchasing department meant that many requisitions were not acted upon for at least several weeks.

The Annual Budget Rush.   The annual budget created two peak loads for purchasing. Many department heads were anxious to spend their full budget before the expiry of the current year. This created a large number of last minute requests. Furthermore, once the new annual budget was approved, this created a great rush of new requisitions. These activities increased the department workload substantially since they necessitated the issuing of formal quotations, bid requests and summaries, and reports to the board.

Departmental Policies and Guidelines.   There was no legal provision which governed the policies and procedures of the purchasing department nor was there a purchasing manual or guidebook available for purchasing staff or using departments. As a result, Hugh was not sure whether all departments were using purchasing and whether the purchasing department left itself open to charges of violating the public trust.

Recommendations.   Hugh Carson knew that Art Simpson was looking forward to his appraisal of the purchasing department. Even though he could see many areas for possible improvement, he was not sure where to begin. Since he had only several days left to prepare the memo Art Simpson had requested, he knew it was time to get his thoughts down on paper.

CHAPTER 14

Acquisition of Capital Assets

The effective acquisition of capital assets presents some unique challenges. Frequently, the sums of money involved are substantial for the individual purchaser and the acquisition becomes a project involving a variety of internal functions. In most organizations the purchase of capital assets requires special budgeting processes and is closely controlled at the top executive level.

The term *capital assets* will be applied broadly to those items in which the cost is more properly chargeable to a capital account than to expense. They are essential *durable* or *capital* goods and include equipment and construction. First the acquisition of equipment will be covered.

NEW EQUIPMENT BUYING

A useful classification of equipment is the division into *multipurpose* and *single purpose*. Multipurpose equipment may have a variety of uses, may be used in many industries, tends to have longer technological life, and may have considerable salvage value. Fork lift trucks, certain classes of computers, and standard lathes are typical examples.

Single-purpose equipment is designed to do one or several operations well, substantially better than a multipurpose piece of equipment could. On the other hand, its specificity limits its potential use, and its usefulness is closely tied to the need for the operations it performs. Such special equipment is often limited to one industry and may even be limited to one customer. The purchaser's specifications are important, requiring extensive consultation between the technical personnel of both buyer and supplier. The salvage value of special equipment may be low, with the drawback that the need for the tasks disappears before the equipment is physically worn out.

Minor or accessory equipment is normally used in an auxiliary capacity and tends to be of much lower dollar value. Its cost may not even be capitalized, and much of it tends to be standardized. Small power packs and motors are typical examples.

Special Problems of Equipment Buying

Equipment procurement raises special problems:

1. The buying of equipment usually requires that substantial amounts of money be expended for a single purchase. Sometimes the sum is so large as to call for a special form of financing, such as a bond issue, leasing, or payment on the installment plan.

2. Because of their comparatively long life, equipment items are likely to be bought less frequently than other types of purchases.

3. The final cost of equipment is more difficult to determine with exactness than, for example, the final cost of raw materials. The initial cost of equipment is but part of the total cost, which involves a whole series of estimates, such as the effects of idle time, of obsolescence, of maintenance and repair, of displaced labor, and even of direct operation factors. Some of these items may never be known exactly, even after experience with the particular piece of equipment in question. Moreover, many of the costs, such as insurance, interest, and obsolescence, continue even when the equipment is not in actual use. The income to be derived is also problematical, and, thus, even when it is possible to compute approximate costs, it is often difficult to determine how soon they will be met. These comments are particularly applicable to nonproductive equipment, such as cranes and hoists.

4. Equipment purchases are often less affected by current price trends than, for instance, raw materials. The demand for equipment more than the demand for any other type of industrial goods is a derived demand. Pricewise, the best time at which to buy is, therefore, particularly hard to determine. Only when the need and the justification of the equipment has been established is there a possibility that its actual purchase may be delayed or hastened by price considerations. Since equipment is not commonly bought until needed, it is seldom bought during periods of business recession, although prices for equipment normally are low at such times and many good arguments can be advanced for buying then. Aside from absence of immediate need, manufacturers in periods of slack business tend to watch their assets carefully. Also, labor may be cheaper during recessions, and there is less incentive to substitute machinery for labor. The reverse conditions prevail in times of prosperity.

5. The purchase of equipment frequently involves problems concerning the wisest method of disposition of the displaced item.

6. Equipment, particularly major installation, may require a significant period of start-up during which extra purchasing support may have to be provided to deal with all kinds of emergencies.

A decision to purchase equipment is likely to require a careful consideration of many factors involving broad management policy. The decision once made may well commit the organization to a series of other decisions of a permanent nature, such as the type of product to be manufactured, allocation of space, the method of its production, and the cost of operation. Put in other words, it is much easier "to get in and out" of a situation involving the purchase of raw materials than one involving the purchase of major equipment. Furthermore, the company's labor and financial policies may be affected. In short, equipment questions are likely to be procurement decisions of prime importance to management.

It is necessary to analyze not only the price of the particular equipment in question but also such elements as plant layout, kind of power used, types of machines used for other operations, and the like. In short, the proposed installation must be looked on as an integral part of an established process; and its coordination with the existing facilities must be obtained, even though extensive changes may be required to effect economical production.

Equipment purchases involve, in part, engineering and production considerations and, in part, factors largely outside the scope of these functions. From the former standpoint, there are six commonly recognized reasons for purchase: economy in operation, increased productivity, better quality, dependability in use, savings in time or labor costs, and durability. To these safety, pollution, and emergency protection should be added.

Beyond these engineering questions are those which only the marketing, purchasing, or financial departments, or general management itself can answer. Are style changes or other modifications in the present product essential or even desirable? Is the market static, contracting, or expanding? Does the company have the funds with which to buy the machine which theoretically is most desirable, or is it necessary, for financial reasons, to be satisfied with something that is perhaps less efficient but of a lower initial cost? What should be done in a case in which the particular equipment most desirable from an engineering standpoint is obtainable only from a manufacturer who is not thoroughly trustworthy or perhaps is on the verge of bankruptcy? Such questions are quite as important in the final decision as are the more purely engineering ones.

For this reason it is sound practice to form a team including representatives from engineering, using departments, finance, marketing, and purchasing to work jointly on major equipment purchases.

In some organizations the volume of equipment purchases is so great that a special person or team of employees in purchasing is assigned the equipment purchasing task exclusively. The title of equipment buyer is a common one in such instances as is manager of equipment purchases.

Importance of Cost Factors

Once the need for new equipment has been determined, one of the first questions to be considered is that of cost. Is the equipment intended for replacement only or to provide additional capacity? What is the installed cost of the equipment? What will start-up costs be? Will its installation create problems of plant layout? What will be the maintenance and repair costs and who will provide repair parts and at what cost? Are accessories required, and if so, what will their cost be? What will be the operating costs, including power and labor? What is the number of machine-hours the equipment will be used? Can the user make the machine or must it be bought outside? At what rate is the machine to be depreciated? What financing costs are involved? If, as is usually the case, the equipment is for production, what is the present cost of producing the product compared with obtaining the item from an outside supplier and of producing the unit with the new equipment?

Life Cycle Costing

The U.S. Department of Defense has strongly encouraged the use of life cycle costing (LCC) as a decision approach to capital investments. The philosophy behind LCC is relatively simple. The total cost of a piece of equipment goes well beyond the purchase price or even its installed cost. What is really of interest is the total cost of performing the intended function over the lifetime of the task or the piece of equipment. Thus, an initial low purchase price may mask a higher operating cost, perhaps occasioned by higher maintenance and downtime costs, more skilled labor, greater material waste, more energy use, or higher waste processing charges. Since the low bid would favor a low initial machine cost, an unfair advantage may accrue to the supplier with possibly the highest life-cycle-cost equipment.

It is the inclusion of every conceivable cost pertaining to the decision that makes the LCC concept easier to grasp theoretically than to practice in real life. Since many of the costs are future ones, possibly even 10 to 15 years hence and of a highly uncertain nature, criticisms of the exactness of LCC are well founded. Fortunately, computer programs are available varying from simple accounting programs, which compute costs from project life cycles, to Monte Carlo simulation of the equipment from conception to disposal. The computer allows for testing of sensitivity, and inputs can be readily changed when necessary. The normal emphasis, particularly in governmental acquisition on the low bid finds, therefore, a serious and preferable alternative in LCC. The experience with LCC has shown in a surprising number of instances that the initial purchase price of equipment may be a relatively low percentage of LCC. For example, computers, if purchased, seldom run over 50 percent and most industrial equipment falls into the 20 to 60 percent range.

Problem of Engineering Service

Most sellers of major equipment maintain an intimate and continuing interest in their equipment after it is sold and installed. Two major questions are involved in providing engineering service: why is the service given and accepted, and what is the cost of such service?

Technical sales service is provided by a vendor to a potential or actual purchaser of equipment, to determine the designs and specifications of the equipment believed best suited to the particular requirements of the buyer and also to ensure that, once bought, the equipment functions properly. It is nearly always related to the "individualized buying problem of particular users." Occasionally, equipment is sold which carries with it a production guarantee, an additional reason for supervising both the installation and the operation of the equipment. Even after this initial period, the seller may provide for regular inspection to ensure the proper operation of the machine.

There is, however, another side to this question of sales service. For one thing, the prospective buyer may ask for and receive a great deal of presale service and advice without real intention of buying or knowing full well that the firm providing the service will under no circumstances receive an order. Not only is such a procedure unethical, but the buyer who pursues it will sooner or later find the organization's reputation for fair dealing has seriously suffered.

The problem of engineering service is really twofold, both phases, however, involving cost. The first phase relates to the method followed by the seller in charging for presale service. Such service is clearly a matter of sales promotion, and when no subsequent sale results or when the profit on the sale is insufficient to cover fully the cost of the service, some other means of recovery must be found. One suggestion for meeting this problem is that a specific charge, either a flat fee or one computed on the basis of actual cost, be made for presale engineering service, with the recipient of the service paying this charge whether or not a purchase is made subsequently.

The second phase of the problem relates to postsale engineering service. The prime abuse of postsale services arises from those firms which insist on furnishing and charging for it whether or not the buyer feels a need for it.

Selection of the Source

Selection of the proper source requires careful consideration in any purchase of major equipment. In the purchase of raw materials and supplies, quick delivery and the availability of a continuous supply are important reasons for choosing a particular supplier. These characteristics are often not so important in equipment purchases. The reliability of the seller and a reasonable price are, of course, important, regardless of what is being bought. But, as contrasted with raw materials, what may be called *cooperation* in selecting the right type of equipment, proper installation, common interests in efficient operation—in short, a long-continuing interest in the product after it is sold—becomes very important. So, too, does the availability of repair parts and of repair services throughout the entire life of the machine. Satisfactory past relationships with the equipment supplier weigh heavily in the placing of future orders.

The interest of operations, engineering, or technical personnel in capital equipment is such that they usually have a strong supplier preference. For large companies, manufacturing equipment in their own shops has always been an alternative. Some even have subsidiaries specializing in equipment design and manufacture. Where secret processes give a manufacturer a competitive edge, such in-house manufacture is almost essential.

Some Legal Questions

Attention should also be directed to the legal questions that arise in connection with equipment buying. The danger of liability for patent infringement constitutes one problem. The extent of liability for accidents to employees is another. Again, the equipment sales contracts and purchase agreements are often long and involved, offering many opportunities for legal controversies. Various forms of insurance coverage are used and are often subject to varying interpretations. Any purchased machine must comply fully with the safety regulations of the state in which it is to be operated, and these safety regulations vary greatly in the different states. Federal Government OSHA (Occupational Safety and Health Act) requirements have to be followed. The question of consequential damages is a particularly touchy one. Should the seller of a key piece of equipment be responsible for the loss of sales and contribution when the machine fails because of a design or fabrication error? Such losses may be huge for the buyer. In one company gross revenue of $1 million per day was lost for six months because of the failure of a new piece of equipment costing $800,000! These and many other situations exist which call for careful scrutiny and interpretation by qualified legal counsel.

Special Budgeting Procedures

When the financial budget is set up, it is customary to make provisions for two types of capital expenditures. The first type covers probable expenditures which, although properly chargeable to some capital account, are still too small to be brought directly to the attention of the finance committee or controller. Customarily, some limit is fixed, such as $2,000 to $5,000.

The second type includes expenditures for larger amounts. The inclusion in the budget normally constitutes neither an authorization to spend that amount of money nor an approval of any specific equipment acquisition. This authorization must be obtained subsequently from the executives concerned, and their specific approval is given only after they have examined carefully a preliminary analysis of the project. A formal appropriation request is called for, giving a detailed description of what is to be bought, estimates of the costs involved, the savings likely to result, the causes which have created the need, the effect of the purchase on the organization as a whole, and whatever other information those initiating the request feel is pertinent. In light of these facts, together with the data regarding other financial requirements of the company and its financial position, a decision is made as to the wisdom of authorizing the particular expenditure under consideration.

Disposition of Obsolete or Replaced Equipment

What to do with old or replaced equipment is an interesting question. One procedure is to trade in the old machine on the new, with the vendor making an allowance and assuming the burden of disposal. A second procedure is to sell the old equipment to a used equipment dealer. A third is to find a direct buyer. A fourth is to sell the old machine as scrap. A fifth is to destroy the machine to assure no one else will have access to it. Some of these procedures are discussed indirectly in Chapter 9, "Disposal of Scrap, Surplus, or Obsolete Material."

PROCUREMENT OF USED EQUIPMENT

In our discussion of equipment purchases thus far, it has been assumed that the buyer was acquiring new equipment. An alternative is the purchase of used equipment, which raises special issues. In general, the same rules of evaluation apply as in the case of new equipment. One important difference, however, may be that, ordinarily, manufacturers' services and guarantees do not apply to such purchases. The value of these intangibles is difficult to determine. Many buyers would say that they are more important with used equipment than with new and that their value may be greater than any differential in price.

Barring other considerations, the decision of whether to trade in or not is largely dependent on which will result in the lowest net cost to the purchaser. Since trade-ins are a form of price concession, they may not accurately reflect current market values of the old equipment. In some industries, old equipment may be in perfect operating condition and its disposal may well create unwanted competition. At other times, it may represent a health or environmental hazard, or contain special secret features. Destruction may be a reasonable solution in all these instances.

In large companies, equipment displaced in one plant may be of use in another within the same organization. It is normal practice for purchasing departments to circulate lists of items available within the organization before searching for other disposal alternatives. Transfer pricing is usually based on book value and the transportation charges are assumed by the receiving plant.

Reasons for Buying Used Equipment

Some of the reasons for the purchase of used equipment follow:

1. When price is important either because the differential between new and used is vital or the buyer's funds are low.
2. For use in a pilot or experimental plant.
3. For use with a special or temporary order over which the entire cost will be amortized.
4. Where the machine will be idle a substantial amount of time.
5. For use of apprentices.
6. For maintenance departments (not production).
7. For faster delivery when time is essential.
8. When a used machine can be easily modernized for relatively little or is already the latest model.
9. When labor costs are unduly high.

Sales Contract Terms

Used equipment may be offered with different contract terms:

1. The equipment may be available "as is," and perhaps "where is." A sale "as is" means that the contract carries essentially "no warranty, guarantee, or representation of any kind, expressed or implied, as to the condition of the item offered for sale." "Where is," of course, is self-explanatory.
2. The equipment may be sold with certain specific guarantees, preferably expressed in writing. This practice is found more generally among used equipment dealers, though they sometimes may offer equipment "as is."
3. Finally, the equipment may be sold "guaranteed and rebuilt." The equipment is invoiced as such; it has been tested; and it carries a binding guarantee of satisfactory performance for not less than 30 days from the date of shipment.

There are various channels through which used equipment is bought and sold. These include the manufacturer who accepted the used equipment as a trade-in, direct sale to user, brokers, auctions, and dealers.

LEASING EQUIPMENT

Many manufacturers of capital equipment lease as well as sell their equipment. Those who advocate leasing point out that leasing involves payments for the use of the assets rather than for the privilege of owning the asset.

Short-term rentals are a special form of lease with which everyone is familiar. Short-term rentals make a lot of sense when limited use of the equipment is foreseen and the capital and/or maintenance cost of the equipment is significant. Often an operator can be obtained along with the piece of equipment rented. The construction industry is a good example where extensive use is made of short-term rentals.

Most lease contracts can be drawn to include an "option to buy" after some stated period. It is important for anyone considering the lease of capital equipment to be sure that the Internal Revenue regulations are understood. On October 15, 1955, the Internal Revenue Service announced its position on ascertaining the tax status of leases:

> In the absence of compelling factors of contrary implication the parties will be considered as having intended a purchase and sale rather than a rental, if one or more of the following conditions are covered in the agreement:
>
> 1. Portions of periodic payments are specifically applicable to any equity to be acquired by the lessees.
> 2. The lessees will acquire title on payment of a stated amount of rentals.
> 3. The total amount which the lessee is required to pay for a relatively short period constitutes an inordinately large proportion of the total sum required to be paid to secure transfer of title.
> 4. The agreed rental payments exceed the current fair-rental values.
> 5. The property may be acquired under a purchase option which is nominal in relation to the value of the property at the time when the option may be exercised, as determined at the time of entering into the original agreement, or which is a relatively small amount when compared with the total payments which are required to be made.
> 6. Some portion of periodic payments is specifically designated as interest or is otherwise recognizable as the equivalent of interest.

Unless the lease rental payments are allowed to be treated as an expense item for income tax purposes, some of the possible advantages of the equipment lease plan may not be realized.

In the past, some large manufacturers of machines and equipment employing advanced technology have preferred to follow a policy of leasing rather than selling their equipment. Government antitrust actions have aimed at giving the user the right to determine whether to lease or purchase. The leasing may be done by the manufacturers of the equipment, by distributors, or by companies organized for the specific purpose of leasing equipment. At times, as in the construction industry, an owner of equipment who has no immediate use for it may lease or rent it to other concerns that may have temporary immediate need for it.

An interesting phenomenon with leasing occurs in large organizations, including public agencies. Since lease costs are normally charged to operating instead of capital budgets, department heads may try to acquire equipment through the back door of leasing when the capital budget does not permit purchase. This can easily lead to abuse and some very high rental costs. In one government agency, the rental of recording equipment over a six-month period equaled the purchase cost. Buyers need to be aware of this practice and on the lookout for costly subterfuges involving leasing.

Advantages and Disadvantages of Leasing

The advantages of leasing may be listed as follows:

1. Lease rentals are expenses for income tax purposes.
2. Small initial outlay (may actually cost less).
3. Availability of expert service.
4. Risk of obsolescence reduced.
5. Adaptability to special jobs and seasonal business.
6. Test period provided before purchase.
7. Burden of investment shifted to supplier.

For example, automobile fleet managers frequently prefer leasing when their fleet is spread across the country and when the leasing company has greater purchasing clout and better disposal ability.

There are certain equally clear disadvantages, however:

1. Final cost may be high.
2. Surveillance by lessor entailed.
3. Less freedom of control and use.

Many leases need to be watched with care since they are one sided in their terms, placing virtually all the risks on the lessee. For instance, what are the arrangements for replacing equipment when it is obsolete or no longer serviceable? Is the lessee free to buy supplies anywhere, such as paper for copying machines? Are the actual charges what they appear to be? Are there onerous limitations on either the maximum or the minimum output or other such operational factors as the number of hours per day or number of shifts the equipment may be used or on using attachments? What limitations, if any, are there to the uses to which the equipment may be put?

Types of Leases

The two main types of leases are the financial and the operational lease. The financial lease may be of the full payout or partial payout variety. In the full payout form the lessee pays the full purchase price of the equipment plus interest and, if applicable, maintenance, service, record keeping, and insurance charges on a regular payment plan. In the partial payout plan, there is a residual value to the equipment at the end of the lease term and the lessee pays for the difference between original cost and residual value plus interest and charges.

The financial lease cost is made up of the lessor's fee, the interest rate, and the depreciation rate of the equipment. The lessor's fee depends on the services offered and may be as low as 0.25 percent of the gross for straight financing without other services. The interest will depend both on the cost of money to the lessor and the credit rating of the lessee. The depreciation normally varies with the type of equipment and its use. For example, trucks are usually depreciated over a five-year period.

The operational lease is in its basic form noncancellable, has a fixed term which is substantially less than the life of the equipment, and a fixed financial commitment which is substantially less than the purchase price of the equipment. Service is the key factor in the operational lease, with the lessor assuming full responsibility for maintenance, obsolescence, insurance, taxes, purchase, and resale of equipment, and so on. The charges for these services must be evaluated by the lessee against other alternatives which may be open.

Categories of Leasing Companies

According to J. P. Matthews,[1] careful analysis of how the lessor will profit from the leasing arrangement is vital in obtaining a satisfactory price. Since most leasing companies have standard procedures for calculating leases but are seldom willing to disclose these or the vital figures behind them, it behooves the buyer to search carefully before signing. Since lessors are more likely to disclose competitors' procedures and figures than their own, the search need not be seen as an impossible task. Matthews identifies four major different structures of leasing relationships, each with its special implications (see Figure 14–1).

The Full-Service Lessor. Full-service lessors are most common in the automotive, office equipment, and industrial equipment fields. The lessor performs all services, purchases the equipment to the buyer's specifications, and has its own source of financing. This type of lessor generally obtains discounts or rebates from the equipment manufacturers which are not disclosed to the lessee. Profits are also obtained on the maintenance and service charges which are included in the lease rate. Care should be taken on long-term leases which contain an escalation provision to allow such escalation only on that portion of the lease on which costs might rise.

The Finance Lease Company. This type of lessor does not purchase or maintain the equipment, so that the lessee deals directly with the equip-

---

[1] J. P. Mathews, "Equipment Leasing: Before the Cash-Flow Analysis, What Else?" *Journal of Purchasing*, February 1974, pp. 5-11.

FIGURE 14–1   Four Leasing Structural Relationships

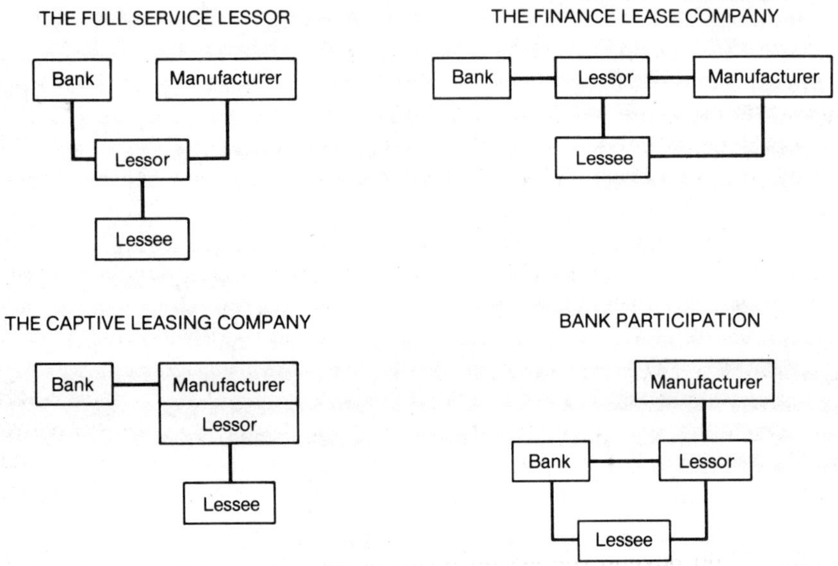

THE FULL SERVICE LESSOR

| Bank | Manufacturer |

Lessor

Lessee

THE FINANCE LEASE COMPANY

| Bank | Lessor | Manufacturer |

Lessee

THE CAPTIVE LEASING COMPANY

| Bank | Manufacturer |

Lessor

Lessee

BANK PARTICIPATION

Manufacturer

| Bank | Lessor |

Lessee

ment manufacturer. The lessor frequently has access to funds at close to prime rate and is able to make its profit by lending above this. Occasionally, if a relatively short lease is involved, the lessor may wish to profit from the resale value of the equipment and may offer unusually low lending rates. A profitable lessor may benefit from the investment tax credits and depreciation which to a less profitable lessee may be meaningless. When a lessee has already reached the limits on its investment tax credits because of large capital expenditures but the lessor is not yet at the limit, leasing may similarly benefit both.

Captive Leasing.   The prime purpose of captive leasing is to encourge the sale and use of the parent's equipment. The reasons why the original manufacturer of equipment may choose to lease rather than to sell are several.

1. To secure either wider distribution or a higher margin.
2. To reduce the credit risk.
3. To sell a full line or to increase the volume of sales of supplies.
4. To control the second-hand market.
5. To stabilize the company's growth through securing distribution in times of recession when sales, especially of new as contrasted with used equipment, are difficult to make.

6. To control servicing.

7. To protect a patent position.

Obviously, a transfer price for the equipment holds between the parent and the lessor. Sometimes a lessor will quote a 2 percent sales tax figure on the rental value when in reality the lessor may only be charged with a use tax which applies to only 50 percent of the rental value. A lessee might expect to gain at least a 1 percent benefit from negotiation here.

Bank Participation.   There are advantages to bank participation in cases where the lessee has a good credit rating. The bank may be willing to finance part of the lease at rates slightly over prime, because it is a low-risk and low-nuisance lease. The lessor looks after the purchasing, servicing, and disposal of the equipment, relieving the bank of tasks it normally has little expertise in.

Lessor Evaluation

Quite aside from any weighing of the specific advantages and disadvantages and beyond the actual terms of the lease, any prospective lessee of equipment needs to exercise the utmost care in passing judgment on the lessor. Is the lessor:

1. Reasonable and fair in dealings with customers?
2. Devoting as much attention and money to research as alleged?
3. Strong financially?
4. If a sole source, prone to be arbitrary in the periodic adjustment of rental and other fees?

The Acquisition of Construction

Construction represents a special class of capital assets. In the first place, land or space needs to be available for construction. Therefore, the question may arise of real estate acquisition with all of the attendant issues of office or plant location involving deeds, access, zoning restrictions, taxes, and availability of services such as water, electricity, and telephone. Other issues may involve distance from customers, suppliers, and labor and transportation access and costs. Obviously, many of these issues are properly the domain of other functions in the organization. In organizations in a rapid expansion mode, such as fast-food chains, or those with substantial land holding, a separate real estate department may manage all real estate acquisition.

In the construction of buildings for offices, production, warehouses, stores, restaurants, maintenance, hotels, education, or research, the intended use of the facility will be the prime concern in its design. It is possible for larger organizations to maintain an in-house architectural and structural, plumbing, air conditioning, and electrical engineering staff. Even in these organizations, the possibility of make or buy exists. A core group of specialists on staff may be augmented with outside consulting assistance when demand peaks occur or special expertise is required. If building needs to be done in a large variety of locations, possibly domestic and foreign, local expertise familiar with climatic conditions, building codes, and construction contractors may be absolutely necessary. It is normal in many construction projects that the cost of the design is a relatively small portion of the total project cost, possibly in the 7 to 12 percent range. Yet, the design itself will be a major determinant of final project cost. Therefore, it is important to examine the question of design acquisition or design management by a set of criteria going well beyond the cost of the design phase itself.

The Traditional Approach to Construction and Pitfalls

In the traditional construction sequence of project concept, capital request, design, construction bids, contractor selection, and construction, many high cost pitfalls exist. Changes during the construction phase are almost invariably expensive and time consuming. The capital approval process is often lengthy and by the time capital is approved, the amount of time available for design, bids, and construction is tight. Rushing through these phases becomes costly and prone to mistakes. The original cost estimate may not be realistic because all details of the design were not yet known, market conditions for construction or labor may have changed, or the project itself may have evolved into a different concept. If construction bids received exceed the original capital request approved, the uncomfortable decision needs to be taken whether to start cost cutting or to engage in a lengthy, and possibly futile, attempt to get approval for more funds.

The intent here is not to paint all construction as a messy and problem-filled area. To the contrary, the existence of all of these possible pitfalls suggests that there is plenty of room for improvement and problem avoidance by sound project management. And, since many of the costs and problems center on the need for outside consultants and contractors, proper supply management is a vital component of successful construction.

Different Approaches to Construction Acquisition

It is not surprising that a number of approaches have evolved to address the key problem areas in construction. Most attempt to ensure proper quality, delivery on time, and cost control. Clearly, even if the traditional approach is followed in all the phases of construction, selection of the right consultants and architects, the right contractors and subtrades with proper coordination and appropriate lead times for all activities will increase the chances of success. Project management techniques like PERT and CPM can assist greatly. By focusing on the activities of the critical path, they permit proper analysis and planning as well as monitoring. Obviously, purchase lead times for various phases are absolutely critical. The availability of a contingency fund to deal with unexpected problems as they arise will also assist in preventing the project from going off schedule. Incentive clauses or bonuses for early or on-time completion and penalty clauses for lateness may also assist in ensuring on-time completion.

In public procurement, the use of bid bonds and performance bonds is intended to ensure contractor commitment and performance.

Some interesting options do exist in construction which do not follow the traditional process. For example, one key issue deals with the question of who is the prime contractor. It is possible to perform this task in-house or to assign responsibility outside. For those organizations without in-house expertise, this question should not even arise. Another possibility is to go to a turnkey project. The purchaser will specify requirements, probably as a set of performance specifications, and a large contractor or a consulting firm will look after all subsequent phases. This clearly places responsibility for quality, delivery, cost, and performance with one party and allows this party to find its own solutions to specific design or construction challenges.

Another option is the request for proposal (RFP) route, rather than having an architect or design engineer produce a specific design. This approach allows the contractors to suggest building materials and a construction design and methodology particularly suited to their own strengths and circumstances.

It is possible and desirable to use value analysis/value engineering techniques during the concept and design steps to ensure that the best value option evolves.

Another option is to select a contractor during the concept stage and use the contractor to design and build to a specific performance, cost, and delivery target. Dramatic savings in time and cost may be possible if the right contractor is selected early on. The new building of the Rotterdam School of Management at Erasmus University was built in less than half the conventional time and at less than half the conventional construction cost using this approach. The contractor chosen had just completed a large apartment block project and was able to use the same construction forms and crews and similar materials on the new school.

On-Site Considerations in Construction

During the construction phase, if it is to be carried out on space owned and operated by the buying organization, special contract provisions may need to deal with issues like identification and security, hours of access to the site, noise, dress, and safety regulations, access to food service, recreational, office, production, and other facilities, deliveries, conduct, cleanliness, etc.

Purchasing Involvement in Construction

In many organizations, construction is largely left to the engineering department and purchasing may or may not send out the request for bids. Meaningful purchasing department involvement will require that the buying staff have special construction expertise. Moreover, as in all other types of purchasing, early purchasing involvement in the project is absolutely necessary, if value analysis, request for proposal, and other innovative supply options should be explored. Since many other functions aside from purchasing and engineering should be involved early in construction planning, the idea of using a task force or project team approach is highly appealing. It is appropriate that the purchasing function be included in such a team.

QUESTIONS FOR REVIEW AND DISCUSSION

1. Why would anyone prefer to lease instead of buy?
2. What are some typical problems encountered in the acquisition of construction?
3. Why is capital asset acquisition different from the purchase of operating supplies?
4. What are the advantages of using a full-service lessor?
5. Why might someone prefer to purchase a used piece of equipment?
6. What are the problems of using life-cycle costing?
7. What could be the disadvantages of buying on a turnkey basis?
8. What contribution can purchasing make in the acquisition of a new computer?
9. Why would a custom piece of equipment be specified when similar standard equipment is available?
10. How can a reasonable value be placed on engineering service supplied by a potential vendor of equipment?

REFERENCES

AMA, *Computer Leasing: Evaluating Criteria for Decision Making*. Chicago, Ill: AMA, 1985.

Auer, Joseph and Charles E. Harrison. *Computer Contract Negotiations*. New York: Van Nostrand, 1981.

        Major Equipment Procurement. New York: Van Nostrand Reinhold Co., 1983.

Basu, S. *Leasing Arrangements: Managerial Decision-Making and Financial Reporting Issues*. Hamilton, Ontario: Society of Management Accountants of Canada, 1980.

Edge, Geoffrey C. and V. Bruce Irvine. *A Practical Approach to the Appraisal of Capital Expenditures*. 2nd ed. Hamilton, Ontario: Society of Management Accountants of Canada, 1981.

Hamel, Henry G. *Leasing in Industry*. New York: National Industrial Conference Board, 1984.

Ibbs, C. William, Jr. "'Or Equal' Clause Procurement in Engineering Construction." *Journal of Purchasing and Materials Management,* Fall 1982.

Ibbs, C. William, Jr. "Owner-Furnished Equipment Procurement." *Journal of Purchasing and Materials Management,* Fall 1982.

Jackson, Donald W. "Life Cycle Costing in Industrial Purchasing." *Journal of Purchasing and Materials Management,* Winter 1980.

Case 14–1

SUFFOLK POWER CORPORATION (AR)

Suffolk Power Corporation was building three additional generating stations to serve its rapidly expanding energy market. To link these stations with the total area grid, a new method of carrying the power lines using ornamental tubular poles instead of towers had been adopted. Suffolk had had no previous operating experience with poles and decided to subcontract the design engineering, fabrication, and erection of the new line.

For the first phase of engineering design, Mr. Carter, the director of purchasing, faced the responsibility of deciding with which supplier the business was to be placed after his staff had developed the information needed. He was aware that Suffolk had only three years in which to complete the entire project, and yet he had to ensure high-quality work.

Company Background

Suffolk Power Corporation had been established before the turn of the century and was now one of the largest power utilities in the eastern United States. It serviced a highly industrialized area from 10 fossil-fueled plants. With assets of over $3 billion and demand doubling every decade, it had already earmarked funds to increase its kilowatt capacity from 8.4 million to 13 million over a four-year period.

The company was well known for its advanced technology and its good public relations. Both purchasing and engineering departments were centralized and located in the head office in the area's largest city. The new construction program was a heavy strain on both the professional and financial resources of the company, placing increased emphasis on the use of qualified people and suppliers outside the corporation.

Transmission Line Background

Although Suffolk was stepping up its older lines to 230 KV, by management decision and in accordance with the technological trend, 345 KV was adopted for the new line. It was to link the new generating stations in Addison, Smithfield, and Mesa Valley with the area grid, some 140 miles all told.

Until now, Suffolk had used structural steel towers exclusively for carrying its power line (See Exhibit 1). These were strong but visually prominent and attracted adverse comments from a public daily growing more aesthetically sophisticated. A relatively new development in the transmission field was the introduction of the ornamental tubular power pole (see Exhibit 2). Approximately 200 miles of line using these poles had been installed with good success in various parts of the country. Most installations were relatively short sections in densely populated areas. A line using poles cost twice as much as the conventional towers but was still substantially cheaper than underground installation. Conscious of the great strides made in power pole design and use, Suffolk management decided to specify poles for the new line.

Because of the volume of conversion and projected expansion work, Mr. Carter and the project engineers knew that the tower manufacturers and erection companies with whom they had dealt in the past would not have the capacity to handle all the elements of the new pole concept. Furthermore, with no experience in 345KV or pole suspension, Suffolk had to rely on the know-how of others for the new line and needed the services and guidance of competent subcontractors.

The total job involved three major phases:

1. Engineering design called for layout as well as a functional pole specification and project guidance.

2. Pole manufacture involved a manufacturing proposal consisting of a specific design to meet the functional specifications as well as manufacturing volume and schedule deadline capabilities.

3. Pole installation involved excavation, foundation setting, pole erection, and line stringing. Preliminary cost estimates for the total project were as follows:

> Phase 1—Engineering—$500,000–$600,000
>
> Phase 2—Pole manufacture—$30 million $56.5 M
>
> Phase 3—Installation—$26 million

Mr. Carter and the chief engineer were not satisfied that any individual supplier could handle the total contract well. They decided, therefore, to subcontract each phase to a reliable source of high expertise within that phase, so that optimum overall benefits would accrue to Suffolk. The first sourcing decision dealt with the engineering phase.

EXHIBIT 1

Design Engineering Selection

All through the spring and half of the summer Oliver Dunn, the buyer, worked with the transmission engineering section of the system engineering department of the company to establish parameters and locate a suitable design source. By late July he was able to make his recommendation to the director of purchases (see Exhibit 3).

It was normal practice at Suffolk to provide a very brief summary for the director

EXHIBIT 2

EXHIBIT 3   Quotation Summary

Description:	Design 140 miles 345 KV transmission line for Addison-Smithfield-Mesa Valley
Recommended vendor:	Pettigrew Associates, New York, N.Y.
Location: Their premises	Using department: General engineering
Buyer: O. Dunn.	Total value: Established $580,000 salaries + burden
P.O. No.:	Date: Approval:

Additional information:

1. The transmission section of our general engineering department is unable to perform the design work of all the planned transmission work for the next three years, and it is necessary to contract some portions of this work. Travers & Bolton are already assigned the conversion of the 120KV to 230, and it is recommended that this 140-mile Addison-Smithfield-Mesa Valley 345 KV be contracted to some competent engineering firm.
2. We had sessions with each of the three below mentioned engineering firms to acquaint them with our needs and learn of their capabilities. The work they will perform is as follows:
   Make route sections; make subsurface investigations; make electrical hardware and general project designs; and furnish miscellaneous specifications, drawings, and technical data required to procure the right of way, hardware, structural steel, and for the awarding of contracts for construction. It is estimated this work will total 12,300 man-hours. There would also be approximately $48,000 worth of computer services and general out-of-pocket expenses in addition to the man-hours.
3. Bid comparison is:

Supplier	Estimated man-hours	Basic average cost per man-hour (w/o fringes)	Approximate fringes (assumed same for all)	Overhead and profit	Estimated $/hour
Travers & Bolton	14,350	$20.00	20%	65.5%	$40.00
Crown Engineering	—	20.00	20	80.0	43.20
Pettigrew Associates	12,190	20.00	20	85.0	44.40

It is recommended that this contract be awarded to Pettigrew even though their cost per hour is higher than the others. Total cost will be influenced by the capability and productivity of the company chosen, and, therefore, Pettigrew may not cost us any more; it is the desire of Suffolk management to have Pettigrew perform such a job with Suffolk as our first experience with them. Both T&B and C.E. have done considerable work for Suffolk.

of purchases on all major contracts. A large file containing detailed information was built up by the buyers and purchasing agents involved. Normally, some preliminary discussions were held as the project progressed, so that Mr. Carter was reasonably informed by the time the official recommendation was prepared. Should he wish to see more information he could request the file at any time.

All three of the engineering firms considered were large and engaged in a wide variety of engineering consulting services. Travers & Bolton and Crown Engineering had both done considerable work for Suffolk in the past and had performed satisfactorily. Pettigrew Associates had its head office in New York and maintained branches in 10 American cities. Pettigrew employed over 3,800 people, had a good credit rating, and had annual sales in excess of $160 million per year. Suffolk had never used Pettigrew in any of its projects. All three engineering firms had some tubular pole experience with short-line sections in other parts of the country. Aside from the design requirements, the consulting engineering firm was also expected to evaluate the bids from pole manufacturing and erection subcontractors.

Case 14-2

THORNETON HOME

In late November, Mr. John Cameron, director of purchasing and supply for the city of Hampton, was reviewing proposals for the Thorneton Home study. Three consulting groups had responded to a request for proposal (RFP) to study the operation of the city-owned old age home. Mr. Cameron knew that his recommendations for selection of a consultant would have to be completed by mid-December.

Thorneton Home

The Thorneton Home for the Aged was opened about thirty years ago for persons requiring nursing care. Thorneton had a bed capacity of 470. Staff totaled 235 with nonmanagement personnel unionized under the District Service Workers Union Local 325.

Day-to-day operations of the Thorneton Home were the responsibility of the Thorneton Home administrator who reported to Mr. Henry Davis, the city's director of social services. Policy and budget plans were developed by Mr. Davis and his staff in conjunction with Thorneton administrative staff and the Thorneton Home Committee of Management (THCM). The THCM consisted of five aldermen who were appointed or volunteered to fill these positions. The THCM reported to another aldermanic committee, with broader community service concerns, called the Committee for Community Services. This committee reviewed major expenditures and decisions impacting on community service policy. All major expenditures were then reviewed by the Board of Control, consisting of the mayor and four elected controllers, prior to being sent to city council for final approval.

As director of social services, Mr. Davis reported to the city administrator, Mr.

EXHIBIT 1   Reporting Structure

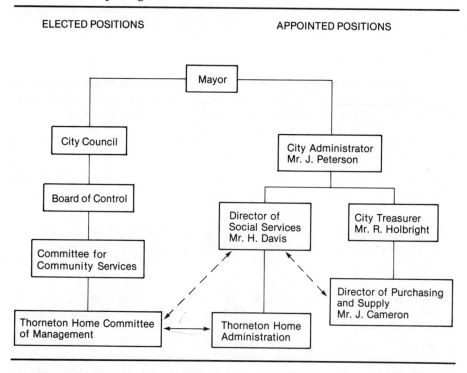

ELECTED POSITIONS   APPOINTED POSITIONS

J. Peterson, who in turn reported to the mayor. The combined elected and appointed reporting structure is shown in Exhibit 1.

Purchasing and Supply Division (PSD)

The PSD had purchasing and disposal authority for the city's engineering, fire, landfill/sanitation departments, social services division, and for city hall building support. The city operated separate purchasing departments in the public utilities commission, the libraries, and the police department. Purchasing authority was granted to the PSD Director and his buyers by municipal bylaw. This bylaw outlined the limits of purchasing authority and formed the basis of the PSD's Policy Manual for Purchasing, Tendering, and Disposal.

The main objective of the PSD was to respond to the needs of other departments and divisions for goods and services at minimum cost, consistent with desired quality, delivery timing, and reliability. The PSD had expertise in the purchasing and tendering of goods and certain services, such as equipment rental, maintenance contracts, and engineering/architectural consulting. However, it had not dealt extensively with management consulting service procurement at that time.

John Cameron became director of PSD two years ago at the age of 35. Prior to this, he was chief buyer and assistant director of purchasing for the city of Forestview, similar in size to Hampton. John reported to the city treasurer, Mr. R. Holbright, and dealt directly with other department and division heads on purchasing matters, as shown in Exhibit 1. He managed a staff of 15, including three buyers.

The Thorneton Home Study

The Thorneton Home had a history of problems related to budgeting and cost control. City council felt that the cost per bed was unnecessarily high, when compared to privately run institutions. Eight months ago the council directed the city administrator, Mr. Peterson, and the director of social services, Mr. Davis, to prepare a report for submission to the Thorneton Home Committee of Management in early June. The report was to contain:

1. An analysis of the comparative costs at Thorneton and other provincial facilities.
2. A review of the feasibility of increasing cost efficiency.
3. A review of the implications of possible alternatives such as:
   a. Contract management.
   b. An in-depth operational review and cost efficiency study carried out by an external agency.

The requested internal report, titled "The Thorneton Home for the Aged, A Review and Alternatives," was tabled on June 9. It revealed that Thorneton costs were approximately 14 percent higher than state averages on a per-bed basis. The report highlighted the difficulties of measuring and controlling costs in the absence of a patient classification system which would enable standard levels of nursing care to be developed. The report recommended an operational review by an outside agency and outlined some general guidelines and objectives. Sections of the internal report, related to these guidelines and objectives, are shown in Exhibit 2.

Council accepted the report's recommendations and directed Messrs. Peterson and Davis to initiate an independent consultant's study of Thorneton. This was not a budgeted expense and the approval of the THCM, the Committee of Community Services, the Board of Control, and city council were necessary prior to letting a consulting contract. Mr. Davis requested the assistance of John Cameron and the PSD in identifying and evaluating potential study participants. John Cameron handled the Thorneton Study personally, since it was beyond the scope of responsibilities and experience of his buyers. He drafted an RFP which is shown in Exhibit 3. In-state consulting organizations were contacted and a list of consulting companies with relevant experience was developed. Five consulting companies were invited to submit proposals.

Pre-bid conferences were held in September. The consulting companies sent representatives for preliminary inspections of Thorneton and for informal discussions of the scope, terms of reference, and evaluation criteria to be used in the proposal evaluation. Three proposals were submitted by closing, on November 17, with the following cost breakdown:

Proposal	Bid
Patientcare Ltd.	$17,500
Clarke-Hamilton Ltd.	23,500
Standardcare Ltd.	38,500

EXHIBIT 2   Thorneton Home

Excerpts from "The Municipal Home for the Aged, A Review and Alternatives." A
report to the Thorneton Committee of Management by J. Peterson, City
Administrator, and H. Davis, Director of Social Services.

Page 29

Increasing levels of care required by Home residents have a major influence on costs,
since care essentially is translated into staff to provide the necessary services. No
objective classification of resident care requirements has ever been carried out at
the Thorneton Home although there is no question that current residents and
even new applicants require much more nursing care than was formerly the case.

Page 33

An operational review could be carried out by an independent consulting firm or the
State's Department of Community and Social Services and would provide a
thorough analysis of options and possible areas for improvement at the Thorneton
Home.
Such an approach would provide a firm basis for the development of strategies for
operational change but would not guarantee implementation of the necessary
changes . . .

Page 34

The overall advantage of an operational review would be the ability to identify, in
depth, problem areas at the Thorneton Home for which change strategies could
be developed by the city. Such strategies might include contract management of
a specific service, for example. This type of analysis would provide solid ground
for future planning. On the negative side of the balance are the costs of such a
study and the necessity to subsequently develop and implement changes for the
identified problem areas.

Patientcare and Standardcare were both large operators of nursing homes;
Clarke-Hamilton was a management consulting firm located 100 miles away.
Prior to evaluating the bids, John summarized the proposals as shown in Exhibit
4. As he sat preparing to evaluate the proposals, John wondered what evaluation
criteria and weightings he should use, keeping in mind the needs of the social services
division and the content of the RFP.
In addition, he knew that his recommendations and justification had to be forwarded to the city administrator by December 19, prior to seeking approval of the
various committees of elected officials.

EXHIBIT 3
Request for Proposal

You are invited to submit a proposal for the purpose of conducting an administrative and operational review of the Thorneton Home for elder citizens. The review is to include all aspects of operation at the home, including but not restricted to assessment of resident care requirements, review of administration, organizational design and staffing. The main sections of the home include laundry and housekeeping, nursing and physiotherapy, dietary, special services, property, building maintenance, and administration. The review is to be conducted by examination and analysis of all relevant documentation, physical tour of the facility and interviews with all levels of staff and administration.

On the basis of the review, you are to develop comprehensive recommendations for introducing improved operating and cost efficiencies for the future operation of the home. All recommendations should offer alternatives, identify savings to be achieved and the related cost in order to implement the recommendations, projected impact on staff and administration and strategies for implementation which are consistent with the city's role as operators of the home, as well as provisions for ensuring the maintenance of the current quality of care.

It is our intent that the cost of the review and subsequent implementation of the recommendations is to be recovered from savings achieved in the operations of the home.

Your Proposal Is to Include the Following Information:

a. Proposed methodology for undertaking the review.
b. Names and qualifications of persons to be involved in the review and development of subsequent recommendations.
c. An estimate of the time required to undertake the review and develop the recommendations.
d. Documentation and references demonstrating your ability to successfully implement recommendations in similar circumstances.
e. Potential cost savings that may be achieved as a result of the review.
f. A copy of any contracts or agreements that are to be entered into as a result of being retained to conduct the review.

It is to be noted that your fee structure including upset limits is to be identified separately, however, included in the operating cost calculations with the savings shown as a net amount.

EXHIBIT 4 Proposals for Thorneton Review

	Patientcare	Clarke-Hamilton	Standardcare
1. Methodology	Require liaison person from city administration to assist team 1. Collect data 2. Review program 3. Conduct interviews 4. Determine and evaluate operational policies 5. Analyze staff and cost 6. Evaluate financial situation 7. Prepare report of funds and recommendations 8. Administration and project control 9. Provide assistance with implementation if required —Intend to utilize Department of Health general guidelines for work standards/patient classifications with judgment applied —May not leave Home with a system to use in the future	Suggest a steering committee be formed from city management and Thorneton administration 1. Discuss terms of review with steering committee 2. Examine pertinent documentation 3. Review all sections 4. Conduct interviews and physical tour 5. Identify opportunities for improvement in all sections 6. Development of detailed recommendations 7. Review recommendations with Management 8. Prepare and present final report 9. Implementation of recommendations if required —Work standard/patient classification to remain in place to be utilized by Home staff to maintain standards at minimal ongoing cost	Maintain contact with Thorneton management staff 1. Review operating statistics 2. Analyze organizational and operating procedures 3. Review and assess level of service in each section 4. Identify problems and potential improvements 5. Develop staffing schedules for comparison against existing and cost effectiveness 6. Identify problems in respect to physical environment 7. Provide draft report 8. Assess availability of skills required to implement 9. Final report and recommendation 10. Assist with implementation if required

EXHIBIT 4 *(continued)*

	Patientcare	Clarke-Hamilton	Standardcare
2. Anticipated Reduction and Implementation Costs	"Patientcare is prepared to estimate that the sum of all proposed operating deficiencies, if implemented, would far exceed the cost of the study and would be at least <u>$350,000</u>."	"The benefits received by our client in terms of reduced operating costs, improved cost effectiveness and operations improvement have invariably outweighed the costs for our services. The benefit to cost ratio from our assignments has varied from 3 to 1 to as much as 30 to 1 or higher."	"With respect to savings, it is difficult to make a definitive statement without having actually completed the study. However, based on previous experience it is expected that savings should be in the order of 8–10 percent of total expenses, which would be approx. $550,000 in the case of the Thorneton Home."
3. Experience	—Functional programming and operation at 11 institutions —List of five (5) other consulting projects —All appear large in scope —Manage nursing homes and chronic hospitals —Own or lease many other facilities	—Operational reviews in 11 Institutions—mainly hospitals with three regional centers —Extensive experience in specific areas again, mainly in hospitals —Experience in implementing two different types of work standard/patient classification systems and MIS systems —Extensive management consulting experience	—Appear to have extensive background in similar situations —Extensive list of 15 facilities either completed or in process —Manage Henford Lodge—150-bed restorative care program —Operational review of Martin Nursing Home —Owns or manages 2,400 nursing home beds and units in this state and Florida

4. References

Church Nursing Home, Dexter
—could not locate in Dexter, or surrounding area

Littlefield Municipal Hospital, Marsland, Saskatchewan
—spoke to administration who advised they consulted on construction of an addition to the hospital. Review only of size, layout, and facilities required. No operational or management review undertaken.

Jedd Park Nursing Home Expansion, Detroit
—could find no home operating under that name in Detroit or surrounding area.

*All other references were either impractical to contact or

Department of Community and Social Services
—Firm conducted operational review at Webster Regional Centre and they were satisfied with their performance. Although not totally implemented, it appeared that they would meet or surpass their estimated savings.

Webster Regional Centre Mgt.
—talked to administrator who was satisfied with the manner in which they conducted their review. Very professional approach with minimum of disruption.

Regional Municipality of Gast City

Greenfield Home for the Aged

Ward Home for the Aged
—Firm completed operational review and currently involved in implementation. Particular emphasis on restorative care techniques in nursing dept. Certain operations being contracted out. Project uncompleted; however, appears they will meet their projected savings of $280,000.

*Due to high cost of service, no further references were checked.

EXHIBIT 4 *(concluded)*

	Patientcare	Clarke-Hamilton	Standardcare
	were areas currently owned or operated by Patientcare. Our requests to visit a Home operated locally by them or to review their patient classification system were discouraged.	—firm performed salary review and reclassification of staff —pleased with performancè and methodology used to approach review. Experienced some minor problems with support in implementation.	
5. Review Team	All appear to possess qualifications and training related to health care environment. (7 individuals)	All appear to possess necessary qualifications and training in health care field. (7 individuals)	All appear to possess necessary qualifications and training related to health care environment. (6 individuals)
6. Time for Review	Approximately six (6) weeks.	Approximately eight (8) weeks.	Commence within ten (10) days; five (5) weeks to complete review.
7. Fee	$17,500—expenses included	Professional Fee $22,000.00 Expenses 1,500.00 $23,500.00	Professional Fee $35,000.00 Expenses 3,000.00 $38,000.00

CHAPTER 15

Acquisition of Services

The effective acquisition of services represents a significant challenge. Thus far, in this text, the prime focus has been on the acquisition of products, raw materials, purchased parts, equipment, and MRO items. Normally, with these requirements it is usually recognized that service is a factor in evaluating the best buy. Service in this context includes, but is not limited to, installation, training of the purchasers, operators or staff, technical advice, maintenance, provision of backup capacity or people, troubleshooting, documentation, quality control assistance, inspection, translation, etc. Almost invariably, however, in this context, the product emphasis is primary and the service dimension secondary in the overall purchase decision. One notable exception, of course, has been the purchase of transportation, a common service purchase covered in Chapter 8.

   Services which may have to be acquired by any organization are extremely diverse. For example, a brief and far from complete listing might include:

Advertising	Interior decorating
Arbitration	Interior space planning
Art	Janitorial
Auditing	Landscaping
Banking	Legal
Communications	Mailing
Computer programming	Maintenance
Consulting in any discipline	Medical
Customs brokerage	Payroll
Design (product, plant and equipment, stationery)	Personnel travel
Engineering design	Protection and security
Fitness	Repair
Food and hospitality services	Reproduction
Household moves	Research studies
Insurance	Snow removal
	Storage

Telephone
Temporary help
Training
Translation

Transport
Utilities
Waste removal

This chapter provides a better framework for dealing with the acquisition of services in the traditional context as well as those situations where the acquisition of a service is primary. This chapter will focus on understanding services better, followed by a discussion of the acquisition process used for services.

What Makes Services Different?

One of the most commonly mentioned special attributes of services deals with the inability to store many services. This attribute arises because many services are processes which may or may not be associated with a product. This implies that timing of the delivery has to coincide with the purchaser's specific needs and that the consequences of improper timing may be very serious. Suppliers, trying to service a variety of customers, need to ensure that sufficient capacity is available to satisfy the needs of all.

The inability to store many services also creates quality assurance difficulties. It may not be possible to inspect a service before its delivery. And, by the time of delivery, it may be too late to do anything about it. Anyone who has ever suffered through a boring speaker or a bad flight may attest to that.

The specification and measurement of quality in a service may present significant difficulties. Frequently, services have both a tangible and an intangible component. In his writing about the hospitality industry, Dr. Martin[1] identified the procedural and the convivial side of hospitality services. The procedural side deals with the ways in which customers' product needs are effectively and efficiently met. The convivial side deals with what the customer expects in addition to satisfactory food and drink. In Dr. Martin's words,

> It deals with the need to be liked, the need to be respected, the need for social interaction, the need to feel important, the need to be relaxed, comfortable, and pampered and the need to enjoy the company of other people in a welcoming environment.[2]

From the restaurant's perspective, conviviality is provided when the service crew shows a genuine personal interest in customers. Such interest is displayed when service personnel are friendly, courteous, and enthusias-

---

[1]William B. Martin, *Quality Service: The Restaurant Manager's Bible* (Cornell University, School of Hotel Administration, Ithaca, N.Y., 1986).

[2]Ibid., p. 33.

tic; when they show they appreciate their customers' patronage; when they are knowledgeable about the products they are selling; when they use sales techniques tactfully and effectively; and when they strive to meet each customer's unique expectations for quality service. In short conviviality means that service personnel have people skills.

Of course, judgment is a third component of the mix. It allows personnel to deal with the unusual events, special requests, and the overall ability to adjust to the circumstances as they arise.

A Framework for Analyzing Services

It is important to recognize that not all services are the same. The variation between services may affect the acquisition perspective. Therefore, various authors have suggested a variety of framework dimensions. From an acquisition point of view the following should be considered: value, repetitiveness, tangibility, direction, production, nature of demand, the nature of delivery, the degree of customization, and the skills required for producing the service. Each of these will be discussed in turn.

It is useful to recognize that, ultimately, the goal of effective acquisition of services is to obtain best value. In this sense there is no difference between the acquisition of services and goods. And the best buy in services represents the appropriate trade-off between quality, delivery, quantity, cost, continuity, flexibility, and other relevant factors. It is in the determination of the need and the ability to assess what should be considered best value in any particular service that the real difficulties arise in the acquisition process.

The Value of the Service

One very broad cut at services would be to classify them as high, medium, or low value. This could be done similarly to the typical ABC analysis. Obviously, from an economic value perspective greater acquisition attention should be spent on the high-value services. Value in this context is probably best expressed as a combination of money spent on this service in one shot, or over a specific time period such as a year. It should also be immediately recognized that some services may require a very careful acquisition process because of the potential impact they could have on the whole organization. For example, the improper removal of asbestos from a building may make the whole building inoperable. A consultant to assist in the long-term strategic planning of the organization may have a very long-term impact.

Degree of Repetitiveness

It is obvious that for the acquisition of repetitive services it may be possible to develop an acquisition system and specialized expertise in the organization. For example, it would be entirely appropriate for a large number of organizations to have specialized buying expertise in the acquisition of maintenance and security services. On the other hand, for unique service requirements, special assistance may have to be sought outside of the organization and the acquisition may have to be handled on a project basis.

Degree of Tangibility

By definition, every service tends to have an intangible dimension, such as the conviviality dimension for the hospitality industry. Even so, some services can be seen as more tangible than others. For example, an architect will produce a drawing or a design which can be examined by others and which will, ultimately, result in a physical structure. Although the structural feature of the physical representation of the design can be examined, the aesthetic features of the design are much more difficult to evaluate and subject to a wide variety of responses. On the other hand, the advice from a consultant on a new marketing strategy may be almost totally intangible.

The development of standards for services in any contract is obviously difficult. Sometimes it is possible to get around this task by using expressions of satisfaction or dissatisfaction by various users or experts as a substitute. For example, how many complaints are received about the cleanliness of the building or how many experts believe the software program to be acceptable? It should be recognized that the selection of experts or evaluators in itself represents a statistical quality problem. Some people may be more eager than others to express their opinions, and their views may not be representative of the whole group. Relying solely on complaints may give a particularly biased response.

One way to deal with the acquisition of intangible services is to substitute qualifications for the people or equipment providing the service. For example, the number of personnel in the organization who have appropriate training in the particular discipline, and the capability of the various pieces of equipment, can be specified ahead of time. Similarly, it may be possible to poll a number of clients of the organization to determine their satisfaction with the particular supplier. Unfortunately, many segments of the service sector tend to be plagued by high turnover and the addition or loss of a few key people can make a significant difference in any one firm. Nevertheless, many important services, such as professional services, are either not plagued by turnover, or are such that turnover is planned for, such as food and janitorial services.

The Direction of the Service

Another aspect of service deals with whether or not it is directed at people. For example, food services are for people; maintenance services may be for buildings or equipment. Once services are directed at people, it is very important to recognize the special needs of the persons who will be most affected by the service. The ultimate user will likely play a major role in both the specification of the service and the assessment as to whether satisfactory quality has, in fact, been received. If services directed at people have an important intangible component, assessment may require a period of exposure of both supplier personnel and purchaser personnel to each other to determine compatibility. In babysitting, is it the parents or the children, or both, who determine the selection?

The Production of the Service

Services can be produced by people or equipment, or a combination of both. Services of low labor intensity may have a high capital or asset component. Typical examples would include real estate and equipment rentals, computer processing, transportation and communication services, as well as custom processing of a machine-intensive nature. In the specification stage understanding the underlying technology or asset base is important. During the acquisition stage potential suppliers can be assessed on the basis of their asset availability and capacity as well as the state of their technology. The delivery of this kind of service is more likely at the location of the vendor's premises or of its equipment, although hookup may be directly to the purchaser's site. Quality monitoring and evaluation may be process oriented with emphasis on the performance of the underlying capital asset.

Services with high labor intensity include activities like hand harvesting, installation and maintenance, education, health support, security, as well as the full range of professional activities like consulting, engineering, accounting, medical, and architectural services. For these activities the quality of the "people component" becomes the primary concern. Services involving largely lower- to medium-skilled people may focus more on cost minimization and efficiency. Services requiring highly skilled individuals may require the purchaser to distinguish between levels of professional skill and may require extensive ongoing communication between requisitioner and purchaser through all phases of the acquisition process.

Nature of Demand

The demand for a particular service may be continuous, periodic, or discreet. The typical example of a continuous service may be insurance or a 24-hour, around-the-clock security service. A discreet or one-shot service may be the acquisition of an interior decorator to suggest a new color scheme for an office complex. The continuous service may permit the opportunity to monitor progress and to make alterations as information about the quality of service becomes evident. For discreet services the monitoring capability may have to be shifted to the various stages in the delivery production, if this is possible. The real problem here may well be that by the time the service is delivered, it is too late to make significant changes. Periodic service may be regular, such as once a week or once a month, such as regular inspections, or may vary with need as in repair services.

The Nature of Service Delivery

The place and nature of service delivery may have significant acquisition repercussions. For example, if the delivery of the service occurs on the premises of the purchaser, the contract agreement may have to address a number of provisions. For example, in construction or installation services, questions of security, access, nature of dress, hours of work, applicability of various codes for health and safety, what working days and hours are applicable, and what equipment and materials are to be provided by whom, are all issues that need to be addressed as part of the contract.

On the other hand, when the service is provided on the supplier's premises or elsewhere, many of these concerns may not arise, provided the service is not directed at personnel of the purchaser.

Degree of Standardization

It makes a substantial difference whether a service is standard or is customized specifically for the purchaser. Generally speaking, the lower the consumer contact, the more standard the service becomes, and, probably, the lower the importance of intangibles. Specification of these kinds of services is probably easier because of the standardization and the common nature of the purchase. With many purchasers in the market, standard specifications are probably available. If there are many suppliers, it may be possible to use competitive bidding techniques, expect quantity discounts, and use a fairly standard type of supplier evaluation.

With highly customized services, the specification process may become much more difficult and the options more difficult to understand. The involvement of the end consumers in this specification process becomes more important. The possibilities of trade-offs in various make or buy suboptions need to be explored before final specification can be agreed to. The acquisition process itself may be less definite as various suppliers may offer substantially different options. Evaluation of supplier performance may have to recognize the purchaser's share of responsibility for quality at the point of delivery.

The Skills Required for the Service

The production of a service may require a full range of skills from unskilled on the one extreme to highly skilled on the other. In services requiring relatively unskilled labor such as grass cutting and other simple maintenance tasks, price emphasis is likely to be high and ease of entry into (and exit from) the service may also be high. On the other extreme, the acquisition of highly skilled services may focus far more on qualifications of the skilled persons, concern over the specific persons who will be performing this service, and recommendations from other skilled persons and users. Frequently, in highly professional services the cost of the professional service may be relatively low compared to the benefit expected. For example, a good design may increase sales substantially; a good architect may be able to design a low-cost, but effective structure; and a good consulting recommendation may turn a whole organization around. It is often very difficult to deal with this trade-off between the estimated cost for the job versus the estimated benefits.

The Acquisition Process for Services

Thus far, the discussion has primarily centered on understanding the nature of the service to be acquired. Next, the acquisition process used for services will be discussed to highlight several dimensions unique to the purchase of services. Four areas of the acquisition process will be covered: 1) need recognition and specification, 2) analysis of supply alternatives, including sourcing, pricing and options, 3) the purchase agreement, including special provisions, and 4) contract administration, including follow-up, quality control, payment, records, and supplier management and evaluation.

1. Need Recognition and Specification

Those in purchasing must understand some very basic questions regarding any service. Typical questions include: Why is this service necessary? What is important about this service? What represents good value? How is quality defined for the service? How is the service produced? And how do we know we received what we expected?

The characteristics of the particular service to be acquired can be checked against those mentioned earlier in this chapter to establish priority and areas of concern. The need for user involvement in need recognition and definition is high in many services because of the user-supplier interface, so common in most services, and the importance of nontangible factors. Careful documentation of need requirements, including the necessity for nontangibles, is the foundation on which a sound acquisition approach is based. Sound documentation will facilitate supplier search and selection, contract content and administration, and quality control. Where possible, measurable attributes or actions which are part of the service need to be identified and quantified. Also, if the service can be broken down into chronological stages, it will be useful to detail progress due dates. For example, for an employee morale survey, the supplier's due dates might be: Overall Research Design—February 1, Questionnaire Design—April 1, Questionnaire Administration—June 1, and Survey Results Report—September 1. It is important to recognize that the accompanying commitments for the purchasing organization need to be agreed to, for example: Overall Research Design Review—January 15, Questionnaire Approval—March 15, Employees Available for Questionnaire Administration—April 1 to June 1, and Preliminary Results Report Review—August 15.

In many services, the need recognition and definition require a dual definition. It is necessary to document exactly what it is that the supplier will provide, and also what the purchaser will do to help the supplier to perform as required.

Value analysis techniques can and should be applied to service need definition. Early involvement of purchasing with users during need recognition and definition will permit the appropriate search for value.

2. Analysis of Supply Alternatives

In the acquisition of services, the analysis of supply alternatives includes sourcing, pricing, and source options, as well as make or buy.

Sourcing

In sourcing, it is useful to recognize that many service organizations are relatively small. Therefore, many of the characteristics of small suppliers discussed in Chapter 6 are likely to be considerations in dealing with service organizations. If the service supplier is small, there is also a high likelihood that it will be a local source.

In sourcing, references from other users may be particularly useful. A typical parallel in consumer buying is the word-of-mouth value for restaurants.

Pricing

Pricing in services may be fixed or variable, by the job or by the hour, day or week. Prices may be obtained by competitive bid if the size of the contract warrants it, sufficient competitors are available, and service description is possible.

Negotiation is another common method for establishing prices and may be the only option in single source situations.

In services, purchasing clout does count and it can be used effectively by the knowledgeable purchaser. Understanding the cost structure of the service will be helpful in revealing negotiation opportunities.

There are a number of situations where it may be difficult to estimate the total time required for a given service task. In professional services it is not unusual to give estimates of professional time required without committing to a specific figure. Most purchasers would probably prefer such contracts to have a "not to exceed limit." Some professionals, such as architects, may quote their fee based on a percentage of the total job cost.

From a purchasing standpoint, this removes the incentive for the architect to seek the best value for the total job.

Requests for proposal are also common in a variety of services where the purchaser believes that supplier ingenuity or skill may reveal options not apparent to the purchaser. Proper briefing of potential bidders is still required so that every supplier fully and correctly understands the need to be fulfilled. The difficulty for purchasers with widely varying proposals is one of assessing which is superior. Moreover, the preparation of such a proposal may be expensive and may have to be paid for by the purchaser to ensure proper competition and proposal quality.

Make or Buy in Services

Almost invariably, the question of make or buy is an important one in the acquisition of services. There appears to be a current trend to subcontracting out services traditionally performed in-house. Typical examples are security, food services, and maintenance, but also legal, engineering, software development, design, and other professional services traditionally performed in-house. Moreover, particularly with services, the option of partially making or partially buying seems to be prevalent. For example, in auditing, the preparation of schedules can be left to the inside accountants, or to the outside auditors. An interior decorator may specify colors and furnishings but leave the purchasing to the procurement department and the painting and the installation to the internal maintenance staff. On the other hand, the whole task could be purchased on a turnkey basis. The repair, disassembly, cleaning and reassembly might be performed in-house whereas regrinding or recalibration of key parts might be done outside. An alert purchaser should always be on the lookout for opportunities to substitute low-cost, in-house work for high-cost outside work. The reverse, of course, also holds true. If inside costs are high and outside costs are low and no other considerations are relevant, it may be much better value to have work done outside. Understanding the full nature of the service and how the various costs are built up for the service is, therefore, an important consideration in assessing the make or buy trade-off.

3. The Purchase Agreement

The purchase agreement for services is usually called a service contract or contract for services. It may be short- or long-term, a standard or custom document.

Services lend themselves to a large variety of contracts. These might include fixed price, unit price, cost plus a percentage fee, cost plus a fixed fee, cost as a percentage of the total project, or incentive contracts, and a variety of other options. Many professional service providers try to use standard contracts agreed to by their professional association. Frequently, the associations even have guidelines as to appropriate fee structures and contracts for a particular kind of work. A purchaser should never feel compelled to accept these contracts as they are.

Most organizations develop contract language over time to suit their own needs and the specific service to be acquired. This tends to result in a wide range of different contracts, each with its own service-specific language. Thus, a security service contract will appear totally different from a contract for corporate maintenance, food services, fax, or marketing consulting. Vendors in each service area will be anxious to suggest the use of their own contracts. In cases of low-value services, using such a standard vendor contract may well be the simplest and least expensive solution.

4. Service Contract Administration

Service contract administration includes follow-up, quality control and supplier evaluation, payment, records, and other aspects of contract administration.

Follow-Up

The follow-up and expediting in services may require internal, as well as supplier checking. Therefore, responsibility for follow-up with the vendor may well be appropriately placed in the user department to help ensure user compliance with prior commitments and deadlines, while follow-up on internal commitments may become a joint responsibility for purchasing as well as the vendor. It is this commonly extensive user interface with vendor personnel during service delivery, and often before, that also affects other aspects of contract administration.

Quality Control and Supplier Evaluation

In highly tangible services, such as construction, quality control can be geared heavily toward the measurement of the tangible, in ways quite similar to standard quality assurance and control.

Two aspects of service, the intangible and the noninventory, can create special quality measurement difficulties. The intangible dimension makes it more difficult to assess proper quality. Were the supplier's personnel sufficiently courteous when dealing with the purchaser's employees? This may be measured by a survey, or by a number of complaints received, but it is important to recognize that any standard will, at best, be imprecise.

Because the delivery of many services prevents storage, it tends to be instantaneous. In other words, quality control will have to be performed while the service delivery is in progress, or afterwards. And, it may be difficult to interrupt the process, even if simultaneous quality control is

possible. Therefore, the quality risk in services may be relatively high compared to the purchase of products.

Quality risk avoidance may be achieved by continuous business with
service suppliers found to be satisfactory in the past, by avoiding repeat
business with suppliers found to be unsatisfactory, by careful checking of
vendors beforehand with other users with similar needs, and careful preser-
vice delivery communications with the vendor and service users to ensure
common understanding of requirements and expectations.

In areas of quality failure, it may not be possible to return the services
for a full refund.

Payment

Payment for services may vary somewhat from payment for goods. Some
services require prepayment, such as an eminent speaker; some immediately
upon delivery, such as hospitality services; whereas others can be delayed.
Small suppliers may find it difficult to offer extended payment terms and
early payment may well be an inducement for price or other concessions
sought by the purchaser. Progress payments are usual for large contracts
spread over time, whereas regular payments are appropriate for such ongoing services as building maintenance or food services.

Records and Other Aspects of Contract Administration

As in all purchases, the need for proper records hardly needs to be
reinforced for the acquisition of services. Part of the difficulty may well be
the feedback loop from user to purchasing and the retrievability of information regarding the service offered. Unless care is taken to preserve this
information, it may well be lost for future reference and consideration.

It is almost inevitable that contract administration for services will
encounter the need for changes subsequent to contract signing. Delivery
dates, the nature of the service, the quality of the service, the place for
delivery, and other aspects may require change. What may seem like an
innocuous change to the purchaser may be very difficult or expensive to the
supplier. For example, a one-week delay in delivery may back the supplier
into a serious capacity constraint. This is one reason why big weddings are
always planned a long time in advance. The reverse may also happen. A
supplier request for change may make life very difficult for the purchaser.
Thus, mechanisms need to be in place, as well as do appropriate representatives of vendor and buyer to deal with changes as necessary. Changes may
be very costly and affect budget status and a host of other dimensions. Before
any changes are agreed to, both purchaser and seller need to assess the
impact on their own organizations and the contract changes arising from
them, including prices. Obviously, if flexibility to change is already foreseen
as important before contract signing, this should be addressed as part of

TABLE 15–1 Brief Summary of Service Characteristics and Acquisition Process Implications

Service Characteristics	Acquisition Process	Need Recognition, Description	Sourcing Alternatives, Pricing, Analysis	Agreement Nature, Contract Provisions	Contract Administration, Follow-up, Q.C., Payment/Records
Value					
High	High attention	Careful Price sensitive Make or buy	Likely negotiated	High attention
Low	Lesser attention	Low acquisition cost Local source	Standard if possible	Low attention
Repetitiveness					
High	Develop standard	Test	Standard longer term	Standardize
Low	Seek expert assistance	Seek expert assistance	Custom or one shot	Custom
Tangibility					
High	Specs important	Pretest, samples	Similar to product purchase	Control for physical characteristics
Low	References User involvement	Personalities important	Specified persons	User involvement high
Direction at					
Equipment	Equipment familiarity	Equipment familiarity	Specified equipment performance	Control process quality
People	User involvement high	User involvement high	People skills important	Control quality at user interface

Production by	Equipment	Specify equipment capability	Specify equipment capability Control for quality	Specify availability	Conditional on equipment use
	People	Specify people capability	Worry about capacity		User provides quality control
Demand	Continuous	Continuity	Reliability and continuity	Complete coverage	Control quality by sampling
	Discrete	Availability during need	Availability during need	Specify delivery	Control quality at delivery
Delivery	At purchaser	User interface important	User interface important	Access clauses	In-house quality control
	At seller	Good description	Location	Purchase access and progress reports	Concern over service completeness
Customization	High	User specification	Custom capability	Special contract	Quality control very specific and may withhold a large % of payment
	Low	Standard specs	Competitive bid	Standard contract	Standard quality control
Skills	High	User specification	Specify specific persons	Availability of individuals	Professional standards, regulations, user involvement
	Low	Standard specs	Competitive bidding	Standard contract	Minimize user hassle

the original need description. Then, in the search for a suitable supplier, flexibility becomes a key sourcing criterion written into the contract itself.

Conclusion

Obviously, it is possible to make a matrix out of these various considerations in service acquisition. A simplified summary is supplied in Table 15–1, highlighting a few significant points in service nature and acquisition. Moreover, as in all other purchases, each service tends to have its own nomenclature, language, tradition, standard practices, technology, etc., which need to be learned by the purchaser.

For those who may look at the purchasing function as a service performed inside one's organization, it is possible to look at the other departments in the organization as requiring this service. How differently would the members of the purchasing department behave if their services were actually bought by the other departments? In a number of organizations, particularly large companies which operate on a decentralized, divisional basis, it is not at all uncommon to charge central purchasing services to specific divisional budgets. Neither is it unusual for the divisions to complain about the size and nature of the charges incurred.

Services are growing rapidly in the economy as a whole. More and more purchasers find themselves involved in the purchase of services. Obviously, the well prepared purchaser can make a significant contribution to the service user by applying sound purchasing theory and practice to the acquisition of services.

QUESTIONS FOR REVIEW AND DISCUSSION

1. What would be a good example of a service high in intangibles, and how would that affect the acquisition process?

2. Why are organizations buying more services outside?

3. What contribution can purchasing make in the acquisition of services?

4. What are the similarities between purchasing operating supplies and purchasing maintenance supplies?

5. Why should it make any difference to the acquisition process whether a service is directed at people or equipment?

6. In professional services, what are some of the different contract options?

7. What are typical quality control difficulties in the acquisition of services?

8. Is make or buy a realistic option in the acquisition of services? Why and how?

9. What process of acquisition might be followed in the purchase of standard services? Can you give an example or two?

10. What are the contract administration implications in the acquisition of services?

REFERENCES

"How to Choose a Computer Maintenance Service."

Martin, William B. *Quality Service: The Restaurant Manager's Bible.* Ithaca, N.Y.: School of Hotel Administration, Cornell University, 1986.

Purchasing World, August 1987.

Sasser, W. Earl. *Management of Service Operations.* Boston, Mass.: Allyn and Bacon, 1978.

Schonberger, Richard J. "Purchasing Intangibles." *Journal of Purchasing and Materials Management,* Fall 1980.

Services Challenge: Integrating for Competitive Advantage. Chicago, Ill.: American Marketing Association, 1987.

Case 15–1

SUFFOLK POWER CORPORATION (CR)

Suffolk Power Corporation was building three additional generating stations to serve the rapidly expanding energy market. To link these stations with the total area grid a new method of carrying the power lines using ornamental tubular poles instead of towers had been adopted. Suffolk lacked experience with poles and decided to subcontract the design engineering, fabrication, and erection of the new line. [For company background and line project information and the selection of engineering consultants see Suffolk Power Corporation (AR) case.]

Having selected its consultants for its first 345KV transmission line and placed its order for the fabrication of the poles and hardware, Suffolk Power was ready to locate a suitable contractor to do the foundation work, erect the poles, and string the lines.

Purchasing and engineering had been pursuing this concurrently with the search for a fabricator, as Suffolk wanted to get started on the line by the fall. Gordon Yarrow, supervisor of materials purchasing, was responsible to the director of purchasing, John Carter, for the negotiations.

Construction Selection

One company, T. D. Rapier, had done almost all Suffolk's transmission work for over the last five years, but, with the consultant's help, a good cross section of qualified line builders had been invited to bid. In addition several foundation companies were asked to quote on the subgrade work. This helped to test the market

EXHIBIT 1   Suffolk Hydro 345KV Transmission Line—
Addison-Smithfield-Mesa Valley

Comparison of Bids

Bidder	Line Construc- tion	Foundation Installation	Total
Line contractors:			
(D)	$15,701,280	$17,693,216	$33,394,496
(E)	12,705,968	14,872,370	27,578,338
(F)	13,796,880	12,592,826	26,389,706
(G) T. D. Rapier	12,495,120	12,664,624	25,159,744
(H) McTaggart Construction	14,477,900	9,224,268	23,702,168
(I)	12,064,024	No bid	2,000,00
Consulting engineer's prior estimate	15,916,800	10,204,800	26,121,600
Foundation contractors:			
(J)		24,591,858	
(K)		12,988,788	
(L)		11,733,792	

Notes:
1. Two line contractors and one foundation contractor declined to bid.
2. The two lowest line constructors, Rapier and McTaggart, were evaluated, plus the possibility of a split award to *(L)* for foundations and *(I)* for above grade work. However, McTaggart is recommended for the following reasons:
   a. Lowest bid.
   b. Highly experienced. Built thousands of miles of line in mountain, desert, and swamp. Experience included 230, 345, 500 and 750KV construction.
   c. Presently working for several other power companies.
   d. Recommended by our design engineers and consultants.
   e. Has done considerable work in this state through a subsidiary, although not for Suffolk.

to determine whether foundation contractors could build foundations cheaper than line builders. Mr. Carter reserved the right to award separate contracts for above- and below- grade work.

Two meetings were held with the bidders, one for the line builders and another for the foundation contractors, at which all aspects of the job were fully discussed. The unit prices were based on current wage rates and working conditions and were subject to adjustment by a percentage equal to .80 times the percentage change in the average wage rates.

By September the consulting engineers were able to provide purchasing with an evaluation of the bidding and computation enabling the attached summary to be compiled (see Exhibit 1).

Case 15–2

THE GRANBY C.E.G.E.P.

Mr. Christyan Lemire, manager of equipment and supply at the Granby C.E.G.E.P., was in the process of deciding how to award a roof repair contract. All of the bids, except one, were above the $300,000 cost estimated by the architect. The bid of Constructoit Ltée was within the budget limits, but Mr. Lemire wondered if the $255,300 quote was too low to be reasonable.

The Granby C.E.G.E.P.

Created in 1970, the Granby C.E.G.E.P., a provincially-funded junior college located about 40 miles southeast of Montreal, Canada, had an enrollment of 1,400 daytime and 1,500 nighttime students. Located in a former high school, the C.E.G.E.P. received its grants directly from the provincial government. Budgets were tight and the college's administration was under considerable pressure to meet the combined challenge of offering quality educational programs and staying within budgets.

Purchasing at the Granby C.E.G.E.P.

Mr. Lemire reported to the director of administrative services, who with two other directors reported to the general director of the college. Mr. Lemire was responsible for both plant and equipment as well as purchases. Purchasing involved acquisition for educational needs such as laboratory, information, physical education, and theatre requirements, as well as the audio visual, maintenance, plumbing and heating support requirements. The physical facilities and the maintenance of plumbing, heating, ventilation, roof, power, windows, lighting, parking, and telephone system were also part of Mr. Lemire's responsibility.

The Roof Repair

Severe water leakage problems had created the need for the roof repair job. Rain water was accumulating in several areas on the roof. Over the years the roof deck had settled, so that the drain pipes were now higher preventing proper drainage.

This case was originally written by Linda Goulet and Francine Blanchette under the direction of Professor Jean Nollet at the Ecole des Hautes Etudes Commerciales de Montréal. It was subsequently translated and modified by Professor Michiel R. Leenders of the School of Business Administration at The University of Western Ontario.

The original case was written with partial funding from the Purchasing Management Association of Canada.

Leaks of water showed up in numerous places and catch basins had to be installed all over the place by the maintenance people. Aside from the inconvenience of these containers, there was considerable danger of water damage to electrical wiring and equipment like computers.

To solve the roof problem the college had first retained the services of a consulting firm specializing in roof design and repairs. A consultant had conducted a full study and submitted his report to Mr. Lemire, recommending complete renovation of one part of the roof and repair of several other sections.

The following step involved the work of an architect who detailed the work to be done. The architect estimated a total cost of $300,000, which was the amount then requested from the provincial authorities. These funds were rapidly approved, as these types of requests were seldom contested by the province.

A request for bids was then published. Interested parties could obtain the necessary drawings and details for $100. A bid bond amount to 10 percent of the bid value was also required. The bid deadline was set for April 18. The work had to be done within the period from May 20 to August 15 and no delay could be tolerated as courses began in the third week of August.

The Bids

Mr. Lemire, his director, the architect, and an engineer from the provincial department of education were all present at the official bid opening. The bid results, in the sequence in which they were opened, were as follows:

Jacques Vidal Inc.	Saint-Jean-sur-le-Richelieu	$317,000
Toutoit Limitée	Montréal	346,410
Couvertures Roy Inc.	Verdun	367,039
Beaudoin Ltée	Sherbrooke	397,186
Chabot & Fils Ltée	Sherbrooke	349,733
Pinet et Guay Ltée	Montréal	369,240
Couvreurs Blais Inc.	Montréal	427,864
Constructoit Ltée	St-Georges-de-Beauce	255,300

The spread between the budget and the bid amounts was unwelcome news to the four persons present at the bid opening. The first bid at $317,000 had seemed to be close to the estimate, but the tension had mounted during the opening session as each subsequent bid seemed to be higher and higher. Especially after the penultimate bid of $427,864, the last bid of $255,300 had come as a complete surprise.

To verify the validity of the bids, the architect subsequently conducted a special technical and legal evaluation. His analysis showed that only one bidder, the first one, Jacques Vidal Inc., had to be disqualified because it did not include a proper authorization from its board of directors. This left Mr. Lemire with seven bids in total with one at $44,700 below budget and the next lowest bid at $46,410 over budget.

Mr. Lemire wondered if the spread in bid price was caused by a poor cost estimate by the architect, or a general padding by the bidders without any collusion. The low bid would permit him to stay within budget guidelines, but he questioned its realism.

He did not want to risk any problems with either the quality or the timing of the job.

Case 15–3

MAYFAIR COUNTY BOARD OF EDUCATION

Fraser Lewis, supervisor of purchasing for the Mayfair County Board of Education (see Exhibit 1), listened thoughtfully to the supervisor of caretaking, Bob Oxford, outline his plans for the cleaning of 10 new and near-new schools:

"As you know, Fraser, we are trying to find a flexible balance in the system between the Caretakers' Association and outside contractors. We find no fault with the association people but, naturally, they want an exclusive if they can get it, even though they are not actually a union. However, this depends on their doing a proper job, and there's nothing like a bit of competition to ensure keeping everyone on his toes. Even if we do contract for schools one to ten, we are large enough to be able to transfer existing staff to other schools without anyone suffering, especially at the rate we are expanding. As you remember, we don't need to employ our own caretaking staff for new schools, under our agreement."

"Fine," said Fraser Lewis. "This will run into quite a bit of money, so we'll have to advertise for bids as well as approach firms we already know. We'll ask for bids on all or some of the schools and reserve the right to accept any combination. I think the board is still sticking to the policy of using our own forces, providing costs are pretty close?"

"That's right," replied the caretaking supervisor. "By the way, I'll send you the usual square footage specification information and work up costs for you when required. As it's nearly April now, perhaps you'll get this rolling quickly?"

"No problem, Bob. Send the material to Lin Godfrey who handles this buying for me."

Fraser Lewis smiled ruefully as he remembered this phone call which had been the starting point of the new cleaning contract. He had a high regard for Bob Oxford, who had formerly managed a national caretaking firm. It was now at the end of November, and the supervisor of caretaking was breathing down his neck. He would have to make a drastic decision soon. He phoned his caretaking buyer. "Lin, let's run through the caretaking file again to refresh my memory. Bob Oxford is furious about the Carlon situation."

"Well, here's the rundown, Fraser," said Godfrey, seating himself and opening a thick file. "On April 9, I advertised for bids. In addition, I sent it to about 15 firms we know. Some we had dealt with, including Carlon, and, of course, we asked for references and supplied complete specs. The prospective contractors had to examine the schools."

"What was Carlon's reputation?" interjected Lewis.

"Well, let's put it this way," said the buyer, "He's done a little for us in the past reasonably well, but he's held some really important contracts for the federal government and quite an array of well-known industrial firms. I'd rate him adequate.

EXHIBIT 1   General Information

The board was one of the largest in the South and fast expanding. It controlled 143 schools with 78,000 pupils. The average cost of a school was $8 million. The operating budget was $125 million; the capital budget about $36 million for new buildings.

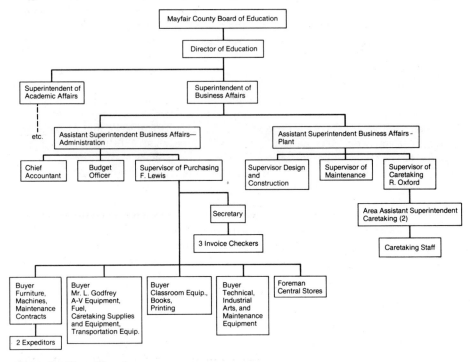

Organization Chart
Purchasing Information

Purchasing expenditures for supplies and equipment were $15 million annually. The bid policy was:

$1,000 and under	Verbal quotation
$1,001–$2,000	Verbal quotation plus written confirmation
$2,001–$10,000	Formal quotation
Over $10,000	Publicly advertise for bids

Usually three quotations were required except when only small amounts were involved or there was too limited a number of suppliers. Public bids were opened by purchasing and the amounts read out to those contractors attending the opening. Mr. Lewis approved all bids and also signed all orders over $10,000. He reported this decision at regular board of trustees meetings.

Unionization of contractors' labor was not demanded.

All things being equal, suppliers in or nearest the boards' territory were favored.

Abnormal bids were only drawn to suppliers' attention if there was an obvious error. Rebidding was permitted once in this event. However, a bidder could withdraw his bid up to the moment of opening.

EXHIBIT 2 Janitorial Service (bid summary in thousands of dollars)

School	Square feet	Present cost	Bidder				Smithers E	Carlon F
			A	B	C	D		
1	180,550	74.8	74.2	72.2	—	69.9	58.7L	66.6
2	173,800	67.4	70.8	—	79.0	67.2	67.2	63.9L
3	169,644	67.6	69.2	72.3	76.7	78.3	58.4L	61.8
4	152,680	61.4	61.6	63.1	—	58.7	48.7L	58.4
5	180,384	69.5	74.6	76.7	82.0	69.4	59.7L	66.6
6	209,801	75.0	89.8	—	—	73.9	67.8L	76.4
7	77,015	31.2	39.2	30.8	—	31.1	30.1L	31.5
8	110,616	37.5	49.2	45.9	—	42.6	36.2L	43.0
9	130,897	—	59.3	—	—	46.7	42.6L	51.2
10	60,500	30.6	39.0	—	—	37.7	28.5	22.4L

Note: Bids recorded April 24.
L = Low bid.

Certainly not by any means low enough to exclude him from consideration, but not a leader like Smithers who walked off with the low bid on eight of the ten original schools. Smithers has done quite a bit of work for us before and always well."

"Did we get the usual bid bonds to ensure that the companies would go ahead if awarded a contract?"

"Yes, for 10 percent of the overall bid."

"And what about performance bonds for 10 percent of the contract value?"

"All O.K.," replied Godfrey, "as far as Smithers is concerned. Actually, Carlon's isn't in our file, but I have Surety's agreement to bond them for performance if they were successful. This was the situation," he continued. "I had all my figures from half a dozen people by April 24 (see Exhibit 2). Some of them go all over the shop. Smithers was lowest on schools 1, 3, 4, 5, 6, 7, 8, and 9 and Carlon on 2 and 10."

"None of the bidders bothered to be present at the opening read-out on May 7, but somehow Carlon knew where he stood. That was obvious from subsequent conversations. It so happened that Carlon was about $3,300 below the next man of School No. 2 and $6,100 lower of School No. 10. In both cases Smithers was the competition." By June 6 we agreed internally to withdraw School No. 2—a large one—because Bob Oxford's cost estimates showed his own forces to be within 2 percent of outside bids. Actually, with your approval I issued the appropriate purchase orders on June 15. We told the board in our recommendation of June 20 that we had given eight schools to Smithers and only one to Carlon.

"When did Carlon react?" asked Mr. Lewis.

"Their sales manager phoned me at the end of June," said the buyer, "and confirmed it on July 6, asking leave to withdraw his quotation" (see Exhibit 3).

"And when did I write him about his obligations?" asked Mr. Lewis. "On July 13," said Mr. Godfrey. "Here it is" (see Exhibit 4).

"Then nothing further transpired until September when Bob Oxford's men noted sloppy work in School No. 10. He sent them a registered letter at the end of that month (see Exhibit 5) and received verbal assurances of improvement but complained

EXHIBIT 3 Letter from Carlon

CARLON CLEANING COMPANY, LIMITED

July 6

Dear Mr. Godfrey:

Referring to our telephone conversation last week, please take note that Carlon Cleaning Company, Ltd., wishes to withdraw its quotation of April 20 covering Janitorial Services to your Public School No. 10.

Our company quoted on the ten schools offered in your tender and was low bid in two cases, Schools Nos. 2 and 10. We would have been able to provide janitorial services had we been awarded both schools, as supervisory and other operating costs could have been split between them. The board's decision not to award us the contract for School No. 2 leaves us little choice but to withdraw our quotation for the remaining School No. 10. Therefore, we are returning your purchase order number 93346 of June 15.

We sincerely hope that our decision will not disqualify our company from any further tender calls of your board.

Thanking you in advance for your understanding.

Yours sincerely,
Carlon Cleaning Company, Limited,

Thomas Inglis,
Sales Manager.

---

again by letter a month later (see Exhibit 6) and got renewed assurance and a very temporary improvement. However, last week he was fed up and sent in one of his assistant superintendents with a team for a detailed inspection which proved the inefficiency of the cleaning. Some floors needed complete refinishing. Bob Oxford is mad. All he wants is to get these blank, blank people out."

"To tell you the truth, Fraser, this Carlon outfit has been around long enough to know what they are doing. I think they're trying to weasel and should be nailed. They know what a performance bond means. We always ask for a performance bond for 10 percent of total contract price. Here is our chance to take advantage of it."

"Thank you, Lin," replied the purchasing supervisor, "I'll think it over."

Fraser Lewis knew that it was bad for a firm's reputation to have to call on surety to make up for a deficiency, yet to release the contractor from his responsibilities would affect the board's posture on future bids. He wondered if all reasonable avenues of avoiding an unpleasant showdown had been explored.

EXHIBIT 4   Reply to Carlon

Mayfair County Board of Education

July 13

Dear Mr. Inglis:

Your letter of July 6, to Mr. L. Godfrey requesting withdrawal of your bid covering Janitorial Services at Public School No. 10 has been referred to me.

I would like to draw to your attention the fact that, included with your bid, was a bid bond that reads in part:

> Now, Therefore the condition of this obligation is such that if the aforesaid Principal shall have the bid accepted within sixty (60) days from the closing date of bid and the said Principal will, within the time required, enter into a formal contract and give a good and sufficient bond to secure the performance of the terms and conditions of the contract, then this obligation shall be null and void; otherwise the Principal and Surety will pay unto the Obligee the difference in money between the amount of the bid of the said Principal and the amount for which the Obligee legally contracts with another party to perform the work if the latter amount be in excess of the former.

> The Surety shall not be liable for a greater sum than the specified penalty of this Bond.

The difference between your tender and the next lowest is $6,100. If the services are not carried out by your company according to specifications, we shall have to refer the matter to your surety company for the extra cost to complete the work. This may not be in your best interest.

Please advise.

Yours truly,

F. Lewis,
Supervisor of Purchasing

EXHIBIT 5   Letter to Carlon

Mayfair County Board of Education

September 27

Re: Contract for Cleaning Services—Public School No. 10

Dear Mr. Dale:

This letter will put on record our experience of the service your company has provided at School No. 10 since the beginning of your contract until the present time.

I personally inspected the interior of this school prior to the commencement of your contract and found it to be in a very clean condition. Since then, a steady deterioration

EXHIBIT 5   *(concluded)*

in the general cleanliness of the school has been noted by the Principal and the Caretaker. Notes have been left daily for your staff to see regarding specific complaints. Your Mr. Johnson was called in by the Principal on September 21, and he agreed that the condition of the interior of the building had deteriorated since your company has assumed the cleaning contract and that some changes would have to be made.

At the Principal's request, Mr. Riddell, Assistant Supervisor of Caretaking, inspected the school this morning. His report to me read as follows:

1. None of the classroom floors had been swept.
2. Desk tops had not been cleaned.
3. Washroom floors had neither been swept or washed.
4. Toilet seats had not been washed.
5. There was no indication that any "spray buffing" had been carried out on the floors the previous night.

This, Mr. Dale, is a very poor situation, and one which requires immediate attention by your company. I would expect an immediate drastic improvement in the quality of the service your company is providing and a firm assurance from yourself that this type of experience will not be repeated.

Yours very truly,

Mayfair County Board of Education.
R. Oxford, Supervisor of Caretaking.

EXHIBIT 6   Letter to Carlon

Mayfair County Board of Education

October 30

Re: Contract Cleaning Services—Public School No. 10

Dear Mr. Dale:

It has again become necessary to write to you regarding the condition of Public School No. 10, where cleaning services are presently being provided by your company. The school premises were inspected once more by my Assistant Supervisor on the morning of October 26. His report follows:

1. Room 29—floor dusty, desk tops dirty, corners dirty.
2. Music Room 28—risers not swept.
3. Large Gym—floor not swept.
4. Locker Rooms—toilets not cleaned, floors not swept.
5. Industrial Arts Room—floor not swept properly, bradley basin not cleaned.
6. Rooms 21–26 inclusive—floors poorly swept, desk tops dirty, chalk ledges dirty, corners of floor dirty.

EXHIBIT 6   *(concluded)*

7. Rooms 12–17 inclusive—desk tops sticky, floors not properly swept.
8. Art Room—floor needs refurbishing.
9. Rooms 3–9 inclusive—floors and desk tops in poor condition (the lunch room is particularly bad).
10. Library—table tops dirty, black base dirty.
11. Office—counter top dirty, dusting could improve.
12. Staff Room—there appeared to be a white film on the floor, tables dirty.
13. Corridors—dull, there is some kind of film all over.
14. The spray buffing program is not being carried out according to specifications.
15. Washrooms—urinals had been poorly cleaned.

As you can see, Mr. Dale, there has been no improvement since my letter of September 27. I would expect you to get in touch with me as soon as possible, as I do not feel that I can authorize payment for your October invoice.

I believe we should also talk about the future of your contract, as no apparent effort is being made by your company to live up to the specifications. You will remember that we offered to cooperate with you in rescheduling your help, receiving your assurance that this would enable you to do a satisfactory job. This has not been the case.

I will await your early reply.

Yours very truly,
Mayfair County Board of Education.
R. Oxford,
Supervisor of Caretaking.

CHAPTER 16

Strategy in Purchasing

Interest in strategic planning, its contribution to an organization's long-term success and survival, the tools for developing the strategic plan, and the substrategies available have drawn much attention over the past two decades.

Certainly the purchasing function, as a major decision area in the allocation of most organizations' resource stream, should be a "major player" in developing an overall strategy. The key question is: How can the purchasing function contribute *effectively* to organizational objectives and strategy? The accompanying question is: How can the organizational objectives and strategy properly reflect the contribution and opportunities offered in the supply arena? (See Figure 16–1.)

DEFINITION OF STRATEGIC PLANNING

There are many definitions of *strategic planning*. One of the pioneers in developing this approach, Peter F. Drucker, defines it as " . . . the continuous process of making present *entrepreneurial (risk taking) decisions* systematically and with the greatest knowledge of their futurity; organizing systematically the *efforts* needed to carry out these decisions; and measuring the results of the decisions against the expectations through *organized systematic feedback.*"[1] He then states the key question in the strategic planning process as "*What do we have to do now* to obtain our objectives tomorrow?"[2]

Thus, a *strategy* is an *action plan* designed to achieve specific *long-term goals and objectives.* The strategy should concentrate on the *key factors necessary* for success and the *major actions* which should be taken now *to assure the future.* It is the process of determining the relationship of the organization to its *environment,* establishing long-term *objectives,* and achieving the desired relationship(s) through efficient and effective *allocation of resources.*

---

[1] Peter F. Drucker, *Management: Tasks, Responsibilities, Practices* (New York: Harper & Row, 1974), p. 125.

[2] Ibid., p. 126.

FIGURE 16–1   Key Strategy Questions

HOW CAN THE SUPPLY FUNCTION CONTRIBUTE EFFECTIVELY TO
ORGANIZATIONAL OBJECTIVES?
OR
HOW CAN THE MANAGER OF PURCHASING MAKE SURE THE SUPPLY
FUNCTION CONTRIBUTES EFFECTIVELY TO ORGANIZATIONAL
OBJECTIVES?

LEVELS OF STRATEGIC PLANNING

To be successful, an organization must approach strategic planning on
three levels:

1. *Corporate.*   These are the decisions and plans which answer the
questions of *what business are we in?*, and *how will we allocate our
resources among these businesses?* For example, is a railroad in the
business of running trains? Or is its business the movement (creating
time and space utility) of things and people?

2. *Unit.*   These decisions mold the plans of a particular business
unit, as necessary to contribute to the corporate strategy.

3. *Function.*   These plans concern the "how" of each functional
area's contribution to the business strategy and involve the allocation
of internal resources.

PURCHASING'S CONTRIBUTION TO BUSINESS STRATEGY

With the problems which have surfaced in the worldwide purchasing
arena over the past two decades (see Chapter 1), and the growing recognition
by top management of the opportunities for attaining greater purchasing
leverage over operating results, purchasing managers relatively recently
have moved into the strategy area. For example, a *Purchasing* magazine
survey found that during the early part of the 1980s about one third of the
purchasing departments became part of the strategic planning effort.[3] The
1988 report of the Center for Advanced Purchasing Studies found that strategic planning is the top area in which purchasing has assumed an increased
role or responsibility since 1980 (cited by 43 percent of the organizations).
That involvement will increase even further in the 1990s.[4]

---

[3]"1980s Bring More Duties to Purchasing Department," *Purchasing,* April 14, 1983, p. 14.
[4]Harold E. Fearon, *Purchasing Organizational Relationships* (Tempe, Ariz.: Center for Advanced Purchasing Studies/National Association of Purchasing Management, 1988), p. 16.

FIGURE 16–2   Supply Strategy Interpreted in Organizational Strategy

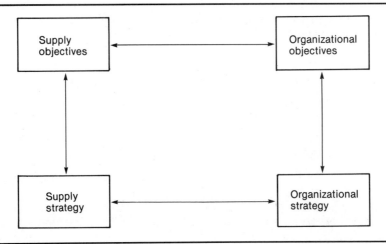

The key question, already mentioned, is how can purchasing contribute effectively to organizational objectives and strategies? The heart of this question lies in the term "effectively." It connotes more than just a response to a directive from top management. It also implies inputs to the strategic planning process so that the units and/or the organizational objectives and strategies include supply opportunities and problems.

This is graphically shown in Figure 16–2 by the use of double arrows between supply objectives and strategy and organizational objectives and strategy.

A somewhat different look at supply strategy is given in Figure 16–3. This shows an effective supply strategy linking both current needs and current markets to future needs and future markets.

One of the significant obstacles to the development of an effective supply strategy lies in the difficulties inherent in translating organizational objectives into supply objectives.

Normally, most organizational objectives can be summarized under four categories:

1. Survival

2. Growth

3. Financial

4. Environmental

Survival is the most basic need of any organization. Growth can be expressed in a variety of ways. For example, growth could be in size of organization in terms of number of employees or assets or number of operating units, or number of countries in which the organization operates,

FIGURE 16–3 Supply Strategy Links Current and Future Markets to Current and Future Needs

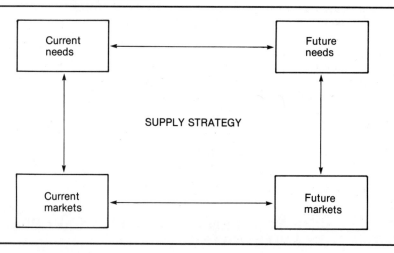

FIGURE 16–4 Normal Organizational and Supply Objectives

NORMAL ORGANIZATION OBJECTIVES
1. Survival
2. Growth
3. Financial
4. Environmental

NORMAL SUPPLY OBJECTIVES
1. Quality
2. Quantity
3. Delivery
4. Price
5. Service

or in market share. Financial objectives could include: total size of budget, surplus or profit, total revenue, return on investment, return on assets, share price, or increases in each of these or any combination. Environmental objectives might include not only traditional environmental concerns like clean air, water, and earth, but also objectives such as the contribution to and fit with values and ideals of the organization's employees and customers, and the laws and aspirations of the countries in which the organization operates. The notion of good citizenship is embodied in this fourth objective.

Unfortunately, typical supply objectives normally are expressed in a totally different language such as: quality and function, delivery, quantity, price, terms and conditions, service, etc. (See Figure 16–4.)

FIGURE 16–5   Potential Business-Strategy Contribution Areas

1. Social issues and trends.
2. Government regulations and controls.
3. Financial planning with suppliers.
4. Product liability exposure.
5. Economic trends and environment.
6. Organizational changes.
7. Product or service line.
8. Competitive intelligence.
9. Technology.
10. Investment.
11. Mergers/acquisition/disinvestment.

THREE MAJOR CHALLENGES IN SETTING SUPPLY OBJECTIVES AND STRATEGIES

The first major challenge facing the supply manager is the effective interpretation of corporate objectives and supply objectives. For example, given the organization's desire to expand rapidly, is supply assurance more important than obtaining "rock bottom" prices?

The second challenge deals with the choice of the appropriate action plan or strategy to achieve the desired objectives. For example, if supply assurance is vital, is it best accomplished by single or dual sourcing, or by making in-house? The U.S. Defense supply planners face this issue. Because of the key role of electronics, does the United States need full chip-making capability domestically?

The third challenge deals with the identification and feedback of supply issues to be integrated into organizational objectives and strategies. For example, because any new technology can be accessed early through supply efforts, how can this be exploited?

The development of a supply strategy requires that the supply manager be in tune with the organization's key objectives and strategies and also be capable of recognizing and grasping opportunities. All three challenges require managerial and strategic skills of the highest order, and the difficulties in meeting these challenges should not be minimized. (See Figure 16–5.)

Social Issues and Trends

During the 1970s and 1980s interest grew rapidly in some of the areas which might be characterized as the social responsibility of firms. For example, during the Nixon administration *Executive Order* 311625 was promulgated to encourage at the federal level minority business enterprises (MBEs), which in turn gave impetus to similar programs in the private sector. This has spawned programs such as Community Economic Development, Public Works Set-Asides, Small Business Administration (SBA) Guaranteed Loans, and MESBICS (Minority Entrepreneurial Small Business Investment Companies). The programs encourage business enterprise on the part of firms and people who, for a variety of reasons, have not been able or permitted to compete effectively in the past. While most of the successes have been in the defense and auto industries, there has been some spillover into other industries, for example, pharmaceuticals, petroleum, food manufacture, insurance, and banking.

Along with the MBE movement, attention has been directed at firms' responsibilities to protect the environment, which has culminated in various federal and state laws and regulations designed to assure that the public's safety and use of air, water, and land are protected. Examples of the concerns are disposal of hazardous wastes, control of smoke and other pollutant emissions from manufacturing processes, flood control as a part of earth movement relating to subdivision construction, reforestation after timber cuts, and embargo of purchases from countries which practice apartheid.

These programs typically are costly to an organization in the short run, but the long-term benefits to the firm, in terms of public attitude and forestalling of potentially damaging, restrictive legislation, may far outweigh the costs.

Purchasing's contribution in the strategy area is to pose questions and supply data, such as:

1. Is there a developing interest on the part of the general public and/or our publics? How potent is this interest? What are the ramifications to our long-term corporate development?

2. What are the direct and indirect costs to our firm from responding to these interests? What are the costs of not responding?

3. How can purchasing respond? What will it do to our short-term material costs? Long-term costs?

4. What risks, for example, supply disruptions, reduction in quality, are involved?

5. What objectives, short-term and long-term, should we set? How will we monitor progress toward these objectives?

Government Regulations and Controls

The firm must be conscious of impending governmental actions and forecast how these might impact the operation. Purchasing should monitor developing trends, forecast the outcomes and potential ramifications, and suggest ways the firm can adjust. If it can anticipate developments, it then can respond in a rational fashion.

The distressing incidents of product contamination in the food and pharmaceutical industry have resulted in a variety of governmental rules and regulations—for example, the Pure Food and Drug Administration—designed to protect the consuming public. These certainly will affect the purchase costs of packaging materials and equipment and the types of materials and equipment required. If purchasing is aware of new developments, technology, and suppliers of such packaging processes, it can understand and be part of a corporate team approach assisting top management in making the strategic decisions necessary to cope with these developments. It might result in product-line changes, such as tablets instead of capsules, or changes in the type of packaging used in presenting the product to the public.

Financial Planning with Suppliers

In most organizations, the dollar cash flow to suppliers is the largest or second largest outflow of funds (in labor-intensive firms, wage and fringe costs may be larger). Thus, the magnitude of purchase dollars has significant implications for the amount of working capital needed. If payment were extended to a 60-day rather than a 30-day basis, that would result in a one-time freeing up of working capital which then might be employed for other purposes. Suppliers would be participating in financing the purchasing firm's operation (a partnership arrangement, so to speak).

Purchasing might investigate the financial implications of stretching out payment arrangements and the feasibility of doing so. Obviously, any such arrangements could be made only with the cooperation of suppliers, and purchasing is in the best position to suggest and evaluate such possibilities. Similarly, an excess of cash might lead purchasing to explore quicker payment to obtain greater discounts. Clearly, any change in the cash discount terms would impact on both the buying and selling organizations' cash flow picture and overall profitability.

Product Liability Exposure

Product safety and product liability considerations have become much more important over the past two decades, due to changes in the liability environment and the ways judges and juries have interpreted the existing laws. Some of the court judgments have had an effect so severe that selling firms have been forced to declare financial bankruptcy, for example, the asbestos producers and sellers of products using asbestos. The concept of "absolute liability" basically says that the seller of a product has total liability to a user of its product if that user is injured, regardless of disclaimers made to the buyer at the time of sale. Since the purchasing department obtains materials and components from a multitude of suppliers, which then are incorporated into an end product, this requires a close working relationship between the buyer and the supplier, and the buyer's own design, engineering, quality assurance, manufacturing, and marketing departments. Purchasing must attempt to assure that the organization is not being unreasonably exposed to potentially disastrous product liability lawsuits.

Purchasing's contribution to the business strategy is to assure that risk is recognized and quantified, and reduced if possible. These considerations should be major inputs to the overall business strategy.

Economic Trends and Environment

Top management needs to be constantly aware of immediate and long-term structural shifts (changes) in the overall economic environment. If, for example, major changes in demand from sectors of business (nationally or internationally) are occurring or projected, this should be taken into account in formulating the overall corporate and/or business strategy.

Purchasing can play a major role in identifying such trends and evaluating their long-term ramifications on the business. Since purchasing obtains a constant flow of information from a variety of external sources (see Figure 3–11 in Chapter 3), and is in almost daily contact with both primary and secondary suppliers, it can serve as a key conduit in obtaining, cataloging, and evaluating the long-term impact of these changes on the business.

Organizational Changes to Facilitate Long-Term Productivity and Efficiency

The traditional organization structures used to manage material flows may need to be revised in the future, to gain the communication and control necessary to facilitate greater productivity and efficiency. Purchasing should be exploring these possible changes and present the alternatives to top management. Such changes normally would impact substantially the relationship between purchasing and other organizational units; any decision to move to one of these newer organizational arrangements would require an overall organization commitment to establish such modified relationships. Four possible changed organizational strategies in which purchasing would play a key role, are:

1. *Materials Management.* In this organizational arrangement (see Chapter 2) all or most of the functions involved with the flow of materials into the organization would be arranged under one responsible manager, normally titled *materials manager.* While the purchasing manager has a key role in such an arrangement, the persons in charge of materials planning and scheduling, incoming transportation, and materials inventory also play a key role.

2. *Project Management.* If key work projects or product lines can

be segregated from other projects or products, the enhanced communication and coordination may favor setting up these operations as self-contained units, each with its own purchasing function.

3. *Logistics Management.* Here, *all* the material flow functions, including the input functions (materials management) and the output functions (physical distribution management) might be included as part of an overall logistics organization. While it may put purchasing in a subordinate role, the resultant synergy may provide major efficiency advantages (see Chapter 2).

4. *JIT Purchasing/Production.* This arrangement effectively couples the purchasing and production/operations functions together with the major suppliers, in effect vertically integrating the organization backwards (in an operational sense). While it requires additional planning resources, the cost/production efficiencies may be substantially greater. Chapter 6 on supplier selection develops more fully the philosophy of this approach.

Product- or Service-Line Decisions

Simply because an organization traditionally has produced and sold a particular product(s) or service(s), this does not mean that it should continue in that mode. Examples of such strategic changes are U.S. Steel's (USX's) movement away from an almost total reliance on basic steel products and into the energy and financial services product lines; General Electric's emphasis on financial service; and American Can Company's (now Primerica) movement out of the container business.

The decision to add or drop a specific product line can be influenced by a myriad of factors, for example, profit margins, return on investment, consumer demand, competition from other firms, and purchased materials availability and cost. Purchasing should continually monitor supply market trends of major purchased raw materials, interpret these trends over the long run, and define the firm's options. Such long-term commodity forecasting normally is done as a part of the purchasing research effort (see Chapter 11 on purchasing research).

Purchasing can make a major contribution to a firm's corporate and/or business strategy by continually keeping in touch with the supply market and factoring in the effect of long-term trends on the firm's position and cost of being in a particular product market. Changes in either long-term supply availability or cost of major raw materials might cause a firm to reevaluate its product-line strategy. For example, continued racial and/or economic problems in the southern African countries which are major suppliers of metals such as chromite, cobalt, gold, or platinum might cause a firm to either consider dropping end product lines dependent on one or more of these raw materials or begin research efforts to develop suitable substitutes for these materials.

Competitive Intelligence

To be successful in today's competitive world, the organization constantly must monitor industry trends and what other organizations are doing and planning to do. Is a key competitor planning to introduce a new product, for example, in the beverage industry, is a competitor going to market a new flavor? Is a competitor going to modify its existing product line? Is it introducing a packaging refinement? Is it withdrawing from a specific product line? The success of an organization is largely due to its ability to anticipate such competitive changes, rather than simply reacting. Similarly, on the public side, how effectively are governments in other parts of the country or world dealing with similar issues?

Because of its many contacts with vendors' sales and technical personnel, purchasing often can get information items that, when pieced together with information and data obtained by other company personnel, will provide advance warning of changes. Such information should be fed by purchasing into the firm's planning process on an organized basis.

Technology

Very few products or services are produced today in exactly the same manner of 10 years ago. In some industries, such as semiconductors, firms compete successfully based on the technology they possess (the production process and the quality assurance system they use) rather than the specific product produced. Staying in the forefront of technology development can give a firm a competitive edge that spells the difference between success and simply a marginal existence.

Purchasing should contribute to technology in three primary ways:

1. By providing information to their own design/process/production people on developments in technology (obtained through their contacts with external information sources). This information can help mold the firm's own technology development.

2. By working with their own suppliers to develop new technology that can be incorporated into the buying firm's operation. In some instances, purchasing can suggest arrangements whereby specific suppliers can share the risk in developing new technology. In some instances these costs are so large that it would not be feasible for the buying company to provide the total developmental resouces on its own.

3. By "locking up" new, advantageous technology through exclusive agreements with suppliers. If this can be done, it may put the firm in a situation where it can produce products or services at lower total cost or with better overall quality performance than can be achieved by competitors.

Investment Decisions

Any organization must continually monitor the rates of return it receives on its use of resources (investments). The cost of capital is constantly changing, and the attractiveness of various investments does not remain static.

While the purchasing department typically will not make the final decisions on where resources will be invested, it is in a position to make sure new alternatives are fed into the development of the organization's strategic plan. For example, the make-or-buy and lease-or-buy alternatives may present some very cost-effective possibilities.

Purchasing is in a position to identify these strategic alternatives and to collect and classify much of the data needed to evaluate each alternative. The make/lease/buy problem, and the role and methodology of purchasing in assessing alternatives, is discussed in Chapter 6, "Supplier Selection and Supplier Relations." Examples of these strategic decision problems, in which purchasing should play a key role, abound:

1. An organization could decide to lease much or all of its transportation equipment (autos, trucks, rail cars), thus freeing up the capital which otherwise would be tied up in that equipment.

2. A university might decide to use the services of an industrial caterer to operate its food service, rather than using its own personnel and equipment.

3. A steel producer has the alternative of buying, rather than making, steel slabs from a primary steel producer and then producing the finished steel products in its own facilities. This could result in a substantially changed cost posture for the steel producer and might allow equipment to be used for other purposes, or permit disinvestment, thus freeing up capital for other uses.

4. A consumer electronics firm might look at the possibility of sourcing out the complete television receiver, rather than buying the components and assembling the set.

Mergers/Acquisitions/Disinvestment

The overall possibilities from vertical integration or disintegration in the production of various products or services are many and have far-reaching consequences. For example, a producer of automobiles currently may buy radios from an outside vendor. A decision could be made to buy a radio producer, thus vertically integrating the production process. Further, the radio producing plant could produce its own semiconductor devices, rather than buying them from a vendor. In the reverse direction, the auto producer now making its own radios might decide to sell off the radio producer and buy out (outsource) the radios from an existing vendor. The merger of DuPont and Conoco was, in a sense, a vertical integration decision, for DuPont gained, as a result of the merger, greater control over the petroleum feedstocks required in the production of many of its chemical lines. The merger of General Electric Company (GE) and Utah International in the 1970s put GE in a position to control a significant amount of the metal-lurgical coal required by Far Eastern steel producers, which then gave them greater assurance of being able to obtain much of the steel needed for the GE production facilities.

Purchasing has the best overall viewpoint of the firm's vendor supply channels and the risks involved in supply movement. It is in a key position to feed this information into the organization's development of an overall strategy to cope with potential problems or opportunities.

STRATEGIC PLANNING IN PURCHASING

Over the past 50 years the purchasing function has evolved from a clerical-type activity to one in which professional purchasing managers per-form the function in an asset management context. This change has stim-ulated the development of strategies to maximize performance.

Following World War II industry began to recognize the profit leverage of purchasing, the effect that purchasing performance has on return on assets (see Chapter 1), and that purchasing should be a profit-contributing function and not merely a routine order-placing activity. The 1970s provided some real shocks to the world business system—material shortages, the energy crises, and rapid price escalation—and a realization that some of the old ways of doing business were outmoded and would not return. These events propelled purchasing into the limelight.[5] Purchasing must now look past the next requisition or the next quarter in the purchase planning of key materials and ask the *what if* questions. Top management in many organizations has recognized the need to integrate long-run purchasing/materials planning into the overall corporate long-term strategic plan.

Today, firms face the challenge of maintaining or regaining position in world competitive markets. The ability to relate effectively to outside en-vironments—(1) social, (2) economic, (3) political and legal, and (4) tech-nological (with its changing materials and processes)—to anticipate changes, to adjust to changes, and to capitalize on opportunity by formu-lating and executing strategic plans, is a major factor in generating future earnings and is critical to survival. Purchasing now must be forward look-ing—it no longer is adequate simply to react to the current situation and problems. If purchasing is primarily in a reactive mode, doing only the urgent things, it will not address the really important issues. Instead, the

---

[5]"The Purchasing Agent Gains More Clout," *Business Week,* January 13, 1975, pp. 62–63.

energies of the people will be dissipated in dealing with immediate problems and ("fire fighting"), which becomes largely a no-win situation.

The events of the decades of the 70s and 80s have established the role of purchasing in strategic planning at the functional level (as well as the strategic business level). For example, a study by *Purchasing* found that between 1979 and 1981, 31 percent of buyers became involved in the strategic planning process.[6] And an August 1985 report of *The Kiplinger Washington Letter* indicated that the role of the purchasing manager is changing, from that of a clerical-type job to a role in top management, with contributions in the areas of cost control, global sourcing, and just-in-time systems. It went on to say that purchasing now can be a path to the CEO's suite.[7]

MAJOR PURCHASING FUNCTIONAL STRATEGY AREAS

A strategy is an action plan designed to permit the achievement of selected goals and objectives. If well developed, the strategy will link the firm to the environment as part of the long-term planning process. An overall purchasing strategy is made up of substrategies, each of which is developed by using all available information in the formulation of a plan directed at the achievement of a *specific* purpose. All purchasing substrategies can be grouped together into five major categories:

1. *Assurance-of-Supply Strategies:* Designed to assure that future supply needs are met at least in terms of quality and quantity. Assurance-of-supply strategies must consider changes in both demand and supply. (Much of the work in purchasing research [see Chapter 11] is focused on providing the relevant information).

2. *Cost-Reduction Strategies:* Designed to reduce the laid-down cost of what is acquired, or the total cost of acquisition and use—life-cycle cost. With changes in the environment and technology, alternatives may be available to reduce an organization's overall operating costs through changes in materials, sources, and purchasing methods.

3. *Supply-Support Strategies:* Designed to maximize the likelihood that the considerable knowledge and capabilities of suppliers are available to the buying organization. For example, better communication systems (perhaps computerized) may be needed between buyer and seller to facilitate the timely notification of changes and to assure that vendor inventory and production goals are consistent with the buying

[6]"1980s Bring More Duties to Purchasing Department."
[7]*The Kiplinger Washington Letter*, August 30, 1985, p. 3.

firm's needs. Buyer and seller also may need better relations for the communication needed to assure higher and/or more consistent quality.

4. *Environmental-Change Strategies:* Designed to anticipate and recognize shifts in the total environment (economic, organizational, people, legal, governmental regulations and controls, and systems availability) so it can turn them to the long-term advantage of the buying organization.

5. *Competitive-Edge Strategies:* Designed to exploit market opportunities and organizational strengths to give the buying organization a significant competitive edge. In the public sector, the term competitive edge may usually be interpreted to mean strong performance in achieving program objectives.

Figure 16–6 is a conceptual flow diagram of the strategic purchasing-planning process. It is important to recognize that the planning process normally focuses on *long-run opportunities* and not primarily on immediate problems.

STRATEGIC COMPONENTS

The number of specific strategic purchasing opportunities which might be addressed in formulating an overall purchasing strategy is limited only by the imagination of the purchasing manager. Any strategy chosen should include a determination of what quality, how much, who, when, what price, where, how, and why. Each of these will be discussed further in turn. (See Figure 16–7.)

What?

Probably the most fundamental question facing an organization under the "what" category is the issue of make-or-buy. Presumably, strong purchasing strengths would favor a buy strategy. Two specific issues not previously discussed in depth include ownership interest in a supplier and backward integration.

Ownership Interest in Supplier. To assure long-term supply in a competitive environment, it may be a good strategy to buy an ownership interest in a key supplier, putting the buyer in a preferred customer position and assuring that the buyer will get a "fair share" (or more) of the supplier's output. If the ownership interest can stand on its own as an investment, this strategy will look even more attractive. The purchase by IBM of a 20 percent equity ownership in Intel Corporation is a good example. Assurance of a large enough supply of microprocessors (which essentially run a personal computer and initially were in short supply) was very important to IBM if

FIGURE 16–6   Strategic Purchasing Planning Process

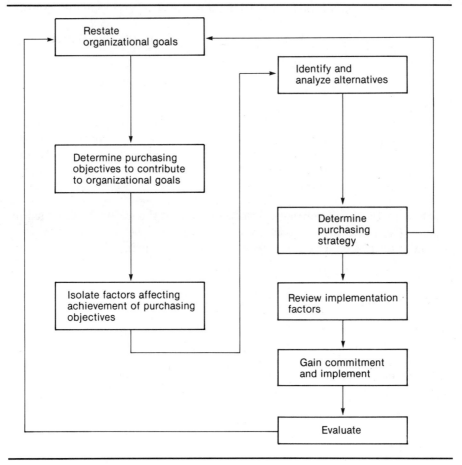

it were to increase output of personal computers fast enough to gain the desired market share.[8] Intel and IBM later entered into an agreement that will allow them to swap computer chip designs and to develop customized chips for use in IBM products. Such an agreement may permit IBM to use customized chips that cannot be copied by firms who make PC "clones," thus making it more difficult for competitors to sell their product against the IBM product line.[9]

---

[8]Thomas C. Hayes, "Intel Copes With a Shortage," *The New York Times,* January 30, 1984, p. 23.

[9]Brenton R. Schlender and Paul B. Carroll, "Intel and IBM Are Set Up to Swap Designs to Create Chips for Future IBM Lines," *The Wall Street Journal,* October 6, 1986, p. 4.

FIGURE 16–7 Supply Strategy Questions

1. WHAT?
   Make or buy
   Standard versus special
   Quality versus cost
2. QUALITY?
   Quality versus cost
   Supplier involvement
3. HOW MUCH?
   Large versus small quantities
   (inventory)
4. WHO?
   Centralize or decentralize
   Quality of staff
   Top management involvement
5. WHEN?
   Now versus later
   Forward buy
6. WHAT PRICE?
   Premium
   Standard
   Lower
   Cost-based
   Market-based
   Lease/Make/Buy
7. WHERE?
   Local, regional
   Domestic, international
   Large versus small

Multiple versus sole source
High versus low supplier turnover
Supplier relations
Supplier certification
Supplier ownership
8. HOW?
   Systems and procedures
   Computerization
   Negotiations
   Competitive bids
   Fixed bids
   Blanket orders/open orders
   Systems contracting
   Blank check system
   Group buying
   Materials requirements planning
   Long-term contracts
   Ethics
   Aggressive or passive
   Purchasing research
   Value analysis
9. WHY?
   Objectives congruent
   Market reasons
   Internal reasons
   1. Outside supply
   2. Inside supply

Backward Vertical Integration. This is a version of "make-or-buy," in which there may be some major, long-term advantages from obtaining control of the production of a key material or component previously bought from a vendor. For example, the General Motors acquisition of Hughes Aircraft Company gave it control of a major manufacturer of electronics components, many of which could be used in the assembly of vehicles. A major purchaser of copper might consider buying a copper mining and refining property. Such backward integration could reduce overall purchase costs, as well as assure availability of needed items in times of severe shortage.

Outsourcing. As referred to in the earlier section under Investment Decisions (p. 616), this is a version of the make-or-buy problem, where a firm elects to buy an item that previously was made in-house. A steel products' producer might decide to buy slabs (the raw material) from another steel producer, and confine its activities to fabrication of the final steel sheets. An auto producer could buy out auto radios, rather than making them in-house. Since a vendor might have greater expertise in a field, this could be a cost-effective strategy. In addition it might free capacity and resources (investment) for use in other, more productive pursuits.

Purchase of Finished Products on an "Our Own Label" Basis. While this is an unusual partnership strategy, in some instances a buying firm may decide to also distribute a purchased product, under its own name, to other firms. This might be attractive because of the price which could be obtained due to the volume, and/or because of the buying firm's ability, due to its size, to support the product after sale. For example, a large purchaser of personal computers might enter into an arrangement with the supplier (manufacturer) to buy and market those same units under its own brand name. Or, a major hospital buying organization might decide, because of the pricing obtained due to its volume, to buy certain products, such as intravenous (IV) solutions, under its own brand name and then act as a distributor of this product to other hospitals, clinics, and doctors' offices. While this is not a typical strategy, it may have income-producing possibilities, and could be considered by a purchasing department that is alert to innovative approaches.

Also included under the heading of what is to be acquired is the issue of whether the organization will lean toward acquiring standard items and materials readily available in the market as opposed to special, custom specified requirements. Standard items may be readily acquired in the marketplace, but they may not afford the organization the competitive edge that special requirements might provide.

Quality?

Part of the what question deals with the quality of the items or services to be acquired. Chapter 4 addresses the various trade-offs possible under quality.

Supplier Quality Assurance Programs. Many firms have concluded that a more consistent quality of end-product output is absolutely essential to the maintenance of, or growth in, market share. To achieve this, suppliers must deliver more consistent quality materials, parts, and components; this also will effect a marked reduction in production costs and in-house quality control administrative costs. Therefore, a strategy of developing suppliers' knowledge of quality requirements and assisting them in implementation of programs to achieve desired results may be needed. Three of the programs which might be used are (1) Zero Defect (ZD) plans, which are basically motivational training programs to convince the supplier and its employees that only the agreed-upon quality should be produced and shipped. "Do it right the first time" is far more cost effective than making corrections after the fact. (2) Process quality control programs, which use statistical control charts to monitor various production processes to isolate developing problems and make needed adjustments (corrections) before bad product is produced. The buying firm may need to assist the supplier with the introduction of the needed statistical techniques, and (3) Quality certification programs, in which the vendor agrees to perform the agreed-upon quality tests and supply the test data, with the shipment, to the buying firm. If the seller does the requisite outgoing quality checks, and can be depended on to do them correctly, the buying firm then can eliminate its incoming inspection procedures and attendant costs. This approach almost always is a key element in any just-in-time purchasing system, as discussed in the following section.

How Much?

Another major component of any supply strategy deals with the question of how much is to be acquired in total and per delivery. Chapter 5 discussed a number of tradeoffs open under quantity. Generally, the trend has been to go toward smaller quantities to be delivered as needed, as opposed to the former stance of buying large quantities at a time to ensure better prices. One option available under the how much question may involve the shifting of inventory.

Shift Inventory to Supplier. The supplier may be able to manage finished goods inventory (which is the buyer's raw material inventory) more effectively than the buyer, due to the supplier's greater knowledge of inventory control procedures for a given line of product. Also, since the vendor may be supplying a common item to several customers, the safety stock required to service a group of customers may be much less than the combined total of the safety stocks if the several customers were to manage their own inventories. This concept is integral to the successful implementation of systems contracting (discussed earlier). From a strategic standpoint, purchasing may wish to analyze its inventory position on all of its major items, with a view to working out a partnership arrangement with key suppliers whereby they agree to maintain the inventory, physically and financially, with delivery as required by the production schedule. An area in the buyer's facility may even be placed under the vendor's control.

Other options are to switch to just-in-time purchasing, or to consignment buying.

Just-in-Time Purchasing. If a vendor can be depended on to deliver needed purchased items, of the agreed-upon quality, in small quantities, and at the specified time, the buying firm can reduce substantially its investment in purchased inventories, enjoy needed continuity of supply, and reduce its receiving and incoming inspection administrative costs. To accomplish this requires a long-term plan and substantial cooperation and understanding between buyer and seller.

Consignment Buying.   In some instances, using the partnership philosophy, a supplier may be induced to maintain an inventory bank in the buyer's facility, under the buyer's control. The buyer assumes responsibility for accounting for withdrawals of stock from that consignment inventory, payment for quantities used, and notification to the supplier of the need to replenish inventory. Verification of quantities remaining in inventory then would be done jointly, at periodic intervals. This strategy has advantages for both supplier (assured volume) and buyer (reduced inventory investment), and often is used in the distribution industry. It can be considered in other industries as well.

Who?

The whole question as to who should do the buying has been extensively addressed in Chapter 2 as part of the organizational issue. The key decisions are whether the supply function should be centralized or not, what the quality of staff should be, and to what extent top management will be involved in the total process. Other options include the choice of materials management and project management.

Materials Management.   Some firms have adopted this organizational strategy (see Chapter 2) to create unified responsibility and more of a partnership philosophy *between the organizational functions* involved in the flow of materials into an organization. While it is not applicable in all organizations, because of differing operating characteristics, it has provided substantial benefits to some organizations, most notably in the airframe, automotive, and electronics industries.

Project Management.   Having purchasing personnel assigned specifically to a research or production project may develop a degree of communication, knowledge, and sense of partnership needed to bring the project to successful fruition. This is a variation of the materials management organizational strategy discussed above.

When?

The question of when to buy is tied very closely to the one of how much. The obvious choices are now versus later. The key strategy issue really lies with the question of forward buying and inventory policy. In the area of commodities, the opportunity exists to go into the futures market and use hedging.

Futures Market (Hedging). The organized commodity exchanges present the opportunity to offset transactions in the spot and future markets to avoid the risk of substantial price fluctuation. Chapters 5 and 7 discuss this strategy that is available to firms that are large buyers of the many basic commodities which are traded continually, or from time to time, on an organized market.

What Price?

It is possible for any organization to follow some specific price strategies. This topic already has been extensively discussed in Chapter 7. Key trade-offs may be whether the organization intends to pursue paying a premium price in return for exceptional service and other commitments from the vendor, a standard price target in line with the rest of the market, or a low price intended to give a cost advantage. Furthermore, the pursuit of a cost-based strategy as opposed to a market-based strategy may require extensive use of ideas like value analysis and intensive negotiation.

Value Analysis/Value Engineering. The "function versus cost" comparison approach has been employed in an organized fashion for many years (since the 1950s). Chapter 11 discusses this approach. The possibilities of reducing costs through changes involving actions such as substitution and standardization are many, and the dollar results can be substantial. As a strategy, it requires a concentrated, organized approach, with a plan, timetable, and assignment of specific responsibility. The assumption that it is an understood part of every buyer's job often turns out to be something for which no one really accepts responsibility.

Another option may be transportation.

Transport Cost Reduction. The efforts to deregulate the domestic system for moving goods has opened up many new transport cost-reduction strategies, such as contract freight services, single transport supplier agreements, negotiated rates, intermodal systems, and use of owned transport facilities and equipment. Only a long-term transport strategy will exploit the cost-saving possibilities. A review of the elements to be considered in developing such a strategy is contained in Chapter 8.

In another vein, lease or buy may offer opportunities.

Lease or Buy. An often overlooked cost reduction strategy is the possibility of leasing equipment and/or facilities from a producer of those items or from a third party (perhaps a financial concern which has purchased equipment from a manufacturer with the intent of then leasing it to the user firm—many of the aircraft used by commercial airline operators are under such an arrangement). In some instances, a firm may decide to enter into the sale of a building or production equipment and then a lease-back arrangement. While the primary purpose of this strategy may be to free up capital for more productive uses (with a higher rate of return), there also may be significant tax benefits. This cost-reduction strategy often is an integral part of a firm's overall financial strategy.

Where?

A vast number of possibilities present themselves under the question of where to buy. Many of these were discussed in Chapter 6 under Source Selection. Obvious trade-offs include local, regional, domestic, or international sourcing; buying from small versus large suppliers; single versus multiple sourcing; and low versus high supplier turnover, as well as supplier certification and supplier ownership. Just a few of these will be discussed here.

Supplier Development. This implies an aggressive search, with the purchaser taking the initiative to create a supplier(s) where none currently exist. It may involve a broad look at technical, financial, and management processes; quality levels; costs; and requirements forecasting and planning. Assistance might be provided to a supplier to get it started, to the long-term benefit of both parties, but the seller must be "sold" this idea. Aggressive supplier development was one of the key factors enabling the computer industry to bring adequate capacity on line to permit mainframe output volume to meet customer demand.

Single Sourcing. Traditional wisdom says that in the case of the major materials and components (or critical purchased items regardless of the monies involved), two or more suppliers should be used to assure continuity of supply. However, splitting the requirements may increase the per-unit price paid, since it denies the benefits of quantity pricing. The price-break benefit may be possible only if the entire quantity is purchased from one vendor. In addition, the single-sourcing strategy may reduce purchasing administrative costs by cutting down the number of individual transactions and obtain faster and more reliable delivery service, since the larger quantity may cause the vendor to value the buyer's account more highly.

This cost reduction strategy may result in increased purchase analysis costs, since the evaluation of a supplier's ability to perform satisfactorily (thus assuring continuity of supply) must be done more completely and accurately—in short, purchasing must reduce the margin for error in the supplier selection process. The cost of these more thorough analysis efforts must be balanced off against the benefits.

Global Sourcing. Over the past decade, the activity in foreign purchasing has increased manyfold, due primarily to two considerations: the increased design, production, and distribution capabilities of foreign suppliers, and the pressures for cost reduction in the manufacturing process. Chapter 12, "Foreign Purchasing," presents the concepts and approaches of global sourcing. Some of the cost reduction substrategies here may address segments such as (1) component buying, in which a firm may elect to contract with a foreign source to supply, on a long-term contract, an entire component or subassembly, such as an automobile engine. This is a version of the make-or-buy strategy. (2) "twin-plant concept," in which two manufacturing plants are built on the border (say in Nogales, Arizona and Nogales, Mexico). Materials are purchased for delivery to the Arizona plant and transferred over the border to the Mexican facility; fabrication/assembly labor applied in the Mexican facility; and the finished components/assemblies moved back across the border to the Arizona plant. Since the labor cost in the foreign plant often is much lower, and import duty is paid only on the labor applied, a substantial reduction in labor cost may result. (3) offsets (see Chapter 12), required to sell product in a foreign market. This puts purchasing right in the middle of designing a distribution strategy where required to sell the dollar value of foreign-produced items which are accepted as part of the offset agreement. (4) exchange rate forecasts required when long-term purchases are made from a foreign supplier, to determine the terms of payment (currency). Exchange rate swings can be large and have a major impact on the purchaser's final cost. One strategy is to spend foreign currency on purchases in the country where that foreign currency is received, if the conversion rate is unfavorable.

Foreign Supplier Facilities in North America.   Major problems in global sourcing, as pointed out in Chapter 12, are time and distance. As a means of minimizing those problems, the buying firm may structure arrangements with foreign suppliers whereby they provide in North America for production; warehousing and distribution; and/or repair, maintenance, and support of product. Since such arrangements are long-term in nature, working them out requires a conscious, strategic purchasing approach.

Long-Term Vendor Forecasting.   The better the buyer understands the situation of the vendor, and changes likely to occur over the next five or so years, the easier it will be to develop a partnership atmosphere. To develop this forecast and understanding will require a good deal of cooperation and vendor furnished information. Some of the areas in which such forecast information is needed are (1) growth plans, in terms of product lines and output capacity, (2) research and development and design capabilities, (3) financial stability and capacity to support new product/application developmental efforts, (4) management strengths and potential, and (5) technological prowess. If the buying firm does develop this long-term understanding with key vendors, it then has a much better basis for formulating a long-term vendor-supply strategy that hopefully will assure supply, at cost-competitive prices.

Minority/Disadvantaged Vendor Development.   Various federal and state programs (see the section on "Social Issues and Trends" earlier in this chapter) have been established to encourage certain types of firms, for example, small business, to pursue economic development more vigorously. If the firm is committed to such economic development, it must develop a strategy to accomplish this. While the overall commitment must come from top management, it is purchasing's role to determine the actions needed to produce the desired results. Normally, a concentrated effort, over a relatively long time period, will be needed if the firm is to provide more than simply "window dressing" for their efforts.

How?

A very large array of options exist under the heading of how to buy. These include, but certainly are not limited to, such areas as systems and procedures, use of the computer, use of negotiations, competitive bids, fixed bids, public opening of bids, blanket orders and open order systems contracting, blank check buying, group buying, materials requirements planning, long-term contracts, the ethics of acquisition, aggressive or passive buying, the use of purchasing research and value analysis, and quality assurance programs. Most of these have been discussed in the earlier chapters in this text. Several will be further highlighted here:

Long-Term Contracting.   Entering into a 5- to 15-year supply contract is almost a decision to make the item, for it melds the supplier's and buyer's operation together in a mutual interdependence, where schedules and plans must be closely coordinated and monitored. The strategic advantages to the buyer are greater supply assurance and stability, and often a lower acquisition-cost base. The supplier gains assured business and operating stability, which should result in a reduction in its long-term cost posture. This may be a sufficient incentive to persuade a supplier to develop and produce a product (supplier development). Before a decision can be made on such a strategic arrangement, long-term projections on costs, advantages, and downside risks must be made.

Commodity Forecasting.   The uncertainty of supply, due to the growth of conglomerates through mergers and acquisitions, and the world geopolitical situation, make it critical for many firms to anticipate changes in the supply environment. If such developments can be anticipated through in-depth commodity-economic research, alternatives to assure supply at a reasonable overall cost can be identified far enough in advance to allow the buyer to take timely action. Many firms now, as a result of the severe materials shortages of the 1970s, do prepare long-term (5 to 20 years) forecasts of commodity supply, demand, and price for their major, "A" purchased items.

Supplier Risk Sharing.   In the development of a major new product, such as a new generation jet aircraft, major investment costs are required. The technological complexity of the product is so great that the risk to, and resources required by, the airframe maker are so large that it can be done successfully only as a partnership arrangement between buyer and seller. Therefore, as a strategy, the purchasing function may need to work out a program with an engine maker which results in, effectively, a joint R & D venture between buyer and supplier.

Supplier/Buyer Data Sharing.   As part of developing a partnership philosophy with key vendors, arrangements must be made to share planning and production information between both buyer and seller. The buyer needs access to the supplier's cost data, production schedules, pricing schedules, inventory availability, and lead times. The seller must have information about the buyer's production plans and schedules, material requirements, and future product and marketing plans. The implementation of an EDI strategy provides an ideal vehicle for these information exchanges.

Electronic Data Interchange (EDI).   As technology in data communication expands and becomes more sophisticated, new opportunities develop to make the interchange of data between buyer and supplier more efficient and effective. The EDI systems discussed in Chapter 3 whereby the purchasing database is tied to a supplier's database through a computer hookup is a good example of how a firm can adjust to changes in the technological environment. Such an adjustment, with its possibly far-reaching administrative and economic advantages, will occur only if the firm establishes a conscious communication strategy which mandates the development and use of such a system. The actions of the U.S. automobile industry, through its Automotive Industry Action Group, in working with the American National Standards Institute to develop a data format standard for EDI applications, is a good example of the strategic approach necessary if a purchasing department is to adjust to and exploit this changed environment in which it now operates.

Why?

Every strategy needs to be examined not only for its various optional components, but also for the reason why it needs to be pursued. The most normal reason for a strategy in supply is to make supply objectives congruent with overall organizational objectives and strategies. Other reasons may include market conditions, both current and future. Furthermore, there may be reasons internal to the organization, both outside of supply and inside supply, to pursue certain strategies. For example, a strong engineering department may afford an opportunity to pursue a strategy based on specially engineered requirements. The availability of excess funds may afford an opportunity to acquire a supplier through backward/vertical integration. The reasons for inside supply may be related to the capability and availability of supply personnel. A highly trained and effective buying group can pursue much more aggressive strategies than one less qualified. Other reasons may include the environment. For example, government regulations and controls in product liability and environmental protection may require the pursuit of certain strategies.

Government Regulations and Controls.   To meet perceived economic problems, the federal government may impose specific economic limitations on the firm's purchasing decision processes. For example, from time to time various price and wage control limitations are imposed; tariff and import regulations and schedules continually are being changed by various governments. Any purchasing strategy must be formulated within this overall structure, if purchasing actions are to meet legal constraints and exploit the ever-changing economic possibilities.

Product Liability.   As Chapter 10 discusses, product safety and product liability considerations have assumed much more importance in the purchasing decision process over the past decade, as various court rulings have interpreted the existing law. The potential financial risk has increased, and the firm must factor this additional legal exposure into its long-term purchase strategy, as it works with suppliers and its own engineering, manufacturing, and marketing functions. As a strategy, with the advice of legal counsel, purchasing will want to transfer product liability to the supplier where possible, to minimize the risk of financial obligation from product liability lawsuits.

Environmental Protection.   Concern has grown markedly about a firm's responsibility to protect the environment (air, water, ground) and has resulted in passage of various environmental protection laws and regulations. This has resulted in suppliers and purchasers having to make many changes in products and services and methods of doing business. For example, in the case of the castings industry, it has resulted in an overall reduction in the number of suppliers and changes in the product line mix of some suppliers. Purchasing, in conjunction with other departments in the firm, must take these constraints into account in establishing its overall acquisition strategy. It may necessitate such things as a long-term strategy to (1) change the supplier base, (2) redesign product to permit substitution of certain materials, or (3) begin manufacture of certain components that previously were bought out.

Waste Disposal.   Purchasing has always been responsible in most firms for the disposal of those residues of the manufacturing process (waste) which have no economic value (see Chapter 9). However, with the changes in materials and technology which have occurred in the post-nuclear era, many waste materials are hazardous in nature and require special disposal procedures. Many localities have enacted regulations to govern transport and disposal procedures, as has the federal government. If a firm generates waste, the purchasing department must factor into its overall disposal strategy the special requirements of environmental protection and hazardous materials.

THE FUTURE

The increasing interest in supply strategies and their potential contribution to organizational objectives and strategies is one of the exciting new developments in the whole field of supply. Fortunately, as this chapter indicates, the number of strategic options open to any supply manager is almost endless. A significant difficulty may exist in making supply strategies congruent with those of the organization as a whole. The long-term perspective required for effective supply strategy development will force supply managers to concentrate more on the future. The coming decade should be a highly rewarding one for those supply managers willing to accept the challenge.

Research Needs

To determine those subject areas which offer the greatest potential for advancing the effectiveness and efficiency of the purchasing function, and improving overall contribution to the organization, the National Association of Purchasing Management conducted a "Research Needs Assessment" in late 1986. From a list of 114 possible topics, 104 senior purchasing/materials managers were interviewed on a one-on-one or small group basis and asked to prioritize the 10 topics having the greatest potential to advance the purchasing function and position it to make the greatest possible contribution to their organization.

The topics identified were, in priority order:

1. Global purchasing strategies.
2. Purchasing's effects on organizational effectiveness, efficiency, and profitability.
3. Purchasing's contributions to organizational strategy.
4. Just-in-time purchasing systems: design and implementation.
5. Cost analysis techniques.
6. Negotiation: planning and practice.
7. Evaluating purchasing performance.
8. Workload assessment: setting performance standards.
9. Data formats for Electronic Data Interchange (EDI).
10. Information support needed for purchasing decisions.

Many of these areas come directly out of the strategy arena, discussed in this chapter. The challenges are great and must be accepted if purchasing is to realize its full potential as a contributor to organizational success.

QUESTIONS FOR REVIEW AND DISCUSSION

1. What factors have caused the current interest in, and attention to, strategic purchasing planning?
2. What role can (should) purchasing play in determining a firm's strategy in the area of social issues and trends?
3. What can purchasing do to assist in minimizing a firm's risk of product liability lawsuits?
4. What type of data would purchasing need to contribute to an organization's strategic plans for merger, acquisition, or disinvestment? How might purchasing obtain such data?
5. Which of the four major categories of purchasing functional strategies can make the greatest contribution to overall purchasing effectiveness?
6. Give some examples of firms which might consider a backward vertical integration strategy. What would the difficulties be in formulating and implementing the strategy?
7. How can the purchasing manager determine which cost-reduction strategies to pursue?
8. Will the foreign purchasing strategy become more or less important in the 1990s?
9. How can purchasing achieve the attitude changes necessary to introduce the several supply-support strategies?
10. What changes in the overall purchasing environment do you predict will have occurred by the year 2000?
11. How can purchasing strategies be related to stages in the product life cycle?

REFERENCES

Browning, John M.; Noel B. Zabriskie; and Alan B. Huellmantel. "Strategic Purchasing Planning." *Journal of Purchasing and Materials Management,* Spring 1983.

Burt, David N. *Proactive Procurement: The Key to Increased Profits, Productivity, and Quality.* Englewood Cliffs, N.J.: Prentice-Hall, 1984.

Corey, E. Raymond. *Procurement Management: Strategy, Organization and Decision-Making.* Boston, Mass.: CBI Publishing Company, 1978.

Hammermesh, Richard G. "Making Planning Strategic." *Harvard Business Review,* July–August, 1986.

Kraljic, Peter. "Purchasing Must Become Supply Management." *Harvard Business Review,* September–October, 1983.

Spekman, Robert E. "A Strategic Approach to Procurement Planning." *Journal of Purchasing and Materials Management,* Winter 1981.

Case 16–1

DIPROD (R)

On June 15, Brent Miller, raw materials buyer, had to prepare his recommendation for DIPROD's annual hexonic acid requirements. Four suppliers had submitted substantially different bids for this annual contract to commence August 1. Brent knew his recommendation would involve a variety of policy considerations and wondered what his best option would be.

Company Background

DIPROD (Canada) was the Canadian subsidiary of a large international chemical company. The company sold both consumer and industrial products and had over the years established an excellent reputation for quality products and marketing effectiveness. This was evidenced by a very substantial growth in total sales and financial success. Total Canadian sales were approximately $800 million and after-tax profits were $40 million. Raw material and packaging costs were about 50 percent of sales.

Purchasing

Brent Miller, a recent graduate of a well-known business school, knew that purchasing was well regarded as a function at DIPROD. The department was staffed with 24 well-qualified persons, including a number of engineering and business graduates at both the undergraduate and masters levels. The department was headed by a director who reported to the president. It was organized along commodity lines and Brent Miller had recently been appointed raw materials buyer reporting to the manager of the chemicals buying group. The hexonic acid contract would have to be approved by the immediate supervisor and the director of the department.

Brent was aware that several DIPROD purchasing policies and practices were of particular importance to his current hexonic contract decision. The purchasing department had worked very hard with suppliers over the years to establish a single-bid policy. It was felt that suppliers should quote their best possible offer on their first and only quote and all suppliers should be willing to live with the consequences of their bid. Long-term supplier relations with the best possible long-term oppor-

EXHIBIT 1   Purchasing Objectives

The basic objectives for the DIPROD purchasing department are:

A. *Assurance of Material Availability*
   The major objective of purchasing must be the guarantee of sufficient supply to support production requirements.
B. *Best Value*
   DIPROD recognizes that value is a combination of price, quality, service, . . . and that maximum profitability can only be obtained through the purchase of optimal value on both a short- and long-term basis.
C. *An Ethical Reputation*
   All dealings must respect all aspects of the law and all business relationships must be founded on a sound ethical approach.
D. *Gathering of Information*
   Purchasing involves a constant search for new ideas and improved products in the changing markets. A responsibility also exists to keep the company informed on industry trends including information on material supply and costs.

---

tunities were considered vital to the procurement strategy. Assured supply for all possible types of market conditions was also of prime concern. Multiple sources were usually favored over single sources where this appeared to be reasonable and where no strong long-term price or other disadvantages were expected. Frequent supplier switching would not be normal, although total volumes placed with suppliers might change depending on past performance and new bids. Brent recognized that any major departure from traditional practice would have to be very carefully justified. Exhibit 1 shows the four prime objectives of the purchasing department and Exhibit 2 contains excerpts from the company's familiarization brochure for new suppliers.

Hexonic Acid—Recent Market History

DIPROD expected to use approximately 3,000 tons of hexonic acid in the following year. Requirements for the past year amounted to 2,750 tons and had been supplied by Canchem and Alfo at 60 and 40 percent.

Hexonic acid was a major raw material in a number of DIPROD products. Its requirements had grown steadily over the years and were expected to remain significant in the years to come. The availability of this material in the marketplace was difficult to predict. The process by which it was produced yielded both hexonic and octonic acids and the market was, therefore, influenced by the demand for either product.

Two years previously there had been major shortages of hexonic acid due to strong European and Japanese demand. Furthermore, capacity expansions had been delayed too long because of depressed prices for hexonic and octonic over the previous years. During this period of shortage both of DIPROD's suppliers, Alfo and Canchem, were caught by the market upsurge. Alfo had just shut down their old Windsor plant and had not yet brought their new Quebec City plant up to design capacity. At the

EXHIBIT 2   Excerpts from Brochure for New Suppliers

The purpose of the information contained herein is to give our suppliers a better understanding of certain policies and practices of DIPROD. We believe it is important that we understand our suppliers and, in turn, that they understand us. As you know DIPROD believes in free enterprise and in competition as the mainspring of a free enterprise system. Many of our basic policies stem from a fundamental belief that competition is the fairest means for DIPROD to purchase the best total value. However, the policies and practices we want to outline here for you relate to DIPROD business ethics and the ethical treatment of suppliers. In brief, fair dealing means these things to us:

1. We live up to our word. We do not mislead. We believe that misrepresentations, phantom prices, chiseling, etc., have no place in our business.
2. We try to be fair in our demands on a supplier and to avoid unreasonable demands for services; we expect to pay our way when special service is required.
3. We try to settle all claims and disputes on a fair and factual basis.
4. We avoid any form of "favored treatment," such as telling a supplier what to quote to get our business or obtaining business by "meeting" an existing price. In addition, all suppliers that could qualify for our business are given identical information and an equal opportunity to quote on our requirements.
5. We do not betray the confidence of a supplier. We believe that it is unethical to talk about a supplier with competitors. New ideas, methods, products, and prices are kept confidential unless disclosure is permitted by the supplier.
6. We believe in giving prompt and courteous attention to all supplier representatives.
7. We are willing to listen to supplier complaints at any level of the buying organization without prejudice concerning the future placement of business.

We also do not believe in reciprocity or in "tie-ins" which require the purchase of one commodity with another.

We believe that supplier relationships should be conducted so that personal obligations, either actual or implied, do not exist. Consequently, we do not accept gifts and we discourage entertainment from suppliers. Similarly, we try to avoid all situations which involve a conflict of personal interest.

The above comments cover the main DIPROD buying policies on both corporate and personal ethics. We sincerely want our relationships with suppliers to be built on respect and good faith, which grow from mutual understanding. Please feel free to discuss with us any points that need clarification.

---

same time, Canchem was in the midst of converting their process to accommodate recent chemical improvements and they, too, found themselves plagued with conversion problems. Both companies were subsidiaries of large American multinational firms. Both were large multiplant companies in Canada and had supplied DIPROD for many years. The parent companies of both Alfo and Canchem had been faced with too high a demand in the United States to be able to afford any material to

EXHIBIT 3   Recent Hexonic Acid Purchases

Period	Total Volume Purchased	Percent Supplier Delivered Cost	Percent Supplier Delivered Cost
Three years ago	1,800 tons	50% Canchem $414/ton	50% Alfo $414/ton
Two years ago	2,200 tons	50% Canchem $588/ton	50% Alfo $542/ton
Last year	2,750 tons	60% Canchem $692/ton	40% Alfo $646/ton

help meet the Canadian commitments of their subsidiaries. As a result, both Canadian suppliers were forced to place many of their customers on allocation. However, through considerable efforts both were able to fulfill all of DIPROD's requirements. The increased prices charged throughout this period fell within the terms of the contracts and were substantially lower than those that would have been incurred if DIPROD would have had to import offshore material. Quotations on such imports had revealed prices ranging from $960 to $1,440 per ton.

The past year was relatively stable with both producers running almost at capacity. DIPROD again had contracted its requirements with Alfo and Canchem, both of whom continued to perform with the same high quality and service to which DIPROD had become accustomed over the years.

For the past year Brent's predecessor had recommended a split in the business of 60 percent to Canchem and 40 percent to Alfo based on a number of factors. Important to the decision at that time was the start-up of the new Alfo plant. The Alfo quotation of $600 per ton offered a lower price per ton than Canchem's at $646 per ton, but it had been uncertain whether the new plant would be able to guarantee more than 40 percent of DIPROD's hexonic requirements. Currently, however, Alfo had brought their plant up to capacity and could certainly supply all of the 6 million pounds required, if called on (see Exhibit 3 for a recent history of hexonic acid purchases).

Brent thought that recently the hexonic acid cycle had turned around. Hexonic demand had eased and now it was octonic acid which was in high demand by the booming paint industry. Recent plant expansions by a number of suppliers had been completed. The overall result seemed to be a building of excess hexonic inventories. Brent believed this would be reflected in a buyer's market in the coming year and looked forward to aggressive quotes from all potential sources.

Meetings with Hexonic Suppliers

An important part of the buyer's job at DIPROD was to become an expert in the materials purchased. Among other things, this meant keeping an open ear to the market and building strong relationships with suppliers. It was the buyer's responsibility to assure that all information between buyer and seller would be completely confidential. The director of purchasing believed it was important to build a reputation that suppliers could trust DIPROD purchasing personnel.

On May 14, Brent had mailed the hexonic inquiry (see Exhibit 4) to the four suppliers he believed had a chance of quoting competitively on the needs of the Hamilton plant. The two current Canadian suppliers, Alfo and Canchem, were in-

EXHIBIT 4   Hexonic Acid Inquiry

P.O. Box 372, Terminal "A"   Toronto, Ontario

                                      May 14

Dear Sir:

Subject: Hexonic Acid

We invite your best quotation to supply all or part of our requirements of Hexonic Acid for the month period beginning next August 1. Please use the attached quote sheets in preparing your reply for the following material:

DIPROD Specification No. 87831 (attached), purchased in tank cars or tank trucks. The total requirement for our Hamilton, Ontario plant is estimated to be 3,000 tons.

Prices

Provide pricing for spot purchases; in addition, indicate any special price arrangement you would offer if we were to agree to purchase this material on a contractual basis. We consider firm prices to be a significant element of value.

If your material is of other than Canadian origin and if Canadian Customs clearance would be the Buyer's responsibility, please include the appropriate fair market value (FMV) within the terms of the Canadian Customs Regulations. Note that the FMV and the selling price can quite properly be different.

In addition to your proposal on the above, we encourage any other proposals which might offer us better value and so enhance your competitive position. We are willing to consider proposals of both a chemical or commercial nature.

Use of the attached quote sheet ensures that we receive the basic information that must be contained in every quote. This format is not intended to restrict your quotation in any way. Please feel free to attach any other additional information that will help us clearly identify the value your company is offering.

To receive consideration your quotation must be in our hands by 4:00 P.M. June 7.

If you have any questions, please don't hesitate to call me at 416-366-5859.

                                      Yours very truly,

                                      B. W. Miller
                                      Buying Department
BWM/em
Att'd.

_____

cluded as well as two American sources. The deadline for bids was June 7, at 4 P.M.

   Brent knew that on receipt of the inquiry, supplier salesmen would be eager to discuss it. Actually, he had two contacts before the inquiry was mailed out.

Meeting with Alfo

Mr. Baker, sales representative of Alfo, met with Brent on April 20. He said that Alfo had unfilled capacity at its new Quebec City plant and he appeared eager to receive an indication of DIPROD's future hexonic requirements. Mr. Baker informed Brent that he was aware of low-priced hexonic on the European market but also made sure to emphasize that it would be uncompetitive in the Canadian market after the cost of duty and freight were added. Brent said it was a published fact that inventories were building in the United States as other hexonic users showed signs of easing their demands. The meeting ended with the assurance from Brent that Mr. Baker would again receive an invitation to quote on the next period's business when it was reviewed in June.

Phone Call by Michigan Chemical

Mr. Wallace, sales representative of Michigan Chemical, assured Brent over the telephone on April 30 that his company would be a contender this year. He said that Michigan Chemical would be represented by their Canadian distributor, Carter Chemicals, Ltd., located in Niagara Falls, Ontario. Brent remembered that Michigan Chemical had a good record with DIPROD (U.S.). According to the U.S. raw materials buying group, Michigan Chemical had supplied close to 99 percent of their commitment in the recent period of shortage. Brent emphasized to Mr. Wallace over the telephone that the present suppliers held the advantage and that he would have to offer better value in order for DIPROD to swing any business away from them. Brent said at the end of the call that Michigan Chemical would receive an inquiry and that their quote would be seriously considered.

Meeting with Canchem

On June 3, Mr. Aldert, sales representative for Canchem, personally brought in his company's quotation and presented the terms to Brent with a distinct air of confidence (see Exhibit 5). Mr. Aldert explained that although his price of $646 per ton was the same as that which DIPROD was currently paying for Canchem material, it remained a competitive price. Brent could not help showing his disappointment to Mr. Aldert and he said that he had expected a more aggressive quote. However, he assured Mr. Aldert that every consideration would be given to Canchem once all the quotations were in by the June 7 deadline.

Meeting with American Chemical Inc. (AMCHEM)

On the morning of June 7, two representatives from AMCHEM delivered their hexonic quotation and explained its contents to Brent. AMCHEM had recently completed a plant expansion at their Cleveland plant and clearly had the ability to supply many times DIPROD's total requirements. Brent thought their quote of $480 per ton appeared very attractive and noted that the price per ton depended on the specific volume allocated to AMCHEM. The price of $480 applied to an annual volume of 1,050 tons. For a volume of 2,250 tons per year the price would be lowered to

EXHIBIT 5   Hexonic Acid Quote Sheet

For all or part of Diprod's requirements of 3,000 tons for the period beginning August 1 to be shipped to our Hamilton plant.

Pricing:

A) On our desired shipment size of tank trucks only.

　　a) spot price __$646.00/ton__

　　　　(i) do you perceive this price to be stable?

　　　　　　__short-term yes__

　　　if not: expected increase

　　　　　　__8% during 2nd or 3rd quarter__

　　　　　　expected decrease

　　　　　　__—__

　　b) contractural purchase price __$646.00/ton__ with __30 day__ price

　　　　adjustments with __30__ days prior notice of change in price.

　　　　i) minimum period (if any): 1 year

　　　　ii) minimum volume (if any): 1,000 tons

Fair Market Value (if applicable):

Manufacturer of this material is confirmed as

　　　　　　__that of Canchem Ltd.__

This material will be shipped from __Kingston, Ontario (plant/warehouse)__

Normal inventory of this material that will be carried at any time, __500 tons__

FOB point: Kingston, Ontario

Freight terms: Freight Collect

Cash terms and discounts: Net 30

Lead time for delivery from receipt of purchase order: 2 weeks

Planned shutdowns: None

Union affiliation at manufacturing plant: Oil & Chemical workers

　　　　i) Union contract expires: August 28, next year.

Material supplied against this quotation will be in accordance with DIPROD Specification No.: 87831

Signed: .... Name of Company ..Canchem Ltd......

Date: ..June 3......................

$474.80. A 15 percent duty would have to be added to the cost of AMCHEM material as well as freight.

When the representatives had left, Brent searched the hexonic material file for any information about past dealings with AMCHEM. He found that DIPROD had been supplied with AMCHEM hexonic seven years previously. At that time AMCHEM apparently had quoted a price below Canchem and Alfo and, as a result, had been allocated a portion of the business. This had the result of sparking aggressiveness into the two Canadian suppliers during the next inquiry. Both fought to gain back the tonnage that had been taken away from them. Apparently, neither Canchem nor Alfo had been aware who their competitor was at the time.

Brent also telephoned the purchasing department of DIPROD (U.S.) in an effort to draw any information about their experience with AMCHEM. Supplier information like this flowed quite freely within the corporation on a need-to-know basis. The U.S. buyer informed Brent that AMCHEM did at one time supply the parent with hexonic and that quality and service were excellent. However, he did caution Brent that during the recent period of shortage AMCHEM did place DIPROD (U.S.) on allocation and as a result fell short of their commitment by a considerable extent.

Meeting with Alfo

Mr. Baker, sales representative of Alfo, presented his company's quote to Brent at 3 P.M., the afternoon of June 7. He explained that the contractual terms and $600 price offered were the same as those under the current contract with Alfo. Brent thanked Mr. Baker for his quotation and told him he would be informed in late June when a decision had been made.

Quotation by Carter Chemical

The quotation from Carter Chemical arrived in the afternoon mail on June 7. The $634 per ton FOB Hamilton plant quote was a pleasant surprise to Brent. He thought that Michigan Chemical had been right when they had said that their distributor would make an aggressive offer. Brent now had received two quotes that offered a better laid-down cost than the two current suppliers.

Visit of Canchem

At 3:45 P.M. on June 7, Brent received another visit from Mr. Aldert of Canchem who had apparently been disheartened after his earlier meeting on June 3. He had obviously gone back to his management, for he now had a new quotation prepared. His new quote offered DIPROD hexonic on a three-year contract for $550 per ton. With freight added, this price appeared to be equal to the lowest that had been received. Brent realized that he had probably inspired Mr. Aldert to resubmit his quotation by the feedback he had given him during their June 3 meeting. With this in mind, Brent was wary of accepting this quotation for fear he would be setting a bad precedent. He told Mr. Aldert that he might not be in a position to accept his bid, but would let him know subsequently. The following day Brent discussed the situation with his superior, Mr. Williams. Mr. Williams retraced the steps Brent had gone through. It had been normal practice at DIPROD to open quotes as they were received. It had also been standard policy not to give suppliers any feedback

EXHIBIT 6   Quotation Summary: Hexonic Acid

	Price		*Terms*
	Spot	*Contract*	
1. Alfo:			
FOB Quebec City	600.00/ton	600.00/ton	Min. period: 1 year
Freight (equal on	46.00	46.00	Min. volume: —
Kingston)	646.00/ton	646.00/ton	Price protection: 90 days
			Notice: 15 days
2. Canchem:			
		(2nd proposal, June 6)	
FOB Kingston	646.00/ton	550.00/ton	Min. period: 3 years
Freight	46.00	46.00	Min. volume: 1,000 tons
	692.00/ton	596.00/ton	Price protection: 30 days
			Notice: 30 days

3. American Chemicals:

	Spot	*Min. 1,050 tons*	*Min. 2,250 tons*	*Terms*
FOB Cleveland	659.00/ton	480.00	474.80	Min. period: 1 year
Duty @ 15%	98.86	72.00	71.20	Min. volume: Stated
Freight	46.00	50.00	50.00	Price protection: Firm
	803.86	602.00	596.00	Notice: —

4. Carter Chemicals: (Michigan Chem material)

	Spot	*Min. 750 tons*	*Terms*
FOB our Hamil-	634.00/ton	634.00/ton	Min. period: 1 year
ton Plant			Min. volume: 750 tons
			Price protection: 90 days
			Notice: 15 days

on their quote until all quotes had been received. Mr. Williams told Brent to think the situation over in his own mind and to make a recommendation on how Canchem's second bid should be treated as part of his hexonic acid contract deliberations.

Quote Summary

Brent prepared a quote summary to put all bids on an equal footing (see Exhibit 6). To be able to compare quotes fairly, it was necessary to examine the laid-down cost of each of the four options. Items like duty and freight could make a significant difference. Brent realized that his final recommendation would have to be based on his calculations as well as his objective view of the current suppliers. He did not have much time left and the unusual situation surrounding Canchem's second bid gave him further concern. Mr. Williams was expecting his written analysis and recommendation no later than June 17.

Case 16-2

Locar Corporation (R)

John Palmer, manager of purchasing for Locar Corporation, became increasingly concerned about the shortage of supply of PL75, a major pipe resin. Several PL75 suppliers had approached Mr. Palmer requesting long-term supply contracts. Mr. Palmer was attempting to assess the advisability of such commitments.

Company Background

Locar, a long-established company in Cincinnati, Ohio, sold industrial piping and plumbing supplies. The company's four plants were located in the eastern United States. A series of regional warehouses provided an extensive distribution system which serviced customers throughout the domestic U.S. market. Total company sales last year exceeded $300 million; piping products totaled $102 million. PL75 pipes and fittings made up 80 percent of piping products sales by Locar. Locar had experienced rapid growth; total company sales had increased at 20 percent a year and were expected to continue at that rate for at least the next four years. The corporate five-year plan called for pipe and fitting sales to exceed $240 million within three years.

PL75 Piping

Locar used PL75 in manufacturing piping products; compounds and stabilizers were added to the PL75 polymer, which was then extruded into pipe and pipe fittings. The manufacturing cost of PL75 pipe amounted to 35 percent of its selling price.

PL75 polymer was a versatile nonburning resin used in significant quantities in nearly every major segment of the pipe market.

Pipes produced from PL75 had remarkable long-life characteristics. Chemically, these pipes had not yet been known to break down or deteriorate. Another reason for the enthusiastic adoption and use of PL75 piping, and plastic piping in general, was the ease of both installing and fastening of the pipe joints with a cement. These characteristics made resin piping far superior to cast iron and copper piping which required soldering. However, PL75 pipe was difficult to stabilize during the extrusion process. The larger the diameter of the pipe or fitting, the more technically competent the extruder had to be. John Palmer believed much of the future market growth would be toward larger pipe sizes and pipe applications which required a high degree of extrusion ability.

The Plastic Pipe Industry

The plastic pipe industry consisted of about 60 companies which shared a business volume of approximately $1,200 million at retail. Of the 60 companies, no more than 25 had any major market impact as plastic pipe manufacturers; as few as six companies had annual volumes exceeding $60 million. The top four companies accounted for approximately half of the plastic pipe market, and were the only ones supplying a complete range of pipe and pipe fittings. Pipe made from PL75 constituted 50 percent of the total plastic pipe market with approximately one third of the industry processing PL75.

Due to a relatively high cost of shipping plastic pipe, many small pipe companies cropped up throughout the country, each serving a small local market, thereby keeping their shipping costs down. There were several other reasons why so many small companies were in the PL75 pipe market. Very little capital was required to become a pipe extruder. Although the more sophisticated equipment, recently introduced, raised the investment requirements, companies still could set up an extrusion line for $80,000 to $100,000. A prospective extruder did not have to be technically proficient. Resin suppliers gave advice about the type of equipment to buy and how it was to be used. Many resin suppliers had, in the past, boasted about the ease of setting up a plastic pipe shop.

As the market matured, small extruders were being forced out of the market, amalgamated, or left to concentrate on a few small sizes of pipe and pipe fittings. In Mr. Palmer's opinion, the future competitive situation in the industry would be based on sales and merchandising strengths rather than on manufacturing capability.

Future Demand for PL75

In the United States, PL75 had experienced an extraordinary growth along with other plastic pipe materials. The problems holding back quick adoption in North America were the need for greater product standardization and the lack of acceptance by local building codes for use of PL75 pipe. Since building standards were normally controlled by local as well as state or federal agencies, the job of gaining plastic piping acceptance was time consuming. Mr. Palmer expected that a steady industry growth would stabilize between 10 and 12 percent per year for PL75 pipe. Some experts in the market predicted a glut on the market of resins, including PL75, within three years, but the manufacturers of PL75 polymer strongly denied this.

Supply of PL75 Polymer

Suppliers of PL75 had built up loyalties with their customers over the years when the market was soft and prices were low. However, since the beginning of the current year they had set quotas for all their present customers, thereby making PL75 still available to many small extruders. Mr. Palmer thought that in a few years these loyalties would be terminated. Other polymer suppliers, who were also extruders of PL75, had stopped selling PL75 polymer during the last year and were using all of their own production.

Suppliers located within a 1,000-mile radius of Locar's plants were considered by Mr. Palmer to be within the maximum shipping distance. Since PL75 was delivered in bulk by rail or truck, all current contracts were FOB Locar plants. Suppliers further than 1,000 miles away would not submit such an FOB quote. Mr. Palmer estimated that within this shipping distance, 15 potential suppliers of PL75 polymer existed. If suppliers were to be switched or lost, freight charges could play a critical role in alternative supplier selections.

EXHIBIT 1   PL75 Purchase Forecasts by Locar (volume—millions pounds)

3 years ago	*			
2 years ago		*		
1 year ago			*	
this year				*
next year				35 million
2 years from now				47 million
3 years from now	20 million	35 million	45 million	60 million

*Year forecast was made.

EXHIBIT 2   PL75 Actual Purchases and Prices per Pound

	Volume (in million pounds)	*Price per pound (paid by Locar)*
15 years ago	3	8
3 years ago	12	20
2 years ago	15	21
1 year ago	20	22
this year	(28) projected to year end	24

Locar Purchases and Suppliers of PL75

Locar started extruding resin pipe 15 years ago. Increasing quantities of PL75 had been purchased since then. Past purchases, future demand, forecasts, and price increases are outlined in Exhibits 1 and 2.

Currently, five companies supplied Locar with PL75. Clark and Solvay had supplied PL75 to Locar for the last 15 years. These two companies also supplied other chemical stabilizers and compounds to Locar in addition to PL75, and were considered by Mr. Palmer to be "old, reliable suppliers." The other three companies had supplied PL75 only and were relatively new, having commenced business with Locar during the last three years. One of these three, Imperial, manufactured PL75 polymer and also extruded industrial food and beverage piping made of PL75. Exhibit 3 outlines the percentages and volumes expected to be supplied by these five companies for this year.

Prices had always been the same from all suppliers. Mr. Palmer noted that with the general tightening of supply, the price had quickly increased to a higher level. Until this year it had been standard industry practice to buy on a hand-to-mouth basis at the current market price.

Long-Term Contract Proposals

In February, Mr. Palmer was stunned by the rapid alteration of the supply situation. Within the same week, three of the present suppliers (Clark, Solvay and

EXHIBIT 3   Current Supply of PL75 to Locar

Company	Current capacity (in million pounds)	Locar purchases (in million pounds)
Clark	85	8.4
Solvay*	60	8.4
Imperial*	20	5.6
Acro	40	2.8
Albis	60	2.8
		28.0

*Capacity available for sale. Other capacity exists which is used within the company.

Imperial) had approached Mr. Palmer with proposals to supply Locar with present and future requirements of PL75.

Clark, a large international producer of a wide range of chemical products, was generally perceived as a leader in the monomer and polymer field. Clark had asked for a five-year contract with escalation clauses for labor, energy, and feedstock based on a current price of 24 cents a pound. Clark pointed out the danger of future capacity shortages by showing Mr. Palmer projected capacity and sales figures. Minimum contract volumes would be based on Clark's present percentage of Locar's total purchases (30 percent) projected over Locar's 60 million pounds forecast. The commitment would be on a firm volume guaranteed contract with an escalated price. Locar would be contractually obligated to pay for that volume at the agreed price. A cancellation penalty was available which would amount to 60 percent of the selling price at the time of cancellation. Clark's sales representative stated that without this long-term contract, no supply guarantees could be given after August of this year.

Solvay, another large international concern, manufactured PL75 polymer as a raw material for some of its own end products as well as selling the polymer on the open market. Solvay's proposal was similar to Clark's except that it asked for a three-year contract instead of a five-year contract.

Imperial, like Solvay, was a large international corporation selling a wide range of end products using PL75 polymer. Imperial asked for a purchase agreement which could be dropped at any time by either party. Mr. Palmer wondered if Imperial's reluctance to offer a long-term contract indicated that Imperial was planning to use all production of PL75 polymer itself within a few years.

Acro and Albis, both small PL75 polymer producers, had not asked for any special considerations and had not initiated discussions of future purchases with Mr. Palmer.

It was clear to Mr. Palmer that the suppliers were trying to protect future capacity increases by signing customers to long-term contracts. Purchasing practice at Locar had never included the use of long-term contracts. Most contracts for materials were on a yearly or monthly basis. During the last few years, contracts for PL75 were short-term, three- or six-month blanket contracts. Availability was such that a telephone call would be all that was required to obtain supply. This situation had changed over the last month with the introduction of quotas by suppliers. Generally, expansion of PL75 production was expected to continue strongly. Mr. Palmer believed that demand would continue to climb as the full potential of PL75 was recognized.

To explore other alternatives during this unusual situation, Mr. Palmer inquired about PL75 polymer production. He learned that bringing a PL75 monomer plant on-stream and producing would take approximately 18 months. Investment would be close to $14 million for a monomer plant with a capacity of 150 million pounds per year. For a polymer plant of 50 million pounds per year capacity, $8 million would be required and $12 million for a 100 million pound capacity plant.

He had also looked into the possibility of contracting PL75 feedstock, which Locar could then provide to its existing five polymer suppliers. Present monomer plants were, however, heavily invested in by the petrochemical companies, making any control over the feedstock difficult. These companies also controlled ethane, itself by a by-product accounting for only 1 percent of their sales, but a major component of the monomer. Unsure about Locar's present suppliers' reactions, Mr. Palmer hesitated to act in this area. He was uncertain about the dangers of becoming too deeply involved in the problems of polymer and monomer producers.

In a recent article, Mr. Palmer had read that a laboratory had successfully developed a better manufacturing method for PL75 monomer. Should this method be proven commercially, it might be expected to reduce the manufacturing cost of PL75 by about two cents per pound three years from now.

On March 5, Clark's sales representative telephoned Mr. Palmer to ask if he could bring his sales manager to a meeting on March 9 to discuss future business. Mr. Palmer knew that the long-term proposals would have to be decided on before then. He was not sure if it was in his company's best interest to make the kind of commitment the suppliers were currently requesting. Nevertheless, he was most anxious to assure adequate supply for the future.

Case 16–3

Mallory Pharmaceuticals Corporation

One afternoon in September, James Wilson, assistant purchasing manager of Mallory Pharmaceuticals Corporation (M.P. Corp.) was discussing the purchase of new packaging materials and contract filling of tablet samples with a supplier's representative. When the details of the packaging purchase order were finalized, Mr. Wilson told the salesman, Fred Brown, of Christie Paper Box Company, that he would send him the purchase order for the packaging components and 25 percent of the contract filling. Mr. Brown replied that Peter O'Toole, of the marketing department, had promised him 100 percent of the contract filling. "This is the first I've heard of that," snapped Mr. Wilson. "It's not marketing's responsibility," he continued, controlling his temper, "to decide what percentages of contract filling a particular supplier will get. Purchasing arranges the contract filling with the suppliers that can give the best quality, delivery, and price."

Mr. Brown, an experienced salesman, remained unperturbed. He replied that he had always dealt with both marketing and purchasing and that sometimes purchasing was not involved at all in the projects. He said that in this case where

EXHIBIT 1   Organization Chart

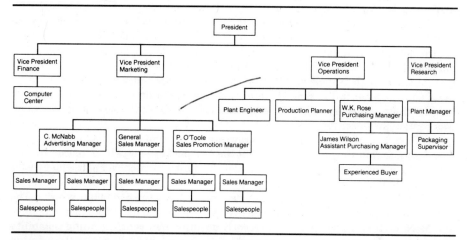

marketing had initiated the contact, he was just keeping purchasing informed of what marketing wanted. Mr. Wilson closed the interview by politely telling the salesman that he would have to clear up the situation between the two company departments. He told Mr. Brown he would let him know how much of the contract packaging he would be getting.

Mr. Wilson, his immediate superior Mr. Rose, and a senior buyer made up the total purchasing staff (see Exhibit 1). One of Mr. Wilson's responsibilities was to handle the purchase of the marketing department's requirements. He also acted as liaison between the department and the production planning, manufacturing, and packaging departments. In recent weeks Mr. Wilson was finding the job more and more frustrating.

The company carried an extensive line of prescription and nonprescription items which were manufactured in Michigan. M.P. Corp. had 10,000 drugstore customers plus hospital and government accounts. Annual sales of close to $40 million were handled by 50 sales representatives from coast to coast. Although the nonprescription items, known as over-the-counter (OTC) products, were promoted directly to the drugstores, most business was generated by convincing the doctors to prescribe M.P. Corp.'s products for their patients. No selling or advertising was directed at the consumer.

The basic idea was that the M.P. sales representative would give samples to a doctor after getting a verbal promise to prescribe. These samples would be used to start the patient on an M.P. product, and the doctor would write a prescription for the patient to pick up at the drugstore. With a large number of similar products on the market, it was a difficult marketing problem to keep M.P.'s brand name in the doctor's mind days or weeks after the salesman's visit. To help solve this problem, salesmen asked the doctors to sign forms requesting additional samples at spaced intervals.

The marketing department had been recently reorganized, and the two new men, P. O'Toole, sales promotion manager, and C. McNabb, advertising manager, were understandably anxious to do a good job.

Unknown to Mr. Wilson, Mr. Brown had worked very closely with Peter O'Toole and Chris McNabb to develop a new sample package design. After at least half a dozen tries, Mr. Brown had come up with an exciting new design which had, in the opinion of O'Toole and McNabb, the potential of a real winner. Not only did they see the new design as extremely promising across a wide range of potential samples, but they also foresaw the possibility that the same design could be used in the regular trade. Both O'Toole and McNabb believed that the new package might stimulate sales substantially. Since both of them had been brought into the company because their predecessors had failed in stimulating sales, the new package design was particularly exciting.

O'Toole and McNabb urged Mr. Brown to make a quick production run of the new design so that they could test market the new package quickly. If market testing proved the design successful, they wanted a substantial switchover subsequently for both sample and production products.

Mr. Brown had tried to get a quick delivery date on the $44,000 test order. The best he could manage was a six-week delivery promise. He had explained to O'Toole and McNabb that his company had recently acquired new contract filling capability with the acquisition of a new machine, which could work in tandem with the printing and package forming equipment. Previously, contract filling was done in a separate department in the plant, necessitating extra work-in-process inventory and double handling. Both O'Toole and McNabb had confirmed to Mr. Brown that this newly acquired capability was of high interest to them. They had also agreed that the $44,000 first order quote was eminently reasonable for both the packaging cost at $35,000 and contract filling at $9,000.

Mr. Brown, as was his custom in previous years, had dealt directly with marketing on the new sample design. After O'Toole and McNabb had given him the order he had dropped by Mr. Wilson's office to let him know what was happening. It came as a complete surprise to him when Mr. Wilson intimated that he might not receive all of the contract filling, since O'Toole and McNabb had already given him the whole order.

The package contract under discussion totaled $44,000 or 0.5 percent of Christie's annual sales of $8 million. In the past, Christie had sold $40,000 worth of materials annually to M.P. Corp. Mr. Brown had designed an attractive new style of sample. Basically, it was a folded card holding strips of tablets which could be pushed through one at a time, as required by the patient.

Although M.P. Corp. did 90 percent of their manufacturing and packaging, they did not have the equipment to strip or heat seal the strip into the folded cards. When goods came in from a contract packager, such as Christie, they were held in inventory until required by marketing.

While Mr. O'Toole and Mr. McNabb had been able to work well together, they were having their difficulties in getting the cooperation of other departments involved. Frequent instances of sample mailings being late or salesmen samples being out of stock continued to plague the success of their program. Delays had been caused by late ordering of components from outside suppliers, shortages of tablets, and computer mailing lists being incorrectly printed. In their attempts to remedy the situation, the marketing men had trampled on a few toes. During attempts to investigate the causes for these delays, the vice president of operations discovered that there were usually good reasons offered by the departments involved.

Purchasing, production, and the computer center pointed out that they could not drop their usual work "every time marketing wanted something in a rush." The feeling expressed by the production planner was typical of most department supervisors. He commented, "It's fine to get out the samples but rather pointless if we are running out of trade size in the meantime. Some of those unusual sample carton constructions slow us up 50 percent."

While it was part of Mr. Wilson's job to coordinate marketing's sample requirements, he was not making much progress. His attempts to get each department to cooperate met with the usual arguments that marketing was only one department and had to wait its turn. Mr. O'Toole and Mr. McNabb at times grew impatient with Mr. Wilson's efforts, and they started to go directly to each department supervisor.

Mr. Wilson felt that the action taken by Mr. O'Toole in telling the supplier how much contract filling business he would get was the last straw. With this in mind he went to see his immediate superior, Mr. Rose, to try to get a policy statement on the matter. He wanted to know where the line was drawn between purchasing's and marketing's responsibility in matters dealing with company suppliers.

Mr. Rose explained that, because marketing promotion expenditures totaled $8.4 million or 21 percent of sales, M.P. Corp., as most other companies in the industry, faced similar purchasing/marketing problems.

If marketing were responsible for their budgets, they had the right to spend $1 each for 10,000 items, or if they wanted, they could buy 5,000 items for $2 each and still stay within their budget. It was a marketing decision whether they were getting better results from the $1 or $2 item. For these items purchasing merely typed a purchase order to confirm the deal already made by marketing with the supplier. This policy applied to nonproduction items, such as calendars, letter openers, diet sheets, patient history cards for doctors, or displays and posters for drugstores. In contrast, production and inventory purchases had last year reached 20 percent of sales dollars.

However, he pointed out that final selection of sources for any purchased items which had to be packaged by the plant had always been the responsibility of the purchasing department. In this particular case there was still a significant inventory of old style samples in the building, which marketing had not considered when they promised Mr. Brown 100 percent of the contract filling. Mr. Wilson felt that placing all the contract filling right away would build up the stock of samples unnecessarily. Besides this, he believed he could negotiate a better price from another reliable supplier and felt that he would give the balance of 75 percent to them.

Marketing, Mr. Rose explained, was only charged for samples as they were shipped to salesmen or mailed out to doctors. Therefore, marketing was not too concerned about inventory levels as long as there were no shortages. Packaging components and bulk products held in inventory were not segregated from trade sizes in the warehouse or in accounting records. Only the finished samples were given a special account number so that the marketing budgets could be debited as the samples were sent out.

Mr. Rose suggested that a marketing-purchasing meeting be held so that each department could state its case. Mr. Wilson wondered how he might best prepare himself for that meeting.

Indexes

Case Index

Subject Index